W9-BZU-170

The Elementary Forms of the Religious Life

The Elementary Forms of the Religious Life

Emile Durkheim

Translated from the French by
Joseph Ward Swain

DOVER PUBLICATIONS, INC.
Mineola, New York

Bibliographical Note

This Dover edition, first published in 2008, is an unabridged republication of the work first published by George Allen & Unwin Ltd., London, in 1915.

Library of Congress Cataloging-in-Publication Data

Durkheim, Émile, 1858–1917.
Formes élémentaires de la vie religieuse. English.
The elementary forms of the religious life / Émile Durkheim ; translated from the French by Joseph Ward Swain.
p. cm.
Originally published: London : G. Allen & Unwin, 1915.
Includes index.
ISBN-13: 978-0-486-45456-6
ISBN-10: 0-486-45456-8
1. Religion. 2. Totemism. I. Swain, Joseph Ward, b. 1891. II. Title.

GN470. D813 2008
306.6—dc22

2007049438

Manufactured in the United States of America
Dover Publications, Inc., 31 East 2nd Street, Mineola, N.Y. 11501

CONTENTS

INTRODUCTION

Subject of our Study: Religious Sociology and the Theory of Knowledge

BOOK I

PRELIMINARY QUESTIONS

CHAPTER I

Definition of Religious Phenomena and of Religion

CHAPTER II

Leading Conceptions of the Elementary Religion

I.—*Animism*

CHAPTER IX

The Idea of Spirits and Gods

BOOK III

THE PRINCIPAL RITUAL ATTITUDES

CHAPTER I

The Negative Cult and its Functions

The Ascetic Rites

CHAPTER II

The Positive Cult

I.—*The Elements of Sacrifice*

CHAPTER III

The Positive Cult—(*continued*)

II.—*Imitative Rites and the Principle of Causality*

CHAPTER IV

The Positive Cult—(*continued*)

III.—*Representative or Commemorative Rites*

CHAPTER V

Piacular Rites and the Ambiguity of the Notion of Sacredness

CONCLUSION

THE ELEMENTARY FORMS OF THE RELIGIOUS LIFE

INTRODUCTION

SUBJECT OF OUR STUDY: RELIGIOUS SOCIOLOGY AND THE THEORY OF KNOWLEDGE

IN this book we propose to study the most primitive and simple religion which is actually known, to make an analysis of it, and to attempt an explanation of it. A religious system may be said to be the most primitive which we can observe when it fulfils the two following conditions: in the first place, when it is found in a society whose organization is surpassed by no others in simplicity;[1] and secondly, when it is possible to explain it without making use of any element borrowed from a previous religion.

We shall set ourselves to describe the organization of this system with all the exactness and fidelity that an ethnographer or an historian could give it. But our task will not be limited to that: sociology raises other problems than history or ethnography. It does not seek to know the passed forms of civilization with the sole end of knowing them and reconstructing them. But rather, like every positive science, it has as its object the explanation of some actual reality which is near to us, and which consequently is capable of affecting our ideas and our acts: this reality is man, and more precisely, the man of to-day, for there is nothing which we are more interested in knowing. Then we are not going to study a very archaic religion simply for the pleasure of telling its peculiarities and its singularities. If we have taken

[1] In the same way, we shall say of these societies that they are primitive, and we shall call the men of these societies primitives. Undoubtedly the expression lacks precision, but that is hardly evitable, and besides, when we have taken pains to fix the meaning, it is not inconvenient.

it as the subject of our research, it is because it has seemed to us better adapted than any other to lead to an understanding of the religious nature of man, that is to say, to show us an essential and permanent aspect of humanity.

But this proposition is not accepted before the raising of strong objections. It seems very strange that one must turn back, and be transported to the very beginnings of history, in order to arrive at an understanding of humanity as it is at present. This manner of procedure seems particularly paradoxical in the question which concerns us. In fact, the various religions generally pass as being quite unequal in value and dignity ; it is said that they do not all contain the same quota of truth. Then it seems as though one could not compare the highest forms of religious thought with the lowest, without reducing the first to the level of the second. If we admit that the crude cults of the Australian tribes can help us to understand Christianity, for example, is that not supposing that this latter religion proceeds from the same mentality as the former, that it is made up of the same superstitions and rests upon the same errors ? This is how the theoretical importance which has sometimes been attributed to primitive religions has come to pass as a sign of a systematic hostility to all religion, which, by prejudging the results of the study, vitiates them in advance.

There is no occasion for asking here whether or not there are scholars who have merited this reproach, and who have made religious history and ethnology a weapon against religion. In any case, a sociologist cannot hold such a point of view. In fact, it is an essential postulate of sociology that a human institution cannot rest upon an error and a lie, without which it could not exist. If it were not founded in the nature of things, it would have encountered in the facts a resistance over which it could never have triumphed. So when we commence the study of primitive religions, it is with the assurance that they hold to reality and express it ; this principle will be seen to re-enter again and again in the course of the analyses and discussions which follow, and the reproach which we make against the schools from which we have separated ourselves is that they have ignored it. When only the letter of the formulæ is considered, these religious beliefs and practices undoubtedly seem disconcerting at times, and one is tempted to attribute them to some sort of a deep-rooted error. But one must know how to go underneath the symbol to the reality which it represents and which gives it its meaning. The most barbarous and the most fantastic rites and the strangest myths translate some human need, some aspect of life, either individual or social. The reasons with which the faithful justify them may be, and generally are, erroneous; but the true reasons do not cease to exist, and it is the duty of science to discover them.

In reality, then, there are no religions which are false. All are true in their own fashion; all answer, though in different ways, to the given conditions of human existence. It is undeniably possible to arrange them in a hierarchy. Some can be called superior to others, in the sense that they call into play higher mental functions, that they are richer in ideas and sentiments, that they contain more concepts with fewer sensations and images, and that their arrangement is wiser. But howsoever real this greater complexity and this higher ideality may be, they are not sufficient to place the corresponding religions in different classes. All are religions equally, just as all living beings are equally alive, from the most humble plastids up to man. So when we turn to primitive religions it is not with the idea of depreciating religion in general, for these religions are no less respectable than the others. They respond to the same needs, they play the same rôle, they depend upon the same causes; they can also well serve to show the nature of the religious life, and consequently to resolve the problem which we wish to study.

But why give them a sort of prerogative? Why choose them in preference to all others as the subject of our study?—It is merely for reasons of method.

In the first place, we cannot arrive at an understanding of the most recent religions except by following the manner in which they have been progressively composed in history. In fact, historical analysis is the only means of explanation which it is possible to apply to them. It alone enables us to resolve an institution into its constituent elements, for it shows them to us as they are born in time, one after another. On the other hand, by placing every one of them in the condition where it was born, it puts into our hands the only means we have of determining the causes which gave rise to it. Every time that we undertake to explain something human, taken at a given moment in history—be it a religious belief, a moral precept, a legal principle, an æsthetic style or an economic system—it is necessary to commence by going back to its most primitive and simple form, to try to account for the characteristics by which it was marked at that time, and then to show how it developed and became complicated little by little, and how it became that which it is at the moment in question. One readily understands the importance which the determination of the point of departure has for this series of progressive explanations, for all the others are attached to it. It was one of Descartes's principles that the first ring has a predominating place in the chain of scientific truths. But there is no question of placing at the foundation of the science of religions an idea elaborated after the cartesian manner, that is to say, a logical concept, a pure possibility, constructed simply by force of thought. What we must find is a concrete reality, and historical and ethnological observation alone can reveal that to us. But even if this cardinal conception is obtained by a different process than that of Descartes, it remains true that it is destined to have a considerable influence on the whole series of propositions which the science establishes. Biological evolution has been conceived quite differently ever since it has been known that monocellular beings do exist. In the same way, the arrangement of religious facts is explained quite differently, according as we put naturism, animism or some other religious form at the beginning of the evolution. Even the most specialized scholars, if they are unwilling to confine themselves to a task of pure erudition, and if they desire to interpret the facts which they analyse, are obliged to choose one of these hypotheses, and make it their starting-point. Whether they desire it or not, the questions which they raise necessarily take the following form : how has naturism or animism been led to take this particular form, here or there, or to enrich itself or impoverish itself in such and such a fashion ? Since it is impossible to avoid taking sides on this initial problem, and since the solution given is destined to affect the whole science, it must be attacked at the outset : that is what we propose to do.

Besides this, outside of these indirect reactions, the study of primitive religions has of itself an immediate interest which is of primary importance.

If it is useful to know what a certain particular religion consists in, it is still more important to know what religion in general is. This is the problem which has aroused the interest of philosophers in all times ; and not without reason, for it is of interest to all humanity. Unfortunately, the method which they generally employ is purely dialectic : they confine themselves to analysing the idea which they make for themselves of religion, except as they illustrate the results of this mental analysis by examples borrowed from the religions which best realize their ideal. But even if this method ought to be abandoned, the problem remains intact, and the great service of philosophy is to have prevented its being suppressed by the disdain of scholars. Now it is possible to attack it in a different way. Since all religions can be compared to each other, and since all are species of the same class, there are necessarily many elements which are common to all. We do not mean to speak simply of the outward and visible characteristics which they all have equally, and which make it possible to give them a provisional definition from the very outset of our researches; the discovery of these apparent signs is relatively easy, for the observation which it demands does not go beneath the surface of things. But these external resemblances suppose others which are profound. At the foundation of all systems of beliefs and of all cults there ought necessarily to be a certain number of fundamental representations or conceptions and of ritual attitudes which, in spite of the diversity of forms which they have taken, have the same objective significance and fulfil the same functions everywhere. These are the permanent elements which constitute that which is permanent and human in religion; they form all the objective contents of the idea which is expressed when one speaks of *religion* in general. How is it possible to pick them out?

Surely it is not by observing the complex religions which appear in the course of history. Every one of these is made up of such a variety of elements that it is very difficult to distinguish what is secondary from what is principal, the essential from the accessory. Suppose that the religion considered is like that of Egypt, India or the classical antiquity. It is a confused mass of many cults, varying according to the locality, the temples, the generations, the dynasties, the invasions, etc. Popular superstitions are there confused with the purest dogmas. Neither the thought nor the activity of the religion is evenly distributed among the believers; according to the men, the environment and the circumstances, the beliefs as well as the rites are thought of in different ways. Here they are priests, there they are monks, elsewhere they are laymen; there are mystics and rationalists, theologians and prophets, etc. In these conditions it is difficult to see what is common to all. In one or another of these systems it is quite possible to find the means of making a profitable study of some particular fact which is specially developed there, such as sacrifice or prophecy, monasticism or the mysteries; but how is it possible to find the common foundation of the religious life underneath the luxuriant vegetation which covers it? How is it possible to find, underneath the disputes of theology, the variations of ritual, the multiplicity of groups and the diversity of individuals, the fundamental states characteristic of religious mentality in general?

Things are quite different in the lower societies. The slighter development of individuality, the small extension of the group, the homogeneity of external circumstances, all contribute to reducing the differences and variations to a minimum. The group has an intellectual and moral conformity of which we find but rare examples in the more advanced societies. Everything is common to all. Movements are stereotyped; everybody performs the same ones in the same circumstances, and this conformity of conduct only translates the conformity of thought. Every mind being drawn into the same eddy, the individual type nearly confounds itself with that of the race. And while all is uniform, all is simple as well. Nothing is deformed like these myths, all composed of one and the same theme which is endlessly repeated, or like these rites made up of a small number of gestures repeated again and again. Neither the popular imagination nor that of the priests has had either the time or the means of refining and transforming the original substance of the religious ideas and practices; these are shown in all their nudity, and offer themselves to an examination, it requiring only the slightest effort to lay them open. That which is accessory or secondary, the development of luxury, has not yet come to hide the principal elements.[1] All is reduced to that which is indispensable, to that without which there could be no religion. But that which is indispensable is also that which is essential, that is to say, that which we must know before all else.

Primitive civilizations offer privileged cases, then, because they are simple cases. That is why, in all fields of human activity, the observations of ethnologists have frequently been veritable revelations, which have renewed the study of human institutions. For example, before the middle of the nineteenth century, everybody was convinced that the father was the essential element of the family; no one had dreamed that there could be a family organization of which the paternal authority was not the keystone. But the discovery of Bachofen came and upset this old conception. Up to very recent times it was regarded as evident that the moral and legal relations of kindred were only another aspect of the psychological relations which result from a common descent; Bachofen and his successors, MacLennan, Morgan and many others still laboured under this misunderstanding. But since we have become acquainted with the nature of the primitive clan, we know that, on the contrary, relationships cannot be explained by consanguinity. To return to religions, the study of only the most familiar ones had led men to believe for a long time that the idea of god was characteristic of everything that is religious. Now the religion which we are going to study presently

[1] But that is not equivalent to saying that all luxury is lacking to the primitive cults. On the contrary, we shall see that in every religion there are beliefs and practices which do not aim at strictly utilitarian ends (Bk. III, ch. iv, § 2). This luxury is indispensable to the religious life; it is at its very heart. But it is much more rudimentary in the inferior religions than in the others, so we are better able to determine its reason for existence here.

is, in a large part, foreign to all idea of divinity; the forces to which the rites are there addressed are very different from those which occupy the leading place in our modern religions, yet they aid us in understanding these latter forces. So nothing is more unjust than the disdain with which too many historians still regard the work of ethnographers. Indeed, it is certain that ethnology has frequently brought about the most fruitful revolutions in the different branches of sociology. It is for this same reason that the discovery of unicellular beings, of which we just spoke, has transformed the current idea of life. Since in these very simple beings, life is reduced to its essential traits, these are less easily misunderstood.

But primitive religions do not merely aid us in disengaging the constituent elements of religion; they also have the great advantage that they facilitate the explanation of it. Since the facts there are simpler, the relations between them are more apparent. The reasons with which men account for their acts have not yet been elaborated and denatured by studied reflection; they are nearer and more closely related to the motives which have really determined these acts. In order to understand an hallucination perfectly, and give it its most appropriate treatment, a physician must know its original point of departure. Now this event is proportionately easier to find if he can observe it near its beginnings. The longer the disease is allowed to develop, the more it evades observation; that is because all sorts of interpretations have intervened as it advanced, which tend to force the original state into the background, and across which it is frequently difficult to find the initial one. Between a systematized hallucination and the first impressions which gave it birth, the distance is often considerable. It is the same thing with religious thought. In proportion as it progresses in history, the causes which called it into existence, though remaining active, are no longer perceived, except across a vast scheme of interpretations which quite transform them. Popular mythologies and subtile theologies have done their work: they have superimposed upon the primitive sentiments others which are quite different, and which, though holding to the first, of which they are an elaborated form, only allow their true nature to appear very imperfectly. The psychological gap between the cause and the effect, between the apparent cause and the effective cause, has become more considerable and more difficult for the mind to leap. The remainder of this book will be an illustration and a verification of this remark on method. It will be seen how, in the primitive religions, the religious fact still visibly carries the mark of its origins: it would have been well-nigh impossible to infer them merely from the study of the more developed religions.

The study which we are undertaking is therefore a way of taking up again, *but under new conditions*, the old problem of the origin of religion. To be sure, if by origin we are to understand the very first beginning, the question has nothing scientific about it, and should be resolutely discarded. There was no given moment when religion began to exist, and there is consequently no need of finding a means of transporting ourselves thither in thought. Like every human institution, religion did not commence anywhere. Therefore, all speculations of this sort are justly discredited; they can only consist in subjective and arbitrary constructions which are subject to no sort of control. But the problem which we raise is quite another one. What we want to do is to find a means of discerning the ever-present causes upon which the most essential forms of religious thought and practice depend. Now for the reasons which were just set forth, these causes are proportionately more easily observable as the societies where they are observed are less complicated. That is why we try to get as near as possible to the origins.[1] It is not that we ascribe particular virtues to the lower religions. On the contrary, they are rudimentary and gross; we cannot make of them a sort of model which later religions only have to reproduce. But even their grossness makes them instructive, for they thus become convenient for experiments, as in them, the facts and their relations are easily seen. In order to discover the laws of the phenomena which he studies, the physicist tries to simplify these latter and rid them of their secondary characteristics. For that which concerns institutions, nature spontaneously makes the same sort of simplifications at the beginning of history. We merely wish to put these to profit. Undoubtedly we can only touch very elementary facts by this method. When we shall have accounted for them as far as possible, the novelties of every sort which have been produced in the course of evolution will not yet be explained. But while we do not dream of denying the importance of the problems thus raised, we think that they will profit by being treated in their turn, and that it is important to take them up only after those of which we are going to undertake the study at present.

[1] It is seen that we give a wholly relative sense to this word " origins," just as to the word " primitive." By it we do not mean an absolute beginning, but the most simple social condition that is actually known or that beyond which we cannot go at present. When we speak of the origins or of the commencement of religious history or thought, it is in this sense that our statements should be understood.

II

But our study is not of interest merely for the science of religion. In fact, every religion has one side by which it overlaps the circle of properly religious ideas, and there, the study of religious phenomena gives a means of renewing the problems which, up to the present, have only been discussed among philosophers.

For a long time it has been known that the first systems of representations with which men have pictured to themselves the world and themselves were of religious origin. There is no religion that is not a cosmology at the same time that it is a speculation upon divine things. If philosophy and the sciences were born of religion, it is because religion began by taking the place of the sciences and philosophy. But it has been less frequently noticed that religion has not confined itself to enriching the human intellect, formed beforehand, with a certain number of ideas; it has contributed to forming the intellect itself. Men owe to it not only a good part of the substance of their knowledge, but also the form in which this knowledge has been elaborated.

At the roots of all our judgments there are a certain number of essential ideas which dominate all our intellectual life; they are what philosophers since Aristotle have called the categories of the understanding: ideas of time, space,[1] class, number, cause, substance, personality, etc. They correspond to the most universal properties of things. They are like the solid frame which encloses all thought; this does not seem to be able to liberate itself from them without destroying itself, for it seems that we cannot think of objects that are not in time and space, which have no number, etc. Other ideas are contingent and unsteady; we can conceive of their being unknown to a man, a society or an epoch; but these others appear to be nearly inseparable from the normal working of the intellect. They are like the framework of the intelligence. Now when primitive religious beliefs are systematically analysed, the principal categories are naturally found. They are born in religion and of religion; they are a product of religious thought. This is a statement that we are going to have occasion to make many times in the course of this work.

[1] We say that time and space are categories because there is no difference between the rôle played by these ideas in the intellectual life and that which falls to the ideas of class or cause (on this point see, Hamelin, *Essai sur les éléments principaux de la représentation*, pp. 63, 76).

This remark has some interest of itself already; but here is what gives it its real importance.

The general conclusion of the book which the reader has before him is that religion is something eminently social. Religious representations are collective representations which express collective realities; the rites are a manner of acting which take rise in the midst of the assembled groups and which are destined to excite, maintain or recreate certain mental states in these groups. So if the categories are of religious origin, they ought to participate in this nature common to all religious facts; they too should be social affairs and the product of collective thought. At least—for in the actual condition of our knowledge of these matters, one should be careful to avoid all radical and exclusive statements—it is allowable to suppose that they are rich in social elements.

Even at present, these can be imperfectly seen in some of them. For example, try to represent what the notion of time would be without the processes by which we divide it, measure it or express it with objective signs, a time which is not a succession of years, months, weeks, days and hours! This is something nearly unthinkable. We cannot conceive of time, except on condition of distinguishing its different moments. Now what is the origin of this differentiation? Undoubtedly, the states of consciousness which we have already experienced can be reproduced in us in the same order in which they passed in the first place; thus portions of our past become present again, though being clearly distinguished from the present. But howsoever important this distinction may be for our private experience, it is far from being enough to constitute the notion or category of time. This does not consist merely in a commemoration, either partial or integral, of our past life. It is an abstract and impersonal frame which surrounds, not only our individual existence, but that of all humanity. It is like an endless chart, where all duration is spread out before the mind, and upon which all possible events can be located in relation to fixed and determined guide lines. It is not *my time* that is thus arranged; it is time in general, such as it is objectively thought of by everybody in a single civilization. That alone is enough to give us a hint that such an arrangement ought to be collective. And in reality, observation proves that these indispensable guide lines, in relation to which all things are temporally located, are taken from social life. The divisions into days, weeks, months, years, etc., correspond to the periodical recurrence of rites, feasts, and public ceremonies.[1] A calendar

[1] See the support given this assertion in Hubert and Mauss, *Mélanges d'Histoire des Religions* (*Travaux de l'Année Sociologique*), chapter on *La Représentation du Temps dans la Religion.*

expresses the rhythm of the collective activities, while at the same time its function is to assure their regularity.[1]

It is the same thing with space. As Hamelin has shown,[2] space is not the vague and indetermined medium which Kant imagined; if purely and absolutely homogeneous, it would be of no use, and could not be grasped by the mind. Spatial representation consists essentially in a primary co-ordination of the data of sensuous experience. But this co-ordination would be impossible if the parts of space were qualitatively equivalent and if they were really interchangeable. To dispose things spatially there must be a possibility of placing them differently, of putting some at the right, others at the left, these above, those below, at the north of or at the south of, east or west of, etc., etc., just as to dispose states of consciousness temporally there must be a possibility of localizing them at determined dates. That is to say that space could not be what it is if it were not, like time, divided and differentiated. But whence come these divisions which are so essential? By themselves, there are neither right nor left, up nor down, north nor south, etc. All these distinctions evidently come from the fact that different sympathetic values have been attributed to various regions. Since all the men of a single civilization represent space in the same way, it is clearly necessary that these sympathetic values, and the distinctions which depend upon them, should be equally universal, and that almost necessarily implies that they be of social origin.[3]

Besides that, there are cases where this social character is made manifest. There are societies in Australia and North America where space is conceived in the form of an immense circle, because the camp has a circular form;[4] and this spatial circle is divided up exactly like the tribal circle, and is in its

[1] Thus we see all the difference which exists between the group of sensations and images which serve to locate us in time, and the category of time. The first are the summary of individual experiences, which are of value only for the person who experienced them. But what the category of time expresses is a time common to the group, a social time, so to speak. In itself it is a veritable social institution. Also, it is peculiar to man; animals have no representations of this sort.

This distinction between the category of time and the corresponding sensations could be made equally well in regard to space or cause. Perhaps this would aid in clearing up certain confusions which are maintained by the controversies of which these questions are the subject. We shall return to this point in the conclusion of the present work (§ 4).

[2] *Op. cit.*, pp. 75 ff.

[3] Or else it would be necessary to admit that all individuals, in virtue of their organo-physical constitution, are spontaneously affected in the same manner by the different parts of space: which is more improbable, especially as in themselves the different regions are sympathetically indifferent. Also, the divisions of space vary with different societies, which is a proof that they are not founded exclusively upon the congenital nature of man.

[4] See Durkheim and Mauss, *De quelques formes primitives de classification*, in *Année Sociologique*, VI, pp. 47 ff.

image. There are as many regions distinguished as there are clans in the tribe, and it is the place occupied by the clans inside the encampment which has determined the orientation of these regions. Each region is defined by the totem of the clan to which it is assigned. Among the Zuñi, for example, the pueblo contains seven quarters; each of these is a group of clans which has had a unity: in all probability it was originally a single clan which was later subdivided. Now their space also contains seven quarters, and each of these seven quarters of the world is in intimate connection with a quarter of the pueblo, that is to say with a group of clans.[1] "Thus," says Cushing, "one division is thought to be in relation with the north, another represents the west, another the south," etc.[2] Each quarter of the pueblo has its characteristic colour, which symbolizes it; each region has its colour, which is exactly the same as that of the corresponding quarter. In the course of history the number of fundamental clans has varied; the number of the fundamental regions of space has varied with them. Thus the social organization has been the model for the spatial organization and a reproduction of it. It is thus even up to the distinction between right and left which, far from being inherent in the nature of man in general, is very probably the product of representations which are religious and therefore collective.[3]

Analogous proofs will be found presently in regard to the ideas of class, force, personality and efficacy. It is even possible to ask if the idea of contradiction does not also depend upon social conditions. What makes one tend to believe this is that the empire which the idea has exercised over human thought has varied with times and societies. To-day the principle of identity dominates scientific thought; but there are vast systems of representations which have played a considerable rôle in the history of ideas where it has frequently been set aside: these are the mythologies, from the grossest up to the most reasonable.[4] There, we are continually coming upon beings which

[1] See Durkheim and Mauss, *De quelques formes primitives de classification*, in *Année Sociologique*, VI, p. 34.

[2] *Zuñi Creation Myths*, in *13th Rep. of the Bureau of Amer. Ethnol.*, pp. 367 ff.

[3] See Hertz, *La prééminence de la main droite. Étude de polarité religieuse*, in the *Revue Philosophique*, Dec., 1909. On this same question of the relations between the representation of space and the form of the group, see the chapter in Ratzel, *Politische Geographie*, entitled *Der Raum in Geist der Völker*.

[4] We do not mean to say that mythological thought ignores it, but that it contradicts it more frequently and openly than scientific thought does. Inversely, we shall show that science cannot escape violating it, though it holds to it far more scrupulously than religion does. On this subject, as on many others, there are only differences of degree between science and religion; but if these differences should not be exaggerated, they must be noted, for they are significant.

have the most contradictory attributes simultaneously, who are at the same time one and many, material and spiritual, who can divide themselves up indefinitely without losing anything of their constitution; in mythology it is an axiom that the part is worth the whole. These variations through which the rules which seem to govern our present logic have passed prove that, far from being engraven through all eternity upon the mental constitution of men, they depend, at least in part, upon factors that are historical and consequently social. We do not know exactly what they are, but we may presume that they exist.[1]

This hypothesis once admitted, the problem of knowledge is posed in new terms.

Up to the present there have been only two doctrines in the field. For some, the categories cannot be derived from experience: they are logically prior to it and condition it. They are represented as so many simple and irreducible data, imminent in the human mind by virtue of its inborn constitution. For this reason they are said to be *a priori*. Others, however, hold that they are constructed and made up of pieces and bits, and that the individual is the artisan of this construction.[2]

But each solution raises grave difficulties.

Is the empirical thesis the one adopted? Then it is necessary to deprive the categories of all their characteristic properties. As a matter of fact they are distinguished from all other knowledge by their universality and necessity. They are the most general concepts which exist, because they are applicable to all that is real, and since they are not attached to any particular object they are independent of every particular subject; they constitute the common field where all minds meet. Further, they must meet there, for reason, which is nothing more than all the fundamental categories taken together, is invested with an authority which we could not set aside if we would. When we attempt to revolt against it, and to free ourselves from some

[1] This hypothesis has already been set forth by the founders of the *Völkerpsychologie*. It is especially remarked in a short article by Windelbrand entitled *Die Erkenntnisslehre unter dem Völkerpsychologischen Gesichtspunke*, in the *Zeitsch. f. Völkerpsychologie*, viii, pp. 166 ff. Cf. a note of Steinthal on the same subject, *ibid.*, pp. 178 ff.

[2] Even in the theory of Spencer, it is by individual experience that the categories are made. The only difference which there is in this regard between ordinary empiricism and evolutionary empiricism is that according to this latter, the results of individual experience are accumulated by heredity. But this accumulation adds nothing essential to them; no element enters into their composition which does not have its origin in the experience of the individual. According to this theory, also, the necessity with which the categories actually impose themselves upon us is the product of an illusion and a superstitious prejudice, strongly rooted in the organism, to be sure, but without foundation in the nature of things.

of these essential ideas, we meet with great resistances. They do not merely depend upon us, but they impose themselves upon us. Now empirical data present characteristics which are diametrically opposed to these. A sensation or an image always relies upon a determined object, or upon a collection of objects of the same sort, and expresses the momentary condition of a particular consciousness; it is essentially individual and subjective. We therefore have considerable liberty in dealing with the representations of such an origin. It is true that when our sensations are actual, they impose themselves upon us *in fact.* But *by right* we are free to conceive them otherwise than they really are, or to represent them to ourselves as occurring in a different order from that where they are really produced. In regard to them nothing is forced upon us except as considerations of another sort intervene. Thus we find that we have here two sorts of knowledge, which are like the two opposite poles of the intelligence. Under these conditions forcing reason back upon experience causes it to disappear, for it is equivalent to reducing the universality and necessity which characterize it to pure appearance, to an illusion which may be useful practically, but which corresponds to nothing in reality; consequently it is denying all objective reality to the logical life, whose regulation and organization is the function of the categories. Classical empiricism results in irrationalism; perhaps it would even be fitting to designate it by this latter name.

In spite of the sense ordinarily attached to the name, the apriorists have more respect for the facts. Since they do not admit it as a truth established by evidence that the categories are made up of the same elements as our sensual representations, they are not obliged to impoverish them systematically, to draw from them all their real content, and to reduce them to nothing more than verbal artifices. On the contrary, they leave them all their specific characteristics. The apriorists are the rationalists; they believe that the world has a logical aspect which the reason expresses excellently. But for all that, it is necessary for them to give the mind a certain power of transcending experience and of adding to that which is given to it directly; and of this singular power they give neither explanation nor justification. For it is no explanation to say that it is inherent in the nature of the human intellect. It is necessary to show whence we hold this surprising prerogative and how it comes that we can see certain relations in things which the examination of these things cannot reveal to us. Saying that only on this condition is experience itself possible changes the problem perhaps, but does not answer it. For the real question is to know how it comes that experience is not sufficient unto itself, but presupposes certain conditions which are exterior and prior to it, and how it happens that these conditions are realized at the moment and in the manner that is desirable. To answer these questions it has sometimes been assumed that above the reason of individuals there is a superior and perfect reason from which the others emanate and from which they get this marvellous power of theirs, by a sort of mystic participation: this is the divine reason. But this hypothesis has at least the one grave disadvantage of being deprived of all experimental control; thus it does not satisfy the conditions demanded of a scientific hypothesis. More than that, the categories of human thought are never fixed in any one definite form; they are made, unmade and remade incessantly; they change with places and times. On the other hand, the divine reason is immutable. How can this immutability give rise to this incessant variability?

Such are the two conceptions that have been pitted against each other for centuries; and if this debate seems to be eternal, it is because the arguments given are really about equivalent. If reason is only a form of individual experience, it no longer exists. On the other hand, if the powers which it has are recognized but not accounted for, it seems to be set outside the confines of nature and science. In the face of these two opposed objections the mind remains uncertain. But if the social origin of the categories is admitted, a new attitude becomes possible, which we believe will enable us to escape both of the opposed difficulties.

The fundamental proposition of the apriorist theory is that knowledge is made up of two sorts of elements, which cannot be reduced into one another, and which are like two distinct layers superimposed one upon the other.[1] Our hypothesis keeps this principle intact. In fact, that knowledge which is called empirical, the only knowledge of which the theorists of empiricism have made use in constructing the reason, is that which is brought into our minds by the direct action of objects. It is composed of individual states which are completely explained[2] by the psychical nature of the individual. If, on the other hand, the categories are, as we believe they are, essentially collective

[1] Perhaps some will be surprised that we do not define the apriorist theory by the hypothesis of innateness. But this conception really plays a secondary part in the doctrine. It is a simple way of stating the impossibility of reducing rational knowledge to empirical data. Saying that the former is innate is only a positive way of saying that it is not the product of experience, such as it is ordinarily conceived.

[2] At least, in so far as there are any representations which are individual and hence wholly empirical. But there are in fact probably none where the two elements are not found closely united.

representations, before all else, they should show the mental states of the group; they should depend upon the way in which this is founded and organized, upon its morphology, upon its religious, moral and economic institutions, etc. So between these two sorts of representations there is all the difference which exists between the individual and the social, and one can no more derive the second from the first than he can deduce society from the individual, the whole from the part, the complex from the simple.[1] Society is a reality *sui generis*; it has its own peculiar characteristics, which are not found elsewhere and which are not met with again in the same form in all the rest of the universe. The representations which express it have a wholly different contents from purely individual ones and we may rest assured in advance that the first add something to the second.

Even the manner in which the two are formed results in differentiating them. Collective representations are the result of an immense co-operation, which stretches out not only into space but into time as well; to make them, a multitude of minds have associated, united and combined their ideas and sentiments; for them, long generations have accumulated their experience and their knowledge. A special intellectual activity is therefore concentrated in them which is infinitely richer and complexer than that of the individual. From that one can understand how the reason has been able to go beyond the limits of empirical knowledge. It does not owe this to any vague mysterious virtue but simply to the fact that according to the well-known formula, man is double. There are two beings in him: an individual being which has its foundation in the organism and the circle of whose activities is therefore strictly limited, and a social being which represents the highest reality in the intellectual and moral order that we can know by observation—I mean society. This duality of our nature has as its consequence in the practical order, the irreducibility of a moral ideal to a utilitarian motive, and in the order of thought, the irreducibility of reason to individual experience. In so far as he belongs to society, the

[1] This irreducibility must not be taken in any absolute sense. We do not wish to say that there is nothing in the empirical representations which shows rational ones, nor that there is nothing in the individual which could be taken as a sign of social life. If experience were completely separated from all that is rational, reason could not operate upon it; in the same way, if the psychic nature of the individual were absolutely opposed to the social life, society would be impossible. A complete analysis of the categories should seek these germs of rationality even in the individual consciousness. We shall have occasion to come back to this point in our conclusion. All that we wish to establish here is that between these indistinct germs of reason and the reason properly so called, there is a difference comparable to that which separates the properties of the mineral elements out of which a living being is composed from the characteristic attributes of life after this has once been constituted.

individual transcends himself, both when he thinks and when he acts.

This same social character leads to an understanding of the origin of the necessity of the categories. It is said that an idea is necessary when it imposes itself upon the mind by some sort of virtue of its own, without being accompanied by any proof. It contains within it something which constrains the intelligence and which leads to its acceptance without preliminary examination. The apriorist postulates this singular quality, but does not account for it; for saying that the categories are necessary because they are indispensable to the functioning of the intellect is simply repeating that they are necessary. But if they really have the origin which we attribute to them, their ascendancy no longer has anything surprising in it. They represent the most general relations which exist between things; surpassing all our other ideas in extension, they dominate all the details of our intellectual life. If men did not agree upon these essential ideas at every moment, if they did not have the same conception of time, space, cause, number, etc., all contact between their minds would be impossible, and with that, all life together. Thus society could not abandon the categories to the free choice of the individual without abandoning itself. If it is to live there is not merely need of a satisfactory moral conformity, but also there is a minimum of logical conformity beyond which it cannot safely go. For this reason it uses all its authority upon its members to forestall such dissidences. Does a mind ostensibly free itself from these forms of thought? It is no longer considered a human mind in the full sense of the word, and is treated accordingly. That is why we feel that we are no longer completely free and that something resists, both within and outside ourselves, when we attempt to rid ourselves of these fundamental notions, even in our own conscience. Outside of us there is public opinion which judges us; but more than that, since society is also represented inside of us, it sets itself against these revolutionary fancies, even inside of ourselves; we have the feeling that we cannot abandon them if our whole thought is not to cease being really human. This seems to be the origin of the exceptional authority which is inherent in the reason and which makes us accept its suggestions with confidence. It is the very authority of society,[1] transferring itself to a certain manner of thought which is the indispensable condition of all common action. The necessity with which the categories are imposed upon us is not

[1] It has frequently been remarked that social disturbances result in multiplying mental disturbances. This is one more proof that logical discipline is a special aspect of social discipline. The first gives way as the second is weakened.

the effect of simple habits whose yoke we could easily throw off with a little effort ; nor is it a physical or metaphysical necessity, since the categories change in different places and times ; it is a special sort of moral necessity which is to the intellectual life what moral obligation is to the will.[1]

But if the categories originally only translate social states, does it not follow that they can be applied to the rest of nature only as metaphors ? If they were made merely to express social conditions, it seems as though they could not be extended to other realms except in this sense. Thus in so far as they aid us in thinking of the physical or biological world, they have only the value of artificial symbols, useful practically perhaps, but having no connection with reality. Thus we come back, by a different road, to nominalism and empiricism.

But when we interpret a sociological theory of knowledge in this way, we forget that even if society is a specific reality it is not an empire within an empire ; it is a part of nature, and indeed its highest representation. The social realm is a natural realm which differs from the others only by a greater complexity. Now it is impossible that nature should differ radically from itself in the one case and the other in regard to that which is most essential. The fundamental relations that exist between things—just that which it is the function of the categories to express—cannot be essentially dissimilar in the different realms. If, for reasons which we shall discuss later,[2] they are more clearly disengaged in the social world, it is nevertheless impossible that they should not be found elsewhere, though in less pronounced forms. Society makes them more manifest but it does not have a monopoly upon them. That is why ideas which have been elaborated on the model of social things can aid us in thinking of another department of nature. It is at least true that if these ideas play the rôle of symbols when they are thus turned aside from their original signification, they are well-founded symbols. If a sort of artificiality enters into them from the mere fact that

[1] There is an analogy between this logical necessity and moral obligation, but there is not an actual identity. To-day society treats criminals in a different fashion than subjects whose intelligence only is abnormal ; that is a proof that the authority attached to logical rules and that inherent in moral rules are not of the same nature, in spite of certain similarities. They are two species of the same class. It would be interesting to make a study on the nature and origin of this difference, which is probably not primitive, for during a long time, the public conscience has poorly distinguished between the deranged and the delinquent. We confine ourselves to signalizing this question. By this example, one may see the number of problems which are raised by the analysis of these notions which generally pass as being elementary and simple, but which are really of an extreme complexity.

[2] This question will be treated again in the conclusion of this work.

they are constructed concepts, it is an artificiality which follows nature very closely and which is constantly approaching it still more closely.[1] From the fact that the ideas of time, space, class, cause or personality are constructed out of social elements, it is not necessary to conclude that they are devoid of all objective value. On the contrary, their social origin rather leads to the belief that they are not without foundation in the nature of things.[2]

Thus renovated, the theory of knowledge seems destined to unite the opposing advantages of the two rival theories, without incurring their inconveniences. It keeps all the essential principles of the apriorists; but at the same time it is inspired by that positive spirit which the empiricists have striven to satisfy. It leaves the reason its specific power, but it accounts for it and does so without leaving the world of observable phenomena. It affirms the duality of our intellectual life, but it explains it, and with natural causes. The categories are no longer considered as primary and unanalysable facts, yet they keep a complexity which falsifies any analysis as ready as that with which the empiricists content themselves. They no longer appear as very simple notions which the first comer can very easily arrange from his own personal observations and which the popular imagination has unluckily complicated, but rather they appear as priceless instruments of thought which the human groups have laboriously forged through the centuries and where they have accumulated the best of their intellectual capital.[3] A complete section of the history of humanity is resumed therein. This is equivalent to saying that to succeed in understanding them and judging them, it is necessary to resort to other means

[1] The rationalism which is imminent in the sociological theory of knowledge is thus midway between the classical empiricism and apriorism. For the first, the categories are purely artificial constructions; for the second, on the contrary, they are given by nature; for us, they are in a sense a work of art, but of an art which imitates nature with a perfection capable of increasing unlimitedly.

[2] For example, that which is at the foundation of the category of time is the rhythm of social life; but if there is a rhythm in collective life, one may rest assured that there is another in the life of the individual, and more generally, in that of the universe. The first is merely more marked and apparent than the others. In the same way, we shall see that the notion of class is founded on that of the human group. But if men form natural groups, it can be assumed that among things there exists groups which are at once analogous and different. Classes and species are natural groups of things.

If it seems to many minds that a social origin cannot be attributed to the categories without depriving them of all speculative value, it is because society is still too frequently regarded as something that is not natural; hence it is concluded that the representations which express it express nothing in nature. But the conclusion is not worth more than the premise.

[3] This is how it is legitimate to compare the categories to tools; for on its side, a tool is material accumulated capital. There is a close relationship between the three ideas of tool, category and institution.

than those which have been in use up to the present. To know what these conceptions which we have not made ourselves are really made of, it does not suffice to interrogate our own consciousnesses; we must look outside of ourselves, it is history that we must observe, there is a whole science which must be formed, a complex science which can advance but slowly and by collective labour, and to which the present work brings some fragmentary contributions in the nature of an attempt. Without making these questions the direct object of our study, we shall profit by all the occasions which present themselves to us of catching at their very birth some at least of these ideas which, while being of religious origin, still remain at the foundation of the human intelligence.

BOOK I

PRELIMINARY QUESTIONS

CHAPTER I

DEFINITION OF RELIGIOUS PHENOMENA AND OF RELIGION[1]

IF we are going to look for the most primitive and simple religion which we can observe, it is necessary to begin by defining what is meant by a religion ; for without this, we would run the risk of giving the name to a system of ideas and practices which has nothing at all religious about it, or else of leaving to one side many religious facts, without perceiving their true nature. That this is not an imaginary danger, and that nothing is thus sacrificed to a vain formalism of method, is well shown by the fact that owing to his not having taken this precaution, a certain scholar to whom the science of comparative religions owes a great deal, Professor Frazer, has not been able to recognize the profoundly religious character of the beliefs and rites which will be studied below, where, according to our view, the initial germ of the religious life of humanity is to be found. So this is a prejudicial question, which must be treated before all others. It is not that we dream of arriving at once at the profound characteristics which really explain religion : these can be determined only at the end of our study. But that which is necessary and possible, is to indicate a certain number of external and easily recognizable signs, which will enable us to recognize religious phenomena wherever they are met with, and which will deter us from confounding them with others. We shall proceed to this preliminary operation at once.

But to attain the desired results, it is necessary to begin by freeing the mind of every preconceived idea. Men have been obliged to make for themselves a notion of what religion is, long before the science of religions started its methodical comparisons. The necessities of existence force all of us, believers and non-believers, to represent in some way these things in

[1] We have already attempted to define religious phenomena in a paper which was published in the *Année Sociologique* (Vol. II, pp. 1 ff.). The definition then given differs, as will be seen, from the one we give to-day. At the end of this chapter (p. 47, n. 1), we shall explain the reasons which have led us to these modifications, but which imply no essential change in the conception of the facts.

the midst of which we live, upon which we must pass judgment constantly, and which we must take into account in all our conduct. However, since these preconceived ideas are formed without any method, according to the circumstances and chances of life, they have no right to any credit whatsoever, and must be rigorously set aside in the examination which is to follow. It is not from our prejudices, passions or habits that we should demand the elements of the definition which we must have; it is from the reality itself which we are going to define.

Let us set ourselves before this reality. Leaving aside all conceptions of religion in general, let us consider the various religions in their concrete reality, and attempt to disengage that which they have in common; for religion cannot be defined except by the characteristics which are found wherever religion itself is found. In this comparison, then, we shall make use of all the religious systems which we can know, those of the present and those of the past, the most primitive and simple as well as the most recent and refined; for we have neither the right nor the logical means of excluding some and retaining others. For those who regard religion as only a natural manifestation of human activity, all religions, without any exception whatsoever, are instructive; for all, after their manner, express man, and thus can aid us in better understanding this aspect of our nature. Also, we have seen how far it is from being the best way of studying religion to consider by preference the forms which it presents among the most civilized peoples.[1]

But to aid the mind in freeing itself from these usual conceptions which, owing to their prestige, might prevent it from seeing things as they really are, it is fitting to examine some of the most current of the definitions in which these prejudices are commonly expressed, before taking up the question on our own account.

I

One idea which generally passes as characteristic of all that is religious, is that of the supernatural. By this is understood all sorts of things which surpass the limits of our knowledge; the supernatural is the world of the mysterious, of the unknowable, of the un-understandable. Thus religion would be a sort of speculation upon all that which evades science or distinct thought in general. "Religions diametrically opposed in their overt dogmas," said Spencer, "are perfectly at one in the tacit

[1] See above, p. 3. We shall say nothing more upon the necessity of these preliminary definitions nor upon the method to be followed to attain them. That is exposed in our *Règles de la Méthode sociologique*, pp. 43 ff. Cf. *Le Suicide*, pp. 1 ff. (Paris, F. Alcan).

conviction that the existence of the world, with all it contains and all which surrounds it, is a mystery calling for an explanation"; he thus makes them consist essentially in "the belief in the omnipresence of something which is inscrutable."[1] In the same manner, Max Müller sees in religion "a struggle to conceive the inconceivable, to utter the unutterable, a longing after the Infinite."[2]

It is certain that the sentiment of mystery has not been without a considerable importance in certain religions, notably in Christianity. It must also be said that the importance of this sentiment has varied remarkably at different moments in the history of Christianity. There are periods when this notion passes to an inferior place, and is even effaced. For example, for the Christians of the seventeenth century, dogma had nothing disturbing for the reason; faith reconciled itself easily with science and philosophy, and the thinkers, such as Pascal, who really felt that there is something profoundly obscure in things, were so little in harmony with their age that they remained misunderstood by their contemporaries.[3] It would appear somewhat hasty, therefore, to make an idea subject to parallel eclipses, the essential element of even the Christian religion.

In all events, it is certain that this idea does not appear until late in the history of religions; it is completely foreign, not only to those peoples who are called primitive, but also to all others who have not attained a considerable degree of intellectual culture. When we see them attribute extraordinary virtues to insignificant objects, and people the universe with singular principles, made up of the most diverse elements and endowed with a sort of ubiquity which is hardly representable, we are undoubtedly prone to find an air of mystery in these conceptions. It seems to us that these men would have been willing to resign themselves to these ideas, so disturbing for our modern reason, only because of their inability to find others which were more rational. But, as a matter of fact, these explanations which surprise us so much, appear to the primitive man as the simplest in the world. He does not regard them as a sort of *ultima ratio* to which the intellect resigns itself only in despair of others, but rather as the most obvious manner of representing and understanding what he sees about him. For him there is nothing strange in the fact that by a mere word or gesture one is able to command

[1] *First Principles*, p. 37.

[2] *Introduction to the Science of Religions*, p. 18. Cf. *Origin and Development of Religion*, p. 23.

[3] This same frame of mind is also found in the scholastic period, as is witnessed by the formula with which philosophy was defined at this time: *Fides quærens intellectum*.

the elements, retard or precipitate the motion of the stars, bring rain or cause it to cease, etc. The rites which he employs to assure the fertility of the soil or the fecundity of the animal species on which he is nourished do not appear more irrational to his eyes than the technical processes of which our agriculturists make use, for the same object, do to ours. The powers which he puts into play by these diverse means do not seem to him to have anything especially mysterious about them. Undoubtedly these forces are different from those which the modern scientist thinks of, and whose use he teaches us; they have a different way of acting, and do not allow themselves to be directed in the same manner; but for those who believe in them, they are no more unintelligible than are gravitation and electricity for the physicist of to-day. Moreover, we shall see, in the course of this work, that the idea of physical forces is very probably derived from that of religious forces; then there cannot exist between the two the abyss which separates the rational from the irrational. Even the fact that religious forces are frequently conceived under the form of spiritual beings or conscious wills, is no proof of their irrationality. The reason has no repugnance *a priori* to admitting that the so-called inanimate bodies should be directed by intelligences, just as the human body is, though contemporary science accommodates itself with difficulty to this hypothesis. When Leibniz proposed to conceive the external world as an immense society of minds, between which there were, and could be, only spiritual relations, he thought he was working as a rationalist, and saw nothing in this universal animism which could be offensive to the intellect.

Moreover, the idea of the supernatural, as we understand it, dates only from to-day; in fact, it presupposes the contrary idea, of which it is the negation; but this idea is not at all primitive. In order to say that certain things are supernatural, it is necessary to have the sentiment that a *natural order of things* exists, that is to say, that the phenomena of the universe are bound together by necessary relations, called laws. When this principle has once been admitted, all that is contrary to these laws must necessarily appear to be outside of nature, and consequently, of reason; for what is natural in this sense of the word, is also rational, these necessary relations only expressing the manner in which things are logically related. But this idea of universal determinism is of recent origin; even the greatest thinkers of classical antiquity never succeeded in becoming fully conscious of it. It is a conquest of the positive sciences; it is the postulate upon which they repose and which they have proved by their progress. Now as long as this was lacking or insufficiently established, the most marvellous events contained nothing which did not appear perfectly conceivable. So long as men did not know the immutability and the inflexibility of the order of things, and so long as they saw there the work of contingent wills, they found it natural that either these wills or others could modify them arbitrarily. That is why the miraculous interventions which the ancients attributed to their gods were not to their eyes miracles in the modern acceptation of the term. For them, they were beautiful, rare or terrible spectacles, or causes of surprise and marvel (*θαύματα, mirabilia, miracula*) ; but they never saw in them glimpses of a mysterious world into which the reason cannot penetrate.

We can understand this mentality the better since it has not yet completely disappeared from our midst. If the principle of determinism is solidly established to-day in the physical and natural sciences, it is only a century ago that it was first introduced into the social sciences, and its authority there is still contested. There are only a small number of minds which are strongly penetrated with this idea that societies are subject to natural laws and form a kingdom of nature. It follows that veritable miracles are believed to be possible there. It is admitted, for example, that a legislator can create an institution out of nothing by a mere injunction of its will, or transform one social system into another, just as the believers in so many religions have held that the divine will created the world out of nothing, or can arbitrarily transmute one thing into another. As far as social facts are concerned, we still have the mentality of primitives. However, if so many of our contemporaries still retain this antiquated conception for sociological affairs, it is not because the life of societies appears obscure and mysterious to them ; on the contrary, if they are so easily contented with these explanations, and if they are so obstinate in their illusions which experience constantly belies, it is because social events seem to them the clearest thing in the world ; it is because they have not yet realized their real obscurity ; it is because they have not yet recognized the necessity of resorting to the laborious methods of the natural sciences to gradually scatter the darkness. The same state of mind is found at the root of many religious beliefs which surprise us by their pseudo-simplicity. It is science and not religion which has taught men that things are complex and difficult to understand.

But the human mind, says Jevons,[1] has no need of a properly scientific culture to notice that determined sequences, or a constant order of succession, exist between facts, or to observe, on the

[1] *Introduction to the History of Religions*, pp. 15 ff.

other hand, that this order is frequently upset. It sometimes happens that the sun is suddenly eclipsed, that rain fails at the time when it is expected, that the moon is slow to reappear after its periodical disappearance, etc. Since these events are outside the ordinary course of affairs, they are attributed to extraordinary exceptional causes, that is to say, in fine, to extra-natural causes. It is under this form that the idea of the supernatural is born at the very outset of history, and from this moment, according to this author, religious thought finds itself provided with its proper subject.

But in the first place, the supernatural cannot be reduced to the unforeseen. The new is a part of nature just as well as its contrary. If we state that in general, phenomena succeed one another in a determined order, we observe equally well that this order is only approximative, that it is not always precisely the same, and that it has all kinds of exceptions. If we have ever so little experience, we are accustomed to seeing our expectations fail, and these deceptions return too often to appear extraordinary to us. A certain contingency is taught by experience just as well as a certain uniformity; then we have no reason for assigning the one to causes and forces entirely different from those upon which the other depends. In order to arrive at the idea of the supernatural, it is not enough, therefore, to be witnesses to unexpected events; it is also necessary that these be conceived as impossible, that is to say, irreconcilable with an order which, rightly or wrongly, appears to us to be implied in the nature of things. Now this idea of a necessary order has been constructed little by little by the positive sciences, and consequently the contrary notion could not have existed before them.

Also, in whatever manner men have represented the novelties and contingencies revealed by experience, there is nothing in these representations which could serve to characterize religion. For religious conceptions have as their object, before everything else, to express and explain, not that which is exceptional and abnormal in things, but, on the contrary, that which is constant and regular. Very frequently, the gods serve less to account for the monstrosities, fantasies and anomalies than for the regular march of the universe, for the movement of the stars, the rhythm of the seasons, the annual growth of vegetation, the perpetuation of species, etc. It is far from being true, then, that the notion of the religions coincides with that of the extraordinary or the unforeseen. Jevons replies that this conception of religious forces is not primitive. Men commenced by imagining them to account for disorders and accidents, and it was only afterwards that they began to utilize them in explaining the uniformities of nature.[1] But it is not clear what could have led men to attribute such manifestly contradictory functions to them. More than that, the hypothesis according to which sacred beings were at first restricted to the negative function of disturbers is quite arbitrary. In fact, we shall see that, even with the most simple religions we know, their essential task is to maintain, in a positive manner, the normal course of life.[2]

So the idea of mystery is not of primitive origin. It was not given to man; it is man who has forged it, with his own hands, along with the contrary idea. This is why it has a place only in a very small number of advanced religions. It is impossible to make it the characteristic mark of religious phenomena without excluding from the definition the majority of the facts to be defined.

II

Another idea by which the attempt to define religion is often made, is that of divinity. "Religion," says M. Réville,[3] "is the determination of human life by the sentiment of a bond uniting the human mind to that mysterious mind whose domination of the world and itself it recognizes, and to whom it delights in feeling itself united." It is certain that if the word divinity is taken in a precise and narrow sense, this definition leaves aside a multitude of obviously religious facts. The souls of the dead and the spirits of all ranks and classes with which the religious imagination of so many different peoples has populated nature, are always the object of rites and sometimes even of a regular cult; yet they are not gods in the proper sense of the term. But in order that the definition may embrace them, it is enough to substitute for the term "gods" the more comprehensive one of "spiritual beings." This is what Tylor does. "The first requisite in a systematic study of the religions of the lower races," he says, "is to lay down a rudimentary definition of religion. By requiring in this definition the belief in a supreme deity . . ., no doubt many tribes may be excluded from the category of religious. But such narrow definition has the fault of identifying religion rather with particular developments. . . . It seems best . . . simply to claim as a minimum definition of Religion, the belief in Spiritual Beings."[4] By spiritual beings must be understood conscious subjects gifted with powers superior to those possessed by common men; this qualification is found

[1] *Introduction to the History of Religions*, p. 23.
[2] See below, Bk. III, ch. ii.
[3] *Prolegomena to the History of Religions*, p. 25 (tr. by Squire).
[4] *Primitive Culture*, I, p. 424. (Fourth edition, 1903.)

in the souls of the dead, geniuses or demons as well as in divinities properly so-called. It is important, therefore, to give our attention at once to the particular conception of religion which is implied in this definition. The relations which we can have with beings of this sort are determined by the nature attributed to them. They are conscious beings; then we can act upon them only in the same way that we act upon consciousnesses in general, that is to say, by psychological processes, attempting to convince them or move them, either with the aid of words (invocations, prayers), or by offerings and sacrifices. And since the object of religion is to regulate our relations with these special beings, there can be no religion except where there are prayers, sacrifices, propitiatory rites, etc. Thus we have a very simple criterium which permits us to distinguish that which is religious from that which is not. It is to this criterium that Frazer,[1] and with him numerous ethnographers,[2] systematically makes reference.

But howsoever evident this definition may appear, thanks to the mental habits which we owe to our religious education, there are many facts to which it is not applicable, but which appertain to the field of religion nevertheless.

In the first place, there are great religions from which the idea of gods and spirits is absent, or at least, where it plays only a secondary and minor rôle. This is the case with Buddhism. Buddhism, says Burnouf, "sets itself in opposition to Brahmanism as a moral system without god and an atheism without Nature."[3] "As it recognizes not a god upon whom man depends," says Barth, "its doctrine is absolutely atheistic,"[4] while Oldenberg, in his turn, calls it "a faith without a god."[5] In fact, all that is essential to Buddhism is found in the four propositions which the faithful call the four noble truths.[6] The first states the existence of suffering as the accompaniment to the perpetual change of things; the second shows desire to be the cause of suffering; the third makes the suppression of desire the only means of suppressing sorrow; the fourth enumerates the three stages through which one must pass to attain this suppression: they are uprightness, meditation, and finally wisdom, the full

[1] Beginning with the first edition of the *Golden Bough*, I, pp. 30–32.

[2] Notably Spencer and Gillen and even Preuss, who gives the name magic to all non-individualized religious forces.

[3] Burnouf, *Introduction à l'histoire du bouddhisme indien*, sec. edit., p. 464. The last word of the text shows that Buddhism does not even admit the existence of an eternal Nature.

[4] Barth, *The Religions of India*, p. 110 (tr. by Wood).

[5] Oldenberg, *Buddha*, p. 53 (tr. by Hoey).

[6] Oldenberg, *ibid.*, pp. 313 ff. Cf. Kern, *Histoire du bouddhisme dans l'Inde*, I, pp. 389 ff.

possession of the doctrine. These three stages once traversed, one arrives at the end of the road, at the deliverance, at salvation by the Nirvâna.

Now in none of these principles is there question of a divinity. The Buddhist is not interested in knowing whence came the world in which he lives and suffers; he takes it as a given fact,[1] and his whole concern is to escape it. On the other hand, in this work of salvation, he can count only upon himself; "he has no god to thank, as he had previously no god to invoke during his struggle."[2] Instead of praying, in the ordinary sense of the term, instead of turning towards a superior being and imploring his assistance, he relies upon himself and meditates. This is not saying "that he absolutely denies the existence of the beings called Indra, Agni and Varuna;[3] but he believes that he owes them nothing and that he has nothing to do with them," for their power can only extend over the goods of this world, which are without value for him. Then he is an atheist, in the sense that he does not concern himself with the question whether gods exist or not. Besides, even if they should exist, and with whatever powers they might be armed, the saint or the emancipated man regards himself superior to them; for that which causes the dignity of beings is not the extent of the action they exercise over things, but merely the degree of their advancement upon the road of salvation.[4]

It is true that Buddha, at least in some divisions of the Buddhist Church, has sometimes been considered as a sort of god. He has his temples; he is the object of a cult, which, by the way, is a very simple one, for it is reduced essentially to the offering of flowers and the adoration of consecrated relics or images. It is scarcely more than a comemorative cult. But more than that, this divinization of Buddha, granting that the term is exact, is peculiar to the form known as Northern Buddhism. "The Buddhist of the South," says Kern, "and the less advanced of the Northern Buddhists can be said, according to data known to-day, to speak of their founder as if he were a man."[5] Of course, they attribute extraordinary powers to Buddha, which are superior to those possessed by ordinary mortals; but it was a very ancient belief in India, and one that

[1] Oldenberg, p. 250; Barth, p. 110.

[2] Oldenberg, p. 314.

[3] Barth, p. 109. In the same way, Burnouf says, "I have the profound conviction that if Çâkya had not found about him a Pantheon already peopled with the gods just named, he would have felt no need of inventing them" (*Introd. à l'hist. du bouddhisme indien*, p. 119).

[4] Burnouf, *op. cit.*, p. 117.

[5] Kern, *op. cit.*, I, p. 289.

is also very general in a host of different religions, that a great saint is endowed with exceptional virtues ;[1] yet a saint is not a god, any more than a priest or magician is, in spite of the superhuman faculties frequently attributed to them. On the other hand, according to the most authorized scholars, all this theism and the complicated mythology which generally accompanies it, are only derived and deviated forms of Buddhism. At first, Buddha was only regarded as " the wisest of men."[2] Burnouf says " the conception of a Buddha who is something more than a man arrived at the highest stage of holiness, is outside the circle of ideas which form the foundation of the simple Sûtras " ;[3] and the same author adds elsewhere that " his humanity is a fact so incontestably recognized by all that the myth-makers, to whom miracles cost so little, have never even had the idea of making a god out of him since his death."[4] So we may well ask if he has ever really divested himself completely of all human character, and if we have a right to make him into a god completely ;[5] in any case, it would have to be a god of a very particular character and one whose rôle in no way resembles that of other divine personalities. For a god is before all else a living being, with whom man should reckon, and upon whom he may count ; but Buddha is dead, he has entered into the Nirvâna, and he can no longer influence the march of human events.[6]

Finally, whatever one may think of the divinity of Buddha, it remains a fact that this is a conception wholly outside the essential part of Buddhism. Buddhism consists primarily in the idea of salvation, and salvation supposes only that one know the good doctrine and practise it. To be sure, this could never have been known if Buddha had not come to reveal it ; but when this revelation had once been made, the work of Buddha was accomplished. From that moment he ceased to be a factor necessary to the religious life. The practice of the four holy truths would be possible, even if the memory of him who revealed

[1] " The belief, universally admitted in India, that great holiness is necessarily accompanied by supernatural faculties, is the only support which he (Çâkya) should find in spirits " (Burnouf, p. 119).

[2] Burnouf, p. 120.

[3] *Ibid.*, p. 107. [4] *Ibid.*, p. 302.

[5] This is what Kern expresses in the following terms : " In certain regards, he is a man ; in certain others, he is not a man ; in others, he is neither the one nor the other " (*op. cit.*, I, p. 290).

[6] " The conception " " was foreign to Buddhism " " that the divine Head of the Community is not absent from his people, but that he dwells powerfully in their midst as their lord and king, so that all cultus is nothing else but the expression of this continuing living fellowship. Buddha has entered into Nirvâna ; if his believers desired to invoke him, he could not hear them " (Oldenberg, p. 369).

them were completely obliterated.[1] It is quite another matter with Christianity, which is inconceivable without the ever-present idea of Christ and his ever-practised cult; for it is by the ever-living Christ, sacrificed each day, that the community of believers continues to communicate with the supreme source of the spiritual life.[2]

All that precedes can be applied equally well to another great religion of India, Jaïnism. The two doctrines have nearly the same conception of the world and of life. " Like the Buddhists," says Barth, " the Jaïnas are atheists. They admit of no creator; the world is eternal; they explicitly deny the possibility of a perfect being from the beginning. The Jina became perfect; he was not always so."

Just as the Buddhists in the north, the Jaïnists, or at least certain of them, have come back to a sort of deism; in the inscriptions of Dekhan there is mention of a *Jinapati*, a sort of supreme Jina, who is called the primary creator; but such language, says the same author, is " in contradiction to the most explicit declarations extracted from their most authorized writings."[3]

Moreover, if this indifference for the divine is developed to such a point in Buddhism and Jaïnism, it is because its germ existed already in the Brahmanism from which the two were derived. In certain of its forms at least, Brahmic speculation ended in " a frankly materialistic and atheistic interpretation of the universe."[4] In time, the numerous divinities which the people of India had originally learned to adore, came to merge themselves into a sort of principal deity, impersonal and abstract, the essence of all that exists. This supreme reality, which no longer has anything of a divine personality about it, is contained within man himself, or rather, man is but one with it, for nothing exists apart from it. To find it, and unite himself to it, one does not have to search some external support outside himself; it is enough to concentrate upon himself and meditate. " If in Buddhism," says Oldenberg, " the proud attempt be made to conceive a deliverance in which man himself delivers himself, to create a faith without a god, it is Brahmanical speculation which has prepared the way for this thought. It thrusts back the idea of a god step by step; the forms of the old gods have

[1] " Buddhist doctrine might be in all its essentials what it actually is, even if the idea of Buddha remained completely foreign to it " (Oldenberg, p. 322).—And whatever is said of the historic Buddha can be applied equally well to the mythological Buddhas.

[2] For the same idea, see Max Müller, *Natural Religion*, pp. 103 ff. and 190.

[3] *Op. cit.*, p. 146.

[4] Barth, in *Encyclopédie des sciences religieuses*, VI, p. 548.

faded away, and besides the Brahma, which is enthroned in its everlasting quietude, highly exalted above the destinies of the human world, there is left remaining, as the sole really active person in the great work of deliverance, man himself."[1] Here, then, we find a considerable portion of religious evolution which has consisted in the progressive recoil of the idea of a spiritual being from that of a deity. Here are great religions where invocations, propitiations, sacrifices and prayers properly so-called are far from holding a preponderating place, and which consequently do not present that distinctive sign by which some claim to recognize those manifestations which are properly called religious.

But even within deistic religions there are many rites which are completely independent of all idea of gods or spiritual beings. In the first place, there are a multitude of interdictions. For example, the Bible orders that a woman live isolated during a determined period each month;[2] a similar isolation is obligatory during the lying-in at child-birth;[3] it is forbidden to hitch an ass and a horse together, or to wear a garment in which the hemp is mixed with flax;[4] but it is impossible to see the part which belief in Jahveh can have played in these interdictions, for he is wholly absent from all the relations thus forbidden, and could not be interested in them. As much can be said for the majority of the dietetic regulations. These prohibitions are not peculiar to the Hebrews, but they are found under diverse forms, but with substantially the same character, in innumerable religions.

It is true that these rites are purely negative, but they do not cease being religious for that. Also there are others which demand active and positive services of the faithful, but which are nevertheless of the same nature. They work by themselves, and their efficacy depends upon no divine power; they mechanically produce the effects which are the reason for their existence. They do not consist either in prayers or offerings addressed to a being upon whose goodwill the expected result depends; this result is obtained by the automatic operation of the ritual. Such is notably the case with the sacrifice of the Vedic religion. "The sacrifice exercises a direct influence upon the celestial phenomena," says Bergaigne;[5] it is all-powerful of itself, and without any divine influence. It is this, for example, which broke open the doors of the cavern where the dawn was imprisoned and which made the light of day burst forth.[6] In the

[1] Oldenberg, *op. cit.*, p. 53.
[2] I Sam. xxi., 6.
[3] Levit. xii.
[4] Deut. xxii., 10 and 11.
[5] *La religion védique*, I, p. 122.
[6] *Ibid.*, p. 133.

same way there are special hymns which, by their direct action, made the waters of heaven fall upon the earth, and *even in spite of the gods.*[1] The practice of certain austerities has the same power. More than that, " the sacrifice is so fully the origin of things *par excellence*, that they have attributed to it not only the origin of man, but even that of the gods. . . . Such a conception may well appear strange. It is explained, however, as being one of the ultimate consequences of the idea of the omnipotence of sacrifice."[2] Thus, in the entire first part of his work, M. Bergaigne speaks only of sacrifices, where divinities play no rôle whatsoever.

Nor is this fact peculiar to the Vedic religion, but is, on the contrary, quite general. In every cult there are practices which act by themselves, by a virtue which is their own, without the intervention of any god between the individual who practises the rite and the end sought after. When, in the so-called Feast of the Tabernacles, the Jew set the air in motion by shaking willow branches in a certain rhythm, it was to cause the wind to rise and the rain to fall; and it was believed that the desired phenomenon would result automatically from the rite, provided it were correctly performed.[3] This is the explanation of the fundamental importance laid by nearly all cults upon the material portion of the ceremonies. This religious formalism—very probably the first form of legal formalism—comes from the fact that since the formula to be pronounced and the movements to be made contain within themselves the source of their efficacy, they would lose it if they did not conform absolutely to the type consecrated by success.

Thus there are rites without gods, and even rites from which gods are derived. All religious powers do not emanate from divine personalities, and there are relations of cult which have other objects than uniting man to a deity. Religion is more than the idea of gods or spirits, and consequently cannot be defined exclusively in relation to these latter.

[1] " No text," says Bergaigne, " bears better witness to the consciousness of a magic action by man upon the waters of heaven than verse x, 32, 7, where this belief is expressed in general terms, applicable to an actual man, as well as to his real or mythological ancestors : ' The ignorant man has questioned the wise ; instructed by the wise, he acts, and here is the profit of his instruction : he obtains the flowing of streams ' " (p. 137).

[2] *Ibid.*, p. 139.

[3] Examples will also be found in Hubert, art. *Magia* in the *Dictionnaire des Antiquités*, VI, p. 1509.

III

These definitions set aside, let us set ourselves before the problem.

First of all, let us remark that in all these formulæ it is the nature of religion as a whole that they seek to express. They proceed as if it were a sort of indivisible entity, while, as a matter of fact, it is made up of parts; it is a more or less complex system of myths, dogmas, rites and ceremonies. Now a whole cannot be defined except in relation to its parts. It will be more methodical, then, to try to characterize the various elementary phenomena of which all religions are made up, before we attack the system produced by their union. This method is imposed still more forcibly by the fact that there are religious phenomena which belong to no determined religion. Such are those phenomena which constitute the matter of folklore. In general, they are the debris of passed religions, inorganized survivals; but there are some which have been formed spontaneously under the influence of local causes. In our European countries Christianity has forced itself to absorb and assimilate them; it has given them a Christian colouring. Nevertheless, there are many which have persisted up until a recent date, or which still exist with a relative autonomy: celebrations of May Day, the summer solstice or the carnival, beliefs relative to genii, local demons, etc., are cases in point. If the religious character of these facts is now diminishing, their religious importance is nevertheless so great that they have enabled Mannhardt and his school to revive the science of religions. A definition which did not take account of them would not cover all that is religious.

Religious phenomena are naturally arranged in two fundamental categories: beliefs and rites. The first are states of opinion, and consist in representations; the second are determined modes of action. Between these two classes of facts there is all the difference which separates thought from action.

The rites can be defined and distinguished from other human practices, moral practices, for example, only by the special nature of their object. A moral rule prescribes certain manners of acting to us, just as a rite does, but which are addressed to a different class of objects. So it is the object of the rite which must be characterized, if we are to characterize the rite itself. Now it is in the beliefs that the special nature of this object is expressed. It is possible to define the rite only after we have defined the belief.

All known religious beliefs, whether simple or complex, present one common characteristic: they presuppose a classification of all the things, real and ideal, of which men think, into two classes or opposed groups, generally designated by two distinct terms which are translated well enough by the words *profane* and *sacred* (*profane, sacré*). This division of the world into two domains, the one containing all that is sacred, the other all that is profane, is the distinctive trait of religious thought; the beliefs, myths, dogmas and legends are either representations or systems of representations which express the nature of sacred things, the virtues and powers which are attributed to them, or their relations with each other and with profane things. But by sacred things one must not understand simply those personal beings which are called gods or spirits; a rock, a tree, a spring, a pebble, a piece of wood, a house, in a word, anything can be sacred. A rite can have this character; in fact, the rite does not exist which does not have it to a certain degree. There are words, expressions and formulæ which can be pronounced only by the mouths of consecrated persons; there are gestures and movements which everybody cannot perform. If the Vedic sacrifice has had such an efficacy that, according to mythology, it was the creator of the gods, and not merely a means of winning their favour, it is because it possessed a virtue comparable to that of the most sacred beings. The circle of sacred objects cannot be determined, then, once for all. Its extent varies infinitely, according to the different religions. That is how Buddhism is a religion: in default of gods, it admits the existence of sacred things, namely, the four noble truths and the practices derived from them.[1]

Up to the present we have confined ourselves to enumerating a certain number of sacred things as examples: we must now show by what general characteristics they are to be distinguished from profane things.

One might be tempted, first of all, to define them by the place they are generally assigned in the hierarchy of things. They are naturally considered superior in dignity and power to profane things, and particularly to man, when he is only a man and has nothing sacred about him. One thinks of himself as occupying an inferior and dependent position in relation to them; and surely this conception is not without some truth. Only there is nothing in it which is really characteristic of the sacred. It is not enough that one thing be subordinated to another for the second to be sacred in regard to the first. Slaves are inferior to their masters,

[1] Not to mention the sage and the saint who practise these truths and who for that reason are sacred.

subjects to their king, soldiers to their leaders, the miser to his gold, the man ambitious for power to the hands which keep it from him; but if it is sometimes said of a man that he makes a religion of those beings or things whose eminent value and superiority to himself he thus recognizes, it is clear that in any case the word is taken in a metaphorical sense, and that there is nothing in these relations which is really religious.[1]

On the other hand, it must not be lost to view that there are sacred things of every degree, and that there are some in relation to which a man feels himself relatively at his ease. An amulet has a sacred character, yet the respect which it inspires is nothing exceptional. Even before his gods, a man is not always in such a marked state of inferiority; for it very frequently happens that he exercises a veritable physical constraint upon them to obtain what he desires. He beats the fetich with which he is not contented, but only to reconcile himself with it again, if in the end it shows itself more docile to the wishes of its adorer.[2] To have rain, he throws stones into the spring or sacred lake where the god of rain is thought to reside; he believes that by this means he forces him to come out and show himself.[3] Moreover, if it is true that man depends upon his gods, this dependence is reciprocal. The gods also have need of man; without offerings and sacrifices they would die. We shall even have occasion to show that this dependence of the gods upon their worshippers is maintained even in the most idealistic religions.

But if a purely hierarchic distinction is a criterium at once too general and too imprecise, there is nothing left with which to characterize the sacred in its relation to the profane except their heterogeneity. However, this heterogeneity is sufficient to characterize this classification of things and to distinguish it from all others, because it is very particular: *it is absolute.* In all the history of human thought there exists no other example of two categories of things so profoundly differentiated or so radically opposed to one another. The traditional opposition of good and bad is nothing beside this; for the good and the bad are only two opposed species of the same class, namely morals, just as sickness and health are two different aspects of the same order of facts, life, while the sacred and the profane have always and everywhere been conceived by the human mind as two distinct classes, as two worlds between which there is nothing in

[1] This is not saying that these relations cannot take a religious character. But they do not do so necessarily.

[2] Schultze, *Fetichismus*, p. 129.

[3] Examples of these usages will be found in Frazer, *Golden Bough*, 2 edit., I, pp. 81 ff.

common. The forces which play in one are not simply those which are met with in the other, but a little stronger ; they are of a different sort. In different religions, this opposition has been conceived in different ways. Here, to separate these two sorts of things, it has seemed sufficient to localize them in different parts of the physical universe ; there, the first have been put into an ideal and transcendental world, while the material world is left in full possession of the others. But howsoever much the forms of the contrast may vary,[1] the fact of the contrast is universal.

This is not equivalent to saying that a being can never pass from one of these worlds into the other : but the manner in which this passage is effected, when it does take place, puts into relief the essential duality of the two kingdoms. In fact, it implies a veritable metamorphosis. This is notably demonstrated by the initiation rites, such as they are practised by a multitude of peoples. This initiation is a long series of ceremonies with the object of introducing the young man into the religious life : for the first time, he leaves the purely profane world where he passed his first infancy, and enters into the world of sacred things. Now this change of state is thought of, not as a simple and regular development of pre-existent germs, but as a transformation *totius substantiae*—of the whole being. It is said that at this moment the young man dies, that the person that he was ceases to exist, and that another is instantly substituted for it. He is re-born under a new form. Appropriate ceremonies are felt to bring about this death and re-birth, which are not understood in a merely symbolic sense, but are taken literally.[2] Does this not prove that between the profane being which he was and the religious being which he becomes, there is a break of continuity ?

This heterogeneity is even so complete that it frequently degenerates into a veritable antagonism. The two worlds are not only conceived of as separate, but as even hostile and jealous rivals of each other. Since men cannot fully belong to one except

[1] The conception according to which the profane is opposed to the sacred, just as the irrational is to the rational, or the intelligible is to the mysterious, is only one of the forms under which this opposition is expressed. Science being once constituted, it has taken a profane character, especially in the eyes of the Christian religions ; from that it appears as though it could not be applied to sacred things.

[2] See Frazer, *On Some Ceremonies of the Central Australian Tribes* in *Australian Association for the Advancement of Science*, 1901, pp. 313 ff. This conception is also of an extreme generality. In India, the simple participation in the sacrificial act has the same effects ; the sacrificer, by the mere act of entering within the circle of sacred things, changes his personality. (See, Hubert and Mauss, *Essai sur le Sacrifice* in the *Année Sociologique*, II, p. 101.)

on condition of leaving the other completely, they are exhorted to withdraw themselves completely from the profane world, in order to lead an exclusively religious life. Hence comes the monasticism which is artificially organized outside of and apart from the natural environment in which the ordinary man leads the life of this world, in a different one, closed to the first, and nearly its contrary. Hence comes the mystic asceticism whose object is to root out from man all the attachment for the profane world that remains in him. From that come all the forms of religious suicide, the logical working-out of this asceticism ; for the only manner of fully escaping the profane life is, after all, to forsake all life.

The opposition of these two classes manifests itself outwardly with a visible sign by which we can easily recognize this very special classification, wherever it exists. Since the idea of the sacred is always and everywhere separated from the idea of the profane in the thought of men, and since we picture a sort of logical chasm between the two, the mind irresistibly refuses to allow the two corresponding things to be confounded, or even to be merely put in contact with each other ; for such a promiscuity, or even too direct a contiguity, would contradict too violently the dissociation of these ideas in the mind. The sacred thing is *par excellence* that which the profane should not touch, and cannot touch with impunity. To be sure, this interdiction cannot go so far as to make all communication between the two worlds impossible ; for if the profane could in no way enter into relations with the sacred, this latter could be good for nothing. But, in addition to the fact that this establishment of relations is always a delicate operation in itself, demanding great precautions and a more or less complicated initiation,[1] it is quite impossible, unless the profane is to lose its specific characteristics and become sacred after a fashion and to a certain degree itself. The two classes cannot even approach each other and keep their own nature at the same time.

Thus we arrive at the first criterium of religious beliefs. Undoubtedly there are secondary species within these two fundamental classes which, in their turn, are more or less incompatible with each other.[2] But the real characteristic of religious phenomena is that they always suppose a bipartite division of the whole universe, known and knowable, into two classes which embrace all that exists, but which radically exclude each other. Sacred

[1] See what was said of the initiation above, p. 39.

[2] We shall point out below how, for example, certain species of sacred things exist, between which there is an incompatibility as all-exclusive as that between the sacred and the profane (Bk. III, ch. v, § 4).

things are those which the interdictions protect and isolate; profane things, those to which these interdictions are applied and which must remain at a distance from the first. Religious beliefs are the representations which express the nature of sacred things and the relations which they sustain, either with each other or with profane things. Finally, rites are the rules of conduct which prescribe how a man should comport himself in the presence of these sacred objects.

When a certain number of sacred things sustain relations of co-ordination or subordination with each other in such a way as to form a system having a certain unity, but which is not comprised within any other system of the same sort, the totality of these beliefs and their corresponding rites constitutes a religion. From this definition it is seen that a religion is not necessarily contained within one sole and single idea, and does not proceed from one unique principle which, though varying according to the circumstances under which it is applied, is nevertheless at bottom always the same: it is rather a whole made up of distinct and relatively individualized parts. Each homogeneous group of sacred things, or even each sacred thing of some importance, constitutes a centre of organization about which gravitate a group of beliefs and rites, or a particular cult; there is no religion, howsoever unified it may be, which does not recognize a plurality of sacred things. Even Christianity, at least in its Catholic form, admits, in addition to the divine personality which, incidentally, is triple as well as one, the Virgin, angels, saints, souls of the dead, etc. Thus a religion cannot be reduced to one single cult generally, but rather consists in a system of cults, each endowed with a certain autonomy. Also, this autonomy is variable. Sometimes they are arranged in a hierarchy, and subordinated to some predominating cult, into which they are finally absorbed; but sometimes, also, they are merely rearranged and united. The religion which we are going to study will furnish us with an example of just this latter sort of organization.

At the same time we find the explanation of how there can be groups of religious phenomena which do not belong to any special religion; it is because they have not been, or are no longer, a part of any religious system. If, for some special reason, one of the cults of which we just spoke happens to be maintained while the group of which it was a part disappears, it survives only in a disintegrated condition. That is what has happened to many agrarian cults which have survived themselves as folk-lore. In certain cases, it is not even a cult, but a simple ceremony or particular rite which persists in this way.[1]

[1] This is the case with certain marriage and funeral rites, for example.

Although this definition is only preliminary, it permits us to see in what terms the problem which necessarily dominates the science of religions should be stated. When we believed that sacred beings could be distinguished from others merely by the greater intensity of the powers attributed to them, the question of how men came to imagine them was sufficiently simple: it was enough to demand which forces had, because of their exceptional energy, been able to strike the human imagination forcefully enough to inspire religious sentiments. But if, as we have sought to establish, sacred things differ in nature from profane things, if they have a wholly different essence, then the problem is more complex. For we must first of all ask what has been able to lead men to see in the world two heterogeneous and incompatible worlds, though nothing in sensible experience seems able to suggest the idea of so radical a duality to them.

IV

However, this definition is not yet complete, for it is equally applicable to two sorts of facts which, while being related to each other, must be distinguished nevertheless: these are magic and religion.

Magic, too, is made up of beliefs and rites. Like religion, it has its myths and its dogmas; only they are more elementary, undoubtedly because, seeking technical and utilitarian ends, it does not waste its time in pure speculation. It has its ceremonies, sacrifices, lustrations, prayers, chants and dances as well. The beings which the magician invokes and the forces which he throws in play are not merely of the same nature as the forces and beings to which religion addresses itself; very frequently, they are identically the same. Thus, even with the most inferior societies, the souls of the dead are essentially sacred things, and the object of religious rites. But at the same time, they play a considerable rôle in magic. In Australia [1] as well as in Melanesia,[2] in Greece as well as among the Christian peoples,[3] the souls of the dead, their bones and their hair, are among the intermediaries used the most frequently by the magician. Demons are also a common instrument for magic action. Now these demons are also beings surrounded with interdictions; they too are separated and live in a world apart, so that it is frequently difficult to

[1] See Spencer and Gillen, *Native Tribes of Central Australia*, pp. 534 ff.; *Northern Tribes of Central Australia*, p. 463; Howitt, *Native Tribes of S.E. Australia*, pp. 359–361.

[2] See Codrington, *The Melanesians*, ch. xii.

[3] See Hubert, art. *Magia* in *Dictionnaire des Antiquités*.

distinguish them from the gods properly so-called.[1] Moreover, in Christianity itself, is not the devil a fallen god, or even leaving aside all question of his origin, does he not have a religious character from the mere fact that the hell of which he has charge is something indispensable to the Christian religion? There are even some regular and official deities who are invoked by the magician. Sometimes these are the gods of a foreign people; for example, Greek magicians called upon Egyptian, Assyrian or Jewish gods. Sometimes, they are even national gods: Hecate and Diana were the object of a magic cult; the Virgin, Christ and the saints have been utilized in the same way by Christian magicians.[2]

Then will it be necessary to say that magic is hardly distinguishable from religion; that magic is full of religion just as religion is full of magic, and consequently that it is impossible to separate them and to define the one without the other? It is difficult to sustain this thesis, because of the marked repugnance of religion for magic, and in return, the hostility of the second towards the first. Magic takes a sort of professional pleasure in profaning holy things;[3] in its rites, it performs the contrary of the religious ceremony.[4] On its side, religion, when it has not condemned and prohibited magic rites, has always looked upon them with disfavour. As Hubert and Mauss have remarked, there is something thoroughly anti-religious in the doings of the magician.[5] Whatever relations there may be between these two sorts of institutions, it is difficult to imagine their not being opposed somewhere; and it is still more necessary for us to find where they are differentiated, as we plan to limit our researches to religion, and to stop at the point where magic commences.

Here is how a line of demarcation can be traced between these two domains.

The really religious beliefs are always common to a determined group, which makes profession of adhering to them and of practising the rites connected with them. They are not merely received individually by all the members of this group; they are something belonging to the group, and they make its unity. The individuals which compose it feel themselves united to each other by the simple fact that they have a common faith. A

[1] For example, in Melanesia, the *tindalo* is a spirit, now religious, now magic (Codrington, pp. 125 ff., 194 ff.).

[2] See Hubert and Mauss, *Théorie Générale de la Magie*, in *Année Sociologique*, vol. VII, pp. 83–84.

[3] For example, the host is profaned in the black mass.

[4] One turns his back to the altar, or goes around the altar commencing by the left instead of by the right.

[5] *Loc. cit.*, p. 19.

society whose members are united by the fact that they think in the same way in regard to the sacred world and its relations with the profane world, and by the fact that they translate these common ideas into common practices, is what is called a Church. In all history, we do not find a single religion without a Church. Sometimes the Church is strictly national, sometimes it passes the frontiers; sometimes it embraces an entire people (Rome, Athens, the Hebrews), sometimes it embraces only a part of them (the Christian societies since the advent of Protestantism); sometimes it is directed by a corps of priests, sometimes it is almost completely devoid of any official directing body.[1] But wherever we observe the religious life, we find that it has a definite group as its foundation. Even the so-called private cults, such as the domestic cult or the cult of a corporation, satisfy this condition; for they are always celebrated by a group, the family or the corporation. Moreover, even these particular religions are ordinarily only special forms of a more general religion which embraces all;[2] these restricted Churches are in reality only chapels of a vaster Church which, by reason of this very extent, merits this name still more.[3]

It is quite another matter with magic. To be sure, the belief in magic is always more or less general; it is very frequently diffused in large masses of the population, and there are even peoples where it has as many adherents as the real religion. But it does not result in binding together those who adhere to it, nor in uniting them into a group leading a common life. *There is no Church of magic.* Between the magician and the individuals who consult him, as between these individuals themselves, there are no lasting bonds which make them members of the same moral community, comparable to that formed by the believers in the same god or the observers of the same cult. The magician has a clientele and not a Church, and it is very possible that his clients have no other relations between each other, or even do not know each other; even the relations which they have with him are generally accidental and transient; they are just like those of a sick man with his physician. The official and public character

[1] Undoubtedly it is rare that a ceremony does not have some director at the moment when it is celebrated; even in the most crudely organized societies, there are generally certain men whom the importance of their social position points out to exercise a directing influence over the religious life (for example, the chiefs of the local groups of certain Australian societies). But this attribution of functions is still very uncertain.

[2] At Athens, the gods to whom the domestic cult was addressed were only specialized forms of the gods of the city (Ζεύς κτήσιος, Ζεύς ἑρκεῖος). In the same way, in the Middle Ages, the patrons of the guilds were saints of the calendar.

[3] For the name Church is ordinarily applied only to a group whose common beliefs refer to a circle of more special affairs.

with which he is sometimes invested changes nothing in this situation; the fact that he works openly does not unite him more regularly or more durably to those who have recourse to his services.

It is true that in certain cases, magicians form societies among themselves: it happens that they assemble more or less periodically to celebrate certain rites in common; it is well known what a place these assemblies of witches hold in European folk-lore. But it is to be remarked that these associations are in no way indispensable to the working of the magic; they are even rare and rather exceptional. The magician has no need of uniting himself to his fellows to practise his art. More frequently, he is a recluse; in general, far from seeking society, he flees it. "Even in regard to his colleagues, he always keeps his personal independence."[1] Religion, on the other hand, is inseparable from the idea of a Church. From this point of view, there is an essential difference between magic and religion. But what is especially important is that when these societies of magic are formed, they do not include all the adherents to magic, but only the magicians; the laymen, if they may be so called, that is to say, those for whose profit the rites are celebrated, in fine, those who represent the worshippers in the regular cults, are excluded. Now the magician is for magic what the priest is for religion, but a college of priests is not a Church, any more than a religious congregation which should devote itself to some particular saint in the shadow of a cloister, would be a particular cult. A Church is not a fraternity of priests; it is a moral community formed by all the believers in a single faith, laymen as well as priests. But magic lacks any such community.[2]

But if the idea of a Church is made to enter into the definition of religion, does that not exclude the private religions which the individual establishes for himself and celebrates by himself? There is scarcely a society where these are not found. Every Ojibway, as we shall see below, has his own personal *manitou*, which he chooses himself and to which he renders special religious services; the Melanesian of the Banks Islands has his *tamaniu*;[3] the Roman, his *genius*;[4] the Christian, his patron saint and guardian angel, etc. By definition all these cults seem to be

[1] Hubert and Mauss, *loc. cit.*, p. 18.

[2] Robertson Smith has already pointed out that magic is opposed to religion, as the individual to the social (*The Religion of the Semites*, 2 edit., pp. 264–265). Also, in thus distinguishing magic from religion, we do not mean to establish a break of continuity between them. The frontiers between the two domains are frequently uncertain.

[3] Codrington, *Trans. and Proc. Roy. Soc. of Victoria*, XVI, p. 136.

[4] Negrioli, *Dei Genii presso i Romani*.

independent of all idea of the group. Not only are these individual religions very frequent in history, but nowadays many are asking if they are not destined to be the pre-eminent form of the religious life, and if the day will not come when there will be no other cult than that which each man will freely perform within himself.[1]

But if we leave these speculations in regard to the future aside for the moment, and confine ourselves to religions such as they are at present or have been in the past, it becomes clearly evident that these individual cults are not distinct and autonomous religious systems, but merely aspects of the common religion of the whole Church, of which the individuals are members. The patron saint of the Christian is chosen from the official list of saints recognized by the Catholic Church ; there are even canonical rules prescribing how each Catholic should perform this private cult. In the same way, the idea that each man necessarily has a protecting genius is found, under different forms, at the basis of a great number of American religions, as well as of the Roman religion (to cite only these two examples) ; for, as will be seen later, it is very closely connected with the idea of the soul, and this idea of the soul is not one of those which can be left entirely to individual choice. In a word, it is the Church of which he is a member which teaches the individual what these personal gods are, what their function is, how he should enter into relations with them and how he should honour them. When a methodical analysis is made of the doctrines of any Church whatsoever, sooner or later we come upon those concerning private cults. So these are not two religions of different types, and turned in opposite directions ; both are made up of the same ideas and the same principles, here applied to circumstances which are of interest to the group as a whole, there to the life of the individual. This solidarity is even so close that among certain peoples,[2] the ceremonies by which the faithful first enter into communication with their protecting geniuses are mixed with rites whose public character is incontestable, namely the rites of initiation.[3]

[1] This is the conclusion reached by Spencer in his *Ecclesiastical Institutions* (ch. xvi), and by Sabatier in his *Outlines of a Philosophy of Religion, based on Psychology and History* (tr. by Seed), and by all the school to which he belongs.

[2] Notably among numerous Indian tribes of North America.

[3] This statement of fact does not touch the question whether exterior and public religion is not merely the development of an interior and personal religion which was the primitive fact, or whether, on the contrary, the second is not the projection of the first into individual consciences. The problem will be directly attacked below (Bk. II, ch. v, § 2, cf. the same book, ch. vi and vii, § 1). For the moment, we confine ourselves to remarking that the individual cult is presented to the observer as an element of, and something dependent upon, the collective cult.

There still remain those contemporary aspirations towards a religion which would consist entirely in internal and subjective states, and which would be constructed freely by each of us. But howsoever real these aspirations may be, they cannot affect our definition, for this is to be applied only to facts already realized, and not to uncertain possibilities. One can define religions such as they are, or such as they have been, but not such as they more or less vaguely tend to become. It is possible that this religious individualism is destined to be realized in facts; but before we can say just how far this may be the case, we must first know what religion is, of what elements it is made up, from what causes it results, and what function it fulfils—all questions whose solution cannot be foreseen before the threshold of our study has been passed. It is only at the close of this study that we can attempt to anticipate the future.

Thus we arrive at the following definition: *A religion is a unified system of beliefs and practices relative to sacred things, that is to say, things set apart and forbidden—beliefs and practices which unite into one single moral community called a Church, all those who adhere to them.* The second element which thus finds a place in our definition is no less essential than the first; for by showing that the idea of religion is inseparable from that of the Church, it makes it clear that religion should be an eminently collective thing.[1]

[1] It is by this that our present definition is connected to the one we have already proposed in the *Année Sociologique*. In this other work, we defined religious beliefs exclusively by their obligatory character; but, as we shall show, this obligation evidently comes from the fact that these beliefs are the possession of a group which imposes them upon its members. The two definitions are thus in a large part the same. If we have thought it best to propose a new one, it is because the first was too formal, and neglected the contents of the religious representations too much. It will be seen, in the discussions which follow, how important it is to put this characteristic into evidence at once. Moreover, if their imperative character is really a distinctive trait of religious beliefs, it allows of an infinite number of degrees; consequently there are even cases where it is not easily perceptible. Hence come difficulties and embarrassments which are avoided by substituting for this criterium the one we now employ.

CHAPTER II

LEADING CONCEPTIONS OF THE ELEMENTARY RELIGION

I.—*Animism*

ARMED with this definition, we are now able to set out in search of this elementary religion which we propose to study.

Even the crudest religions with which history and ethnology make us acquainted are already of a complexity which corresponds badly with the idea sometimes held of primitive mentality. One finds there not only a confused system of beliefs and rites, but also such a plurality of different principles, and such a richness of essential notions, that it seems impossible to see in them anything but the late product of a rather long evolution. Hence it has been concluded that to discover the truly original form of the religious life, it is necessary to descend by analysis beyond these observable religions, to resolve them into their common and fundamental elements, and then to seek among these latter some one from which the others were derived.

To the problem thus stated, two contrary solutions have been given.

There is no religious system, ancient or recent, where one does not meet, under different forms, two religions, as it were, side by side, which, though being united closely and mutually penetrating each other, do not cease, nevertheless, to be distinct. The one addresses itself to the phenomena of nature, either the great cosmic forces, such as winds, rivers, stars or the sky, etc., or else the objects of various sorts which cover the surface of the earth, such as plants, animals, rocks, etc.; for this reason it has been given the name of *naturism*. The other has spiritual beings as its object, spirits, souls, geniuses, demons, divinities properly so-called, animated and conscious agents like man, but distinguished from him, nevertheless, by the nature of their powers and especially by the peculiar characteristic that they do not affect the senses in the same way: ordinarily they are not visible to human eyes. This religion of spirits is called *animism*. Now, to explain the universal co-existence of these two sorts of cults, two contradictory theories have been proposed. For some, animism is the primitive religion, of which naturism is only a secondary and derived form. For the others, on the contrary, it is the nature cult which was the point of departure for religious evolution; the cult of spirits is only a peculiar case of that.

These two theories are, up to the present, the only ones by which the attempt has been made to explain rationally[1] the origins of religious thought. Thus the capital problem raised by the history of religions is generally reduced to asking which of these two solutions should be chosen, or whether it is not better to combine them, and in that case, what place must be given to each of the two elements.[2] Even those scholars who do not admit either of these hypotheses in their systematic form, do not refuse to retain certain propositions upon which they rest.[3] Thus we have a certain number of theories already made, which must be submitted to criticism before we take up the study of the facts for ourselves. It will be better understood how indispensable it is to attempt a new one, when we have seen the insufficiency of these traditional conceptions.

I

It is Tylor who formed the animist theory in its essential outlines.[4] Spencer, who took it up after him, did not reproduce it without introducing certain modifications.[5] But in general the questions are posed by each in the same terms, and the solutions accepted are, with a single exception, identically the same. Therefore we can unite these two doctrines in the exposition which follows, if we mark, at the proper moment, the place where the two diverge from one another.

[1] We thus leave aside here those theories which, in whole or in part, make use of super-experimental data. This is the case with the theory which Andrew Lang exposed in his book, *The Making of Religion*, and which Father Schmidt has taken up again, with variations of detail, in a series of articles on *The Origin of the Idea of God* (*Anthropos*, 1908, 1909). Lang does not set animism definitely aside, but in the last analysis, he admits a sense or intuition of the divine directly. Also, if we do not consider it necessary to expose and discuss this conception in the present chapter, we do not intend to pass it over in silence; we shall come to it again below, when we shall ourselves explain the facts upon which it is founded (Bk. II, ch. ix, § 4).

[2] This is the case, for example, of Fustel de Coulanges who accepts the two conceptions together (*The Ancient City*, Bk. I and Bk. III, ch. ii).

[3] This is the case with Jevons, who criticizes the animism taught by Tylor, but accepts his theories on the origin of the idea of the soul and the anthropomorphic instinct of man. Inversely, Usener, in his *Götternamen*, rejects certain hypotheses of Max Müller which will be described below, but admits the principal postulates of naturism.

[4] *Primitive Culture*, chs. xi–xviii.

[5] *Principles of Sociology*, Parts I and VI.

In order to find the elementary form of the religious life in these animistic beliefs and practices, three *desiderata* must be satisfied: first, since according to this hypothesis, the idea of the soul is the cardinal idea of religion, it must be shown how this is formed without taking any of its elements from an anterior religion; secondly, it must be made clear how souls become the object of a cult and are transformed into spirits; and thirdly and finally, since the cult of these spirits is not all of any religion, it remains to be explained how the cult of nature is derived from it.

According to this theory, the idea of the soul was first suggested to men by the badly understood spectacle of the double life they ordinarily lead, on the one hand, when awake, on the other, when asleep. In fact, for the savage,[1] the mental representations which he has while awake and those of his dreams are said to be of the same value: he objectifies the second like the first, that is to say, that he sees in them the images of external objects whose appearance they more or less accurately reproduce. So when he dreams that he has visited a distant country, he believes that he really was there. But he could not have gone there, unless two beings exist within him: the one, his body, which has remained lying on the ground and which he finds in the same position on awakening; the other, during this time, has travelled through space. Similarly, if he seems to talk with one of his companions who he knows was really at a distance, he concludes that the other also is composed of two beings: one which sleeps at a distance, and another which has come to manifest himself by means of the dream. From these repeated experiences, he little by little arrives at the idea that each of us has a double, another self, which in determined conditions has the power of leaving the organism where it resides and of going roaming at a distance.

Of course, this double reproduces all the essential traits of the perceptible being which serves it as external covering; but at the same time it is distinguished from this by many characteristics. It is more active, since it can cover vast distances in an instant. It is more malleable and plastic; for, to leave the body, it must pass out by its apertures, especially the mouth and nose. It is represented as made of matter, undoubtedly, but of a matter much more subtile and etherial than any which we

[1] This is the word used by Tylor. It has the inconvenience of seeming to imply that men, in the proper sense of the term, existed before there was a civilization. However, there is no proper term for expressing the idea; that of primitive, which we prefer to use, lacking a better, is, as we have said, far from satisfactory.

know empirically. This double is the soul. In fact, it cannot be doubted that in numerous societies the soul has been conceived in the image of the body; it is believed that it reproduces even the accidental deformities such as those resulting from wounds or mutilations. Certain Australians, after having killed their enemy, cut off his right thumb, so that his soul, deprived of its thumb also, cannot throw a javelin and revenge itself. But while it resembles the body, it has, at the same time, something half spiritual about it. They say that "it is the finer or more aeriform part of the body," that "it has no flesh nor bone nor sinew"; that when one wishes to take hold of it, he feels nothing; that it is "like a purified body."[1]

Also, other facts of experience which affect the mind in the same way naturally group themselves around this fundamental fact taught by the dream: fainting, apoplexy, catalepsy, ecstasy, in a word, all cases of temporary insensibility. In fact, they all are explained very well by the hypothesis that the principle of life and feeling is able to leave the body momentarily. Also, it is natural that this principle should be confounded with the double, since the absence of the double during sleep daily has the effect of suspending thought and life. Thus diverse observations seem to agree mutually and to confirm the idea of the constitutional duality of man.[2]

But the soul is not a spirit. It is attached to a body which it can leave only by exception; in so far as it is nothing more than that, it is not the object of any cult. The spirit, on the other hand, though generally having some special thing as its residence, can go away at will, and a man can enter into relations with it only by observing ritual precautions. The soul can become a spirit, then, only by transforming itself: the simple application of these preceding ideas to the fact of death produced this metamorphosis quite naturally. For a rudimentary intelligence, in fact, death is not distinguished from a long fainting swoon or a prolonged sleep; it has all their aspects. Thus it seems that it too consists in a separation of the soul and the body, analogous to that produced every night; but as in such cases, the body is not reanimated, the idea is formed of a separation without an assignable limit of time. When the body is once destroyed—and funeral rites have the object of hastening this destruction—the separation is taken as final. Hence come spirits detached from any organism and left free in space. As

[1] Tylor, *op. cit.*, I, pp. 455 f.

[2] See Spencer, *Principles of Sociology*, I, pp. 143 ff., and Tylor, *op. cit.*, I, pp. 434 ff., 445 ff.

their number augments with time, a population of souls forms around the living population. These souls of men have the needs and passions of men; they seek to concern themselves with the life of their companions of yesterday, either to aid them or to injure them, according to the sentiments which they have kept towards them. According to the circumstances, their nature makes them either very precious auxiliaries or very redoubtable adversaries. Owing to their extreme fluidity, they can even enter into the body, and cause all sorts of disorders there, or else increase its vitality. Thus comes the habit of attributing to them all those events of life which vary slightly from the ordinary: there are very few of these for which they cannot account. Thus they constitute a sort of ever-ready supply of causes which never leaves one at a loss when in search of explanations. Does a man appear inspired, does he speak with energy, is it as though he were lifted outside himself and above the ordinary level of men? It is because a good spirit is in him and animates him. Is he overtaken by an attack or seized by madness? It is because an evil spirit has entered into him and brought him all this trouble. There are no maladies which cannot be assigned to some influence of this sort. Thus the power of souls is increased by all that men attribute to them, and in the end men find themselves the prisoners of this imaginary world of which they are, however, the authors and the models. They fall into dependence upon these spiritual forces which they have created with their own hands and in their own image. For if souls are the givers of health and sickness, of goods and evils to this extent, it is wise to conciliate their favour or appease them when they are irritated; hence come the offerings, prayers, sacrifices, in a word, all the apparatus of religious observances.[1]

Here is the soul transformed. From a simple vital principle animating the body of a man, it has become a spirit, a good or evil genius, or even a deity, according to the importance of the effects with which it is charged. But since it is death which brought about this apotheosis, it is to the dead, to the souls of ancestors, that the first cult known to humanity was addressed. Thus the first rites were funeral rites; the first sacrifices were food offerings destined to satisfy the needs of the departed; the first altars were tombs.[2]

But since these spirits were of human origin, they interested themselves only in the life of men and were thought to act only upon human events. It is still to be explained how other spirits

[1] Tylor, II, pp. 113 ff.

[2] Tylor, I, pp. 481 ff.

were imagined to account for the other phenomena of the universe and how the cult of nature was subsequently formed beside that of the ancestors.

For Tylor, this extension of animism was due to the particular mentality of the primitive who, like an infant, cannot distinguish the animate and the inanimate. Since the first beings of which the child commences to have an idea are men, that is, himself and those around him, it is upon this model of human nature that he tends to think of everything. The toys with which he plays, or the objects of every sort which affect his senses, he regards as living beings like himself. Now the primitive thinks like a child. Consequently, he also is inclined to endow all things, even inanimate ones, with a nature analogous to his own. Then if, for the reasons exposed above, he once arrives at the idea that man is a body animated by a spirit, he must necessarily attribute a duality of this sort and souls like his own even to inert bodies themselves. Yet the sphere of action of the two could not be the same. The souls of men have a direct influence only upon the world of men: they have a marked preference for the human organism, even when death has given them their liberty. On the other hand, the souls of things reside especially in these things, and are regarded as the productive causes of all that passes there. The first account for health and sickness, skilfulness or unskilfulness, etc.; by the second are explained especially the phenomena of the physical world, the movement of water-courses or the stars, the germination of plants, the reproduction of animals, etc. Thus the first philosophy of man, which is at the basis of the ancestor-cult, is completed by a philosophy of the world.

In regard to these cosmic spirits, man finds himself in a state of dependence still more evident than that in regard to the wandering doubles of his ancestors. For he could have only ideal and imaginary relations with the latter, but he depends upon things in reality; to live, he has need of their concurrence; he then believes that he has an equal need of the spirits which appear to animate these things and to determine their diverse manifestations. He implores their assistance, he solicits them with offerings and prayers, and the religion of man is thus completed in a religion of nature.

Herbert Spencer objects against this explanation that the hypothesis upon which it rests is contradicted by the facts. It is held, he says, that there is a time when men do not realize the differences which separate the animate from the inanimate. Now, as one advances in the animal scale, he sees the ability to make this distinction develop. The superior animals do not confound an object which moves of itself and whose movements are adapted to certain ends, with those which are mechanically moved from without. "Amusing herself with a mouse she has caught, the cat, if it remains long stationary, touches it with her paw to make it run. Obviously the thought is that a living thing disturbed will try to escape."[1] Even the primitive men could not have an intelligence inferior to that of the animals which preceded them in evolution; then it cannot be for lack of discernment that they passed from the cult of ancestors to the cult of things.

According to Spencer, who upon this point, but upon this point only, differs from Tylor, this passage was certainly due to a confusion, but to one of a different sort. It was, in a large part at least, the result of numerous errors due to language. In many inferior societies it is a very common custom to give to each individual, either at his birth or later, the name of some animal, plant, star or natural object. But as a consequence of the extreme imprecision of his language, it is very difficult for a primitive to distinguish a metaphor from the reality. He soon lost sight of the fact that these names were only figures, and taking them literally, he ended by believing that an ancestor named "Tiger" or "Lion" was really a tiger or a lion. Then the cult of which the ancestor was the object up to that time, was changed over to the animal with which he was thereafter confounded; and as the same substitution went on for the plants, the stars and all the natural phenomena, the religion of nature took the place of the old religion of the dead. Besides this fundamental confusion, Spencer signalizes others which aided the action of the first from time to time. For example, the animals which frequent the surroundings of the tombs or houses of men have been taken for their reincarnated souls, and adored under this title;[2] or again, the mountain which tradition made the cradle of the race was finally taken for the ancestor of the race; it was thought that men were descended from it because their ancestors appeared coming from it, and it was consequently treated as an ancestor itself.[3] But according to the statement of Spencer, these accessory causes had only a secondary influence; that which principally determined the institution of naturism was "the literal interpretation of metaphorical names."[4]

We had to mention this theory to have our exposition of animism complete; but it is too inadequate for the facts, and too universally abandoned to-day to demand that we stop any longer for it. In order to explain a fact as general as the religion

[1] *Principles of Sociology*, I, p. 126.
[2] *Ibid.*, pp. 322 ff. [3] *Ibid.*, pp. 366–367. [4] *Ibid.*, p. 346. Cf. p. 384.

of nature by an illusion, it would be necessary that the illusion invoked should have causes of an equal generality. Now even if misunderstandings, such as those of which Spencer gives some rare illustrations, could explain the transformation of the cult of ancestors into that of nature, it is not clear why this should be produced with a sort of universality. No psychical mechanism necessitated it. It is true that because of its ambiguity, the word might lead to an equivocation ; but on the other hand, all the personal souvenirs left by the ancestor in the memories of men should oppose this confusion. Why should the tradition which represented the ancestor such as he really was, that is to say, as a man who led the life of a man, everywhere give way before the prestige of a word ? Likewise, one should have a little difficulty in admitting that men were born of a mountain or a star, of an animal or a plant ; the idea of a similar exception to the ordinary conceptions of generation could not fail to raise active resistance. Thus, it is far from true that the error found a road all prepared before it, but rather, all sorts of reasons should have kept it from being accepted. It is difficult to understand how, in spite of all these obstacles, it could have triumphed so generally.

II

The theory of Tylor, whose authority is always great, still remains. His hypotheses on the dream and the origin of the ideas of the soul and of spirits are still classic ; it is necessary, therefore, to test their value.

First of all, it should be recognized that the theorists of animism have rendered an important service to the science of religions, and even to the general history of ideas, by submitting the idea of the soul to historical analysis. Instead of following so many philosophers and making it a simple and immediate object of consciousness, they have much more correctly viewed it as a complex whole, a product of history and mythology. It cannot be doubted that it is something essentially religious in its nature, origin and functions. It is from religion that the philosophers received it ; it is impossible to understand the form in which it is represented by the thinkers of antiquity, if one does not take into account the mythical elements which served in its formation.

But if Tylor has had the merit of raising this problem, the solution he gives raises grave difficulties.

First of all, there are reservations to be made in regard to the very principle which is at the basis of this theory. It is taken for granted that the soul is entirely distinct from the body, that it is its double, and that within it or outside of it, it normally lives its own autonomous life. Now we shall see[1] that this conception is not that of the primitive, or at least, that it only expresses one aspect of his idea of the soul. For him, the soul, though being under certain conditions independent of the organism which it animates, confounds itself with this latter to such an extent that it cannot be radically separated from it: there are organs which are not only its appointed seat, but also its outward form and material manifestation. The notion is therefore more complex than the doctrine supposes, and it is doubtful consequently whether the experiences mentioned are sufficient to account for it; for even if they did enable us to understand how men have come to believe themselves double, they cannot explain how this duality does not exclude, but rather, implies a deeper unity and an intimate interpenetration of the two beings thus differentiated.

But let us admit that the idea of the soul can be reduced to the idea of a double, and then see how this latter came to be formed. It could not have been suggested to men except by the experience of dreams. That they might understand how they could see places more or less distant during sleep, while their bodies remained lying on the ground, it would seem that they were led to conceive of themselves as two beings: on the one hand, the body, and on the other, a second self, able to leave the organism in which it lives and to roam about in space. But if this hypothesis of a double is to be able to impose itself upon men with a sort of necessity, it should be the only one possible, or at least, the most economical one. Now as a matter of fact, there are more simple ones which, it would seem, might have occurred to the mind just as naturally. For example, why should the sleeper not imagine that while asleep he is able to see things at a distance? To imagine such a power would demand less expense to the imagination than the construction of this complex notion of a double, made of some etherial, semi-invisible substance, and of which direct experience offers no example. But even supposing that certain dreams rather naturally suggest the animistic explanation, there are certainly many others which are absolutely incompatible with it. Often our dreams are concerned with passed events; we see again the things which we saw or did yesterday or the day before or even during our youth, etc.; dreams of this sort are frequent and hold a rather considerable place in our nocturnal life. But the idea of a double cannot account for them. Even if the double

[1] See below, Bk. II, ch. viii.

can go from one point to another in space, it is not clear how it could possibly go back and forth in time. Howsoever rudimentary his intelligence may be, how could a man on awakening believe that he had really been assisting at or taking part in events which he knows passed long before? How could he imagine that during his sleep he lived a life which he knows has long since gone by? It would be much more natural that he should regard these renewed images as merely what they really are, that is, as souvenirs like those which he has during the day, but ones of a special intensity.

Moreover, in the scenes of which we are the actors and witnesses while we sleep, it constantly happens that one of our contemporaries has a rôle as well as ourselves: we think we see and hear him in the same place where we see ourselves. According to the animists, the primitive would explain this by imagining that his double was visited by or met with those of certain of his companions. But it would be enough that on awakening he question them, to find that their experiences do not coincide with his. During this same time, they too have had dreams, but wholly different ones. They have not seen themselves participating in the same scene; they believe that they have visited wholly different places. Since such contradictions should be the rule in these cases, why should they not lead men to believe that there had probably been an error, that they had merely imagined it, that they had been duped by illusions? This blind credulity which is attributed to the primitive is really too simple. It is not true that he must objectify all his sensations. He cannot live long without perceiving that even when awake his senses sometimes deceive him. Then why should he believe them more infallible at night than during the day? Thus we find that there are many reasons opposing the theory that he takes his dreams for the reality and interprets them by means of a double of himself.

But more than that, even if every dream were well explained by the hypothesis of a double, and could not be explained otherwise, it would remain a question why men have attempted to explain them. Dreams undoubtedly constitute the matter of a possible problem. But we pass by problems every day which we do not raise, and of which we have no suspicion until some circumstance makes us feel the necessity of raising them. Even when the taste for pure speculation is aroused, reflection is far from raising all the problems to which it could eventually apply itself; only those attract it which present a particular interest. Especially, when it is a question of facts which always take place in the same manner, habit easily numbs curiosity, and we do not even dream of questioning them. To shake off this torpor, it is necessary that practical exigencies, or at least a very pressing theoretical interest, stimulate our attention and turn it in this direction. That is why, at every moment of history, there have been so many things that we have not tried to understand, without even being conscious of our renunciation. Up until very recent times, it was believed that the sun was only a few feet in diameter. There is something incomprehensible in the statement that a luminous disc of such slight dimensions could illuminate the world: yet for centuries men never thought of resolving this contradiction. The fact of heredity has been known for a long time, but it is very recently that the attempt has been made to formulate its theory. Certain beliefs were even admitted which rendered it wholly unintelligible: thus in many Australian societies of which we shall have occasion to speak, the child is not physiologically the offspring of its parents.[1] This intellectual laziness is necessarily at its maximum among the primitive peoples. These weak beings, who have so much trouble in maintaining life against all the forces which assail it, have no means for supporting any luxury in the way of speculation. They do not reflect except when they are driven to it. Now it is difficult to see what could have led them to make dreams the theme of their meditations. What does the dream amount to in our lives? How little is the place it holds, especially because of the very vague impressions it leaves in the memory, and of the rapidity with which it is effaced from remembrance, and consequently, how surprising it is that a man of so rudimentary an intelligence should have expended such efforts to find its explanation! Of the two existences which he successively leads, that of the day and that of the night, it is the first which should interest him the most. Is it not strange that the second should have so captivated his attention that he made it the basis of a whole system of complicated ideas destined to have so profound an influence upon his thought and conduct?

Thus all tends to show that, in spite of the credit it still enjoys, the animistic theory of the soul must be revised. It is true that to-day the primitive attributes his dreams, or at least certain of them, to displacements of his double. But that does not say that the dream actually furnished the materials out of which the idea of the double or the soul was first constructed; it might have been applied afterwards to the phenomena of dreams, ecstasy and possession, without having been derived from them. It is very frequent that, after it has been formed, an idea is

[1] See Spencer and Gillen, *The Native Tribes of Central Australia*, pp. 123–127; Strehlow, *Die Aranda- und Loritja-Stämme in Zentral Australien*, II, pp. 52 ff.

employed to co-ordinate or illuminate—with a light frequently more apparent than real—certain facts with which it had no relation at first, and which would never have suggested it themselves. God and the immortality of the soul are frequently proven to-day by showing that these beliefs are implied in the fundamental principles of morality; as a matter of fact, they have quite another origin. The history of religious thought could furnish numerous examples of these retrospective justifications, which can teach us nothing of the way in which the ideas were formed, nor of the elements out of which they are composed.

It is also probable that the primitive distinguishes between his dreams, and does not interpret them all in the same way. In our European societies the still numerous persons for whom sleep is a sort of magico-religious state in which the mind, being partially relieved of the body, has a sharpness of vision which it does not enjoy during waking moments, do not go to the point of considering all their dreams as so many mystic intuitions: on the contrary, along with everybody else, they see in the majority of their dreams only profane conditions, vain plays of images, or simple hallucinations. It might be supposed that the primitive should make analogous distinctions. Codrington says distinctly that the Melanesians do not attribute all their dreams indiscriminately to the wanderings of their souls, but merely those which strike their imagination forcibly:[1] undoubtedly by that should be understood those in which the sleeper imagines himself in relations with religious beings, good or evil geniuses, souls of the dead, etc. Similarly, the Dieri in Australia sharply distinguish ordinary dreams from those nocturnal visions in which some deceased friend or relative shows himself to them. In the first, they see a simple fantasy of their imagination; they attribute the second to the action of an evil spirit.[2] All the facts which Howitt mentions as examples to show how the Australian attributes to the soul the power of leaving the body, have an equally mystic character. The sleeper believes himself transported into the land of the dead or else he converses with a dead companion.[3] These dreams are frequent among the primitives.[4] It is probably

[1] *The Melanesians*, pp. 249–250.

[2] Howitt, *The Native Tribes of South-Eastern Australia*, p. 358.

[3] *Ibid.*, pp. 434–442.

[4] Of the negroes of southern Guinea, Tylor says that "their sleeping hours are characterized by almost as much intercourse with the dead as their waking are with the living" (*Primitive Culture*, I, p. 443). In regard to these peoples, the same author cites this remark of an observer: "*All their dreams* are construed into visits from the spirits of their deceased friends" (*ibid.*, p. 443). This statement is certainly exaggerated; but it is one more proof of the frequency of

upon these facts that the theory is based. To account for them, it is admitted that the souls of the dead come back to the living during their sleep. This theory was the more readily accepted because no fact of experience could invalidate it. But these dreams were possible only where the ideas of spirits, souls and a land of the dead were already existent, that is to say, where religious evolution was relatively advanced. Thus, far from having been able to furnish to religion the fundamental notion upon which it rests, they suppose a previous religious system, upon which they depended.[1]

III

We now arrive at that which constitutes the very heart of the doctrine.

Wherever this idea of a double may come from, it is not sufficient, according to the avowal of the animists themselves, to explain the formation of the cult of the ancestors which they would make the initial type of all religions. If this double is to become the object of a cult, it must cease to be a simple reproduction of the individual, and must acquire the characteristics necessary to put it in the rank of sacred beings. It is death, they say, which performs this transformation. But whence comes the virtue which they attribute to this? Even were the analogy of sleep and death sufficient to make one believe that the soul survives the body (and there are reservations to be made on this point), why does this soul, by the mere fact that it is now detached from the organism, so completely change its nature? If it was only a profane thing, a wandering vital principle, during life, how does it become a sacred thing all at once, and

mystic dreams among the primitives. The etymology which Strehlow proposes for the Arunta word *altjirerama*, which means " to dream," also tends to confirm this theory. This word is composed of *altjira*, which Strehlow translates by " god " and *rama*, which means " see." Thus a dream would be the moment when a man is in relations with sacred beings (*Die Aranda- und Loritja-Stämme*, I, p. 2).

[1] Andrew Lang, who also refuses to admit that the idea of the soul was suggested to men by their dream experiences, believes that he can derive it from other empirical data: these are the data of spiritualism (telepathy, distance-seeing, etc.). We do not consider it necessary to discuss the theory such as it has been exposed in his book *The Making of Religion*. It reposes upon the hypothesis that spiritualism is a fact of constant observation, and that distance-seeing is a real faculty of men, or at least of certain men, but it is well known how much this theory is scientifically contested. What is still more contestable is that the facts of spiritualism are apparent enough and of a sufficient frequency to have been able to serve as the basis for all the religious beliefs and practices which are connected with souls and spirits. The examination of these questions would carry us too far from what is the object of our study. It is still less necessary to engage ourselves in this examination, since the theory of Lang remains open to many of the objections which we shall address to that of Tylor in the paragraphs which follow.

the object of religious sentiments ? Death adds nothing essential to it, except a greater liberty of movement. Being no longer attached to a special residence, from now on, it can do at any time what it formerly did only by night ; but the action of which it is capable is always of the same sort. Then why have the living considered this uprooted and vagabond double of their former companion as anything more than an equal ? It was a fellow-creature, whose approach might be inconvenient ; it was not a divinity.[1]

It seems as though death ought to have the effect of weakening vital energies, instead of strengthening them. It is, in fact, a very common belief in the inferior societies that the soul participates actively in the life of the body. If the body is wounded, it is wounded itself and in a corresponding place. Then it should grow old along with the body. In fact, there are peoples who do not render funeral honours to men arrived at senility ; they are treated as if their souls also had become senile.[2] It even happens that they regularly put to death, before they arrive at old age, certain privileged persons, such as kings or priests, who are supposed to be the possessors of powerful spirits whose protection the community wishes to keep. They thus seek to keep the spirit from being affected by the physical decadence of its momentary keepers ; with this end in view, they take it from the organism where it resides before age can have weakened it, and they transport it, while it has as yet lost nothing of its vigour, into a younger body where it will be able to keep its vitality intact.[3] So when death results from sickness or old age, it seems as though the soul could retain only a diminished power ; and if it is only its double, it is difficult to see how it could survive at all, after the body is once definitely dissolved. From this point of view, the idea of survival is intelligible only with great difficulty. There is a logical and psychological gap between the idea of a double at liberty and that of a spirit to which a cult is addressed.

This interval appears still more considerable when we realize what an abyss separates the sacred world from the profane ;

[1] Jevons has made a similar remark. With Tylor, he admits that the idea of the soul comes from dreams, and that after it was created, men projected it into things. But, he adds, the fact that nature has been conceived as animated like men does not explain how it became the object of a cult. " The man who believes the bowing tree or the leaping flame to be a living thing like himself, does not therefore believe it to be a supernatural being—rather, so far as it is like himself, it, like himself, is not supernatural " (*Introduction to the History of Religions*, p. 55).

[2] See Spencer and Gillen, *Nor. Tr.*, p. 506, and *Nat. Tr.*, p. 512.

[3] This is the ritual and mythical theme which Frazer studies in his *Golden Bough*.

it becomes evident that a simple change of degree could not be enough to make something pass from one category into the other. Sacred beings are not distinguished from profane ones merely by the strange or disconcerting forms which they take or by the greater powers which they enjoy; between the two there is no common measure. Now there is nothing in the notion of a double which could account for so radical a heterogeneity. It is said that when once freed from the body, the spirit can work all sorts of good or evil for the living, according to the way in which it regards them. But it is not enough that a being should disturb his neighbourhood to seem to be of a wholly different nature from those whose tranquillity it menaces. To be sure, in the sentiment which the believer feels for the things he adores, there always enters in some element of reserve and fear; but this is a fear *sui generis,* derived from respect more than from fright, and where the dominating emotion is that which *la majesté* inspires in men. The idea of majesty is essentially religious. Then we have explained nothing of religion until we have found whence this idea comes, to what it corresponds and what can have aroused it in the mind. Simple souls of men cannot become invested with this character by the simple fact of being no longer incarnate.

This is clearly shown by an example from Melanesia. The Melanesians believe that men have souls which leave the body at death; it then changes its name and becomes what they call a *tindalo*, a *natmat,* etc. Also, they have a cult of the souls of the dead: they pray to them, invoke them and make offerings and sacrifices to them. But every *tindalo* is not the object of these ritual practices; only those have this honour which come from men to whom public opinion attributed, during life, the very special virtue which the Melanesians call the *mana*. Later on, we shall have occasion to fix precisely the meaning which this word expresses; for the time being, it will suffice to say that it is the distinctive character of every sacred being. As Codrington says, "it is what works to effect anything which is beyond the ordinary power of men, outside the common processes of nature."[1] A priest, a sorcerer or a ritual formula have mana as well as a sacred stone or spirit. Thus the only tindalo to which religious services are rendered are those which were already sacred of themselves, when their proprietor was still alive. In regard to the other souls, which come from ordinary men, from the crowd of the profane, the same author says that they are "nobodies alike before and after death."[2] By itself, death has no deifying virtue. Since it

[1] *The Melanesians*, p. 119. [2] *Ibid.*, p. 125.

brings about in a more or less complete and final fashion the separation of the soul from profane things, it can well reinforce the sacred character of the soul, if this already exists, but it cannot create it.

Moreover, if, as the hypothesis of the animists supposes, the first sacred beings were really the souls of the dead and the first cult that of the ancestors, it should be found that the lower the societies examined are, the more the place given to this cult in the religious life. But it is rather the contrary which is true. The ancestral cult is not greatly developed, or even presented under a characteristic form, except in advanced societies like those of China, Egypt or the Greek and Latin cities; on the other hand, it is completely lacking in the Australian societies which, as we shall see, represent the lowest and simplest form of social organization which we know. It is true that funeral rites and rites of mourning are found there; but these practices do not constitute a cult, though this name has sometimes wrongfully been given them. In reality, a cult is not a simple group of ritual precautions which a man is held to take in certain circumstances; it is a system of diverse rites, festivals and ceremonies which *all have this characteristic, that they reappear periodically*. They fulfil the need which the believer feels of strengthening and reaffirming, at regular intervals of time, the bond which unites him to the sacred beings upon which he depends. That is why one speaks of marriage rites but not of a marriage cult, of rites of birth but not of a cult of the new-born child; it is because the events on the occasion of which these rites take place imply no periodicity. In the same way, there is no cult of the ancestors except when sacrifices are made on the tombs from time to time, when libations are poured there on certain more or less specific dates, or when festivals are regularly celebrated in honour of the dead. But the Australian has no relations of this sort with his dead. It is true that he must bury their remains according to a ritual, mourn for them during a prescribed length of time and in a prescribed manner, and revenge them if there is occasion to.[1] But when he has once accomplished these pious tasks, when the bones are once dry and the period of mourning is once accomplished, then all is said and done, and the survivors have no more duties towards their relatives who exist no longer. It is true that there is a way in which the dead continue to hold a place in the lives of

[1] There are sometimes, as it seems, even funeral offerings. (See Roth, *Superstition, Magic and Medicine*, in *North Queensland Ethnog.*, Bulletin No. 5, § 69 c., and *Burial Customs*, in *ibid.*, No. 10, in *Records of the Australian Museum*, Vol. VI, No. 5, p. 395). But these offerings are not periodical.

their kindred, even after the mourning is finished. It is sometimes the case that their hair or certain of their bones are kept, because of special virtues which are attached to them.[1] But by that time they have ceased to exist as persons, and have fallen to the rank of anonymous and impersonal charms. In this condition they are the object of no cult; they serve only for magical purposes.

However, there are certain Australian tribes which periodically celebrate rites in honour of fabulous ancestors whom tradition places at the beginning of time. These ceremonies generally consist in a sort of dramatic representation in which are rehearsed the deeds which the myths ascribe to these legendary heroes.[2] But the personages thus represented are not men who, after living the life of men, have been transformed into a sort of god by the fact of their death. They are considered to have exercised superhuman powers while alive. To them is attributed all that is grand in the history of the tribe, or even of the whole world. It is they who in a large measure made the earth such as it is, and men such as they are. The haloes with which they are still decorated do not come to them merely from the fact that they are ancestors, that is to say, in fine, that they are dead, but rather from the fact that a divine character is and always has been attributed to them; to use the Melanesian expression, it is because they are constitutionally endowed with mana. Consequently, there is nothing in these rites which shows that death has the slightest power of deification. It cannot even be correctly said of certain rites that they form an ancestor-cult, since they are not addressed to ancestors as such. In order to have a real cult of the dead, it is necessary that after death real ancestors, the relations whom men really lose every day, become the object of the cult; let us repeat it once more, there are no traces of any such cult in Australia.

Thus the cult which, according to this hypothesis, ought to be the predominating one in inferior societies, is really non-existent there. In reality, the Australian is not concerned with his dead, except at the moment of their decease and during the time which immediately follows. Yet these same peoples, as we shall see, have a very complex cult for sacred beings of a wholly different nature, which is made up of numerous ceremonies and frequently occupying weeks or even entire months. It cannot be admitted that the few rites which the Australian performs when he happens to lose one of his relatives were the origin of these permanent cults which return regularly every

[1] Spencer and Gillen, *Nat. Tr.*, pp. 538, 553, and *Nor. Tr.*, pp. 463, 543, 547.
[2] See especially, Spencer and Gillen, *Northern Tribes*, ch. vi, vii, ix.

year and which take up a considerable part of his existence. The contrast between the two is so great that we may even ask whether the first were not rather derived from the second, and if the souls of men, far from having been the model upon which the gods were originally imagined, have not rather been conceived from the very first as emanations from the divinity.

IV

From the moment that the cult of the dead is shown not to be primitive, animism lacks a basis. It would then seem useless to discuss the third thesis of the system, which concerns the transformation of the cult of the dead into the cult of nature. But since the postulate upon which it rests is also found in certain historians of religion who do not admit the animism properly so-called, such as Brinton,[1] Lang,[2] Réville,[3] and even Robertson Smith himself,[4] it is necessary to make an examination of it.

This extension of the cult of the dead to all nature is said to come from the fact that we instinctively tend to represent all things in our own image, that is to say, as living and thinking beings. We have seen that Spencer has already contested the reality of this so-called instinct. Since animals clearly distinguish living bodies from dead ones, it seemed to him impossible that man, the heir of the animals, should not have had this same faculty of discernment from the very first. But howsoever certain the facts cited by Spencer may be, they have not the demonstrative value which he attributes to them. His reasoning supposes that all the faculties, instincts and aptitudes of the animal have passed integrally into man; now many errors have their origin in this principle which is wrongfully taken as a proven truth. For example, since sexual jealousy is generally very strong among the higher animals, it has been concluded that it ought to be found among men with the same intensity from the very beginnings of history.[5] But it is well known to-day that men can practise a sexual communism which would be impossible if this jealousy were not capable of attenuating itself and even of disappearing when necessary.[6] The fact is

[1] *The Religions of Primitive Peoples*, pp. 47 ff.
[2] *Myth, Ritual and Religions*, p. 123.
[3] *Les Religions des peuples non civilisés*, II, *Conclusion*.
[4] *The Religion of the Semites*, 2 ed., pp. 126, 132.
[5] This is the reasoning of Westermarck (*Origins of Human Marriage*, p. 6).
[6] By sexual communism we do not mean a state of promiscuity where man knows no matrimonial rules: we believe that such a state has never existed. But it has frequently happened that groups of men have been regularly united to one or several women.

that man is not merely an animal with certain additional qualities: he is something else. Human nature is the result of a sort of recasting of the animal nature, and in the course of the various complex operations which have brought about this recasting, there have been losses as well as gains. How many instincts have we not lost? The reason for this is that men are not only in relations with the physical environment, but also with a social environment infinitely more extended, more stable and more active than the one whose influence animals undergo. To live, they must adapt themselves to this. Now in order to maintain itself, society frequently finds it necessary that we should see things from a certain angle and feel them in a certain way; consequently it modifies the ideas which we would ordinarily make of them for ourselves and the sentiments to which we would be inclined if we listened only to our animal nature; it alters them, even going so far as to put the contrary sentiments in their place. Does it not even go so far as to make us regard our own individual lives as something of little value, while for the animal this is the greatest of things?[1] Then it is a vain enterprise to seek to infer the mental constitution of the primitive man from that of the higher animals.

But if the objection of Spencer does not have the decisive value which its author gives it, it is equally true that the animist theory can draw no authority from the confusions which children seem to make. When we hear a child angrily apostrophize an object which he has hit against, we conclude that he thinks of it as a conscious being like himself; but that is interpreting his words and acts very badly. In reality, he is quite a stranger to the very complicated reasoning attributed to him. If he lays the blame on the table which has hurt him, it is not because he supposes it animated and intelligent, but because it has hurt him. His anger, once aroused by the pain, must overflow; so it looks for something upon which to discharge itself, and naturally turns toward the thing which has provoked it, even though this has no effect. The action of an adult in similar circumstances is often as slightly reasonable. When we are violently irritated, we feel the need of inveighing, of destroying, though we attribute no conscious ill-will to the objects upon which we vent our anger. There is even so little confusion that when the emotion of a child is calmed, he can very well distinguish a chair from a person: he does not act in at all the same way towards the two. It is a similar reason which explains his tendency to treat his playthings as if they were living beings. It is his extremely intense need of playing which thus finds a

[1] See our *Suicide*, pp. 233 ff.

means of expressing itself, just as in the other case the violent sentiments caused by pain created an object out of nothing. In order that he may consciously play with his jumping-jack, he imagines it a living person. This illusion is the easier for him because imagination is his sovereign mistress; he thinks almost entirely with images, and we know how pliant images are, bending themselves with docility before every exigency of the will. But he is so little deceived by his own fiction that he would be the first to be surprised if it suddenly became a reality, and his toy bit him![1]

Let us therefore leave these doubtful analogies to one side. To find out if men were primitively inclined to the confusions imputed to them, we should not study animals or children of to-day, but the primitive beliefs themselves. If the spirits and gods of nature were really formed in the image of the human soul, they should bear traces of their origin and bring to mind the essential traits of their model. The most important characteristic of the soul is that it is conceived as the internal principle which animates the organism: it is that which moves it and makes it live, to such an extent that when it withdraws itself, life ceases or is suspended. It has its natural residence in the body, at least while this exists. But it is not thus with the spirits assigned to the different things in nature. The god of the sun is not necessarily in the sun, nor is the spirit of a certain rock in the rock which is its principal place of habitation. A spirit undoubtedly has close relations with the body to which it is attached, but one employs a very inexact expression when he says that it is its soul. As Codrington says,[2] "there does not appear to be anywhere in Melanesia a belief in a spirit which animates any natural object, a tree, waterfall, storm or rock, so as to be to it what the soul is believed to be to the body of man. Europeans, it is true, speak of the spirits of the sea or of the storm or of the forest; but the native idea which they represent is that ghosts haunt the sea and the forest, having power to raise storms and strike a traveller with disease." While the soul is essentially within the body, the spirit passes the major portion of its time outside the object which serves as its base. This is one difference which does not seem to show that the second idea was derived from the first.

From another point of view, it must be added that if men were really forced to project their own image into things, then the first sacred beings ought to have been conceived in their likeness. Now anthropomorphism, far from being primitive, is

[1] Spencer, *Principles of Sociology*, I, pp. 129 f.
[2] *The Melanesians*, p. 123.

rather the mark of a relatively advanced civilization. In the beginning, sacred beings are conceived in the form of an animal or vegetable, from which the human form is only slowly disengaged. It will be seen below that in Australia, it is animals and plants which are the first sacred beings. Even among the Indians of North America, the great cosmic divinities, which commence to be the object of a cult there, are very frequently represented in animal forms.[1] "The difference between the animal, man and the divine being," says Réville, not without surprise, "is not felt in this state of mind, and generally it might be said that *it is the animal form which is the fundamental one.*"[2] To find a god made up entirely of human elements, it is necessary to advance nearly to Christianity. Here, God is a man, not only in the physical aspect in which he is temporarily made manifest, but also in the ideas and sentiments which he expresses. But even in Greece and Rome, though the gods were generally represented with human traits, many mythical personages still had traces of an animal origin: thus there is Dionysus, who is often met with in the form of a bull, or at least with the horns of a bull; there is Demeter, who is often represented with a horse's mane, there are Pan and Silenus, there are the Fauns, etc.[3] It is not at all true that man has had such an inclination to impose his own form upon things. More than that, he even commenced by conceiving of himself as participating closely in the animal nature. In fact, it is a belief almost universal in Australia, and very widespread among the Indians of North America, that the ancestors of men were beasts or plants, or at least that the first men had, either in whole or in part, the distinctive characters of certain animal or vegetable species. Thus, far from seeing beings like themselves everywhere, men commenced by believing themselves to be in the image of some beings from which they differed radically.

V

Finally, the animistic theory implies a consequence which is perhaps its best refutation.

If it were true, it would be necessary to admit that religious beliefs are so many hallucinatory representations, without any objective foundation whatsoever. It is supposed that they are all derived from the idea of the soul because one sees only a

[1] Dorsey, *A Study of Siouan Cults*, in *XIth Annual Report of the Bureau of Amer. Ethnology*, pp. 431 ff., and *passim*.

[2] *La religion des peuples non civilisés*, I, p. 248.

[3] V. W. de Visser, *De Graecorum diis non referentibus speciem humanam.* Cf. P. Perdrizet, *Bulletin de correspondance hellénique*, 1899, p. 635.

magnified soul in the spirits and gods. But according to Tylor and his disciples, the idea of the soul is itself constructed entirely out of the vague and inconsistent images which occupy our attention during sleep : for the soul is the double, and the double is merely a man as he appears to himself while he sleeps. From this point of view, then, sacred beings are only the imaginary conceptions which men have produced during a sort of delirium which regularly overtakes them every day, though it is quite impossible to see to what useful ends these conceptions serve, nor what they answer to in reality. If a man prays, if he makes sacrifices and offerings, if he submits to the multiple privations which the ritual prescribes, it is because a sort of constitutional eccentricity has made him take his dreams for perceptions, death for a prolonged sleep, and dead bodies for living and thinking beings. Thus not only is it true, as many have held, that the forms under which religious powers have been represented to the mind do not express them exactly, and that the symbols with the aid of which they have been thought of partially hide their real nature, but more than that, behind these images and figures there exists nothing but the nightmares of primitive minds. In fine, religion is nothing but a dream, systematized and lived, but without any foundation in reality.[1] Thence it comes about that the theorists of animism, when looking for the origins of religious thought, content themselves with a small outlay of energy. When they think that they have explained how men have been induced to imagine beings of a strange, vaporous form, such as those they see in their dreams, they think the problem is resolved.

In reality, it is not even approached. It is inadmissible that systems of ideas like religions, which have held so considerable a place in history, and to which, in all times, men have come to receive the energy which they must have to live, should be made up of a tissue of illusions. To-day we are beginning to

[1] However, according to Spencer, there is a germ of truth in the belief in spirits: this is the idea that " the power which manifests itself inside the consciousness is a different form of power from that manifested outside the consciousness " (*Ecclesiastical Institutions*, § 659). Spencer understands by this that the notion of force in general is the sentiment of the force which we have extended to the entire universe ; this is what animism admits implicitly when it peoples nature with spirits analogous to our own. But even if this hypothesis in regard to the way in which the idea of force is formed were true—and it requires important reservations which we shall make (Bk. III, ch. iii, § 3)—it has nothing religious about it ; it belongs to no cult. It thus remains that the system of religious symbols and rites, the classification of things into sacred and profane, all that which is really religious in religion, corresponds to nothing in reality. Also, this germ of truth, of which he speaks, is still more a germ of error, for if it be true that the forces of nature and those of the mind are related, they are profoundly distinct, and one exposes himself to grave misconceptions in identifying them.

realize that law, morals and even scientific thought itself were born of religion, were for a long time confounded with it, and have remained penetrated with its spirit. How could a vain fantasy have been able to fashion the human consciousness so strongly and so durably ? Surely it ought to be a principle of the science of religions that religion expresses nothing which does not exist in nature ; for there are sciences only of natural phenomena. The only question is to learn from what part of nature these realities come and what has been able to make men represent them under this singular form which is peculiar to religious thought. But if this question is to be raised, it is necessary to commence by admitting that they are real things which are thus represented. When the philosophers of the eighteenth century made religion a vast error imagined by the priests, they could at least explain its persistence by the interest which the sacerdotal class had in deceiving the people. But if the people themselves have been the artisans of these systems of erroneous ideas at the same time that they were its dupes, how has this extraordinary dupery been able to perpetuate itself all through the course of history ?

One might even demand if under these conditions the words of science of religions can be employed without impropriety. A science is a discipline which, in whatever manner it is conceived, is always applied to some real data. Physics and chemistry are sciences because physico-chemical phenomena are real, and of a reality which does not depend upon the truths which these sciences show. There is a psychological science because there are really consciousnesses which do not hold their right of existence from the psychologist. But on the contrary, religion could not survive the animistic theory and the day when its truth was recognized by men, for they could not fail to renounce the errors whose nature and origin would thus be revealed to them. What sort of a science is it whose principal discovery is that the subject of which it treats does not exist ?

CHAPTER III

LEADING CONCEPTIONS OF THE ELEMENTARY RELIGION—*continued*

II.—*Naturism*

THE spirit of the naturistic school is quite different.

In the first place, it is recruited in a different environment. The animists are, for the most part, ethnologists or anthropologists. The religions which they have studied are the crudest which humanity has ever known. Hence comes the extraordinary importance which they attribute to the souls of the dead, to spirits and to demons, and, in fact, to all spiritual beings of the second order: it is because these religions know hardly any of a higher order.[1] On the contrary, the theories which we are now going to describe are the work of scholars who have concerned themselves especially with the great civilizations of Europe and Asia.

Ever since the work of the Grimm brothers, who pointed out the interest that there is in comparing the different mythologies of the Indo-European peoples, scholars have been struck by the remarkable similarities which these present. Mythical personages were identified who, though having different names, symbolized the same ideas and fulfilled the same functions; even the names were frequently related, and it has been thought possible to establish the fact that they are not unconnected with one another. Such resemblances seemed to be explicable only by a common origin. Thus they were led to suppose that these conceptions, so varied in appearance, really came from one common source, of which they were only diversified forms, and which it was not impossible to discover. By the comparative method, they believed one should be able to go back, beyond these great religions, to a much more ancient system of ideas, and to the really primitive religion, from which the others were derived.

The discovery of the Vedas aided greatly in stimulating these ambitions. In the Vedas, scholars had a written text, whose antiquity was undoubtedly exaggerated at the moment of its

[1] This is undoubtedly what explains the sympathy which folk-lorists like Mannhardt have felt for animistic ideas. In popular religions as in inferior religions, these spiritual beings of a second order hold the first place.

discovery, but which is surely one of the most ancient which we have at our disposition in an Indo-European language. Here they were enabled to study, by the ordinary methods of philology, a literature as old as or older than Homer, and a religion which was believed more primitive than that of the ancient Germans. A document of such value was evidently destined to throw a new light upon the religious beginnings of humanity, and the science of religions could not fail to be revolutionized by it.

The conception which was thus born was so fully demanded by the state of the science and by the general march of ideas, that it appeared almost simultaneously in two different lands. In 1856, Max Müller exposed its principles in his *Oxford Essays.*[1] Three years later appeared the work of Adalbert Kuhn on *The Origin of Fire and the Drink of the Gods,*[2] which was clearly inspired by the same spirit. When once set forth, the idea spread very rapidly in scientific circles. To the name of Kuhn is closely associated that of his brother-in-law Schwartz, whose work on *The Origin of Mythology,*[3] followed closely upon the preceding one. Steinthal and the whole German school of *Völkerpsychologie* attached themselves to the same movement. The theory was introduced into France in 1863 by M. Michel Bréal.[4] It met so little resistance that, according to an expression of Gruppe,[5] " a time came when, aside from certain classical philologists, to whom Vedic studies were unknown, all the mythologists had adopted the principles of Max Müller or Kuhn as their point of departure." [6] It is therefore important to see what they really are, and what they are worth.

Since no one has presented them in a more systematic form than Max Müller, it is upon his work that we shall base the description which follows.[7]

[1] In the essay entitled *Comparative Mythology* (pp. 47 ff).

[2] *Herabkunft des Feuers und Göttertranks,* Berlin, 1859 (a new edition was given by Ernst Kuhn in 1886). Cf. *Der Schuss des Wilden Jägers auf den Sonnenhirsch,* Zeitschrift f. d. Phil., I, 1869, pp. 89–169. *Entwickelungsstufen des Mythus,* Abhandl. d. Berl. Akad., 1873.

[3] *Der Ursprung der Mythologie,* Berlin, 1860.

[4] In his book *Hercule et Cacus. Étude de mythologie comparée.* Max Müller's *Comparative Mythology* is there signalized as a work " which marks a new epoch in the history of Mythology " (p. 12).

[5] *Die Griechischen Kulte und Mythen,* I, p. 78.

[6] Among others who have adopted this conception may be cited Renan. See his *Nouvelles études d'histoire religieuse,* 1884, p. 31.

[7] Aside from the *Comparative Mythology,* the works where Max Müller has exposed his general theories on religion are : *Hibbert Lectures* (1878) under the title *The Origin and Development of Religion* ; *Natural Religion* (1889) ; *Physical Religion* (1890) ; *Anthropological Religion* (1892) ; *Theosophy, or Psychological Religion* (1893) ; *Contributions to the Science of Mythology* (1897). Since his mythological theories are closely related to his philosophy of language, these works should be consulted in connection with the ones consecrated to language or logic, especially *Lectures on the Science of Language,* and *The Science of Thought.*

I

We have seen that the postulate at the basis of animism is that religion, at least in its origin, expresses no physical reality. But Max Müller commences with the contrary principle. For him, it is an axiom that religion reposes upon an experience, from which it draws all its authority. "Religion," he says, "if it is to hold its place as a legitimate element of our consciousness, must, like all other knowledge, begin with sensuous experience."[1] Taking up the old empirical adage, "*Nihil est in intellectu quod non ante fuerit in sensu*," he applies it to religion and declares that there can be nothing in beliefs which was not first perceived. So here is a doctrine which seems to escape the grave objection which we raised against animism. From this point of view, it seems that religion ought to appear, not as a sort of vague and confused dreaming, but as a system of ideas and practices well founded in reality.

But which are these sensations which give birth to religious thought? That is the question which the study of the Vedas is supposed to aid in resolving.

The names of the gods are generally either common words, still employed, or else words formerly common, whose original sense it is possible to discover. Now both designate the principal phenomena of nature. Thus *Agni*, the name of one of the principal divinities of India, originally signified only the material fact of fire, such as it is ordinarily perceived by the senses and without any mythological addition. Even in the Vedas, it is still employed with this meaning; in any case, it is well shown that this signification was primitive by the fact that it is conserved in other Indo-European languages: the Latin *ignis*, the Lithuanian *ugnis*, the old Slav *ogny* are evidently closely related to Agni. Similarly, the relationship of the Sanskrit *Dyaus*, the Greek *Zeus*, the Latin *Jovis* and the *Zio* of High German is to-day uncontested. This proves that these different words designate one single and the same divinity, whom the different Indo-European peoples recognized as such before their separation. Now Dyaus signifies the bright sky. These and other similar facts tend to show that among these peoples the forms and forces of nature were the first objects to which the religious sentiment attached itself: they were the first things to be deified. Going one step farther in his generalization, Max Müller thought that he was prepared to conclude that the religious evolution of humanity in general had the same point of departure.

[1] *Natural Religion*, p. 114.

It is almost entirely by considerations of a psychological sort that he justifies these inferences. The varied spectacles which nature offers man seemed to him to fulfil all the conditions necessary for arousing religious ideas in the mind directly. In fact, he says, " at first sight, nothing seemed less natural than nature. Nature was the greatest surprise, a terror, a marvel, a standing miracle, and it was only on account of their permanence, constancy, and regular recurrence that certain features of that standing miracle were called natural, in the sense of foreseen, common, intelligible. . . . It was that vast domain of surprise, of terror, of marvel, of miracle, the unknown, as distinguished from the known, or, as I like to express it, the infinite, as distinct from the finite, which supplied from the earliest times the impulse to religious thought and language." [1] In order to illustrate his idea, he applies it to a natural force which holds a rather large place in the Vedic religion, fire. He says, " if you can for a moment transfer yourselves to that early stage of life to which we must refer not only the origin, but likewise the early phases of Physical Religion, you can easily understand what an impression the first appearance of fire must have made on the human mind. Fire was not given as something permanent or eternal, like the sky, or the earth, or the water. In whatever way it first appeared, whether through lightning or through the friction of the branches of trees, or through the sparks of flints, it came and went, it had to be guarded, it brought destruction, but at the same time, it made life possible in winter, it served as a protection during the night, it became a weapon of defence and offence, and last, not least, it changed man from a devourer of raw flesh into an eater of cooked meat. At a later time it became the means of working metal, of making tools and weapons, it became an indispensable factor in all mechanical and artistic progress, and has remained so ever since. What should we be without fire even now ? " [2] The same author says in another work that a man could not enter into relations with nature without taking account of its immensity, of its infiniteness. It surpasses him in every way. Beyond the distances which he perceives, there are others which extend without limits ; each moment of time is preceded and followed by a time to which no limit can be assigned ; the flowing river manifests an infinite force, since nothing can exhaust it.[3] There is no aspect of nature which is not fitted to awaken within us this overwhelming sensation of an infinity which surrounds us and dominates us.[4] It is from this sensation that religions are derived.[5]

[1] *Physical Religion*, pp. 119–120. [2] *Ibid.*, p. 121 ; cf. p. 304.
[3] *Natural Religion*, pp. 121 ff., and 149–155.
[4] " The overwhelming pressure of the infinite " (*ibid.*, p. 138).
[5] *Ibid.*, pp. 195–196.

However, they are there only in germ.[1] Religion really commences only at the moment when these natural forces are no longer represented in the mind in an abstract form. They must be transformed into personal agents, living and thinking beings, spiritual powers or gods; for it is to beings of this sort that the cult is generally addressed. We have seen that animism itself has been obliged to raise this question, and also how it has answered it: man seems to have a sort of native incapacity for distinguishing the animate from the inanimate and an irresistible tendency to conceive the second under the form of the first. Max Müller rejects any such solution.[2] According to him it is language which has brought about this metamorphosis, by the action which it exercises upon thought.

It is easily explained how men, being perplexed by the marvellous forces upon which they feel that they depend, have been led to reflect upon them, and how they have asked themselves what these forces are and have made an effort to substitute for the obscure sensation which they primitively had of them, a clearer idea and a better defined concept. But as our author very justly says,[3] this idea and concept are impossible without the word. Language is not merely the external covering of a thought; it also is its internal framework. It does not confine itself to expressing this thought after it has once been formed; it also aids in making it. However, its nature is of a different sort, so its laws are not those of thought. Then since it contributes to the elaboration of this latter, it cannot fail to do it violence to some extent, and to deform it. It is a deformation of this sort which is said to have created the special characteristic of religious thought.

Thinking consists in arranging our ideas, and consequently in classifying them. To think of fire, for example, is to put it into a certain category of things, in such a way as to be able to say that it is this or that, or this and not that. But classifying is also naming, for a general idea has no existence and reality except in and by the word which expresses it and which alone makes its individuality. Thus the language of a people always has an influence upon the manner in which new things, recently learned, are classified in the mind and are subsequently thought of; these new things are thus forced to adapt themselves to pre-existing forms. For this reason, the language which men spoke when they

[1] Max Müller even goes so far as to say that until thought has passed this first stage, it has very few of the characteristics which we now attribute to religion (*Physic. Rel.*, p. 120).

[2] *Physic. Rel.*, p. 128.

[3] *The Science of Thought*, p. 30.

undertook to construct an elaborated representation of the universe marked the system of ideas which was then born with an indelible trace.

Nor are we without some knowledge of this language, at least in so far as the Indo-European peoples are concerned. Howsoever distant it may be from us, souvenirs of it remain in our actual languages which permit us to imagine what it was: these are the roots. These stems, from which are derived all the words which we employ and which are found at the basis of all the Indo-European languages, are regarded by Max Müller as so many echoes of the language which the corresponding peoples spoke before their separation, that is to say, at the very moment when this religion of nature, which is to be explained, was being formed. Now these roots present two remarkable characteristics, which, it is true, have as yet been observed only in this particular group of languages, but which our author believes to be present equally in the other linguistic families.[1]

In the first place, the roots are general; that is to say that they do not express particular things and individuals, but types, and even types of an extreme generality. They represent the most general themes of thought; one finds there, as though fixed and crystallized, those fundamental categories of the intellect which at every moment in history dominate the entire mental life, the arrangement of which philosophers have many times attempted to reconstruct.[2]

Secondly, the types to which they correspond are types of action, and not of objects. They translate the most general manners of acting which are to be observed among living beings and especially among men; they are such actions as striking, pushing, rubbing, lying down, getting up, pressing, mounting, descending, walking, etc. In other words, men generalized and named their principal ways of acting before generalizing and naming the phenomena of nature.[3]

Owing to their extreme generality, these words could easily be extended to all sorts of objects which they did not originally include; it is even this extreme suppleness which has permitted them to give birth to the numerous words which are derived from them. Then when men, turning towards things, undertook to name them, that they might be able to think about them, they applied these words to them, though they were in no way designed for them. But, owing to their origin, these were able to designate the forces of nature only by means of their manifestations

[1] *Natural Religion*, pp. 393 ff.

[2] *Physic. Rel.*, p. 133; *The Science of Thought*, p. 219; *Lectures on the Science of Language*, II, pp. 1 ff.

[3] *The Science of Thought*, p. 272.

which seemed the nearest to human actions: a thunderbolt was called *something* that tears up the soil or that spreads fire; the wind, *something* that sighs or whistles; the sun, *something* that throws golden arrows across space; a river, *something* that flows, etc. But since natural phenomena were thus compared to human acts, this *something* to which they were attached was necessarily conceived under the form of personal agents, more or less like men. It was only a metaphor, but it was taken literally; the error was inevitable, for science, which alone could dispel the illusion, did not yet exist. In a word, since language was made of human elements, translating human states, it could not be applied to nature without transforming it.[1] Even to-day, remarks M. Bréal, it forces us in a certain measure to represent things from this angle. "We do not express an idea, even one designating a simple quality, without giving it a gender, that is to say, a sex; we cannot speak of an object, even though it be considered in a most general fashion, without determining it by an article; every subject of a sentence is presented as an active being, every idea as an action, and every action, be it transitory or permanent, is limited in its duration by the tense in which we put the verb."[2] Our scientific training enables us to rectify the errors which language might thus suggest to us; but the influence of the word ought to be all-powerful when it has no check. Language thus superimposes upon the material world, such as it is revealed to our senses, a new world, composed wholly of spiritual beings which it has created out of nothing and which have been considered as the causes determining physical phenomena ever since.

But its action does not stop there. When words were once forged to represent these personalities which the popular imagination had placed behind things, a reaction affected these words themselves: they raised all sorts of questions, and it was to resolve these problems that myths were invented. It happened that one object received a plurality of names, corresponding to the plurality of aspects under which it was presented in experience; thus there are more than twenty words in the Vedas for the sky. Since these words were different, it was believed that they corresponded to so many distinct personalities. But at the same time, it was strongly felt that these same personalities had an air of relationship. To account for that, it was imagined that they formed a single family; genealogies, a civil condition and a history were invented for them. In other cases, different things were designated by the same term: to explain these

[1] *The Science of Thought*, I, p. 327; *Physic. Rel.*, pp. 125 ff.
[2] *Mélanges de mythologie et de linguistique*, p. 8.

homonyms, it was believed that the corresponding things were transformations of each other, and new fictions were invented to make these metamorphoses intelligible. Or again, a word which had ceased to be understood, was the origin of fables designed to give it a meaning. The creative work of language continued then, making constructions ever more and more complex, and then mythology came to endow each god with a biography, ever more and more extended and complete, the result of all of which was that the divine personalities, at first confounded with things, finally distinguished and determined themselves.

This is how the notion of the divine is said to have been constructed. As for the religion of ancestors, it was only a reflection of this other.[1] The idea of the soul is said to have been first formed for reasons somewhat analogous to those given by Tylor, except that according to Max Müller, they were designed to account for death, rather than for dreams.[2] Then, under the influence of diverse, partially accidental, circumstances,[3] the souls of men, being once disengaged from the body, were drawn little by little within the circle of divine beings, and were thus finally deified themselves. But this new cult was the product of only a secondary formation. This is proven by the fact that deified men have generally been imperfect gods or demi-gods, whom the people have always been able to distinguish from the genuine deities.[4]

II

This doctrine rests, in part, upon a certain number of linguistic postulates which have been and still are very much questioned. Some have contested the reality of many of the similarities which Max Müller claimed to have found between the names of the gods in the various European languages. The interpretation which he gave them has been especially doubted: it has been asked if these names, far from being the mark of a very primitive

[1] *Anthropological Religion*, pp. 128–130.

[2] This explanation is not as good as that of Tylor. According to Max Müller, men could not admit that life stopped with death; therefore they concluded that there were two beings within them, one of which survived the body. But it is hard to see what made them think that life continued after the body was decomposed.

[3] For the details, see *Anthrop. Rel.*, pp. 351 ff.

[4] *Anthrop. Rel.*, p. 130.—This is what keeps Max Müller from considering Christianity the climax of all this development. The religion of ancestors, he says, supposes that there is something divine in man. Now is that idea not the one at the basis of the teaching of Christ? (*ibid.*, pp. 378 ff.). It is useless to insist upon the strangeness of the conception which makes Christianity the latest of the cults of the dead.

religion, are not the slow product, either of direct borrowings or of natural intercourse with others.[1] Also, it is no longer admitted that the roots once existed in an isolated state as autonomous realities, nor that they allow us to reconstruct, even hypothetically, the original language of the Indo-Europeans.[2] Finally, recent researches would tend to show that the Vedic divinities did not all have the exclusively naturistic character attributed to them by Max Müller and his school.[3] But we shall leave aside those questions, the discussion of which requires a special competence as a philologist, and address ourselves directly to the general principles of the system. It will be important here not to confound the naturistic theory with these controverted postulates; for this is held by numbers of scholars who do not make language play the predominating rôle attributed to it by Max Müller.

That men have an interest in knowing the world which surrounds them, and consequently that their reflection should have been applied to it at an early date, is something that everyone will readily admit. Co-operation with the things with which they were in immediate connection was so necessary for them that they could not fail to seek a knowledge of their nature. But if, as naturism pretends, it is of these reflections that religious thought was born, it is impossible to explain how it was able to survive the first attempts made, and the persistence with which it has maintained itself becomes unintelligible. If we have need of knowing the nature of things, it is in order to act upon them in an appropriate manner. But the conception of the universe given us by religion, especially in its early forms, is too greatly mutilated to lead to temporarily useful practices. Things become nothing less than living and thinking beings, minds or personalities like those which the religious imagination has made into the agents of cosmic phenomena. It is not by conceiving of them under this form or by treating them according to this conception that men could make them work for their ends. It is not by addressing prayers to them, by celebrating them in feasts and sacrifices, or by imposing upon themselves fasts and privations, that men can deter them from working harm or oblige them to serve their own designs. Such processes could succeed only very exceptionally and, so to speak, miraculously. If, then, religion's reason for existence was to give us a conception of the

[1] See the discussion of the hypothesis in Gruppe, *Griechishen Kulte und Mythen*, pp. 79–184.

[2] See Meillet, *Introduction à l'étude comparative des langues indo-européennes*, p. 119.

[3] Oldenberg, *Die Religion des Vedas*, pp. 59 ff.; Meillet, *Le dieu Iranien Mythra*, in *Journal Asiatique*, X, No. 1, July-August, 1907, pp. 143 ff.

world which would guide us in our relations with it, it was in no condition to fulfil its function, and people would not have been slow to perceive it: failures, being infinitely more frequent than successes, would have quickly shown them that they were following a false route, and religion, shaken at each instant by these repeated contradictions, would not have been able to survive.

It is undeniably true that errors have been able to perpetuate themselves in history; but, except under a union of very exceptional circumstances, they can never perpetuate themselves thus unless they were *true practically*, that is to say, unless, without giving us a theoretically exact idea of the things with which they deal, they express well enough the manner in which they affect us, either for good or for bad. Under these circumstances, the actions which they determine have every chance of being, at least in a general way, the very ones which are proper, so it is easily explained how they have been able to survive the proofs of experience.[1] But an error and especially a system of errors which leads to, and can lead to nothing but mistaken and useless practices, has no chance of living. Now what is there in common between the rites with which the believer tries to act upon nature and the processes by which science has taught us to make use of it, and which we now know are the only efficacious ones? If that is what men demanded of religion, it is impossible to see how it could have maintained itself, unless clever tricks had prevented their seeing that it did not give them what they expected from it. It would be necessary to return again to the over simple explanations of the eighteenth century.[2]

Thus it is only in appearance that naturism escapes the

[1] In this category are a large number of the maxims of popular wisdom.

[2] It is true that this argument does not touch those who see in religion a code (especially of hygiene) whose provisions, though placed under the sanction of imaginary beings, are nevertheless well founded. But we shall not delay to discuss a conception so insupportable, and which has, in fact, never been sustained in a systematic manner by persons somewhat informed upon the history of religions. It is difficult to see what good the terrible practices of the initiation bring to the health which they threaten; what good the dietetic restrictions, which generally deal with perfectly clean animals, have hygienically; how sacrifices, which take place far from a house, make it more solid, etc. Undoubtedly there are religious precepts which at the same time have a practical utility; but they are lost in the mass of others, and even the services which they render are frequently not without some drawbacks. If there is a religiously enforced cleanliness, there is also a religious filthiness which is derived from these same principles. The rule which orders a corpse to be carried away from the camp because it is the seat of a dreaded spirit is undoubtedly useful. But the same belief requires the relatives to anoint themselves with the liquids which issue from a corpse in putrefaction, because they are supposed to have exceptional virtues.—From this point of view, magic has served a great deal more than religion.

objection which we recently raised against animism. It also makes religion a system of hallucinations, since it reduces it to an immense metaphor with no objective value. It is true that it gives religion a point of departure in reality, to wit, in the sensations which the phenomena of nature provoke in us ; but by the bewitching action of language, this sensation is soon transformed into extravagant conceptions. Religious thought does not come in contact with reality, except to cover it at once with a thick veil which conceals its real forms : this veil is the tissue of fabulous beliefs which mythology brought forth. Thus the believer, like the delirious man, lives in a world peopled with beings and things which have only a verbal existence. Max Müller himself recognized this, for he regarded myths as the product of a disease of the intellect. At first, he attributed them to a disease of language, but since language and the intellect are inseparable for him, what is true of the one is true of the other. " When trying to explain the inmost nature of mythology," he says, " I called it a disease of Language rather than of Thought. . . . After I had fully explained in my *Science of Thought* that language and thought are inseparable, and that a disease of language is therefore the same thing as a disease of thought, no doubt ought to have remained as to what I meant. To represent the supreme God as committing every kind of crime, as being deceived by men, as being angry with his wife and violent with his children, is surely a proof of a disease, of an unusual condition of thought, or, to speak more clearly, of real madness." [1] And this argument is not valid merely against Max Müller and his theory, but against the very principle of naturism, in whatever way it may be applied. Whatever we may do, if religion has as its principal object the expression of the forces of nature, it is impossible to see in it anything more than a system of lying fictions, whose survival is incomprehensible.

Max Müller thought he escaped this objection, whose gravity he felt, by distinguishing radically between mythology and religion, and by putting the first outside the second. He claims the right of reserving the name of religion for only those beliefs which conform to the prescriptions of a sane moral system and a rational theology. The myths were parasitic growths which, under the influence of language, attached themselves upon these fundamental conceptions, and denatured them. Thus the belief in Zeus was religious in so far as the Greeks considered him the supreme God, father of humanity, protector of laws, avenger of crimes, etc. ; but all that which concerned

[1] *Contributions to the Science of Mythology*, I, pp. 68 f.

the biography of Zeus, his marriages and his adventures, was only mythology.[1]

But this distinction is arbitrary. It is true that mythology has an æsthetic interest as well as one for the history of religions; but it is one of the essential elements of the religious life, nevertheless. If the myth were withdrawn from religion, it would be necessary to withdraw the rite also; for the rites are generally addressed to definite personalities who have a name, a character, determined attributes and a history, and they vary according to the manner in which these personalities are conceived. The cult rendered to a divinity depends upon the character attributed to him; and it is the myth which determines this character. Very frequently, the rite is nothing more than the myth put in action; the Christian communion is inseparable from the myth of the Last Supper, from which it derives all its meaning. Then if all mythology is the result of a sort of verbal delirium, the question which we raised remains intact: the existence, and especially the persistence of the cult become inexplicable. It is hard to understand how men have continued to do certain things for centuries without any object. Moreover, it is not merely the peculiar traits of the divine personalities which are determined by mythology; the very idea that there are gods or spiritual beings set above the various departments of nature, in no matter what manner they may be represented, is essentially mythical.[2] Now if all that which appertains to the notion of gods conceived as cosmic agents is blotted out of the religions of the past, what remains? The idea of a divinity in itself, of a transcendental power upon which man depends and upon which he supports himself? But that is only an abstract and philosophic conception which has been fully realized in no historical religion; it is without interest for the science of religions.[3] We must therefore avoid distinguishing between religious beliefs, keeping some because they seem to us

[1] *Lectures on the Science of Language*, II, p. 456 ff.; *Physic. Rel.*, pp. 276 ff.—Also Bréal, *Mélanges*, p. 6, "To bring the necessary clarity into this question of the origin of mythology, it is necessary to distinguish carefully the *gods*, which are the immediate product of the human intelligence, from the *fables*, which are its indirect and involuntary product."

[2] Max Müller recognized this. See *Physic. Rel.*, p. 132, and *Comparative Mythology*, p. 58. "The gods are *nomina* and not *numina*, names without being and not beings without name."

[3] It is true that Max Müller held that for the Greeks, "Zeus was, and remained, in spite of all mythological obscurations, the name of the Supreme Deity" (*Science of Language*, II, p. 478). We shall not dispute this assertion, though it is historically contestable; but in any case, this conception of Zeus could never have been more than a glimmer in the midst of all the other religious beliefs of the Greeks.

Besides this, in a later work, Max Müller went so far as to make even the notion of god in general the product of a wholly verbal process and thus of a mythological elaboration (*Physic. Rel.*, p. 138).

to be true and sane and rejecting others because they shock and disconcert us. All myths, even those which we find the most unreasonable, have been believed.[1] Men have believed in them no less firmly than in their own sensations; they have based their conduct upon them. In spite of appearances, it is therefore impossible that they should be without objective foundation.

However, it will be said that in whatever manner religions may be explained, it is certain that they are mistaken in regard to the real nature of things: science has proved it. The modes of action which they counsel or prescribe to men can therefore rarely have useful effects: it is not by lustrations that the sick are cured nor by sacrifices and chants that the crops are made to grow. Thus the objection which we have made to naturism would seem to be applicable to all possible systems of explanation.

Nevertheless, there is one which escapes it. Let us suppose that religion responds to quite another need than that of adapting ourselves to sensible objects: then it will not risk being weakened by the fact that it does not satisfy, or only badly satisfies, this need. If religious faith was not born to put man in harmony with the material world, the injuries which it has been able to do him in his struggle with the world do not touch it at its source, because it is fed from another.

If it is not for these reasons that a man comes to believe, he should continue to believe even when these reasons are contradicted by the facts. It is even conceivable that faith should be strong enough, not only to support these contradictions, but also even to deny them and to keep the believer from seeing their importance; this is what succeeds in rendering them inoffensive for religion. When the religious sentiment is active, it will not admit that religion can be in the wrong, and it readily suggests explanations which make it appear innocent; if the rite does not produce the desired results, this failure is imputed either to some fault of execution, or to the intervention of another, contrary deity. But for that, it is necessary that these religious ideas have their source in another sentiment than that betrayed by these deceptions of experience, or else whence could come their force of resistance?

[1] Undoubtedly outside the real myths there were always fables which were not believed, or at least were not believed in the same way and to the same degree, and hence had no religious character. The line of demarcation between fables and myths is certainly floating and hard to determine. But this is no reason for making all myths stories, any more than we should dream of making all stories myths. There is at least one characteristic which in a number of cases suffices to differentiate the religious myth: that is its relation to the cult.

III

But more than that, even if men had really had reasons for remaining obstinate, in spite of all their mistakes, in expressing cosmic phenomena in religious terms, it is also necessary that these be of a nature to suggest such an interpretation. Now when could they have gotten such a property? Here again we find ourselves in the presence of one of those postulates which pass as evident only because they have not been criticized. It is stated as an axiom that in the natural play of physical forces there is all that is needed to arouse within us the idea of the sacred; but when we closely examine the proofs of this proposition, which, by the way, are sufficiently brief, we find that they reduce to a prejudice.

They talk about the marvel which men should feel as they discover the world. But really, that which characterizes the life of nature is a regularity which approaches monotony. Every morning the sun mounts in the horizon, every evening it sets; every month the moon goes through the same cycle; the river flows in an uninterrupted manner in its bed; the same seasons periodically bring back the same sensations. To be sure, here and there an unexpected event sometimes happens: the sun is eclipsed, the moon is hidden behind clouds, the river overflows. But these momentary variations could only give birth to equally momentary impressions, the remembrance of which is gone after a little while; they could not serve as a basis for these stable and permanent systems of ideas and practices which constitute religions. Normally, the course of nature is uniform, and uniformity could never produce strong emotions. Representing the savage as filled with admiration before these marvels transports much more recent sentiments to the beginnings of history. He is much too accustomed to it to be greatly surprised by it. It requires culture and reflection to shake off this yoke of habit and to discover how marvellous this regularity itself is. Besides, as we have already remarked,[1] admiring an object is not enough to make it appear sacred to us, that is to say, to mark it with those characteristics which make all direct contact with it appear a sacrilege and a profanation. We misunderstand what the religious sentiment really is, if we confound it with every impression of admiration and surprise.

But, they say, even if it is not admiration, there is a certain impression which men cannot help feeling in the presence of nature. He cannot come in contact with it, without realizing

[1] See above, p. 28.

that it is greater than he. It overwhelms him by its immensity. This sensation of an infinite space which surrounds him, of an infinite time which has preceded and will follow the present moment, and of forces infinitely superior to those of which he is master, cannot fail, as it seems, to awaken within him the idea that outside of him there exists an infinite power upon which he depends. And this idea enters as an essential element into our conception of the divine.

But let us bear in mind what the question is. We are trying to find out how men came to think that there are in reality two categories of things, radically heterogeneous and incomparable to each other. Now how could the spectacle of nature give rise to the idea of this duality? Nature is always and everywhere of the same sort. It matters little that it extends to infinity: beyond the extreme limit to which my eyes can reach, it is not different from what it is here. The space which I imagine beyond the horizon is still space, identical with that which I see. The time which flows without end is made up of moments identical with those which I have passed through. Extension, like duration, repeats itself indefinitely; if the portions which I touch have of themselves no sacred character, where did the others get theirs? The fact that I do not see them directly, is not enough to transform them.[1] A world of profane things may well be unlimited; but it remains a profane world. Do they say that the physical forces with which we come in contact exceed our own? Sacred forces are not to be distinguished from profane ones simply by their greater intensity, they are different; they have special qualities which the others do not have. Quite on the contrary, all the forces manifested in the universe are of the same nature, those that are within us just as those that are outside of us. And especially, there is no reason which could have allowed giving a sort of pre-eminent dignity to some in relation to others. Then if religion really was born because of the need of assigning causes to physical phenomena, the forces thus imagined would have been no more sacred than those conceived by the scientist to-day to account for the same facts.[2]

[1] More than that, in the language of Max Müller, there is a veritable abuse of words. Sensuous experience, he says, implies, at least in certain cases, " beyond the known, *something unknown, something which I claim the liberty to call infinite* " (*Natural Rel.*, p. 195; cf. p. 218). The unknown is not necessarily the infinite, any more than the infinite is necessarily the unknown if it is in all points the same, and consequently like the part which we know. It would be necessary to prove that the part of it which we perceive differs in nature from that which we do not perceive.

[2] Max Müller involuntarily recognizes this in certain passages. He confesses that he sees little difference between Agni, the god of fire, and the notion of ether, by which the modern physicist explains light and heat (*Phys. Rel.*, pp. 126 f.). Also, he connects the notion of divinity to that of agency (p. 138) or

This is as much as to say that there would have been no sacred beings and therefore no religion.

But even supposing that this sensation of being "overwhelmed" were really able to suggest religious ideas, it could not have produced this effect upon the primitive, for he does not have it. He is in no way conscious that cosmic forces are so superior to his own. Since science has not yet taught him modesty, he attributes to himself an empire over things which he really does not have, but the illusion of which is enough to prevent his feeling dominated by them. As we have already pointed out, he thinks that he can command the elements, release the winds, compel the rain to fall, or stop the sun, by a gesture, etc.[1] Religion itself contributes to giving him this security, for he believes that it arms him with extended powers over nature. His rites are, in part, means destined to aid him in imposing his will upon the world. Thus, far from being due to the sentiment which men should have of their littleness before the universe, religions are rather inspired by the contrary sentiment. Even the most elevated and idealistic have the effect of reassuring men in their struggle with things: they teach that faith is, of itself, able "to move mountains," that is to say, to dominate the forces of nature. How could they give rise to this confidence if they had had their origin in a sensation of feebleness and impotency?

Finally, if the objects of nature really became sacred because of their imposing forms or the forces which they manifest, then the sun, the moon, the sky, the mountains, the sea, the winds, in a word, the great cosmic powers, should have been the first to be raised to this dignity; for there are no others more fitted to appeal to the senses and the imagination. But as a matter of fact, they were divinized but slowly. The first beings to which the cult is addressed—the proof will be found in the chapters which follow—are humble vegetables and animals, in relation to which men could at least claim an equality: they are ducks, rabbits, kangaroos, lizards, worms, frogs, etc. Their objective qualities surely were not the origin of the religious sentiments which they inspired.

of a causality which is not natural and profane. The fact that religion represents the causes thus imagined, under the form of personal agents, is not enough to explain how they got a sacred character. A personal agent can be profane, and also, many religious forces are essentially impersonal.

[1] We shall see below, in speaking of the efficacy of rites and faith, how these illusions are to be explained (Bk. III, ch. ii).

CHAPTER IV

TOTEMISM AS AN ELEMENTARY RELIGION

History of the Question.—Method of Treating it

HOWSOEVER opposed their conclusions may seem to be, the two systems which we have just studied agree upon one essential point: they state the problem in identical terms. Both undertake to construct the idea of the divine out of the sensations aroused in us by certain natural phenomena, either physical or biological. For the animists it is dreams, for the naturists, certain cosmic phenomena, which served as the point of departure for religious evolution. But for both, it is in the nature, either of man or of the universe, that we must look for the germ of the grand opposition which separates the profane from the sacred.

But such an enterprise is impossible: it supposes a veritable creation *ex nihilo*. A fact of common experience cannot give us the idea of something whose characteristic is to be outside the world of common experience. A man, as he appears to himself in his dreams, is only a man. Natural forces, as our senses perceive them, are only natural forces, howsoever great their intensity may be. Hence comes the common criticism which we address to both doctrines. In order to explain how these pretended data of religious thought have been able to take a sacred character which has no objective foundation, it would be necessary to admit that a whole world of delusive representations has superimposed itself upon the other, denatured it to the point of making it unrecognizable, and substituted a pure hallucination for reality. Here, it is the illusions of the dream which brought about this transfiguration; there, it is the brilliant and vain company of images evoked by the word. But in one case as in the other, it is necessary to regard religion as the product of a delirious imagination.

Thus one positive conclusion is arrived at as the result of this critical examination. Since neither man nor nature have of themselves a sacred character, they must get it from another source. Aside from the human individual and the physical world, there should be some other reality, in relation to which this variety of delirium which all religion is in a sense, has a significance and an objective value. In other words, beyond those which we have called animistic and naturistic, there should be another sort of cult, more fundamental and more primitive, of which the first are only derived forms or particular aspects.

In fact, this cult does exist: it is the one to which ethnologists have given the name of totemism.

I

It was only at the end of the eighteenth century that the word totem appeared in ethnographical literature. It is found for the first time in the book of an Indian interpreter, J. Long, which was published in London in 1791.[1] For nearly a half a century, totemism was known only as something exclusively American.[2] It was only in 1841 that Grey, in a passage which has remained celebrated,[3] pointed out the existence of wholly similar practices in Australia. From that time on, scholars began to realize that they were in the presence of a system of a certain generality.

But they saw there only an essentially archaic institution, an ethnographical curiosity, having no great interest for the historian. MacLennan was the first who undertook to attach totemism to the general history of humanity. In a series of articles in the *Fortnightly Review*,[4] he set himself to show that totemism was not only a religion, but one from which were derived a multitude of beliefs and practices which are found in much more advanced religious systems. He even went so far as to make it the source of all the animal-worshipping and plant-worshipping cults which are found among ancient peoples. Certainly this extension of totemism was abusive. The cults of animals and plants depend upon numerous causes which cannot be reduced to one, without the error of too great simplicity. But this error, by its very exaggerations, had at least the advantage, that it put into evidence the historical importance of totemism.

Students of American totemism had already known for a

[1] *Voyages and Travels of an Indian Interpreter*.

[2] This idea was so common that even M. Réville continued to make America the classic land of totemism (*Religions des peuples non civilisés*, I, p. 242).

[3] *Journals of Two Expeditions in North-West and Western Australia*, II, p. 228.

[4] *The Worship of Animals and Plants. Totems and Totemism* (1869, 1870).

long time that this form of religion was most intimately united to a determined social organization, that its basis is the division of the social group into clans.[1] In 1877, in his *Ancient Society*,[2] Lewis H. Morgan undertook to make a study of it, to determine its distinctive characteristics, and at the same time to point out its generality among the Indian tribes of North and Central America. At nearly the same moment, and even following the direct suggestion of Morgan, Fison and Howitt [3] established the existence of the same social system in Australia, as well as its relations with totemism.

Under the influence of these directing ideas, observations could be made with better method. The researches which the American Bureau of Ethnology undertook, played an important part in the advance of these studies.[4] By 1887, the documents were sufficiently numerous and significant to make Frazer consider it time to unite them and present them to us in a systematic form. Such is the object of his little book *Totemism*,[5] where the system is studied both as a religion and as a legal institution. But this study was purely descriptive; no effort was made to explain totemism [6] or to understand its fundamental notions.

Robertson Smith is the first who undertook this work of elaboration. He realized more clearly than any of his predecessors how rich this crude and confused religion is in germs for the future. It is true that MacLennan had already connected it with the great religions of antiquity; but that was merely because he thought he had found here and there the cult of animals or plants. Now if we reduce totemism to a sort of animal or plant worship, we have seen only its most superficial aspect: we have even misunderstood its real nature. Going

[1] This idea is found already very clearly expressed in a study by Gallatin entitled *Synopsis of the Indian Tribes* (*Archæologia Americana*, II, pp. 109 ff.), and in a notice by Morgan in the *Cambrian Journal*, 1860, p. 149.

[2] This work had been prepared for and preceded by two others by the same author: *The League of the Iroquois* (1851), and *Systems of Consanguinity and Affinity of the Human Family* (1871).

[3] *Kamilaroi and Kurnai*, 1880.

[4] In the very first volumes of the *Annual Report of the Bureau of American Ethnology* are found the study of Powell, *Wyandot Government* (I, p. 59), that of Cushing, *Zuñi Fetiches* (II, p. 9), Smith, *Myths of the Iroquois* (*ibid.*, p. 77), and the important work of Dorsey, *Omaha Sociology* (III, p. 211), which are also contributions to the study of totemism.

[5] This first appeared, in an abridged form, in the *Encyclopædia Britannica* (9th ed.).

[6] In his *Primitive Culture*, Tylor had already attempted an explanation of totemism, to which we shall return presently, but which we shall not give here; for by making totemism only a particular case of the ancestor-cult, he completely misunderstood its importance. In this chapter we mention only those theories which have contributed to the progress of the study of totemism.

beyond the mere letter of the totemic beliefs, Smith set himself to find the fundamental principles upon which they depend. In his book upon *Kinship and Marriage in Early Arabia*,[1] he had already pointed out that totemism supposes a likeness in nature, either natural or acquired, of men and animals (or plants). In his *The Religion of the Semites*,[2] he makes this same idea the first origin of the entire sacrificial system: it is to totemism that humanity owes the principle of the communion meal. It is true that the theory of Smith can now be shown one-sided; it is no longer adequate for the facts actually known; but for all that, it contains an ingenious theory and has exercised a most fertile influence upon the science of religions. The *Golden Bough* [3] of Frazer is inspired by these same ideas, for totemism, which MacLennan had attached to the religions of classical antiquity, and Smith to the religions of the Semitic peoples, is here connected to the European folk-lore. The schools of MacLennan and Morgan are thus united to that of Mannhardt.[4]

During this time, the American tradition continued to develop with an independence which it has kept up until very recent times. Three groups of societies were the special object of the researches which were concerned with totemism. These are, first, certain tribes of the North-west, the Tlinkit, the Haida, the Kwakiutl, the Salish and the Tsimshian; then, the great nation of the Sioux; and finally, the Pueblo Indians in the south-western part of the United States. The first were studied principally by Dall, Krause, Boas, Swanton, Hill Tout; the second by Dorsey; the last by Mindeleff, Mrs. Stevenson and Cushing.[5] But however rich the harvest of facts thus gathered in all parts of the country may have been, the documents at our disposal were still fragmentary. Though the American religions contain numerous traces of totemism, they have passed the stage of real totemism. On the other hand, observations in Australia had brought little more than scattered beliefs and isolated rites, initiation rituals and interdictions relative to totemism. It was with facts taken from all these sources that Frazer attempted to draw a picture of totemism in its entirety. Whatever may be the incontestable merit of the reconstruction undertaken in

[1] Published at Cambridge, 1885.

[2] First edition, 1889. This is the arrangement of a course given at the University of Aberdeen in 1888. Cf. the article *Sacrifice* in the *Encyclopædia Britannica* (9th edition).

[3] London, 1890. A second edition in three volumes has since appeared (1900) and a third in five volumes is already in course of publication.

[4] In this connection must be mentioned the interesting work of Sidney Hartland, *The Legend of Perseus*, 3 vols., 1894–1896.

[5] We here confine ourselves to giving the names of the authors; their works will be indicated below, when we make use of them.

such circumstances, it could not help being incomplete and hypothetical. A totemic religion in complete action had not yet been observed.

It is only in very recent years that this serious deficiency has been repaired. Two observers of remarkable ability, Baldwin Spencer and F. J. Gillen, discovered [1] in the interior of the Australian continent a considerable number of tribes whose basis and unity was founded in totemic beliefs. The results of their observations have been published in two works, which have given a new life to the study of totemism. The first of these, *The Native Tribes of Central Australia*,[2] deals with the more central of these tribes, the Arunta, the Luritcha, and a little farther to the south, on the shores of Lake Eyre, the Urabunna. The second, which is entitled *The Northern Tribes of Central Australia*,[3] deals with the societies north of the Urabunna, occupying the territory between MacDonnell's Range and Carpenter Gulf. Among the principal of these we may mention the Unmatjera, the Kaitish, the Warramunga, the Worgaia, the Tjingilli, the Binbinga, the Walpari, the Gnanji and finally, on the very shores of the gulf, the Mara and the Anula.[4]

More recently, a German missionary, Carl Strehlow, who has also passed long years in these same Central Australian societies,[5] has commenced to publish his own observations on two of these tribes, the Aranda and the Loritja (the Arunta and Luritcha of

[1] If Spencer and Gillen have been the first to study these tribes in a scientific and thorough manner, they were not the first to talk about them. Howitt had already described the social organization of the Wuaramongo (Warramunga of Spencer and Gillen) in 1888 in his *Further Notes on the Australian Classes* in *The Journal of the Anthropological Institute* (hereafter, *J.A.I.*), pp. 44 f. The Arunta had already been briefly studied by Schulze (*The Aborigines of the Upper and Middle Finke River*, in *Transactions of the Royal Society of South Australia*, Vol. XIV, fasc. 2): the organization of the Chingalee (the Tjingilli of Spencer and Gillen), the Wombya, etc., by Mathews (*Wombya Organization of the Australian Aborigines*, in *American Anthropologist*, New Series, Vol. II, p. 494; *Divisions of some West Australian Tribes*, *ibid.*, p. 185; *Proceedings Amer. Philos. Soc.*, XXXVII, pp. 151–152, and *Journal Roy. Soc. of N.S. Wales*, XXXII, p. 71 and XXXIII, p. 111). The first results of the study made of the Arunta had also been published already in the *Report on the Work of the Horn Scientific Expedition to Central Australia*, Pt. IV (1896). The first part of this *Report* is by Stirling, the second by Gillen; the entire publication was placed under the direction of Baldwin Spencer.

[2] London, 1899. Hereafter, *Native Tribes* or *Nat. Tr.*

[3] London, 1904. Hereafter, *Northern Tribes* or *Nor. Tr.*

[4] We write the Arunta, the Anula, the Tjingilli, etc., without adding the characteristic *s* of the plural. It does not seem very logical to add to these words, which are not European, a grammatical sign which would have no meaning except in our languages. Exceptions to this rule will be made when the name of the tribe has obviously been Europeanized (the Hurons for example).

[5] Strehlow has been in Australia since 1892; at first he lived among the Dieri, and from them he went to the Arunta.

Spencer and Gillen).[1] Having well mastered the language spoken by these peoples,[2] Strehlow has been able to bring us a large number of totemic myths and religious songs, which are given us, for the most part, in the original text. In spite of some differences of detail which are easily explained and whose importance has been greatly exaggerated,[3] we shall see that the observations of Strehlow, though completing, making more precise and sometimes even rectifying those of Spencer and Gillen, confirm them in all that is essential.

These discoveries have given rise to an abundant literature to which we shall have occasion to return. The works of Spencer and Gillen especially have exercised a considerable influence, not only because they were the oldest, but also because the facts were there presented in a systematic form, which was of a nature to give a direction to later studies,[4] and to stimulate speculation. Their results were commented upon, discussed and interpreted in all possible manners. At this same time, Howitt, whose fragmentary studies were scattered in a number of different publications,[5] undertook to do for the southern tribes what Spencer and Gillen had done for those of the centre. In his *Native Tribes of South-East Australia*,[6] he gives us a view of the social organization of the peoples who occupy Southern Australia, New South Wales, and a good part of Queensland. The progress thus realized suggested to Frazer the idea of completing his *Totemism* by a sort of compendium[7] where would be brought

[1] *Die Aranda- und Loritja-Stämme in Zentral Australien*. Four fascicules have been published up to the present. The last appeared at the moment when the present book was finished, so it could not be used. The two first have to do with the myths and legends, and the third with the cult. It is only just to add to the name of Strehlow that of von Leonhardi, who has had a great deal to do with this publication. Not only has he charged himself with editing the manuscripts of Strehlow, but by his judicious questions he has led the latter to be more precise on more than one point. It would be useful also to consult an article which von Leonhardi gave the *Globus*, where numerous extracts from his correspondence with Strehlow will be found (*Ueber einige religiöse und totemistische Vorstellungen der Aranda und Loritja in Zentral Australien*, in *Globus*, XCI, p. 285). Cf. an article on the same subject by N. W. Thomas in *Folk-lore*, XVI, pp. 428 ff.

[2] Spencer and Gillen are not ignorant of it, but they are far from possessing it as thoroughly as Strehlow.

[3] Notably by Klaatsch, *Schlussbericht über meine Reise nach Australien*, in *Zeitschrift f. Ethnologie*, 1907, pp. 635 ff.

[4] The book of K. Langloh Parker, *The Euahlayi Tribe*, that of Eylmann, *Die Eingeborenen der Kolonie Südaustralien*; that of John Mathews, *Two Representative Tribes of Queensland*, and certain recent articles of Mathews all show the influence of Spencer and Gillen.

[5] A list of these publications will be found in the preface to his *Nat. Tr.*, pp. 8–9.

[6] London, 1904. Hereafter we shall cite this work by the abbreviation *Nat. Tr.*, but always mentioning the name of Howitt, to distinguish it from the first work of Spencer and Gillen, which we abbreviate in the same manner.

[7] *Totemism and Exogamy*, 4 vols., London, 1910. The work begins with a re-edition of *Totemism*, reproduced without any essential changes.

together all the important documents which are concerned either with the totemic religion or the family and matrimonial organization which, rightly or wrongly, is believed to be connected with this religion. The purpose of this book is not to give us a general and systematic view of totemism, but rather to put the materials necessary for a construction of this sort at the disposition of scholars.[1] The facts are here arranged in a strictly ethnographical and geographical order: each continent, and within the continent, each tribe or ethnic group is studied separately. Though so extended a study, where so many diverse peoples are successively passed in review, could hardly be equally thorough in all its parts, still it is a useful hand-book to consult, and one which can aid greatly in facilitating researches.

II

From this historical résumé it is clear that Australia is the most favourable field for the study of totemism, and therefore we shall make it the principal area of our observations.

In his *Totemism*, Frazer sought especially to collect all the traces of totemism which could be found in history or ethnography. He was thus led to include in his study societies the nature and degree of whose culture differs most widely: ancient Egypt,[2] Arabia and Greece,[3] and the southern Slavs[4] are found there, side by side with the tribes of Australia and America. This manner of procedure is not at all surprising for a disciple of the anthropological school. For this school does not seek to locate religions in the social environments of which they are a part,[5] and to differentiate them according to the different environments to which they are thus connected. But rather, as is indicated by the name which it has taken to itself, its purpose is to go beyond the national and historical differences to the universal and really human bases of the religious life. It is supposed that man has a religious nature of himself, in virtue of his

[1] It is true that at the end and at the beginning there are some general theories on totemism, which will be described and discussed below. But these theories are relatively independent of the collection of facts which accompanies them, for they had already been published in different articles in reviews, long before this work appeared. These articles are reproduced in the first volume (pp. 89–172).

[2] *Totemism*, p. 12. [3] *Ibid.*, p. 15. [4] *Ibid.*, p. 32.

[5] It should be noted that in this connection, the more recent work, *Totemism and Exogamy*, shows an important progress in the thought as well as the method of Frazer. Every time that he describes the religious or domestic institutions of a tribe, he sets himself to determine the geographic and social conditions in which this tribe is placed. Howsoever summary these analyses may be, they bear witness nevertheless to a rupture with the old methods of the anthropological school.

own constitution, and independently of all social conditions, and they propose to study this.[1] For researches of this sort, all peoples can be called upon equally well. It is true that they prefer the more primitive peoples, because this fundamental nature is more apt to be unaltered here; but since it is found equally well among the most civilized peoples, it is but natural that they too should be called as witnesses. Consequently, all those who pass as being not too far removed from the origins, and who are confusedly lumped together under the rather imprecise rubric of *savages*, are put on the same plane and consulted indifferently. Since from this point of view, facts have an interest only in proportion to their generality, they consider themselves obliged to collect as large a number as possible of them; the circle of comparisons could not become too large.

Our method will not be such a one, for several reasons.

In the first place, for the sociologist as for the historian, social facts vary with the social system of which they form a part; they cannot be understood when detached from it. This is why two facts which come from two different societies cannot be profitably compared merely because they seem to resemble each other; it is necessary that these societies themselves resemble each other, that is to say, that they be only varieties of the same species. The comparative method would be impossible, if social types did not exist, and it cannot be usefully applied except within a single type. What errors have not been committed for having neglected this precept! It is thus that facts have been unduly connected with each other which, in spite of exterior resemblances, really have neither the same sense nor the same importance: the primitive democracy and that of to-day, the collectivism of inferior societies and actual socialistic tendencies, the monogamy which is frequent in Australian tribes and that sanctioned by our laws, etc. Even in the work of Frazer such confusions are found. It frequently happens that he assimilates simple rites of wild-animal-worship to practices that are really totemic, though the distance, sometimes very great, which separates the two social systems would exclude all idea of assimilation. Then if we do not wish to fall into these same errors, instead of scattering our researches over all the societies possible, we must concentrate them upon one clearly determined type.

It is even necessary that this concentration be as close as possible. One cannot usefully compare facts with which he is

[1] Undoubtedly we also consider that the principal object of the science of religions is to find out what the religious nature of man really consists in. However, as we do not regard it as a part of his constitutional make-up, but rather as the product of social causes, we consider it impossible to find it, if we leave aside his social environment.

not perfectly well acquainted. But when he undertakes to include all sorts of societies and civilizations, one cannot know any of them with the necessary thoroughness ; when he assembles facts from every country in order to compare them, he is obliged to take them hastily, without having either the means or the time to carefully criticize them. Tumultuous and summary comparisons result, which discredit the comparative method with many intelligent persons. It can give serious results only when it is applied to so limited a number of societies that each of them can be studied with sufficient precision. The essential thing is to choose those where investigations have the greatest chance to be fruitful.

Also, the value of the facts is much more important than their number. In our eyes, the question whether totemism has been more or less universal or not, is quite secondary.[1] If it interests us, it does so before all because in studying it we hope to discover relations of a nature to make us understand better what religion is. Now to establish these relations it is neither necessary nor always useful to heap up numerous experiences upon each other ; it is much more important to have a few that are well studied and really significant. One single fact may make a law appear, where a multitude of imprecise and vague observations would only produce confusion. In every science, the scholar would be overwhelmed by the facts which present themselves to him, if he did not make a choice among them. It is necessary that he distinguish those which promise to be the most instructive, that he concentrate his attention upon these, and that he temporarily leave the others to one side.

That is why, with one reservation which will be indicated below, we propose to limit our research to Australian societies. They fulfil all the conditions which were just enumerated. They are perfectly homogeneous, for though it is possible to distinguish varieties among them, they all belong to one common type. This homogeneity is even so great that the forms of social organization are not only the same, but that they are even designated by identical or equivalent names in a multitude of tribes, sometimes very distant from each other.[2] Also, Australian totemism is the variety for which our documents are the most complete. Finally, that which we propose to study in this work is the most primitive and simple religion which it is possible to find. It is therefore natural that to discover it, we address ourselves

[1] We cannot repeat too frequently that the importance which we attach to totemism is absolutely independent of whether it was ever universal or not.

[2] This is the case with the phratries and matrimonial classes ; on this point, see Spencer and Gillen, *Northern Tribes*, ch. iii ; Howitt, *Native Tribes*, pp. 109 and 137–142 ; Thomas, *Kinship and Marriage in Australia*, ch. vi and vii.

to societies as slightly evolved as possible, for it is evidently there that we have the greatest chance of finding it and studying it well. Now there are no societies which present this characteristic to a higher degree than the Australian ones. Not only is their civilization most rudimentary—the house and even the hut are still unknown—but also their organization is the most primitive and simple which is actually known; it is that which we have elsewhere called *organization on a basis of clans.*[1] In the next chapter, we shall have occasion to restate its essential traits.

However, though making Australia the principal field of our research, we think it best not to leave completely aside the societies where totemism was first discovered, that is to say, the Indian tribes of North America.

This extension of the field of comparison has nothing about it which is not legitimate. Undoubtedly these people are more advanced than those of Australia. Their civilization has become much more advanced: men there live in houses or under tents, and there are even fortified villages. The size of the society is much greater, and centralization, which is completely lacking in Australia, is beginning to appear there; we find vast confederations, such as that of the Iroquois, under one central authority. Sometimes a complicated system of differentiated classes arranged in a hierarchy is found. However, the essential lines of the social structure remain the same as those in Australia; it is always the organization on a basis of clans. Thus we are not in the presence of two different types, but of two varieties of a single type, which are still very close to each other. They represent two successive moments of a single evolution, so their homogeneousness is still great enough to permit comparisons.

Also, these comparisons may have their utility. Just because their civilization is more advanced than that of the Australians, certain phases of the social organization which is common to both can be studied more easily among the first than among the second. As long as men are still making their first steps in the art of expressing their thought, it is not easy for the observer to perceive that which moves them; for there is nothing to translate clearly that which passes in these obscure minds which have only a confused and ephemeral knowledge of themselves. For example, religious symbols then consist only in formless combinations of lines and colours, whose sense it is not easy to divine, as we shall see. There are many gestures and movements by which interior states express themselves; but being

[1] *Division du Travail social*, 3rd ed., p. 150.

essentially ephemeral, they readily elude observation. That is why totemism was discovered earlier in America than in Australia; it was much more visible there, though it held relatively less place in the totality of the religious life. Also, wherever beliefs and institutions do not take a somewhat definite material form, they are more liable to change under the influence of the slightest circumstances, or to become wholly effaced from the memory. Thus the Australian clans frequently have something floating and Protean about them, while the corresponding organization in America has a greater stability and more clearly defined contours. Thus, though American totemism is further removed from its origins than that of Australia, still there are important characteristics of which it has better kept the memory.

In the second place, in order to understand an institution, it is frequently well to follow it into the advanced stages of its evolution; [1] for sometimes it is only when it is fully developed that its real signification appears with the greatest clearness. In this way also, American totemism, since it has a long history behind it, could serve to clarify certain aspects of Australian totemism.[2] At the same time, it will put us in a better condition to see how totemism is bound up with the forms which follow, and to mark its place in the general historical development of religion.

So in the discussions which follow, we shall not forbid ourselves the use of certain facts borrowed from the Indian societies of North America. But we are not going to study American totemism here; [3] such a study must be made directly and by itself, and cannot be mixed with the one which we are undertaking; it raises other problems and implies a wholly different set of special investigations. We shall have recourse to American facts merely in a supplementary way, and only when they seem to be able to make us understand Australian facts to advantage. It is these latter which constitute the real and immediate object of our researches.[4]

[1] It is to be understood that this is not always the case. It frequently happens, as we have already said, that the simpler forms aid to a better understanding of the more complex. On this point, there is no rule of method which is applicable to every possible case.

[2] Thus the individual totemism of America will aid us in understanding the function and importance of that in Australia. As the latter is very rudimentary, it would probably have passed unobserved.

[3] Besides, there is not one unique type of totemism in America, but several different species which must be distinguished.

[4] We shall leave this field only very exceptionally, and when a particularly instructive comparison seems to us to impose itself.

BOOK II

THE ELEMENTARY BELIEFS

CHAPTER I

TOTEMIC BELIEFS

The Totem as Name and as Emblem

OWING to its nature, our study will include two parts. Since every religion is made up of intellectual conceptions and ritual practices, we must deal successively with the beliefs and rites which compose the totemic religion. These two elements of the religious life are too closely connected with each other to allow of any radical separation. In principle, the cult is derived from the beliefs, yet it reacts upon them; the myth is frequently modelled after the rite in order to account for it, especially when its sense is no longer apparent. On the other hand, there are beliefs which are clearly manifested only through the rites which express them. So these two parts of our analysis cannot fail to overlap. However, these two orders of facts are so different that it is indispensable to study them separately. And since it is impossible to understand anything about a religion while unacquainted with the ideas upon which it rests, we must seek to become acquainted with these latter first of all.

But it is not our intention to retrace all the speculations into which the religious thought, even of the Australians alone, has run. The things we wish to reach are the elementary notions at the basis of the religion, but there is no need of following them through all the development, sometimes very confused, which the mythological imagination of these peoples has given them. We shall make use of myths when they enable us to understand these fundamental ideas better, but we shall not make mythology itself the subject of our studies. In so far as this is a work of art, it does not fall within the jurisdiction of the simple science of religions. Also, the intellectual evolution from which it results is of too great a complexity to be studied indirectly and from a foreign point of view. It constitutes a very difficult problem which must be treated by itself, for itself and with a method peculiar to itself.

Among the beliefs upon which totemism rests, the most important are naturally those concerning the totem; it is with these that we must begin.

I

At the basis of nearly all the Australian tribes we find a group which holds a preponderating place in the collective life: this is the clan. Two essential traits characterize it.

In the first place, the individuals who compose it consider themselves united by a bond of kinship, but one which is of a very special nature. This relationship does not come from the fact that they have definite blood connections with one another; they are relatives from the mere fact that they have the same name. They are not fathers and mothers, sons or daughters, uncles or nephews of one another in the sense which we now give these words; yet they think of themselves as forming a single family, which is large or small according to the dimensions of the clan, merely because they are collectively designated by the same word. When we say that they regard themselves as a single family, we do so because they recognize duties towards each other which are identical with those which have always been incumbent upon kindred: such duties as aid, vengeance, mourning, the obligation not to marry among themselves, etc.

By this first characteristic, the clan does not differ from the Roman *gens* or the Greek γένος; for this relationship also came merely from the fact that all the members of the *gens* had the same name,[1] the *nomen gentilicium*. And in one sense, the *gens* is a clan; but it is a variety which should not be confounded with the Australian clan.[2] This latter is distinguished by the fact that its name is also the name of a determined species of material things with which it believes that it has very particular relations, the nature of which we shall presently describe; they are especially relations of kinship. The species of things which serves to designate the clan collectively is called its *totem*. The totem of the clan is also that of each of its members.

Each clan has its totem, which belongs to it alone; two different clans of the same tribe cannot have the same. In fact, one is a member of a clan merely because he has a certain name. All who bear this name are members of it for that very reason; in whatever manner they may be spread over the tribal territory,

[1] This is the definition given by Cicero: *Gentiles sunt qui inter se eodem nomine sunt* (*Top.* 6). (Those are of the same *gens* who have the same name among themselves.)

[2] It may be said in a general way that the clan is a family group, where kinship results solely from a common name; it is in this sense that the *gens* is a clan. But the totemic clan is a particular sort of the class thus constituted.

they all have the same relations of kinship with one another.[1] Consequently, two groups having the same totem can only be two sections of the same clan. Undoubtedly, it frequently happens that all of a clan does not reside in the same locality, but has representatives in several different places. However, this lack of a geographical basis does not cause its unity to be the less keenly felt.

In regard to the word totem, we may say that it is the one employed by the Ojibway, an Algonquin tribe, to designate the sort of thing whose name the clan bears.[2] Although this expression is not at all Australian,[3] and is found only in one single society in America, ethnographers have definitely adopted it, and use it to denote, in a general way, the system which we are describing. Schoolcraft was the first to extend the meaning of the word thus and to speak of a "totemic system." [4] This extension, of which there are examples enough in ethnography, is not without inconveniences. It is not normal for an institution of this importance to bear a chance name, taken from a strictly local dialect, and bringing to mind none of the distinctive characteristics of the thing it designates. But to-day this way of employing the word is so universally accepted that it would be an excess of purism to rise against this usage.[5]

In a very large proportion of the cases, the objects which serve as totems belong either to the animal or the vegetable kingdom, but especially to the former. Inanimate things are much more rarely employed. Out of more than 500 totemic names collected by Howitt among the tribes of south-eastern Australia, there are scarcely forty which are not the names of plants or animals; these are the clouds, rain, hail, frost, the

[1] In a certain sense, these bonds of solidarity extend even beyond the frontiers of the tribe. When individuals of different tribes have the same totem, they have peculiar duties towards each other. This fact is expressly stated for certain tribes of North America (see Frazer, *Totemism and Exogamy*, III, pp. 57, 81, 299, 356–357). The texts relative to Australia are less explicit. However, it is probable that the prohibition of marriage between members of a single totem is international.

[2] Morgan, *Ancient Society*, p. 165.

[3] In Australia the words employed differ with the tribes. In the regions observed by Grey, they said *Kobong*; the Dieri say *Murdu* (Howitt, *Nat Tr.*, p. 91); the Narrinyeri, *Ngaitye* (Talpin, *in* Curr, II, p. 244); the Warramunga, *Mungái* or *Mungáii* (*Nor. Tr.*, p. 754), etc.

[4] *Indian Tribes of the United States*, IV, p. 86.

[5] This fortune of the word is the more regrettable since we do not even know exactly how it is written. Some write *totam*, others *toodaim*, or *dodaim*, or *ododam* (see Frazer, *Totemism*, p. 1). Nor is the meaning of the word determined exactly. According to the report of the first observer of the Ojibway, J. Long, the word *totam* designated the protecting genius, the individual totem, of which we shall speak below (Bk. II, ch. iv) and not the totem of the clan. But the accounts of other explorers say exactly the contrary (on this point, see Frazer, *Totemism and Exogamy*, III, pp. 49–52).

moon, the sun, the wind, the autumn, the summer, the winter, certain stars, thunder, fire, smoke, water or the sea. It is noticeable how small a place is given to celestial bodies and, more generally, to the great cosmic phenomena, which were destined to so great a fortune in later religious development. Among all the clans of which Howitt speaks, there were only two which had the moon as totem,[1] two the sun,[2] three a star,[3] three the thunder,[4] two the lightning.[5] The rain is a single exception ; it, on the contrary, is very frequent.[6]

These are the totems which can be spoken of as normal. But totemism has its abnormalities as well. It sometimes happens that the totem is not a whole object, but the part of an object. This fact appears rather rarely in Australia ;[7] Howitt cites only one example.[8] However, it may well be that this is found with a certain frequency in the tribes where the totemic groups are excessively subdivided ; it might be said that the totems had to break themselves up in order to be able to furnish names to these numerous divisions. This is what seems to have taken place among the Arunta and the Loritja. Strehlow has collected 442 totems in these two societies, of which many are not an animal species, but some particular organ of the animal of the species, such as the tail or stomach of an opossum, the fat of the kangaroo, etc.[9]

We have seen that normally the totem is not an individual, but a species or a variety : it is not such and such a kangaroo or crow, but the kangaroo or crow in general. Sometimes, however, it is a particular object. First of all, this is necessarily the case when the thing serving as totem is unique in its class, as the sun, the moon, such or such a constellation, etc. It also happens that clans take their names from certain geographical irregularities or depressions of the land, from a certain ant-hill, etc. It is true

[1] The *Wotjobaluk* (p. 121) and the *Buandik* (p. 123).

[2] The same.

[3] The *Wolgal* (p. 102), the *Wotjobaluk* and the *Buandik*.

[4] The *Muruburra* (p. 117), the *Wotjobaluk* and the *Buandik*.

[5] The *Buandik* and the *Kaiabara* (p. 116). It is to be remarked that all the examples come from only five tribes.

[6] Thus, out of 204 kinds of totems, collected by Spencer and Gillen out of a large number of tribes, 188 are animals or plants. The inanimate objects are the boomerang, cold weather, darkness, fire, lightning, the moon, red ochre, resin, salt water, the evening star, a stone, the sun, water, the whirlwind, the wind and hail-stones (*Nor. Tr.*, p. 773. Cf. Frazer, *Totemism and Exogamy*, I, pp. 253–254).

[7] Frazer (*Totemism*, pp. 10 and 13) cites a rather large number of cases and puts them in a special group which he calls *split-totems*, but these are taken from tribes where totemism is greatly altered, such as in Samoa or the tribes of Bengal.

[8] Howitt, *Nat. Tr.*, p. 107.

[9] See the tables collected by Strehlow, *op. cit.*, II, pp. 61–72 (cf. III, pp. xiii–xvii). It is remarkable that these fragmentary totems are taken exclusively from animal totems.

that we have only a small number of examples of this in Australia; but Strehlow does mention some.[1] But the very causes which have given rise to these abnormal totems show that they are of a relatively recent origin. In fact, what has made certain geographical features of the land become totems is that a mythical ancestor is supposed to have stopped there or to have performed some act of his legendary life there.[2] But at the same time, these ancestors are represented in the myths as themselves belonging to clans which had perfectly regular totems, that is to say, ones taken from the animal or vegetable kingdoms. Therefore, the totemic names thus commemorating the acts and performances of these heroes cannot be primitive; they belong to a form of totemism that is already derived and deviated. It is even permissible to ask if the meteorological totems have not a similar origin; for the sun, the moon and the stars are frequently identified with the ancestors of the mythological epoch.[3]

Sometimes, but no less exceptionally, it is an ancestor or a group of ancestors which serves as totem directly. In this case, the clan takes its name, not from a thing or a species of real things, but from a purely mythical being. Spencer and Gillen had already mentioned two or three totems of this sort. Among the Warramunga and among the Tjingilli there are clans which bear the name of an ancestor named Thaballa who seems to be gaiety incarnate.[4] Another Warramunga clan bears the name of a huge fabulous serpent named Wollunqua, from which the clan considers itself descended.[5] We owe other similar facts to Strehlow.[6] In any case, it is easy enough to see what probably took place. Under the influence of diverse causes and by the very development of mythological thought, the collective and impersonal totem became effaced before certain mythical personages who advanced to the first rank and became totems themselves.

[1] Strehlow, II, pp. 52 and 72.

[2] For example, one of these totems is a cave where an ancestor of the Wild Cat totem rested; another is a subterranean gallery which an ancestor of the Mouse clan dug, etc. (*ibid.*, p. 72).

[3] *Nat. Tr.*, pp. 561 ff. Strehlow, II, p. 71, note 2. Howitt, *Nat. Tr.*, pp. 426 ff.; *On Australian Medicine Men*, *J.A.I.*, XVI, p. 53; *Further Notes on the Australian Class Systems*, *J.A.I.*, XVIII, pp. 63 ff.

[4] Thaballa means "laughing boy," according to the translation of Spencer and Gillen. The members of the clan which bear this name think they hear him laughing in the rocks which are his residence (*Nor. Tr.*, pp. 207, 215, 226 note). According to a myth given on p. 422, there was an initial group of mythical Thaballa (cf. p. 208). The clan of the Kati, "full-grown men," as Spencer and Gillen say, seems to be of the same sort (*Nor. Tr.*, p. 207).

[5] *Nor. Tr.*, pp. 226 ff.

[6] Strehlow, II, pp. 71 f. He mentions a totem of the Loritja and Arunta which is very close to the serpent Wollunqua: it is the totem of a mythical water-snake.

Howsoever interesting these different irregularities may be, they contain nothing which forces us to modify our definition of a totem. They are not, as has sometimes been believed,[1] different varieties of totems which are more or less irreducible into each other or into the normal totem, such as we have defined it. They are merely secondary and sometimes even aberrant forms of a single notion which is much more general, and there is every ground for believing it the more primitive.

The manner in which the name is acquired is more important for the organization and recruiting of the clan than for religion; it belongs to the sociology of the family rather than to religious sociology.[2] So we shall confine ourselves to indicating summarily the most essential principles which regulate the matter.

In the different tribes, three different systems are in use.

In a great number, or it might even be said, in the greater number of the societies, the child takes the totem of its mother, by right of birth: this is what happens among the Dieri and the Urabunna of the centre of Southern Australia; the Wotjobaluk and the Gournditch-Mara of Victoria; the Kamilaroi, the Wiradjuri, the Wonghibon and the Euahlayi of New South Wales; and the Wakelbura, the Pitta-Pitta and the Kurnandaburi of Queensland, to mention only the most important names. In this case, owing to a law of exogamy, the mother is necessarily of a different totem from her husband, and on the other hand, as she lives in his community, the members of a single totem are necessarily dispersed in different localities according to the chances of their marriages. As a result, the totemic group lacks a territorial base.

Elsewhere the totem is transmitted in the paternal line. In this case, if the child remains with his father, the local group is largely made up of people belonging to a single totem; only the married women there represent foreign totems. In other words, each locality has its particular totem. Up until recent times, this scheme of organization was found in Australia only among the tribes where totemism was in decadence, such as the Narrinyeri, where the totem has almost no religious character at all

[1] This is the case with Klaatsch, in the article already cited (see above, p. 92, n. 3).

[2] As we indicated in the preceding chapter, totemism is at the same time of interest for the question of religion and that of the family, for the clan is a family. In the lower societies, these two problems are very closely connected. But both are so complex that it is indispensable to treat them separately. Also, the primitive family organization cannot be understood before the primitive religious beliefs are known; for the latter serve as the basis of the former. This is why it is necessary to study totemism as a religion before studying the totemic clan as a family group.

any more.[1] It was therefore possible to believe that there was a close connection between the totemic system and descent in the uterine line. But Spencer and Gillen have observed, in the northern part of central Australia, a whole group of tribes where the totemic religion is still practised but where the transmission of the totem is in the paternal line: these are the Warramunga, the Quanji, the Umbia, the Binbinga, the Mara and the Anula.[2]

Finally, a third combination is the one observed among the Arunta and Loritja. Here the totem of the child is not necessarily either that of the mother or that of the father; it is that of a mythical ancestor who came, by processes which the observers recount in different ways,[3] and mysteriously fecundated the mother at the moment of conception. A special process makes it possible to learn which ancestor it was and to which totemic group he belonged.[4] But since it was only chance which determined that this ancestor happened to be near the mother, rather than another, the totem of the child is thus found to depend finally upon fortuitous circumstances.[5]

Outside of and above the totems of clans there are totems of phratries which, though not differing from the former in nature, must none the less be distinguished from them.

A phratry is a group of clans which are united to each other by particular bonds of fraternity. Ordinarily the Australian tribe is divided into two phratries between which the different clans are distributed. Of course there are some tribes where this organization has disappeared, but everything leads us to believe that it was once general. In any case, there are no tribes in Australia where the number of phratries is greater than two.

Now in nearly all the cases where the phratries have a name

[1] See Taplin, *The Narrinyeri Tribe*, in Curr, II, pp. 244 f.; Howitt, *Nat. Tr.*, p. 131.

[2] *Nor. Tr.*, pp. 163, 169, 170, 172. It is to be noted that in all these tribes, except the Mara and the Anula, the transmission of the totem in the paternal line is only a general rule, which has exceptions.

[3] According to Spencer and Gillen (*Nat. Tr.*, pp. 123 ff.), the soul of the ancestor becomes reincarnate in the body of the mother and becomes the soul of the child; according to Strehlow (II, pp. 51 ff.), the conception, though being the work of the ancestor, does not imply any reincarnation; but in neither interpretation does the totem of the child necessarily depend upon that of the parents.

[4] *Nat. Tr.*, p. 133; Strehlow, II, p. 53.

[5] It is in large part the locality where the mother believes that she conceived which determines the totem of the child. Each totem, as we shall see, has its centre and the ancestors preferably frequent the places serving as centres for their respective totems. The totem of the child is therefore that which belongs to the place where the mother believes that she conceived. As this should generally be in the vicinity of the place which serves as totemic centre for her husband, the child should generally follow the totem of his father. It is undoubtedly this which explains why the greater part of the inhabitants of a given locality belong to the same totem (*Nat. Tr.*, p. 9).

whose meaning has been established, this name is that of an animal; it would therefore seem that it is a totem. This has been well demonstrated in a recent work by A. Lang.[1] Thus, among the Gournditch (Victoria), the phratries are called Krokitch and Kaputch; the former of the words designates the white cockatoo and the latter the black cockatoo.[2] The same expressions are found again among the Buandik and the Wotjobaluk.[3] Among the Wurunjerri, the names employed are Bunjil and Waang, which designate the eagle-hawk and the crow.[4] The words Mukwara and Kilpara are used for the same purpose in a large number of tribes of New South Wales;[5] they designate the same birds.[6] It is also the eagle-hawk and the crow which have given their names to the two phratries of the Ngarigo and the Wolgal.[7] Among the Kuinmurbura, it is the white cockatoo and the crow.[8] Many other examples might be cited. Thus we are led to regard the phratry as an ancient clan which has been dismembered; the actual clans are the product of this dismemberment, and the solidarity which unites them is a souvenir of their primitive unity.[9] It is true that in certain tribes, the phratries no longer have special names, as it seems; in others where these names exist, their meaning is no longer known, even to the members. But there is nothing surprising in this. The phratries are certainly a primitive institution, for they are everywhere in a state of regression; their descendants the clans have passed to the first rank. So it is but natural that the names which they bore should have been effaced from memory little by little, when they were no longer understood; for they must belong to a very archaic language no longer in use. This is proved by the fact that in many cases where we know the animal whose name the phratry bears, the word designating this animal in the current language is very different from the one employed here.[10]

[1] *The Secret of the Totem*, pp. 159 ff. Cf. Fison and Howitt, *Kamilaroi and Kurnai*, pp. 40 f.; John Mathews, *Eaglehawk and Crow*; Thomas, *Kinship and Marriage in Australia*, pp. 52 ff.

[2] Howitt, *Nat. Tr.*, p. 124.

[3] Howitt, pp. 121, 123, 124; Curr, III, p. 461.

[4] Howitt, p. 126.

[5] Howitt, pp. 98 ff.

[6] Curr, II, p. 165; Brough Smyth, I, p. 423; Howitt, *op. cit.*, p. 429.

[7] Howitt, pp. 101, 102.

[8] J. Mathews, *Two Representative Tribes of Queensland*, p. 139.

[9] Still other reasons could be given in support of this hypothesis, but it would be necessary to bring in considerations relative to the organization of the family, and we wish to keep these two studies separate. Also this question is only of secondary interest to our subject.

[10] For example, Mukwara, which is the name of a phratry among the Barkinji, the Paruinji and the Milpulko, designates the eagle-hawk, according to Brough Smyth; now one of the clans of this phratry has the eagle-hawk as totem. But here the animal is designated by the word Bilyara. Many cases of the same thing are cited by Lang, *op. cit.*, p. 162.

Between the totem of the phratry and the totems of the clans there exists a sort of relation of subordination. In fact, in principle each clan belongs to one and only one phratry; it is very exceptional that it has representatives in the other phratry. This is not met with at all except among certain central tribes, notably the Arunta;[1] also even where, owing to disturbing influences, overlappings of this sort have taken place, the great part of the clan is included entirely within one or the other of the two groups of the tribe; only a small minority is to be found in the other one.[2] As a rule then, the two phratries do not overlap each other; consequently, the list of totems which an individual may have is predetermined by the phratry to which he belongs. In other words, the phratry is like a species of which the clans are varieties. We shall presently see that this comparison is not purely metaphorical.

In addition to the phratries and clans, another secondary group is frequently met with in Australian societies, which is not without a certain individuality: these are the matrimonial classes.

By this name they designate certain subdivisions of the phratry, whose number varies with the tribe: there are sometimes two and sometimes four per phratry.[3] Their recruiting and operation are regulated by the two following principles. In the first place, each generation in a phratry belongs to different clans from the immediately preceding one. Thus, when there are only two classes per phratry, they necessarily alternate with each other every generation. The children make up the class of which their parents are not members; but grandchildren are of the same class as their grandparents. Thus, among the Kamilaroi, the Kupathin phratry has two classes, Ippai and Kumbo; the Dilby phratry, two others which are called Murri and Kubbi. As descent is in the uterine line, the child is in the phratry of its mother; if she is a Kupathin, the child will be one also. But if she is of the Ippai class, he will be a Kumbo; if the child is a girl, her children will again be in the Ippai class.

[1] Spencer and Gillen, *Nat. Tr.*, p. 115. According to Howitt (*op. cit.*, pp. 121 and 454), among the Wotjobaluk, the clan of the pelican is found in the two phratries equally. This fact seems doubtful to us. It is very possible that the two clans may have two varieties of pelicans as totems. Information given by Mathews on the same tribe seems to point to this (*Aboriginal Tribes of N.S. Wales and Victoria*, in *Journal and Proceedings of the Royal Society of N.S. Wales*, 1904, pp. 287 f.).

[2] In connection with this question, see our memoir on *Le Totémisme*, in the *Année Sociologique*, Vol. V, pp. 82 ff.

[3] On the question of Australian matrimonial classes in general, see our memoir on *La Prohibition de l'inceste*, in the *Année Soc.*, I, pp. 9 ff., and especially for the tribes with eight classes, *L'Organisation matrimoniale des sociétés Australiennes*, in *Année Soc.*, VIII, pp. 118–147.

Likewise, the children of the women of the Murri class will be in the Kubbi class, and the children of the Kubbi women will be Murri again. When there are four classes per phratry, instead of two, the system is naturally more complex, but the principle is the same. The four classes form two couples of two classes each, and these two classes alternate with each other every generation in the manner just indicated. Secondly, the members of one class can in principle [1] marry into only one of the classes of the other phratry. The Ippai must marry into the Kubbi class and the Murri into the Kumbo class. It is because this organization profoundly affects matrimonial relations that we give the group the name of matrimonial class.

Now it may be asked whether these classes do not sometimes have totems like the phratries and clans.

This question is raised by the fact that in certain tribes of Queensland, each matrimonial class has dietetic restrictions that are peculiar to it. The individuals who compose it must abstain from eating the flesh of certain animals which the others may consume freely.[2] Are these animals not totems?

But dietetic restrictions are not the characteristic marks of totemism. The totem is a name first of all, and then, as we shall see, an emblem. Now in the societies of which we just spoke, there are no matrimonial classes which bear the name of an animal or plant, or which have an emblem.[3] Of course it is possible that these restrictions are indirectly derived from totemism. It might be supposed that the animals which these interdictions protect were once the totems of clans which have since disappeared, while the matrimonial classes remained. It is certain that they have a force of endurance which the clans do not have. Then these interdictions, deprived of their original

[1] This principle is not maintained everywhere with an equal strictness. In the central tribes of eight classes notably, beside the class with which marriage is regularly permitted, there is another with which a sort of secondary concubinage is allowed (Spencer and Gillen, *Nor. Tr.*, p. 106). It is the same with certain tribes of four classes. Each class has a choice between the two classes of the other phratry. This is the case with the Kabi (see Mathews, *in* Curr, III, 162).

[2] See Roth, *Ethnological Studies among the North-West-Central Queensland Aborigines*, pp. 56 ff.; Palmer, *Notes on some Australian Tribes*, *J.A.I.*, XIII (1884), pp. 302 ff.

[3] Nevertheless, some tribes are cited where the matrimonial classes bear the names of animals or plants: this is the case with the Kabi (Mathew, *Two Representative Tribes*, p. 150), the tribes observed by Mrs. Bates (*The Marriage Laws and Customs of the West Australian Aborigines*, in *Victorian Geographical Journal*, XXIII–XXIV, p. 47), and perhaps in two tribes observed by Palmer. But these facts are very rare and their significance badly established. Also, it is not surprising that the classes, as well as the sexual groups, should sometimes adopt the names of animals. This exceptional extension of the totemic denominations in no way modifies our conception of totemism.

field, may have spread themselves out over the entire class, since there were no other groups to which they could be attached. But it is clear that if this regulation was born of totemism, it represents only an enfeebled and denatured form of it.[1]

All that has been said of the totem in Australian societies is equally applicable to the Indian tribes of North America. The only difference is that among these latter, the totemic organization has a strictness of outline and a stability which are not found in Australia. The Australian clans are not only very numerous, but in a single tribe their number is almost unlimited. Observers cite some of them as examples, but without ever succeeding in giving us a complete list. This is because the list is never definitely terminated. The same process of dismemberment which broke up the original phratries and give birth to clans properly so-called still continues within these latter ; as a result of this progressive crumbling, a clan frequently has only a very small effective force.[2] In America, on the contrary, the totemic system has better defined forms. Although the tribes there are considerably larger on the average, the clans are less numerous. A single tribe rarely has more than a dozen of them,[3] and frequently less ; each of them is therefore a much more important group. But above all, their number is fixed ; they know their exact number, and they it tell to us.[4]

[1] Perhaps the same explanation is applicable to certain other tribes of the South-East and the East where, if we are to believe the informers of Howitt, totems specially attached to each matrimonial class are to be found. This is the case among the Wiradjuri, the Wakelbura and the Bunta-Murra on the Bulloo River (Howitt, *Nat. Tr.*, pp. 210, 221, 226). However, the evidence collected is suspect, according to his own admission. In fact, it appears from the lists which he has drawn up, that many totems are found equally in the two classes of the same phratry.

The explanation which we propose, after Frazer (*Totemism and Exogamy*, pp. 531 ff.), raises one difficulty. In principle, each clan and consequently each totem, is represented equally in the two classes of a single phratry, since one of the classes is that of the children and the other that of the parents from whom the former get their totems. So when the clans disappeared, the totemic interdictions which survived should have remained in both matrimonial classes, while in the actual cases cited, each class has its own. Whence comes this differentiation ? The example of the Kaiabara (a tribe of southern Queensland) allows us to see how it may have come about. In this tribe, the children have the totem of their mother, but it is particularized by some distinctive mark. If the mother has the black eagle-hawk as totem, the child has the white eagle-hawk (Howitt, *Nat. Tr.*, p. 229). This appears to be the beginning of a tendency for the totems to differentiate themselves according to the matrimonial classes.

[2] A tribe of only a few hundred members frequently has fifty or sixty clans, or even many more. On this point, see Durkheim and Mauss, *De quelques formes primitives de classification*, in the *Année Sociologique*, Vol. VI, p. 28, n. 1.

[3] Except among the Pueblo Indians of the South-West, where they are more numerous. See Hodge, *Pueblo Indian Clans*, in *American Anthropologist*, 1st series, Vol. IX, pp. 345 ff. It may always be asked whether the groups which have these totems are clans or sub-clans.

[4] See the tables arranged by Morgan, *Ancient Society*, pp. 153–185.

This difference is due to the superiority of their social economy. From the moment when these tribes were observed for the first time, the social groups were strongly attached to the soil, and consequently better able to resist the decentralizing forces which assailed them. At the same time, the society had too keen a sentiment of its unity to remain unconscious of itself and of the parts out of which it was composed. The example of America thus enables us to explain even better the organization at the base of the clans. We would take a mistaken view, if we judged this only on the present conditions in Australia. In fact, it is in a state of change and dissolution there, which is not at all normal; it is much rather the product of a degeneration which we see, due both to the natural decay of time and the disorganizing effect of the whites. To be sure, it is hardly probable that the Australian clans ever had the dimensions and solid structure of the American ones. But there must have been a time when the distance between them was less considerable than it is to-day, for the American societies would never have succeeded in making so solid a structure if the clans had always been of so fluid and inconsistent a nature.

This greater stability has even enabled the archaic system of phratries to maintain itself in America with a clearness and a relief no longer to be found in Australia. We have just seen that in the latter continent the phratry is everywhere in a state of decadence; very frequently it is nothing more than an anonymous group; when it has a name, this is either no longer understood, or in any case, it cannot mean a great deal to the native, since it is borrowed from a foreign language, or from one no longer spoken. Thus we have been able to infer the existence of totems for phratries only from a few survivals, which, for the most part, are so slightly marked that they have escaped the attention of many observers. In certain parts of America, on the contrary, this institution has retained its primitive importance. The tribes of the North-west coast, the Tlinkit and the Haida especially, have now attained a relatively advanced civilization; yet they are divided into two phratries which are subdivided into a certain number of clans: the phratries of the Crow and the Wolf among the Tlinkit,[1] of the Eagle and the Crow among the Haida.[2] And this division is not merely nominal; it corresponds to an ever-existing state of tribal customs and is deeply marked with the tribal life. The moral distance separating the clans is

[1] Krause, *Die Tlinkit-Indianer*, p. 112; Swanton, *Social Condition, Beliefs and Linguistic Relationship of the Tlingit Indians*, in *XXVIth Rep.*, p. 308.

[2] Swanton, *Contributions to the Ethnology of the Haida*, p. 62.

very slight in comparison with that separating the phratries.[1] The name of each is not a word whose sense is forgotten or only vaguely known; it is a totem in the full sense of the term; they have all its essential attributes, such as will be described below.[2] Consequently, upon this point also, American tribes must not be neglected, for we can study the totems of phratries directly there, while Australia offers only obscure vestiges of them.

II

But the totem is not merely a name; it is an emblem, a veritable coat-of-arms whose analogies with the arms of heraldry have often been remarked. In speaking of the Australians, Grey says, "each family adopt an animal or vegetable as their crest and sign,"[3] and what Grey calls a family is incontestably a clan. Also Fison and Howitt say, "the Australian divisions show that the totem is, in the first place, the badge of a group."[4] Schoolcraft says the same thing about the totems of the Indians of North America. "The totem is in fact a design which corresponds to the heraldic emblems of civilized nations, and each person is authorized to bear it as a proof of the identity of the family to which it belongs. This is proved by the real etymology of the word, which is derived from *dodaim*, which means village or the residence of a family group."[5] Thus when the Indians entered into relations with the Europeans and contracts were formed between them, it was with its totem that each clan sealed the treaties thus concluded.[6]

The nobles of the feudal period carved, engraved and designed in every way their coats-of-arms upon the walls of their castles, their arms, and every sort of object that belonged to them; the blacks of Australia and the Indians of North America do the

[1] "The distinction between the two clans is absolute in every respect," says Swanton, p. 68; he gives the name clan to what we call phratries. The two phratries, he says elsewhere, are like two foreign nations in their relations to each other.

[2] Among the Haida at least, the totem of the real clans is altered more than that of the phratries. In fact, usage permits a clan to sell or give away the right of bearing its totem, as a result of which each clan has a number of totems, some of which it has in common with other clans (see Swanton, pp. 107 and 268). Since Swanton calls the phratries clans, he is obliged to give the name of *family* to the real clans, and of *household* to the regular families. But the real sense of his terminology is not to be doubted.

[3] *Journals of two Expeditions in N.W. and W. Australia*, II, p. 228.

[4] *Kamilaroi and Kurnai*, p. 165.

[5] *Indian Tribes*, I, p. 420; cf. I, p. 52. This etymology is very doubtful. Cf. *Handbook of American Indians North of Mexico* (*Smithsonian Inst. Bur. of Ethnol.*, Pt. II, *s.v.*, Totem, p. 787).

[6] Schoolcraft, *Indian Tribes*, III, 184; Garrick Mallery, *Picture Writing of the American Indians*, in *Tenth Report*, 1893, p. 377.

same thing with their totems. The Indians who accompanied Samuel Hearne painted their totems on their shields before going into battle.[1] According to Charlevoix, in time of war, certain tribes of Indians had veritable ensigns, made of bits of bark fastened to the end of a pole, upon which the totems were represented.[2] Among the Tlinkit, when a conflict breaks out between two clans, the champions of the two hostile groups wear helmets over their heads, upon which are painted their respective totems.[3] Among the Iroquois, they put the skin of the animal which serves as totem upon each wigwam, as a mark of the clan.[4] According to another observer, the animal was stuffed and set up before the door.[5] Among the Wyandot, each clan has its own ornaments and its distinctive paintings.[6] Among the Omaha, and among the Sioux generally, the totem is painted on the tent.[7]

Wherever the society has become sedentary, where the tent is replaced by the house, and where the plastic arts are more fully developed, the totem is engraved upon the woodwork and upon the walls. This is what happens, for example, among the Haida, the Tsimshian, the Salish and the Tlinkit. "A very particular ornament of the house, among the Tlinkit," says Krause, "is the totemic coat-of-arms." Animal forms, sometimes combined with human forms, are engraved upon the posts at the sides of the door of entry, which are as high as 15 yards; they are generally painted with very bright colours.[8] However, these totemic decorations are not very numerous in the Tlinkit village; they are found almost solely before the houses of the chiefs and rich men. They are much more frequent in the neighbouring tribe of the Haida; here there are always several for each house.[9] With its many sculptured posts arising on every hand, sometimes to a great height, a Haida village gives the impression of a sacred city, all bristling with belfries or little minarets.[10] Among the Salish, the totem is frequently represented upon the interior walls of the house.[11] Elsewhere, it

[1] Hearne, *Journey to the Northern Ocean*, p. 148 (quoted from Frazer, *Totemism*, p. 30).

[2] Charlevoix, *Histoire et description de la Nouvelle France*, V, p. 329.

[3] Krause, *Tlinkit-Indianer*, p. 248.

[4] Erminnie A. Smith, *Myths of the Iroquois*, in *Sec. Rep. of the Bur. of Ethnol.*, p. 78.

[5] Dodge, *Our Wild Indians*, p. 225.

[6] Powell, *Wyandot Government*, in *First Rep. of the Bur. of Ethnol.*, 1881, p. 64.

[7] Dorsey, *Omaha Sociology*, in *Third Rep.*, pp. 229, 240, 248.

[8] Krause, *op. cit.*, pp. 130 f.

[9] Krause, p. 308.

[10] See a photograph of a Haida village in Swanton, *op. cit.*, Pl. IX. Cf. Tylor, *Totem Post of the Haida Village of Masset*, *J.A.I.*, New Series I, p. 133.

[11] Hill Tout, *Report on the Ethnology of the Statlumh of British Columbia*, *J.A.I.*, XXXV, p. 155.

is found upon the canoes, the utensils of every sort and the funeral piles.[1]

The preceding examples are taken exclusively from the Indians of North America. This is because sculpture, engravings and permanent figurations are not possible except where the technique of the plastic arts has reached a degree of perfection to which the Australian tribes have not yet attained. Consequently the totemic representations of the sort which we just mentioned are rarer and less apparent in Australia than in America. However, cases of them are cited. Among the Warramunga, at the end of the burial ceremonies, the bones of the dead man are interred, after they have been dried and reduced to powder; beside the place where they are deposited, a figure representing the totem is traced upon the ground.[2] Among the Mara and the Anula, the body is placed in a piece of hollow wood decorated with designs characteristic of the totem.[3] In New South Wales, Oxley found engravings upon the trees near the tomb where a native was buried [4] to which Brough Smyth attributes a totemic character. The natives of the Upper Darling carve totemic images upon their shields.[5] According to Collins, nearly all the utensils are covered with ornaments which probably have the same significance; figures of the same sort are found upon the rocks.[6] These totemic designs may even be more frequent than it seems, for, owing to reasons which will be discussed below, it is not always easy to see what their real meaning is.

These different facts give us an idea of the considerable place held by the totem in the social life of the primitives. However, up to the present, it has appeared to us as something relatively outside of the man, for it is only upon external things that we have seen it represented. But totemic images are not placed only upon the walls of their houses, the sides of their canoes, their arms, their utensils and their tombs; they are also found on the bodies of the men. They do not put their coat-of-arms merely upon the things which they possess, but they put it upon their persons; they imprint it upon their flesh, it becomes a

[1] Krause, *op. cit.*, p. 230; Swanton, *Haida*, pp. 129, 135 ff.; Schoolcraft, *op. cit.*, I, pp. 52–53, 337, 356. In the latter case the totem is represented upside down, in sign of mourning. Similar usages are found among the Creek (C. Swan, *in* Schoolcraft, V, p. 265) and the Delaware (Heckewelder, *An Account of the History, Manners and Customs of the Indian Nations who once inhabited Pennsylvania*, pp. 246–247).

[2] Spencer and Gillen, *Nor. Tr.*, pp. 168, 537, 540.

[3] *Ibid.*, p. 174.

[4] Brough Smyth, *The Aborigines of Victoria*, I, p. 99 n.

[5] Brough Smyth, I, p. 284. Strehlow cites a fact of the same sort among the Arunta (III, p. 68).

[6] *An Account of the English Colony in N.S. Wales*, II, p. 381.

part of them, and this world of representations is even by far the more important one.

In fact, it is a very general rule that the members of each clan seek to give themselves the external aspect of their totem. At certain religious festivals among the Tlinkit, the person who is to direct the ceremonies wears a garment which represents, either wholly or in part, the body of the animal whose name he bears.[1] These same usages are also found in all the North-West of America.[2] They are found again among the Minnitaree, when they go into combat,[3] and among the Indians of the Pueblos.[4] Elsewhere, when the totem is a bird, men wear the feathers of this bird on their heads.[5] Among the Iowa, each clan has a special fashion of cutting the hair. In the Eagle clan, two large tufts are arranged on the front of the head, while there is another one behind; in the Buffalo clan, they are arranged in the form of horns.[6] Among the Omaha, analogous arrangements are found: each clan has its own head-dress. In the Turtle clan, for example, the hair is all shaved off, except six bunches, two on each side of the head, one in front, and one behind, in such a way as to imitate the legs, the head and the tail of the animal.[7]

But it is more frequently upon the body itself that the totemic mark is stamped: for this is a way of representation within the capacity of even the least advanced societies. It has sometimes been asked whether the common rite of knocking out a young man's two upper teeth at the age of puberty does not have the object of reproducing the form of the totem. The fact is not established, but it is worth mentioning that the natives themselves sometimes explain the custom thus. For example, among the Arunta, the extraction of teeth is practised only in the clans of the rain and of water; now according to tradition, the object of this operation is to make their faces look like certain black clouds with light borders which are believed to announce the speedy arrival of rain, and which are therefore considered things of the same family.[8] This is a proof that the native himself is conscious that the object of these deformations is to give him, at least conventionally, the aspect of his totem. Among these

[1] Krause, p. 237.

[2] Swanton, *Social Condition, Beliefs and Linguistic Relationship of the Tlingit Indians*, in *XXVIth Rep.*, pp. 435 ff.; Boas, *The Social Organization and Secret Societies of the Kwakiutl Indians*, p. 358.

[3] Frazer, *Totemism*, p. 26.

[4] Bourke, *The Snake Dance of the Moquis of Arizona*, p. 229; J. W. Fewkes, *The Group of Tusayan Ceremonials called Katcinas*, in *XVth Rep.*, 1897, pp. 151–263.

[5] Müller, *Geschichte der Amerikanischen Urreligionen*, p. 327.

[6] Schoolcraft, *op. cit.*, III, p. 269.

[7] Dorsey, *Omaha Sociol.*, *Third Rep.*, pp. 229, 238, 240, 245.

[8] Spencer and Gillen, *Nat. Tr.*, p. 451.

same Arunta, in the course of the rites of sub-incision, certain gashes are cut upon the sisters and the future wife of the novice; scars result from these, whose form is also represented upon a certain sacred object of which we shall speak presently and which is called the *churinga;* as we shall see, the lines thus drawn upon the *churinga* are emblematic of the totem.[1] Among the Kaitish, the euro is believed to be closely connected with the rain;[2] the men of the rain clan wear little ear-rings made of euro teeth.[3] Among the Yerkla, during the initiation the young man is given a certain number of slashes which leave scars; the number and form of these varies with the totems.[4] An informer of Fison mentions the same fact in the tribes observed by him.[5] According to Howitt, a relationship of the same sort exists among the Dieri between certain arrangements of scars and the water totem.[6] Among the Indians of the North-West, it is a very general custom for them to tattoo themselves with the totem.[7]

But even if the tattooings which are made by mutilations or scars do not always have a totemic significance,[8] it is different with simple designs drawn upon the body: they are generally representations of the totem. It is true that the native does not carry them every day. When he is occupied with purely economic occupations, or when the small family groups scatter to hunt or fish, he does not bother with all this paraphernalia, which is quite complicated. But when the clans unite to live a common life and to assist at the religious ceremonies together, then he must adorn himself. As we shall see, each of the ceremonies concerns a particular totem, and in theory the rites which are connected with a totem can be performed only by the men of that totem. Now those who perform,[9] who take the part of

[1] Spencer and Gillen, *Nat. Tr.*, p. 257.

[2] The meaning of these relations will be seen below (Bk. II, ch. iv).

[3] Spencer and Gillen, *Nor. Tr.*, p. 296.

[4] Howitt, *Nat. Tr.*, pp. 744–746; cf. p. 129.

[5] *Kamilaroi and Kurnai*, p. 66 n. It is true that other informers contest this fact.

[6] Howitt, *Nat. Tr.*, p. 744.

[7] Swanton, *Contributions to the Ethnology of the Haida*, pp. 41 ff., Pl. XX and XXI; Boas, *The Social Organization of the Kwakiutl*, p. 318; Swanton, *Tlingit*, Pl. XVI ff.—In one place, outside the two ethnographic regions which we are specially studying, these tattooings are put on the animals which belong to the clan. The Bechuana of South Africa are divided into a certain number of clans; there are the people of the crocodile, the buffalo, the monkey, etc. Now the crocodile people, for example, make an incision in the ears of their cattle whose form is like the jaws of this animal (Casalis, *Les Basoutos*, p. 221). According to Robertson Smith, the same custom existed among the ancient Arabs (*Kinship and Marriage in Early Arabia*, pp. 212–214).

[8] However, according to Spencer and Gillen, there are some which have no religious sense (see *Nat. Tr.*, pp. 41 f.; *Nor. Tr.*, pp. 45, 54–56).

[9] Among the Arunta, this rule has exceptions which will be explained below.

officiants, and sometimes even those who assist as spectators, always have designs representing the totem on their bodies.[1] One of the principal rites of initiation, by which a young man enters into the religious life of the tribe, consists in painting the totemic symbol on his body.[2] It is true that among the Arunta the design thus traced does not always and necessarily represent the totem of the initiated;[3] but these are exceptions, due, undoubtedly, to the disturbed state of the totemic organization of this tribe.[4] Also, even among the Arunta, at the most solemn moment of the initiation, which is its crown and consecration, when the neophyte is allowed to enter the sanctuary where all the sacred objects belonging to the clan are preserved, an emblematic painting is placed upon him; this time, it is the

[1] Spencer and Gillen, *Nat. Tr.*, p. 162; *Nor. Tr.*, pp. 179, 259, 292, 295 f.; Schulze, *loc. cit.*, p. 221. The thing thus represented is not always the totem itself, but one of those things which, being associated to this totem, are regarded as being in the same family of things.

[2] This is the case, for example, among the Warramunga, the Walpari, the Wulmala, the Tjingilli, the Umbaia and the Unmatjera (*Nor. Tr.*, 339, 348). Among the Warramunga, at the moment when the design is executed, the performers address the initiated with the following words: " That mark belongs to your place; do not look out along another place." " This means," say Spencer and Gillen, " that the young man must not interfere with ceremonies belonging to other totems than his own: it also indicates the very close association which is supposed to exist between a man and his totem and any spot especially connected with the totem " (*Nor. Tr.*, p. 584 and n.). Among the Warramunga, the totem is transmitted from father to child, so each locality has its own.

[3] Spencer and Gillen, *Nat. Tr.*, pp. 215, 241, 376.

[4] It will be remembered (see above, p. 107) that in this tribe, the child may have a different totem than his father, his mother, or his relatives in general. Now the relatives on both sides are the performers designated for the ceremonies of initiation. Consequently, since in principle a man can have the quality of performer or officiant only for the ceremonies of his own totem, it follows that in certain cases the rites by which the young man is initiated must be in connection with a totem that is not his own. That is why the paintings made on the body of the novice do not necessarily represent his own totem: cases of this sort will be found in Spencer and Gillen, *Nat. Tr.*, p. 229. That there is an anomaly here is well shown by the fact that the circumcision falls to the totem which predominates in the local group of the initiate, that is to say, to the one which would be the totem of the initiate himself, if the totemic organization were not disturbed, if among the Arunta it were what it is among the Warramunga (see Spencer and Gillen, *ibid.*, p. 219).

The same disturbance has had another consequence. In a general way, its effect is to extend a little the bonds attaching each totem to a special group, since each totem may have members in all the local groups possible, and even in the two phratries. The idea that these ceremonies of a totem might be celebrated by an individual of another totem—an idea which is contrary to the very principles of totemism, as we shall see better after a while—has thus been accepted without too much resistance. It has been admitted that a man to whom a spirit revealed the formula for a ceremony had the right of presiding over it, even when he was not of the totem in question himself (*Nat. Tr.*, p. 519). But that this is an exception to the rule and the product of a sort of toleration is proved by the fact that the beneficiary of the formula does not have the free disposition of it; if he transmits it—and these transmissions are frequent—it can be only to a member of the totem which the rite concerns (*Nat. Tr.*, *ibid.*).

totem of the young man which is thus represented.[1] The bonds which unite the individual to his totem are even so strong that in the tribes on the North-west coast of North America, the emblem of the clan is painted not only upon the living but also upon the dead: before a corpse is interred, they put the totemic mark upon it.[2]

III

These totemic decorations enable us to see that the totem is not merely a name and an emblem. It is in the course of the religious ceremonies that they are employed; they are a part of the liturgy; so while the totem is a collective label, it also has a religious character. In fact, it is in connection with it, that things are classified as sacred or profane. It is the very type of sacred thing.

The tribes of Central Australia, especially the Arunta, the Loritja, the Kaitish, the Unmatjera, and the Ilpirra,[3] make constant use of certain instruments in their rites which are called the *churinga* by the Arunta, according to Spencer and Gillen, or the *tjurunga*, according to Strehlow.[4] They are pieces of wood or bits of polished stone, of a great variety of forms, but generally oval or oblong.[5] Each totemic group has a more or less important collection of these. *Upon each of these is engraved a design representing the totem of this same group.*[6] A certain number of the churinga have a hole at one end, through which goes a thread made of human hair or that of an opossum. Those which are made of wood and are pierced in this way serve for exactly the same purposes as those instruments of the cult to which English ethnographers have given the name of "bull-roarers." By means of the thread by which they are suspended, they are whirled rapidly in the air in such a way as to produce a sort of humming identical with that made by the toys of this name still used by our children; this deafening noise has a ritual

[1] *Nat. Tr.*, p. 140. In this case, the novice keeps the decoration with which he has thus been adorned until it disappears of itself by the effect of time.

[2] Boas, *General Report on the Indians of British Columbia* in *British Association for the Advancement of Science, Fifth Rep. of the Committee on the N.W. Tribes of the Dominion of Canada*, p. 41.

[3] There are also some among the Warramunga, but in smaller numbers than among the Arunta; they do not figure in the totemic ceremonies, though they do have a place in the myths (*Nor. Tr.*, p. 163).

[4] Other names are used by other tribes. We give a generic sense to the Arunta term because it is in this tribe that the churinga have the most important place and have been studied the best.

[5] Strehlow, II, p. 81.

[6] There are a few which have no apparent design (see Spencer and Gillen, *Nat. Tr.*, p. 144).

significance and accompanies all ceremonies of any importance. These sorts of churinga are real bull-roarers. But there are others which are not made of wood and are not pierced; consequently they cannot be employed in this way. Nevertheless, they inspire the same religious sentiments.

In fact, every churinga, for whatever purpose it may be employed, is counted among the eminently sacred things; there are none which surpass it in religious dignity. This is indicated even by the word which is used to designate them. It is not only a substantive but also an adjective meaning sacred. Also, among the several names which each Arunta has, there is one so sacred that it must not be revealed to a stranger; it is pronounced but rarely, and then in a low voice and a sort of mysterious murmur. Now this name is called the *aritna churinga* (aritna means name).[1] In general, the word churinga is used to designate all ritual acts; for example, *ilia churinga* signifies the cult of the emu.[2] Churinga, when used substantively, therefore designates the thing whose essential characteristic is sacredness. Profane persons, that is to say, women and young men not yet initiated into the religious life, may not touch or even see the churinga; they are only allowed to look at it from a distance, and even this is only on rare occasions.[3]

The churinga are piously kept in a special place, which the Arunta call the *ertnatulunga*.[4] This is a cave or a sort of cavern hidden in a deserted place. The entrance is carefully closed by means of stones so cleverly placed that a stranger going past it could not suspect that the religious treasury of the clan was so near to him. The sacred character of the churinga is so great that it communicates itself to the locality where they are stored: the women and the uninitiated cannot approach it. It is only after their initiation is completely finished that the young men have access to it: there are some who are not esteemed worthy

[1] *Nat. Tr.*, pp. 139 and 648; Strehlow, II, p. 75.

[2] Strehlow, who writes *tjurunga*, gives a slightly different translation to the word. "This word," he says, "means that which is secret and personal (*der eigene geheime*). *Tju* is an old word which means hidden or secret, and *runga* means that which is my own." But Kempe, who has more authority than Strehlow in this matter, translates *tju* by great, powerful, sacred (Kempe, *Vocabulary of the Tribes inhabiting Macdonell Ranges*, s.v. *Tju*, in *Transactions of the R. Society of Victoria*, Vol. XIII). At bottom, the translation of Strehlow is not so different from the other as might appear at first glance, for what is secret is hidden from the knowledge of the profane, that is, it is sacred. As for the meaning given to *runga*, it appears to us very doubtful. The ceremonies of the emu belong to all the members of that clan; all may participate in them; therefore they are not personal to any one of them.

[3] *Nat. Tr.*, pp. 130–132; Strehlow, II, p. 78. A woman who has seen a churinga or a man who has shown one to her are both put to death.

[4] Strehlow calls this place, defined in exactly the same terms as by Spencer and Gillen, *arknanaua* instead of *ertnatulunga* (Strehlow, II, p. 78).

of this favour except after years of trial.[1] The religious nature radiates to a distance and communicates itself to all the surroundings: everything near by participates in this same nature and is therefore withdrawn from profane touch. Is one man pursued by another? If he succeeds in reaching the ertnatulunga, he is saved; he cannot be seized there.[2] Even a wounded animal which takes refuge there must be respected.[3] Quarrels are forbidden there. It is a place of peace, as is said in the Germanic societies; it is a sanctuary of the totemic group, it is a veritable place of asylum.

But the virtues of the churinga are not manifested merely by the way in which it keeps the profane at a distance. If it is thus isolated, it is because it is something of a high religious value whose loss would injure the group and the individuals severely. It has all sorts of marvellous properties: by contact it heals wounds, especially those resulting from circumcision;[4] it has the same power over sickness;[5] it is useful for making the beard grow;[6] it confers important powers over the totemic species, whose normal reproduction it ensures;[7] it gives men force, courage and perseverance, while, on the other hand, it depresses and weakens their enemies. This latter belief is so firmly rooted that when two combatants stand pitted against one another, if one sees that the other has brought churinga against him, he loses confidence and his defeat is certain.[8] Thus there is no ritual instrument which has a more important place in the religious ceremonies.[9] By means of various sorts of anointings, their powers are communicated either to the officiants or to the assistants; to bring this about, they are rubbed over the members and stomach of the faithful after being covered with grease;[10] or sometimes they are covered with a down which flies away and scatters itself in every direction when they are

[1] *Nor. Tr.*, p. 270; *Nat. Tr.*, p. 140.

[2] *Nat. Tr.*, p. 135.

[3] Strehlow, II, p. 78. However, Strehlow says that if a murderer takes refuge near an ertnatulunga, he is unpityingly pursued there and put to death. We find some difficulty in conciliating this fact with the privilege enjoyed by animals, and ask ourselves if the rigour with which a criminal is treated is not something recent and should not be attributed to a weakening of the taboo which originally protected the ertnatulunga.

[4] *Nat. Tr.*, p. 248.

[5] *Ibid.*, pp. 545 f. Strehlow, II, p. 79. For example, the dust detached by rubbing a churinga with a stone, when dissolved in water, forms a potion which restores health to sick persons.

[6] *Nat. Tr.*, pp. 545 f. Strehlow (II, p. 79) contests this fact.

[7] For example, the churinga of the yam totem, if placed in the soil, make the yams grow (*Nor. Tr.*, p. 275). It has the same power over animals (Strehlow, II, pp. 76, 78; III, pp. 3, 7).

[8] *Nat. Tr.*, p. 135; Strehlow, II, p. 79.

[9] *Nor. Tr.*, p. 278.

[10] *Ibid.*, p. 180.

whirled ; this is a way of disseminating the virtues which are in them.[1]

But they are not useful merely to individuals ; the fate of the clan as a whole is bound up with theirs. Their loss is a disaster ; it is the greatest misfortune which can happen to the group.[2] Sometimes they leave the ertnatulunga, for example when they are loaned to other groups.[3] Then follows a veritable public mourning. For two weeks, the people of the totem weep and lament, covering their bodies with white clay just as they do when they have lost a relative.[4] And the churinga are not left at the free disposition of everybody ; the ertnatulunga where they are kept is placed under the control of the chief of the group. It is true that each individual has special rights to some of them ; [5] yet, though he is their proprietor in a sense, he cannot make use of them except with the consent and under the direction of the chief. It is a collective treasury ; it is the sacred ark of the clan.[6] The devotion of which they are the object shows the high price that is attached to them. The respect with which they are handled is shown by the solemnity of the movements.[7] They are taken care of, they are greased, rubbed, polished, and when they are moved from one locality to another, it is in the midst of ceremonies which bear witness to the fact that this displacement is regarded as an act of the highest importance.[8]

Now in themselves, the churinga are objects of wood and stone like all others ; they are distinguished from profane things of the same sort by only one particularity : this is that the totemic mark is drawn or engraved upon them. So it is this mark and this alone which gives them their sacred character. It is true that according to Spencer and Gillen, the churinga serve as the residence of an ancestor's soul and that it is the presence of this soul which confers these properties.[9] While

[1] *Nor. Tr.*, pp. 272 f.

[2] *Nat. Tr.*, p. 135.

[3] One group borrows the churinga of another with the idea that these latter will communicate some of the virtues which are in them and that their presence will quicken the vitality of the individuals and of the group (*Nat. Tr.*, pp. 158 ff.).

[4] *Ibid.*, p. 136.

[5] Each individual is united by a particular bond to a special churinga which assures him his life, and also to those which he has received as a heritage from his parents.

[6] *Nat. Tr.*, p. 154 ; *Nor. Tr.*, p. 193. The churinga are so thoroughly collective that they take the place of the " message-sticks " with which the messengers of other tribes are provided, when they are sent to summon foreign groups to a ceremony (*Nat. Tr.*, pp. 141 f.).

[7] *Ibid.*, p. 326. It should be remarked that the bull-roarers are used in the same way (Mathews, *Aboriginal Tribes of N.S. Wales and Victoria*, in *Jour. of Roy. Soc. of N.S. Wales*, XXXVIII, pp. 307 f.).

[8] *Nat. Tr.*, pp. 161, 259 ff.

[9] *Ibid.*, p. 138.

declaring this interpretation inexact, Strehlow, in his turn, proposes another which does not differ materially from the other: he claims that the churinga are considered the image of the ancestor's body, or the body itself.[1] So, in any case, it would be sentiments inspired by the ancestor which fix themselves upon the material object, and convert it into a sort of fetish. But in the first place, both conceptions,—which, by the way, scarcely differ except in the letter of the myth,—have obviously been made up afterwards, to account for the sacred character of the churinga. In the constitution of these pieces of wood and bits of stone, and in their external appearance, there is nothing which predestines them to be considered the seat of an ancestral soul, or the image of his body. So if men have imagined this myth, it was in order to explain the religious respect which these things inspired in them, and the respect was not determined by the myth. This explanation, like so many mythological explanations, resolves the question only by repeating it in slightly different terms; for saying that the churinga is sacred and saying that it has such and such a relation with a sacred being, is merely to proclaim the same fact in two different ways; it is not accounting for them. Moreover, according to the avowal of Spencer and Gillen, there are some churinga among the Arunta which are made by the old men of the group, to the knowledge of and before the eyes of all;[2] these obviously do not come from the great ancestors. However, except for certain differences of degree, they have the same power as the others and are preserved in the same manner. Finally, there are whole tribes where the churinga is never associated with a spirit.[3] Its religious nature comes to it, then, from some other source, and whence could it come, if not from the totemic stamp which it bears? It is to this image, therefore, that the demonstrations of the rite are really addressed; it is this which sanctifies the object upon which it is carved.

Among the Arunta and the neighbouring tribes, there are two other liturgical instruments closely connected with the totem

[1] Strehlow, I, *Vorwort. in fine*; II, pp. 76, 77 and 82. For the Arunta, it is the body of the ancestor itself; for the Loritja, it is only an image.

[2] When a child has just been born, the mother shows the father the spot where she believes that the soul of the ancestor entered her. The father, accompanied by a few relatives, goes to this spot and looks for the churinga which the ancestor is believed to have left at the moment that he reincarnated himself. If it is found there, some old man of the group undoubtedly put it there (this is the hypothesis of Spencer and Gillen). If they do not find it, a new churinga is made in a determined manner (*Nat. Tr.*, p. 132. Cf. Strehlow, II, p. 80).

[3] This is the case among the Warramunga, the Urabunna, the Worgaia, the Umbaia, the Tjingilli and the Guangi (*Nor. Tr.*, pp. 258, 275 f.). Then, say Spencer and Gillen, "*they were regarded as of especial value because of their association with a totem*" (*ibid.*, p. 276). There are examples of the same fact among the Arunta (*Nat. Tr.*, 156).

and the churinga itself, which ordinarily enters into their composition: they are the *nurtunja* and the *waninga*.

The nurtunja,[1] which is found among the northern Arunta and their immediate neighbours,[2] is made up principally of a vertical support which is either a single lance, or several lances united into a bundle, or of a simple pole.[3] Bunches of grass are fastened all around it by means of belts or little cords made of hair. Above this, down is placed, arranged either in circles or in parallel lines which run from the top to the bottom of the support. The top is decorated with the plumes of an eagle-hawk. This is only the most general and typical form; in particular cases, it has all sorts of variations.[4].

The waninga, which is found only among the southern Arunta, the Urabunna and the Loritja, has no one unique model either. Reduced to its most essential elements, it too consists in a vertical support, formed by a long stick or by a lance several yards high, with sometimes one and sometimes two cross-pieces.[5] In the former case, it has the appearance of a cross. Cords made either of human hair or opossum or bandicoot fur diagonally cross the space included between the arms of the cross and the extremities of the central axis; as they are quite close to each other, they form a network in the form of a lozenge. When there are two cross-bars, these cords go from one to the other and from these to the top and bottom of the support. They are sometimes covered with a layer of down, thick enough to conceal the foundation. Thus the waninga has the appearance of a veritable flag.[6]

Now the nurtunja and the waninga, which figure in a multitude of important rites, are the object of a religious respect quite like that inspired by the churinga. The process of their manufacture and erection is conducted with the greatest solemnity. Fixed in the earth, or carried by an officiant, they mark the central point of the ceremony: it is about them that the dances take place and the rites are performed. In the course of the initiation, the

[1] Strehlow writes *tnatanja* (I, pp. 4–5).

[2] The Kaitish, the Ilpirra, the Unmatjera; but it is rare among the latter.

[3] The pole is sometimes replaced by very long churinga, placed end to end.

[4] Sometimes another smaller one is hung from the top of the nurtunja. In other cases, the nurtunja is in the form of a cross or a T. More rarely, the central support is lacking (*Nat. Tr.*, pp. 298–300, 360–364, 627).

[5] Sometimes there are even three of these cross-bars.

[6] *Nat. Tr.*, pp. 231–234, 306–310, 627. In addition to the nurtunja and the waninga, Spencer and Gillen distinguish a third sort of sacred post or flag, called the kanana (*Nat. Tr.*, pp. 364, 370, 629), whose functions they admit they have been unable to determine. They merely note that it "is regarded as something common to the members of all the totems." According to Strehlow (II, p. 23, n. 2) the kanana of which Spencer and Gillen speak, is merely the nurtunja of the Wild Cat totem. As this animal is the object of a tribal cult, the veneration of which it is the object might easily be common to all the clans.

novice is led to the foot of a nurtunja erected for the occasion. Someone says to him, "There is the nurtunja of your father; many young men have already been made by it." After that, the initiate must kiss the nurtunja.[1] By this kiss, he enters into relations with the religious principle which resides there; it is a veritable communion which should give the young man the force required to support the terrible operation of sub-incision.[2] The nurtunja also plays a considerable rôle in the mythology of these societies. The myths relate that in the fabulous times of the great ancestors, the territory of the tribe was overrun in every direction by companies composed exclusively of individuals of the same totem.[3] Each of these troops had a nurtunja with it. When it stopped to camp, before scattering to hunt, the members fixed their nurtunja in the ground, from the top of which their churinga was suspended.[4] That is equivalent to saying that they confided the most precious things they had to it. It was at the same time a sort of standard which served as a rallying-centre for the group. One cannot fail to be struck by the analogies between the nurtunja and the sacred post of the Omaha.[5]

Now its sacred character can come from only one cause: that is that it represents the totem materially. The vertical lines or rings of down which cover it, and even the cords of different colours which fasten the arms of the waninga to the central axis, are not arranged arbitrarily, according to the taste of the makers; they must conform to a type strictly determined by tradition which, in the minds of the natives, represents the totem.[6] Here we cannot ask, as we did in the case of the churinga, whether the veneration accorded to this instrument of the cult is not merely the reflex of that inspired by the ancestors; for it is a rule that each nurtunja and each waninga last only during the ceremony where they are used. They are made all over again every time that it is necessary, and when the rite is once accomplished, they are stripped of their ornaments and the elements out of which they are made are scattered.[7] They are nothing more than images—and temporary images at that—

[1] *Nor. Tr.*, p. 342; *Nat. Tr.*, p. 309.

[2] *Nat. Tr.*, p. 255. [3] *Ibid.*, ch. x and xi. [4] *Ibid.*, pp. 138, 144.

[5] See Dorsey, *Siouan Cults, XIth Rep.*, p. 413; *Omaha Sociology, Third Rep.*, p. 234. It is true that there is only one sacred post for the tribe, while there is a nurtunja for each clan. But the principle is the same.

[6] *Nat. Tr.*, pp. 232, 308, 313, 334, etc.; *Nor. Tr.*, 182, 186, etc.

[7] *Nat. Tr.*, p. 346. It is true that some say that the nurtunja represents the lance of the ancestor who was at the head of each clan in Alcheringa times. But it is only a symbolic representation of it; it is not a sort of relic, like the churinga, which is believed to come from the ancestor himself. Here the secondary character of the explanation is very noticeable.

of the totem, and consequently it is on this ground, and on this ground alone, that they play a religious rôle.

So the churinga, the nurtunja and the waninga owe their religious nature solely to the fact that they bear the totemic emblem. It is the emblem that is sacred. It keeps this character, no matter where it may be represented. Sometimes it is painted upon rocks; these paintings are called *churinga ilkinia,* sacred drawings.[1] The decorations with which the officiants and assistants at the religious ceremonies adorn themselves have the same name: women and children may not see them.[2] In the course of certain rites, the totem is drawn upon the ground. The way in which this is done bears witness to the sentiments inspired by this design, and the high value attributed to it; it is traced upon a place that has been previously sprinkled, and saturated with human blood,[3] and we shall presently see that the blood is in itself a sacred liquid, serving for pious uses only. When the design has been made, the faithful remain seated on the ground before it, in an attitude of the purest devotion.[4] If we give the word a sense corresponding to the mentality of the primitive, we may say that they adore it. This enables us to understand how the totemic blazon has remained something very precious for the Indians of North America: it is always surrounded with a sort of religious halo.

But if we are seeking to understand how it comes that these totemic representations are so sacred, it is not without interest to see what they consist in.

Among the Indians of North America, they are painted, engraved or carved images which attempt to reproduce as faithfully as possible the external aspect of the totemic animal. The means employed are those which we use to-day in similar circumstances, except that they are generally cruder. But it is not the same in Australia, and it is in the Australian societies that we must seek the origin of these representations. Although the Australian may show himself sufficiently capable of imitating the forms of things in a rudimentary way,[5] sacred representations generally seem to show no ambitions in this line: they consist essentially in geometrical designs drawn upon the churinga, the nurtunga, rocks, the ground, or the human body. They are either straight or curved lines, painted in different ways,[6] and

[1] *Nat. Tr.*, pp. 614 ff., esp. p. 617; *Nor. Tr.*, p. 749.

[2] *Nat. Tr.*, p. 624. [3] *Ibid.*, p. 179. [4] *Ibid.*, p. 181.

[5] See the examples given in Spencer and Gillen, *Nat. Tr.*, Fig. 131. Here are designs, many of which evidently have the object of representing animals, plants, the heads of men, etc., though of course all are very conventional.

[6] *Nat. Tr.*, p. 617; *Nor. Tr.*, p. 716 ff.

the whole having only a conventional meaning. The connection between the figure and the thing represented is so remote and indirect that it cannot be seen, except when it is pointed out. Only the members of the clan can say what meaning is attached to such and such combinations of lines.[1] Men and women are generally represented by semicircles, and animals by whole circles or spirals,[2] the tracks of men or animals by lines of points, etc. The meaning of the figures thus obtained is so arbitrary that a single design may have two different meanings for the men of two different totems, representing one animal here, and another animal or plant there. This is perhaps still more apparent with the nurtunja and waninga. Each of them represents a different totem. But the few and simple elements which enter into their composition do not allow a great variety of combinations. The result is that two nurtunja may have exactly the same appearance, and yet express two things as different as a gum tree and an emu.[3] When a nurtunja is made, it is given a meaning which it keeps during the whole ceremony, but which, in the last resort, is fixed by convention.

These facts prove that if the Australian is so strongly inclined to represent his totem, it is in order not to have a portrait of it before his eyes which would constantly renew the sensation of it ; it is merely because he feels the need of representing the idea which he forms of it by means of material and external signs, no matter what these signs may be. We are not yet ready to attempt to understand what has thus caused the primitive to write his idea of his totem upon his person and upon different objects, but it is important to state at once the nature of the need which has given rise to these numerous representations.[4]

[1] *Nat. Tr.*, p. 145 ; Strehlow, II, p. 80.

[2] *Nat. Tr.*, p. 151.

[3] *Ibid.*, p. 346.

[4] It cannot be doubted that these designs and paintings also have an æsthetic character ; here is the first form of art. Since they are also, and even above all, a written language, it follows that the origins of design and those of writing are one. It even becomes clear that men commenced designing, not so much to fix upon wood or stone beautiful forms which charm the senses, as to translate his thought into matter (*cf.* Schoolcraft, *Indian Tribes*, I, p. 405 ; Dorsey, *Siouan Cults*, pp. 394 ff.).

CHAPTER II

TOTEMIC BELIEFS—*continued*

The Totemic Animal and Man

BUT totemic images are not the only sacred things. There are real things which are also the object of rites, because of the relations which they have with the totem: before all others, are the beings of the totemic species and the members of the clan.

I

First of all, since the designs which represent the totem arouse religious sentiments, it is natural that the things whose aspect these designs reproduce should have this same property, at least to a certain degree.

For the most part, these are animals or plants. The profane function of vegetables and even of animals is ordinarily to serve as food; then the sacred character of the totemic animal or plant is shown by the fact that it is forbidden to eat them. It is true that since they are sacred things, they can enter into the composition of certain mystical repasts, and we shall see, in fact, that they sometimes serve as veritable sacraments; yet normally they cannot be used for everyday consumption. Whoever oversteps this rule, exposes himself to grave dangers. It is not that the group always intervenes to punish this infraction artificially; it is believed that the sacrilege produces death automatically. A redoubtable principle is held to reside in the totemic plant or animal, which cannot enter into the profane organism without disorganizing it or destroying it.[1] In certain tribes at least, only the old men are free from this prohibition;[2] we shall see the reason for this later.

However, if this prohibition is formal in a large number of

[1] See the cases in Taplin, *The Narrinyeri*, p. 63; Howitt, *Nat. Tr.*, pp. 146, 769; Fison and Howitt, *Kamilaroi and Kurnai*, p. 169; Roth, *Superstition, Magic and Medicine*, § 150; Wyatt, *Adelaide and Encounter Bay Tribe*, in Woods, p. 168; Meyer, *ibid.*, p. 186.

[2] This is the case with the Warramunga (*Nor. Tr.*, p. 168).

tribes [1]—with certain exceptions which will be mentioned later —it is incontestable that it tends to weaken as the old totemic organization is disturbed. But the restrictions which remain even then prove that these attenuations are not admitted without difficulty. For example, when it is permitted to eat the plant or animal that serves as totem, it is not possible to do so freely; only a little bit may be taken at a time. To go beyond this amount is a ritual fault that has grave consequences.[2] Elsewhere, the prohibition remains intact for the parts that are regarded as the most precious, that is to say, as the most sacred; for example, the eggs or the fat.[3] In still other parts, consumption is not allowed except when the animal in question has not yet reached full maturity.[4] In this case, they undoubtedly think that its sacred character is not yet complete. So the barrier which isolates and protects the totemic being yields but slowly and with active resistance, which bears witness to what it must have been at first.

It is true that according to Spencer and Gillen these restrictions are not the remnants of what was once a rigorous prohibition now losing hold, but the beginnings of an interdiction which is only commencing to establish itself. These writers hold [5] that at first there was a complete liberty of consumption and that the limitations which were presently brought are relatively recent. They think they find the proof of their theory in the two following facts. In the first place, as we just said, there are solemn occasions when the members of the clan or their chief not only may, but must eat the totemic animal or plant. Moreover, the myths relate that the great ancestors, the founders of the clans, ate their totems regularly: now, it is said, these stories cannot be understood except as an echo of a time when the present prohibitions did not exist.

But the fact that in the course of certain solemn ceremonies a consumption of the totem, and a moderate one at that, is ritually required in no way implies that it was once an ordinary article of food. Quite on the contrary, the food that one eats at a mystical repast is essentially sacred, and consequently forbidden to the profane. As for the myths, a somewhat summary critical method is employed, if they are so readily given the

[1] For example, among the Warramunga, the Urabunna, the Wonghibon, the Yuin, the Wotjobaluk, the Buandik, Ngeumba, etc.

[2] Among the Kaitish, if a man of the clan eats too much of his totem, the members of the other phratry have recourse to a magic operation which is expected to kill him (*Nor. Tr.*, p. 284; cf. *Nat. Tr.*, p. 204; Langloh Parker, *The Euahlayi Tribe*, p. 20).

[3] *Nat. Tr.*, p. 202, n.; Strehlow, II, p. 58.

[4] *Nor. Tr.*, p. 173.

[5] *Nat. Tr.*, pp. 207 ff.

value of historical documents. In general, their object is to interpret existing rites rather than to commemorate past events; they are an explanation of the present much more than a history. In this case, the traditions according to which the ancestors of the fabulous epoch ate their totem are in perfect accord with the beliefs and rites which are always in force. The old men and those who have attained a high religious dignity are freed from the restrictions under which ordinary men are placed:[1] they can eat the sacred thing because they are sacred themselves; this rule is in no way peculiar to totemism, but it is found in all the most diverse religions. Now the ancestral heroes were nearly gods. It is therefore still more natural that they should eat the sacred food;[2] but that is no reason why the same privilege should be awarded to the simple profane.[3]

However, it is neither certain nor even probable that the prohibition was ever absolute. It seems to have always been suspended in case of necessity, as, for example, when a man is famished and has nothing else with which to nourish himself.[4] A stronger reason for this is found when the totem is a form of nourishment which a man cannot do without. Thus there are a great many tribes where water is a totem; a strict prohibition is manifestly impossible in this case. However, even here, the privilege granted is submitted to certain restrictions which greatly limit its use and which show clearly that it goes against a recognized principle. Among the Kaitish and the Warramunga, a man of this totem is not allowed to drink water freely; he may not take it up himself; he may receive it only from the hands of a third party who must belong to the phratry of which he is not a member.[5] The complexity of this procedure and the embarrassment which results from it are still another proof that access to the sacred thing is not free. This same rule is applied in certain central tribes every time that the totem is eaten, whether from

[1] See above, p. 128.

[2] It should also be borne in mind that in these myths the ancestors are never represented as nourishing themselves *regularly* with their totem. Consumption of this sort is, on the contrary, the exception. Their ordinary food, according to Strehlow, was the same as that of the corresponding animal (see Strehlow, I, p. 4).

[3] Also, this whole theory rests upon an entirely arbitrary hypothesis: Spencer and Gillen, as well as Frazer, admit that the tribes of central Australia, and especially the Arunta, represent the most archaic and consequently the purest form of totemism. We shall presently say why this conjecture seems to us to be contrary to all probability. It is even probable that these authors would not have accepted their thesis so readily if they had not refused to regard totemism as a religion and if they had not consequently misunderstood the sacred character of the totem.

[4] Taplin, *The Narrinyeri*, p. 64; Howitt, *Nat. Tr.*, pp. 145 and 147; Spencer and Gillen, *Nat. Tr.*, p. 202; Grey, *loc. cit.*; Curr, III, p. 462.

[5] *Nor. Tr.*, pp. 160, 167. It is not enough that the intermediary be of another totem: as we shall see, every totem of a phratry is forbidden in a certain measure for the members of the phratry who are of a different totem.

necessity or any other cause. It should also be added that when this formality is not possible, that is, when a man is alone or with members of his own phratry only, he may, on necessity, do without an intermediary. It is clear that the prohibition is susceptible of various moderations.

Nevertheless, it rests upon ideas so strongly ingrained in the mind that it frequently survives its original cause for being. We have seen that in all probability, the different clans of a phratry are only subdivisions of one original clan which has been dismembered. So there was a time when all the clans, being welded together, had the same totem; consequently, wherever the souvenir of this common origin is not completely effaced, each clan continues to feel itself united to the others and to consider that their totems are not completely foreign to it. For this reason an individual may not eat freely of the totems held by the different clans of the phratry of which he is a member; he may touch them only if the forbidden plant or animal is given him by a member of the other phratry.[1]

Another survival of the same sort is the one concerning the maternal totem. There are strong reasons for believing that at first, the totem was transmitted in the uterine line. Therefore, wherever descent in the paternal line has been introduced, this probably took place only after a long period, during which the opposite principle was applied and the child had the totem of his mother along with all the restrictions attached to it. Now in certain tribes where the child inherits the paternal totem to-day, some of the interdictions which originally protected the totem of his mother still survive: he cannot eat it freely.[2] In the present state of affairs, however, there is no longer anything corresponding to this prohibition.

[1] *Nor. Tr.*, p. 167. We can now explain more easily how it happens that when an interdiction is not observed, it is the other phratry which revenges this sacrilege (see above, p. 129, n. 2). It is because it has an interest in seeing that the rule is observed. In fact, they believe that when the rule is broken, the totemic species may not reproduce abundantly. Now the members of the other phratry consume it regularly: therefore it is they who are affected. That is why they revenge themselves.

[2] This is the case among the Loritja (Strehlow, II, pp. 60, 61), the Worgaia, the Warramunga, the Walpari, the Mara, the Anula and the Binbinga (*Nor. Tr.*, pp. 166, 167, 171, 173). It may be eaten by a Warramunga or a Walpari, but only when offered by a member of the other phratry. Spencer and Gillen remark (p. 167, n.), that in this regard the paternal and the maternal totems appear to be under different rules. It is true that in both cases the offer must come from the other phratry. But when it is a question of the paternal totem, or the totem properly so-called, this phratry is the one to which the totem does not belong; for the maternal totem, the contrary is the case. Probably the principle was first established for the former, then mechanically extended to the other, though the situation was different. When the rule had once become established that the prohibition protecting the totem could be neglected only on the invitation of the other phratry, it was applied also to the maternal totem.

To this prohibition of eating is frequently added that of killing the totem, or picking it, when it is a plant.[1] However, here also there are exceptions and tolerations. These are especially in the case of necessity, when the totem is a dangerous animal,[2] for example, or when the man has nothing to eat. There are even tribes where men are forbidden to hunt the animals whose names they bear, on their own accounts, but where they may kill them for others.[3] But the way in which this act is generally accomplished clearly indicates that it is something illicit. One excuses himself as though for a fault, and bears witness to the chagrin which he suffers and the repugnance which he feels,[4] while precautions are taken that the animal may suffer as little as possible.[5]

In addition to these fundamental interdictions, certain cases of a prohibition of contact between a man and his totem are cited. Thus among the Omaha, in the clan of the Elk, no one may touch any part of the body of a male elk ; in the sub-clan of the Buffalo, no one is allowed to touch the head of this animal.[6] Among the Bechuana, no man dares to clothe himself in the skin of his totem.[7] But these cases are rare ; and it is natural that they should be exceptional, for normally a man must wear the image of his totem or something which brings it to mind. The tattooings and the totemic costumes would not be possible if all contact were forbidden. It has also been remarked that this prohibition has not been found in Australia, but only in those societies where totemism has advanced far from its original form ; it is therefore probably of late origin and due perhaps to the influence of ideas that are really not totemic at all.[8]

[1] For example, among the Warramunga (*Nor. Tr.*, p. 166), the Wotjobaluk, the Buandik, the Kurnai (Howitt, pp. 146 f.) and the Narrinyeri (Taplin, *The Narrinyeri*, p. 63).

[2] Even this is not always the case. An Arunta of the Mosquito totem must not kill this insect, even when it bothers him : he must confine himself to driving it away (Strehlow, II, p. 58 ; cf. Taplin, p. 63).

[3] Among the Kaitish and the Unmatjera (*Nor. Tr.*, p. 160). It even happens that in certain cases an old man gives a young one of a different totem one of his churinga, so that he may kill the donor's totem more easily (*ibid.*, p. 272).

[4] Howitt, *Nat. Tr.*, p. 146 ; Grey, *op. cit.*, II, p. 228 ; Casalis, *Basoutos*, p. 221. Among these latter, " one must be purified after committing such a sacrilege."

[5] Strehlow, II, pp. 58, 59, 61.

[6] Dorsey, *Omaha Sociology, IIIrd Rep.*, pp. 225, 231.

[7] Casalis, *ibid.*

[8] Even among the Omaha, it is not certain that the interdictions of contact, certain examples of which we have just cited, are really of a totemic nature, for many of them have no direct connection with the animal that serves as totem of the clan. Thus in the sub-clan of the Eagle, the characteristic interdiction is against touching the head of a buffalo (Dorsey, *op. cit.*, p. 239) ; in another sub-clan with the same totem, they must not touch verdigris, charcoal, etc. (*ibid.*, p. 245).

We do not mention other interdictions mentioned by Frazer, such as those of naming or looking at the animal or plant, for it is still less certain that they are of totemic origin, except perhaps for certain facts observed among the

If we now compare these various interdictions with those whose object is the totemic emblem, contrarily to all that could be foreseen, it appears that these latter are more numerous, stricter, and more severely enforced than the former. The figures of all sorts which represent the totem are surrounded with a respect sensibly superior to that inspired by the very being whose form these figures reproduce. The churinga, the nurtunja and the waninga can never be handled by the women or the uninitiated, who are even allowed to catch glimpses of it only very exceptionally, and from a respectful distance. On the other hand, the plant or animal whose name the clan bears may be seen and touched by everybody. The churinga are preserved in a sort of temple, upon whose threshold all noises from the profane life must cease ; it is the domain of sacred things. On the contrary, the totemic animals and plants live in the profane world and are mixed up with the common everyday life. Since the number and importance of the interdictions which isolate a sacred thing, and keep it apart, correspond to the degree of sacredness with which it is invested, we arrive at the remarkable conclusion that *the images of totemic beings are more sacred than the beings themselves*. Also, in the ceremonies of the cult, it is the churinga and the nurtunja which have the most important place ; the animal appears there only very exceptionally. In a certain rite, of which we shall have occasion to speak,[1] it serves as the substance for a religious repast, but it plays no active rôle. The Arunta dance around the nurtunja, and assemble before the image of their totem to adore it, but a similar demonstration is never made before the totemic being itself. If this latter were the primarily sacred object, it would be with it, the sacred animal or plant, that the young initiate would communicate when he is introduced into the religious life ; but we have seen that on the contrary, the most solemn moment of the initiation is the one when the novice enters into the sanctuary of the churinga. It is with them and the nurtunja that he communicates. The representations of the totem are therefore more actively powerful than the totem itself.

Bechuana (*Totemism*, pp. 12–13). Frazer admits too readily—and in this regard, he has imitators—that the prohibitions against eating or touching an animal depend upon totemic beliefs. However, there is one case in Australia, where the sight of the animal seems to be forbidden. According to Strehlow (II, p. 59), among the Arunta and the Loritja, a man who has the moon as totem must not look at it very long, or he would be likely to die at the hand of an enemy. But we believe that this is a unique case. We must not forget, also, that astronomical totems were probably not primitive in Australia, so this prohibition may be the product of a complex elaboration. This hypothesis is confirmed by the fact that among the Euahlayi, looking at the moon is forbidden to all mothers and children, no matter what their totems may be (L. Parker, *The Euahlayi*, p. 53).

[1] See Bk. III, ch. ii, § 2.

II

We must now determine the place of man in the scheme of religious things.

By the force of a whole group of acquired habits and of language itself, we are inclined to consider the common man, the simple believer, as an essentially profane being. It may well happen that this conception is not literally true for any religion;[1] in any case, it is not applicable to totemism. Every member of the clan is invested with a sacred character which is not materially inferior to that which we just observed in the animal. This personal sacredness is due to the fact that the man believes that while he is a man in the usual sense of the word, he is also an animal or plant of the totemic species.

In fact, he bears its name; this identity of name is therefore supposed to imply an identity of nature. The first is not merely considered as an outward sign of the second; it supposes it logically. This is because the name, for a primitive, is not merely a word or a combination of sounds; it is a part of the being, and even something essential to it. A member of the Kangaroo clan calls himself a kangaroo; he is therefore, in one sense, an animal of this species. "The totem of any man," say Spencer and Gillen, "is regarded as the same thing as himself; a native once said to us when we were discussing the matter with him, 'That one,' pointing to his photograph which we had taken, 'is the same thing as me; so is a kangaroo' (his totem)."[2] So each individual has a double nature: two beings coexist within him, a man and an animal.

In order to give a semblance of intelligibility to this duality, so strange for us, the primitive has invented myths which, it is true, explain nothing and only shift the difficulty, but which, by shifting it, seem at least to lessen the logical scandal. With slight variations of detail, all are constructed on the same plan: their object is to establish genealogical connections between the man and the totemic animal, making the one a relative of the other. By this common origin, which, by the way, is represented in various manners, they believe that they account for their common nature. The Narrinyeri, for example, have imagined that certain of the first men had the power of transforming

[1] Perhaps there is no religion which makes man an exclusively profane being. For the Christian, the soul which each of us has within him and which constitutes the very essence of our being, has something sacred about it. We shall see that this conception of the soul is as old as religious thought itself. The place of man in the hierarchy of sacred things is more or less elevated.

[2] *Nat. Tr.*, p. 202.

themselves into beasts.[1] Other Australian societies place at the beginning of humanity either strange animals from which the men were descended in some unknown way,[2] or mixed beings, half-way between the two kingdoms,[3] or else unformed creatures, hardly representable, deprived of all determined organs, and even of all definite members, and the different parts of whose bodies were hardly outlined.[4] Mythical powers, sometimes conceived under the form of animals, then intervened and made men out of these ambiguous and innumerable beings which Spencer and Gillen say represent " stages in the transformation of animals and plants into human beings." [5] These transformations are represented to us under the form of violent and, as it were, surgical operations. It is under the blows of an axe or, if the operator is a bird, blows of the beak, that the human individual was carved out of this shapeless mass, his members separated from each other, his mouth opened and his nostrils pierced.[6] Analogous legends are found in America, except that owing to the more highly developed mentality of these peoples, the representations which they employ do not contain confusions so troublesome for the mind. Sometimes it is a legendary personage who, by an act of his power, metamorphosed the animal who gives its name to the clan into a man.[7] Sometimes the myth attempts to explain how, by a series of nearly natural events and a sort of spontaneous evolution, the animal transformed himself little by little, and finally took a human form.[8]

[1] Taplin, *The Narrinyeri*, pp. 59–61.

[2] Among certain clans of the Warramunga, for example (*Nor. Tr.*, p. 162).

[3] Among the Urabunna (*Nor. Tr.*, p. 147). Even when they tell us that the first beings were men, these are really only semi-human, and have an animal nature at the same time. This is the case with certain Unmatjera (*ibid.*, pp. 153–154). Here we find ways of thought whose confusion disconcerts us, but which must be accepted as they are. We would denature them if we tried to introduce a clarity that is foreign to them (cf. *Nat. Tr.*, p. 119).

[4] Among the Arunta (*Nat. Tr.*, pp. 388 ff.); and among certain Unmatjera (*Nor. Tr.*, p. 153).

[5] *Nat. Tr.*, p. 389. Cf. Strehlow, I, pp. 2–7.

[6] *Nat. Tr.*, p. 389; Strehlow, I, pp. 2 ff. Undoubtedly there is an echo of the initiation rites in this mythical theme. The initiation also has the object of making the young man into a complete man, and on the other hand, it also implies actual surgical operations (circumcision, sub-incision, the extraction of teeth, etc.). The processes which served to form the first men would naturally be conceived on the same model.

[7] This the case with the nine clans of the Moqui (Schoolcraft, *Indian Tribes*, IV, p. 86), the Crain clan among the Ojibway (Morgan, *Ancient Society*, p. 180), and the Nootka clans (Boas, *VIth Rep. on the N.W. Tribes of Canada*, p. 43), etc.

[8] It is thus that the Turtle clan of the Iroquois took form. A group of turtles had been forced to leave the lake where they dwelt and seek another home. One of them, which was larger than the others, stood this exercise very badly owing to the heat. It made such violent efforts that it got out of its shell. The process of transformation, being once commenced, went on by itself and the turtle finally became a man who was the ancestor of the clan (Erminnie A. Smith,

It is true that there are societies (the Haida, Tlinkit, Tsimshian) where it is no longer admitted that man was born of an animal or plant; but the idea of an affinity between the animals of the totemic species and the members of the clan has survived there nevertheless, and expresses itself in myths which, though differing from the preceding, still retain all that is essential in them. Here is one of the fundamental themes. The ancestor who gives his name to the clan is here represented as a human being, but who, in the course of various wanderings, has been led to live for a while among the fabulous animals of the very species which gave the clan its name. As the result of this intimate and prolonged connection, he became so like his new companions that when he returned to men, they no longer recognized him. He was therefore given the name of the animal which he resembled. It is from his stay in this mythical land that he brought back the totemic emblem, together with the powers and virtues believed to be attached to it.[1] Thus in this case, as in the others, men are believed to participate in the nature of the animal, though this participation may be conceived in slightly different forms.[2]

So man also has something sacred about him. Though diffused

The Myths of the Iroquois, IInd Report, p. 77). The Crab clan of the Choctaw was formed in a similar manner. Some men surprised a certain number of crabs that lived in the neighbourhood, took them home with them, taught them to talk and to walk, and finally adopted them into their society (Catlin, *North American Indians*, II, p. 128).

[1] For example, here is a legend of the Tsimshian. In the course of a hunt, an Indian met a black bear which took him to its home, and taught him to catch salmon and build canoes. The man stayed with the bear for two years, and then returned to his native village. But the people were afraid of him, because he was just like a bear. He could not talk or eat anything except raw food. Then he was rubbed with magic herbs and gradually regained his original form. After that, whenever he was in trouble, he called upon his bear friends, who came to aid him. He built a house and painted a bear on the foundation. His sister made a blanket for the dance, upon which a bear was designed. That is why the descendants of this sister had the bear as their emblem (Boas, *Kwakiutl*, p. 323. Cf. *Vth Rep. on the N.W. Tribes of Canada*, pp. 23, 29 ff.; Hill Tout, *Report on the Ethnology of the Statlumh of British Columbia*, in *J.A.I.*, 1905, XXXV, p. 150).

Thus we see the inconveniences in making this mystical relationship between the man and the animal the distinctive characteristic of totemism, as M. Van Gennep proposes (*Totémisme et méthode comparative*, in *Revue de l'histoire des religions*, Vol. LVIII, July, 1908, p. 55). This relationship is a mythical representation of otherwise profound facts; but it may be omitted without causing the disappearance of the essential traits of totemism. Undoubtedly there are always close bonds between the people of the clan and the totemic animal, but these are not necessarily bonds of blood-relationship, though they are frequently conceived in this form.

[2] There are also some Tlinkit myths in which the relationship of descent between the man and the animal is still more carefully stated. It is said that the clan is descended from a mixed union, if we may so speak, that is to say, one where either the husband or the wife was an animal of the species whose name the clan bears (see Swanton, *Social Condition, Beliefs, etc., of the Tlinkit Indians*, *XXVIth Rep.*, pp. 415–418).

into the whole organism, this characteristic is especially apparent in certain privileged places. There are organs and tissues that are specially marked out: these are particularly the blood and the hair.

In the first place, human blood is so holy a thing that in the tribes of Central Australia, it frequently serves to consecrate the most respected instruments of the cult. For example, in certain cases, the nurtunja is regularly anointed from top to bottom with the blood of a man.[1] It is upon ground all saturated with blood that the men of the Emu, among the Arunta, trace their sacred images.[2] We shall presently see that streams of blood are poured upon the rocks which represent the totemic animals and plants.[3] There is no religious ceremony where blood does not have some part to play.[4] During the initiation, the adults open their veins and sprinkle the novice with their blood; and this blood is so sacred a thing that women may not be present while it is flowing; the sight of it is forbidden them, just as the sight of a churinga is.[5] The blood lost by a young initiate during the very violent operations he must undergo has very particular virtues: it is used in various ceremonies.[6] That which flows during the sub-incision is piously kept by the Arunta and buried in a place upon which they put a piece of wood warning passers-by of the sacredness of the spot; no woman should approach it.[7] The religious nature of blood also explains the equal importance, religiously, of the red ochre, which is very frequently employed in ceremonies; they rub the churinga with it and use it in ritual decorations.[8] This is due to the fact that because of its colour, it is regarded as something kindred to blood. Many deposits of red ochre which are found in the Arunta territory are even supposed to be the coagulated blood which certain heroines of the mythical period shed on to the soil.[9]

Hair has similar properties. The natives of the centre wear belts made of human hair, whose religious functions we have already pointed out: they are also used to wrap up certain

[1] *Nat. Tr.*, p. 284. [2] *Ibid.*, p. 179.

[3] See Bk. III, ch. ii. Cf. *Nat. Tr.*, pp. 184, 201.

[4] *Ibid.*, pp. 204, 262, 284.

[5] Among the Dieri and the Parnkalla. See Howitt, *Nat. Tr.*, pp. 658, 661, 668, 669–671.

[6] Among the Warramunga, the blood from the circumcision is drunk by the mother (*Nor. Tr.*, p. 352). Among the Binbinga, the blood on the knife which was used in the sub-incision must be licked off by the initiate (*ibid.*, p. 368). In general, the blood coming from the genital organs is regarded as especially sacred (*Nat. Tr.*, p. 464; *Nor. Tr.*, p. 598).

[7] *Nat. Tr.*, p. 268. [8] *Ibid.*, pp. 144, 568.

[9] *Ibid.*, pp. 442, 464. This myth is quite common in Australia.

instruments of the cult.[1] Does one man loan another one of his churinga? As a sign of acknowledgment, the second makes a present of hair to the first; these two sorts of things are therefore thought to be of the same order and of equivalent value.[2] So the operation of cutting the hair is a ritual act, accompanied by definite ceremonies: the individual operated upon must squat on the ground, with his face turned in the direction of the place where the fabulous ancestors from which the clan of his mother is believed to be descended, are thought to have camped.[3] For the same reason, as soon as a man is dead, they cut his hair off and put it away in some distant place, for neither women nor the non-initiated have the right of seeing it: it is here, far from profane eyes, that the belts are made.[4]

Other organic tissues might be mentioned which have similar properties, in varying degrees: such are the whiskers, the foreskin, the fat of the liver, etc.[5] But it is useless to multiply examples. Those already given are enough to prove that there is something in man which holds profane things at a distance and which possesses a religious power; in other words, the human organism conceals within its depths a sacred principle, which visibly comes to the surface in certain determined cases. This principle does not differ materially from that which causes the religious character of the totem. In fact, we have just seen that the different substances in which it incarnates itself especially enter into the ritual composition of the objects of the cult (nurtunja, totemic designs), or else are used in the anointings whose object is to renew the virtues either of the churinga or of the sacred rocks; they are things of the same species.

Sometimes the religious dignity which is inherent in each member of the clan on this account is not equal for all. Men possess it to a higher degree than women; in relation to them, women are like profane beings.[6] Thus, every time that there is

[1] *Nat. Tr.*, p. 627. [2] *Ibid.*, p. 466.

[3] *Ibid.* It is believed that if all these formalities are not rigorously observed, grave calamities will fall upon the individual.

[4] *Nat. Tr.*, p. 538; *Nor. Tr.*, p. 604.

[5] After the foreskin has been detached by circumcision, it is sometimes hidden, just like the blood; it has special virtues; for example, it assures the fecundity of certain animal and vegetable species (*Nor. Tr.*, pp. 353 f.). The whiskers are mixed with the hair, and treated as such (*ibid.*, pp. 604, 544). They also play a part in the myths (*ibid.*, p. 158). As for the fat, its sacred character is shown by the use made of it in certain funeral rites.

[6] This is not saying that the woman is absolutely profane. In the myths, at least among the Arunta, she plays a religious rôle much more important than she does in reality (*Nat. Tr.*, pp. 195 f.). Even now she takes part in certain initiation rites. Finally, her blood has religious virtues (see *Nat. Tr.*, p. 464; cf. *La prohibition de l'inceste et ses origines*, *Année Sociol.*, I, pp. 41 ff.).

It is upon this complex situation of the woman that the exogamic restrictions depend. We do not speak of them here because they concern the problem of domestic and matrimonial organization more directly than the present one.

an assembly, either of the totemic group or of the tribe, the men have a separate camp, distinct from that of the women, and into which these latter may not enter: they are separated off.[1] But there are also differences in the way in which men are marked with a religious character. The young men not yet initiated are wholly deprived of it, since they are not admitted to the ceremonies. It is among the old men that it reaches its greatest intensity. They are so very sacred that certain things forbidden to ordinary people are permissible for them: they may eat the totemic animal more freely and, as we have seen, there are even some tribes where they are freed from all dietetic restrictions.

So we must be careful not to consider totemism a sort of animal worship. The attitude of a man towards the animals or plants whose name he bears is not at all that of a believer towards his god, for he belongs to the sacred world himself. Their relations are rather those of two beings who are on the same level and of equal value. The most that can be said is that in certain cases, at least, the animal seems to occupy a slightly more elevated place in the hierarchy of sacred things. It is because of this that it is sometimes called the father or the grandfather of the men of the clan, which seems to show that they feel themselves in a state of moral dependence in regard to it.[2] But in other, and perhaps even more frequent cases, it happens that the expressions used denote rather a sentiment of equality. The totemic animal is called the friend or the elder brother of its human fellows.[3] Finally, the bonds which exist between them and it are much more like those which unite the members of a single family; the animals and the men are made of the same flesh, as the Buandik say.[4] On account of this kinship, men regard the animals of the totemic species as kindly associates upon whose aid they think they can rely. They call them to their aid [5] and they come, to direct their blows in the hunt and to give warning of whatever dangers there may be.[6]

[1] *Nat. Tr.*, p. 460.

[2] Among the Wakelbura, according to Howitt, p. 146; among the Bechuana, according to Casalis, *Basoutos*, p. 221.

[3] Among the Buandik and Kurnai (Howitt, *ibid.*); among the Arunta (Strehlow, II, p. 58).

[4] Howitt, *ibid.*

[5] In the Tully River district, says Roth (*Superstition, Magic and Medicine*, in *North Queensland Ethnography*, No. 5, § 74), as an individual goes to sleep or gets up in the morning, he pronounces in a rather low voice the name of the animal after which he is named himself. The purpose of this practice is to make the man clever or lucky in the hunt, or be forewarned of the dangers to which he may be exposed from this animal. For example, a man who has a species of serpent as his totem is protected from bites if this invocation has been made regularly.

[6] Taplin, *Narrinyeri*, p. 64; Howitt, *Nat. Tr.*, p. 147; Roth, *loc. cit.*

In return for this, men treat them with regard and are never cruel to them ;[1] but these attentions in no way resemble a cult.

Men sometimes even appear to have a mysterious sort of property-right over their totems. The prohibition against killing and eating them is applied only to members of the clan, of course ; it could not be extended to other persons without making life practically impossible. If, in a tribe like the Arunta, where there is such a host of different totems, it were forbidden to eat, not only the animal or plant whose name one bears, but also all the animals and all the plants which serve as totems to other clans, the sources of food would be reduced to nothing. Yet there are tribes where the consumption of the totemic plant or animal is not allowed without restrictions, even to foreigners. Among the Wakelbura, it must not take place in the presence of men of this totem.[2] In other places, their permission must be given. For example, among the Kaitish and the Unmatjera, whenever a man of the Emu totem happens to be in a place occupied by a grass-seed clan, and gathers some of these seed, before eating them he must go to the chief and say to him, " I have gathered these seeds in your country." To this the chief replies, " All right ; you may eat them." But if the Emu man ate them before demanding permission, it is believed that he would fall sick and run the risk of dying.[3] There are even cases where the chief of the group must take a little of the food and eat it himself : it is a sort of payment which must be made.[4] For the same reason, the churinga gives the hunter a certain power over the corresponding animal : by rubbing his body with a Euro churinga, for example, a man acquires a greater chance of catching euros.[5] This is the proof that the fact of participating in the nature of a totemic being confers a sort of eminent right over this latter. Finally, there is one tribe in northern Queensland, the Karingbool, where the men of the totem are the only ones who have a right to kill the animal or, if the totem is a tree, to peel off its bark. Their aid is indispensable to all others who want to use the flesh of this animal or the wood of this tree for their own personal ends.[6] So they appear as proprietors, though it is quite evidently over a special sort of property, of which we find it hard to form an idea.

[1] Strehlow, II, p. 58.
[2] Howitt, p. 148.
[3] *Nor. Tr.*, pp. 159–160.
[4] *Ibid.*
[5] *Ibid.*, p. 225 ; *Nat. Tr.*, pp. 202, 203.
[6] A. L. P. Cameron, *On Two Queensland Tribes*, in *Science of Man, Australasian Anthropological Journal*, 1904, VII, 28, col. 1.

CHAPTER III

TOTEMIC BELIEFS—*continued*

The Cosmological System of Totemism and the Idea of Class

WE are beginning to see that totemism is a much more complex religion than it first appeared to be. We have already distinguished three classes of things which it recognizes as sacred, in varying degrees: the totemic emblem, the animal or plant whose appearance this emblem reproduces, and the members of the clan. However, this list is not yet complete. In fact, a religion is not merely a collection of fragmentary beliefs in regard to special objects like those we have just been discussing. To a greater or less extent, all known religions have been systems of ideas which tend to embrace the universality of things, and to give us a complete representation of the world. If totemism is to be considered as a religion comparable to the others, it too should offer us a conception of the universe. As a matter of fact, it does satisfy this condition.

I

The fact that this aspect of totemism has generally been neglected is due to the too narrow notion of the clan which has been prevalent. Ordinarily it is regarded as a mere group of human beings. Being a simple subdivision of the tribe, it seems that like this, it is made up of nothing but men. But in reasoning thus, we substitute our European ideas for those which the primitive has of man and of society. For the Australian, things themselves, everything which is in the universe, are a part of the tribe; they are constituent elements of it and, so to speak, regular members of it; just like men, they have a determined place in the general scheme of organization of the society. "The South Australian savage," says Fison, "looks upon the universe as the Great Tribe, to one of whose divisions he himself belongs; and all things, animate and inanimate, which belong to his class are parts of the body corporate whereof he himself is a part."[1] As a consequence of this principle, whenever the tribe is divided into two phratries, all known things are distributed between them. "All nature," says Palmer, in speaking of the Bellinger River tribe, "is also divided into class [phratry] names. . . . The sun and moon and stars

[1] *Kamilaroi and Kurnai*, p. 170.

are said . . . to belong to classes [phratries] just as the blacks themselves."[1] The Port Mackay tribe in Queensland has two phratries with the names Yungaroo and Wootaroo, as do the neighbouring tribes. Now as Bridgmann says, "all things, animate and inanimate, are divided by these tribes into two classes, named Yungaroo and Wootaroo."[2] Nor does the classification stop here. The men of each phratry are distributed among a certain number of clans; likewise, the things attributed to each phratry are in their turn distributed among the clans of which the phratry is composed. A certain tree, for example, will be assigned to the Kangaroo clan, and to it alone; then, just like the human members of the clan, it will have the Kangaroo as totem; another will belong to the Snake clan; clouds will be placed under one totem, the sun under another, etc. All known things will thus be arranged in a sort of tableau or systematic classification embracing the whole of nature.

We have given a certain number of these classifications elsewhere;[3] at present we shall confine ourselves to repeating a few of these as examples. One of the best known of these is the one found in the Mount Gambier tribe. This tribe includes two phratries, named respectively the Kumite and the Kroki; each of these, in its turn, is subdivided into five clans. Now "everything in nature belongs to one or another of these ten clans";[4] Fison and Howitt say that they are all "included" within it. In fact, they are classified under these ten totems just like species in their respective classes. This is well shown by the following table based on information gathered by Curr and by Fison and Howitt.[5]

PHRATRIES.	CLANS.	THINGS CLASSED IN EACH CLAN.
KUMITE	Fish-hawk	Smoke, honeysuckle, certain trees, etc.
	Pelican	Blackwood-trees, dogs, fire, frost, etc.
	Crow	Rain, thunder, lightning, clouds, hail, winter, etc.
	Black cockatoo	The stars, the moon, etc.
	A non-poisonous snake	Fish, seal, eel, the stringybark-tree, etc.
KROKI	Tea-tree	Duck, crayfish, owls, etc.
	An edible root	Bustard, quail, a small kangaroo, etc.
	A white crestless cockatoo	Kangaroo, the summer, the sun, wind, the autumn, etc.
	Details are lacking for the fourth and fifth Kroki clans.	

[1] *Notes on some Australian Tribes*, *J.A.I.*, XIII, p. 300.

[2] In Curr, *Australian Race*, III, p. 45; Brough Smyth, *The Aborigines of Victoria*, I, p. 91; Fison and Howitt, *Kamilaroi and Kurnai*, p. 168.

[3] Durkheim and Mauss, *De quelques formes primitives de classification*, in *Année Sociol.*, VI, pp. 1 ff.

[4] Curr, III, p. 461.

[5] Curr and Fison were both informed by the same person, D. S. Stewart.

The list of things attached to each clan is quite incomplete; Curr himself warns us that he has limited himself to enumerating some of them. But through the work of Mathews and of Howitt[1] we have more extended information to-day on the classification adopted by the Wotjobaluk tribe, which enables us to understand better how a system of this kind is able to include the whole universe, as known to the natives. The Wotjobaluk also are divided into two phratries called Gurogity and Gumaty (Krokitch and Gamutch according to Howitt[2]); not to prolong this enumeration, we shall content ourselves with indicating, after Mathews, the things classed in some of the clans of the Gurogity phratry.

In the clan of the Yam are classified the plain-turkey, the native cat, the *mopoke*, the *dyim-dyim* owl, the *mallee* hen, the rosella parrot, the peewee.

In the Mussel[3] clan are the grey emu, the porcupine, the curlew, the white cockatoo, the wood-duck, the *mallee* lizard, the stinking turtle, the flying squirrel, the ring-tail opossum, the bronze-wing pigeon, the *wijuggla*.

In the Sun clan are the bandicoot, the moon, the kangaroo-rat, the black and white magpies, the opossum, the *ngŭrt* hawk, the gum-tree grub, the wattle-tree grub, the planet Venus.

In the clan of the Warm Wind[4] are the grey-headed eagle-hawk, the carpet snake, the smoker parrot, the shell parrot, the *murrakan* hawk, the *dikkomur* snake, the ring-neck parrot, the *mirudai* snake, the shingle-back lizard.

If we remember that there are many other clans (Howitt names twelve and Mathews fourteen and adds that his list is incomplete[5]), we will understand how all the things in which the native takes an interest find a natural place in these classifications.

Similar arrangements have been observed in the most diverse

[1] Mathews, *Aboriginal Tribes of N.S. Wales and Victoria*, in *Journal and Proceedings of the Royal Society of N.S. Wales*, XXXVIII, pp. 287 f.; Howitt, *Nat. Tr.*, p. 121.

[2] The feminine form of the names given by Mathews is Gurogigurk and Gamatykurk. These are the forms which Howitt reproduces, with a slightly different orthography. The names are also equivalent to those used by the Mount Gambier tribe (Kumite and Kroki).

[3] The native name of this clan is Dyàlup, which Mathews does not translate. This word appears to be identical with Jallup, by which Howitt designates a sub-clan of the same tribe, and which he translates "mussel." That is why we think we can hazard this translation.

[4] This is the translation of Howitt; Mathews renders the word (Wartwurt, "heat of the midday sun."

[5] The tables of Mathews and Howitt disagree on many important points. It even seems that clans attributed by Howitt to the Kroki phratry are given to the Gamutch phratry by Mathews, and inversely. This proves the great difficulties that these observations present. But these differences are without interest for our present question.

parts of the Australian continent; in South Australia, in Victoria, and in New South Wales (among the Euahlayi[1]); very clear traces of it are found in the central tribes.[2] In Queensland, where the clans seem to have disappeared and where the matrimonial classes are the only subdivisions of the phratry, things are divided up among these classes. Thus, the Wakelbura are divided into two phratries, Mallera and Wutaru; the classes of the first are called Kurgilla and Banbe, those of the second, Wungo and Obu. Now to the Banbe belong the opossum, the kangaroo, the dog, honey of little bees, etc.; to the Wungo are attributed the emu, the bandicoot, the black duck, the black snake, the brown snake; to the Obu, the carpet snake, the honey of stinging bees, etc.; to the Kurgilla, the porcupine, the turkey of the plains, water, rain, fire, thunder, etc.[3]

This same organization is found among the Indians of North America. The Zuñi have a system of classification which, in its essential lines, is in all points comparable to the one we have just described. That of the Omaha rests on the same principles as that of the Wotjobaluk.[4] An echo of these same ideas survives even into the more advanced societies. Among the Haida, all the gods and mythical beings who are placed in charge of the different phenomena of nature are classified in one or the other of the two phratries which make up the tribe just like men; some are Eagles, the others, Crows.[5] Now the gods of things are only another aspect of the things which they govern.[6] This mythological classification is therefore merely another form of the preceding one. So we may rest assured that this way of conceiving the world is independent of all ethnic or geographic particularities; and at the same time it is clearly seen to be closely united to the whole system of totemic beliefs.

II

In the paper to which we have already made allusion several times, we have shown what light these facts throw upon the way in which the idea of kind or class was formed in humanity. In fact, these systematic classifications are the first we meet with

[1] Mrs. Langloh Parker, *The Euahlayi Tribe*, pp. 12 ff.

[2] The facts will be found below.

[3] Carr, III, p. 27. Cf. Howitt, *Nat. Tr.*, p. 112. We are merely mentioning the most characteristic facts. For details, one may refer to the memoir already mentioned on *Les classifications primitives*.

[4] *Ibid.*, pp. 34 ff.

[5] Swanton, *The Haida*, pp. 13–14, 17, 22.

[6] This is especially clear among the Haida. Swanton says that with them every animal has two aspects. First, it is an ordinary animal to be hunted and eaten; but it is also a supernatural being in the animal's form, upon which men depend. The mythical beings corresponding to cosmic phenomena have the same ambiguity (Swanton, *ibid.*, 16, 14, 25).

in history, and we have just seen that they are modelled upon the social organization, or rather that they have taken the forms of society as their framework. It is the phratries which have served as classes, and the clans as species. It is because men were organized that they have been able to organize things, for in classifying these latter, they limited themselves to giving them places in the groups they formed themselves. And if these different classes of things are not merely put next to each other, but are arranged according to a unified plan, it is because the social groups with which they commingle themselves are unified and, through their union, form an organic whole, the tribe. The unity of these first logical systems merely reproduces the unity of the society. Thus we have an occasion for verifying the proposition which we laid down at the commencement of this work, and for assuring ourselves that the fundamental notions of the intellect, the essential categories of thought, may be the product of social factors. The above-mentioned facts show clearly that this is the case with the very notion of category itself.

However, it is not our intention to deny that the individual intellect has of itself the power of perceiving resemblances between the different objects of which it is conscious. Quite on the contrary, it is clear that even the most primitive and simple classifications presuppose this faculty. The Australian does not place things in the same clan or in different clans at random. For him as for us, similar images attract one another, while opposed ones repel one another, and it is on the basis of these feelings of affinity or of repulsion that he classifies the corresponding things in one place or another.

There are also cases where we are able to perceive the reasons which inspired this. The two phratries were very probably the original and fundamental bases for these classifications, which were consequently bifurcate at first. Now, when a classification is reduced to two classes, these are almost necessarily conceived as antitheses; they are used primarily as a means of clearly separating things between which there is a very marked contrast. Some are set at the right, the others at the left. As a matter of fact this is the character of the Australian classifications. If the white cockatoo is in one phratry, the black one is in the other; if the sun is on one side, the moon and the stars of night are on the opposite side.[1] Very frequently the beings which serve as the totems of the two phratries have contrary colours.[2]

[1] See above, p. 142. This is the case among the Gournditch-mara (Howitt, *Nat. Tr.*, p. 124), in the tribes studied by Cameron near the Dead Lake, and among the Wotjobaluk (*ibid.*, pp. 125, 250).

[2] J. Mathews, *Two Representative Tribes*, p. 139; Thomas, *Kinship and Marriage*, pp. 53 f.

These oppositions are even met with outside of Australia. Where one of the phratries is disposed to peace, the other is disposed to war;[1] if one has water as its totem, the other has earth.[2] This is undoubtedly the explanation of why the two phratries have frequently been thought of as naturally antagonistic to one another. They say that there is a sort of rivalry or even a constitutional hostility between them.[3] This opposition of things has extended itself to persons; the logical contrast has begotten a sort of social conflict.[4]

It is also to be observed that within each phratry, those things have been placed in a single clan which seem to have the greatest affinity with that serving as totem. For example, the moon has been placed with the black cockatoo, but the sun, together with the atmosphere and the wind, with the white cockatoo. Or again, to a totemic animal has been united all that serves him as food,[5] as well as the animals with which he has the closest connection.[6] Of course, we cannot always understand the obscure psychology which has caused many of these connections and distinctions, but the preceding examples are enough to show that a certain intuition of the resemblances and differences presented by things

[1] Among the Osage, for example (see Dorsey, *Siouan Sociology*, in *XVth Rep.*, pp. 233 ff.

[2] At Mabuiag, an island in Torrès' Strait (Haddon, *Head Hunters*, p. 132), the same opposition is found between the two phratries of the Arunta: one includes the men of a water totem, the other those of earth (Strehlow, I, p. 6).

[3] Among the Iroquois there is a sort of tournament between the two phratries (Morgan, *Ancient Society*, p. 94). Among the Haida, says Swanton, the members of the two phratries of the Eagle and the Crow "are frequently considered as avowed enemies. Husband and wife (who must be of different phratries) do not hesitate to betray each other" (*The Haida*, p. 62). In Australia this hostility is carried into the myths. The two animals serving the phratries as totems are frequently represented as in a perpetual war against each other (see J. Mathews, *Eaglehawk and Crow, a study of Australian Aborigines*, pp. 14 ff.). In games, each phratry is the natural rival of the other (Howitt, *Nat. Tr.*, p. 770).

[4] So Thomas has wrongly urged against our theory of the origin of the phratries its inability to explain their opposition (*Kinship and Marriage*, p. 69). We do not believe that it is necessary to connect this opposition to that of the profane and the sacred (see Hertz, *La prééminence de la main droite*, in the *Revue Philosophique*, Dec., 1909, p. 559). The things of one phratry are not profane for the other; both are a part of the same religious system (see below, p. 155).

[5] For example, the clan of the Tea-tree includes the grasses, and consequently herbivorous animals (see *Kamilaroi and Kurnai*, p. 169). This is undoubtedly the explanation of a particularity of the totemic emblems of North America pointed out by Boas. "Among the Tlinkit," he says, "and all the other tribes of the coast, the emblem of a group includes the animals serving as food to the one whose name the group bears" (*Fifth Rep. of the Committee, etc., British Association for the Advancement of Science*, p. 25).

[6] Thus, among the Arunta, frogs are connected with the totem of the gum-tree, because they are frequently found in the cavities of this tree; water is related to the water-hen; with the kangaroo is associated a sort of parrot frequently seen flying about this animal (Spencer and Gillen, *Nat. Tr.*, pp. 146–147, 448).

has played an important part in the genesis of these classifications.

But the feeling of resemblances is one thing and the idea of class is another. The class is the external framework of which objects perceived to be similar form, in part, the contents. Now the contents cannot furnish the frame into which they fit. They are made up of *vague and fluctuating* images, due to the superimposition and partial fusion of a *determined number of individual images*, which are found to have common elements; the framework, on the contrary, is a *definite form*, with fixed outlines, but which may be applied to an *undetermined number of things*, perceived or not, actual or possible. In fact, every class has possibilities of extension which go far beyond the circle of objects which we know, either from direct experience or from resemblance. This is why every school of thinkers has refused, and not with good reason, to identify the idea of class with that of a generic image. The generic image is only the indistinctly-bounded residual representation left in us by similar representations, when they are present in consciousness simultaneously; the class is a logical symbol by means of which we think distinctly of these similarities and of other analogous ones. Moreover, the best proof of the distance separating these two notions is that an animal is able to form generic images though ignorant of the art of thinking in classes and species.

The idea of class is an instrument of thought which has obviously been constructed by men. But in constructing it, we have at least had need of a model; for how could this idea ever have been born, if there had been nothing either in us or around us which was capable of suggesting it to us? To reply that it was given to us *a priori* is not to reply at all; this lazy man's solution is, as has been said, the death of analysis. But it is hard to see where we could have found this indispensable model except in the spectacle of the collective life. In fact, a class is not an ideal, but a clearly defined group of things between which internal relationships exist, similar to those of kindred. Now the only groups of this sort known from experience are those formed by men in associating themselves. Material things may be able to form collections of units, or heaps, or mechanical assemblages with no internal unity, but not groups in the sense we have given the word. A heap of sand or a pile of rock is in no way comparable to that variety of definite and organized society which forms a class. In all probability, we would never have thought of uniting the beings of the universe into homogeneous groups, called classes, if we had not had the example of human societies before our eyes, if we had not even commenced by making things themselves members of men's society, and also if human groups and logical groups had not been confused at first.[1]

It is also to be borne in mind that a classification is a system whose parts are arranged according to a hierarchy. There are dominating members and others which are subordinate to the first; species and their distinctive properties depend upon classes and the attributes which characterize them; again, the different species of a single class are conceived as all placed on the same level in regard to each other. Does someone prefer to regard them from the point of view of the understanding? Then he represents things to himself in an inverse order: he puts at the top the species that are the most particularized and the richest in reality, while the types that are most general and the poorest in qualities are at the bottom. Nevertheless, all are represented in a hierarchic form. And we must be careful not to believe that the expression has only a metaphorical sense here: there are really relations of subordination and co-ordination, the establishment of which is the object of all classification, and men would never have thought of arranging their knowledge in this way if they had not known beforehand what a hierarchy was. But neither the spectacle of physical nature nor the mechanism of mental associations could furnish them with this knowledge. The hierarchy is exclusively a social affair. It is only in society that there are superiors, inferiors and equals. Consequently, even if the facts were not enough to prove it, the mere analysis of these ideas would reveal their origin. We have taken them from society, and projected them into our conceptions of the world. It is society that has furnished the outlines which logical thought has filled in.

III

But these primitive classifications have a no less direct interest for the origins of religious thought.

They imply that all the things thus classed in a single clan or a single phratry are closely related both to each other and to the thing serving as the totem of this clan or phratry. When an Australian of the Port Mackay tribe says that the sun, snakes, etc., are of the Yungaroo phratry, he does not mean merely to apply a common, but none the less a purely conventional, nomenclature to

[1] One of the signs of this primitive lack of distinction is that territorial bases are sometimes assigned to the classes just as to the social divisions with which they were at first confounded. Thus, among the Wotjobaluk in Australia and the Zuñi in America, things are ideally distributed among the different regions of space, just as the clans are. Now this regional distribution of things and that of the clans coincide (see *De quelques formes primitives de classification*, pp. 34 ff.). Classifications keep something of this special character even among relatively advanced peoples, as for example, in China (*ibid.*, pp. 55 ff.).

these different things; the word has an objective signification for him. He believes that "alligators really *are* Yungaroo and that kangaroos are Wootaroo. The sun *is* Yungaroo, the moon Wootaroo, and so on for the constellations, trees, plants, etc."[1] An internal bond attaches them to the group in which they are placed; they are regular members of it. It is said that they belong to the group,[2] just exactly as the individual men make a part of it; consequently, the same sort of a relation unites them to these latter. Men regard the things in their clan as their relatives or associates; they call them their friends and think that they are made out of the same flesh as themselves.[3] Therefore, between the two there are elective affinities and quite special relations of agreement. Things and people have a common name, and in a certain way they naturally understand each other and harmonize with one another. For example, when a Wakelbura of the Mallera phratry is buried, the scaffold upon which the body is exposed "must be made of the wood of some tree belonging to the Mallera phratry."[4] The same is true for the branches that cover the corpse. If the deceased is of the Banbe class, a Banbe tree must be used. In this same tribe, a magician can use in his art only those things which belong to his own phratry;[5] since the others are strangers to him, he does not know how to make them obey him. Thus a bond of mystic sympathy unites each individual to those beings, whether living or not, which are associated with him; the result of this is a belief in the possibility of deducing what he will do or what he has done from what they are doing. Among these same Wakelbura, when a man dreams that he has killed an animal belonging to a certain social division, he expects to meet a man of this same division the next day.[6] Inversely, the things attributed to a clan or phratry cannot be used against the members of this clan or phratry. Among the Wotjobaluk, each phratry has its own special trees. Now in hunting an animal of the Gurogity phratry, only arms whose wood is taken from trees of the other phratry may be used, and *vice versa;* otherwise the hunter is sure to miss his aim.[7] The native is convinced that the arrow would turn of itself and refuse, so to speak, to hit a kindred and friendly animal.

[1] Bridgmann, *in* Brough Smyth, *The Aborigines of Victoria*, I, p. 91.

[2] Fison and Howitt, *Kamilaroi and Kurnai*, p. 168; Howitt, *Further Notes on the Australian Class Systems*, *J.A.I.*, XVIII, p. 60.

[3] Curr, III, p. 461. This is about the Mount Gambier tribe.

[4] Howitt, *On some Australian Beliefs*, *J.A.I.*, XIII, p. 191, n. 1.

[5] Howitt, *Notes on Australian Message Sticks*, *J.A.I.*, XVIII, p. 326; *Further Notes*, *J.A.I.*, XVIII, p. 61, n. 3.

[6] Curr, III, p. 28.

[7] Mathews, *Ethnological Notes on the Aboriginal Tribes of N.S. Wales and Victoria*, in *Journ. and Proceed. of the Royal Soc. of N.S. Wales*, XXXVIII, p. 294.

Thus the men of the clan and the things which are classified in it form by their union a solid system, all of whose parts are united and vibrate sympathetically. This organization, which at first may have appeared to us as purely logical, is at the same time moral. A single principle animates it and makes its unity: this is the totem. Just as a man who belongs to the Crow clan has within him something of this animal, so the rain, since it is of the same clan and belongs to the same totem, is also necessarily considered as being " the same thing as a crow "; for the same reason, the moon is a black cockatoo, the sun a white cockatoo, every black-nut tree a pelican, etc. All the beings arranged in a single clan, whether men, animals, plants or inanimate objects, are merely forms of the totemic being. This is the meaning of the formula which we have just cited and this is what makes the two really of the same species: all are really of the same flesh in the sense that all partake of the nature of the totemic animal. Also, the qualifiers given them are those given to the totem.[1] The Wotjobaluk give the name *Mir* both to the totem and to the things classed with it.[2] It is true that among the Arunta, where visible traces of classification still exist, as we shall see, different words designate the totem and the other beings placed with it; however, the name given to these latter bears witness to the close relations which unite them to the totemic animal. It is said that they are its *intimates*, its *associates*, its *friends*; it is believed that they are inseparable from it.[3] So there is a feeling that these are very closely related things.

But we also know that the totemic animal is a sacred being. All the things that are classified in the clan of which it is the emblem have this same character, because in one sense, they are animals of the same species, just as the man is. They, too, are sacred, and the classifications which locate them in relation to the other things of the universe, by that very act give them a place in the religious world. For this reason, the animals or plants among these may not be eaten freely by the human members of the clan. Thus in the Mount Gambier tribe, the men whose totem is a certain non-poisonous snake must not merely refrain from eating the flesh of this snake; that of seals, eels, etc., is also forbidden to them.[4] If, driven by necessity, they do eat some of it, they must at least attenuate the sacrilege by expiatory rites, just as if they had eaten the totem itself.[5] Among the

[1] Cf. Curr, III, p. 461; and Howitt, *Nat. Tr.*, p. 146. The expressions *Tooman* and *Wingo* are applied to the one and the other.

[2] Howitt, *Nat. Tr.*, p. 123.

[3] Spencer and Gillen, *Nat. Tr.*, pp. 447 ff.; cf. Strehlow, III, pp. xii ff.

[4] Fison and Howitt, *Kamilaroi and Kurnai*, p. 169.

[5] Curr, III, p. 462.

Euahlayi, where it is permitted to use the totem, but not to abuse it, the same rule is applied to the other members of the clan.[1] Among the Arunta, the interdictions protecting the totemic animal extend over the associated animals;[2] and in any case, particular attention must be given to these latter.[3] The sentiments inspired by the two are identical.[4]

But the fact that the things thus attached to the totem are not of a different nature from it, and consequently have a religious character, is best proved by the fact that on certain occasions they fulfil the same functions. They are accessory or secondary totems, or, according to an expression now consecrated by usage, they are sub-totems.[5] It is constantly happening in the clans that under the influence of various sympathies, particular affinities are forming, smaller groups and more limited associations arise, which tend to lead a relatively autonomous life and to form a new subdivision like a sub-clan within the larger one. In order to distinguish and individualize itself, this sub-clan needs a special totem or, consequently, a sub-totem.[6] Now the totems of these secondary groups are chosen from among the things classified under the principal totem. So they are always almost totems and the slightest circumstance is enough to make them actually so. There is a latent totemic nature in them, which shows itself as soon as conditions permit

[1] Mrs. Parker, *The Euahlayi Tribe*, p. 20.

[2] Spencer and Gillen, *Nor. Tr.*, p. 151; *Nat. Tr.*, p. 447; Strehlow, III, p. xii.

[3] Spencer and Gillen, *Nat. Tr.*, p. 449.

[4] However, there are certain tribes in Queensland where the things thus attributed to a social group are not forbidden for the members of the group: this is notably the case with the Wakelbura. It is to be remembered that in this society, it is the matrimonial classes that serve as the framework of the classification (see above, p. 144). Not only are the men of one class allowed to eat the animals attributed to this class, but *they may eat no others*. All other food is forbidden them (Howitt, *Nat. Tr.*, p. 113; Curr, III, p. 27).

But we must not conclude from this that these animals are considered profane. In fact, it should be noticed that the individual not only has the privilege of eating them, but that he is compelled to do so, for he cannot nourish himself otherwise. Now the imperative nature of this rule is a sure sign that we are in the presence of things having a religious nature, only this has given rise to a positive obligation rather than the negative one known as an interdiction. Perhaps it is not quite impossible to see how this deviation came about. We have seen above (p. 140) that every individual is thought to have a sort of property-right over his totem and consequently over the things dependent upon it. Perhaps, under the influence of special circumstances, this aspect of the totemic relation was developed, and they naturally came to believe that only the members of the clan had the right of disposing of their totem and all that is connected with it, and that others, on the contrary, did not have the right of touching it. Under these circumstances, a tribe could nourish itself only on the food attributed to it.

[5] Mrs. Parker uses the expression "multiplex totems."

[6] As examples, see the Euahlayi tribe in Mrs. Parker's book (pp. 15 ff.) and the Wotjobaluk (Howitt, *Nat. Tr.*, pp. 121 ff.; cf. the above-mentioned article of Mathews).

it or demand it. It thus happens that a single individual has two totems, a principal totem common to the whole clan and a sub-totem which is special to the sub-clan of which he is a member. This is something analogous to the *nomen* and *cognomen* of the Romans.[1]

Sometimes we see a sub-clan emancipate itself completely and become an autonomous group and an independent clan ; then, the sub-totem, on its side, becomes a regular totem. One tribe where this process of segmentation has been pushed to the limit, so to speak, is the Arunta. The information contained in the first book of Spencer and Gillen showed that there were some sixty totems among the Arunta ;[2] but the recent researches of Strehlow have shown the number to be much larger. He counted no less than 442.[3] Spencer and Gillen did not exaggerate at all when they said, " In fact, there is scarcely an object, animate or inanimate, to be found in the country occupied by the natives which does not give its name to some totemic group."[4] Now this multitude of totems, whose number is prodigious when compared to the population, is due to the fact that under special circumstances, the original clans have divided and sub-divided infinitely ; consequently nearly all the sub-totems have passed to the stage of totems.

This has been definitely proved by the observations of Strehlow. Spencer and Gillen cited only certain isolated cases of associated totems.[5] Strehlow has shown that this is in reality an absolutely general organization. He has been able to draw up a table where nearly all the totems of the Arunta are classified according to this principle : all are attached, either as associates or as auxiliaries, to some sixty principal totems.[6] The first are believed to be in the service of the second.[7] This state of

[1] See the examples in Howitt, *Nat. Tr.*, p. 122.

[2] See our *De quelques formes primitives de classification*, p. 28, n. 2.

[3] Strehlow, II, pp. 61–72.

[4] *Nat. Tr.*, p. 112.

[5] See especially *Nat. Tr.*, p. 447, and *Nor. Tr.*, p. 151.

[6] Strehlow, III, pp. xiii–xviii. It sometimes happens that the same secondary totems are attached to two or three principal totems at the same time. This is undoubtedly because Strehlow has not been able to establish with certainty which is the principal totem.

Two interesting facts which appear from this table confirm certain propositions which we had already formulated. First, the principal totems are nearly all animals, with but rare exceptions. Also, stars are always only secondary or associated totems. This is another proof that these latter were only slowly advanced to the rank of totems and that at first the principal totems were preferably chosen from the animal kingdom.

[7] According to the myth, the associate totems served as food to the men of the principal totem in the fabulous times, or, when these are trees, they gave their shade (Strehlow, III, p. xii ; Spencer and Gillen, *Nat. Tr.*, p. 403). The fact that the associate totems are believed to have been eaten does not imply that they are considered profane ; for in the mythical period, the principal totem itself was consumed by the ancestors, the founders of the clan, according to the belief.

dependence is very probably the echo of a time when the "allies" of to-day were only sub-totems, and consequently when the tribe contained only a small number of clans subdivided into subclans. Numerous survivals confirm this hypothesis. It frequently happens that two groups thus associated have the same totemic emblem: now this unity of emblem is explicable only if the two groups were at first only one.[1] The relation of the two clans is also shown by the part and the interest that each one takes in the rites of the other. The two cults are still only imperfectly separated; this is very probably because they were at first completely intermingled.[2] Tradition explains the bonds which unite them by imagining that formerly the two clans occupied neighbouring places.[3] In other cases, the myth says expressly that one of them was derived from the other. It is related that at first the associated animal belonged to the species still serving as principal totem; it differentiated itself at a later period. Thus the chantunga birds, which are associated with the witchetly grub to-day, were witchetly grubs in fabulous times, who later transformed themselves into birds. Two species which are now attached to the honey-ant were formerly honey-ants, etc.[4] This transformation of a sub-totem into a totem goes on by imperceptible degrees, so that in certain cases the situation is undecided, and it is hard to say whether one is dealing with a principal totem or a secondary one.[5] As Howitt says in regard to the Wotjobaluk, there are sub-totems which are totems in formation.[6] Thus the different things classified in a clan constitute, as it were, so many nuclei around which new totemic cults are able to form. This is the best proof of the religious sentiments which they inspire. If they did not have a sacred character, they could not be promoted so easily to the same dignity as the things which are sacred before all others, the regular totems.

So the field of religious things extends well beyond the limits within which it seemed to be confined at first. It embraces not only the totemic animals and the human members of the clan; but since no known thing exists that is not classified in a clan and under a totem, there is likewise nothing which does not receive

[1] Thus in the Wild Cat clan, the designs carved on the churinga represent the Hakea tree, which is a distinct totem to-day (Spencer and Gillen, *Nat. Tr.*, pp. 147 f.). Strehlow (III, p. xii, n. 4) says that this is frequent.

[2] Spencer and Gillen, *Nor. Tr.*, p. 182; *Nat. Tr.*, pp. 151 and 297.

[3] *Nat. Tr.*, pp. 151 and 158.

[4] *Ibid.*, pp. 448 and 449.

[5] Thus Spencer and Gillen speak of a pigeon called Inturrita, sometimes as a principal totem (*Nat. Tr.*, p. 410), sometimes as an associate totem (*ibid.*, p. 448).

[6] Howitt, *Further Notes*, pp. 63–64.

to some degree something of a religious character. When, in the religions which later come into being, the gods properly so-called appear, each of them will be set over a special category of natural phenomena, this one over the sea, that one over the air, another over the harvest or over fruits, etc., and each of these provinces of nature will be believed to draw what life there is in it from the god upon whom it depends. This division of nature among the different divinities constitutes the conception which these religions give us of the universe. Now so long as humanity has not passed the phase of totemism, the different totems of the tribe fulfil exactly the same functions that will later fall upon the divine personalities. In the Mount Gambier tribe, which we have taken as our principal example, there are ten clans; consequently the entire world is divided into ten classes, or rather into ten families, each of which has a special totem as its basis. It is from this basis that the things classed in the clan get all their reality, for they are thought of as variant forms of the totemic being; to return to our example, the rain, thunder, lightning, clouds, hail and winter are regarded as different sorts of crows. When brought together, these ten families of things make up a complete and systematic representation of the world; and this representation is religious, for religious notions furnish its basis. Far from being limited to one or two categories of beings, the domain of totemic religion extends to the final limits of the known universe. Just like the Greek religion, it puts the divine everywhere; the celebrated formula παντὰ πλήρη θεῶν (everything is full of the gods), might equally well serve it as motto.

However, if totemism is to be represented thus, the notion of it which has long been held must be modified on one essential point. Until the discoveries of recent years, it was made to consist entirely in the cult of one particular totem, and it was defined as the religion of the clan. From this point of view, each tribe seemed to have as many totemic religions, each independent of the others, as it had different clans. This conception was also in harmony with the idea currently held of the clan; in fact, this was regarded as an autonomous society,[1] more or less closed to other similar societies, or having only external and superficial relations with these latter. But the reality is more complex. Undoubtedly, the cult of each totem has its home in the corresponding clan; it is there, and only there, that it is celebrated; it is members of the clan who have charge of it;

[1] Thus it comes about that the clan has frequently been confounded with the tribe. This confusion, which frequently introduces trouble into the writings of ethnologists, has been made especially by Curr (I, pp. 61 ff.).

it is through them that it is transmitted from one generation to another, along with the beliefs which are its basis. But it is also true that the different totemic cults thus practised within a single tribe do not have a parallel development, though remaining ignorant of each other, as if each of them constituted a complete and self-sufficing religion. On the contrary, they mutually imply each other; they are only the parts of a single whole, the elements of a single religion. The men of one clan never regard the beliefs of neighbouring clans with that indifference, scepticism or hostility which one religion ordinarily inspires for another which is foreign to it; they partake of these beliefs themselves. The Crow people are also convinced that the Snake people have a mythical serpent as ancestor, and that they owe special virtues and marvellous powers to this origin. And have we not seen that at least in certain conditions, a man may eat a totem that is not his own only after he has observed certain ritual formalities? Especially, he must demand the permission of the men of this totem, if any are present. So for him also, this food is not entirely profane; he also admits that there are intimate affinities between the members of a clan of which he is not a member and the animal whose name they bear. Also, this community of belief is sometimes shown in the cult. If in theory the rites concerning a totem can be performed only by the men of this totem, nevertheless representatives of different clans frequently assist at them. It sometimes happens that their part is not simply that of spectators; it is true that they do not officiate, but they decorate the officiants and prepare the service. They themselves have an interest in its being celebrated; therefore, in certain tribes, it is they who invite the qualified clan to proceed with the ceremonies.[1] There is even a whole cycle of rites which must take place in the presence of the assembled tribe: these are the totemic ceremonies of initiation.[2]

Finally, the totemic organization, such as we have just described it, must obviously be the result of some sort of an indistinct understanding between all the members of the tribe. It is impossible that each clan should have made its beliefs in an absolutely independent manner; it is absolutely necessary that the cults of the different totems should be in some way adjusted to each other, since they complete one another exactly. In fact, we have seen that normally a single totem is not repeated twice in the same tribe, and that the whole universe is divided up among the totems thus constituted in such a way that the same object is not found in two different clans. So methodical

[1] This is the case especially among the Warramunga (*Nor. Tr.*, p. 298).

[2] See, for example, Spencer and Gillen, *Nat. Tr.*, p. 380 and *passim*.

a division could never have been made without an agreement, tacit or planned, in which the whole tribe participated. So the group of beliefs which thus arise are partially (but only partially) a tribal affair.[1]

To sum up, then, in order to form an adequate idea of totemism, we must not confine ourselves within the limits of the clan, but must consider the tribe as a whole. It is true that the particular cult of each clan enjoys a very great autonomy ; we can now see that it is within the clan that the active ferment of the religious life takes place. But it is also true that these cults fit into each other and the totemic religion is a complex system formed by their union, just as Greek polytheism was made by the union of all the particular cults addressed to the different divinities. We have just shown that, thus understood, totemism also has it cosmology.

[1] One might even ask if tribal totems do not exist sometimes. Thus, among the Arunta, there is an animal, the wild cat, which serves as totem to a particular clan, but which is forbidden for the whole tribe ; even the people of other clans can eat it only very moderately (*Nat. Tr.*, p. 168). But we believe that it would be an abuse to speak of a tribal totem in this case, for it does not follow from the fact that the free consumption of an animal is forbidden that this is a totem. Other causes can also give rise to an interdiction. The religious unity of the tribe is undoubtedly real, but this is affirmed with the aid of other symbols. We shall show what these are below (Bk. II, ch. ix).

CHAPTER IV

TOTEMIC BELIEFS—*end*

The Individual Totem and the Sexual Totem

UP to the present, we have studied totemism only as a public institution: the only totems of which we have spoken are common to a clan, a phratry or, in a sense, to a tribe; [1] an individual has a part in them only as a member of a group. But we know that there is no religion which does not have an individual aspect. This general observation is applicable to totemism. In addition to the impersonal and collective totems which hold the first place, there are others which are peculiar to each individual, which express his personality, and whose cult he celebrates in private.

I

In certain Australian tribes, and in the majority of the Indian tribes of North America,[2] each individual personally sustains relations with some determined object, which are comparable to those which each clan sustains with its totem. This is sometimes an inanimate being or an artificial object; but it is generally an animal. In certain cases, a special part of the organism, such as the head, the feet or the liver, fulfils this office.[3]

The name of the thing also serves as the name of the individual. It is his personal name, his forename, which is added to that of the collective totem, as the *praenomen* of the Romans was to the *nomen gentilicium*. It is true that this fact is not reported except in a certain number of societies,[4] but it is probably general. In

[1] The totems belong to the tribe in the sense that this is interested as a body in the cult which each clan owes to its totem.

[2] Frazer has made a very complete collection of the texts relative to individual totemism in North America (*Totemism and Exogamy*, III, pp. 370–456).

[3] For example, among the Hurons, the Iroquois, the Algonquins (Charlevoix, *Histoire de la Nouvelle France*, VI, pp. 67–70; Sagard, *Le grand voyage au pays des Hurons*, p. 160), or among the Thompson Indians (Teit, *The Thompson Indians of British Columbia*, p. 355).

[4] This is the case of the Yuin (Howitt, *Nat. Tr.*, p. 133), the Kurnai (*ibid.*, p. 135), several tribes of Queensland (Roth, *Superstition, Magic and Medicine, North Queensland Ethnography*, Bulletin No. 5, p. 19; Haddon, *Head-Hunters*, p. 193); among the Delaware (Heckewelder, *An Account of the History . . . of the Indian Nations*, p. 238), among the Thompson Indians (Teit, *op. cit.*, p. 355), and among the Salish Statlumh (Hill Tout, *Rep. of the Ethnol. of the Statlumh*, *J.A.I.*, XXXV, pp. 147 ff.).

fact, we shall presently show that there is an identity of nature between the individual and the thing ; now an identity of nature implies one of name. Being given in the course of especially important religious ceremonies, this forename has a sacred character. It is not pronounced in the ordinary circumstances of profane life. It even happens that the word designating this object in the ordinary language must be modified to a greater or less extent if it is to serve in this particular case.[1] This is because the terms of the usual language are excluded from the religious life.

In certain American tribes, at least, this name is reinforced by an emblem belonging to each individual and representing, under various forms, the thing designated by the name. For example, each Mandan wears the skin of the animal of which he is the namesake.[2] If it is a bird, he decorates himself with its feathers.[3] The Hurons and Algonquins tattoo their bodies with its image.[4] It is represented on their arms.[5] Among the northwestern tribes, the individual emblem, just like the collective emblem of the clan, is carved or engraved on the utensils, houses,[6] etc. ; it serves as a mark of ownership.[7] Frequently the two coats-of-arms are combined together, which partially explains the great diversity of aspects presented by the totemic escutcheons among these peoples.[8]

Between the individual and his animal namesake there exist the very closest bonds. The man participates in the nature of the animal ; he has its good qualities as well as its faults. For example, a man having the eagle as his coat-of-arms is believed to possess the gift of seeing into the future ; if he is named after a bear, they say that he is apt to be wounded in combat, for the bear is heavy and slow and easily caught ;[9] if the animal is despised, the man is the object of the same sentiment.[10] The relationship of the two is even so close that it is believed that in certain circumstances, especially in case of danger, the man can take the form of the animal.[11] Inversely, the animal is

[1] Hill Tout, *loc. cit.*, p. 154.
[2] Catlin, *Manners and Customs*, etc., London, 1876, I, p. 36.
[3] *Lettres édifiantes et curieuses*, new edition, VI, pp. 172 ff.
[4] Charlevoix, *op. cit.*, VI, p. 69.
[5] Dorsey, *Siouan Cults*, *XIth Rep.*, p. 443.
[6] Boas, *Kwakiutl*, p. 323.
[7] Hill Tout, *loc. cit.*, p. 154.
[8] Boas, *Kwakiutl*, p. 323.
[9] Miss Fletcher, *The Import of the Totem, a Study from the Omaha Tribe* (*Smithsonian Rep. for* 1897, p. 583).—Similar facts will be found in Teit, *op. cit.*, pp. 354, 356 ; Peter Jones, *History of the Ojibway Indians*, p. 87.
[10] This is the case, for example, with the dog among the Salish Statlumh, owing to the condition of servitude in which it lives (Hill Tout, *loc. cit.*, p. 153).
[11] Langloh Parker, *Euahlayi*, p. 21.

regarded as a double of the man, as his *alter ego.*[1] The association of the two is so close that their destinies are frequently thought to be bound up together: nothing can happen to one without the other's feeling a reaction.[2] If the animal dies, the life of the man is menaced. Thus it comes to be a very general rule that one should not kill the animal, nor eat its flesh. This interdiction, which, when concerning the totem of the clan, allows of all sorts of attenuations and modifications, is now much more formal and absolute.[3]

On its side, the animal protects the man and serves him as a sort of patron. It informs him of possible dangers and of the way of escaping them;[4] they say that it is his friend.[5] Since it frequently happens to possess marvellous powers, it communicates them to its human associate, who believes in them, even under the proof of bullets, arrows, and blows of every sort.[6] This confidence of an individual in the efficacy of his protector is so great that he braves the greatest dangers and accomplishes the most disconcerting feats with an intrepid serenity: faith gives him the necessary courage and strength.[7] However, the relations of a man with his patron are not purely and simply those of dependence. He, on his side, is able to act upon the animal. He gives it orders; he has influence over it. A Kurnai having the shark as ally and friend believes that he can disperse the sharks who menace a boat, by means of a charm.[8] In other cases, the relations thus contracted are believed to confer upon the man a special aptitude for hunting the animal with success.[9]

[1] "The spirit of a man," says Mrs. Parker (*ibid.*), "is in his Yuanbeai (his individual totem), and his Yuanbeai is in him."

[2] Langloh Parker, *Euahlayi*, p. 20. It is the same among certain Salish (Hill Tout, *Ethn. Rep. on the Stseelis and Skaulits Tribes, J.A.I.*, XXXIV, p. 324). The fact is quite general among the Indians of Central America (Brinton, *Nagualism, a Study in Native American Folklore and History*, in *Proceed. of the Am. Philos. Soc.*, XXXIII, p. 32).

[3] Parker, *ibid.*; Howitt, *Nat. Tr.*, p. 147; Dorsey, *Siouan Cults*, *XIth Rep.*, p. 443. Frazer has made a collection of the American cases and established the generality of the interdiction (*Totemism and Exogamy*, III, p. 450). It is true that in America, as we have seen, the individual must kill the animal whose skin serves to make what ethnologists call his medicine-sack. But this usage has been observed in five tribes only; it is probably a late and altered form of the institution.

[4] Howitt, *Nat. Tr.*, pp. 135, 147, 387; *Australian Medicine Men, J.A.I.*, XVI, p. 34; Teit, *The Shuswap*, p. 607.

[5] Meyer, *Manners and Customs of the Aborigines of the Encounter Bay Tribe*, in Woods, p. 197.

[6] Boas, *VIth Rep. on the North-West Tribes of Canada*, p. 93; Teit, *The Thompson Indians*, p. 336; Boas, *Kwakiutl*, p. 394.

[7] Facts will be found in Hill Tout, *Rep. of the Ethnol. of the Statlumh, J.A.I.*, XXXV, pp. 144, 145. Cf. Langloh Parker, *op. cit.*, p. 29.

[8] According to information given by Howitt in a personal letter to Frazer (*Totemism and Exogamy*, I, p. 495, and n. 2).

[9] Hill Tout, *Ethnol. Rep. on the Stseelis and Skaulits Tribes, J.A.I.*, XXXIV, p. 324.

The very nature of these relations seems clearly to imply that the being to which each individual is thus associated is only an individual itself, and not a species. A man does not have a species as his *alter ego*. In fact, there are cases where it is certainly a certain determined tree, rock or stone that fulfils this function.[1] It must be thus every time that it is an animal, and that the existences of the animal and the man are believed to be connected. A man could not be united so closely to a whole species, for there is not a day nor, so to speak, an instant when the species does not lose some one of its members. Yet the primitive has a certain incapacity for thinking of the individual apart from the species; the bonds uniting him to the one readily extend to the other; he confounds the two in the same sentiment. Thus the entire species becomes sacred for him.[2]

This protector is naturally given different names in different societies: *nagual* among the Indians of Mexico,[3] *manitou* among the Algonquins and *okki* among the Hurons,[4] *snam* among certain Salish,[5] *sulia* among others,[6] *budjan* among the Yuin,[7] *yunbeai* among the Euahlayi,[8] etc. Owing to the importance of these beliefs and practices among the Indians of North America, some have proposed creating a word *nagualism* or *manitouism* to designate them.[9] But in giving them a special and distinctive name, we run the risk of misunderstanding their relations with the rest of totemism. In fact, the same principle is applied in the one case to the clan and in the other to the individual. In both cases we find the same belief that there are vital connections

[1] Howitt, *Australian Medicine Men*, *J.A.I.*, XVI, p. 34; Lafitau, *Mœurs des Sauvages Amériquains*, I, p. 370; Charlevoix, *Histoire de la Nouvelle France*, VI, p. 68. It is the same with the *atai* and *tamaniu* in Mota (Codrington, *The Melanesians*, pp. 250 f.).

[2] Thus the line of demarcation between the animal protectors and fetishes, which Frazer has attempted to establish, does not exist. According to him, fetishism commences when the protector is an individual object and not a class (*Totemism*, p. 56); but it frequently happens in Australia that a determined animal takes this part (see Howitt, *Australian Medicine Men*, *J.A.I.*, XVI, p. 34). The truth is that the ideas of fetish and fetishism do not correspond to any definite thing.

[3] Brinton, *Nagualism*, in *Proceed. Amer. Philos. Soc.*, XXXIII, p. 32.

[4] Charlevoix, VI, p. 67.

[5] Hill Tout, *Rep. on the Ethnol. of the Statlumh of British Columbia*, *J.A.I.*, XXXV, p. 142.

[6] Hill Tout, *Ethnol. Rep. on the Stseelis and Skaulits Tribes*, *J.A.I.*, XXXIV, pp. 311 ff.

[7] Howitt, *Nat. Tr.*, p. 133.

[8] Langloh Parker, *op. cit.*, p. 20.

[9] J. W. Powell, *An American View of Totemism*, in *Man*, 1902, No. 84; Tylor, *ibid.*, No. 1; Andrew Lang has expressed analogous ideas in *Social Origins*, pp. 133–135. Also Frazer himself, turning from his former opinion, now thinks that until we are better acquainted with the relations existing between collective totems and " guardian spirits," it would be better to designate them by different names (*Totemism and Exogamy*, III, p. 456).

between the things and the men, and that the former are endowed with special powers, of which their human allies may also enjoy the advantage. We also find the same custom of giving the man the name of the thing with which he is associated and of adding an emblem to this name. The totem is the patron of the clan, just as the patron of the individual is his personal totem. So it is important that our terminology should make the relationship of the two systems apparent; that is why we, with Frazer, shall give the name *individual totemism* to the cult rendered by each individual to his patron. A further justification of this expression is found in the fact that in certain cases the primitive himself uses the same word to designate the totem of the clan and the animal protector of the individual.[1] If Tylor and Powell have rejected this term and demanded different ones for these two sorts of religious institutions, it is because the collective totem is, in their opinion, only a name or label, having no religious character.[2] But we, on the contrary, know that it is a sacred thing, and even more so than the protecting animal. Moreover, the continuation of our study will show how these two varieties of totemism are inseparable from each other.[3]

Yet, howsoever close the kinship between these two institutions may be, there are important differences between them. While the clan believes that it is the offspring of the animal or plant serving it as totem, the individual does not believe that he has any relationship of descent with his personal totem. It is a friend, an associate, a protector; but it is not a relative. He takes advantage of the virtues it is believed to possess; but he is not of the same blood. In the second place, the members of a clan allow neighbouring clans to eat of the animal whose name they bear collectively, under the simple condition that the necessary formalities shall be observed. But, on the contrary, the individual respects the species to which his personal totem belongs and also protects it against strangers, at least in those parts where the destiny of the man is held to be bound up with that of the animal.

But the chief difference between these two sorts of totems is in the manner in which they are acquired.

The collective totem is a part of the civil status of each individual: it is generally hereditary; in any case, it is birth

[1] This is the case in Australia among the Yuin (Howitt, *Nat. Tr.*, p. 81), and the Narrinyeri (Meyer, *Manners and Customs of the Aborigines of the Encounter Bay Tribe*, in Woods, pp. 197 ff.).

[2] "The totem resembles the patron of the individual no more than an escutcheon resembles the image of a saint," says Tylor (*op. cit.*, p. 2). Likewise, if Frazer has taken up the theory of Tylor, it is because he refuses all religious character to the totem of the clan (*Totemism and Exogamy*, III, p. 452).

[3] See below, chapter ix of this book.

which designates it, and the wish of men counts for nothing. Sometimes the child has the totem of his mother (Kamilaroi, Dieri, Urabunna, etc.) ; sometimes that of his father (Narrinyeri, Warramunga, etc.) ; sometimes the one predominating in the locality where his mother conceived (Arunta, Loritja). But, on the contrary, the individual totem is acquired by a deliberate act :[1] a whole series of ritual operations are necessary to determine it. The method generally employed by the Indians of North America is as follows. About the time of puberty, as the time for initiation approaches, the young man withdraws into a distant place, for example, into a forest. There, during a period varying from a few days to several years, he submits himself to all sorts of exhausting and unnatural exercises. He fasts, mortifies himself and inflicts various mutilations upon himself. Now he wanders about, uttering violent cries and veritable howls ; now he lies extended, motionless and lamenting, upon the ground. Sometimes he dances, prays and invokes his ordinary divinities. At last, he thus gets himself into an extreme state of super-excitation, verging on delirium. When he has reached this paroxysm, his representations readily take on the character of hallucinations. " When," says Heckewelder, " a boy is on the eve of being initiated, he is submitted to an alternating régime of fasts and medical treatment ; he abstains from all food and takes the most powerful and repugnant drugs : at times, he drinks intoxicating concoctions until his mind really wanders. Then he has, or thinks he has, visions and extraordinary dreams to which he was of course predisposed by all this training. He imagines himself flying through the air, advancing under the ground, jumping from one mountain-top to another across the valleys, and fighting and conquering giants and monsters." [2] If in these circumstances he sees, or, as amounts to the same thing, he thinks he sees, while dreaming or while awake, an animal appearing to him in an attitude seeming to

[1] Yet according to one passage in Mathews, the individual totem is hereditary among the Wotjobaluk. " Each individual," he says, " claims some animal, plant or inanimate object as his special and personal totem, which he inherits from his mother " (*Journ. and Proc. of the Roy. Soc. of N.S. Wales*, XXXVIII, p. 291). But it is evident that if all the children in the same family had the personal totem of their mother, neither they nor she would really have personal totems at all. Mathews probably means to say that each individual chooses his individual totem from the list of things attributed to the clan of his mother. In fact, we shall see that each clan has its individual totems which are its exclusive property ; the members of the other clans cannot make use of them. In this sense, birth determines the personal totem to a certain extent, but to a certain extent only.

[2] Heckewelder, *An Account of the History, Manners and Customs of the Indian Nations who once inhabited Pennsylvania*, in *Transactions of the Historical and Literary Committee of the American Philosophical Society*, I, p. 238.

show friendly intentions, then he imagines that he has discovered the patron he awaited.[1]

Yet this procedure is rarely employed in Australia.[2] On this continent, the personal totem seems to be imposed by a third party, either at birth [3] or at the moment of initiation.[4] Generally it is a relative who takes this part, or else a personage invested with special powers, such as an old man or a magician. Sometimes divination is used for this purpose. For example, on Charlotte Bay, Cape Bedford or the Proserpine River, the grandmother or some other old woman takes a little piece of umbilical cord to which the placenta is still attached and whirls it about quite violently. Meanwhile the other old women propose different names. That one is adopted which happens to be pronounced just at the moment when the cord breaks.[5] Among the Yarraikanna of Cape York, after a tooth has been knocked out of the young initiate, they give him a little water to rinse his mouth and ask him to spit in a bucket full of water. The old men carefully examine the clot formed by the blood and saliva thus spit out, and the natural object whose shape it resembles becomes the personal totem of the young man.[6] In other cases, the totem is transmitted from one individual to another, for example from father to son, or uncle to nephew.[7] This method is also used in America. In a case reported by Hill Tout, the operator was a shaman,[8] who wished to transmit his totem to his nephew. " The uncle took the symbol of his *snam* (his personal totem), which in this case was a dried bird's skin, and bade his nephew breathe upon it. He then blew upon it also himself, uttered some mystic words and the dried skin seemed to Paul (the nephew) to become a living bird, which flew about them a moment or two

[1] See Dorsey, *Siouan Cults, XIth Rep.*, p. 507; Catlin, *op. cit.*, I, p. 37; Miss Fletcher, *The Import of the Totem*, in *Smithsonian Rep.* for 1897, p. 580; Teit, *The Thompson Indians*, pp. 317–320; Hill Tout, *J.A.I.*, XXXV, p. 144.

[2] But some examples are found. The Kurnai magicians see their personal totems revealed to them in dreams (Howitt, *Nat. Tr.*, p. 387; *On Australian Medicine Men*, in *J.A.I.*, XVI, p. 34). The men of Cape Bedford believe that when an old man dreams of something during the night, this thing is the personal totem of the first person he meets the next day (W. E. Roth, *Superstition, Magic and Medicine*, p. 19). But it is probable that only supplementary and accessory totems are acquired in this way; for in this same tribe another process is used at the moment of initiation, as we said in the text.

[3] In certain tribes of which Roth speaks (*ibid.*); also in certain tribes near to Maryborough (Howitt, *Nat. Tr.*, p. 147).

[4] Among the Wiradjuri (Howitt, *Nat. Tr.*, p. 406; *On Australian Medicine Men*, in *J.A.I.*, XVI, p. 50).

[5] Roth, *loc. cit.*

[6] Haddon, *Head Hunters*, pp. 193 ff.

[7] Among the Wiradjuri (same references as above, n. 4).

[8] In general, it seems as though these transmissions from father to son never take place except when the father is a shaman or a magician. This is also the case among the Thompson Indians (Teit, *The Thompson Indians*, p. 320) and the Wiradjuri, of whom we just spoke.

and then finally disappeared. Paul was then instructed by his uncle to procure that day a bird's skin of the same kind as his uncle's and wear it on his person. This he did, and that night he had a dream, in which the *snam* appeared to him in the shape of a human being, disclosed to him its mystic name by which it might be summoned, and promised him protection." [1]

Not only is the individual totem acquired and not given, but ordinarily the acquisition of one is not obligatory. In the first place, there are a multitude of tribes in Australia where the custom seems to be absolutely unknown.[2] Also, even where it does exist, it is frequently optional. Thus among the Euahlayi, while all the magicians have individual totems from which they get their powers, there are a great number of laymen who have none at all. It is a favour given by the magician, but which he reserves for his friends, his favourites and those who aspire to becoming his colleagues.[3] Likewise, among certain Salish, persons desiring to excel especially either in fighting or in hunting, or aspirants to the position of shaman, are the only ones who provide themselves with protectors of this sort.[4] So among certain peoples, at least, the individual totem seems to be considered an advantage and convenient thing rather than a necessity. It is a good thing to have, but a man can do without one. Inversely, a man need not limit himself to a single totem; if he wishes to be more fully protected, nothing hinders his seeking and acquiring several,[5] and if the one he has fulfils its part badly, he can change it.[6]

But while it is more optional and free, individual totemism contains within it a force of resistance never attained by the totemism of the clan. One of the chief informers of Hill Tout was a baptized Salish; however, though he had sincerely abandoned the faith of his fathers, and though he had become a model catechist, still his faith in the efficacy of the personal totems remained unshaken.[7] Similarly, though no visible traces of collective totemism remain in civilized countries, the idea that there is a connection between each individual and some

[1] Hill Tout (*J.A.I.*, XXXV, pp. 146 f.). The essential rite is the blowing upon the skin: if this were not done correctly, the transmission would not take place. As we shall presently see, the breath is the soul. When both breathe upon the skin of the animal, the magician and the recipient each exhale a part of their souls, which are thus fused, while partaking at the same time of the nature of the animal, who also takes part in the ceremony in the form of its symbol.

[2] N. W. Thomas, *Further Remarks on Mr. Hill Tout's Views on Totemism*, in *Man*, 1904, p. 85.

[3] Langloh Parker, *op. cit.*, pp. 20, 29.

[4] Hill Tout, in *J.A.I.*, XXXV, pp. 143 and 146; *ibid.*, XXXIV, p. 324.

[5] Parker, *op. cit.*, p. 30; Teit, *The Thompson Indians*, p. 320; Hill Tout, in *J.A.I.*, XXXV, p. 144.

[6] Charlevoix, VI, p. 69.

[7] Hill Tout, *ibid.*, p. 145.

animal, plant or other object, is at the bottom of many customs still observable in many European countries.[1]

II

Between collective totemism and individual totemism there is an intermediate form partaking of the characteristics of each: this is sexual totemism. It is found only in Australia and in a small number of tribes. It is mentioned especially in Victoria and New South Wales.[2] Mathews, it is true, claims to have observed it in all the parts of Australia that he has visited, but he gives no precise facts to support this affirmation.[3]

Among these different peoples, all the men of the tribe on the one hand, and all the women on the other, to whatever special clan they may belong, form, as it were, two distinct and even antagonistic societies. Now each of these two sexual corporations believes that it is united by mystical bonds to a determined animal. Among the Kurnai, all the men think they are brothers, as it were, of the emu-wren (Yeerŭng), all the women, that they are as sisters of the linnet (Djeetgŭn); all the men are Yeerŭng and all the women are Djeetgŭn. Among the Wotjobaluk and the Wurunjerri, it is the bat and the *nightjar* (a species of screech-owl) respectively who take this rôle. In other tribes, the woodpecker is substituted for the *nightjar*. Each sex regards the animal to which it is thus related as a sort of protector which must be treated with the greatest regard; it is also forbidden to kill and eat it.[4]

Thus this protecting animal plays the same part in relation to the sexual society that the totem of the clan plays to this latter group. So the expression sexual totemism, which we borrow from Frazer,[5] is justified. This new sort of totem resembles that of the clan particularly in that it, too, is collective; it belongs to all the people of one sex indiscriminately. It also resembles this form in that it implies a relationship of descent and consanguinity between the animal patron and the

[1] Thus at the birth of a child, a tree is planted which is cared for piously; for it is believed that its fate and the child's are united. Frazer, in his *Golden Bough*, gives a number of customs and beliefs translating this same idea in different ways. (Cf. Hartland, *Legend of Perseus*, II, pp. 1–55.)

[2] Howitt, *Nat. Tr.*, pp. 148 ff.; Fison and Howitt, *Kamilaroi and Kurnai*, pp. 194, 201 ff.; Dawson, *Australian Aborigines*, p. 52. Petrie also mentions it in Queensland (*Tom Petrie's Reminiscences of Early Queensland*, pp. 62 and 118).

[3] *Journ. and Proc. of the Roy. Soc. of N.S. Wales*, XXXVIII, p. 339. Must we see a trace of sexual totemism in the following custom of the Warramunga? When a dead person is buried, a bone of the arm is kept. If it is a woman, the feathers of an emu are added to the bark in which it is wrapped up; if it is a man, the feathers of an owl (*Nor. Tr.*, p. 169).

[4] Some cases are cited where each sexual group has two sexual totems; thus the Wurunjerri unite the sexual totems of the Kurnai (the emu-wren and the linnet) to those of the Wotjobaluk (the bat and the *nightjar* owl). See Howitt, *Nat. Tr.*, p. 150.

[5] *Totemism*, p. 51.

corresponding sex: among the Kurnai, all the men are believed to be descended from Yeerŭng and all the women from Djeetgŭn.[1] The first observer to point out this curious institution described it, in 1834, in the following terms: "Tilmun, a little bird the size of a thrush (it is a sort of woodpecker), is supposed by the women to be the first maker of women. These birds are held in veneration by the women only."[2] So it was a great ancestor. But in other ways, this same totem resembles the individual totem. In fact, it is believed that each member of a sexual group is personally united to a determined individual of the corresponding animal species. The two lives are so closely associated that the death of the animal brings about that of the man. "The life of a bat," say the Wotjobaluk, "is the life of a man."[3] That is why each sex not only respects its own totem, but forces the members of the other to do so as well. Every violation of this interdiction gives rise to actual bloody battles between the men and the women.[4]

Finally, the really original feature of these totems is that they are, in a sense, a sort of tribal totems. In fact, they result from men's representing the tribe as descended as a whole from one couple of mythical beings. Such a belief seems to demonstrate clearly that the tribal sentiment has acquired sufficient force to resist, at least to a considerable extent, the particularism of the clans. In regard to the distinct origins assigned to men and to women, it must be said that its cause is to be sought in the separate conditions in which the men and the women live.[5]

It would be interesting to know how the sexual totems are related to the totems of the clans, according to the theory of the Australians, what relations there were between the two ancestors thus placed at the commencement of the tribe, and from which one each special clan is believed to be descended. But the ethnographical data at our present disposal do not allow us to resolve these questions. Moreover, however natural and even necessary it may appear to us, it is very possible that the natives never raised it. They do not feel the need of co-ordinating and systematizing their beliefs as strongly as we do.[6]

[1] *Kamilaroi and Kurnai*, p. 215.

[2] Threlkeld, quoted by Mathews, *loc. cit.*, p. 339.

[3] Howitt, *Nat. Tr.*, pp. 148, 151.

[4] *Kamilaroi and Kurnai*, pp. 200–203; Howitt, *Nat. Tr.*, p. 149; Petrie, *op. cit.*, p. 62. Among the Kurnai, these bloody battles frequently terminate in marriages of which they are, as it were, a sort of ritual precursor. Sometimes they are merely plays (Petrie, *loc. cit.*).

[5] On this point, see our study on *La Prohibition de l'inceste et ses origines*, in the *Année Sociologique*, I, pp. 44 ff.

[6] However, as we shall presently see (ch. ix), there is a connection between the sexual totems and the great gods.

CHAPTER V

ORIGINS OF THESE BELIEFS

Critical Examination of Preceding Theories

THE beliefs which we have just summarized are manifestly of a religious nature, since they imply a division of things into sacred and profane. It is certain that there is no thought of spiritual beings, and in the course of our exposition we have not even had occasion to pronounce the words, spirits, genii or divine personalities. But if certain writers, of whom we shall have something more to say presently, have, for this reason, refused to regard totemism as a religion, it is because they have an inexact notion of what religious phenomena are.

On the other hand, we are assured that this religion is the most primitive one that is now observable and even, in all probability, that has ever existed. In fact, it is inseparable from a social organization on a clan basis. Not only is it impossible, as we have already pointed out, to define it except in connection with the clan, but it even seems as though the clan could not exist, in the form it has taken in a great number of Australian societies, without the totem. For the members of a single clan are not united to each other either by a common habitat or by common blood, as they are not necessarily consanguineous and are frequently scattered over different parts of the tribal territory. Their unity comes solely from their having the same name and the same emblem, their believing that they have the same relations with the same categories of things, their practising the same rites, or, in a word, from their participating in the same totemic cult. Thus totemism and the clan mutually imply each other, in so far, at least, as the latter is not confounded with the local group. Now the social organization on a clan basis is the simplest which we know. In fact, it exists in all its essential elements from the moment when the society includes two primary clans; consequently, we may say that there are none more rudimentary, as long as societies reduced to a single clan have not been discovered, and we believe that up to the present no traces of such have been found. A religion so closely connected to a social system surpassing all others in simplicity may well be regarded as the most elementary religion we can possibly know. If we succeed in discovering the origins of the beliefs which we have just analysed, we shall very probably discover at the same time the causes leading to the rise of the religious sentiment in humanity.

But before treating this question for ourselves, we must examine the most authorized solutions of it which have already been proposed.

I

In the first place, we find a group of scholars who believe that they can account for totemism by deriving it from some previous religion.

For Tylor [1] and Wilken,[2] totemism is a special form of the cult of the ancestors; it was the widespread doctrine of the transmigration of souls that served as a bridge between these two religious systems. A large number of peoples believe that after death, the soul does not remain disincarnate for ever, but presently animates another living body; on the other hand, "the lower psychology, drawing no definite line of demarcation between the souls of men and of beasts, can at least admit without difficulty the transmigration of human souls into the bodies of the lower animals." [3] Tylor cites a certain number of cases.[4] Under these circumstances, the religious respect inspired by the ancestor is quite naturally attached to the animal or plant with which he is presently confounded. The animal thus serving as a receptacle for a venerated being becomes a holy thing, the object of a cult, that is, a totem, for all the descendants of the ancestor, who form the clan descended from him.

Facts pointed out by Wilken among the societies of the Malay Archipelago would tend to prove that it really was in this manner that the totemic beliefs originated. In Java and Sumatra, crocodiles are especially honoured; they are regarded as benevolent protectors who must not be killed; offerings are made to them. Now the cult thus rendered to them is due to their being supposed to incarnate the souls of ancestors. The Malays of the Philippines consider the crocodile their grandfather; the tiger is treated in the same way for the same reasons. Similar beliefs have been observed among the Bantous.[5] In Melanesia

[1] *Primitive Culture*, I, p. 402; II, p. 237; *Remarks on Totemism, with especial reference to some modern theories concerning it*, in *J.A.I.*, XXVIII, and I, New Series, p. 138.

[2] *Het Animisme bij den Volken van den indischen Archipel*, pp. 69–75.

[3] Tylor, *Primitive Culture*, II, p. 6.

[4] Tylor, *ibid.*, II, pp. 6–18.

[5] G. McCall Theal, *Records of South-Eastern Africa*, VII. We are acquainted with this work only through an article by Frazer, *South African Totemism*, published in *Man*, 1901, No. 111.

it sometimes happens that an influential man, at the moment of death, announces his desire to reincarnate himself in a certain animal or plant; it is easily understood how the object thus chosen as his posthumous residence becomes sacred for his whole family.[1] So, far from being a primitive fact, totemism would seem to be the product of a more complex religion which preceded it.[2]

But the societies from which these facts were taken had already arrived at a rather advanced stage of culture; in any case, they had passed the stage of pure totemism. They have families and not totemic clans.[3] Even the majority of the animals to which religious honours are thus rendered are venerated, not by special groups of families, but by the tribes as a whole. So if these beliefs and practices do have some connection with ancient totemic cults, they now represent only altered forms of them [4] and are consequently not very well fitted for showing us their origins. It is not by studying an institution at the moment when it is in full decadence that we can learn how it was formed. If we want to know how totemism originated, it is neither in Java nor Sumatra nor Melanesia that we must study it, but in Australia. Here we find neither a cult of the dead[5] nor the doctrine of transmigration. Of course they believe that the mythical heroes, the founders of the clan, reincarnate themselves periodically; *but this is in human bodies only;* each birth, as we shall see, is the product of one of these reincarnations. So if the animals of the totemic species are the object of rites, it is not because the ancestral souls are believed to reside in them. It is true that the first ancestors are frequently represented under the form of an animal, and this very common representation is an important fact for which we must account; but it was not the belief in metempsychosis which gave it birth, for this belief is unknown among Australian societies.

Moreover, far from being able to explain totemism, this belief takes for granted one of the fundamental principles upon which this rests; that is to say, it begs the question to be explained. It, just as much as totemism, implies that man is

[1] Codrington, *The Melanesians*, pp. 32 f., and a personal letter by the same author cited by Tylor in *J.A.I.*, XXVIII, p. 147.

[2] This is practically the solution adopted by Wundt (*Mythus und Religion*, II, p. 269).

[3] It is true that according to Tylor's theory, a clan is only an enlarged family; therefore whatever may be said of one of these groups is, in his theory, applicable to the other (*J.A.I.*, XXVIII, p. 157). But this conception is exceedingly contestable; only the clan presupposes a totem, which has its whole meaning only in and through the clan.

[4] For this same conception, see A. Lang, *Social Origins*, p. 150.

[5] See above, p. 63.

considered a close relative of the animal; for if these two kingdoms were clearly distinguished in the mind, men would never believe that a human soul could pass so easily from one into the other. It is even necessary that the body of the animal be considered its true home, for it is believed to go there as soon as it regains its liberty. Now while the doctrine of transmigration postulates this singular affinity, it offers no explanation of it. The only explanation offered by Tylor is that men sometimes resemble in certain traits the anatomy and physiology of the animal. "The half-human features and actions and characters of animals are watched with wondering sympathy by the savage, as by the child. The beast is the very incarnation of familiar qualities of man: and such names as lion, bear, fox, owl, parrot, viper, worm, when we apply them as epithets to men, condense into a word some leading features of a human life."[1] But even if these resemblances are met with, they are uncertain and exceptional; before all else, men resemble their relatives and companions, and not plants and animals. Such rare and questionable analogies could not overcome such unanimous proofs, nor could they lead a man to think of himself and his forefathers in forms contradicted by daily experience. So this question remains untouched, and as long as it is not answered, we cannot say that totemism is explained.[2]

Finally, this whole theory rests upon a fundamental misunderstanding. For Tylor as for Wundt, totemism is only a particular case of the cult of animals.[3] But we, on the contrary, know that

[1] *Primitive Culture*, II, p. 17.

[2] Wundt, who has revived the theory of Tylor in its essential lines, has tried to explain this mysterious relationship of the man and the animal in a different way: it was the sight of the corpse in decomposition which suggested the idea. When they saw worms coming out of the body, they thought that the soul was incarnate in them and escaped with them. Worms, and by extension, reptiles (snakes, lizards, etc.), were therefore the first animals to serve as receptacles for the souls of the dead, and consequently they were also the first to be venerated and to play the rôle of totems. It was only subsequently that other animals and plants and even inanimate objects were elevated to the same dignity. But this hypothesis does not have even the shadow of a proof. Wundt affirms (*Mythus und Religion*, II, p. 296) that reptiles are much more common totems than other animals; from this, he concludes that they are the most primitive. But we cannot see what justifies this assertion, in the support of which the author cites no facts. The lists of totems gathered either in Australia or in America do not show that any special species of animal has played a preponderating rôle. Totems vary from one region to another with the flora and fauna. Moreover, if the circle of possible totems was so closely limited at first, we cannot see how totemism was able to satisfy the fundamental principle which says that the two clans or sub-clans of a tribe must have two different totems.

[3] "Sometimes men adore certain animals," says Tylor, "because they regard them as the reincarnation of the divine souls of the ancestors; this belief is a sort of bridge between the cult rendered to shades and that rendered to animals" (*Primitive Culture*, II, p. 805, cf. 309, *in fine*). Likewise, Wundt presents totemism as a section of animalism (II, p. 234).

it is something very different from a sort of animal-worship.[1] The animal is never adored; the man is nearly its equal and sometimes even treats it as his possession, so far is he from being subordinate to it like a believer before his god. If the animals of the totemic species are really believed to incarnate the ancestors, the members of foreign clans would not be allowed to eat their flesh freely. In reality, it is not to the animal as such that the cult is addressed, but to the emblem and the image of the totem. Now between this religion of the emblem and the ancestor-cult, there is no connection whatsoever.

While Tylor derives totemism from the ancestor-cult, Jevons derives it from the nature-cult,[2] and here is how he does so.

When, under the impulse of the surprise occasioned by the irregularities observed in the course of phenomena, men had once peopled the world with supernatural beings,[3] they felt the need of making agreements with these redoubtable forces with which they had surrounded themselves. They understood that the best way to escape being overwhelmed by them was to ally themselves to some of them, and thus make sure of their aid. But at this period of history men knew no other form of alliance and association than the one resulting from kinship. All the members of a single clan aid each other mutually because they are kindred or, as amounts to the same thing, because they think they are; on the other hand, different clans treat each other as enemies because they are of different blood. So the only way of assuring themselves of the support of these supernatural beings was to adopt them as kindred and to be adopted by them in the same quality: the well-known processes of the blood-covenant permitted them to attain this result quite easily. But since at this period, the individual did not yet have a real personality, and was regarded only as a part of his group, or clan, it was the clan as a whole, and not the individual, which collectively contracted this relationship. For the same reason, it was contracted, not with a particular object, but with the natural group or species of which this object was a part; for men think of the world as they think of themselves, and just as they could not conceive themselves apart from their clans, so they were unable to conceive of anything else as distinct from the species to which it belonged. Now a species of things united to a clan by a bond of kinship is, says Jevons, a totem.

In fact, it is certain that totemism implies the close association of a clan to a determined category of objects. But that this

[1] See above, p. 139.

[2] *Introduction to the History of Religions*, pp. 97 ff.

[3] See above, p. 28.

association was contracted with a deliberate design and in the full consciousness of an end sought after, as Jevons would have us believe, is a statement having but little harmony with what history teaches. Religions are too complex, and answer to needs that are too many and too obscure, to have their origin in a premeditated act of the will. And while it sins through over-simplicity, this hypothesis is also highly improbable. It says that men sought to assure themselves of the aid of the supernatural beings upon which things depend. Then they should preferably have addressed themselves to the most powerful of these, and to those whose protection promised to be the most beneficial.[1] But quite on the contrary, the beings with whom they have formed this mystic kinship are often among the most humble which exist. Also, if it were only a question of making allies and defenders, they would have tried to make as many as possible ; for one cannot be defended too well. Yet as a matter of fact, each clan systematically contents itself with a single totem, that is to say, with one single protector, leaving the other clans to enjoy their own in perfect liberty. Each group confines itself within its own religious domain, never seeking to trespass upon that of its neighbours. This reserve and moderation are inexplicable according to the hypothesis under consideration.

II

Moreover, all these theories are wrong in omitting one question which dominates the whole subject. We have seen that there are two sorts of totemism : that of the individual and that of the clan. There is too evident a kinship between the two for them not to have some connection with each other. So we may well ask if one is not derived from the other, and, in the case of an affirmative answer, which is the more primitive ; according to the solution accepted, the problem of the origins of totemism will be posed in different terms. This question becomes all the more necessary because of its general interest. Individual totemism is an individual aspect of the totemic cult. Then if it was the primitive fact, we must say that religion is born in the consciousness of the individual, that before all else, it answers to individual aspirations, and that its collective form is merely secondary.

The desire for an undue simplicity, with which ethnologists and sociologists are too frequently inspired, has naturally led many scholars to explain, here as elsewhere, the complex by the

[1] Jevons recognizes this himself, saying, " It is to be presumed that in the choice of an ally he would prefer . . . the kind or species which possessed the greatest power " (p. 101).

simple, the totem of the group by that of the individual. Such, in fact, is the theory sustained by Frazer in his *Golden Bough*,[1] by Hill Tout,[2] by Miss Fletcher,[3] by Boas [4] and by Swanton.[5] It has the additional advantage of being in harmony with the conception of religion which is currently held; this is quite generally regarded as something intimate and personal. From this point of view, the totem of the clan can only be an individual totem which has become generalized. Some eminent man, having found from experience the value of a totem he chose for himself by his own free will, transmitted it to his descendants; these latter, multiplying as time went on, finally formed the extended family known as a clan, and thus the totem became collective.

Hill Tout believes that he has found a proof supporting this theory in the way totemism has spread among certain societies of North-western America, especially among the Salish and certain Indians on the Thompson River. Individual totemism and the clan totemism are both found among these peoples; but they either do not co-exist in the same tribe, or else, when they do co-exist, they are not equally developed. They vary in an inverse proportion to each other; where the clan totem tends to become the general rule, the individual totem tends to disappear, and *vice versa*. Is that not as much as to say that the first is a more recent form of the second, which excludes it by replacing it? [6] Mythology seems to confirm this interpretation. In these same societies, in fact, the ancestor of the clan is not a totemic animal; the founder of the group is generally represented in the form of a human being who, at a certain time, had entered into familiar relations with a fabulous animal from whom he received his totemic emblem. This emblem, together with the special powers which are attached to it, was then passed on to the descendants of this mythical hero by right of heritage. So these people themselves seem to consider the collective totem as an individual one, perpetuated in the same family.[7]

[1] 2nd Edition, III, pp. 416 ff.; see especially p. 419, n. 5. In more recent articles, to be analysed below, Frazer exposes a different theory, but one which does not, in his opinion, completely exclude the one in the *Golden Bough*.

[2] *The Origin of the Totemism of the Aborigines of British Columbia*, in *Proc. and Transact. of the Roy. Soc. of Canada*, 2nd series, VII, § 2, pp. 3 ff. Also, *Report on the Ethnology of the Statlumh, J.A.I.*, XXXV, p. 141. Hill Tout has replies to various objections made to his theory in Vol. IX of the *Transact. of the Roy. Soc. of Canada*, pp. 61–99.

[3] Alice C. Fletcher, *The Import of the Totem*, in *Smithsonian Report for* 1897, pp. 577–586.

[4] *The Kwakiutl Indians*, pp. 323 ff., 336–338, 393.

[5] *The Development of the Clan System*, in *Amer. Anthrop.*, N.S. VI, 1904, pp. 477–486.

[6] *J.A.I.*, XXXV, p. 142.

[7] *Ibid.*, p. 150. Cf. *Vth Rep. on the . . . N.W. Tribes of Canada, B.A.A.S.*, p. 24. A myth of this sort has been quoted above.

Moreover, it still happens to-day that a father transmits his own totem to his children. So if we imagine that the collective totem had, in a general way, this same origin, we are assuming that the same thing took place in the past which is still observable to-day.[1]

It is still to be explained whence the individual totem comes. The reply given to this question varies with different authors.

Hill Tout considers it a particular case of fetishism. Feeling himself surrounded on all sides by dreaded spirits, the individual experienced that sentiment which we have just seen Jevons attribute to the clan: in order that he might continue to exist, he sought some powerful protector in this mysterious world. Thus the use of a personal totem became established.[2] For Frazer, this same institution was rather a subterfuge or trick of war, invented by men that they might escape from certain dangers. It is known that according to a belief which is very widespread in a large number of inferior societies, the human soul is able, without great inconvenience, to quit the body it inhabits for a while; howsoever far away it may be, it continues to animate this body by a sort of detached control. Then, in certain critical moments, when life is supposed to be particularly menaced, it may be desirable to withdraw the soul from the body and lead it to some place or into some object where it will be in greater security. In fact, there are a certain number of practices whose object is to withdraw the soul in order to protect it from some danger, either real or imaginary. For example, at the moment when men are going to enter a newly-built house, a magician removes their souls and puts them in a sack, to be saved and returned to their proprietors after the door-sill has been crossed. This is because the moment when one enters a new house is exceptionally critical; one may have disturbed, and consequently offended, the spirits who reside in the ground and especially under the sill, and if precautions are not taken, these could make a man pay dearly for his audacity. But when this danger is once passed, and one has been able to anticipate their anger and even to make sure of their favour through the accomplishment of certain rites, the souls may safely retake their accustomed place.[3] It is this same belief which gave birth to the personal totem. To protect themselves from sorcery, men thought it wise to hide their souls in the anonymous crowd of some species of animal or vegetable. But after these relations had once been

[1] *J.A.I.*, XXXV, p. 147.

[2] *Proc. and Transact.*, *etc.*, VII, § 2, p. 12.

[3] See *The Golden Bough*,[2] III, pp. 351 ff. Wilken had already pointed out similar facts in *De Simsonsage*, in *De Gids*, 1890; *De Betrekking tusschen Menschen-Dieren en Plantenleven*, in *Indische Gids*, 1884, 1888; *Ueber das Haaropfer*, in *Revue Coloniale Internationale*, 1886–1887.

established, each individual found himself closely united to the animal or plant where his own vital principle was believed to reside. Two beings so closely united were finally thought to be practically indistinguishable: men believed that each participated in the nature of the other. When this belief had once been accepted, it facilitated and hastened the transformation of the personal totem into an hereditary, and consequently a collective, totem; for it seemed quite evident that this kinship of nature should be transmitted hereditarily from father to child.

We shall not stop to discuss these two explanations of the individual totem at length: they are ingenious fabrications of the mind, but they completely lack all positive proof. If we are going to reduce totemism to fetishism, we must first establish that the latter is prior to the former; now, not merely is no fact brought forward to support this hypothesis, but it is even contradicted by everything that we know. The ill-determined group of rites going under the name of fetishism seem to appear only among peoples who have already attained to a certain degree of civilization; but it is a species of cult unknown in Australia. It is true that some have described the churinga as a fetish; [1] but even supposing that this qualification were justified, it would not prove the priority which is postulated. Quite on the contrary, the churinga presupposes totemism, since it is essentially an instrument of the totemic cult and owes the virtues attributed to it to totemic beliefs alone.

As for the theory of Frazer, it presupposes a thoroughgoing idiocy on the part of the primitive which known facts do not allow us to attribute to him. He does have a logic, however strange this may at times appear; now unless he were completely deprived of it, he could never be guilty of the reasoning imputed to him. Nothing could be more natural than that he should believe it possible to assure the survival of his soul by hiding it in a secret and inaccessible place, as so many heroes of myths and legends are said to have done. But why should he think it safer in the body of an animal than in his own? Of course, if it were thus lost in space, it might have a chance to escape the spells of a magician more readily, but at the same time it would be prepared for the blows of hunters. It is a strange way of sheltering it to place it in a material form exposing it to risks at every instant.[2] But above all, it is inconceivable that a whole people should allow themselves to be carried into such an

[1] For example, Eylmann in *Die Eingeborenen der Kolonie Südaustralien*, p. 199.

[2] Mrs. Parker says in connection with the Euahlayi, that if the Yunbeai does "confer exceptional force, it also exposes one to exceptional dangers, for all that hurts the animal wounds the man" (*Euahlayi*, p. 29).

aberration.[1] Finally, in a very large number of cases, the function of the individual totem is very different from that assigned it by Frazer ; before all else, it is a means of conferring extraordinary powers upon magicians, hunters or warriors.[2] As to the kinship of the man and the thing, with all the inconveniences it implies, it is accepted as a consequence of the rite ; but it is not desired in its and for itself.

There is still less occasion for delaying over this controversy since it concerns no real problem. What we must know before everything else is whether or not the individual totem is really a primitive fact, from which the collective totem was derived ; for, according to the reply given to this question, we must seek the home of the religious life in one or the other of two opposite directions.

Against the hypothesis of Hill Tout, Miss Fletcher, Boas and Frazer there is such an array of decisive facts that one is surprised that it has been so readily and so generally accepted.

In the first place, we know that a man frequently has the greatest interest not only in respecting, but also in making his companions respect the species serving him as personal totem ; his own life is connected with it. Then if collective totemism were only a generalized form of individual totemism, it too should repose upon this same principle. Not only should the men of a clan abstain from killing and eating their totem-animal themselves, but they should also do all in their power to force this same abstention upon others. But as a matter of fact, far from imposing such a renunciation upon the whole tribe, each clan, by rites which we shall describe below, takes care that the plant or animal whose name it bears shall increase and prosper,

[1] In a later work (*The Origin of Totemism*, in *The Fortnightly Review*, May, 1899, pp. 844–845), Frazer raises this objection himself. " If," he says, " I deposit my soul in a hare, and my brother John (a member of another clan) shoots that hare, roasts and swallows it, what becomes of my soul ? To meet this obvious danger it is necessary that John should know the state of my soul, and that, knowing it, he should, whenever he shoots a hare, take steps to extract and restore to me my soul before he cooks and dines upon the animal." Now Frazer believes that he has found this practice in use in Central Australia. Every year, in the course of a ceremony which we shall describe presently, when the animals of the new generation arrive at maturity, the first game to be killed is presented to men of that totem, who eat a little of it ; and it is only after this that the men of the other clans may eat it freely. This, says Frazer, is a way of returning to the former the souls they may have confided to these animals. But, aside from the fact that this interpretation of the fact is wholly arbitrary, it is hard not to find this way of escaping the danger rather peculiar. This ceremony is annual ; long days may have elapsed since the animal was killed. During all this time, what has become of the soul which it sheltered and the individual whose life depended on this soul ? But it is superfluous to insist upon all the inconceivable things in this explanation.

[2] Parker, *op. cit.*, p. 20 ; Howitt, *Australian Medicine Men*, in *J.A.I.*, XVI, pp. 34, 49 f. ; Hill Tout, *J.A.I.*, XXXV, p. 146.

so as to assure an abundant supply of food for the other clans. So we must at least admit that in becoming collective, individual totemism was transformed profoundly, and we must therefore account for this transformation.

In the second place, how is it possible to explain, from this point of view, the fact that except where totemism is in full decay, two clans of a single tribe always have different totems? It seems that nothing prevents two or several members of a single tribe, even when there is no kinship between them, from choosing their personal totem in the same animal species and passing it on to their descendants. Does it not happen to-day that two distinct families have the same name? The carefully regulated way in which the totems and sub-totems are divided up, first between the two phratries and then among the various clans of the phratry, obviously presupposes a social agreement and a collective organization. This is as much as to say that totemism is something more than an individual practice spontaneously generalized.

Moreover, collective totemism cannot be deduced from individual totemism except by a misunderstanding of the differences separating the two. The one is acquired by the child at birth; it is a part of his civil status. The other is acquired during the course of his life; it presupposes the accomplishment of a determined rite and a change of condition. Some seek to diminish this distance by inserting between the two, as a sort of middle term, the right of each possessor of a totem to transmit it to whomsoever he pleases. But wherever these transfers do take place, they are rare and relatively exceptional acts; they cannot be performed except by magicians or other personages invested with special powers; [1] in any case, they are possible only through ritual ceremonies which bring about the change. So it is necessary to explain how this prerogative of a few became the right of all; how that which at first implied a profound change in the religious and moral constitution of the individual, was able to become an element of this constitution; and finally, how a transmission which at first was the consequence of a rite was later believed to operate automatically from the nature of things and without the intervention of any human will.

In support of his interpretation, Hill Tout claims that certain myths give the totem of the clan an individual origin: they tell how the totemic emblem was acquired by some special individual, who then transmitted it to his descendants. But in

[1] According to Hill Tout himself, " The gift or transmission (of a personal totem) can only be made or effected by certain persons, such as shamans, or those who possess great mystery power " (*J.A.I.*, p. 146). Cf. Langloh Parker, *op. cit.*, pp. 29–30.

the first place, it is to be remarked that these myths are all taken from the Indian tribes of North America, which are societies arrived at a rather high degree of culture. How could a mythology so far removed from the origins of things aid in reconstituting the primitive form of an institution with any degree of certainty? There are many chances for intermediate causes to have gravely disfigured the recollection which these people have been able to retain. Moreover, it is very easy to answer these myths with others, which seem much more primitive and whose signification is quite different. The totem is there represented as the very being from whom the clan is descended. So it must be that it constitutes the substance of the clan; men have it within them from their birth; it is a part of their very flesh and blood, so far are they from having received it from without.[1] More than that, the very myths upon which Hill Tout relies contain an echo of this ancient conception. The founder who gave his name to the clan certainly had a human form; but he was a man who, after living among animals of a certain species, finally came to resemble them. This is undoubtedly because a time came when the mind was too cultivated to admit any longer, as it had formerly done, that men might have been born of animals; so the animal ancestor, now become inconceivable, is replaced by a human being; but the idea persists that this man had acquired certain characteristics of the animal either by imitation or by some other process. Thus even this late mythology bears the mark of a more remote epoch when the totem of the clan was never regarded as a sort of individual creation.

But this hypothesis does not merely raise grave logical difficulties; it is contradicted directly by the following facts.

If individual totemism were the initial fact, it should be more developed and apparent, the more primitive the societies are, and inversely, it should lose ground and disappear before the other among the more advanced peoples. Now it is the contrary which is true. The Australian tribes are far behind those of North America; yet Australia is the classic land of collective totemism. *In the great majority of the tribes, it alone is found, while we do not know a single one where individual totemism alone is practised.*[2] This latter is found in a characteristic form only in an infinitesimal number of tribes.[3] Even where it is met with

[1] Cf. Hartland, *Totemism and some recent Discoveries*, in *Folk-Lore*, XI, pp. 59 ff.

[2] Except perhaps the Kurnai; but even in this tribe, there are sexual totems in addition to the personal ones.

[3] Among the Wotjobaluk, the Buandik, the Wiradjuri, the Yuin and the tribes around Maryborough (Queensland). See Howitt, *Nat. Tr.*, pp. 114–147; Mathews, *J. of the R. Soc. of N.S. Wales*, XXXVIII, p. 291. Cf. Thomas, *Further Notes on Mr. Hill Tout's Views on Totemism*, in *Man*, 1904, p. 85.

it is generally in a rudimentary form. It is made up of individual and optional practices having no generality. Only magicians are acquainted with the art of creating mysterious relationships with species of animals to which they are not related by nature. Ordinary people do not enjoy this privilege.[1] In America, on the contrary, the collective totem is in full decadence; in the societies of the North-west especially, its religious character is almost gone. Inversely, the individual totem plays a considerable rôle among these same peoples. A very great efficacy is attributed to it; it has become a real public institution. This is because it is the sign of a higher civilization. This is undoubtedly the explanation of the inversion of these two forms of totemism, which Hill Tout believes he has observed among the Salish. If in those parts where collective totemism is the most fully developed the other form is almost lacking, it is not because the second has disappeared before the first, but rather, because the conditions necessary for its existence have not yet been fully realized.

But a fact which is still more conclusive is that individual totemism, far from having given birth to the totemism of the clan, presupposes this latter. It is within the frame of collective totemism that it is born and lives: it is an integral part of it. In fact, in those very societies where it is preponderating, the novices do not have the right of taking any animal as their individual totem; to each clan a certain definite number of species are assigned, outside of which it may not choose. In return, those belonging to it thus are its exclusive property; members of other clans may not usurp them.[2] They are thought to have relations of close dependence upon the one serving as totem to the clan as a whole. There are even cases where it is quite possible to observe these relations: the individual aspect represents a part or a particular aspect of the collective totem.[3] Among the Wotjobaluk, each member of the clan considers the

[1] This is the case with the Euahlayi and the facts of personal totemism cited by Howitt, *Australian Medicine Men*, in *J.A.I.*, XVI, pp. 34, 35, 49–50.

[2] Miss Fletcher, *A Study of the Omaha Tribe*, in *Smithsonian Report for* 1897, p. 586; Boas, *The Kwakiutl*, p. 322. Likewise, *Vth Rep. of the Committee . . . of the N.W. Tribes of the Dominion of Canada, B.A.A.S.*, p. 25; Hill Tout, *J.A.I.*, XXXV, p. 148.

[3] The proper names of the *gentes*, says Boas in regard to the Tlinkit, are derived from their respective totems, each *gens* having its special names. The connection between the name and the (collective) totem is not very apparent sometimes, but it always exists (*Vth Rep. of the Committee, etc.*, p. 25). The fact that individual forenames are the property of the clan, and characterize it as surely as the totem, is also found among the Iroquois (Morgan, *Ancient Society*, p. 78), the Wyandot (Powell, *Wyandot Government*, in *Ist Rep.*, p. 59), the Shawnee, Sauk and Fox (Morgan, *Ancient Society*, pp. 72, 76–77) and the Omaha (Dorsey, *Omaha Sociology*, in *IIIrd Rep.*, pp. 227 ff.). Now the relation between forenames and personal totems is already known (see above, p. 157).

personal totems of his companions as being his own after a fashion;[1] so they are probably sub-totems. Now the sub-totem supposes the totem, as the species supposes the class. Thus the first form of individual religion met with in history appears, not as the active principle of all public religion, but, on the contrary, as a simple aspect of this latter. The cult which the individual organizes for himself in his own inner conscience, far from being the germ of the collective cult, is only this latter adapted to the personal needs of the individual.

III

In a more recent study,[2] which the works of Spencer and Gillen suggested to him, Frazer has attempted to substitute a new explanation of totemism for the one he first proposed, and which we have just been discussing. It rests on the postulate that the totemism of the Arunta is the most primitive which we know; Frazer even goes so far as to say that it scarcely differs from the really and absolutely original type.[3]

The singular thing about it is that the totems are attached neither to persons nor to determined groups of persons, but to localities. In fact, each totem has its centre at some definite spot. It is there that the souls of the first ancestors, who founded the totemic group at the beginning of time, are believed to have their preferred residence. It is there that the sanctuary is located where the churinga are kept; there the cult is celebrated. It is also this geographical distribution of totems which determines the manner in which the clans are recruited. The child has neither the totem of his father nor that of his mother, but the one whose centre is at the spot where the mother believes that she felt the first symptoms of approaching maternity. For it is said that the Arunta is ignorant of the exact relation existing between generation and the sexual act;[4] he thinks that every

[1] "For example," says Mathews, "if you ask a Wartwurt man what totem he is, he will first tell his personal totem, and will probably then enumerate those of his clan" (*Jour. of the Roy. Soc. of N.S. Wales*, XXXVIII, p. 291).

[2] *The Beginnings of Religion and Totemism among the Australian Aborigines*, in *Fortnightly Review*, July, 1905, pp. 162 ff., and Sept., p. 452. Cf. the same author, *The Origin of Totemism, ibid.*, April, 1899, p. 648, and May, p. 835. These latter articles, being slightly older, differ from the former on one point, but the foundation of the theory is not essentially different. Both are reproduced in *Totemism and Exogamy*, I, pp. 89–172. In the same sense, see Spencer and Gillen, *Some Remarks on Totemism as applied to Australian Tribes*, in *J.A.I.*, 1899, pp. 275–280, and the remarks of Frazer on the same subject, *ibid.*, pp. 281–286.

[3] "Perhaps we may . . . say that it is but one remove from the original pattern, the absolutely original form of totemism" (*Fortnightly Review*, Sept., 1905, p. 455).

[4] On this point, the testimony of Strehlow (II, p. 52) confirms that of Spencer and Gillen. For a contrary opinion, see A. Lang, *The Secret of the Totem*, p. 190.

conception is due to a sort of mystic fecundation. According to him, it is due to the entrance of the soul of an ancestor into the body of a woman and its becoming the principle of a new life there. So at the moment when a woman feels the first tremblings of the child, she imagines that one of the souls whose principal residence is at the place where she happens to be, has just entered into her. As the child who is presently born is merely the reincarnation of this ancestor, he necessarily has the same totem; thus his totem is determined by the locality where he is believed to have been mysteriously conceived.

Now, it is this local totemism which represents the original form of totemism; at most, it is separated from this by a very short step. This is how Frazer explains its genesis.

At the exact moment when the woman realizes that she is pregnant, she must think that the spirit by which she feels herself possessed has come to her from the objects about her, and especially from one of those which attract her attention at the moment. So if she is engaged in plucking a plant, or watching an animal, she believes that the soul of this plant or animal has passed into her. Among the things to which she will be particularly inclined to attribute her condition are, in the first place, the things she has just eaten. If she has recently eaten emu or yam, she will not doubt that an emu or yam has been born in her and is developing. Under these conditions, it is evident how the child, in his turn, will be considered a sort of yam or emu, how he regards himself as a relative of the plant or animal of the same species, how he has sympathy and regard for them, how he refuses to eat them, etc.[1] From this moment, totemism exists in its essential traits: it is the native's theory of conception that gave rise to it, so Frazer calls this primitive totemism *conceptional*.

It is from this original type that all the other forms of totemism are derived. "When several women had, one after the other, felt the first premonitions of maternity at the same spot and under the same circumstances, the place would come to be regarded as haunted by spirits of a peculiar sort; and so the whole country might in time be dotted over with totem centres and distributed into totem districts."[2] This is how the local totemism of the Arunta originated. In order that the totems

[1] A very similar idea had already been expressed by Haddon in his *Address to the Anthropological Section* (*B.A.A.S.*, 1902, pp. 8 ff.). He supposes that at first, each local group had some food which was especially its own. The plant or animal thus serving as the principal item of food became the totem of the group.

All these explanations naturally imply that the prohibitions against eating the totemic animal were not primitive, but were even preceded by a contrary prescription.

[2] *Fortnightly Review*, Sept., 1905, p. 458.

may subsequently be detached from their territorial base, it is sufficient to think that the ancestral souls, instead of remaining immutably fixed to a determined spot, are able to move freely over the surface of the territory and that in their voyages they follow the men and women of the same totem as themselves. In this way, a woman may be impregnated by her own totem or that of her husband, though residing in a different totemic district. According to whether it is believed that it is the ancestor of the husband or of the wife who thus follow the family about, seeking occasions to reincarnate themselves, the totem of the child will be that of his father or mother. In fact, it is in just this way that the Guanji and Umbaia on the one hand, and the Urabunna on the other, explain their systems of filiation.

But this theory, like that of Tylor, rests upon a begging of the question. If he is to imagine that human souls are the souls of animals or plants, one must believe beforehand that men take either from the animal or vegetable world whatever is most essential in them. Now this belief is one of those at the foundation of totemism. To state it as something evident is therefore to take for granted that which is to be explained.

Moreover, from this point of view, the religious character of the totem is entirely inexplicable, for the vague belief in an obscure kinship between the man and the animal is not enough to found a cult. This confusion of distinct kingdoms could never result in dividing the world into sacred and profane. It is true that, being consistent with himself, Frazer refuses to admit that totemism is a religion, under the pretext that he finds in it neither spiritual beings, nor prayers, nor invocations, nor offerings, etc. According to him, it is only a system of magic, by which he means a sort of crude and erroneous science, a first effort to discover the laws of things.[1] But we know how inexact this conception, both of magic and of religion, is. We have a religion as soon as the sacred is distinguished from the profane, and we have seen that totemism is a vast system of sacred things. If we are to explain it, we must therefore show how it happened that these things were stamped with this character.[2] But he does not even raise this problem.

But this system is completely overthrown by the fact that the postulate upon which it rests can no longer be sustained. The whole argument of Frazer supposes that the local totemism of the Arunta is the most primitive we know, and especially

[1] *Fortn. Rev.*, May, 1899, p. 835, and July, 1905, pp. 162 ff.

[2] Though considering totemism only a system of magic, Frazer recognizes that the first germs of a real religion are sometimes found in it (*Fortn. Rev.*, July, 1905, p. 163). On the way in which he thinks religion developed out of magic, see *The Golden Bough*,[2] I, pp. 75–78.

that it is clearly prior to hereditary totemism, either in the paternal or the maternal line. Now as soon as the facts contained in the first volume of Spencer and Gillen were at our disposal, we were able to conjecture that there had been a time in the history of the Arunta people when the totems, instead of being attached to localities, were transmitted hereditarily from mother to child.[1] This conjecture is definitely proved by the new facts discovered by Strehlow,[2] which only confirm the previous observations of Schulze.[3] In fact, both of these authors tell us that even now, in addition to his local totem, each Arunta has another which is completely independent of all geographical conditions, and which belongs to him as a birthright: it is his mother's. This second totem, just like the first, is considered a powerful friend and protector by the natives, which looks after their food, warns them of possible dangers, etc. They have the right of taking part in its cult. When they are buried, the corpse is laid so that the face is turned towards the region of the maternal totemic centre. So after a fashion this centre is also that of the deceased. In fact it is given the name *tmara altjira*, which is translated: camp of the totem which is associated with me. So it is certain that among the Arunta, hereditary totemism in the uterine line is not later than local totemism, but, on the contrary, must have preceded it. For to-day, the maternal totem has only an accessory and supplementary rôle; it is a second totem, which explains how it was able to escape observation as attentive and careful as that of Spencer and Gillen. But in order that it should be able to retain this secondary place, being employed along with the local totem, there must have been a time when it held the primary place in the religious life. It is, in part, a fallen totem, but one recalling an epoch when the totemic organization of the Arunta was very different from what it is to-day. So the whole superstructure of Frazer's system is undermined at its foundation.[4]

[1] *Sur le totemisme*, in *Année Soc.*, V, pp. 82–121. Cf., on this same question, Hartland, *Presidential Address*, in *Folk-Lore*, XI, p. 75; A. Lang, *A Theory of Arunta Totemism*, in *Man*, 1904, No. 44; *Conceptional Totemism and Exogamy*, *ibid.*, 1907, No. 55; *The Secret of the Totem*, ch. iv; N. W. Thomas, *Arunta Totemism*, in *Man*, 1904, No. 68; P. W. Schmidt, *Die Stellung der Aranda unter der Australischen Stämmen*, in *Zeitschrift für Ethnologie*, 1908, pp. 866 ff.

[2] *Die Aranda*, II, pp. 57–58.

[3] Schulze, *loc. cit.*, pp. 238–239.

[4] In the conclusion of *Totemism and Exogamy* (IV, pp. 58–59), Frazer says, it must be admitted, that there is a totemism still more ancient than that of the Arunta: it is the one observed by Rivers in the Banks Islands (*Totemism in Polynesia and Melanesia*, in *J.A.I.*, XXXIX, p. 172). Among the Arunta it is the spirit of an ancestor who is believed to impregnate the mother; in the Banks Islands, it is the spirit of an animal or vegetable, as the theory supposes. But as the ancestral spirits of the Arunta have an animal or vegetable form, the difference is slight. Therefore we have not mentioned it in our exposition.

IV

Although Andrew Lang has actively contested this theory of Frazer's, the one he proposes himself in his later works,[1] resembles it on more than one point. Like Frazer, he makes totemism consist in the belief in a sort of consubstantiality of the man and the animal. But he explains it differently.

He derives it entirely from the fact that the totem is a name. As soon as human groups were founded,[2] each one felt the need of distinguishing between the neighbouring groups with which it came into contact and, with this end in view, it gave them different names. The names were preferably chosen from the surrounding flora and fauna because animals and plants can easily be designated by movements or represented by drawings.[3] The more or less precise resemblances which men may have with such and such objects determined the way in which these collective denominations were distributed among the groups.[4]

Now, it is a well-known fact that " to the early mind names, and the things known by names, are in a mystic and transcendental connection of *rapport*."[5] For example, the name of an individual is not considered as a simple word or conventional sign, but as an essential part of the individual himself. So if it were the name of an animal, the man would have to believe that he himself had the most characteristic attributes of this same animal. This theory would become better and better accredited as the historic origins of these denominations became more remote and were effaced from the memory. Myths arose to make this strange ambiguity of human nature more easily representable in the mind. To explain this, they imagined that the animal was the ancestor of the men, or else that the two were descended from a common ancestor. Thus came the conception of bonds of kinship uniting each clan to the animal species whose name it bore. With the origins of this fabulous kinship once explained, it seems to our author that totemism no longer contains a mystery.

[1] *Social Origins*, London, 1903, especially ch. viii, entitled *The Origin of Totem Names and Beliefs*, and *The Secret of the Totem*, London, 1905.

[2] In his *Social Origins* especially, Lang attempts to reconstitute by means of conjecture the form which these primitive groups should have; but it seems superfluous to reproduce these hypotheses, which do not affect his theory of totemism.

[3] On this point, Lang approaches the theory of Julius Pickler (see Pickler and Szomolo, *Der Ursprung des Totemismus. Ein Beitrag zur materialistirchen Geschichtstheorie*, Berlin, 36 pp. in 8vo). The difference between the two hypotheses is that Pickler attributes a higher importance to the pictorial representation of the name than to the name itself.

[4] *Social Origins*, p. 166.

[5] *The Secret of the Totem*, p. 121; cf. pp. 116, 117.

But whence comes the religious character of the totemic beliefs and practices? For the fact that a man considers himself an animal of a certain species does not explain why he attributes marvellous powers to this species, and especially why he renders a cult to the images symbolizing it.—To this question Lang gives the same response as Frazer: he denies that totemism is a religion. "I find in Australia," he says, "no example of religious practices such as praying to, nourishing or burying the totem." [1] It was only at a later epoch, when it was already established, that totemism was drawn into and surrounded by a system of conceptions properly called religious. According to a remark of Howitt,[2] when the natives undertake the explanation of the totemic institutions, they do not attribute them to the totems themselves nor to a man, but to some supernatural being such as Bunjil or Baiame. "Accepting this evidence," says Lang, "one source of the 'religious' character of totemism is at once revealed. The totemist obeys the decree of Bunjil, or Baiame, as the Cretans obeyed the divine decrees given by Zeus to Minos." Now according to Lang the idea of these great divinities arose outside of the totemic system; so this is not a religion in itself; it has merely been given a religious colouring by contact with a genuine religion.

But these very myths contradict Lang's conception of totemism. If the Australians had regarded totemism as something human and profane, it would never have occurred to them to make a divine institution out of it. If, on the other hand, they have felt the need of connecting it with a divinity, it is because they have seen a sacred character in it. So these mythological interpretations prove the religious nature of totemism, but do not explain it.

Moreover, Lang himself recognizes that this solution is not sufficient. He realizes that totemic things are treated with a religious respect; [3] that especially the blood of an animal, as well as that of a man, is the object of numerous interdictions, or, as he says, taboos which this comparatively late mythology cannot explain.[4] Then where do they come from? Here are the words with which Lang answers this question: "As soon as the animal-named groups evolved the universally diffused beliefs about the *wakan* or *mana*, or mystically sacred quality of the blood as the life, they would also develop the various taboos." [5] The words *wakan* and *mana*, as we shall see in the

[1] *The Secret of the Totem*, p. 136.
[2] *J.A.I.*, Aug., 1888, pp. 53–54; cf. *Nat. Tr.*, pp. 89, 488, 498.
[3] "With reverence," as Lang says (*The Secret of the Totem*, p. 111).
[4] Lang adds that these taboos are the basis of exogamic practices.
[5] *Ibid.*, p. 125.

following chapter, involve the very idea of *sacredness* itself; the one is taken from the language of the Sioux, the other from that of the Melanesian peoples. To explain the sacred character of totemic things by postulating this characteristic, is to answer the question by the question. What we must find out is whence this idea of *wakan* comes and how it comes to be applied to the totem and all that is derived from it. As long as these two questions remain unanswered, nothing is explained.

V

We have now passed in review all the principal explanations which have been given for totemic beliefs,[1] leaving to each of them its own individuality. But now that this examination is finished, we may state one criticism which addresses itself to all these systems alike.

If we stick to the letter of the formulæ, it seems that these may be arranged in two groups. Some (Frazer, Lang) deny the religious character of totemism; in reality, that amounts to denying the facts. Others recognize this, but think that they can explain it by deriving it from an anterior religion out of which totemism developed. But as a matter of fact, this distinction is only apparent: the first group is contained within the second. Neither Frazer nor Lang have been able to maintain their principle systematically and explain totemism as if it were not a religion. By the very force of facts, they have been compelled to slip ideas of a religious nature into their explanations. We have just seen how Lang calls in the idea of sacredness, which is the cardinal idea of all religion. Frazer, on his side, in each of the theories which he has successively proposed, appeals openly to the idea of souls or spirits; for according to him, totemism came from the fact that men thought they could deposit their souls in safety in some external object, or else that they attributed conception to a sort of spiritual fecundation of which a spirit was the agent. Now a soul, and still more, a spirit, are sacred things and the object of rites; so the ideas expressing them are essentially religious and it is therefore in vain that Frazer makes totemism a mere system of magic, for he succeeds in explaining it only in the terms of another religion.

We have already pointed out the insufficiencies of animism and naturism; so one may not have recourse to them, as Tylor

[1] However, we have not spoken of the theory of Spencer. But this is because it is only a part of his general theory of the transformation of the ancestor-cult into the nature-cult. As we have described that already, it is not necessary to repeat it.

and Jevons do, without exposing himself to these same objections. Yet neither Frazer nor Lang seems to dream of the possibility of another hypothesis.[1] On the other hand, we know that totemism is tightly bound up with the most primitive social system which we know, and in all probability, of which we can conceive. To suppose that it has developed out of another religion, differing from it only in degree, is to leave the data of observation and enter into the domain of arbitrary and unverifiable conjectures. If we wish to remain in harmony with the results we have already obtained, it is necessary that while affirming the religious nature of totemism, we abstain from deriving it from another different religion. There can be no hope of assigning it non-religious ideas as its cause. But among the representations entering into the conditions from which it results, there may be some which directly suggest a religious nature of themselves. These are the ones we must look for.

[1] Except that Lang ascribes another source to the idea of the great gods: as we have already said, he believes that this is due to a sort of primitive revelation. But Lang does not make use of this idea in his explanation of totemism.

CHAPTER VI

ORIGINS OF THESE BELIEFS—*continued*

The Notion of the Totemic Principle, or Mana, and the Idea of Force

SINCE individual totemism is later than the totemism of the clan, and even seems to be derived from it, it is to this latter form that we must turn first of all. But as the analysis which we have just made of it has resolved it into a multiplicity of beliefs which may appear quite heterogeneous, before going farther, we must seek to learn what makes its unity.

I

We have seen that totemism places the figured representations of the totem in the first rank of the things it considers sacred; next come the animals or vegetables whose name the clan bears, and finally the members of the clan. Since all these things are sacred in the same way, though to different degrees, their religious character can be due to none of the special attributes distinguishing them from each other. If a certain species of animal or vegetable is the object of a reverential fear, this is not because of its special properties, for the human members of the clan enjoy this same privilege, though to a slightly inferior degree, while the mere image of this same plant or animal inspires an even more pronounced respect. The similar sentiments inspired by these different sorts of things in the mind of the believer, which give them their sacred character, can evidently come only from some common principle partaken of alike by the totemic emblems, the men of the clan and the individuals of the species serving as totem. In reality, it is to this common principle that the cult is addressed. In other words, totemism is the religion, not of such and such animals or men or images, but of an anonymous and impersonal force, found in each of these beings but not to be confounded with any of them. No one possesses it entirely and all participate in it. It is so completely independent of the particular subjects in whom it incarnates itself, that it precedes them and survives them. Individuals die, generations pass and are replaced by others; but this force always remains actual, living and the same. It animates the generations of to-day as it animated those of yesterday and as it will animate those of to-morrow. Taking the words in a large sense, we may say that it is the god adored by each totemic cult. Yet it is an impersonal god, without name or history, immanent in the world and diffused in an innumerable multitude of things.

But even now we have only an imperfect idea of the real ubiquity of this quasi-divine entity. It is not merely found in the whole totemic species, the whole clan and all the objects symbolizing the totem: the circle of its action extends beyond that. In fact, we have seen that in addition to the eminently holy things, all those attributed to the clan as dependencies of the principal totem have this same character to a certain degree. They also have something religious about them, for some are protected by interdictions, while others have determined functions in the ceremonies of the cult. Their religiousness does not differ in kind from that of the totem under which they are classified; it must therefore be derived from the same source. So it is because the totemic god—to use again the metaphorical expression which we have just employed—is in them, just as it is in the species serving as totem and in the men of the clan. We may see how much it differs from the beings in which it resides from the fact that it is the soul of so many different beings.

But the Australian does not represent this impersonal force in an abstract form. Under the influence of causes which we must seek, he has been led to conceive it under the form of an animal or vegetable species, or, in a word, of a visible object. This is what the totem really consists in: it is only the material form under which the imagination represents this immaterial substance, this energy diffused through all sorts of heterogeneous things, which alone is the real object of the cult. We are now in a better condition for understanding what the native means when he says that the men of the Crow phratry, for example, are crows. He does not exactly mean to say that they are crows in the vulgar and empiric sense of the term, but that the same principle is found in all of them, which is their most essential characteristic, which they have in common with the animals of the same name and which is thought of under the external form of a crow. Thus the universe, as totemism conceives it, is filled and animated by a certain number of forces which the imagination represents in forms taken, with only a few exceptions, from the animal or vegetable kingdoms: there are as many of them as there are clans in the tribe, and each of them is also found in certain categories of things, of which it is the essence and vital principle.

When we say that these principles are forces, we do not take the word in a metaphorical sense; they act just like veritable forces. In one sense, they are even material forces which mechanically engender physical effects. Does an individual come in contact with them without having taken proper precautions? He receives a shock which might be compared to the effect of an electric discharge. Sometimes they seem to conceive of these as a sort of fluid escaping by points.[1] If they are introduced into an organism not made to receive them, they produce sickness and death by a wholly automatic action.[2] Outside of men, they play the rôle of vital principle; it is by acting on them, we shall see,[3] that the reproduction of the species is assured. It is upon them that the universal life reposes.

But in addition to this physical aspect, they also have a moral character. When someone asks a native why he observes his rites, he replies that his ancestors always have observed them, and he ought to follow their example.[4] So if he acts in a certain way towards the totemic beings, it is not only because the forces resident in them are physically redoubtable, but because he feels himself morally obliged to act thus; he has the feeling that he is obeying an imperative, that he is fulfilling a duty. For these sacred beings, he has not merely fear, but also respect. Moreover, the totem is the source of the moral life of the clan. All the beings partaking of the same totemic principle consider that owing to this very fact, they are morally bound to one another; they have definite duties of assistance, vendetta, etc., towards each other; and it is these duties which constitute kinship. So while the totemic principle is a totemic force, it is also a moral power; so we shall see how it easily transforms itself into a divinity properly so-called.

Moreover, there is nothing here which is special to totemism. Even in the most advanced religions, there is scarcely a god who has not kept something of this ambiguity and whose functions are not at once cosmic and moral. At the same time that it is a spiritual discipline, every religion is also a means enabling men to face the world with greater confidence. Even for the Christian, is not God the Father the guardian of the physical order as well as the legislator and the judge of human conduct?

[1] For example, in a Kwakiutl myth, an ancestral hero pierces the head of an enemy by pointing a finger at him (Boas, *Vth Rep. on the North. Tribes of Canada*, *B.A.A.S.*, 1889, p. 30).

[2] References supporting this assertion will be found on p. 128, n. 1, and p. 320, n. 1.

[3] See Bk. III, ch. ii.

[4] See, for example, Howitt, *Nat. Tr.*, p. 482; Schürmann, *The Aboriginal Tribes of Port Lincoln*, in Woods, *Nat. Tr. of S. Australia*, p. 231.

II

Perhaps someone will ask whether, in interpreting totemism thus, we do not endow the native with ideas surpassing the limits of his intellect. Of course we are not prepared to affirm that he represents these forces with the relative clarity which we have been able to give to them in our analysis. We are able to show quite clearly that this notion is implied by the whole system of beliefs which it dominates; but we are unable to say how far it is conscious and how far, on the contrary, it is only implicit and confusedly felt. There is no way of determining just what degree of clarity an idea like this may have in obscure minds. But it is well shown, in any case, that this in no way surpasses the capacities of the primitive mind, and on the contrary, the results at which we have just arrived are confirmed by the fact that either in the societies closely related to these Australian tribes, or even in these tribes themselves, we find, in an explicit form, conceptions which differ from the preceding only by shades and degrees.

The native religions of Samoa have certainly passed the totemic phase. Real gods are found there, who have their own names, and, to a certain degree, their own personal physiognomy. Yet the traces of totemism are hardly contestable. In fact, each god is attached to a group, either local or domestic, just as the totem is to its clan.[1] Then, each of these gods is thought of as immanent in a special species of animal. But this does not mean that he resides in one subject in particular: he is immanent in all at once; he is diffused in the species as a whole. When an animal dies, the men of the group who venerate it weep for it and render pious duties to it, because a god inhabits it; but the god is not dead. He is eternal, like the species. He is not even confused with the present generation; he has already been the soul of the preceding one, as he will be the soul of the one which is to follow.[2] So he has all the characteristics of the totemic principle. He is the totemic principle, re-clothed in a slightly personal form by the imagination. But still, we must not exaggerate a personality which is hardly reconcilable with this diffusion and ubiquity. If its contours were clearly defined, it could never spread out thus and enter into such a multitude of things.

[1] Frazer has even taken many facts from Samoa which he presents as really totemic (See *Totemism*, pp. 6, 12–15, 24, etc.). It is true that we have charged Frazer with not being critical enough in the choice of his examples, but so many examples would obviously have been impossible if there had not really been important survivals of totemism in Samoa.

[2] See Turner, *Samoa*, p. 21 and ch. iv and v.

However, it is incontestable that in this case the idea of an impersonal religious force is beginning to change; but there are other cases where it is affirmed in all its abstract purity and even reaches a higher degree of generality than in Australia. If the different totemic principles to which the various clans of a single tribe address themselves are distinct from each other, they are, none the less, comparable to each other at bottom; for all play the same rôle in their respective spheres. There are societies which have had the feeling of this unity with nature and have consequently advanced to the idea of a unique religious force of which all other sacred principles are only expressions and which makes the unity of the universe. As these societies are still thoroughly impregnated with totemism, and as they remain entangled in a social organization identical with that of the Australians, we may say that totemism contained this idea in potentiality.

This can be observed in a large number of American tribes, especially those belonging to the great Sioux family: the Omaha, Ponka, Kansas, Osage, Assiniboin, Dakota, Iowa, Winnebago, Mandan, Hidatsa, etc. Many of these are still organized in clans, as the Omaha[1] and the Iowa;[2] others were so not long since, and, says Dorsey, it is still possible to find among them "all the foundations of the totemic system, just as in the other societies of the Sioux."[3] Now among these peoples, above all the particular deities to whom men render a cult, there is a pre-eminent power to which all the others have the relation of derived forms, and which is called *wakan*.[4] Owing to the preponderating place thus assigned to this principle in the Siouan pantheon, it is sometimes regarded as a sort of sovereign god, or a Jupiter or Jahveh, and travellers have frequently translated wakan by "great spirit." This is misrepresenting its real nature gravely. The wakan is in no way a personal being; the natives do not represent it in a determined form. According to an observer cited by Dorsey, "they say that they have never seen the wakanda, so they cannot pretend to personify it."[5] It is not even possible

[1] Alice Fletcher, *A Study of the Omaha Tribe*, in *Smithsonian Rep.* for 1897, pp. 582 f.

[2] Dorsey, *Siouan Sociology*, in *XVth Rep.*, p. 238.

[3] *Ibid.*, p. 221.

[4] Riggs and Dorsey, *Dakota-English Dictionary*, in *Contrib. N. Amer. Ethnol.*, VII, p. 508. Many observers cited by Dorsey identify the word wakan with the words wakanda and wakanta, which are derived from it, but which really have a more precise signification.

[5] *XIth Rep.*, p. 372, § 21. Miss Fletcher, while recognizing no less clearly the impersonal character of the wakanda, adds nevertheless that a certain anthropomorphism has attached to this conception. But this anthropomorphism concerns the various manifestations of the wakanda. Men address the trees or rocks where they think they perceive the wakanda, as if they were personal beings. But the wakanda itself is not personified (*Smithsonian Rep. for* 1897, p. 579).

to define it by determined attributes and characteristics. " No word," says Riggs, " can explain the meaning of this term among the Dakota. It embraces all mystery, all secret power, all divinity."[1] All the beings which the Dakota reveres, " the earth, the four winds, the sun, the moon and the stars, are manifestations of this mysterious life and power " which enters into all. Sometimes it is represented in the form of a wind, as a breath having its seat in the four cardinal points and moving everything :[2] sometimes it is a voice heard in the crashing of the thunder ;[3] the sun, moon and stars are wakan.[4] But no enumeration could exhaust this infinitely complex idea. It is not a definite and definable power, the power of doing this or that ; it is Power in an absolute sense, with no epithet or determination of any sort. The various divine powers are only particular manifestations and personifications of it ; each of them is this power seen under one of its numerous aspects.[5] It is this which made one observer say, " He is a protean god ; he is supposed to appear to different persons in different forms."[6] Nor are the gods the only beings animated by it : it is the principle of all that lives or acts or moves. " All life is wakan. So also is everything which exhibits power, whether in action, as the winds and drifting clouds, or in passive endurance, as the boulder by the wayside."[7]

Among the Iroquois, whose social organization has an even more pronouncedly totemic character, this same idea is found again ; the word *orenda* which expresses it is the exact equivalent of the wakan of the Sioux. " The savage man," says Hewitt, " conceived the diverse bodies collectively constituting his environment to possess inherently mystic potence . . . (whether they be) the rocks, the waters, the tides, the plants and the trees, the animals and man, the wind and the storms, the clouds and the thunders and the lightnings,"[8] etc. " This potence is held to be the property of all things . . . and by the inchoate mentation of man is regarded as the efficient cause of all phenomena, all the activities of his environment."[9] A sorcerer or shaman has orenda, but as much would be said of a man succeeding in his enterprises. At bottom, there is nothing in the world which does not have its quota of orenda ; but the quantities vary. There are some beings, either men or things, which are favoured ; there are others which are relatively disinherited, and the universal life

[1] Riggs, *Tah-Koo Wah-Kon*, pp. 56–57, quoted from Dorsey, *XIth Rep.*, p. 433, § 95.

[2] *XIth Rep.*, p. 380, § 33.

[3] *Ibid.*, p. 381, § 35.

[4] *Ibid.*, p. 376, § 28 ; p. 378, § 30 ; cf. p. 449, § 138.

[5] *Ibid.*, p. 432, § 95.

[6] *Ibid.*, p. 431, § 92.

[7] *Ibid.*, p. 433, § 95.

[8] *Orenda and a Definition of Religion*, in *American Anthropologist*, 1902, p. 33.

[9] *Ibid.*, p. 36.

consists in the struggles of these orenda of unequal intensity. The more intense conquer the weaker. Is one man more successful than his companions in the hunt or at war? It is because he has more orenda. If an animal escapes from a hunter who is pursuing it, it is because the orenda of the former was the more powerful.

This same idea is found among the Shoshone under the name of *pokunt*, among the Algonquin under the name of *manitou*,[1] of *nauala* among the Kwakiutl,[2] of *yek* among the Tlinkit[3] and of *sgâna* among the Haida.[4] But it is not peculiar to the Indians of North America; it is in Melanesia that it was studied for the first time. It is true that in certain of the islands of Melanesia, social organization is no longer on a totemic basis; but in all, totemism is still visible,[5] in spite of what Codrington has said about it. Now among these peoples, we find, under the name of *mana*, an idea which is the exact equivalent of the wakan of the Sioux and the orenda of the Iroquois. The definition given by Codrington is as follows: " There is a belief in a force altogether distinct from physical power, which acts in all ways for good and evil; and which it is of the greatest advantage to possess or control. This is Mana. I think I know what our people mean by it. . . . It is a power or influence, not physical and in a way supernatural; but it shows itself in physical force, or in any kind of power or excellence which a man possesses. This mana is not fixed in anything, and can be conveyed in almost anything. . . . All Melanesian religion consists, in fact, in getting this mana for one's self, or getting it used for one's benefit."[6] Is this not the same notion of an anonymous and diffused force, the germs of which we recently found in the totemism of Australia? Here is the same impersonality; for, as Codrington says, we must be careful not to regard it as a sort of supreme being; any such idea is " absolutely foreign " to Melanesian thought. Here is the same ubiquity; the mana is located nowhere definitely and it is everywhere. All forms of life and all the effects of the action,

[1] Tesa, *Studi del Thavenet*, p. 17.

[2] Boas, *Kwakiutl*, p. 695.

[3] Swanton, *Social Condition, etc., of the Tlinkit Indians, XXVIth Rep.*, 1905, p. 451, n. 2.

[4] Swanton, *Contributions to the Ethnology of the Haida*, p. 14; cf. *Social Condition, etc.*, p. 479.

[5] In certain Melanesian societies (Banks Islands, North New Hebrides) the two exogamic phratries are found which characterize the Australian organization (Codrington, *The Melanesians*, pp. 23 ff.). In Florida, there are regular totems, called *butos* (*ibid.*, p. 31). An interesting discussion of this point will be found in Lang, *Social Origins*, pp. 176 ff. On the same subject, and in the same sense, see W. H. R. Rivers, *Totemism in Polynesia and Melanesia*, in *J.A.I.*, XXXIX, pp. 156 ff.

[6] *The Melanesians*, p. 118, n. 1. Cf. Parkinson, *Dreissig Jahre in der Südsee*, pp. 178, 392, 394, etc.

either of men or of living beings or of simple minerals, are attributed to its influence.[1]

Therefore there is no undue temerity in attributing to the Australians an idea such as the one we have discovered in our analysis of totemic beliefs, for we find it again, but abstracted and generalized to a higher degree, at the basis of other religions whose roots go back into a system like the Australian one and which visibly bear the mark of this. The two conceptions are obviously related; they differ only in degree, while the mana is diffused into the whole universe, what we call the god or, to speak more precisely, the totemic principle, is localized in the more limited circle of the beings and things of certain species. It is mana, but a little more specialized; yet as a matter of fact, this specialization is quite relative.

Moreover, there is one case where this connection is made especially apparent. Among the Omaha, there are totems of all sorts, both individual and collective; [2] but both are only particular forms of wakan. "The foundation of the Indian's faith in the efficacy of the totem," says Miss Fletcher, "rested upon his belief concerning nature and life. This conception was complex and involved two prominent ideas: First, that all things, animate and inanimate, were permeated by a common life; and second, that this life could not be broken, but was continuous." [3] Now this common principle of life is the wakan. The totem is the means by which an individual is put into relations with this source of energy; if the totem has any powers, it is because it incarnates the wakan. If a man who has violated the interdictions protecting his totem is struck by sickness or death, it is because this mysterious force against which he has thus set himself, that is, the wakan, reacts against him with a force proportionate to the shock received.[4] Also, just as the totem is wakan, so the wakan, in its turn, sometimes shows its totemic origin by the way in which it is conceived. In fact, Say says that among the Dakota the "wahconda" is manifested sometimes in the form of a grey bear, sometimes of a bison, a beaver or some other animal.[5] Undoubtedly, this formula cannot be accepted without reserve. The wakan repels all personification

[1] An analysis of this idea will be found in Hubert and Mauss, *Théorie Générale de la Magie*, in *Année Sociol.*, VII, p. 108.

[2] There are not only totems of clans but also of guilds (A. Fletcher, *Smithsonian Rep. for* 1897, pp. 581 ff.).

[3] Fletcher, *op. cit.*, pp. 578 f.

[4] *Ibid.*, p. 583. Among the Dakota, the totem is called Wakan. See Riggs and Dorsey, *Dakota Grammar, Texts and Ethnol.*, in *Contributions N. Amer. Ethn.*, 1893, p. 219.

[5] *James's Account of Long's Expedition in the Rocky Mountains*, I, p. 268. (Quoted by Dorsey, *XIth Rep.*, p. 431, § 92.)

and consequently it is hardly probable that it has ever been thought of in its abstract generality with the aid of such definite symbols. But Say's remark is probably applicable to the particular forms which it takes in specializing itself in the concrete reality of life. Now if there is a possibility that there was a time when these specializations of the wakan bore witness to such an affinity for an animal form, that would be one more proof of the close bonds uniting this conception to the totemic beliefs.[1]

It is possible to explain why this idea has been unable to reach the same degree of abstraction in Australia as in the more advanced societies. This is not merely due to the insufficient aptitude of the Australian for abstracting and generalizing: before all, it is the nature of the social environment which has imposed this particularism. In fact, as long as totemism remains at the basis of the cultural organization, the clan keeps an autonomy in the religious society which, though not absolute, is always very marked. Of course we can say that in one sense each totemic group is only a chapel of the tribal Church; but it is a chapel enjoying a large independence. The cult celebrated there, though not a self-sufficing whole, has only external relations with the others; they interchange without intermingling; the totem of the clan is fully sacred only for this clan. Consequently the groups of things attributed to each clan, which are a part of it in the same way the men are, have the same individuality and autonomy. Each of them is represented as irreducible into similar groups, as separated from them by a break of continuity, and as constituting a distinct realm. Under these circumstances, it would occur to no one that these heterogeneous worlds were different manifestations of one and the same fundamental force; on the contrary, one might suppose that each of them corresponded to an organically different mana whose action could not extend beyond the clan and the circle of things attributed to it. The idea of a single and universal mana could be born only at the moment when the tribal religion developed above that of the clans and absorbed them more or less completely. It is along with the feeling of the tribal unity that the feeling of the substantial unity of the world awakens. As we shall presently show,[2] it is true that the Australian societies are already acquainted with a cult that is common to the tribe as a whole. But if this cult represents the highest form of the

[1] We do not mean to say that in principle every representation of religious forces in an animal form is an index of former totemism. But when we are dealing with societies where totemism is still apparent, as is the case with the Dakota, it is quite natural to think that these conceptions are not foreign to it.

[2] See below, same book, ch. ix, § 4, pp. 285 ff.

Australian religions, it has not succeeded in touching and modifying the principles upon which they repose : totemism is essentially a federative religion which cannot go beyond a certain degree of centralization without ceasing to be itself.

One characteristic fact clearly shows the fundamental reason which has kept the idea of the mana so specialized in Australia. The real religious forces, those thought of in the form of totems, are not the only ones with which the Australian feels himself obliged to reckon. There are also some over which magicians have particular control. While the former are theoretically considered healthful and beneficent, the second have it as their especial function to cause sickness and death. And at the same time that they differ so greatly in the nature of their effects, they are contrasted also by the relations which they sustain with the social organization. A totem is always a matter of the clan ; but on the contrary, magic is a tribal and even an intertribal institution. Magic forces do not belong to any special portion of the tribe in particular. All that is needed to make use of them is the possession of efficient recipes. Likewise, everybody is liable to feel their effects and consequently should try to protect himself against them. These are vague forces, specially attached to no determined social division, and even able to spread their action beyond the tribe. Now it is a remarkable fact that among the Arunta and Loritja, they are conceived as simple aspects and particular forms of a unique force, called in Arunta *Arungquiltha* or *Arúnkulta*.[1] " This is a term," say Spencer and Gillen, " of somewhat vague import, but always associated at bottom with the possession of *supernatural evil power*. . . . The name is applied indiscriminately to the evil influence or to the object in which it is, for the time being, or permanently, resident."[2] " By arúnkulta," says Strehlow, " the native signifies a force which suddenly stops life and brings death to all who come in contact with it."[3] This name is given to the bones and pieces of wood from which evil-working charms are derived, and also to poisonous animals and vegetables. So it may accurately be called a harmful mana. Grey mentions an absolutely identical notion among the tribes he observed.[4] Thus among these different peoples, while the properly religious

[1] The first spelling is that of Spencer and Gillen ; the second, that of Strehlow.

[2] *Nat. Tr.*, p. 548, n. 1. It is true that Spencer and Gillen add : " The idea can be best expressed by saying that an Arungquiltha object is possessed of an evil spirit." But this free translation of Spencer and Gillen is their own unjustified interpretation. The idea of the arungquiltha in no way implies the existence of spiritual beings, as is shown by the context and Strehlow's definition.

[3] *Die Aranda*, II, p. 76, n.

[4] Under the name Boyl-ya (see Grey, *Journal of Two Expeditions*, II, pp. 337–338).

forces do not succeed in avoiding a certain heterogeneity, magic forces are thought of as being all of the same nature; the mind represents them in their generic unity. This is because they rise above the social organization and its divisions and subdivisions, and move in a homogeneous and continuous space where they meet with nothing to differentiate them. The others, on the contrary, being localized in definite and distinct social forms, are diversified and particularized in the image of the environment in which they are situated.

From this we can see how thoroughly the idea of an impersonal religious force enters into the meaning and spirit of Australian totemism, for it disengages itself with clarity as soon as no contrary cause opposes it. It is true that the arungquiltha is purely a magic force. But between religious forces and magic forces there is no difference of kind: [1] sometimes they are even designated by the same name: in Melanesia, the magicians and charms have mana just like the agents and rites of the regular cult; [2] the word oranda is employed in the same way by the Iroquois.[3] So we can legitimately infer the nature of the one from that of the other.[4]

III

The results to which the above analysis has led us do not concern the history of totemism only, but also the genesis of religious thought in general.

Under the pretext that in early times men were dominated by their senses and the representations of their senses, it has frequently been held that they commenced by representing the divine in the concrete form of definite and personal beings. The facts do not confirm this presumption. We have just described a systematically united scheme of religious beliefs which we have good reason to regard as very primitive, yet we

[1] See above, p. 42. Spencer and Gillen recognize this implicitly when they say that the arungquiltha is a "supernatural force." Cf. Hubert and Mauss, *Théorie Générale de la Magie*, in *Année Sociol.*, VII, p. 119.

[2] Codrington, *The Melanesians*, pp. 191 ff.

[3] Hewitt, *loc. cit.*, p. 38.

[4] There is even ground for asking whether an analogous notion is completely lacking in Australia. The word churinga, or tjurunga as Strehlow writes, has a very great similarity, with the Arunta. Spencer and Gillen say that it designates "all that is secret or sacred. It is applied both to the object and to the quality it possesses" (*Nat. Tr.*, p. 648, s.v. churinga). This is almost a definition of mana. Sometimes Spencer and Gillen even use this word to designate religious power or force in a general way. While describing a ceremony among the Kaitish, they say that the officiant is "*full of churinga*," that is to say, they continue, of the "magic power emanating from the objects called churinga." Yet it does not seem that the notion of churinga has the same clarity and precision as that of the mana in Melanesia or of the wakan among the Sioux.

have met with no personalities of this sort. The real totemic cult is addressed neither to certain determined animals nor to certain vegetables nor even to an animal or vegetable species, but to a vague power spread through these things.[1] Even in the most advanced religions which have developed out of totemism, such as those which we find among the North American Indians, this idea, instead of being effaced, becomes more conscious of itself; it is declared with a clarity it did not have before, while at the same time, it attains a higher generality. It is this which dominates the entire religious system.

This is the original matter out of which have been constructed those beings of every sort which the religions of all times have consecrated and adored. The spirits, demons, genii and gods of every sort are only the concrete forms taken by this energy, or "potentiality," as Hewitt calls it,[2] in individualizing itself, in fixing itself upon a certain determined object or point in space, or in centring around an ideal and legendary being, though one conceived as real by the popular imagination. A Dakota questioned by Miss Fletcher expressed this essential consubstantiability of all sacred things in language that is full of relief. "Every thing as it moves, now and then, here and there, makes stops. The bird as it flies stops in one place to make its nest, and in another to rest in its flight. A man when he goes forth stops when he wills. So the god has stopped. The sun, which is so bright and beautiful, is one place where he has stopped. The trees, the animals, are where he has stopped, and the Indian thinks of these places and sends his prayers to reach the place where the god has stopped and to win help and a blessing."[3] In other words, the wakan (for this is what he was talking about) comes and goes through the world, and sacred things are the points upon which it alights. Here we are, for once, just as far from naturism as from animism. If the sun, the moon and the stars have been adored, they have not owed this honour to their intrinsic nature or their distinctive properties, but to the fact that they are thought to participate in this force which alone is able to give things a sacred character, and which is also found in a multitude of other beings, even the smallest. If the souls of the dead have been the object of rites, it is not because they are believed to be made out of some fluid and impalpable substance, nor is it because they resemble the shadow cast by a body or its

[1] Yet we shall see below (this book, ch. viii and ix) that totemism is not foreign to all ideas of a mythical personality. But we shall show that these conceptions are the product of secondary formations: far from being the basis of the beliefs we have just analysed, they are derived from them.

[2] *Loc cit.*, p. 38.

[3] *Rep. Peabody Museum*, III, p. 276, n. (quoted by Dorsey, *XIth Rep.*, p. 435).

reflection on a surface of water. Lightness and fluidity are not enough to confer sanctity; they have been invested with this dignity only in so far as they contained within them something of this same force, the source of all religiosity.

We are now in a better condition to understand why it has been impossible to define religion by the idea of mythical personalities, gods or spirits; it is because this way of representing religious things is in no way inherent in their nature. What we find at the origin and basis of religious thought are not determined and distinct objects and beings possessing a sacred character of themselves; they are indefinite powers, anonymous forces, more or less numerous in different societies, and sometimes even reduced to a unity, and whose impersonality is strictly comparable to that of the physical forces whose manifestations the sciences of nature study. As for particular sacred things, they are only individualized forms of this essential principle. So it is not surprising that even in the religions where there are avowed divinities, there are rites having an efficient virtue in themselves, independently of all divine intervention. It is because this force may be attached to words that are pronounced or movements that are made just as well as to corporal substances; the voice or the movements may serve as its vehicle, and it may produce its effects through their intermediacy, without the aid of any god or spirit. Even should it happen to concentrate itself especially in a rite, this will become a creator of divinities from that very fact.[1] This is why there is scarcely a divine personality who does not retain some impersonality. Those who represent it most clearly in a concrete and visible form, think of it, at the same time, as an abstract power which cannot be defined except by its own efficacy, or as a force spread out in space and which is contained, at least in part, in each of its effects. It is the power of producing rain or wind, crops or the light of day; Zeus is in each of the raindrops which falls, just as Ceres is in each of the sheaves of the harvest.[2] As a general rule, in fact, this efficacy is so imperfectly determined that the believer is able to form only a very vague notion of it. Moreover, it is this indecision which has made possible these syncretisms and duplications in the course of which gods are broken up, dismembered and confused in every way. Perhaps there is not a single religion in which the original mana, whether unique or multiform, has been

[1] See above, p. 35.

[2] In the expressions such as *Ζεὺς ὕει* or *Ceres succiditur*, it is shown that this conception survived in Greece as well as in Rome. In his *Götternamen*, Usener has clearly shown that the primitive gods of Greece and Rome were impersonal forces thought of only in terms of their attributes.

resolved entirely into a clearly defined number of beings who are distinct and separate from each other; each of them always retains a touch of impersonality, as it were, which enables it to enter into new combinations, not as the result of a simple survival but because it is the nature of religious forces to be unable to individualize themselves completely.

This conception, to which we have been led by the study of totemism alone, has the additional recommendation that many scholars have recently adopted it quite independently of one another, as a conclusion from very different sorts of studies. There is a tendency towards a spontaneous agreement on this point which should be remarked, for it is a presumption of objectivity.

As early as 1899, we pointed out the impossibility of making the idea of a mythical personality enter into the definition of religious phenomena.[1] In 1900, Marrett showed the existence of a religious phase which he called *preanimistic*, in which the rites are addressed to impersonal forces like the Melanesian mana and the wakan of the Omaha and Dakota.[2] However, Marrett did not go so far as to maintain that always and in every case the idea of a spirit is logically and chronologically posterior to that of mana and is derived from it; he even seemed disposed to admit that it has sometimes appeared independently and consequently, that religious thought flows from a double source.[3] On the other hand, he conceived the mana as an inherent property of things, as an element of their appearance; for, according to him, this is simply the character which we attribute to everything out of the ordinary, and which inspires a sentiment of fear or admiration.[4] This practically amounts to a return to the naturist theory.[5]

A little later, MM. Hubert and Mauss, while attempting to formulate a general theory of magic, established the fact that magic as a whole reposes on the notion of mana.[6] The close kinship of the magic rite and the religious rite being known, it was even possible to foresee that the same theory should be applied to religion. This was sustained by Preuss in a series of

[1] *Définition du phénomène religieux*, in *Année Sociol.*, II, pp. 14–16.

[2] *Preanimistic Religion*, in *Folk-Lore*, 1900, pp. 162–182.

[3] *Ibid.*, p. 179. In a more recent work, *The Conception of Mana* (in *Transactions of the Third International Congress for the History of Religions*, II, pp. 54 ff.), Marrett tends to subordinate still further the animistic conception of mana, but his thought on this point remains hésitating and very reserved.

[4] *Ibid.*, p. 168.

[5] This return of preanimism to naturism is still more marked in Clodd, *Preanimistic Stages of Religion* (*Trans. Third Inter. Congress for the H. of Rel.*, I, p. 33).

[6] *Théorie générale de la Magie*, in *Année Sociol.*, VII, pp. 108 ff.

articles in the *Globus* [1] that same year. Relying chiefly upon facts taken from American civilizations, Preuss set out to prove that the ideas of the soul and spirit were not developed until after those of power and impersonal force, that the former are only a transformation of the latter, and that up to a relatively late date they retain the marks of their original impersonality. In fact, he shows that even in the advanced religions, they are represented in the form of vague emanations disengaging themselves automatically from the things in which they reside, and even tending to escape by all the ways that are open to them: the mouth, the nose and all the other openings of the body, the breath, the look, the word, etc. At the same time, Preuss pointed out their Protean forms and their extreme plasticity which permits them to give themselves successively and almost concurrently to the most varied uses.[2] It is true that if we stick to the letter of the terminology employed by this author, we may believe that for him the forces have a magic, not a religious nature: he calls them charms (*Zauber*, *Zauberkräfte*). But it is evident that in expressing himself thus, he does not intend to put them outside of religion; for it is in the essentially religious rites that he shows their action, for example, in the great Mexican ceremonies.[3] If he uses these expressions, it is undoubtedly because he knows no others which mark better the impersonality of these forces and the sort of mechanism with which they operate.

Thus this same idea tends to come to light on every side.[4] The impression becomes more and more prevalent that even the most elementary mythological constructions are secondary products [5] which cover over a system of beliefs, at once simpler and more obscure, vaguer and more essential, which form the solid foundations upon which the religious systems are built. It is this primitive foundation which our analysis of totemism has enabled us to reach. The various writers whose studies we have just mentioned arrived at this conclusion only through

[1] *Der Ursprung der Religion und Kunst*, in *Globus*, 1904, Vol. LXXXVI, pp. 321, 355, 376, 389; 1905, Vol. LXXXVII, pp. 333, 347, 380, 394, 413.

[2] *Globus*, LXXXVII, p. 381.

[3] He clearly opposes them to all influences of a profane nature (*Globus*, LXXXVI, p. 379a).

[4] It is found even in the recent theories of Frazer. For if this scholar denies to totemism all religious character, in order to make it a sort of magic, it is just because the forces which the totemic cult puts into play are impersonal like those employed by the magician. So Frazer recognizes the fundamental fact which we have just established. But he draws different conclusions because he recognizes religion only where there are mythical personalities.

[5] However, we do not take this word in the same sense as Preuss and Marrett. According to them, there was a time in religious evolution when men knew neither souls nor spirits: a *preanimistic* phase. But this hypothesis is very questionable: we shall discuss this point below (Bk. II, ch. viii and ix).

facts taken from very diverse religions, some of which even correspond to a civilization that is already far advanced: such is the case, for example, with the Mexican religions, of which Preuss makes great use. So it might be asked if this theory is equally applicable to the most simple religions. But since it is impossible to go lower than totemism, we are not exposed to this risk of error, and at the same time, we have an opportunity of finding the initial notion from which the ideas of wakan and mana are derived: this is the notion of the totemic principle.[1]

IV

But this notion is not only of primary importance because of the rôle it has played in the development of religious ideas; it also has a lay aspect in which it is of interest for the history of scientific thought. It is the first form of the idea of force.

In fact, the wakan plays the same rôle in the world, as the Sioux conceives it, as the one played by the forces with which science explains the diverse phenomena of nature. This, however, does not mean that it is thought of as an exclusively physical energy; on the contrary, in the next chapter we shall see that the elements going to make up this idea are taken from the most diverse realms. But this very compositeness of its nature enables it to be utilized as a universal principle of explanation. It is from it that all life comes;[2] "all life is wakan"; and by this word life, we must understand everything that acts and reacts, that moves and is moved, in both the mineral and biological kingdoms. The wakan is the cause of all the movements which take place in the universe. We have even seen that the orenda of the Iroquois is "the efficient cause of all the phenomena and all the activities which are manifested around men." It is a power "inherent in all bodies and all things."[3] It is the orenda which makes the wind blow, the sun lighten and heat the earth, or animals reproduce and which makes men strong, clever and intelligent. When the Iroquois says that the life of all nature is the product of the conflicts aroused between the unequally intense orenda of the different beings, he only expresses, in his own language, this modern idea that the world is a system

[1] On this same question, see an article of Alessandro Bruno, *Sui fenomeni magico-religiosi della communità primitive*, in *Rivista italiana di Sociologia*, XII Year, Fasc. IV–V, pp. 568 ff., and an unpublished communication made by W. Bogoras to the XIV Congress of the Americanists, held at Stuttgart in 1904. This communication is analysed by Preuss in the *Globus*, LXXXVI, p. 201.

[2] "All things," says Miss Fletcher, "are filled with a common principle of life," *Smiths. Rep. for* 1897, p. 579.

[3] Hewitt, in *American Anthropologist*, 1902, p. 36.

of forces limiting and containing each other and making an equilibrium.

The Melanesian attributes this same general efficacy to his mana. It is owing to his mana that a man succeeds in hunting or fighting, that gardens give a good return or that flocks prosper. If an arrow strikes its mark, it is because it is charged with mana; it is the same cause which makes a net catch fish well, or a canoe ride well on the sea,[1] etc. It is true that if certain phrases of Codrington are taken literally, mana should be the cause to which is attributed "everything which is beyond the ordinary power of men, outside the common processes of nature."[2] But from the very examples which he cites, it is quite evident that the sphere of the mana is really much more extended. In reality, it serves to explain usual and everyday phenomena; there is nothing superhuman or supernatural in the fact that a ship sails or a hunter catches game, etc. However, among these events of daily life, there are some so insignificant and familiar that they pass unperceived: they are not noticed and consequently no need is felt of explaining them. The concept of mana is applied only to those that are important enough to cause reflection, and to awaken a minimum of interest and curiosity; but they are not marvellous for all that. And what is true of the mana as well as the orenda and wakan, may be said equally well of the totemic principle. It is through this that the life of the men of the clan and the animals or plants of the totemic species, as well as all the things which are classified under the totem and partake of its nature, is manifested.

So the idea of force is of religious origin. It is from religion that it has been borrowed, first by philosophy, then by the sciences. This has already been foreseen by Comte and this is why he made metaphysics the heir of "theology." But he concluded from this that the idea of force is destined to disappear from science; for, owing to its mystic origins, he refused it all objective value. But we are going to show that, on the contrary, religious forces are real, howsoever imperfect the symbols may be, by the aid of which they are thought of. From this it will follow that the same is true of the concept of force in general.

[1] *The Melanesians*, pp. 118–120.

[2] *Ibid.*, p. 119.

CHAPTER VII

ORIGINS OF THESE BELIEFS—*end*

Origin of the Idea of the Totemic Principle or Mana

THE proposition established in the preceding chapter determines the terms in which the problem of the origins of totemism should be posed. Since totemism is everywhere dominated by the idea of a quasi-divine principle, imminent in certain categories of men and things and thought of under the form of an animal or vegetable, the explanation of this religion is essentially the explanation of this belief; to arrive at this, we must seek to learn how men have been led to construct this idea and out of what materials they have constructed it.

I

It is obviously not out of the sensations which the things serving as totems are able to arouse in the mind; we have shown that these things are frequently insignificant. The lizard, the caterpillar, the rat, the ant, the frog, the turkey, the bream-fish, the plum-tree, the cockatoo, etc., to cite only those names which appear frequently in the lists of Australian totems, are not of a nature to produce upon men these great and strong impressions which in a way resemble religious emotions and which impress a sacred character upon the objects they create. It is true that this is not the case with the stars and the great atmospheric phenomena, which have, on the contrary, all that is necessary to strike the imagination forcibly; but as a matter of fact, these serve only very exceptionally as totems. It is even probable that they were very slow in taking this office.[1] So it is not the intrinsic nature of the thing whose name the clan bears that marked it out to become the object of a cult. Also, if the sentiments which it inspired were really the determining cause of the totemic rites and beliefs, it would be the pre-eminently sacred thing; the animals or plants employed as totems would play an eminent part in the religious life. But we know that the

[1] See above, p. 103.

centre of the cult is actually elsewhere. It is the figurative representations of this plant or animal and the totemic emblems and symbols of every sort, which have the greatest sanctity; so it is in them that is found the source of that religious nature, of which the real objects represented by these emblems receive only a reflection.

Thus the totem is before all a symbol, a material expression of something else.[1] But of what?

From the analysis to which we have been giving our attention, it is evident that it expresses and symbolizes two different sorts of things. In the first place, it is the outward and visible form of what we have called the totemic principle or god. But it is also the symbol of the determined society called the clan. It is its flag; it is the sign by which each clan distinguishes itself from the others, the visible mark of its personality, a mark borne by everything which is a part of the clan under any title whatsoever, men, beasts or things. So if it is at once the symbol of the god and of the society, is that not because the god and the society are only one? How could the emblem of the group have been able to become the figure of this quasi-divinity, if the group and the divinity were two distinct realities? The god of the clan, the totemic principle, can therefore be nothing else than the clan itself, personified and represented to the imagination under the visible form of the animal or vegetable which serves as totem.

But how has this apotheosis been possible, and how did it happen to take place in this fashion?

II

In a general way, it is unquestionable that a society has all that is necessary to arouse the sensation of the divine in minds, merely by the power that it has over them; for to its members it is what a god is to his worshippers. In fact, a god is, first of all, a being whom men think of as superior to themselves, and upon whom they feel that they depend. Whether it be a conscious personality, such as Zeus or Jahveh, or merely abstract forces such as those in play in totemism, the worshipper, in the one case as in the other, believes himself held to certain manners of acting which are imposed upon him by the nature of the sacred principle with which he feels that he is in communion. Now society also gives us the sensation of a perpetual dependence. Since it has a nature which is peculiar to itself and different from our individual nature, it pursues ends which

[1] Pickler, in the little work above mentioned, had already expressed, in a slightly dialectical manner, the sentiment that this is what the totem essentially is.

are likewise special to it ; but, as it cannot attain them except through our intermediacy, it imperiously demands our aid. It requires that, forgetful of our own interests, we make ourselves its servitors, and it submits us to every sort of inconvenience, privation and sacrifice, without which social life would be impossible. It is because of this that at every instant we are obliged to submit ourselves to rules of conduct and of thought which we have neither made nor desired, and which are sometimes even contrary to our most fundamental inclinations and instincts.

Even if society were unable to obtain these concessions and sacrifices from us except by a material constraint, it might awaken in us only the idea of a physical force to which we must give way of necessity, instead of that of a moral power such as religions adore. But as a matter of fact, the empire which it holds over consciences is due much less to the physical supremacy of which it has the privilege than to the moral authority with which it is invested. If we yield to its orders, it is not merely because it is strong enough to triumph over our resistance ; it is primarily because it is the object of a venerable respect.

We say that an object, whether individual or collective, inspires respect when the representation expressing it in the mind is gifted with such a force that it automatically causes or inhibits actions, *without regard for any consideration relative to their useful or injurious effects*. When we obey somebody because of the moral authority which we recognize in him, we follow out his opinions, not because they seem wise, but because a certain sort of physical energy is imminent in the idea that we form of this person, which conquers our will and inclines it in the indicated direction. Respect is the emotion which we experience when we feel this interior and wholly spiritual pressure operating upon us. Then we are not determined by the advantages or inconveniences of the attitude which is prescribed or recommended to us ; it is by the way in which we represent to ourselves the person recommending or prescribing it. This is why commands generally take a short, peremptory form leaving no place for hesitation ; it is because, in so far as it is a command and goes by its own force, it excludes all idea of deliberation or calculation ; it gets its efficacy from the intensity of the mental state in which it is placed. It is this intensity which creates what is called a moral ascendancy.

Now the ways of action to which society is strongly enough attached to impose them upon its members, are, by that very fact, marked with a distinctive sign provocative of respect. Since they are elaborated in common, the vigour with which they have been thought of by each particular mind is retained in all the other minds, and reciprocally. The representations which express them within each of us have an intensity which no purely private states of consciousness could ever attain; for they have the strength of the innumerable individual representations which have served to form each of them. It is society who speaks through the mouths of those who affirm them in our presence; it is society whom we hear in hearing them; and the voice of all has an accent which that of one alone could never have.[1] The very violence with which society reacts, by way of blame or material suppression, against every attempted dissidence, contributes to strengthening its empire by manifesting the common conviction through this burst of ardour.[2] In a word, when something is the object of such a state of opinion, the representation which each individual has of it gains a power of action from its origins and the conditions in which it was born, which even those feel who do not submit themselves to it. It tends to repel the representations which contradict it, and it keeps them at a distance; on the other hand, it commands those acts which will realize it, and it does so, not by a material coercion or by the perspective of something of this sort, but by the simple radiation of the mental energy which it contains. It has an efficacy coming solely from its psychical properties, and it is by just this sign that moral authority is recognized. So opinion, primarily a social thing, is a source of authority, and it might even be asked whether all authority is not the daughter of opinion.[3] It may be objected that science is often the antagonist of opinion, whose errors it combats and rectifies. But it cannot succeed in this task if it does not have sufficient authority, and it can obtain this authority only from opinion itself. If a people did not have faith in science, all the scientific demonstrations in the world would be without any influence whatsoever over their minds. Even to-day, if science happened to resist a very strong current of public opinion, it would risk losing its credit there.[4]

[1] See our *Division du travail social*, 3rd ed., pp. 64 ff.

[2] *Ibid.*, p. 76.

[3] This is the case at least with all moral authority recognized as such by the group as a whole.

[4] We hope that this analysis and those which follow will put an end to an inexact interpretation of our thought, from which more than one misunderstanding has resulted. Since we have made constraint the *outward sign* by which social facts can be the most easily recognized and distinguished from the facts of individual psychology, it has been assumed that according to our opinion, physical constraint is the essential thing for social life. As a matter of fact, we have never considered it more than the material and apparent expression of an interior and profound fact which is wholly ideal: this is *moral authority*. The problem of sociology—if we can speak of *a* sociological problem—consists in seeking, among the different forms of external constraint, the different sorts of moral authority corresponding to them and in discovering the causes which have determined these latter. The particular question which we are treating in this present work has as its principal object, the discovery of the form under

Since it is in spiritual ways that social pressure exercises itself, it could not fail to give men the idea that outside themselves there exist one or several powers, both moral and, at the same time, efficacious, upon which they depend. They must think of these powers, at least in part, as outside themselves, for these address them in a tone of command and sometimes even order them to do violence to their most natural inclinations. It is undoubtedly true that if they were able to see that these influences which they feel emanate from society, then the mythological system of interpretations would never be born. But social action follows ways that are too circuitous and obscure, and employs psychical mechanisms that are too complex to allow the ordinary observer to see whence it comes. As long as scientific analysis does not come to teach it to them, men know well that they are acted upon, but they do not know by whom. So they must invent by themselves the idea of these powers with which they feel themselves in connection, and from that, we are able to catch a glimpse of the way by which they were led to represent them under forms that are really foreign to their nature and to transfigure them by thought.

But a god is not merely an authority upon whom we depend; it is a force upon which our strength relies. The man who has obeyed his god and who, for this reason, believes the god is with him, approaches the world with confidence and with the feeling of an increased energy. Likewise, social action does not confine itself to demanding sacrifices, privations and efforts from us. For the collective force is not entirely outside of us; it does not act upon us wholly from without; but rather, since society cannot exist except in and through individual consciousnesses,[1] this force must also penetrate us and organize itself within us; it thus becomes an integral part of our being and by that very fact this is elevated and magnified.

There are occasions when this strengthening and vivifying action of society is especially apparent. In the midst of an assembly animated by a common passion, we become susceptible of acts and sentiments of which we are incapable when reduced

which that particular variety of moral authority which is inherent in all that is religious has been born, and out of what elements it is made. It will be seen presently that even if we do make social pressure one of the distinctive characteristics of sociological phenomena, we do not mean to say that it is the only one. We shall show another aspect of the collective life, nearly opposite to the preceding one, but none the less real (see p. 212).

[1] Of course this does not mean to say that the collective consciousness does not have distinctive characteristics of its own (on this point, see *Représentations individuelles et représentations collectives*, in *Revue de Métaphysique et de Morale*, 1898, pp. 273 ff.).

to our own forces ; and when the assembly is dissolved and when, finding ourselves alone again, we fall back to our ordinary level, we are then able to measure the height to which we have been raised above ourselves. History abounds in examples of this sort. It is enough to think of the night of the Fourth of August, 1789, when an assembly was suddenly led to an act of sacrifice and abnegation which each of its members had refused the day before, and at which they were all surprised the day after.[1] This is why all parties, political, economic or confessional, are careful to have periodical reunions where their members may revivify their common faith by manifesting it in common. To strengthen those sentiments which, if left to themselves, would soon weaken, it is sufficient to bring those who hold them together and to put them into closer and more active relations with one another. This is the explanation of the particular attitude of a man speaking to a crowd, at least if he has succeeded in entering into communion with it. His language has a grandiloquence that would be ridiculous in ordinary circumstances ; his gestures show a certain domination ; his very thought is impatient of all rules, and easily falls into all sorts of excesses. It is because he feels within him an abnormal over-supply of force which overflows and tries to burst out from him ; sometimes he even has the feeling that he is dominated by a moral force which is greater than he and of which he is only the interpreter. It is by this trait that we are able to recognize what has often been called the demon of oratorical inspiration. Now this exceptional increase of force is something very real ; it comes to him from the very group which he addresses. The sentiments provoked by his words come back to him, but enlarged and amplified, and to this degree they strengthen his own sentiment. The passionate energies he arouses re-echo within him and quicken his vital tone. It is no longer a simple individual who speaks ; it is a group incarnate and personified.

Beside these passing and intermittent states, there are other more durable ones, where this strengthening influence of society makes itself felt with greater consequences and frequently even with greater brilliancy. There are periods in history when, under the influence of some great collective shock, social interactions have become much more frequent and active. Men look for each other and assemble together more than ever. That general effervescence results which is characteristic of revo-

[1] This is proved by the length and passionate character of the debates where a legal form was given to the resolutions made in a moment of collective enthusiasm. In the clergy as in the nobility, more than one person called this celebrated night the dupe's night, or, with Rivarol, the St. Bartholomew of the estates (see Stoll, *Suggestion und Hypnotismus in der Völkerpsychologie*, 2nd ed., p. 618, n. 2).

lutionary or creative epochs. Now this greater activity results in a general stimulation of individual forces. Men see more and differently now than in normal times. Changes are not merely of shades and degrees; men become different. The passions moving them are of such an intensity that they cannot be satisfied except by violent and unrestrained actions, actions of superhuman heroism or of bloody barbarism. This is what explains the Crusades,[1] for example, or many of the scenes, either sublime or savage, of the French Revolution.[2] Under the influence of the general exaltation, we see the most mediocre and inoffensive bourgeois become either a hero or a butcher.[3] And so clearly are all these mental processes the ones that are also at the root of religion that the individuals themselves have often pictured the pressure before which they thus gave way in a distinctly religious form. The Crusaders believed that they felt God present in the midst of them, enjoining them to go to the conquest of the Holy Land; Joan of Arc believed that she obeyed celestial voices.[4]

But it is not only in exceptional circumstances that this stimulating action of society makes itself felt; there is not, so to speak, a moment in our lives when some current of energy does not come to us from without. The man who has done his duty finds, in the manifestations of every sort expressing the sympathy, esteem or affection which his fellows have for him, a feeling of comfort, of which he does not ordinarily take account, but which sustains him, none the less. The sentiments which society has for him raise the sentiments which he has for himself. Because he is in moral harmony with his comrades, he has more confidence, courage and boldness in action, just like the believer who thinks that he feels the regard of his god turned graciously towards him. It thus produces, as it were, a perpetual sustenance for our moral nature. Since this varies with a multitude of external circumstances, as our relations with the groups about us are more or less active and as these groups themselves vary, we cannot fail to feel that this moral support depends upon an external cause; but we do not perceive where this cause is nor what it is. So we ordinarily think of it under the form of a moral power which, though immanent in us, represents within us something not ourselves: this is the moral conscience, of which, by the way, men have never made even a slightly distinct representation except by the aid of religious symbols.

[1] See Stoll, *op. cit.*, pp. 353 ff.

[2] *Ibid.*, pp. 619, 635.

[3] *Ibid.*, pp. 622 ff.

[4] The emotions of fear and sorrow are able to develop similarly and to become intensified under these same conditions. As we shall see, they correspond to quite another aspect of the religious life (Bk. III, ch. v).

In addition to these free forces which are constantly coming to renew our own, there are others which are fixed in the methods and traditions which we employ. We speak a language that we did not make; we use instruments that we did not invent; we invoke rights that we did not found; a treasury of knowledge is transmitted to each generation that it did not gather itself, etc. It is to society that we owe these varied benefits of civilization, and if we do not ordinarily see the source from which we get them, we at least know that they are not our own work. Now it is these things that give man his own place among things; a man is a man only because he is civilized. So he could not escape the feeling that outside of him there are active causes from which he gets the characteristic attributes of his nature and which, as benevolent powers, assist him, protect him and assure him of a privileged fate. And of course he must attribute to these powers a dignity corresponding to the great value of the good things he attributes to them.[1]

Thus the environment in which we live seems to us to be peopled with forces that are at once imperious and helpful, august and gracious, and with which we have relations. Since they exercise over us a pressure of which we are conscious, we are forced to localize them outside ourselves, just as we do for the objective causes of our sensations. But the sentiments which they inspire in us differ in nature from those which we have for simple visible objects. As long as these latter are reduced to their empirical characteristics as shown in ordinary experience, and as long as the religious imagination has not metamorphosed them, we entertain for them no feeling which resembles respect, and they contain within them nothing that is able to raise us outside ourselves. Therefore, the representations which express them appear to us to be very different from those aroused in us by collective influences. The two form two distinct and separate mental states in our consciousness, just as do the two forms of life to which they correspond. Consequently, we get the impression that we are in relations with two distinct sorts of reality and that a sharply drawn line of demarcation separates them from each other: on the one hand is the world of profane things, on the other, that of sacred things.

Also, in the present day just as much as in the past, we see society constantly creating sacred things out of ordinary ones. If it

[1] This is the other aspect of society which, while being imperative, appears at the same time to be good and gracious. It dominates us and assists us. If we have defined the social fact by the first of these characteristics rather than the second, it is because it is more readily observable, for it is translated into outward and visible signs; but we have never thought of denying the second (see our *Règles de la Méthode Sociologique*, preface to the second edition, p. xx, n.1).

happens to fall in love with a man and if it thinks it has found in him the principal aspirations that move it, as well as the means of satisfying them, this man will be raised above the others and, as it were, deified. Opinion will invest him with a majesty exactly analogous to that protecting the gods. This is what has happened to so many sovereigns in whom their age had faith: if they were not made gods, they were at least regarded as direct representatives of the deity. And the fact that it is society alone which is the author of these varieties of apotheosis, is evident since it frequently chances to consecrate men thus who have no right to it from their own merit. The simple deference inspired by men invested with high social functions is not different in nature from religious respect. It is expressed by the same movements: a man keeps at a distance from a high personage; he approaches him only with precautions; in conversing with him, he uses other gestures and language than those used with ordinary mortals. The sentiment felt on these occasions is so closely related to the religious sentiment that many peoples have confounded the two. In order to explain the consideration accorded to princes, nobles and political chiefs, a sacred character has been attributed to them. In Melanesia and Polynesia, for example, it is said that an influential man has *mana*, and that his influence is due to this *mana*.[1] However, it is evident that his situation is due solely to the importance attributed to him by public opinion. Thus the moral power conferred by opinion and that with which sacred beings are invested are at bottom of a single origin and made up of the same elements. That is why a single word is able to designate the two.

In addition to men, society also consecrates things, especially ideas. If a belief is unanimously shared by a people, then, for the reason which we pointed out above, it is forbidden to touch it, that is to say, to deny it or to contest it. Now the prohibition of criticism is an interdiction like the others and proves the presence of something sacred. Even to-day, howsoever great may be the liberty which we accord to others, a man who should totally deny progress or ridicule the human ideal to which modern societies are attached, would produce the effect of a sacrilege. There is at least one principle which those the most devoted to the free examination of everything tend to place above discussion and to regard as untouchable, that is to say, as sacred: this is the very principle of free examination.

[1] Codrington, *The Melanesians*, pp. 50, 103, 120. It is also generally thought that in the Polynesian languages, the word *mana* primitively had the sense of authority (see Tregear, *Maori Comparative Dictionary*, s.v.).

This aptitude of society for setting itself up as a god or for creating gods was never more apparent than during the first years of the French Revolution. At this time, in fact, under the influence of the general enthusiasm, things purely laïcal by nature were transformed by public opinion into sacred things: these were the Fatherland, Liberty, Reason.[1] A religion tended to become established which had its dogmas,[2] symbols,[3] altars [4] and feasts.[5] It was to these spontaneous aspirations that the cult of Reason and the Supreme Being attempted to give a sort of official satisfaction. It is true that this religious renovation had only an ephemeral duration. But that was because the patriotic enthusiasm which at first transported the masses soon relaxed.[6] The cause being gone, the effect could not remain. But this experiment, though short-lived, keeps all its sociological interest. It remains true that in one determined case we have seen society and its essential ideas become, directly and with no transfiguration of any sort, the object of a veritable cult.

All these facts allow us to catch glimpses of how the clan was able to awaken within its members the idea that outside of them there exist forces which dominate them and at the same time sustain them, that is to say in fine, religious forces: it is because there is no society with which the primitive is more directly and closely connected. The bonds uniting him to the tribe are much more lax and more feebly felt. Although this is not at all strange or foreign to him, it is with the people of his own clan that he has the greatest number of things in common; it is the action of this group that he feels the most directly; so it is this also which, in preference to all others, should express itself in religious symbols.

But this first explanation has been too general, for it is applicable to every sort of society indifferently, and consequently to every sort of religion. Let us attempt to determine exactly what form this collective action takes in the clan and how it arouses the sensation of sacredness there. For there is no place where it is more easily observable or more apparent in its results.

III

The life of the Australian societies passes alternately through two distinct phases.[7] Sometimes the population is broken up into little groups who wander about independently of one another,

[1] See Albert Mathiez, *Les origines des cultes révolutionnaires* (1789–1792).
[2] *Ibid.*, p. 24. [3] *Ibid.*, pp. 29, 32. [4] *Ibid.*, p. 30. [5] *Ibid.*, p. 46.
[6] See Mathiez, *La Théophilanthropie et la Culte décadaire*, p. 36.
[7] See Spencer and Gillen, *Nor. Tr.*, p. 33.

in their various occupations ; each family lives by itself, hunting and fishing, and in a word, trying to procure its indispensable food by all the means in its power. Sometimes, on the contrary, the population concentrates and gathers at determined points for a length of time varying from several days to several months. This concentration takes place when a clan or a part of the tribe [1] is summoned to the gathering, and on this occasion they celebrate a religious ceremony, or else hold what is called a corrobbori [2] in the usual ethnological language.

These two phases are contrasted with each other in the sharpest way. In the first, economic activity is the preponderating one, and it is generally of a very mediocre intensity. Gathering the grains or herbs that are necessary for food, or hunting and fishing are not occupations to awaken very lively passions.[3] The dispersed condition in which the society finds itself results in making its life uniform, languishing and dull.[4] But when a corrobbori takes place, everything changes. Since the emotional and passional faculties of the primitive are only imperfectly placed under the control of his reason and will, he easily loses control of himself. Any event of some importance puts him quite outside himself. Does he receive good news ? There are at once transports of enthusiasm. In the contrary conditions, he is to be seen running here and there like a madman, giving himself up to all sorts of immoderate movements, crying, shrieking, rolling in the dust, throwing it in every direction, biting himself, brandishing his arms in a furious manner, etc.[5] The very fact of the concentration acts as an exceptionally powerful stimulant. When they are once come together, a sort of electricity is formed by their collecting which quickly transports them to an extraordinary degree of exaltation. Every sentiment expressed finds a place without resistance in all the minds, which are very open to outside impressions ; each re-echoes the others, and is re-echoed

[1] There are even ceremonies, for example, those which take place in connection with the initiation, to which members of foreign tribes are invited. A whole system of messages and messengers is organized for these convocations, without which the great solemnities could not take place (see Howitt, *Notes on Australian Message-Sticks and Messengers*, in *J.A.I.*, 1889 ; *Nat. Tr.*, pp. 83, 678–691 ; Spencer and Gillen, *Nat. Tr.*, p. 159 ; *Nor. Tr.*, p. 551).

[2] The corrobbori is distinguished from the real religious ceremonies by the fact that it is open to women and uninitiated persons. But if these two sorts of collective manifestations are to be distinguished, they are, none the less, closely related. We shall have occasion elsewhere to come back to this relationship and to explain it.

[3] Except, of course, in the case of the great bush-beating hunts.

[4] " The peaceful monotony of this part of his life," say Spencer and Gillen (*Nor. Tr.*, p. 33).

[5] Howitt, *Nat. Tr.*, p. 683. He is speaking of the demonstrations which take place when an ambassador sent to a group of foreigners returns to camp with news of a favourable result. Cf. Brough Smyth, I, p. 138 ; Schulze, *loc. cit.*, p. 222.

by the others. The initial impulse thus proceeds, growing as it goes, as an avalanche grows in its advance. And as such active passions so free from all control could not fail to burst out, on every side one sees nothing but violent gestures, cries, veritable howls, and deafening noises of every sort, which aid in intensifying still more the state of mind which they manifest. And since a collective sentiment cannot express itself collectively except on the condition of observing a certain order permitting co-operation and movements in unison, these gestures and cries naturally tend to become rhythmic and regular; hence come songs and dances. But in taking a more regular form, they lose nothing of their natural violence; a regulated tumult remains tumult. The human voice is not sufficient for the task; it is reinforced by means of artificial processes: boomerangs are beaten against each other; bull-roarers are whirled. It is probable that these instruments, the use of which is so general in the Australian religious ceremonies, are used primarily to express in a more adequate fashion the agitation felt. But while they express it, they also strengthen it. This effervescence often reaches such a point that it causes unheard-of actions. The passions released are of such an impetuosity that they can be restrained by nothing. They are so far removed from their ordinary conditions of life, and they are so thoroughly conscious of it, that they feel that they must set themselves outside of and above their ordinary morals. The sexes unite contrarily to the rules governing sexual relations. Men exchange wives with each other. Sometimes even incestuous unions, which in normal times are thought abominable and are severely punished, are now contracted openly and with impunity.[1] If we add to all this that the ceremonies generally take place at night in a darkness pierced here and there by the light of fires, we can easily imagine what effect such scenes ought to produce on the minds of those who participate. They produce such a violent super-excitation of the whole physical and mental life that it cannot be supported very long: the actor taking the principal part finally falls exhausted on the ground.[2]

To illustrate and make specific this necessarily schematic picture, let us describe certain scenes taken from Spencer and Gillen.

[1] See Spencer and Gillen, *Nat. Tr.*, pp. 96 f.; *Nor. Tr.*, p. 137; Brough Smyth, II, p. 319.—This ritual promiscuity is found especially in the initiation ceremonies (Spencer and Gillen, *Nat. Tr.*, pp. 267, 381; Howitt, *Nat. Tr.*, p. 657), and in the totemic ceremonies (*Nor. Tr.*, pp. 214, 298, 237). In these latter, the ordinary exogamic rules are violated. Sometimes among the Arunta, unions between father and daughter, mother and son, and brothers and sisters (that is in every case, relationship by blood) remain forbidden (*Nat. Tr.*, pp. 96 f.).

[2] Howitt, *Nat. Tr.*, pp. 535, 545. This is extremely common.

One of the most important religious ceremonies among the Warramunga is the one concerning the snake Wollunqua. It consists in a series of ceremonies lasting through several days. On the fourth day comes the following scene.

According to the ceremonial used among the Warramunga, representatives of the two phratries take part, one as officiants, the other as preparers and assistants. Only the members of the Uluuru phratry are qualified to celebrate the rite, but the members of the Kingilli phratry must decorate the actors, make ready the place and the instruments, and play the part of an audience. In this capacity, they were charged with making a sort of mound in advance out of wet sand, upon which a design is marked with red down which represents the snake Wollunqua. The real ceremony only commenced after nightfall. Towards ten or eleven o'clock, the Uluuru and Kingilli men arrived on the ground, sat down on the mound and commenced to sing. Everyone was evidently very excited. A little later in the evening, the Uluuru brought up their wives and gave them over to the Kingilli,[1] who had intercourse with them. Then the recently initiated young men were brought in and the whole ceremony was explained to them in detail, and until three o'clock in the morning singing went on without a pause. Then followed a scene of the wildest excitement. While fires were lighted on all sides, making the whiteness of the gum-trees stand out sharply against the surrounding darkness, the Uluuru knelt down one behind another beside the mound, then rising from the ground they went around it, with a movement in unison, their two hands resting upon their thighs, then a little farther on they knelt down again, and so on. At the same time they swayed their bodies, now to the right and now to the left, while uttering at each movement a piercing cry, a veritable yell, "*Yrrsh! Yrrsh! Yrrsh!*" In the meantime the Kingilli, in a state of great excitement, clanged their boomerangs and their chief was even more agitated than his companions. When the procession of the Uluuru had twice gone around the mound, quitting the kneeling position, they sat down and commenced to sing again; at moments the singing died away, then suddenly took up again. When day commenced to dawn, all leaped to their feet; the fires that had gone out were relighted and the Uluuru, urged on by the Kingilli, attacked the mound furiously with boomerangs, lances and clubs; in a few minutes it was torn to pieces. The fires died away and profound silence reigned again.[2]

[1] These women were Kingilli themselves, so these unions violated the exogamic rules.

[2] *Nor. Tr.*, p. 237.

A still more violent scene at which these same observers assisted was in connection with the fire ceremonies among the Warramunga.

Commencing at nightfall, all sorts of processions, dances and songs had taken place by torchlight; the general effervescence was constantly increasing. At a given moment, twelve assistants each took a great lighted torch in their hands, and one of them holding his like a bayonet, charged into a group of natives. Blows were warded off with clubs and spears. A general mêlée followed. The men leaped and pranced about, uttering savage yells all the time; the burning torches continually came crashing down on the heads and bodies of the men, scattering lighted sparks in every direction. "The smoke, the blazing torches, the showers of sparks falling in all directions and the masses of dancing, yelling men," say Spencer and Gillen, "formed altogether a genuinely wild and savage scene of which it is impossible to convey any adequate idea in words."[1]

One can readily conceive how, when arrived at this state of exaltation, a man does not recognize himself any longer. Feeling himself dominated and carried away by some sort of an external power which makes him think and act differently than in normal times, he naturally has the impression of being himself no longer. It seems to him that he has become a new being: the decorations he puts on and the masks that cover his face figure materially in this interior transformation, and to a still greater extent, they aid in determining its nature. And as at the same time all his companions feel themselves transformed in the same way and express this sentiment by their cries, their gestures and their general attitude, everything is just as though he really were transported into a special world, entirely different from the one where he ordinarily lives, and into an environment filled with exceptionally intense forces that take hold of him and metamorphose him. How could such experiences as these, especially when they are repeated every day for weeks, fail to leave in him the conviction that there really exist two heterogeneous and mutually incomparable worlds? One is that where his daily life drags wearily along; but he cannot penetrate into the other without at once entering into relations with extraordinary powers that excite him to the point of frenzy. The first is the profane world, the second, that of sacred things.

So it is in the midst of these effervescent social environments and out of this effervescence itself that the religious idea seems

[1] *Nor. Tr.*, p. 391. Other examples of this collective effervescence during the religious ceremonies will be found in *Nat. Tr.*, pp. 244–246, 365–366, 374, 509–510 (this latter in connection with a funeral rite). Cf. *Nor. Tr.*, pp. 213, 351.

to be born. The theory that this is really its origin is confirmed by the fact that in Australia the really religious activity is almost entirely confined to the moments when these assemblies are held. To be sure, there is no people among whom the great solemnities of the cult are not more or less periodic ; but in the more advanced societies, there is not, so to speak, a day when some prayer or offering is not addressed to the gods and some ritual act is not performed. But in Australia, on the contrary, apart from the celebrations of the clan and tribe, the time is nearly all filled with lay and profane occupations. Of course there are prohibitions that should be and are preserved even during these periods of temporal activity ; it is never permissible to kill or eat freely of the totemic animal, at least in those parts where the interdiction has retained its original vigour ; but almost no positive rites are then celebrated, and there are no ceremonies of any importance. These take place only in the midst of assembled groups. The religious life of the Australian passes through successive phases of complete lull and of super-excitation, and social life oscillates in the same rhythm. This puts clearly into evidence the bond uniting them to one another, but among the peoples called civilized, the relative continuity of the two blurs their relations. It might even be asked whether the violence of this contrast was not necessary to disengage the feeling of sacredness in its first form. By concentrating itself almost entirely in certain determined moments, the collective life has been able to attain its greatest intensity and efficacy, and consequently to give men a more active sentiment of the double existence they lead and of the double nature in which they participate.

But this explanation is still incomplete. We have shown how the clan, by the manner in which it acts upon its members, awakens within them the idea of external forces which dominate them and exalt them ; but we must still demand how it happens that these forces are thought of under the form of totems, that is to say, in the shape of an animal or plant.

It is because this animal or plant has given its name to the clan and serves it as emblem. In fact, it is a well-known law that the sentiments aroused in us by something spontaneously attach themselves to the symbol which represents them. For us, black is a sign of mourning ; it also suggests sad impressions and ideas. This transference of sentiments comes simply from the fact that the idea of a thing and the idea of its symbol are closely united in our minds ; the result is that the emotions provoked by the one extend contagiously to the other. But this contagion, which takes place in every case to a certain degree, is much more complete and more marked when the symbol is something simple, definite and easily representable, while the thing itself, owing to its dimensions, the number of its parts and the complexity of their arrangement, is difficult to hold in the mind. For we are unable to consider an abstract entity, which we can represent only laboriously and confusedly, the source of the strong sentiments which we feel. We cannot explain them to ourselves except by connecting them to some concrete object of whose reality we are vividly aware. Then if the thing itself does not fulfil this condition, it cannot serve as the accepted basis of the sentiments felt, even though it may be what really aroused them. Then some sign takes its place ; it is to this that we connect the emotions it excites. It is this which is loved, feared, respected ; it is to this that we are grateful ; it is for this that we sacrifice ourselves. The soldier who dies for his flag, dies for his country ; but as a matter of fact, in his own consciousness, it is the flag that has the first place. It sometimes happens that this even directly determines action. Whether one isolated standard remains in the hands of the enemy or not does not determine the fate of the country, yet the soldier allows himself to be killed to regain it. He loses sight of the fact that the flag is only a sign, and that it has no value in itself, but only brings to mind the reality that it represents ; it is treated as if it were this reality itself.

Now the totem is the flag of the clan. It is therefore natural that the impressions aroused by the clan in individual minds—impressions of dependence and of increased vitality—should fix themselves to the idea of the totem rather than that of the clan : for the clan is too complex a reality to be represented clearly in all its complex unity by such rudimentary intelligences. More than that, the primitive does not even see that these impressions come to him from the group. He does not know that the coming together of a number of men associated in the same life results in disengaging new energies, which transform each of them. All that he knows is that he is raised above himself and that he sees a different life from the one he ordinarily leads. However, he must connect these sensations to some external object as their cause. Now what does he see about him ? On every side those things which appeal to his senses and strike his imagination are the numerous images of the totem. They are the waninga and the nurtunja, which are symbols of the sacred being. They are churinga and bull-roarers, upon which are generally carved combinations of lines having the same significance. They are the decorations covering the different parts of his body, which are totemic marks. How could this image, repeated everywhere and in all sorts of forms, fail to stand out with exceptional relief in his mind? Placed thus in the centre of the scene, it becomes representative. The sentiments experienced fix themselves upon it, for it is the only concrete object upon which they can fix themselves. It continues to bring them to mind and to evoke them even after the assembly has dissolved, for it survives the assembly, being carved upon the instruments of the cult, upon the sides of rocks, upon bucklers, etc. By it, the emotions experienced are perpetually sustained and revived. Everything happens just as if they inspired them directly. It is still more natural to attribute them to it for, since they are common to the group, they can be associated only with something that is equally common to all. Now the totemic emblem is the only thing satisfying this condition. By definition, it is common to all. During the ceremony, it is the centre of all regards. While generations change, it remains the same; it is the permanent element of the social life. So it is from it that those mysterious forces seem to emanate with which men feel that they are related, and thus they have been led to represent these forces under the form of the animate or inanimate being whose name the clan bears.

When this point is once established, we are in a position to understand all that is essential in the totemic beliefs.

Since religious force is nothing other than the collective and anonymous force of the clan, and since this can be represented in the mind only in the form of the totem, the totemic emblem is like the visible body of the god. Therefore, it is from it that those kindly or dreadful actions seem to emanate, which the cult seeks to provoke or prevent; consequently, it is to it that the cult is addressed. This is the explanation of why it holds the first place in the series of sacred things.

But the clan, like every other sort of society, can live only in and through the individual consciousnesses that compose it. So if religious force, in so far as it is conceived as incorporated in the totemic emblem, appears to be outside of the individuals and to be endowed with a sort of transcendence over them, it, like the clan of which it is the symbol, can be realized only in and through them; in this sense, it is imminent in them and they necessarily represent it as such. They feel it present and active within them, for it is this which raises them to a superior life. This is why men have believed that they contain within them a principle comparable to the one residing in the totem, and consequently, why they have attributed a sacred character to themselves, but one less marked than that of the emblem. It is because the emblem is the pre-eminent source of the religious life; the man participates in it only indirectly, as he is well aware; he takes into account the fact that the force that transports him into the world of sacred things is not inherent in him, but comes to him from the outside.

But for still another reason, the animals or vegetables of the totemic species should have the same character, and even to a higher degree. If the totemic principle is nothing else than the clan, it is the clan thought of under the material form of the totemic emblem; now this form is also that of the concrete beings whose name the clan bears. Owing to this resemblance, they could not fail to evoke sentiments analogous to those aroused by the emblem itself. Since the latter is the object of a religious respect, they too should inspire respect of the same sort and appear to be sacred. Having external forms so nearly identical, it would be impossible for the native not to attribute to them forces of the same nature. It is therefore forbidden to kill or eat the totemic animal, since its flesh is believed to have the positive virtues resulting from the rites; it is because it resembles the emblem of the clan, that is to say, it is in its own image. And since the animal naturally resembles the emblem more than the man does, it is placed on a superior rank in the hierarchy of sacred things. Between these two beings there is undoubtedly a close relationship, for they both partake of the same essence: both incarnate something of the totemic principle. However, since the principle itself is conceived under an animal form, the animal seems to incarnate it more fully than the man. Therefore, if men consider it and treat it as a brother, it is at least as an elder brother.[1]

But even if the totemic principle has its preferred seat in a determined species of animal or vegetable, it cannot remain localized there. A sacred character is to a high degree contagious;[2] it therefore spreads out from the totemic being to everything that is closely or remotely connected with it. The religious sentiments inspired by the animal are communicated to the substances upon which it is nourished and which serve to make or remake its flesh and blood, to the things that resemble it, and to the different beings with which it has constant relations. Thus, little by little, sub-totems are attached to the totems and from

[1] Thus we see that this fraternity is the logical consequence of totemism, rather than its basis. Men have not imagined their duties towards the animals of the totemic species because they regarded them as kindred, but have imagined the kinship to explain the nature of the beliefs and rites of which they were the object. The animal was considered a relative of the man because it was a sacred being like the man, but it was not treated as a sacred being because it was regarded as a relative.

[2] See below, Bk. III, ch. i, § 3.

the cosmological systems expressed by the primitive classifications. At last, the whole world is divided up among the totemic principles of each tribe.

We are now able to explain the origin of the ambiguity of religious forces as they appear in history, and how they are physical as well as human, moral as well as material. They are moral powers because they are made up entirely of the impressions this moral being, the group, arouses in those other moral beings, its individual members; they do not translate the manner in which physical things affect our senses, but the way in which the collective consciousness acts upon individual consciousnesses. Their authority is only one form of the moral ascendancy of society over its members. But, on the other hand, since they are conceived of under material forms, they could not fail to be regarded as closely related to material things.[1] Therefore they dominate the two worlds. Their residence is in men, but at the same time they are the vital principles of things. They animate minds and discipline them, but it is also they who make plants grow and animals reproduce. It is this double nature which has enabled religion to be like the womb from which come all the leading germs of human civilization. Since it has been made to embrace all of reality, the physical world as well as the moral one, the forces that move bodies as well as those that move minds have been conceived in a religious form. That is how the most diverse methods and practices, both those that make possible the continuation of the moral life (law, morals, beaux-arts) and those serving the material life (the natural, technical and practical sciences), are either directly or indirectly derived from religion.[2]

IV

The first religious conceptions have often been attributed to feelings of weakness and dependence, of fear and anguish which seized men when they came into contact with the world. Being the victims of nightmares of which they were themselves

[1] At the bottom of this conception there is a well-founded and persistent sentiment. Modern science also tends more and more to admit that the duality of man and nature does not exclude their unity, and that physical and moral forces, though distinct, are closely related. We undoubtedly have a different conception of this unity and relationship than the primitive, but beneath these different symbols, the truth affirmed by the two is the same.

[2] We say that this derivation is sometimes indirect on account of the industrial methods which, in a large number of cases, seem to be derived from religion through the intermediacy of magic (see Hubert and Mauss, *Théorie générale de la Magie*, *Année Sociol.*, VII, pp. 144 ff.); for, as we believe, magic forces are only a special form of religious forces. We shall have occasion to return to this point several times.

the creators, they believed themselves surrounded by hostile and redoubtable powers which their rites sought to appease. We have now shown that the first religions were of a wholly different origin. The famous formula *Primus in orbe deos fecit timor* is in no way justified by the facts. The primitive does not regard his gods as foreigners, enemies or thoroughly and necessarily malevolent beings whose favours he must acquire at any price ; quite on the contrary, they are rather friends, kindred or natural protectors for him. Are these not the names he gives to the beings of the totemic species ? The power to which the cult is addressed is not represented as soaring high above him and overwhelming him by its superiority ; on the contrary, it is very near to him and confers upon him very useful powers which he could never acquire by himself. Perhaps the deity has never been nearer to men than at this period of history, when it is present in the things filling their immediate environment and is, in part, imminent in himself. In fine, the sentiments at the root of totemism are those of happy confidence rather than of terror and compression. If we set aside the funeral rites—the sober side of every religion—we find the totemic cult celebrated in the midst of songs, dances and dramatic representations. As we shall see, cruel expiations are relatively rare ; even the painful and obligatory mutilations of the initiations are not of this character. The terrible and jealous gods appear but slowly in the religious evolution. This is because primitive societies are not those huge Leviathans which overwhelm a man by the enormity of their power and place him under a severe discipline ; [1] he gives himself up to them spontaneously and without resistance. As the social soul is then made up of only a small number of ideas and sentiments, it easily becomes wholly incarnate in each individual consciousness. The individual carries it all inside of him ; it is a part of him and consequently, when he gives himself up to the impulses inspired by it, he does not feel that he is giving way before compulsion, but that he is going where his nature calls him.[2]

This way of understanding the origins of religious thought escapes the objections raised against the most accredited classical theories.

We have seen how the naturists and animists pretend to construct the idea of sacred beings out of the sensations evoked in us by different phenomena of the physical or biological order,

[1] At least after he is once adult and fully initiated, for the initiation rites, introducing the young man to the social life, are a severe discipline in themselves.

[2] Upon this particular aspect of primitive societies, see our *Division du travail social*, 3rd ed., pp. 123, 149, 173 ff.

and we have shown how this enterprise is impossible and even self-contradictory. Nothing is worth nothing. The impressions produced in us by the physical world can, by definition, contain nothing that surpasses this world. Out of the visible, only the visible can be made; out of that which is heard, we cannot make something not heard. Then to explain how the idea of sacredness has been able to take form under these conditions, the majority of the theorists have been obliged to admit that men have superimposed upon reality, such as it is given by observation, an unreal world, constructed entirely out of the fantastic images which agitate his mind during a dream, or else out of the frequently monstrous aberrations produced by the mythological imagination under the bewitching but deceiving influence of language. But it remained incomprehensible that humanity should have remained obstinate in these errors through the ages, for experience should have very quickly proven them false.

But from our point of view, these difficulties disappear. Religion ceases to be an inexplicable hallucination and takes a foothold in reality. In fact, we can say that the believer is not deceived when he believes in the existence of a moral power upon which he depends and from which he receives all that is best in himself: this power exists, it is society. When the Australian is carried outside himself and feels a new life flowing within him whose intensity surprises him, he is not the dupe of an illusion; this exaltation is real and is really the effect of forces outside of and superior to the individual. It is true that he is wrong in thinking that this increase of vitality is the work of a power in the form of some animal or plant. But this error is merely in regard to the letter of the symbol by which this being is represented to the mind and the external appearance which the imagination has given it, and not in regard to the fact of its existence. Behind these figures and metaphors, be they gross or refined, there is a concrete and living reality. Thus religion acquires a meaning and a reasonableness that the most intransigent rationalist cannot misunderstand. Its primary object is not to give men a representation of the physical world; for if that were its essential task, we could not understand how it has been able to survive, for, on this side, it is scarcely more than a fabric of errors. Before all, it is a system of ideas with which the individuals represent to themselves the society of which they are members, and the obscure but intimate relations which they have with it. This is its primary function; and though metaphorical and symbolic, this representation is not unfaithful. Quite on the contrary, it translates everything essential in the relations which are to be explained : for it is an eternal truth that outside of us there exists something greater than us, with which we enter into communion.

That is why we can rest assured in advance that the practices of the cult, whatever they may be, are something more than movements without importance and gestures without efficacy. By the mere fact that their apparent function is to strengthen the bonds attaching the believer to his god, they at the same time really strengthen the bonds attaching the individual to the society of which he is a member, since the god is only a figurative expression of the society. We are even able to understand how the fundamental truth thus contained in religion has been able to compensate for the secondary errors which it almost necessarily implies, and how believers have consequently been restrained from tearing themselves off from it, in spite of the misunderstandings which must result from these errors. It is undeniably true that the recipes which it recommends that men use to act upon things are generally found to be ineffective. But these checks can have no profound influence, for they do not touch religion in its fundamentals.[1]

However, it may be objected that even according to this hypothesis, religion remains the object of a certain delirium. What other name can we give to that state when, after a collective effervescence, men believe themselves transported into an entirely different world from the one they have before their eyes ?

It is certainly true that religious life cannot attain a certain degree of intensity without implying a psychical exaltation not far removed from delirium. That is why the prophets, the founders of religions, the great saints, in a word, the men whose religious consciousness is exceptionally sensitive, very frequently give signs of an excessive nervousness that is even pathological : these physiological defects predestined them to great religious rôles. The ritual use of intoxicating liquors is to be explained in the same way.[2] Of course this does not mean that an ardent religious faith is necessarily the fruit of the drunkenness and mental derangement which accompany it ; but as experience soon informed people of the similarities between the mentality of a delirious person and that of a seer, they sought to open a way to the second by artificially exciting the first. But if, for this reason, it may be said that religion is not without a certain delirium, it must be added that this delirium, if it has the causes which we have attributed to it, *is well-founded*. The images out

[1] We provisionally limit ourselves to this general indication : we shall return to this idea and give more explicit proof, when we speak of the rites (Bk. III).

[2] On this point, see Achelis, *Die Ekstase*, Berlin, 1902, especially ch. i.

of which it is made are not pure illusions like those the naturists and animists put at the basis of religion; they correspond to something in reality. Of course it is only natural that the moral forces they express should be unable to affect the human mind powerfully without pulling it outside itself and without plunging it into a state that may be called *ecstatic*, provided that the word be taken in its etymological sense (ἔκστασις); but it does not follow that they are imaginary. Quite on the contrary, the mental agitation they cause bears witness to their reality. It is merely one more proof that a very intense social life always does a sort of violence to the organism, as well as to the individual consciousness, which interferes with its normal functioning. Therefore it can last only a limited length of time.[1]

Moreover, if we give the name delirious to every state in which the mind adds to the immediate data given by the senses and projects its own sentiments and feelings into things, then nearly every collective representation is in a sense delirious; religious beliefs are only one particular case of a very general law. Our whole social environment seems to us to be filled with forces which really exist only in our own minds. We know what the flag is for the soldier; in itself, it is only a piece of cloth. Human blood is only an organic liquid, but even to-day we cannot see it flowing without feeling a violent emotion which its physico-chemical properties cannot explain. From the physical point of view, a man is nothing more than a system of cells, or from the mental point of view, than a system of representations; in either case, he differs only in degree from animals. Yet society conceives him, and obliges us to conceive him, as invested with a character *sui generis* that isolates him, holds at a distance all rash encroachments and, in a word, imposes respect. This dignity which puts him into a class by himself appears to us as one of his distinctive attributes, although we can find nothing in the empirical nature of man which justifies it. A cancelled postage stamp may be worth a fortune; but surely this value is in no way implied in its natural properties. In a sense, our representation of the external world is undoubtedly a mere fabric of hallucinations, for the odours, tastes and colours that we put into bodies are not really there, or at least, they are not such as we perceive them. However, our olfactory, gustatory and visual sensations continue to correspond to certain objective states of the things represented; they express in their way the properties, either of material particles or of ether waves, which certainly have their origin in the bodies which we perceive

[1] Cf. Mauss, *Essai sur les variations saisonnières des sociétés eskimos*, in *Année Sociol.*, IX, p. 127.

as fragrant, sapid or coloured. But collective representations very frequently attribute to the things to which they are attached qualities which do not exist under any form or to any degree. Out of the commonest object, they can make a most powerful sacred being.

Yet the powers which are thus conferred, though purely ideal, act as though they were real; they determine the conduct of men with the same degree of necessity as physical forces. The Arunta who has been rubbed with his churinga feels himself stronger; he is stronger. If he has eaten the flesh of an animal which, though perfectly healthy, is forbidden to him, he will feel himself sick, and may die of it. Surely the soldier who falls while defending his flag does not believe that he sacrifices himself for a bit of cloth. This is all because social thought, owing to the imperative authority that is in it, has an efficacy that individual thought could never have; by the power which it has over our minds, it can make us see things in whatever light it pleases; it adds to reality or deducts from it according to the circumstances. Thus there is one division of nature where the formula of idealism is applicable almost to the letter: this is the social kingdom. Here more than anywhere else, the idea is the reality. Even in this case, of course, idealism is not true without modification. We can never escape the duality of our nature and free ourselves completely from physical necessities: in order to express our own ideas to ourselves, it is necessary, as has been shown above, that we fix them upon material things which symbolize them. But here the part of matter is reduced to a minimum. The object serving as support for the idea is not much in comparison with the ideal superstructure, beneath which it disappears, and also, it counts for nothing in the superstructure. This is what that pseudo-delirium consists in, which we find at the bottom of so many collective representations: it is only a form of this essential idealism.[1] So it is not properly called a delirium, for the ideas thus objectified are well founded, not in the nature of the material things upon which they settle themselves, but in the nature of society.

We are now able to understand how the totemic principle,

[1] Thus we see how erroneous those theories are which, like the geographical materialism of Ratzel (see especially his *Politische Geographie*), seek to derive all social life from its material foundation (either economic or territorial). They commit an error precisely similar to the one committed by Maudsley in individual psychology. Just as this latter reduced all the psychical life of the individual to a mere epiphenomenon of his physiological basis, they seek to reduce the whole psychical life of the group to its physical basis. But they forget that ideas are realities and forces, and that collective representations are forces even more powerful and active than individual representations. On this point, see our *Représentations individuelles et représentations collectives*, in the *Revue de Métaphysique et de Morale*, May, 1898.

and in general, every religious force, comes to be outside of the object in which it resides.[1] It is because the idea of it is in no way made up of the impressions directly produced by this thing upon our senses or minds. Religious force is only the sentiment inspired by the group in its members, but projected outside of the consciousnesses that experience them, and objectified. To be objectified, they are fixed upon some object which thus becomes sacred ; but any object might fulfil this function. In principle, there are none whose nature predestines them to it to the exclusion of all others ; but also there are none that are necessarily impossible.[2] Everything depends upon the circumstances which lead the sentiment creating religious ideas to establish itself here or there, upon this point or upon that one. Therefore, the sacred character assumed by an object is not implied in the intrinsic properties of this latter : *it is added to them.* The world of religious things is not one particular aspect of empirical nature ; *it is superimposed upon it.*

This conception of the religious, finally, allows us to explain an important principle found at the bottom of a multitude of myths and rites, and which may be stated thus : when a sacred thing is subdivided, each of its parts remains equal to the thing itself. In other words, as far as religious thought is concerned, the part is equal to the whole ; it has the same powers, the same efficacy. The debris of a relic has the same virtue as a relic in good condition. The smallest drop of blood contains the same active principle as the whole thing. The soul, as we shall see, may be broken up into nearly as many pieces as there are organs or tissues in the organism ; each of these partial souls is worth a whole soul. This conception would be inexplicable if the sacredness of something were due to the constituent properties of the thing itself ; for in that case, it should vary with this thing, increasing and decreasing with it. But if the virtues it is believed to possess are not intrinsic in it, and if they come from certain sentiments which it brings to mind and symbolizes, though these originate outside of it, then, since it has no need of determined dimensions to play this rôle of reminder, it will have the same value whether it is entire or not. Since the part makes us think of the whole, it evokes the same sentiments as the whole. A mere fragment of the flag represents the fatherland just as well as the flag itself : so it is sacred in the same way and to the same degree.[3]

[1] See above, pp. 188 and 194.

[2] Even the *excreta* have a religious character. See Preuss, *Der Ursprung der Religion und Kunst*, especially ch. ii, entitled *Der Zauber der Defäkation* (*Globus*, LXXXVI, pp. 325 ff.).

[3] This principle has passed from religion into magic : it is the *totem ex parte* of the alchemists.

V

But if this theory of totemism has enabled us to explain the most characteristic beliefs of this religion, it rests upon a fact not yet explained. When the idea of the totem, the emblem of the clan, is given, all the rest follows; but we must still investigate how this idea has been formed. This is a double question and may be subdivided as follows: What has led the clan to choose an emblem? and why have these emblems been borrowed from the animal and vegetable worlds, and particularly from the former?

That an emblem is useful as a rallying-centre for any sort of a group it is superfluous to point out. By expressing the social unity in a material form, it makes this more obvious to all, and for that very reason the use of emblematic symbols must have spread quickly when once thought of. But more than that, this idea should spontaneously arise out of the conditions of common life; for the emblem is not merely a convenient process for clarifying the sentiment society has of itself: it also serves to create this sentiment; it is one of its constituent elements.

In fact, if left to themselves, individual consciousnesses are closed to each other; they can communicate only by means of signs which express their internal states. If the communication established between them is to become a real communion, that is to say, a fusion of all particular sentiments into one common sentiment, the signs expressing them must themselves be fused into one single and unique resultant. It is the appearance of this that informs individuals that they are in harmony and makes them conscious of their moral unity. It is by uttering the same cry, pronouncing the same word, or performing the same gesture in regard to some object that they become and feel themselves to be in unison. It is true that individual representations also cause reactions in the organism that are not without importance; however, they can be thought of apart from these physical reactions which accompany them or follow them, but which do not constitute them. But it is quite another matter with collective representations. They presuppose that minds act and react upon one another; they are the product of these actions and reactions which are themselves possible only through material intermediaries. These latter do not confine themselves to revealing the mental state with which they are associated; they aid in creating it. Individual minds cannot come in contact and communicate with each other except by coming out of themselves; but they cannot do this except by movements. So it is the homogeneity of these movements that gives the group consciousness of itself and consequently makes it exist. When this homogeneity is once established and these movements have once taken a stereotyped form, they serve to symbolize the corresponding representations. But they symbolize them only because they have aided in forming them.

Moreover, without symbols, social sentiments could have only a precarious existence. Though very strong as long as men are together and influence each other reciprocally, they exist only in the form of recollections after the assembly has ended, and when left to themselves, these become feebler and feebler; for since the group is now no longer present and active, individual temperaments easily regain the upper hand. The violent passions which may have been released in the heart of a crowd fall away and are extinguished when this is dissolved, and men ask themselves with astonishment how they could ever have been so carried away from their normal character. But if the movements by which these sentiments are expressed are connected with something that endures, the sentiments themselves become more durable. These other things are constantly bringing them to mind and arousing them; it is as though the cause which excited them in the first place continued to act. Thus these systems of emblems, which are necessary if society is to become conscious of itself, are no less indispensable for assuring the continuation of this consciousness.

So we must refrain from regarding these symbols as simple artifices, as sorts of labels attached to representations already made, in order to make them more manageable: they are an integral part of them. Even the fact that collective sentiments are thus attached to things completely foreign to them is not purely conventional: it illustrates under a conventional form a real characteristic of social facts, that is, their transcendence over individual minds. In fact, it is known that social phenomena are born, not in individuals, but in the group. Whatever part we may take in their origin, each of us receives them from without.[1] So when we represent them to ourselves as emanating from a material object, we do not completely misunderstand their nature. Of course they do not come from the specific thing to which we connect them, but nevertheless, it is true that their origin is outside of us. If the moral force sustaining the believer does not come from the idol he adores or the emblem he venerates, still it is from outside of him, as he is well aware. The objectivity of its symbol only translates its externalness.

Thus social life, in all its aspects and in every period of its history, is made possible only by a vast symbolism. The material

[1] On this point see *Règles de la méthode sociologique*, pp. 5 ff.

emblems and figurative representations with which we are more especially concerned in our present study, are one form of this; but there are many others. Collective sentiments can just as well become incarnate in persons or formulæ: some formulæ are flags, while there are persons, either real or mythical, who are symbols. But there is one sort of emblem which should make an early appearance without reflection or calculation: this is tattooing. Indeed, well-known facts demonstrate that it is produced almost automatically in certain conditions. When men of an inferior culture are associated in a common life, they are frequently led, by an instinctive tendency, as it were, to paint or cut upon the body, images that bear witness to their common existence. According to a text of Procopius, the early Christians printed on their skin the name of Christ or the sign of the cross;[1] for a long time, the groups of pilgrims going to Palestine were also tattooed on the arm or wrist with designs representing the cross or the monogram of Christ.[2] This same usage is also reported among the pilgrims going to certain holy places in Italy.[3] A curious case of spontaneous tattooing is given by Lombroso: twenty young men in an Italian college, when on the point of separating, decorated themselves with tattoos recording, in various ways, the years they had spent together.[4] The same fact has frequently been observed among the soldiers in the same barracks, the sailors in the same boat, or the prisoners in the same jail.[5] It will be understood that especially where methods are still rudimentary, tattooing should be the most direct and expressive means by which the communion of minds can be affirmed. The best way of proving to one's self and to others that one is a member of a certain group is to place a distinctive mark on the body. The proof that this is the reason for the existence of the totemic image is the fact, which we have already mentioned, that it does not seek to reproduce the aspect of the thing it is supposed to represent. It is made up of lines and points to which a wholly conventional significance is attributed.[6] Its object is not to represent or bring to mind a determined object, but to bear witness to the fact that a certain number of individuals participate in the same moral life.

Moreover, the clan is a society which is less able than any other to do without an emblem or symbol, for there is almost

[1] Procopius of Gaza, *Commentarii in Isaiam*, 496.

[2] See Thévenot, *Voyage au Levant*, Paris, 1689, p. 638. The fact was still found in 1862.

[3] Lacassagne, *Les Tatouages*, p. 10.

[4] Lombroso, *L'homme criminel*, I, p. 292.

[5] Lombroso, *ibid.*, I, pp. 268, 285, 291 f.; Lacassagne, *op. cit.*, p. 97.

[6] See above, p. 127.

no other so lacking in consistency. The clan cannot be defined by its chief, for if central authority is not lacking, it is at least uncertain and unstable.[1] Nor can it be defined by the territory it occupies, for the population, being nomad,[2] is not closely attached to any special locality. Also, owing to the exogamic law, husband and wife must be of different totems; so wherever the totem is transmitted in the maternal line—and this system of filiation is still the most general one [3]—the children are of a different clan from their father, though living near to him. Therefore we find representatives of a number of different clans in each family, and still more in each locality. The unity of the group is visible, therefore, only in the collective name borne by all the members, and in the equally collective emblem reproducing the object designated by this name. A clan is essentially a reunion of individuals who bear the same name and rally around the same sign. Take away the name and the sign which materializes it, and the clan is no longer representable. Since the group is possible only on this condition, both the institution of the emblem and the part it takes in the life of the group are thus explained.

It remains to ask why these names and emblems were taken almost exclusively from the animal and vegetable kingdoms, but especially from the former.

It seems probable to us that the emblem has played a more important part than the name. In any case, the written sign still holds a more central place in the life of the clan to-day than does the spoken sign. Now the basis of an emblematic image can be found only in something susceptible of being represented by a design. On the other hand, these things had to be those with which the men of the clan were the most immediately and habitually coming in contact. Animals fulfilled this condition to a pre-eminent degree. For these nations of hunters and fishers, the animal constituted an essential element of the economic environment. In this connection plants had only a secondary place, for they can hold only a secondary place

[1] For the authority of the chiefs, see Spencer and Gillen, *Nat. Tr.*, p. 10; *Nor. Tr.*, p. 25; Howitt, *Nat. Tr.*, pp. 295 ff.

[2] At least in Australia. In America, the population is more generally sedentary; but the American clan represents a relatively advanced form of organization.

[3] To make sure of this, it is sufficient to look at the chart arranged by Thomas, *Kinship and Marriage in Australia*, p. 40. To appreciate this chart properly, it should be remembered that the author has extended, for a reason unknown to us, the system of totemic filiation in the paternal line clear to the western coast of Australia, though we have almost no information about the tribes of this region, which is, moreover, largely a desert.

as food as long as they are not cultivated. Moreover, the animal is more closely associated with the life of men than the plant is, if only because of the natural kinship uniting these two to each other. On the other hand, the sun, moon and stars are too far away, they give the effect of belonging to another world.[1] Also, as long as the constellations were not distinguished and classified, the starry vault did not offer a sufficient diversity of clearly differentiated things to be able to mark all the clans and sub-clans of a tribe ; but, on the contrary, the variety of the flora, and especially of the fauna, was almost inexhaustible. Therefore celestial bodies, in spite of their brilliancy and the sharp impression they make upon the senses, were unfitted for the rôle of totems, while animals and plants seemed predestined to it.

An observation of Strehlow even allows us to state precisely the way in which these emblems were probably chosen. He says that he has noticed that the totemic centres are generally situated near a mountain, spring or gorge where the animals serving as totems to the group gather in abundance, and he cites a certain number of examples of this fact.[2] Now these totemic centres are surely the consecrated places where the meetings of the clan are held. So it seems as though each group had taken as its insignia the animal or plant that was the commonest in the vicinity of the place where it had the habit of meeting.[3]

VI

This conception of totemism will give us the explanation of a very curious trait of human mentality which, even though more marked formerly than to-day, has not yet disappeared and which, in any case, has been of considerable importance in the history of human thought. It will furnish still another occasion for showing how logical evolution is closely connected with religious evolution and how it, like this latter, depends upon social conditions.[4]

[1] The stars are often regarded, even by the Australians, as the land of souls and mythical personages, as will be established in the next chapter : that means that they pass as being a very different world from that of the living.

[2] *Op. cit.*, I, p. 4. Cf. Schulze, *loc. cit.*, p. 243.

[3] Of course it is to be understood that, as we have already pointed out (see above, p. 155), this choice was not made without a more or less formal agreement between the groups that each should take a different emblem from its neighbours.

[4] The mental state studied in this paragraph is identical to the one called by Lévy-Bruhl the law of participation (*Les fonctions mentales dans les sociétés inférieures*, pp. 76 ff.). The following pages were written when this work appeared and we publish them without change ; we confine ourselves to adding certain explanations showing in what we differ from M. Lévy-Bruhl in our understanding of the facts.

If there is one truth which appears to be absolutely certain to-day, it is that beings differing not only in their outward appearance but also in their most essential properties, such as minerals, plants, animals and men, cannot be considered equivalent and interchangeable. Long usage, which scientific culture has still more firmly embedded in our minds, has taught us to establish barriers between the kingdoms, whose existence transformism itself does not deny; for though this admits that life may have arisen from non-living matter and men from animals, still, it does not fail to recognize the fact that living beings, once formed, are different from minerals, and men different from animals. Within each kingdom the same barriers separate the different classes: we cannot conceive of one mineral having the same distinctive characteristics as another, or of one animal species having those of another species. But these distinctions, which seem so natural to us, are in no way primitive. In the beginning, all the kingdoms are confounded with each other. Rocks have a sex; they have the power of begetting; the sun, moon and stars are men or women who feel and express human sentiments, while men, on the contrary, are thought of as animals or plants. This state of confusion is found at the basis of all mythologies. Hence comes the ambiguous character of the beings portrayed in the mythologies; they can be classified in no definite group, for they participate at the same time in the most opposed groups. It is also readily admitted that they can go from one into another; and for a long time men believed that they were able to explain the origin of things by these transmutations.

That the anthropomorphic instinct, with which the animists have endowed primitive men, cannot explain their mental condition is shown by the nature of the confusions of which they are guilty. In fact, these do not come from the fact that men have immoderately extended the human kingdom to the point of making all the others enter into it, but from the fact that they confound the most disparate kingdoms. They have not conceived the world in their own image any more than they have conceived themselves in the world's image: they have done both at the same time. Into the idea they have formed of things, they have undoubtedly made human elements enter; but into the idea they have formed of themselves, they have made enter elements coming from things.

Yet there is nothing in experience which could suggest these connections and confusions. As far as the observation of the senses is able to go, everything is different and disconnected. Nowhere do we really see beings mixing their natures and metamorphosing themselves into each other. It is therefore necessary that some exceptionally powerful cause should have intervened to transfigure reality in such a way as to make it appear under an aspect that is not really its own.

It is religion that was the agent of this transfiguration ; it is religious beliefs that have substituted for the world, as it is perceived by the senses, another different one. This is well shown by the case of totemism. The fundamental thing in this religion is that the men of the clan and the different beings whose form the totemic emblems reproduce pass as being made of the same essence. Now when this belief was once admitted, the bridge between the different kingdoms was already built. The man was represented as a sort of animal or plant ; the plants and animals were thought of as the relatives of men, or rather, all these beings, so different for the senses, were thought of as participating in a single nature. So this remarkable aptitude for confusing things that seem to be obviously distinct comes from the fact that the first forces with which the human intellect has peopled the world were elaborated by religion. Since these were made up of elements taken from the different kingdoms, men conceived a principle common to the most heterogeneous things, which thus became endowed with a sole and single essence.

But we also know that these religious conceptions are the result of determined social causes. Since the clan cannot exist without a name and an emblem, and since this emblem is always before the eyes of men, it is upon this, and the objects whose image it is, that the sentiments which society arouses in its members are fixed. Men were thus compelled to represent the collective force, whose action they felt, in the form of the thing serving as flag to the group. Therefore, in the idea of this force were mixed up the most different kingdoms ; in one sense, it was essentially human, since it was made up of human ideas and sentiments ; but at the same time, it could not fail to appear as closely related to the animate or inanimate beings who gave it its outward form. Moreover, the cause whose action we observe here is not peculiar to totemism ; there is no society where it is not active. In a general way, a collective sentiment can become conscious of itself only by being fixed upon some material object ;[1] but by this very fact, it participates in the nature of this object, and reciprocally, the object participates in its nature. So it was social necessity which brought about the fusion of notions appearing distinct at first, and social life has facilitated this fusion by the great mental effervescences it

[1] See above, p. 230.

determines.[1] This is one more proof that logical understanding is a function of society, for it takes the forms and attitudes that this latter presses upon it.

It is true that this logic is disconcerting for us. Yet we must be careful not to depreciate it : howsoever crude it may appear to us, it has been an aid of the greatest importance in the intellectual evolution of humanity. In fact, it is through it that the first explanation of the world has been made possible. Of course the mental habits it implies prevented men from seeing reality as their senses show it to them ; but as they show it, it has the grave inconvenience of allowing of no explanation. For to explain is to attach things to each other and to establish relations between them which make them appear to us as functions of each other and as vibrating sympathetically according to an internal law founded in their nature. But sensations, which see nothing except from the outside, could never make them disclose these relations and internal bonds ; the intellect alone can create the notion of them. When I learn that A regularly precedes B, my knowledge is increased by a new fact ; but my intelligence is not at all satisfied with a statement which does not show its reason. I commence to *understand* only if it is possible for me to conceive B in a way that makes it appear to me as something that is not foreign to A, and as united to A by some relation of kinship. The great service that religions have rendered to thought is that they have constructed a first representation of what these relations of kinship between things may be. In the circumstances under which it was attempted, the enterprise could obviously attain only precarious results. But then, does it ever attain any that are definite, and is it not always necessary to reconsider them ? And also, it is less important to succeed than to try. The essential thing was not to leave the mind enslaved to visible appearances, but to teach it to dominate them and to connect what the senses separated ; for from the moment when men have an idea that there are internal connections between things, science and philosophy become possible. Religion opened up the way for them. But if it has been able to play this part, it is only because it is a social affair. In order to make a law for the impressions of the senses and to substitute a new way of representing reality for them,

[1] Another cause has contributed much to this fusion ; this is the extreme contagiousness of religious forces. They seize upon every object within their reach, whatever it may be. Thus a single religious force may animate the most diverse things which, by that very fact, become closely connected and classified within a single group. We shall return again to this contagiousness, when we shall show that it comes from the social origins of the idea of sacredness (Bk. III, ch. i, *in fine*).

thought of a new sort had to be founded: this is collective thought. If this alone has had this efficacy, it is because of the fact that to create a world of ideals through which the world of experienced realities would appear transfigured, a super-excitation of the intellectual forces was necessary, which is possible only in and through society.

So it is far from true that this mentality has no connection with ours. Our logic was born of this logic. The explanations of contemporary science are surer of being objective because they are more methodical and because they rest on more carefully controlled observations, but they do not differ in nature from those which satisfy primitive thought. To-day, as formerly, to explain is to show how one thing participates in one or several others. It has been said that the participations of this sort implied by the mythologies violate the principle of contradiction and that they are by that opposed to those implied by scientific explanations.[1] Is not the statement that a man is a kangaroo or the sun a bird, equal to identifying the two with each other? But our manner of thought is not different when we say of heat that it is a movement, or of light that it is a vibration of the ether, etc. Every time that we unite heterogeneous terms by an internal bond, we forcibly identify contraries. Of course the terms we unite are not those which the Australian brings together; we choose them according to different criteria and for different reasons; but the processes by which the mind puts them in connection do not differ essentially.

It is true that if primitive thought had that sort of general and systematic indifference to contradictions which has been attributed to it,[2] it would be in open contradiction on this point with modern thought, which is always careful to remain consistent with itself. But we do not believe that it is possible to characterize the mentality of inferior societies by a single and exclusive inclination for indistinction. If the primitive confounds things which we distinguish, he also distinguishes things which we connect together, and he even conceives these distinctions in the form of sharp and clear-cut oppositions. Between two things which are classified in two different phratries, there is not only separation, but even antagonism.[3] For this reason, the same Australian who confounds the sun and the white cockatoo, opposes this latter to the black cockatoo as to its contrary. The two seem to him to belong to two separate classes between which there is nothing in common. A still more marked opposition is that existing between sacred things

[1] Lévy-Bruhl, *op. cit.*, pp. 77 ff. [2] *Ibid.*, p. 79.
[3] See above, p. 146.

and profane things. They repel and contradict each other with so much force that the mind refuses to think of them at the same time. They mutually expel each other from the consciousness.

Thus between the logic of religious thought and that of scientific thought there is no abyss. The two are made up of the same elements, though inequally and differently developed. The special characteristic of the former seems to be its natural taste for immoderate confusions as well as sharp contrasts. It is voluntarily excessive in each direction. When it connects, it confounds; when it distinguishes, it opposes. It knows no shades and measures, it seeks extremes; it consequently employs logical mechanisms with a certain awkwardness, but it ignores none of them.

CHAPTER VIII

THE IDEA OF THE SOUL

IN the preceding chapters we have been studying the fundamental principles of the totemic religion. We have seen that no idea of soul or spirit or mythical personality is to be found among these. Yet, even if the idea of spiritual beings is not at the foundation of totemism or, consequently, of religious thought in general, still, there is no religion where this notion is not met with. So it is important to see how it is formed. To make sure that it is the product of a secondary formation, we must discover the way in which it is derived from the more essential conceptions which we have just described and explained.

Among the various spiritual beings, there is one which should receive our attention first of all because it is the prototype after which the others have been constructed: this is the soul.

I

Just as there is no known society without a religion, so there exist none, howsoever crudely organized they may be, where we do not find a whole system of collective representations concerning the soul, its origin and its destiny. So far as we are able to judge from the data of ethnology, the idea of the soul seems to have been contemporaneous with humanity itself, and it seems to have had all of its essential characteristics so well formulated at the very outset that the work of the more advanced religions and philosophy has been practically confined to refining it, while adding nothing that is really fundamental. In fact, all the Australian societies admit that every human body shelters an interior being, the principle of the life which animates it: this is the soul. It sometimes happens, it is true, that women form an exception to this general rule: there are tribes where they are believed to have no souls.[1] If Dawson is to be believed, it is the same with young children in the

[1] This is the case with the Gnanji; see *Nor. Tr.*, pp. 170, 546; cf. a similar case in Brough Smyth, II, p. 269.

tribes that he has observed.[1] But these are exceptional and probably late cases ; [2] the last one even seems to be suspect and may well be due to an erroneous interpretation of the facts.[3]

It is not easy to determine the idea which the Australian makes of the soul, because it is so obscure and floating ; but we should not be surprised at this. If someone asked our own contemporaries, or even those of them who believe most firmly in the existence of the soul, how they represented it, the replies that he would receive would not have much more coherence and precision. This is because we are dealing with a very complex notion, into which a multitude of badly analysed impressions enter, whose elaboration has been carried on for centuries, though men have had no clear consciousness of it. Yet from this come the most essential, though frequently contradictory, characteristics by which it is defined.

In some cases they tell us that it has the external appearance of the body.[4] But sometimes it is also represented as having the size of a grain of sand ; its dimensions are so reduced that it can pass through the smallest crevices or the finest tissues.[5] We shall also see that it is represented in the appearance of animals. This shows that its form is essentially inconsistent and undetermined ; [6] it varies from one moment to another with the demands of circumstances or according to the exigencies of the myth and the rite. The substance out of which it is made is no less indefinable. It is not without matter, for it has a form, howsoever vague this may be. And in fact, even during this life, it has physical needs : it eats, and inversely, it may be eaten. Sometimes it leaves the body, and in the course of its

[1] *Australian Aborigines*, p. 51.

[2] There certainly was a time when the Gnanji women had souls, for a large number of women's souls still exist to-day. However, they never reincarnate themselves ; since in this tribe the soul animating a new-born child is an old reincarnated soul, it follows from the fact that women's souls do not reincarnate themselves, that women cannot have a soul. Moreover, it is possible to explain whence this absence of reincarnation comes. Filiation among the Gnanji, after having been uterine, is now in the paternal line : a mother no longer transmits her totem to her child. So the woman no longer has any descendants to perpetuate her ; she is the *finis familiæ suæ*. To explain this situation, there are only two possible hypotheses ; either women have no souls, or else they are destroyed after death. The Gnanji have adopted the former of these two explanations ; certain peoples of Queensland have preferred the latter (see Roth, *Superstition, Magic and Medicine*, in *N. Queensland Ethnog.*, No. 5, § 68).

[3] " The children below four or five years of age have neither soul nor future life," says Dawson. But the fact he thus relates is merely the absence of funeral rites for young children. We shall see the real meaning of this below.

[4] Dawson, p. 51 ; Parker, *The Euahlayi*, p. 35 ; Eylmann, p. 188.

[5] *Nor. Tr.*, p. 542 ; Schürmann, *The Aboriginal Tribes of Port Lincoln*, in Woods, p. 235.

[6] This is the expression used by Dawson, p. 50.

travels it occasionally nourishes itself on foreign souls.[1] After it has once been completely freed from the organism, it is thought to lead a life absolutely analogous to the one it led in this world; it eats, drinks, hunts, etc.[2] When it flutters among the branches of trees, it causes rustlings and crackings which even profane ears hear.[3] But at the same time, it is believed to be invisible to the vulgar.[4] It is true that magicians or old men have the faculty of seeing souls; but it is in virtue of special powers which they owe either to age or to a special training that they perceive things which escape our senses. According to Dawson, ordinary individuals enjoy the same privilege at only one moment of their existence: when they are on the eve of a premature death. Therefore this quasi-miraculous vision is considered a sinister omen. Now, invisibility is generally considered one of the signs of spirituality. So the soul is conceived as being immaterial to a certain degree, for it does not affect the senses in the way bodies do: it has no bones, as the tribes of the Tully River say.[5] In order to conciliate all these opposed characteristics, they represent it as made of some infinitely rare and subtle matter, like something ethereal,[6] and comparable to a shadow or breath.[7]

It is distinct and independent of the body, for during this life it can leave it at any moment. It does leave it during sleep, fainting spells, etc.[8] It may even remain absent for some time without entailing death; however, during these absences life is weakened and even stops if the soul does not return home.[9] But it is especially at death that this distinction and independence manifest themselves with the greatest clarity. While the body no longer exists and no visible traces of it remain, the soul continues to live: it leads an autonomous existence in another world.

But howsoever real this duality may be, it is in no way absolute. It would show a grave misunderstanding to represent the body

[1] Strehlow, I, p. 15, n. 1; Schulze, *loc. cit.*, p. 246; this is the theme of the myth of the vampire.

[2] Strehlow, I, p. 15; Schulze, p. 244; Dawson, p. 51. It is true that it is sometimes said that souls have nothing corporeal; according to certain testimony collected by Eylmann (p. 188), they are *ohne Fleisch und Blut*. But these radical negations leave us sceptical. The fact that offerings are not made to the souls of the dead in no way implies, as Roth thinks (*Superstition, Magic*, etc., § 65), that they do not eat.

[3] Roth, *ibid.*, § 65; *Nor. Tr.*, p. 530. It sometimes happens that the soul emits odours (Roth, *ibid.*, § 68).

[4] Roth, *ibid.*, § 67; Dawson, p. 51.

[5] Roth, *ibid.*, § 65.

[6] Schürmann, *Aborig. Tr. of Port Lincoln*, in Woods, p. 235.

[7] Parker, *The Euahlayi*, pp. 29, 35; Roth, *ibid.*, §§ 65, 67, 68.

[8] Roth, *ibid.*, § 65; Strehlow, I, p. 15.

[9] Strehlow, I, p. 14, n. 1.

as a sort of habitat in which the soul resides, but with which it has only external relations. Quite on the contrary, it is united to it by the closest bonds; it is separable from it only imperfectly and with difficulty. We have already seen that it has, or at least is able to have, its external aspect. Consequently, everything that hurts the one hurts the other; every wound of the body spreads to the soul.[1] It is so intimately associated with the life of the organism that it grows with it and decays with it. This is why a man who has attained a certain age enjoys privileges refused to young men; it is because the religious principle within him has acquired greater force and efficacy as he has advanced in life. But when senility sets in, and the old man is no longer able to take a useful part in the great religious ceremonies in which the vital interests of the tribe are concerned, this respect is no longer accorded to him. It is thought that weakness of the body is communicated to the soul. Having the same powers no longer, he no longer has a right to the same prestige.[2]

There is not only a close union of soul and body, but there is also a partial confusion of the two. Just as there is something of the body in the soul, since it sometimes reproduces its form, so there is something of the soul in the body. Certain regions and certain products of the organism are believed to have a special affinity with it: such is the case with the heart, the breath, the placenta,[3] the blood,[4] the shadow,[5] the liver, the fat of the liver, the kidneys,[6] etc. These various material substrata are not mere habitations of the soul; they are the soul itself seen from without. When blood flows, the soul escapes with it. The soul is not in the breath; it is the breath. It and the part of the body where it resides are only one. Hence comes the conception according to which a man has a number of souls. Being dispersed in various parts of the organism, the soul is differentiated and broken up into fragments. Each organ has individualized, as it were, the portion of the soul which it contains, and which has thus become a distinct entity. The soul of

[1] Frazer, *On Certain Burial Customs, as Illustrative of the Primitive Theory of the Soul*, in *J.A.I.*, XV, p. 66.

[2] This is the case with the Kaitish and the Unmatjera; see *Nor. Tr.*, p. 506; and *Nat. Tr.*, p. 512.

[3] Roth, *ibid.*, §§ 65, 66, 67, 68.

[4] Roth, *ibid.*, § 68; this says that when someone faints after a loss of blood, it is because the soul is gone. Cf. Parker, *The Euahlayi*, p. 38.

[5] Parker, *The Euahlayi*, pp. 29, 35; Roth, *ibid.*, § 65.

[6] Strehlow, I, pp. 12, 14. In these passages he speaks of evil spirits which kill little children and eat their souls, livers and fat, or else their souls, livers and kidneys. The fact that the soul is thus put on the same plane as the different viscera and tissues and is made a food like them shows the close connection it has with them. Cf. Schulze, p. 245.

the heart could not be that of the breath or the shadow or the placenta. While they are all related, still they are to be distinguished, and even have different names.[1]

Moreover, even if the soul is localized especially in certain parts of the organism, it is not absent from the others. In varying degrees, it is diffused through the whole body, as is well shown by the funeral rites. After the last breath has been expired and the soul is believed to be gone, it seems as though it should profit by the liberty thus regained, to move about at will and to return as quickly as possible to its real home, which is elsewhere. Nevertheless, it remains near to the corpse; the bond uniting them has been loosened, but not broken. A whole series of special rites are necessary to induce it to depart definitely. It is invited to go by gestures and significant movements.[2] The way is laid open for it, and outlets are arranged so that it can go more easily.[3] This is because it has not left the body entirely; it was too closely united to it to break away all at once. Hence comes the very frequent rite of funeral anthropophagy; the flesh of the dead is eaten because it is thought to contain a sacred principle, which is really nothing more than the soul.[4] In order to drive it out definitely, the flesh is melted, either by submitting it to the heat of the sun,[5] or to that of an artificial fire.[6] The soul departs with the liquids which result. But even the dry bones still retain some part of it. Therefore they can be used as sacred objects or instruments of magic; [7] or if someone wishes to give complete liberty to the principle which they contain, he breaks these.[8]

But a moment does arrive when the final separation is accomplished; the liberated soul takes flight. But by nature it is so intimately associated with the body that this removal cannot take place without a profound change in its condition. So it takes a new name also.[9] Although keeping all the distinctive traits of the individual whom it animated, his humours and his good

[1] For example, among the peoples on the Pennefather River (Roth, *ibid.*, § 68), there is a name for the soul residing in the heart (*Ngai*), another for the one in the placenta (*Cho-i*), and a third for the one which is confounded with the breath (*Wanji*). Among the Euahlayi, there are three or even four souls (Parker, *The Euahlayi*, p. 35).

[2] See the description of the *Urpmilchima* rite among the Arunta (*Nat. Tr.*, pp. 503 ff.).

[3] Spencer and Gillen, *Nat. Tr.*, pp. 497 and 508.

[4] *Nor. Tr.*, pp. 547, 548.

[5] *Ibid.*, pp. 506, 527 ff.

[6] Meyer, *The Encounter Bay Tribe*, in Woods, p. 198.

[7] *Nor. Tr.*, pp. 551, 463; *Nat. Tr.*, p. 553.

[8] *Nor. Tr.*, p. 540.

[9] Among the Arunta and Loritja, for example (Strehlow, I, p. 15, n. 2; II, p. 77). During life, the soul is called *gumna*, and *ltana* after death. The *ltana* of Strehlow is identical with the *ulthana* of Spencer and Gillen (*Nat. Tr.*, pp. 514 ff.). The same is true of the tribes on the Bloomfield River (Roth, *Superstition*, etc., § 66).

and bad qualities,[1] still it has become a new being. From that moment a new existence commences for it.

It goes to the land of souls. This land is conceived differently by different tribes; sometimes different conceptions are found existing side by side in the same society. For some, it is situated under the earth, where each totemic group has its part. This is at the spot where the first ancestors, the founders of the clan, entered the ground at a certain time, and where they live since their death. In the subterranean world there is a geographical disposition of the dead corresponding to that of the living. There, the sun always shines and rivers flow which never run dry. Such is the conception which Spencer and Gillen attribute to the central tribes, Arunta,[2] Warramunga,[3] etc. It is found again among the Wotjobaluk.[4] In other places, all the dead, no matter what their totems may have been, are believed to live together in the same place, which is more or less vaguely localized as beyond the sea, in an island,[5] or on the shores of a lake.[6] Sometimes, finally, it is into the sky, beyond the clouds, that the souls are thought to go. "There," says Dawson, "there is a delectable land, abounding in kangaroos and game of every sort, where men lead a happy life. Souls meet again there and recognize one another."[7] It is probable that certain of the features of this picture have been taken from the paradise of the Christian missionaries;[8] but the idea that souls, or at least some souls, enter the skies after death appears to be quite indigenous; for it is found again in other parts of the continent.[9]

In general, all the souls meet the same fate and lead the same life. However, a different treatment is sometimes accorded them based on the way they have conducted themselves upon earth, and we can see the first outlines of these two distinct and even opposed compartments into which the world to come will later be divided. The souls of those who have excelled, during life, as hunters, warriors, dancers, etc., are not confounded

[1] Eylmann, p. 188.

[2] *Nat. Tr.*, pp. 524, 491, 496.

[3] *Nor. Tr.*, pp. 542, 504.

[4] Mathews, *Ethnol. Notes on the Aboriginal Tribes of N.S. Wales and Victoria*, in *Journal and Proc. of the Roy. Soc. of N.S. Wales*, XXXVIII, p. 287.

[5] Strehlow, I, pp. 15 ff. Thus, according to Strehlow, the dead live in an island in the Arunta theory, but according to Spencer and Gillen, in a subterranean place. It is probable that the two myths coexist and are not the only ones. We shall see that even a third has been found. On this conception of an island of the dead, see Howitt, *Nat. Tr.*, p. 498; Schürmann, *Aborig. Tr. of Port Lincoln*, in Woods, p. 235; Eylmann, p. 189.

[6] Schulze, p. 244.

[7] Dawson, p. 51.

[8] In these same tribes evident traces of a more ancient myth will be found, according to which the dead live in a subterranean place (Dawson, *ibid.*).

[9] Taplin, *The Narrinyeri*, pp. 18 f.; Howitt, *Nat. Tr.*, p. 473; Strehlow, I, p. 16.

with the common horde of the others ; a special place is granted to them.[1] Sometimes, this is the sky.[2] Strehlow even says that according to one myth, the souls of the wicked are devoured by dreadful spirits, and destroyed.[3] Nevertheless, these conceptions always remain very vague in Australia ; [4] they begin to have a clarity and determination only in the more advanced societies, such as those of America.[5]

II

Such are the beliefs relative to the soul and its destiny, in their most primitive form, and reduced to their most essential traits. We must now attempt to explain them. What is it that has been able to lead men into thinking that there are two beings in them, one of which possesses these very special characteristics which we have just enumerated ? To find the reply to this question, let us begin by seeking the origin attributed to this spiritual principle by the primitive himself : if it is well analysed, his own conception will put us on the way towards the solution.

Following out the method which we have set before ourselves, we shall study these ideas in a determined group of societies where they have been observed with an especial precision ; these are the tribes of Central Australia. Though not narrow, the area of our observations will be limited. But there is good reason for believing that these same ideas are quite generally held, in various forms, even outside of Australia. It is also to be noted that the idea of the soul, as it is found among these central tribes, does not differ specifically from the one found in other tribes ; it has the same essential characteristics everywhere. As one effect always has the same cause, we may well think that this idea, which is everywhere the same, does not result from one cause here and another there. So the origin which we shall be led to attribute to it as a result of our study of these particular tribes with which we are going to deal, ought to be equally true for the others. These tribes will give us a chance to make an experiment, as it were, whose results, like those of every well-made experiment, are susceptible of generalization. The homogeneity of the Australian civilization would of itself

[1] Howitt, *Nat. Tr.*, p. 498.

[2] Strehlow, I, p. 16 ; Eylmann, p. 189 ; Howitt, *Nat. Tr.*, p. 473.

[3] These ar[illegible] the spirits of the ancestors of a special clan, the clan of a certain poisonous gland (*Giftdrüsenmänner*).

[4] Sometimes the work of the missionaries is evident. Dawson speaks of a real hell opposed to paradise ; but he too tends to regard this as a European importation.

[5] Dorsey, *XIth Rep.*, pp. 419–420, 422, 485. Cf. Marillier, *La survivance de l'âme et l'idée de justice chez les peuples non-civilisés, Rapport de l'École des Hautes Études*, 1893.

be enough to justify this generalization ; but we shall be careful to verify it afterwards with facts taken from other peoples, both in Australia and America.

As the conceptions which are going to furnish us with the basis of our demonstration have been reported in different terms by Spencer and Gillen on the one hand and Strehlow on the other, we must give these two versions one after the other. We shall see that when they are well understood, they differ in form more than in matter, and that they both have the same sociological significance.

According to Spencer and Gillen, the souls which, in each generation, come to animate the bodies of newly-born children, are not special and original creations ; all these tribes hold that there is a definite stock of souls, whose number cannot be augmented at all,[1] and which reincarnate themselves periodically. When an individual dies, his soul quits the body in which it dwelt, and after the mourning is accomplished, it goes to the land of the souls ; but after a certain length of time, it returns to incarnate itself again, and these reincarnations are the cause of conception and birth. At the beginning of things, it was these fundamental souls which animated the first ancestors, the founders of the clan. At an epoch, beyond which the imagination does not go and which is considered the very beginning of time, there were certain beings who were not derived from any others. For this reason, the Arunta call them the *Altjirangamitjina*,[2] the uncreated ones, those who exist from all eternity, and, according to Spencer and Gillen, they give the name *Alcheringa* [3] to the period when these fabulous beings are thought to have lived. Being organized in totemic clans just as the men of to-day are, they passed their time in travels, in the course of which they accomplished all sorts of prodigious actions, the memory of which is preserved in the myths. But a moment arrived when this terrestrial life came to a close ; singly or in groups, they entered into the earth. But their souls live for ever ; they are immortal. They even continue to frequent the places where the existence of their former hosts came to an end. Moreover, owing to the memories attached to them, these places have a sacred character ; it is here that the oknanikilla are located, the sorts of sanctuaries where the churinga of the clan is kept, and the centres of the different totemic cults. When one of the souls which wander about these sanctuaries enters into the body of a woman, the result is a conception and

[1] They may be doubled temporarily, as we shall see in the next chapter : but these duplications add nothing to the number of the souls capable of reincarnation.

[2] Strehlow, I, p. 2.

[3] *Nat. Tr.*, p. 73, n. 1

later a birth.[1] So each individual is considered as a new appearance of a determined ancestor: it is this ancestor himself, come back in a new body and with new features. Now, what were these ancestors?

In the first place, they were endowed with powers infinitely superior to those possessed by men to-day, even the most respected old men and the most celebrated magicians. They are attributed virtues which we may speak of as miraculous: "They could travel on, or above, or beneath the ground; by opening a vein in the arm, each of them could flood whole tracts of country or cause level plains to arise; in rocky ranges they could make pools of water spring into existence, or could make deep gorges and gaps through which to traverse the ranges, and where they planted their sacred poles (nurtunja), there rocks or trees arose to mark the spot."[2] It is they who gave the earth the form it has at present. They created all sorts of beings, both men and animals. They are nearly gods. So their souls also have a divine character. And since the souls of men are these ancestral souls reincarnated in the human body, these are sacred beings too.

In the second place, these ancestors were not men in the proper sense of the word, but animals or vegetables, or perhaps mixed beings in which the animal or vegetable element predominated: "In the Alcheringa," say Spencer and Gillen, "lived ancestors who, in the native mind, are so intimately associated with the animals or plants the name of which they bear that an Alcheringa man of, say, the kangaroo totem may sometimes be spoken of either as a man-kangaroo or a kangaroo-man. The identity of the human individual is often sunk in that of the animal or plant from which he is supposed to have originated."[3] Their immortal souls necessarily have the same nature; in them, also, the human element is wedded to the animal element, with a certain tendency for the latter to predominate over the former. So they are made of the same substance as the totemic principle, for we know that the special characteristic of this is to present this double nature, and to synthesize and confound the two realms in itself.

Since no other souls than these exist, we reach the conclusion that, in a general way, the soul is nothing other than the totemic principle incarnate in each individual. And there is nothing to

[1] On this set of conceptions, see *Nat. Tr.*, pp. 119, 123–127, 387 ff.; *Nor. Tr.*, pp. 145–174. Among the Gnanji, it is not necessarily near the oknanikilla that the conception takes place. But they believe that each couple is accompanied in its wanderings over the continent by a swarm of souls of the husband's totem. When the time comes, one of these souls enters the body of the wife and fertilizes it, wherever she may be (*Nor. Tr.*, p. 169).

[2] *Nat. Tr.*, pp. 512 f.; cf. ch. x and xi.

[3] *Nat. Tr.*, p. 119.

surprise us in this derivation. We already know that this principle is immanent in each of the members of the clan. But in penetrating into these individuals, it must inevitably individualize itself. Because the consciousnesses, of which it becomes thus an integral part, differ from each other, it differentiates itself according to their image ; since each has its own physiognomy, it takes a distinct physiognomy in each. Of course it remains something outside of and foreign to the man, but the portion of it which each is believed to possess cannot fail to contract close affinities with the particular subject in which it resides ; it becomes his to a certain extent. Thus it has two contradictory characteristics, but whose coexistence is one of the distinctive features of the notion of the soul. To-day, as formerly, the soul is what is best and most profound in ourselves, and the pre-eminent part of our being ; yet it is also a passing guest which comes from the outside, which leads in us an existence distinct from that of the body, and which should one day regain its entire independence. In a word, just as society exists only in and through individuals, the totemic principle exists only in and through the individual consciousnesses whose association forms the clan. If they did not feel it in them it would not exist ; it is they who put it into things. So it must of necessity be divided and distributed among them. Each of these fragments is a soul.

A myth which is found in a rather large number of the societies of the centre, and which, moreover, is only a particular form of the preceding ones, shows even better that this is really the matter out of which the idea of the soul is made. In these tribes, tradition puts the origin of each clan, not in a number of ancestors, but in only two,[1] or even in one.[2] This unique being, as long as he remained single, contained the totemic principle within him integrally, for at this moment there was nothing to which this principle could be communicated. Now, according to this same tradition, all the human souls which exist, both those which now animate the bodies of men and those which are at present unemployed, being held in reserve for the future, have issued from this unique personage ; they are made of his substance. While travelling over the surface of the ground, or moving about, or shaking himself, he made them leave his body and planted them in the various places he is believed to have passed over. Is this not merely a symbolic way of saying that they are parts of the totemic divinity ?

[1] Among the Kaitish (*Nor. Tr.*, p. 154) and the Urabunna (*Nor. Tr.*, p. 146).

[2] This is the case among the Warramunga and the related tribes, the Walpari, Wulmala, Worgaia, Tjingilli (*Nor. Tr.*, p. 161), and also the Umbaia and the Gnanji (*ibid.*, p. 170).

But this conclusion presupposes that the tribes of which we have just been speaking admit the doctrine of reincarnation. Now according to Strehlow, this doctrine is unknown to the Arunta, the society which Spencer and Gillen have studied the longest and the best. If, in this particular case, these two observers have misunderstood things to such an extent, their whole testimony would become suspect. So it is important to determine the actual extent of this divergence.

According to Strehlow, after the soul has once been definitely freed from the body by the rites of mourning, it never reincarnates itself again. It goes off to the isles of the dead, where it passes its days in sleeping and its nights in dancing, until it returns again to earth. Then it comes back into the midst of the living and plays the rôle of protecting genius to the young sons, or if such are lacking, to the grandsons whom the dead man left behind him ; it enters their body and aids their growth. It remains thus in the midst of its former family for a year or two, after which it goes back to the land of the souls. But after a certain length of time it goes away once more to make another sojourn upon earth, which is to be the last. A time will come when it must take up again, and with no hope of return this time, the route to the isles of the dead ; then, after various incidents, the details of which it is useless to relate, a storm will overtake it, in the course of which it will be struck by a flash of lightning. Thus its career is definitely terminated.[1]

So it cannot reincarnate itself ; nor can conceptions and births be due to the reincarnation of souls which periodically commence new existences in new bodies. It is true that Strehlow, as Spencer and Gillen, declares that for the Arunta commerce of the sexes is in no way the determining condition of generation,[2] which is considered the result of mystic operations, but different from the ones which the other observers told us about. It takes place in one or the other of the two following ways :

Wherever an ancestor of the Alcheringa[3] times is believed to have entered into the ground, there is either a stone or a tree representing his body. The tree or rock which has this mystic relation with the departed hero is called *nanja* according to

[1] Strehlow, I, pp. 15–16. For the Loritja, see Strehlow, p. 7.

[2] Strehlow even goes so far as to say that sexual relations are not even thought to be a necessary condition or sort of preparation for conception (II, p. 52, n. 7). It is true that he adds a few lines below that the old men know perfectly well the connection which unites sexual intercourse and generation, and that as far as animals are concerned, the children themselves know it. This lessens the value of his first assertion a little.

[3] In general, we employ the terminology of Spencer and Gillen rather than that of Strehlow because it is now consecrated by long usage.

Spencer and Gillen,[1] or *ngarra* according to Strehlow.[2] Sometimes it is a water-hole which is believed to have been formed in this way. Now, on each of these trees or rocks and in each of these water-holes, there live embryo children, called *ratapa*,[3] which belong to exactly the same totem as the corresponding ancestor. For example, on a gum-tree representing an ancestor of the kangaroo totem there are ratapa, all of which have the kangaroo as their totem. If a woman happens to pass it, and she is of the matrimonial class to which the mothers of these ratapa should belong,[4] one of them may enter her through the hip. The woman learns of this act by the characteristic pains which are the first symptoms of pregnancy. The child thus conceived will of course belong to the same totem as the ancestor upon whose mystical body he resided before becoming incarnate.[5]

In other cases, the process employed is slightly different: the ancestor himself acts in person. At a given moment he leaves his subterranean retreat and throws on to the passing woman a little churinga of a special form, called *namatuna*.[6] The churinga enters the body of the woman and takes a human form there, while the ancestor disappears again into the earth.[7]

These two ways of conception are believed to be equally frequent. The features of the child will reveal the manner in which he was conceived; according to whether his face is broad or long, they say that he is the incarnation of a ratapa or a namatuna. Beside these two means of fecundation, Strehlow places a third, which, however, is much more rare. After his namatuna has penetrated into the body of the woman, the ancestor himself enters her and voluntarily submits to a new birth. So in this case, the conception is due to a real reincarnation of the ancestor. But this is very exceptional, and when a man who

[1] *Nat. Tr.*, pp. 124, 513.

[2] I, p. 5. *Ngarra* means eternal, according to Strehlow. Among the Loritja, only rocks fulfil this function.

[3] Strehlow translates it by *Kinderkeime* (children-germs). It is not true that Spencer and Gillen have ignored the myth of the *ratapa* and the customs connected with it. They explicitly mention it in *Nat. Tr.*, pp. 336 ff. and 552. They noticed, at different points of the Arunta territory, the existence of rocks called *Erathipa* from which the *spirit children*, or the children's souls, disengage themselves, to enter the bodies of women and fertilize them. According to Spencer and Gillen, *Erathipa* means child, though, as they add, it is rarely used in this sense in ordinary conversation (*ibid.*, p. 338).

[4] The Arunta are divided into four or eight matrimonial classes. The class of a child is determined by that of his father; inversely, that of the latter may be deduced from the former (see Spencer and Gillen, *Nat. Tr.*, pp. 70 ff.; Strehlow, I, pp. 6 ff.). It remains to be seen how the ratapa has a matrimonial class; we shall return to this point again.

[5] Strehlow, II, p. 52. It happens sometimes, though rarely, that disputes arise over the nature of the child's totem. Strehlow cites such a case (II, p. 53).

[6] This is the same word as the *namatwinna* found in Spencer and Gillen (*Nat. Tr.*, p. 541).

[7] Strehlow, II, p. 53.

has been conceived thus dies, the ancestral soul which animated him goes away, just like ordinary souls, to the isles of the dead where, after the usual delays, it is definitely annihilated. So it cannot undergo any further reincarnations.[1]

Such is the version of Strehlow.[2] In the opinion of this author it is radically opposed to that of Spencer and Gillen. But in reality it differs only in the letter of the formulæ and symbols, while in both cases we find the same mythical theme in slightly different forms.

In the first place, all the observers agree that every conception is the result of an incarnation. Only according to Strehlow, that which is incarnated is not a soul but a ratapa or a namatuna. But what is a ratapa? Strehlow says that it is a complete embryo, made up of a soul and a body. But the soul is always represented in material forms; it sleeps, dances, hunts, eats, etc. So it, too, has a corporal element. Inversely, the ratapa is invisible to ordinary men; no one sees it as it enters the body of the woman;[3] this is equivalent to saying that it is made of a matter quite similar to that of the soul. So it hardly seems possible to differentiate the two clearly in this regard. In reality, these are mythical beings which are obviously conceived after the same model. Schulze calls them the souls of children.[4] Moreover, the ratapa, just like the soul, sustains the closest relations with the ancestor of which the sacred tree or rock is the materialized form. It is of the same totem as this ancestor, of the same phratry and of the same matrimonial class.[5] Its place in the social organization of the tribe is the very one that its ancestor is believed to have held before it. It bears the same name,[6] which is a proof that these two personalities are at least very closely related to one another.

But there is more than this; this relationship even goes as far as a complete identification. In fact, it is on the mystic body of the ancestor that the ratapa is formed; it comes from this; it is like a detached portion of it. So it really is a part of the

[1] Strehlow, II, p. 56.

[2] Mathews attributes a similar theory of conception to the Tjingilli (*alias* Chingalee) (*Proc. Roy. Geogr. Trans. and Soc. Queensland*, XXII (1907), pp. 75–76).

[3] It sometimes happens that the ancestor who is believed to have thrown the namatuna shows himself to the woman in the form of an animal or a man; this is one more proof of the affinity of the ancestral soul for a material form.

[4] Schulze, *loc. cit.*, p. 237.

[5] This results from the fact that the ratapa can incarnate itself only in the body of a woman belonging to the same matrimonial class as the mother of the mythical ancestor. So we cannot understand how Strehlow could say (I, p. 42, *Anmerkung*) that, except in one case, the myths do not attribute determined matrimonial classes to the Alcheringa ancestors. His own theory of conception proves the contrary (cf. II, pp. 53 ff.).

[6] Strehlow, II, p. 58.

ancestor which penetrates into the womb of the mother and which becomes the child. Thus we get back to the conception of Spencer and Gillen : birth is due to the reincarnation of an ancestral personage. Of course it is not the entire person that is reincarnated, it is only an emanation from him. But this difference has only a secondary interest, for when a sacred being divides and duplicates itself, all of its essential characteristics are to be found again in each of the fragments into which it is broken up. So really the Alcheringa ancestor is entire in each part of himself which becomes a ratapa.[1]

The second mode of conception distinguished by Strehlow has the same significance. In fact, the churinga, and more especially the particular churinga that is called the namatuna, is considered a transformation of the ancestor ; according to Strehlow,[2] it is his body, just as the nanja tree is. In other words, the personality of the ancestor, his churinga and his nanja tree, are sacred things, inspiring the same sentiments and to which the same religious value is attributed. So they transmute themselves into one another : in the spot where an ancestor lost his churinga, a sacred tree or rock has come out of the soil, just the same as in those places where he entered the ground himself.[3] So there is a mythological equivalence of a person of the Alcheringa and his churinga ; consequently, when the former throws a namatuna into the body of a woman, it is as if he entered into it himself. In fact, we have seen that sometimes he does enter in person after the namatuna ; according to other stories he precedes it ; it might be said that he opens up the way for it.[4] The fact that these two themes exist side by side in the same myth completes the proof that one is only a doublet of the other.

Moreover, in whatever way the conception may have taken place, there can be no doubt that each individual is united to some determined ancestor of the Alcheringa by especially close

[1] The difference between the two versions becomes still smaller and is reduced to almost nothing, if we observe that, when Spencer and Gillen tell us that the ancestral soul is incarnated in the woman, the expressions they use are not to be taken literally. It is not the whole soul which comes to fertilize the mother, but only an emanation from this soul. In fact, according to their own statement, a soul equal or even superior in power to the one that is incarnated continues to live in the nanja tree or rock (see *Nat. Tr.*, p. 514) ; we shall have occasion to come back to this point again (cf. below, p. 275).

[2] II, pp. 76, 81. According to Spencer and Gillen, the churinga is not the soul of the ancestor, but the object in which his soul resides. At bottom, these two mythological interpretations are identical, and it is easy to see how one has been able to pass into the other : the body is the place where the soul resides.

[3] Strehlow, I, p. 4.

[4] Strehlow, I, pp. 53 f. In these stories, the ancestor begins by introducing himself into the body of the woman and causing there the troubles characteristic of pregnancy. Then he goes out, and only then does he leave his namatuna.

bonds. In the first place, each man has his appointed ancestor; two persons cannot have the same one simultaneously. In other words, a being of the Alcheringa never has more than one representative among the living.[1] More than that, the one is only an aspect of the other. In fact, as we already know, the churinga left by the ancestor expresses his personality; if we adopt the interpretation of Strehlow, which, perhaps, is the more satisfactory, we shall say that it is his body. But this same churinga is related in the same way to the individual who is believed to have been conceived under the influence of this ancestor, and who is the fruit of his mystic works. When the young initiate is introduced into the sanctuary of the clan, he is shown the churinga of his ancestor, and someone says to him, "You are this body; you are the same thing as this."[2] So, in Strehlow's own expression, the churinga is "the body common to the individual and his ancestor."[3] Now if they are to have the same body it is necessary that on one side at least their two personalities be confounded. Strehlow recognizes this explicitly, moreover, when he says, "By the tjurunga (churinga) the individual is united to his personal ancestor."[4]

So for Strehlow as well as for Spencer and Gillen, there is a mystic, religious principle in each new-born child, which emanates from an ancestor of the Alcheringa. It is this principle which forms the essence of each individual, therefore it is his soul, or in any case the soul is made of the same matter and the same substance. Now it is only upon this one fundamental fact that we have relied in determining the nature and origin of the idea of the soul. The different metaphors by means of which it may have been expressed have only a secondary interest for us.[5]

Far from contradicting the data upon which our theory rests, the recent observations of Strehlow bring new proofs confirming it. Our reasoning consisted in inferring the totemic nature of the human soul from the totemic nature of the ancestral

[1] Strehlow, II, p. 76.

[2] *Ibid.*, p. 81. This is the word for word translation of the terms employed, as Strehlow gives them: *Dies du Körper bist*; *dies du der nämliche*. In the myth, a civilizing hero, Mangarkunjerkunja, says as he presents to each man the churinga of his ancestor: "You are born of this churinga" (*ibid.*, p. 76).

[3] Strehlow, II, p. 76.

[4] Strehlow, *ibid.*

[5] At bottom, the only real difference between Strehlow and Spencer and Gillen is the following one. For these latter, the soul of the individual, after death, returns to the nanja tree, where it is again confounded with the ancestor's soul (*Nat. Tr.*, p. 513); for Strehlow, it goes to the isle of the dead, where it is finally annihilated. In neither myth does it survive individually. We are not going to seek the cause of this divergence. It is possible that there has been an error of observation on the part of Spencer and Gillen, who do not speak of the isle of the dead. It is also possible that the myth is not the same among the eastern Arunta, whom Spencer and Gillen observed particularly, as in the other parts of the tribe.

soul, of which the former is an emanation and a sort of replica. Now, some of the new facts which we owe to Strehlow show this character of both even more categorically than those we had at our disposal before do. In the first place, Strehlow, like Spencer and Gillen, insists on "the intimate relations uniting each ancestor to an animal, to a plant, or to some other natural object." Some of these Altjirangamitjina (these are Spencer and Gillen's men of the Alcheringa) "should," he says, "be manifested directly as animals; others take the animal form in a way."[1] Even now they are constantly transforming themselves into animals.[2] In any case, whatever external aspect they may have, "the special and distinctive qualities of the animal clearly appear in each of them." For example, the ancestors of the Kangaroo clan eat grass just like real kangaroos, and flee before the hunter; those of the Emu clan run and feed like emus,[3] etc. More than that, those ancestors who had a vegetable as totem become this vegetable itself on death.[4] Moreover, this close kinship of the ancestor and the totemic being is so keenly felt by the natives that it is shown even in their terminology. Among the Arunta, the child calls the totem of his mother, which serves him as a secondary totem,[5] *altjira*. As filiation was at first in the uterine line, there was once a time when each individual had no other totem than that of his mother; so it is very probable that the term *altjira* then designated the real totem. Now this clearly enters into the composition of the word which means great ancestor, *altjirangamitjina*.[6]

The idea of the totem and that of the ancestor are even so closely kindred that they sometimes seem to be confounded. Thus, after speaking of the totem of the mother, or *altjira*, Strehlow goes on to say, "This altjira appears to the natives in dreams and gives them warnings, just as it takes information concerning them to their sleeping friends."[7] This *altjira*, which speaks and which is attached to each individual personally, is evidently an ancestor; yet it is also an incarnation of the totem. A certain text in Roth, which speaks of invocations addressed to the totem, should certainly be interpreted in this sense.[8] So it appears that the totem is sometimes represented in the mind in the form of a group of ideal beings or mythical personages who are more or less indistinct from the ancestors. In a word, the ancestors are the fragments of the totem.[9]

[1] Strehlow, II, p. 51. [2] *Ibid.*, II, p. 56. [3] *Ibid.*, I, pp. 3–4.
[4] *Ibid.*, II, p. 61. [5] See above, p. 183. [6] Strehlow, II, p. 57; I, p. 2.
[7] Strehlow, II, p. 57. [8] Roth, *Superstition, Magic*, etc., § 74.
[9] In other words, the totemic species is made up of the group of ancestors and the mythological species much more than of the regular animal or vegetable species.

But if the ancestor is so readily confused with the totemic being, the individual soul, which is so near the ancestral soul, cannot do otherwise. Moreover, this is what actually results from the close union of each man with his churinga. In fact, we know that the churinga represents the personality of the individual who is believed to have been born of it;[1] but it also expresses the totemic animal. When the civilizing hero, Mangarkunjerkunja, presented each member of the Kangaroo clan with his personal totem, he spoke as follows: "Here is the body of a kangaroo."[2] Thus the churinga is at once the body of the ancestor, of the individual himself and of the totemic animal; so, according to a strong and very just expression of Strehlow, these three beings form a "solid unity."[3] They are almost equivalent and interchangeable terms. This is as much as to say that they are thought of as different aspects of one and the same reality, which is also defined by the distinctive attributes of the totem. Their common essence is the totemic principle. The language itself expresses this identity. The word ratapa, and the *aratapi* of the Loritja language, designate the mythical embryo which is detached from the ancestor and which becomes the child; now these same words also designate the totem of this same child, such as is determined by the spot where the mother believes that she conceived.[4]

III

Up to the present we have studied the doctrine of reincarnation only in the tribes of Central Australia; therefore the bases upon which our inference rests may be deemed too narrow. But in the first place, for the reasons which we have pointed out, the experiment holds good outside of the societies which we have observed directly. Also, there are abundant facts proving that the same or analogous conceptions are found in the most diverse parts of Australia or, at least, have left very evident traces there. They are found even in America.

Howitt mentions them among the Dieri of South Australia.[5] The word *Mura-mura*, which Gason translates with Good Spirit and which he thinks expresses a belief in a god creator,[6] is really a collective word designating the group of ancestors placed by the myth at the beginning of the tribe. They continue to exist

[1] See above, p. 254. [2] Strehlow, II, p. 76. [3] Strehlow, *ibid.*

[4] Strehlow, II, pp. 57, 60, 61. Strehlow calls the list of totems the list of ratapa.

[5] Howitt, *Nat. Tr.*, pp. 475 ff.

[6] *The Manners and Customs of the Dieyerie Tribe of Australian Aborigines*, in Curr, II, p. 47.

to-day as formerly. "They are believed to live in trees, which are sacred for this reason." Certain irregularities of the ground, rocks and springs are identified with these Mura-mura,[1] which consequently resemble the Altjirangamitjina of the Arunta in a singular way. The Kurnai of Gippsland, though retaining only vestiges of totemism, also believe in the existence of ancestors called *Muk-Kurnai,* and which they think of as beings intermediate between men and animals.[2] Among the Nimbaldi, Taplin has observed a theory of conception similar to that which Strehlow attributes to the Arunta.[3] We find this belief in reincarnation held integrally by the Wotjobaluk in Victoria. "The spirits of the dead," says Mathews, "assemble in the *miyur*[4] of their respective clans; they leave these to be born again in human form when a favourable occasion presents itself."[5] Mathews even affirms that "the belief in the reincarnation or transmigration of souls is strongly enrooted in all the Australian tribes."[6]

If we pass to the northern regions we find the pure doctrine of the Arunta among the Niol-Niol in the north-west; every birth is attributed to the incarnation of a pre-existing soul, which introduces itself into the body of a woman.[7] In northern Queensland myths, differing from the preceding only in form, express exactly the same ideas. Among the tribes on the Pennefather River it is believed that every man has two souls: the one, called *ngai,* resides in the heart; the other, called *choi,* remains in the placenta. Soon after birth the placenta is buried in a consecrated place. A particular genius, named Anje-a, who has charge of the phenomena of procreation, comes to get this *choi* and keeps it until the child, being grown up, is married When the time comes to give him a son, Anje-a takes a bit of the choi of this man, places it in the embryo he is making, and inserts it into the womb of the mother. So it is out of the soul of the father that that of the child is made. It is true that the child does not receive the paternal soul integrally at first, for the *ngai* remains in the heart of the father as long as he lives. But when he dies the *ngai,* being liberated, also incarnates itself in the bodies of the children; if there are several children it is divided equally among them. Thus there is a perfect spiritual

[1] Howitt, *Nat. Tr.*, p. 482. [2] *Ibid.*, p. 487.

[3] Taplin, *Folk-Lore, Customs, Manners, etc., of the South Australian Aborig.*, p. 88.

[4] The clan of each ancestor has its special camp underground; this camp is the miyur.

[5] Mathews, in *Jour. of Roy. Soc. of N.S. Wales*, XXXVIII, p. 293. He points out the same belief among other tribes of Victoria (*ibid.*, p. 197).

[6] Mathews, *ibid.*, p. 349.

[7] J. Bishop, *Die Niol-Niol*, in *Anthropos*, III, p. 35.

continuity between the generations ; it is the same soul which is transmitted from a father to his children and from these to their children, and this unique soul, always remaining itself in spite of its successive divisions and subdivisions, is the one which animated the first ancestor at the beginning of all things.[1] Between this theory and the one held by the central tribes there is only one difference of any importance ; this is that the reincarnation is not the work of the ancestors themselves but that of a special genius who takes charge of this function professionally. But it seems probable that this genius is the product of a syncretism which has fused the numerous figures of the first ancestors into one single being. This hypothesis is at least made probable by the fact that the words Anje-a and Anjir are evidently very closely related ; now the second designates the first man, the original ancestor from whom all men are descended.[2]

These same ideas are found again among the Indian tribes of America. Krauss says that among the Tlinkit, the souls of the departed are believed to come back to earth and introduce themselves into the bodies of the pregnant women of their families. " So when a woman dreams, during pregnancy, of some deceased relative, she believes that the soul of this latter has penetrated into her. If the young child has some characteristic mark which the dead man had before, they believe that it is the dead man himself come back to earth, and his name is given to the child." [3] This belief is also general among the Haida. It is the shaman who reveals which relative it was who reincarnated himself in the child and what name should consequently be given to him.[4] Among the Kwakiutl it is believed that the latest member of a family who died comes back to life in the person of the first child to be born in that family.[5] It is the same with the Hurons, the Iroquois, the Tinneh, and many other tribes of the United States.[6]

The universality of these conceptions extends, of course, to the conclusion which we have deduced from them, that is, to the explanation of the idea of the soul which we have proposed. Its general acceptability is also proved by the following facts.

[1] Roth, *Superstition*, etc., § 68 ; cf. § 69a, gives a similar case from among the natives on the Proserpine River. To simplify the description, we have left aside the complications due to differences of sex. The souls of daughters are made out of the choi of their mother, though these share with their brothers the ngai of their father. This peculiarity, coming perhaps from two systems of filiation which have been in use successively, has nothing to do with the principle of the perpetuity of the soul.

[2] *Ibid.*, p. 16. [3] *Die Tlinkit-Indianer*, p. 282.

[4] Swanton, *Contributions to the Ethnology of the Haida*, pp. 117 ff.

[5] Boas, *Sixth Rep. of the Comm. on the N.W. Tribes of Canada*, p. 59.

[6] Lafitau, *Mœurs des sauvages Amériquains*, II, p. 434 ; Petitot, *Monographie des Dénè-Dindjié*, p. 59.

We know [1] that each individual contains within him something of that anonymous force which is diffused in the sacred species; he is a member of this species himself. But as an empirical and visible being, he is not, for, in spite of the symbolic designs and marks with which he decorates his body, there is nothing in him to suggest the form of an animal or plant. So it must be that there is another being in him, in whom he recognizes himself, but whom he represents in the form of an animal or vegetable species. Now is it not evident that this double can only be the soul, since the soul is, of itself, already a double of the subject whom it animates? The justification of this identification is completed by the fact that the organs where the fragment of the totemic principle contained in each individual incarnates itself the most eminently are also those where the soul resides. This is the case with the blood. The blood contains something of the nature of the totem, as is proved by the part it takes in the totemic ceremonies.[2] But at the same time, the blood is one of the seats of the soul; or rather, it is the soul itself, seen from without. When blood flows, life runs out and, in the same process, the soul escapes. So the soul is confused with the sacred principle which is imminent in the blood.

Regarding matters from another point of view, if our explanation is well-founded, the totemic principle, in penetrating into the individual as we suppose, should retain a certain amount of autonomy there, since it is quite distinct from the subject in whom it is incarnated. Now this is just what Howitt claims to have observed among the Yuin: "That in this tribe the totem is thought to be in some way part of a man is clearly seen by the case of Umbara, before mentioned, who told me that, many years ago, someone of the Lace-lizard totem sent it while he was asleep, and that it went down his throat and almost ate his totem, which was in his breast, so that he nearly died." [3] So it is quite true that the totem is broken up in individualizing itself and that each of the bits thus detached plays the part of a spirit or soul residing in the body.[4]

But there are other more clearly demonstrative facts. If the soul is only the totemic principle individualized, it should have, in certain cases at least, rather close relations with the animal or vegetable species whose form is reproduced by the totem.

[1] See above, pp. 134 ff.

[2] See above, p. 137.

[3] Howitt, *Nat. Tr.*, p. 147; cf. *ibid.*, p. 769.

[4] Strehlow (I, p. 15, n. 2) and Schulze (*loc. cit.*, p. 246) speak of the soul, as Howitt here speaks of the totem, as leaving the body to go to eat another soul. Likewise, as we have seen above, the altjira or maternal totem shows itself in dreams, just as a soul or spirit does.

And, in fact, "the Geawe-Gal (a tribe of New South Wales) had a superstition that everyone had within himself an affinity to the spirit of some bird, beast or reptile. Not that he sprung from the creature in any way, but that the spirit which was in him was akin to that of the creature."[1]

There are even cases where the soul is believed to emanate directly from the animal or vegetable serving as totem. Among the Arunta, according to Strehlow, when a woman has eaten a great deal of fruit, it is believed that she will give birth to a child who will have this fruit as totem. If, at the moment when she felt the first tremblings of the child, she was looking at a kangaroo, it is believed that the ratapa of the kangaroo has entered her body and fertilized her.[2] H. Basedow reported the same fact from the Wogait.[3] We know, also, that the ratapa and the soul are almost indistinguishable things. Now, such an origin could never have been attributed to the soul if men did not think that it was made out of the same substances as the plants and animals of the totemic species.

Thus the soul is frequently represented in an animal form. It is known that in inferior societies, death is never considered a natural event, due to the action of purely physical causes; it is generally attributed to the evil workings of some sorcerer. In a large number of Australian societies, in order to determine who is the responsible author of this murder, they work on the principle that the soul of the murderer must inevitably come to visit its victim. Therefore, the body is placed upon a scaffolding; then, the ground under the corpse and all around it is carefully smoothed off so that the slightest mark becomes easily perceptible. They return the next day; if an animal has passed by there during the interval, its tracks are readily recognizable. Their form reveals the species to which it belongs, and from that, they infer the social group of which the guilty man is a member. They say that it is a man of such a class or such a clan,[4] according

[1] Fison and Howitt, *Kurnai and Kamilaroi*, p. 280.

[2] *Globus*, Vol. CXI, p. 289. In spite of the objections of Leonhardi, Strehlow maintains his affirmations on this point (see Strehlow, III, p. xi). Leonhardi finds a contradiction between this assertion and the theory according to which the ratapa emanate from trees, rocks or churinga. But the totemic animal incarnates the totem just as much as the nanja-tree or rock does, so they may fulfil the same function. The two things are mythological equivalents.

[3] *Notes on the West Coastal Tribes of the Northern Territory of S. Australia*, in *Trans. of the Roy. Soc. of S. Aust.*, XXXI (1907), p. 4. Cf. *Man*, 1909, No. 86.

[4] Among the Wakelbura, where, according to Curr and Howitt, each matrimonial class has its own totems, the animal shows the class (see Curr, III, p. 28); among the Buandik, it reveals the clan (Mrs. James S. Smith, *The Buandik Tribes of S. Australian Aborigines*, p, 128). Cf. Howitt, *On Some Australian Beliefs*, in *J.A.I.*, XIII, p. 191; XIV, p. 362; Thomas, *An American View of Totemism*, in *Man*, 1902, No. 85; Mathews, *Journ. of the Roy. Soc. of N.S. Wales*, XXXVIII, pp. 347–348; Brough Smyth, I, p. 110; *Nor. Tr.*, p. 513.

to whether the animal is the totem of this or that class or clan. So the soul is believed to have come in the form of the totemic animal.

In other societies where totemism has weakened or disappeared, the soul still continues to be thought of in an animal form. The natives of Cape Bedford (North Queensland) believe that the child, at the moment of entering the body of its mother, is a curlew if it is a girl, or a snake if it is a boy.[1] It is only later that it takes a human form. Many of the Indians of North America, says the Prince of Wied, say that they have an animal in their bodies.[2] The Bororo of Brazil represent the soul in the form of a bird, and therefore believe that they are birds of the same variety.[3] In other places, it is thought of as a snake, a lizard, a fly, a bee, etc.[4]

But it is especially after death that this animal nature of the soul is manifested. During life, this characteristic is partially veiled, as it were, by the very form of the human body. But when death has once set it free, it becomes itself again. Among the Omaha, in at least two of the Buffalo clans, it is believed that the souls of the dead go to rejoin the buffalo, their ancestors.[5] The Hopi are divided into a certain number of clans, whose ancestors were animals or beings with animal forms. Now Schoolcraft tells us that they say that at death, they take their original form again; each becomes a bear or deer, according to the clan to which he belongs.[6] Very frequently the soul is believed to reincarnate itself in the body of an animal.[7] It is probably from this that the widely-spread doctrine of metempsychosis was derived. We have already seen how hard pressed Tylor is to account for it.[8] If the soul is an essentially human

[1] Roth, *Superstition*, etc., § 83. This is probably a form of sexual totemism.

[2] Prinz zu Wied, *Reise in das innere Nord-Amerika*, II, p. 190.

[3] K. von den Steinen, *Unter den Naturvölkern Zentral-Bräsiliens*, 1894, pp. 511, 512.

[4] See Frazer, *Golden Bough*[2], I, pp. 250, 253, 256, 257, 258.

[5] *Third Rep.*, pp. 229, 233. [6] *Indian Tribes*, IV, p. 86.

[7] For example, among the Batta of Sumatra (see *Golden Bough*[2], III, p. 420), in Melanesia (Codrington, *The Melanesians*, p. 178), in the Malay Archipelago (Tylor, *Remarks on Totemism*, in *J.A.I.*, New Series, I, p. 147). It is to be remarked that the cases where the soul clearly presents itself after death in an animal form all come from the societies where totemism is more or less perverted. This is because the idea of the soul is necessarily ambiguous wherever the totemic beliefs are relatively pure, for totemism implies that it participate in the two kingdoms at the same time. So it cannot become either one or the other exclusively, but takes one aspect or the other, according to the circumstances. As totemism develops, this ambiguity becomes less necessary, while at the same time, spirits more actively demand attention. Then the marked affinities of the soul for the animal kingdom are manifested, especially after it is freed from the human body.

[8] See above, p. 170. On the generality of the doctrine of metempsychosis, see Tylor, II, pp. 8 ff.

principle, what could be more curious than this marked predilection which it shows, in so large a number of societies, for the animal form ? On the other hand, everything is explained if, by its very constitution, the soul is closely related to the animal, for in that case, when it returns to the animal world at the close of this life, it is only returning to its real nature. Thus the generality of the belief in metempsychosis is a new proof that the constituent elements of the idea of the soul have been taken largely from the animal kingdom, as is presupposed by the theory which we have just set forth.

IV

Thus the notion of the soul is a particular application of the beliefs relative to sacred beings. This is the explanation of the religious character which this idea has had from the moment when it first appeared in history, and which it still retains to-day. In fact, the soul has always been considered a sacred thing ; on this ground, it is opposed to the body which is, in itself, profane. It is not merely distinguished from its material envelope as the inside from the outside ; it is not merely represented as made out of a more subtle and fluid matter ; but more than this, it inspires those sentiments which are everywhere reserved for that which is divine. If it is not made into a god, it is at least regarded as a spark of the divinity. This essential characteristic would be inexplicable if the idea of the soul were only a pre-scientific solution given to the problem of dreams ; for there is nothing in the dream to awaken religious emotions, so the cause by which these are explained could not have such a character. But if the soul is a part of the divine substance, it represents something not ourselves that is within us ; if it is made of the same mental matter as the sacred beings, it is natural that it should become the object of the same sentiments.

And the sacred character which men thus attribute to themselves is not the product of a pure illusion either ; like the notions of religious force and of divinity, the notion of the soul is not without a foundation in reality. It is perfectly true that we are made up of two distinct parts, which are opposed to one another as the sacred to the profane, and we may say that, in a certain sense, there is divinity in us. For society, this unique source of all that is sacred, does not limit itself to moving us from without and affecting us for the moment ; it establishes itself within us in a durable manner. It arouses within us a whole world of ideas and sentiments which express it but which, at the same time, form an integral and permanent part of ourselves. When the Australian goes away from a religious ceremony, the representations which this communal life has aroused or re-aroused within him are not obliterated in a second. The figures of the great ancestors, the heroic exploits whose memory these rites perpetuate, the great deeds of every sort in which he, too, has participated through the cult, in a word, all these numerous ideals which he has elaborated with the co-operation of his fellows, continue to live in his consciousness and, through the emotions which are attached to them and the ascendancy which they hold over his entire being, they are sharply distinguished from the vulgar impressions arising from his daily relations with external things. Moral ideas have the same character. It is society which forces them upon us, and as the respect inspired by it is naturally extended to all that comes from it, its imperative rules of conduct are invested, by reason of their origin, with an authority and a dignity which is shared by none of our internal states : therefore, we assign them a place apart in our psychical life. Although our moral conscience is a part of our consciousness, we do not feel ourselves on an equality with it. In this voice which makes itself heard only to give us orders and establish prohibitions, we cannot recognize our own voices ; the very tone in which it speaks to us warns us that it expresses something within us that is not of ourselves. This is the objective foundation of the idea of the soul : those representations whose flow constitutes our interior life are of two different species which are irreducible one into another. Some concern themselves with the external and material world ; others, with an ideal world to which we attribute a moral superiority over the first. So we are really made up of two beings facing in different and almost contrary directions, one of whom exercises a real pre-eminence over the other. Such is the profound meaning of the antithesis which all men have more or less clearly conceived between the body and the soul, the material and the spiritual beings who coexist within us. Moralists and preachers have often maintained that no one can deny the reality of duty and its sacred character without falling into materialism. And it is true that if we have no idea of moral and religious imperatives, our psychical life will all be reduced to one level,[1] all our states of consciousness

[1] Even if we believe that religious and moral representations constitute the essential elements of the idea of the soul, still we do not mean to say that they are the only ones. Around this central nucleus are grouped other states of consciousness having this same character, though to a slighter degree. This is the case with all the superior forms of the intellectual life, owing to the special price and dignity attributed to them by society. When we devote our lives to science or art, we feel that we are moving in a circle of things that are above bodily sensations, as we shall have occasion to show more precisely in our conclusion. This is why the highest functions of the intelligence have always been considered specific manifestations of the soul. But they would probably not have been enough to establish the idea of it.

will be on the same plane, and all feeling of duality will perish. To make this duality intelligible, it is, of course, in no way necessary to imagine a mysterious and unrepresentable substance, under the name of the soul, which is opposed to the body. But here, as in regard to the idea of sacredness, the error concerns the letter of the symbol employed, not the reality of the fact symbolized. It remains true that our nature is double; there really is a particle of divinity in us because there is within us us a particle of these great ideas which are the soul of the group.

So the individual soul is only a portion of the collective soul of the group; it is the anonymous force at the basis of the cult, but incarnated in an individual whose personality it espouses; it is *mana* individualized. Perhaps dreams aided in determining certain secondary characteristics of the idea. The inconsistency and instability of the images which fill our minds during sleep, and their remarkable aptitude for transforming themselves into one another, may have furnished the model for this subtile, transparent and Protean matter out of which the soul is believed to be made. Also, the facts of swooning, catalepsy, etc., may have suggested the idea that the soul was mobile, and quitted the body temporarily during this life; this, in its turn, has served to explain certain dreams. But all these experiences and observations could have had only a secondary and complimentary influence, whose very existence it is difficult to establish. All that is really essential in the idea comes from elsewhere.

But does not this genesis of the idea of the soul misunderstand its essential characteristic? If the soul is a particular form of the impersonal principle which is diffused in the group, the totemic species and all the things of every sort which are attached to these, at bottom it is impersonal itself. So, with differences only of degree, it should have the same properties as the force of which it is a special form, and particularly, the same diffusion, the same aptitude for spreading itself contagiously and the same ubiquity. But quite on the contrary, the soul is voluntarily represented as a concrete, definite being, wholly contained within itself and not communicable to others; it is made the basis of our personality.

But this way of conceiving the soul is the product of a late and philosophic elaboration. The popular representation, as it is spontaneously formed from common experience, is very different, especially at first. For the Australian, the soul is a very vague thing, undecided and wavering in form, and spread over the whole organism. Though it manifests itself especially at certain points, there are probably none from which it is totally absent. So it has a diffusion, a contagiousness and an omnipresence comparable to those of the *mana*. Like the mana, it is able to divide and duplicate itself infinitely, though remaining entire in each of its parts; it is from these divisions and duplications that the plurality of souls is derived. On the other hand, the doctrine of reincarnation, whose generality we have established, shows how many impersonal elements enter into the idea of the soul and how essential those are. For if the same soul is going to clothe a new personality in each generation, the individual forms in which it successively develops itself must all be equally external to it, and have nothing to do with its true nature. It is a sort of generic substance which individualizes itself only secondarily and superficially. Moreover, this conception of the soul is by no means completely gone. The cult of relics shows that for a host of believers even to-day, the soul of a saint, with all its essential powers, continues to adhere to his different bones; and this implies that he is believed to be able to diffuse himself, subdivide himself and incorporate himself in all sorts of different things simultaneously.

Just as the characteristic attributes of the mana are found in the soul, so secondary and superficial changes are enough to enable the mana to individualize itself in the form of a soul. We pass from the first idea to the second with no break of continuity. Every religious force which is attached in a special way to a determined being participates in the characteristics of this being, takes on its appearance and becomes its spiritual double. Tregear, in his Maori-Polynesian dictionary, has thought it possible to connect the word *mana* with another group of words, such as *manawa*, *manamana*, etc., which seem to belong to the same family, and which signify heart, life, consciousness.[1] Is this not equivalent to saying that some sort of kinship ought to exist between the corresponding ideas as well, that is to say, between the idea of impersonal force and those of internal life, mental force and, in a word, of the soul? This is why the question whether the churinga is sacred because it serves as the residence of a soul, as Spencer and Gillen believe, or because it has impersonal virtues, as Strehlow thinks, seems to us to have little interest and to be without sociological importance. Whether the efficacy of a sacred object is represented in an abstract form in the mind or is attributed to some personal agent does not really matter. The psychological roots of both beliefs are identical: an object

[1] F. Tregear, *The Maori-Polynesian Comparative Dictionary*, pp. 203–205.

is sacred because it inspires, in one way or another, a collective sentiment of respect which removes it from profane touches. In order to explain this sentiment, men sometimes fall back on to a vague and imprecise cause, and sometimes on to a determined spiritual being endowed with a name and a history; but these different interpretations are superadded to one fundamental phenomenon which is the same in both cases.

This, moreover, is what explains the singular confusions, examples of which we have met with as we have progressed. The individual, the soul of the ancestor which he reincarnates or from which his own is an emanation, his churinga and the animals of the totemic species are, as we have said, partially equivalent and interchangeable things. This is because in certain connections, they all affect the collective consciousness in the same way. If the churinga is sacred, it is because of the collective sentiments of respect inspired by the totemic emblem carved upon its surface; now the same sentiment attaches itself to the animals or plants whose outward form is reproduced by the totem, to the soul of the individual, for it is thought of in the form of the totemic being, and finally to the ancestral soul, of which the preceding one is only a particular aspect. So all these various objects, whether real or ideal, have one common element by which they arouse a single affective state in the mind, and through this, they become confused. In so far as they are expressed by one and the same representation, they are indistinct. This is how the Arunta has come to regard the churinga as the body common to the individual, the ancestor and even the totemic being. It is his way of expressing the identity of the sentiments of which these different things are the object.

However, it does not follow from the fact the idea of the soul is derived from the idea of mana that the first has a relatively later origin, or that there was a period in history when men were acquainted with religious forces only in their impersonal forms. When some wish to designate by the word preanimist an historical period during which animism was completely unknown, they build up an arbitrary hypothesis; [1] for there is no people among whom the ideas of the soul and of mana do not coexist side by side. So there is no ground for imagining that they were formed at two distinct times; everything, on the contrary, goes to show that the two are coeval. Just as there is no society without individuals, so those impersonal forces which are disengaged from the group cannot establish themselves

[1] This is the thesis of Preuss in his articles in the *Globus* which we have cited several times. It seems that M. Lévy-Bruhl also tends towards this conception (see his *Fonctions mentales*, etc., pp. 92–93).

without incarnating themselves in the individual consciousnesses where they individualize themselves. In reality, we do not have two different developments, but two different aspects of one and the same development. It is true that they do not have an equal importance ; one is more essential than the other. The idea of mana does not presuppose the idea of the soul ; for if the mana is going to individualize itself and break itself up into the particular souls, it must first of all exist, and what it is in itself does not depend upon the forms it takes when individualized. But on the contrary, the idea of the soul cannot be understood except when taken in connection with the idea of mana. So on this ground, it is possible to say that it is the result of a secondary formation ; but we are speaking of a secondary formation in the logical, not the chronological, sense of the word.

V

But how does it come that men have believed that the soul survives the body and is even able to do so for an indefinite length of time ?

From the analysis which we have made, it is evident that the belief in immortality has not been established under the influence of moral ideas. Men have not imagined the prolongation of their existence beyond the tomb in order that a just retribution for moral acts may be assured in another life, if it fails in this one ; for we have seen that all considerations of this sort are foreign to the primitive conception of the beyond.

Nor is the other hypothesis any better, according to which the other life was imagined as a means of escaping the agonizing prospect of annihilation. In the first place, it is not true that the need of personal survival was actively felt at the beginning. The primitive generally accepts the idea of death with a sort of indifference. Being trained to count his own individuality for little, and being accustomed to exposing his life constantly, he gives it up easily enough.[1] More than that, the immortality promised by the religions he practices is not personal. In a large number of cases, the soul does not continue the personality of the dead man, or does not continue it long, for, forgetful of its previous existence, it goes away, after a while, to animate another body and thus becomes the vivifying principle of a new personality. Even among the most advanced peoples, it was only a pale and sad existence that shades led in Sheol or Erebus, and could hardly attenuate the regrets occasioned by the memories of the life lost.

[1] On this point, see our *Suicide*, pp. 233 ff.

A more satisfactory explanation is the one attaching the conception of a posthumous life to the experiences of dreams. Our dead friends and relatives reappear to us in dreams: we see them act, we hear them speak; it is natural to conclude that they continue to exist. But if these observations were able to confirm the idea after it had once been born, they hardly seem capable of creating it out of nothing. Dreams in which we see departed persons living again are too rare and too short and leave only too vague recollections of themselves, to have been able to suggest so important a system of beliefs to men all by themselves. There is a remarkable lack of proportion between the effect and the cause to which it is attributed.

What makes this question embarrassing is the fact that in itself, the idea of the soul does not imply that of its survival, but rather seems to exclude it. In fact, we have seen that the soul, though being distinguished from the body, is believed, nevertheless, to be closely united to it: it ages along with the body, it feels a reaction from all the maladies that fall upon the body; so it would seem natural that it should die with the body. At least, men ought to have believed that it ceased to exist from the moment when it definitely lost its original form, and when it was no longer what it had been. Yet it is at just this moment that a new life opens out before it.

The myths which we have already described give the only possible explanation of this belief. We have seen that the souls of new-born children are either emanations of the ancestral souls, or these souls themselves reincarnated. But in order that they may either reincarnate themselves, or periodically give off new emanations, they must have survived their first holders. So it seems as though they admitted the survival of the dead in order to explain the birth of the living. The primitive does not have the idea of an all-powerful god who creates souls out of nothing. It seems to him that souls cannot be made except out of souls. So those who are born can only be new forms of those who have been; consequently, it is necessary that these latter continue to exist in order that others may be born. In fine, the belief in the immortality of the soul is the only way in which men were able to explain a fact which could not fail to attract their attention; this fact is the perpetuity of the life of the group. Individuals die, but the clan survives. So the forces which give it life must have the same perpetuity. Now these forces are the souls which animate individual bodies; for it is in them and through them that the group is realized. For this reason, it is necessary that they endure. It is even necessary that in enduring, they remain always the same; for, as the clan always keeps its characteristic appearance, the spiritual substance out of which it is made must be thought of as qualitatively invariable. Since it is always the same clan with the same totemic principle, it is necessary that the souls be the same, for souls are only the totemic principle broken up and particularized. Thus there is something like a germinative plasm, of a mystic order, which is transmitted from generation to generation and which makes, or at least is believed to make, the spiritual unity of the clan through all time. And this belief, in spite of its symbolic character, is not without a certain objective truth. For though the group may not be immortal in the absolute sense of the word, still it is true that it endures longer than the individuals and that it is born and incarnated afresh in each new generation.

A fact confirms this interpretation. We have seen that according to the testimony of Strehlow, the Arunta distinguish two sorts of souls: on the one hand are those of the ancestors of the Alcheringa, on the other, those of the individuals who actually compose the active body of the tribe at each moment in history. The second sort only survive the body for a relatively short time; they are soon totally annihilated. Only the former are immortal; as they are uncreated, so they do not perish. It is also to be noticed that they are the only ones whose immortality is necessary to explain the permanence of the group; for it is upon them, and upon them alone, that it is incumbent to assure the perpetuity of the clan, for every conception is their work. In this connection, the others have no part to play. So souls are not said to be immortal except in so far as this immortality is useful in rendering intelligible the continuity of the collective life.

Thus the causes leading to the first beliefs in a future life had no connections with the functions to be filled at a later period by the institutions beyond the tomb. But when that had once appeared, they were soon utilized for other purposes besides those which had been their original reasons for existence. Even in the Australian societies, we see them beginning to organize themselves for this other purpose. Moreover, there was no need of any fundamental transformation for this. How true it is that the same social institution can successively fulfil different functions without changing its nature!

VI

The idea of the soul was for a long time, and still is in part, the popular form of the idea of personality.[1] So the genesis

[1] It may be objected perhaps that unity is the characteristic of the personality, while the soul has always been conceived as multiple, and as capable of dividing and subdividing itself almost to infinity. But we know to-day that the

of the former of these ideas should aid us in understanding how the second one was formed.

From what has already been said, it is clear that the notion of person is the product of two sorts of factors. One of these is essentially impersonal: it is the spiritual principle serving as the soul of the group. In fact, it is this which constitutes the very substance of individual souls. Now this is not the possession of any one in particular: it is a part of the collective patrimony; in it and through it, all consciousnesses communicate. But on the other hand, in order to have separate personalities, it is necessary that another factor intervene to break up and differentiate this principle: in other words, an individualizing factor is necessary. It is the body that fulfils this function. As bodies are distinct from each other, and as they occupy different points of space and time, each of them forms a special centre about which the collective representations reflect and colour themselves differently. The result is that even if all the consciousnesses in these bodies are directed towards the same world, to wit, the world of the ideas and sentiments which brings about the moral unity of the group, they do not all see it from the same angle; each one expresses it in its own fashion.

Of these two equally indispensable factors, the former is certainly not the less important, for this is the one which furnishes the original matter for the idea of the soul. Perhaps some will be surprised to see so considerable a rôle attributed to the impersonal element in the genesis of the idea of personality. But the philosophical analysis of the idea of person, which has gone far ahead of the sociological analysis, has reached analogous results on this point. Among all the philosophers, Leibniz is one of those who have felt most vividly what a personality is; for before all, the nomad is a personal and autonomous being. Yet, for Leibniz, the contents of all the monads is identical. In fact, all are consciousnesses which express one and the same object, the world; and as the world itself is only a system of representations, each particular consciousness is really only the reflection of the universal consciousness. However, each one expresses it from its own point of view, and in its own manner. We know how this difference of perspectives comes from the

unity of the person is also made up of parts and that it, too, is capable of dividing and decomposing. Yet the notion of personality does not vanish because of the fact that we no longer think of it as a metaphysical and indivisible atom. It is the same with the popular conceptions of personality which find their expression in the idea of the soul. These show that men have always felt that the human personality does not have that absolute unity attributed to it by certain metaphysicians.

fact that the monads are situated differently in relation to each other and to the whole system which they constitute.

Kant expresses the same sentiment, though in a different form. For him, the corner-stone of the personality is the will. Now the will is the faculty of acting in conformity with reason, and the reason is that which is most impersonal within us. For reason is not my reason ; it is human reason in general. It is the power which the mind has of rising above the particular, the contingent and the individual, to think in universal forms. So from this point of view, we may say that what makes a man a personality is that by which he is confounded with other men, that which makes him a man, not a certain man. The senses, the body and, in a word, all that individualizes, is, on the contrary, considered as the antagonist of the personality by Kant.

This is because individuation is not the essential characteristic of the personality. A person is not merely a single subject distinguished from all the others. It is especially a being to which is attributed a relative autonomy in relation to the environment with which it is most immediately in contact. It is represented as capable of moving itself, to a certain degree : this is what Leibniz expressed in an exaggerated way when he said that the monad was completely closed to the outside. Now our analysis permits us to see how this conception was formed and to what it corresponds.

In fact, the soul, a symbolic representation of the personality, has the same characteristic. Although closely bound to the body, it is believed to be profoundly distinct from it and to enjoy, in relation to it, a large degree of independence. During life, it may leave it temporarily, and it definitely withdraws at death. Far from being dependent upon the body, it dominates it from the higher dignity which is in it. It may well take from the body the outward form in which it individualizes itself, but it owes nothing essential to it. Nor is the autonomy which all peoples have attributed to the soul a pure illusion ; we know now what its objective foundation is. It is quite true that the elements which serve to form the idea of the soul and those which enter into the representation of the body come from two different sources that are independent of one another. One sort are made up of the images and impressions coming from all parts of the organism ; the others consist in the ideas and sentiments which come from and express society. So the former are not derived from the latter. There really is a part of ourselves which is not placed in immediate dependence upon the organic factor : this is all that which represents society in us.

The general ideas which religion or science fix in our minds, the mental operations which these ideas suppose, the beliefs and sentiments which are at the basis of our moral life, and all these superior forms of psychical activity which society awakens in us, these do not follow in the trail of our bodily states, as our sensations and our general bodily consciousness do. As we have already shown, this is because the world of representations in which social life passes is superimposed upon its material substratum, far from arising from it; the determinism which reigns there is much more supple than the one whose roots are in the constitution of our tissues and it leaves with the actor a justified impression of the greatest liberty. The medium in which we thus move is less opaque and less resistant: we feel ourselves to be, and we are, more at our ease there. In a word, the only way we have of freeing ourselves from physical forces is to oppose them with collective forces.

But whatever we receive from society, we hold in common with our companions. So it is not at all true that we are more personal as we are more individualized. The two terms are in no way synonymous: in one sense, they oppose more than they imply one another. Passion individualizes, yet it also enslaves. Our sensations are essentially individual; yet we are more personal the more we are freed from our senses and able to think and act with concepts. So those who insist upon all the social elements of the individual do not mean by that to deny or debase the personality. They merely refuse to confuse it with the fact of individuation.[1]

[1] For all this, we do not deny the importance of the individual factor: this is explained from our point of view just as easily as its contrary. If the essential element of the personality is the social part of us, on the other hand there can be no social life unless distinct individuals are associated, and this is richer the more numerous and different from each other they are. So the individual factor is a condition of the impersonal factor. And the contrary is no less true, for society itself is an important source of individual differences (see our *Division du travail social*, 3rd. ed., pp. 267 ff.).

CHAPTER IX

THE IDEA OF SPIRITS AND GODS

WHEN we come to the idea of the soul, we have left the circle of purely impersonal forces. But above the soul the Australian religions already recognize mythical personalities of a superior order: spirits, civilizing heroes and even gods who are properly so-called. While it will be unnecessary to enter into the detail of the mythologies, we must at least seek the form in which these three categories of spiritual beings are presented in Australia, and the way in which they are connected with the whole religious system.

I

A soul is not a spirit. In fact, it is shut up in a determined organism; though it may leave it at certain moments, it is ordinarily a prisoner there. It definitely escapes only at death, and we have already seen the difficulties under which the separation is accomplished. A spirit, on the contrary, though often tied by the closest bonds to some particular object, such as a spring, a rock, a tree, a star, etc., and though residing there by preference, may go away at will and lead an independent existence in free space. So it has a more extended circle of action. It can act upon the individuals who approach it or whom it approaches. The soul, on the contrary, has almost no influence except over the body it animates; it is very exceptional that it succeeds in influencing outside objects during the course of its terrestrial life.

But if the soul does not have the distinctive characteristics of the spirit, it acquires them, at least in part, at death. In fact, when it has been disincarnated, so long as it does not descend into a body again, it has the same liberty of movement as a spirit. Of course, after the rites of mourning have been accomplished, it is thought to go to the land of souls, but before this it remains about the tomb for a rather long time. Also, even after it has definitely departed, it is believed to prowl about in the brush near the camp.[1] It is generally represented as a rather beneficent being, especially for the surviving members of its family; we have seen that the soul of the father comes to aid the growth of his children or his grandchildren. But it also happens sometimes that it shows signs of a veritable cruelty; everything depends upon its humour and the manner in which it is treated by the living.[2] So it is recommended, especially to women and children, not to venture outside of the camp during the night so as not to expose oneself to dangerous encounters.[3]

However, a ghost is not a real spirit. In the first place, it generally has only a limited power of action; also, it does not have a definite province. It is a vagabond, upon whom no determined task is incumbent, for the effect of death has been to put it outside of all regular forms; as regards the living, it is a sort of a exile. A spirit, on the other hand, always has a power of a certain sort and it is by this that it is defined; it is set over a certain order of cosmic or social phenomena; it has a more or less precise function to fulfil in the system of the universe.

But there are some souls which satisfy this double condition and which are consequently spirits, in the proper sense of the word. These are the souls of the mythical personages whom popular imagination has placed at the beginning of time, the Altjirangamitjina or the men of the Alcheringa among the Arunta; the Mura-mura among the tribes of Lake Eyre; the Muk-Kurnai among the Kurnai, etc. In one sense, they are still souls, for they are believed to have formerly animated bodies from which they separated themselves at a certain moment. But even when they led a terrestrial life, they already had, as we have seen, exceptional powers; they had a mana superior to that of ordinary men, and they have kept it. Also, they are charged with definite functions.

In the first place, whether we accept the version of Spencer and Gillen or that of Strehlow, it is to them that the care of assuring the periodical recruiting of the clan falls. They have charge of the phenomena of conception.

Even when the conception has been accomplished, the task of the ancestor is not yet completed. It is his duty to guard over the new-born child. Later, when the child has become a man, he accompanies him in the hunt, brings game to him, warns him by dreams of the dangers he may run, protects him

[1] Roth, *Superstition, Magic*, etc., §§ 65, 68; Spencer and Gillen, *Nat. Tr.*, pp. 514, 516.

[2] Spencer and Gillen, *Nat. Tr.*, pp. 521, 515; Dawson, *Austral. Aborig.*, p. 58; Roth, *op. cit.*, § 67.

[3] Spencer and Gillen, *Nat. Tr.*, p. 517.

against his enemies, etc. On this point, Strehlow is entirely in accord with Spencer and Gillen.[1] It is true that someone may ask how it is possible, according to the version of these latter, for the ancestor to fulfil this function; for, since he reincarnates himself at the moment of conception, it seems as though he should be confounded with the soul of the child and should therefore be unable to protect it from without. But the fact is that he does not reincarnate himself entirely; he merely duplicates himself. One part of him enters the body of the woman and fertilizes her; another part continues to exist outside and, under the special name of Arumburinga, fulfils the office of guardian genius.[2]

Thus we see how great a kinship there is between this ancestral spirit and the *genius* of the Latins or the *δαίμων* of the Greeks.[3] The identification of function is complete. In fact, at first the genius is the one who begets, *qui gignit;* he expresses and personifies the powers of generation.[4] But at the same time, he is the protector and director of the particular individual to whose person he is attached.[5] He is finally confused with the personality itself of this individual; he represents the totality of the proclivities and tendencies which characterize him and give him a distinctive appearance among other men.[6] Hence come the well-known expressions *indulgere genio, defraudere genium* with the sense of *to follow one's natural temperament.* At bottom, the *genius* is another form or double of the soul of the individual. This is proved by the partial synonomy of *genius* and *manes.*[7] The manes is the genius after death; but it is also all that survives of the dead man, that is to say, his soul. In the same way, the soul of the Arunta and the ancestral spirit which serves as his genius are only two different aspects of one and the same being.

But it is not only in relation to persons that the ancestor has a definite situation; he also has one in relation to things. Though he is believed to have his real residence under the ground, they think that he is always haunting the place where his nanja-tree or rock is, or the water-hole which was spontaneously formed at the exact spot where he disappeared into the ground, having terminated his first existence. As this tree or rock is

[1] Strehlow, II, p. 76 and n. 1; Spencer and Gillen, *Nat. Tr.*, pp. 514, 516.

[2] Spencer and Gillen, *Nat. Tr.*, p. 513.

[3] On this question, see Negrioli, *Dei Genii presso i Romani*; the articles *Daimon* and *Genius* in the *Dict. of Antiq.*; Preller, *Romische Mythologie*, II, pp. 195 ff.

[4] Negrioli, *ibid.*, p. 4.

[5] *Ibid.*, p. 8.

[6] *Ibid.*, p. 7.

[7] *Ibid.*, p. 11. Cf. Samter, *Der Ursprung der Larencultus*, in *Archiv f. Religions-wissenschaft*, 1907, pp. 368–393.

believed to represent the body of the hero, they imagine that the soul itself is constantly coming back there, and lives there more or less permanently; it is by the presence of this soul that they explain the religious respect inspired by these localities. No one can break the branch of a nanja-tree without a risk of falling sick.[1] "Formerly the act of breaking it down or injuring it was punished with death. An animal or bird taking refuge there could not be killed. Even the surrounding bushes had to be respected: the grass could not be burned, the rocks also had to be treated with respect. It was forbidden to remove them or break them."[2] As this sacred character is attributed to the ancestor, he appears as the spirit of this tree or rock, of this water-hole or spring.[3] If the spring is thought of as having some connection with rain,[4] he will become a spirit of rain. Thus, the same souls which serve as protecting geniuses for men also fulfil cosmic functions at the same time. It is undoubtedly in this sense that we must understand the text of Roth where he says that in northern Queensland, the spirits of nature are the souls of the dead who have chosen to live in the forests or caves.[5]

So we have here some spiritual beings that are different from the wandering souls with no definite powers. Strehlow calls them gods;[6] but this expression is inexact, at least in the great majority of cases. If it were true, then in a society like the Arunta where each one has his protecting ancestor, there would be as many or more gods than there are individuals. It would merely introduce confusion into our terminology to give the name of god to a sacred being with only one worshipper. It may be, of course, that the figure of the ancestor grows to a point where it resembles a real divinity. Among the Warramunga, as we have already pointed out,[7] the clan as a whole is thought to be descended from one sole and unique ancestor. It is easily seen how this collective ancestor might, under certain circumstances, become the object of a collective devotion. To choose a notable example, this is what has happened to the snake Wollunqua.[8] This mythical beast, from whom the clan of the same name is held to be descended, continues to live, they believe, in water-holes which are therefore surrounded

[1] Schulze, *loc. cit.*, p. 237.

[2] Strehlow, I, p. 5. Cf. Spencer and Gillen, *Nat. Tr.*, p. 133; Gason, in Curr, II, p. 69.

[3] See the case of a Mura-mura who is considered the spirit of certain hot springs, in Howitt, *Nat. Tr.*, p. 482.

[4] *Nor. Tr.*, pp. 313 f.; Mathews, *Journ. of the Roy. Soc. of N.S. Wales*, XXXVIII, p. 351. Among the Dieri there is also a Mura-mura whose function is to produce rain (Howitt, *Nat. Tr.*, pp. 798 f.).

[5] Roth, *Superstition*, etc., § 67. Cf. Dawson, p. 59.

[6] Strehlow, I, pp. 2 ff.

[7] See above, p. 249.

[8] *Nor. Tr.*, ch. vii.

with a religious respect. Thus it becomes the object of a cult which the clan celebrates collectively: through determined rites, they attempt to please him and to win his favours, and they address to him all sorts of prayers, etc. So we may say that he is like a god of the clan. But this is a very exceptional case, or even, according to Spencer and Gillen, a unique one Normally, the word " spirits " is the only one suitable for designating these ancestral personages.

As to the manner in which this conception has been formed, we may say that it is evident from what has preceded.

As we have already shown, the existence of individual souls, when once admitted, cannot be understood unless one imagines an original supply of fundamental souls at the origin of things, from which all the others were derived. Now these architype souls had to be conceived as containing within them the source of all religious efficacy; for, since the imagination does not go beyond them, it is from them and only from them that all sacred things are believed to come, both the instruments of the cult, the members of the clan and the animals of the totemic species. They incarnate all the sacredness diffused in the whole tribe and the whole world, and so they are attributed powers noticeably superior to those enjoyed by the simple souls of men. Moreover, time by itself increases and reinforces the sacred character of things. A very ancient churinga inspires much more respect than a new one, and is supposed to have more virtues.[1] The sentiments of veneration of which it has been the object during the series of successive generations who have handled it are, as it were, accumulated in it. For the same reason, the personages who for centuries have been the subject of myths respectfully passed on from mouth to mouth, and periodically put into action by the rites, could not fail to take a very especial place in the popular imagination.

But how does it happen that, instead of remaining outside of the organized society, they have become regular members of it?

This is because each individual is the double of an ancestor. Now when two beings are related as closely as this, they are naturally conceived as incorporated together; since they participate in the same nature, it seems as though that which affects one ought to affect the other as well. Thus the group of mythical ancestors became attached to the society of the living; the same interests and the same passions were attributed to each; they were regarded as associates. However, as the former had a higher dignity than the latter, this association takes, in the

[1] Spencer and Gillen, *Nor. Tr.*, p. 277.

public mind, the form of an agreement between superiors and inferiors, between patrons and clients, benefactors and recipients. Thus comes this curious idea of a protecting genius who is attached to each individual.

The question of how this ancestor came to have relations not only with men, but also with things, may appear more embarrassing; for, at the first glance, we do not see what connection there can be between a personage of this sort and a rock or tree. But a fact which we owe to Strehlow furnishes us with a solution of this problem, which is at least probable.

These trees and rocks are not situated at any point in the tribal territory, but, for the most part, they are grouped around the sanctuaries, called ertnatulunga by Spencer and Gillen and arknanaua by Strehlow, where the churinga of the clan is kept.[1] We know the respect with which these localities are enhaloed from the mere fact that the most precious instruments of the cult are there. Each of these spreads sanctity all about it. It is for this reason that the neighbouring trees and rocks appear sacred, that it is forbidden to destroy or harm them, and that all violence used against them is a sacrilege. This sacred character is really due to a simple phenomenon of psychic contagiousness; but in order to explain it, the native must admit that these different objects have relations with the different beings in whom he sees the source of all religious power, that is to say, with the ancestors of the Alcheringa. Hence comes the system of myths of which we have spoken. They imagined that each ertnatulunga marked the spot where a group of ancestors entered into the ground. The mounds or trees which covered the ground were believed to represent their bodies. But as the soul retains, in a general way, a sort of affinity for the body in which it dwelt, they were naturally led to believe that these ancestral souls continued to frequent these places where their material envelope remained. So they were located in the rocks, the trees or the water-holes. Thus each of them, though remaining attached to some determined individual, became transformed into a sort of *genius loci* and fulfilled its functions.[2]

[1] Strehlow, I, p. 5.

[2] It is true that some nanja-trees and rocks are not situated around the ertnatulunga; they are scattered over different parts of the tribal territory. It is said that these are places where an isolated ancestor disappeared into the ground, lost a member, let some blood flow, or lost a churinga which was transformed into a tree or rock. But these totemic sites have only a secondary importance; Strehlow calls them *kleinere Totemplätze* (I, pp. 4–5). So it may be that they have taken this character only by analogy with the principal totemic centres. The trees and rocks which, for some reason or other, remind one of those found in the neighbourhood of an ertnatulunga, inspire analogous sentiments, so the myth which was formed in regard to the latter was extended to the former.

The conceptions thus elucidated enable us to understand a form of totemism which we have left unexplained up to the present: this is individual totemism.

An individual totem is defined, in its essence, by the two following characteristics: (1) it is a being in an animal or vegetable form whose function is to protect an individual; (2) the fate of this individual and that of his patron are closely united: all that touches the latter is sympathetically communicated to the former. Now the ancestral spirits of which we have just been speaking answer to this same definition. They also belong, at least in part, to the animal or vegetable kingdoms. They, too, are protecting geniuses. Finally, a sympathetic bond unites each individual to his protecting ancestor. In fact, the nanja-tree, representing the mystical body of this ancestor, cannot be destroyed without the man's feeling himself menaced. It is true that this belief is losing its force to-day, but Spencer and Gillen have observed it, and in any case, they are of the opinion that formerly it was quite general.[1]

The identity of these two conceptions is found even in their details.

The ancestral souls reside in trees or rocks which are considered sacred. Likewise, among the Euahlayi, the spirit of the animal serving as individual totem is believed to inhabit a tree or stone.[2] This tree or stone is sacred; no one may touch it except the proprietor of the totem; when it is a stone or rock, this interdiction is still absolute.[3] The result is that they are veritable places of refuge.

Finally, we have seen that the individual soul is only another aspect of the ancestral spirit, according to Strehlow, this serves after a fashion, as a second self.[4] Likewise, following an expression of Mrs. Parker, the individual totem of the Euahlayi, called Yunbeai, is the *alter ego* of the individual: "The soul of a man is in his Yunbeai and the soul of his Yunbeai is in him." [5] So at bottom, it is one soul in two bodies. The kinship of these two notions is so close that they are sometimes expressed by one and the same word. This is the case in Melanesia and in Polynesia: *atai* in the island Mota, *tamaniu* in the island Aurora, and *talegia* in Motlaw all designate both the soul of the individual and his personal totem.[6] It is the same with *aitu* in Samoa.[7]

[1] *Nat. Tr.*, p. 139.

[2] Parker, *The Euahlayi*, p. 21. The tree serving for this use is generally one of those figuring among the sub-totems of the individual. As a reason for this choice, they say that as it is of the same family as the individual, it should be better disposed to giving him aid (*ibid.*, p. 29).

[3] *Ibid.*, p. 36. [4] Strehlow, II, p. 81. [5] Parker, *op. cit.*, p. 21.

[6] Codrington, *The Melanesians*, pp. 249–253. [7] Turner, *Samoa*, p. 17.

This is because the individual totem is merely the outward and visible form of the ego or the personality, of which the soul is the inward and invisible form.[1]

Thus the individual totem has all the essential characteristics of the protecting ancestor and fills the same rôle: this is because it has the same origin and proceeds from the same idea.

Each of them, in fact, consists in a duplication of the soul. The totem, as the ancestor, is the soul of the individual, but externalized and invested with powers superior to those it is believed to possess while within the organism. Now this duplication is the result of a psychological necessity; for it only expresses the nature of the soul which, as we have seen, is double. In one sense, it is ours: it expresses our personality. But at the same time, it is outside of us, for it is only the reaching into us of a religious force which is outside of us. We cannot confound ourselves with it completely, for we attribute to it an excellence and a dignity by which it rises far above us and our empirical individuality. So there is a whole part of ourselves which we tend to project into the outside. This way of thinking of ourselves is so well established in our nature that we cannot escape it, even when we attempt to regard ourselves without having recourse to any religious symbols. Our moral consciousness is like a nucleus about which the idea of the soul forms itself; yet when it speaks to us, it gives the effect of an outside power, superior to us, which gives us our law and judges us, but which also aids and sustains us. When we have it on our side, we feel ourselves to be stronger against the trials of life, and better assured of triumphing over them, just as the Australian who, when trusting in his ancestor or his personal totem, feels himself more valiant against his enemies.[2] So there is something objective at the basis of these conceptions, whether we have in mind the Roman *genius*, the individual totem, or the Alcheringa ancestor; and this is why they have survived, in various forms, up to the present day. Everything goes just as if we really had two souls; one which is within us, or rather, which is us; the other which is above us, and whose function it is to control and

[1] These are the very words used by Codrington (p. 251).

[2] This close connection between the soul, the guardian genius and the moral conscience of the individual is especially apparent among certain peoples of Indonesia. " One of the seven souls of the Tobabatak is buried with the placenta; though preferring to live in this place, it may leave it to warn the individual or to manifest its approbation when he does well. So in one sense, it plays the rôle of a moral conscience. However, its communications are not confined to the domain of moral facts. It is called the younger brother of the soul, as the placenta is called the younger brother of the child. . . . In war, it inspires the man with courage to march against the enemy " (Warneck, *Der bataksche Ahnen und Geistercult*, in *Allg. Missionszeitschrift*, Berlin, 1904. p. 10. Cf. Kruijt, *Het Animisme in den indischen Archipel*, p. 25).

assist the first one. Frazer thought that the individual totem was an external soul; but he believed that this exteriority was the result of an artifice and a magic ruse. In reality, it is implied in the very constitution of the idea of the soul.[1]

II

The spirits of which we have just been speaking are essentially benefactors. Of course they punish a man if he does not treat them in a fitting manner; [2] but it is not their function to work evil.

However, a spirit is in itself just as capable of doing evil as good. This is why we find a class of evil geniuses forming itself naturally, in opposition to these auxiliary and protecting spirits, which enables men to explain the permanent evils that they have to suffer, their nightmares [3] and illnesses,[4] whirlwinds and tempests,[5] etc. Of course this is not saying that all these human miseries have appeared as things too abnormal to be explained in any way except by supernatural forces; but it is saying that these forces are thought of under a religious form. As it is a religious principle which is considered the source of life, so, all the events which disturb or destroy life ought logically to be traced to a principle of the same sort.

These harmful spirits seem to have been conceived on the

[1] It still remains to be investigated how it comes that after a certain moment in evolution, this duplication of the soul was made in the form of an individual totem rather than of a protecting ancestor. Perhaps this question has an ethnological rather than a sociological interest. However, the manner in which this substitution was probably effected may be represented as follows.

The individual totem commenced by playing a merely complimentary rôle. Those individuals who wished to acquire powers superior to those possessed by everybody, did not and could not content themselves with the mere protection of the ancestor; so they began to look for another assistant of the same sort. Thus it comes about that among the Euahlayi, the magicians are the only ones who have or who can procure individual totems. As each one has a collective totem in addition, he finds himself having many souls. But there is nothing surprising in this plurality of souls: it is the condition of a superior power.

But when collective totemism once begins to lose ground, and when the conception of the protecting ancestor consequently begins to grow dim in the mind, another method must be found for representing the double nature of the soul, which is still felt. The resulting idea was that, outside of the individual soul, there was another, charged with watching over the first one. Since this protecting power was no longer demonstrated by the very fact of birth, men found it natural to employ, for its discovery, means analogous to those used by magicians to enter into communion with the forces of whose aid they thus assured themselves.

[2] For example, see Strehlow, II, p. 82.

[3] Wyatt, *Adelaide and Encounter Bay Tribes*, in Woods, p. 168.

[4] Taplin, *The Narrinyeri*, pp. 62 f.; Roth, *Superstition*, etc., § 116; Howitt, *Nat. Tr.*, pp. 356, 358; Strehlow, pp. 11–12.

[5] Strehlow, I, pp. 13–14; Dawson, p. 49.

same model as the good spirits of which we have just been speaking. They are represented in an animal form, or one that is half-animal, half-man;[1] but men are naturally inclined to give them enormous dimensions and a repulsive aspect.[2] Like the souls of the ancestors, they are believed to inhabit trees, rocks, water-holes and subterranean caverns.[3] Taking the Arunta as a particular example, Spencer and Gillen say expressly that these evil geniuses, known under the name of Oruncha, are beings of the Alcheringa.[4] Many are represented as the souls of persons who had led a terrestrial life.[5] Among the personages of the fabulous epoch, there were, in fact, many different temperaments: some had cruel and evil instincts which they retained;[6] others were naturally of a bad constitution; they were thin and emaciated; so after they had entered into the ground, the nanja rocks to which they gave birth were considered the homes of dangerous influences.[7]

Yet they are distinguished by special characteristics from their confrères, the heroes of the Alcheringa. They do not reincarnate themselves; among living men, there is no one who represents them; they are without human posterity.[8] When, judging from certain signs, they believe that a child is the result of their work, it is put to death as soon as born.[9] Also, these belong to no determined totemic group; they are outside the social organization.[10] By all these traits, they are recognized as magic powers rather than religious ones. And in fact, it is especially with the magician that they have relations; very frequently it is from them that he gets his powers.[11] So we have now arrived at the point where the world of religion stops and that of magic commences; and as this latter is

[1] Strehlow, I, pp. 11–14; Eylmann, pp. 182, 185; Spencer and Gillen, *Nor. Tr.*, p. 211; Schürmann, *The Aborig. Tr. of Port Lincoln*, in Woods, p. 239.

[2] Eylmann, p. 182.

[3] Mathews, *Journ. of the Roy. Soc. of N.S. Wales*, XXXVIII, p. 345; Fison and Howitt, *Kamilaroi and Kurnai*, p. 467; Strehlow, I, p. 11.

[4] *Nat. Tr.*, pp. 390–391. Strehlow calls these evil spirits *Erintja*; but this word is evidently equivalent to Oruncha. Yet there is a difference in the ways the two are presented to us. According to Spencer and Gillen, the Oruncha are malicious rather than evil; they even say (p. 328) that the Arunta know no necessarily evil spirits. On the contrary, the regular business of Strehlow's Erintja is to do evil. Judging from certain myths given by Spencer and Gillen (*Nat. Tr.*, p. 390), they seem to have touched up the figures of the Oruncha a little: these were originally ogres (*ibid.*, p. 331).

[5] Roth, *Superstition*, etc., § 115; Eylmann, p. 190.

[6] *Nat. Tr.*, pp. 390 f. [7] *Ibid.*, p. 551.

[8] *Ibid.*, pp. 326 f.

[9] Strehlow, I, p. 14. When there are twins, the first one is believed to have been conceived in this manner.

[10] Spencer and Gillen, *Nat. Tr.*, p. 327.

[11] Howitt, *Nat. Tr.*, pp. 358, 381, 385; Spencer and Gillen, *Nat. Tr.*, p. 334; *Nor. Tr.*, pp. 501, 530.

outside the field of our research, we need not push our researches further.[1]

III

The appearance of the notion of spirits marks an important step in advance in the individualization of religious forces.

However, the spiritual beings of whom we have been speaking up to the present are as yet only secondary personages. They are either evil-working geniuses who belong to magic rather than religion, or else, being attached to determined individuals or places, they cannot make their influence felt except within a circle of a very limited radius. So they can only be the objects of private and local rites. But after the idea has once been established, it naturally spreads to the higher spheres of the religious life, and thus mythical personalities of a superior order are born.

Though the ceremonies of the different clans differ from one another, they all belong to the same religion, none the less ; also, a certain number of essential similarities exist between them. Since all the clans are only parts of one and the same tribe, the unity of the tribe cannot fail to make itself felt through this diversity of particular cults. In fact, there is no totemic group that does not have churinga and bull-roarers, and these are used everywhere in the same way. The organization of the tribe into phratries, matrimonial classes and clans, and the exogamic interdictions attached to them, are veritable tribal institutions. The initiation celebrations all include certain fundamental practices, the extraction of a tooth, circumcision, subincision, etc., which do not vary with the totems within a single tribe. The uniformity on this point is the more easily established as the initiation always takes place in the presence of the tribe, or at least, before an assembly to which the different clans have been summoned. The reason for this is that the object of the initiation is to introduce the neophyte into the religious life, not merely of the clan into which he was born, but of the tribe as a whole ; so it is necessary that the various aspects of the tribal religion be represented before him and take place, in a way, under his very eyes. It is on this occasion that the moral and religious unity of the tribe is affirmed the best.

Thus, in each society there are a certain number of rites

[1] As the magician can either cause or cure sickness, we sometimes find, besides these magical spirits whose function is to do evil, others who forestall or neutralize the evil influence of the former. Cases of this sort will be found in *Nor. Tr.*, pp. 501–502. The fact that the latter are magic just as much as the former is well shown by the fact that the two have the same name, among the Arunta. So they are different aspects of a single magic power.

which are distinguished from all the others by their homogeneity and their generality. So noticeably a harmony seemed to be explicable only by a unity of origin. So they imagined that each group of similar rites had been founded by one and the same ancestor, who came to reveal them to the tribe as a whole. Thus, among the Arunta, it was an ancestor of the Wild Cat clan, named Putiaputia,[1] who is thought to have taught men the way of making churinga and using it ritually; among the Warramunga, it was Murtu-murtu;[2] among the Urabunna, Witurna;[3] it was Atnatu among the Kaitish[4] and Tendun among the Kurnai.[5] Likewise, the practice of circumcision is attributed by the eastern Dieri and many other tribes[6] to two special Muramura, and by the Arunta to a hero of the Alcheringa, of the Lizard totem, named Mangarkunjerkunja.[7] To this same personage are ascribed the foundation of the matrimonial institutions and the social organization they imply, the discovery of fire, the invention of the spear, the buckler, the boomerang, etc. It also happens very frequently that the inventor of the bull-roarer is also considered the founder of the rites of initiation.[8]

These special ancestors cannot be put in the same rank as the others. On the one hand, the sentiments of veneration which they inspire are not limited to one clan, but are common to the whole tribe. On the other hand, it is to them that men ascribe all that is most esteemed in the tribal civilization. For this double reason, they became the object of a special consideration. For example, they say of Atnatu that he was born in heaven at an epoch even prior to the times of the Alcheringa, that he made himself and that he gave himself the name he bears. The stars are his wives and daughters. Beyond the heaven where he lives, there is another one with another sun. His name is sacred, and should never be pronounced before women or non-initiated persons.[9]

[1] Strehlow, I, p. 9. Putiaputia is not the only personage of this sort of whom the Arunta myths speak: certain portions of the tribe give a different name to the hero to whom the same invention is ascribed. We must not forget that the extent of the territory occupied by the Arunta prevents their mythology from being completely homogeneous.

[2] Spencer and Gillen, *Nor. Tr.*, p. 493.

[3] *Ibid.*, p. 498.

[4] *Ibid.*, pp. 498 f.

[5] Howitt, *Nat. Tr.*, p. 135.

[6] *Ibid.*, pp. 476 ff.

[7] Strehlow, I, pp. 6–8. The work of Mangarkunjerkunja must be taken up again later among other heroes; for, according to a belief that is not confined to the Arunta, a time came when men forgot the teaching of their first initiators and became corrupt.

[8] This is the case, for example, of Atnatu (Spencer and Gillen, *Nor. Tr.*, p. 153) and the Witurna (*Nor. Tr.*, p. 498), If Tendun did not establish these rites, it is he who is charged with the direction of their celebration (Howitt, *Nat. Tr.*, p. 670).

[9] *Nor. Tr.*, p. 499.

Yet, howsoever great the prestige enjoyed by these personages may be, there was no occasion for founding special rites in their honour; for they themselves are only rites personified. They have no other reason for existence than to explain existing practices; they are only another aspect of these. The churinga and the ancestor who invented it are only one; sometimes, both have the same name.[1] When someone makes the bull-roarer resound, they say that it is the voice of the ancestor making himself heard.[2] But, for the very reason that each of these heroes is confounded with the cult he is believed to have founded, they believe that he is attentive to the way in which it is celebrated. He is not satisfied unless the worshippers fulfil their duties exactly; he punishes those who are negligent.[3] So he is thought of as the guardian of the rite, as well as its founder, and for this reason, he becomes invested with a veritable moral rôle.[4]

IV

However, this mythological formation is not the highest which is to be found among the Australians. There are at least a certain number of tribes who have arrived at a conception of a god who, if not unique, is at least supreme, and to whom is attributed a pre-eminent position among all the other religious entities.

The existence of this belief was pointed out long ago by different observers;[5] but it is Howitt who has contributed the most to establishing its relative generality. In fact, he has verified it over a very extended geographical area embracing the State of Victoria and New South Wales and even extending up to Queensland.[6] In all this entire region, a considerable number of tribes believe in the existence of a veritable tribal divinity, who has different names, according to the district. The ones most frequently employed are Bunjil or Punjil,[7] Daramulun[8]

[1] Howitt, *Nat. Tr.*, p. 493; *Kamilaroi and Kurnai*, pp. 197 and 247; Spencer and Gillen, *Nor. Tr.*, p. 492.

[2] For example, see *Nor. Tr.*, p. 499.

[3] *Nor. Tr.*, pp. 338, 347, 499.

[4] It is true that Spencer and Gillen maintain that these mythical beings play no moral rôle (*Nor. Tr.*, p. 493); but this is because they give too narrow a meaning to the word. Religious duties are duties: so the fact of looking after the manner in which these are observed concerns morals, especially because all morals have a religious character at this period.

[5] The fact was observed as early as 1845 by Eyre, *Journals*, etc., II, p. 362, and, before Eyre, by Henderson, *Observations on the Colonies of N.S. Wales and Van Diemen's Land*, p. 147.

[6] *Nat. Tr.*, pp. 488–508.

[7] Among the Kulin, Wotjobaluk and Woëworung (Victoria).

[8] Among the Yuin, Ngarrigo and Wolgal (New South Wales).

and Baiame.[1] But we also find Nuralie or Nurelle,[2] Kohin [3] and Mangan-ngaua.[4] The same conception is found again farther west, among the Narrinyeri, where the great god is called Nurunderi or Ngurrunderi.[5] Among the Dieri, it is probable that there is one of the Mura-mura, or ordinary ancestors, who enjoys a sort of supremacy over the others.[6] Finally, in opposition to the affirmations of Spencer and Gillen, who declare that they have observed no belief in a real divinity among the Arunta,[7] Strehlow assures us that this people, as well as the Loritja, recognize, under the name Altjira, a veritable "good god." [8]

The essential characteristics of this personage are the same everywhere. It is an immortal, and even an eternal being, for it was not derived from any other. After having lived on earth for a certain length of time, he ascended to heaven, or else was taken up there,[9] and continues to live there, surrounded by his family, for generally he is said to have one or several wives, children and brothers,[10] who sometimes assist him in his functions. Under the pretext of a visit he is said to have made to them, he and his family are frequently identified with certain stars.[11]

[1] Among the Kamilaroi and Euahlayi (northern part of New South Wales); and more to the centre, in the same province, among the Wonghibon and the Wiradjuri.

[2] Among the Wiimbaio and the tribes on the lower Murray (Ridley, *Kamilaroi*, p. 137; Brough Smyth, I, pp. 423, n., 431).

[3] Among the tribes on the Herbert River (Howitt, *Nat. Tr.*, p. 498).

[4] Among the Kurnai.

[5] Taplin, p. 55; Eylmann, p. 182.

[6] It is undoubtedly to this supreme Mura-mura that Gason makes allusion in the passage already cited (Curr, II, p. 55).

[7] *Nat. Tr.*, p. 246.

[8] Between Baiame, Bunjil and Daramulun on the one hand, and Altjira on the other, there is the difference that the latter is completely foreign to all that concerns humanity; he did not make man and does not concern himself with what they do. The Arunta have neither love nor fear for him. But when this conception is carefully observed and analysed, it is hard to admit that it is primitive; for if the Altjira plays no rôle, explains nothing, serves for nothing, what made the Arunta imagine him? Perhaps it is necessary to consider him as a sort of Baiame who has lost his former prestige, as an ancient god whose memory is fading away. Perhaps, also, Strehlow has badly interpreted the testimony he has gathered. According to Eylmann, who, it is to be admitted, is neither a very competent nor a very sure observer, Altjira made men (*op. cit.*, p. 134). Moreover, among the Loritja, the corresponding personage, Tukura, is believed to celebrate the initiation ceremonies himself.

[9] For Bunjil, see Brough Smyth, I, p. 417; for Baiame, see Ridley, *Kamilaroi*, p. 136; for Daramulun, see Howitt, *Nat. Tr.*, p. 495.

[10] On the composition of Bunjil's family, for example, see Howitt, *Nat. Tr.*, pp. 128, 129, 489, 491; Brough Smyth, I, pp. 417, 423; for Baiame's, see L. Parker, *The Euahlayi*, pp. 7, 66, 103; Howitt, *Nat. Tr.*, pp. 502, 585, 407; for Nurunderi's, Taplin, *The Narrinyeri*, pp. 57 f. Of course, there are all sorts of variations in the ways in which the families of these great gods are conceived. The personage who is a brother here, is a son there. The number and names of the wives vary with the locality.

[11] Howitt, *Nat. Tr.*, p. 128.

Moreover, they attribute to him a power over stars. It is he who regulates the journey of the sun and moon ; [1] he gives them orders.[2] It is he who makes the lightning leap from the clouds and who throws the thunder-bolts.[3] Since he is the thunder, he is also connected with the rain : [4] it is to him that men address themselves when there is a scarcity of water, or when too much falls.[5]

They speak of him as a sort of creator : he is called the father of men and they say that he made them. According to a legend current around Melbourne, Bunjil made the first man in the following manner. He made a little statue out of white clay ; then, after he had danced all around it several times and had breathed into its nostrils, the statue became animated and commenced to walk about.[6] According to another myth, he lighted the sun ; thus the earth became heated and men came out of it.[7] At the same time that he made men,[8] this divine personage made the animals and trees ; [9] it is to him that men owe all the arts of life, arms, language and tribal rites.[10] He is the benefactor of humanity. Even yet, he plays the rôle of a sort of providence for them. It is he who supplies his worshippers with all that is necessary for their existence.[11] He is in communication with them, either directly or through intermediaries.[12] But being at the same time guardian of the morals of the tribe, he treats them severely when these are violated.[13] If we are to believe certain observers, he will even fulfil the office of judge, after this life ; he will separate the good from the bad, and will not reward the ones like the others.[14] In any case, they are often represented as ruling the land of the dead,[15] and as gathering the souls together when they arrive in the beyond.[16]

[1] Brough Smyth, I, pp. 430, 431.
[2] *Ibid.*, I, p. 432, n.
[3] Howitt, *Nat. Tr.*, pp. 498, 538 ; Mathews, *Jour. of the Roy. Soc. of N.S. Wales*, XXXVIII, p. 343 ; Ridley, p. 136.
[4] Howitt, *Nat. Tr.*, p. 538 ; Taplin, *The Narrinyeri*, pp. 57–58.
[5] L. Parker, *The Euahlayi*, p. 8.
[6] Brough Smyth, I, p. 424.
[7] Howitt, *Nat. Tr.*, p. 492.
[8] According to certain myths, he made men but not women ; this is related of Bunjil. But then, the origin of women is attributed to his son-brother, Pallyan (Brough Smyth, I, pp. 417 and 423).
[9] Howitt, *Nat. Tr.*, pp. 489, 492 ; Mathews, *Journ. of the Roy. Soc. of N.S. Wales*, XXXVIII, p. 340.
[10] L. Parker, *The Euahlayi*, p. 7 ; Howitt, *Nat. Tr.*, p. 630.
[11] Ridley, *Kamilaroi*, p. 136 ; L. Parker, *The Euahlayi*, p. 114.
[12] L. Parker, *More Austr. Leg. Tales*, pp. 84–89, 90–91.
[13] Howitt, *Nat. Tr.*, pp. 495, 498, 543, 563, 564 ; Brough Smyth, I, p. 429 ; L. Parker, *The Euahlayi*, pp. 79.
[14] Ridley, p. 137.
[15] L. Parker, *The Euahlayi*, pp. 90–91.
[16] Howitt, *Nat. Tr.*, p. 495 ; Taplin, *The Narrinyeri*, p. 58.

As the initiation is the principal form of the tribal cult, it is to the rites of initiation that he is attached especially; he is their centre. He is very frequently represented by an image cut on a piece of bark or soaked into the ground. They dance around it; they sing in its honour; they even address real prayers to it.[1] They explain to the young men who the personage is whom this image represents; they tell them his secret name, which the women and the uninitiated cannot know; they relate to them his history and the part attributed to him in the life of the tribe. At other times they raise their hands towards the heaven where he is thought to dwell, or else they point their arms or the ritual instruments they have in hand in this direction;[2] this is a way of entering into communication with him. They feel his presence everywhere. He watches over the neophyte when he has withdrawn into the forest.[3] He is attentive to the manner in which the ceremonies are celebrated. The initiation is his cult. So he gives special attention to seeing that these are carried out exactly: if there are any faults or negligences, he punishes them in a terrible manner.[4]

Moreover, the authority of each of these supreme gods is not limited to a single tribe; it is recognized equally by a number of neighbouring tribes. Bunjil is adored in nearly all of Victoria, Baiame in a considerable portion of New South Wales, etc.; this is why there are so few gods for a relatively extended geographical area. So the cults of which they are the object have an international character. It even happens sometimes that mythologies intermingle, combine and make mutual borrowings. Thus the majority of the tribes who believe in Baiame also admit the existence of Daramulun; however, they accord him a slighter dignity. They make him a son or brother of Baiame, and subordinate to this latter.[5] Thus the faith in Daramulun has spread in diverse forms, into all of New South Wales. So it is far from true that religious internationalism is a peculiarity of the most recent and advanced religions. From the dawn of history, religious beliefs have manifested a tendency to overflow out of one strictly limited political society; it is as though they had a natural aptitude for crossing frontiers, and for diffusing and internationalizing themselves. Of course there have been

[1] Howitt, *Nat. Tr.*, pp. 538, 543, 553, 555, 556; Mathews, *loc. cit.*, p. 318; L. Parker, *The Euahlayi*, pp. 6, 79, 80.

[2] Howitt, *Nat. Tr.*, pp. 498, 528.

[3] Howitt, *ibid.*, p. 493; L. Parker, *The Euahlayi*, p. 76.

[4] L. Parker, *The Euahlayi*, p. 76; Howitt, *Nat. Tr.*, pp. 493, 612.

[5] Ridley, *Kamilaroi*, p. 153; L. Parker, *The Euahlayi*, p. 67; Howitt, *Nat Tr.*, p. 585; Mathews, *loc. cit.*, p. 343. In opposition to Baiame, Daramulun is sometimes presented as a necessarily evil spirit (L. Parker, *loc. cit.*; Ridley, in Brough Smyth, II, p. 285).

peoples and times when this spontaneous aptitude has been held in check by opposed social necessities; but that does not keep it from being real and, as we see, very primitive.

To Tylor this conception has appeared to be a part of so elevated a theology that he refuses to see in it anything but the product of a European importation: he would have it be a more or less denatured Christian idea.[1] Andrew Lang, on the contrary, considers them autochthonous;[2] but as he also admits that it is contrasted with all the other Australian beliefs and rests on completely different principles, he concludes that the religions of Australia are made up of two heterogeneous systems, superimposed one upon the other, and consequently derived from a double origin. On the one hand, there were ideas relative to totems and spirits, which had been suggested to men by the sight of certain natural phenomena. But at the same time, by a sort of intuition as to the nature of which he refuses to make himself clear,[3] the human intelligence succeeded at the first onset in conceiving a unique god, creator of the world and legislator of the moral order. Lang even estimates that this idea was purer of foreign elements at the beginning, and especially in Australia, than in the civilizations which immediately followed. With time, it was covered over and obscured little by little by the ever-growing mass of animistic and totemic superstitions. Thus it underwent a sort of progressive degeneration up to the day when, as the effect of a privileged culture, it succeeded in coming into its own and restated itself again with more force and clarity than it had in the first place.[4]

But the facts allow neither the sceptical hypothesis of Tylor nor the theological interpretation of Lang.

In the first place, it is certain to-day that the ideas relative to the great tribal god are of indigenous origin. They were

[1] *J.A.I.*, XXI, pp. 292 ff.

[2] *The Making of Religion*, pp. 187–293.

[3] Lang, *ibid.*, p. 331. The author confines himself to stating that the hypothesis of St. Paul does not appear to him "the most unsatisfactory."

[4] The thesis of Lang has been taken up again by Father Schmidt in the *Anthropos* (1908–1909). Replying to Sydney Hartland, who had criticized Lang's theory in an article entitled *The "High Gods" of Australia*, in *Folk-Lore* (Vol. IX, pp. 290 ff.), Father Schmidt undertook to show that Baiame, Bunjil, etc., are eternal gods, creators, omnipotent, omniscient and guardians of the moral order. We are not going to enter into this discussion, which seems to have neither interest nor importance. If these different adjectives are given a relative sense, in harmony with the Australian mind, we are quite ready to accept them, and have even used them ourselves. From this point of view, omnipotent means having more power than the other sacred beings; omniscient, seeing things that escape the vulgar and even the greatest magicians; guardian of the moral order, one causing the rules of Australian morality to be respected, howsoever much these may differ from our own. But if they want to give these words meanings which only a spiritualistic Christian could attach to them, it seems useless to discuss an opinion so contrary to the principles of the historical method.

observed before the influence of the missionaries had as yet had time to make itself felt.[1] But it does not follow that it is necessary to attribute them to a mysterious revelation. Far from being derived from a different source than the regular totemic beliefs, they are, on the contrary, only the logical working-out of these beliefs and their highest form.

We have already seen how the notion of mythical ancestors is implied in the very principles upon which totemism rests, for each of them is a totemic being. Now, though the great gods are certainly superior to these, still, there are only differences of degree between them ; we pass from the first to the second with no break of continuity. In fact, a great god is himself an ancestor of especial importance. They frequently speak to us about him as though he were a man, endowed, to be sure, with more than human powers, but one who lived a human life upon the earth.[2] He is pictured as a great hunter,[3] a powerful magician,[4] or the founder of the tribe.[5] He was the first man.[6] One legend even represents him in the form of a worn-out old man who could hardly move about.[7] If a supreme god named Mura-mura has existed among the Dieri, the very word is significant, for it serves to designate the class of the ancestors. Likewise, Nuralie, the name of a great god among the tribes on the Murray River, is sometimes used as a collective expression which is applied to the group of mythical beings whom tradition places at the origin of things.[8] They are personages wholly comparable to those of the Alcheringa.[9] In Queensland, we have already met with a god Anjea or Anjir, who made men but who seems, nevertheless, to be only the first man.[10]

A fact that has aided Australian thought to pass from the numerous ancestral geniuses to the idea of the tribal god is that between the two extremes a middle term has been inserted, which has served as a transition : these are the civilizing heroes. The fabulous beings whom we call by this name are really simple

[1] On this question, see N. W. Thomas, *Baiame and Bell-bird—A Note on Australian Religion*, in *Man*, 1905, No. 28. Cf. Lang, *Magic and Religion*, p. 25. Waitz had already upheld the original character of this conception in his *Anthropologie d. Naturvölker*, pp. 796–798.

[2] Dawson, p. 49 ; Meyer, *Encounter Bay Tribe*, in Woods, pp. 205, 206 ; Howitt, *Nat. Tr.*, pp. 481, 491, 492, 494 ; Ridley, *Kamilaroi*, p. 136.

[3] Taplin, *The Narrinyeri*, pp. 55–56.

[4] L. Parker, *More Austr. Leg. Tales*, p. 94.

[5] Brough Smyth, I, pp. 425–427.

[6] Taplin, *ibid.*, p. 60.

[7] Taplin, *ibid.*, p. 61.

[8] " The world was created by beings called Nuralie ; these beings, who had already long existed, had the forms of crows or of eagle-hawks " (Brough Smyth, I, pp. 423–424).

[9] " Bayamee," says Mrs. Parker, " is for the Euahlayi what the Alcheringa is for the Arunta " (*The Euahlayi*, p. 6).

[10] See above, pp. 257 f.

ancestors to whom mythology has attributed an eminent place in the history of the tribe, and whom it has, for this reason, set above the others. We have even seen that they ordinarily form a part of the totemic organization: Mangarkunjerkunja belongs to the Lizard totem and Putiaputia to the Wild Cat totem. But on the other hand, the functions which they are believed to fulfil, or to have fulfilled, are closely similar to those incumbent upon a great god. He, too, is believed to have introduced the arts of civilization among men, to have been the founder of the principal social institutions and the revealer of the great religious ceremonies which still remain under his control. If he is the father of men, it is because he manufactured them rather than begat them: but Mangarkunjerkunja also made them. Before his time, there were no men, but only unformed masses of flesh, in which the different members and even the different individuals were not yet separated from one another. It was he who cut up this original matter and made real human beings out of it.[1] Between this mode of fabrication and the one the myth we have spoken of attributes to Bunjil, there are only shades of difference. Moreover, the bonds uniting these two sorts of figures to each other are well shown by the fact that a relationship of descent is sometimes established between them. Among the Kurnai, the hero of the bull-roarer, Tundun, is the son of the great god Mungan-ngaua.[2] Likewise, among the Euahlayi, Daramulun, the son or brother of Baiame, is identical with Gayandi who is the equivalent of the Tundun of the Kurnai.[3] Of course it is not necessary to conclude from these facts that the great god is nothing more than a civilizing hero. There are cases where these two personages are carefully differentiated. But if they are not confounded, they are at least relatives. So it sometimes happens that we find it hard to distinguish them; there are some who could be classified equally well in one category or the other. Thus, we have spoken of Atnatu as a civilizing hero; but he comes very near to being a great god.

The notion of a supreme god even depends so closely upon the entire system of the totemic beliefs that it still bears their mark. Tundun is a divine hero, as we have just seen, who is very close to the tribal divinity; now among the Kurnai, the

[1] In another myth, reported by Spencer and Gillen, a wholly analogous rôle is filled by two personages living in heaven, named Ungambikula (*Nat. Tr.*, pp. 388 ff.).

[2] Howitt, *Nat. Tr.*, p. 493.

[3] Parker, *The Euahlayi*, pp. 62–66, 67. This is because the great god is connected with the bull-roarer, which is identified with the thunder; for the roaring of this ritual instrument is connected with the rolling of thunder.

same word means totem.[1] Similarly, among the Arunta, Altjira is the name of a great god; it is also the name of the maternal totem.[2] But there is more to be said than this; many great gods have an obviously totemic aspect. Daramulun is an eagle-hawk; [3] his mother, an emu.[4] It is also under the features of an emu that Baiame is represented.[5] The Altjira of the Arunta has the legs of an emu.[6] Before being the name of a great god, Nuralie designated, as we just saw, the ancestor-founders of the tribe; now some of these were crows, the others hawks.[7] According to Howitt,[8] Bunjil is always represented in a human form; however, the same word serves to designate the totem of a phratry, the eagle-hawk. At least one of his sons is among the totems included in the phratry to which he has given, or from which he has taken his name.[9] His brother is Pallyan, the bat; now this latter serves as sexual totem for the men in many tribes in Victoria.[10]

We can even go farther and state more definitely the connection which these great gods have with the totemic system. We have just seen that Bunjil is the totem of a phratry. Daramulun, like Bunjil, is an eagle-hawk, and we know that this bird is the totem of phratries in a large number of south-eastern tribes.[11] We have already pointed out that Nuralie seems to have originally been a collective term designating indistinctly either eagle-hawks or crows; now in the tribes where this myth has been observed, the crow is the totem of one of the two phratries, the eagle-hawk, that of the other.[12] Also, the legendary history of the great gods resembles that of the totems of the phratries very closely. The myths, and sometimes the rites, commemorate the struggles which each of these divinities fought against a carnivorous bird, over which it triumphed only with the greatest difficulty. Bunjil, the first man, after making the second man, Karween, entered into a conflict with him, and in the course of a sort of duel, he wounded him severely and changed

[1] Howitt, *Nat. Tr.*, p. 135. The word meaning totem is written *thundung* by Howitt.

[2] Strehlow, I, pp. 1–2 and II, p. 59. It will be remembered that, among the Arunta, the maternal totem was quite probably the real totem at first.

[3] Howitt, *Nat. Tr.*, p. 555.

[4] *Ibid.*, pp. 546, 560.

[5] Ridley, *Kamilaroi*, pp. 136, 156. He is represented in this form during the initiation rites of the Kamilaroi. According to another legend, he is a black swan (L. Parker, *More Aust. Leg. Tales*, p. 94).

[6] Strehlow, I, p. 1.

[7] Brough Smyth, I, pp. 423–424.

[8] *Nat. Tr.*, p. 492.

[9] Howitt, *Nat. Tr.*, p. 128.

[10] Brough Smyth, I, pp. 417–423.

[11] See above, p. 108.

[12] There are phratries bearing the names Kilpara (crow) and Mukwara. This is the explanation of the myth itself, which is reported by Brough Smyth (I, pp. 423–424).

him into a crow.[1] The two species of Nurtalie are represented as two hostile groups which were originally in a constant state of war.[2] Baiame, on his side, had to fight against Mullian, the cannibal eagle-hawk, who, by the way, is identical with Daramulun.[3] Now, as we have seen, there is also a sort of constitutional hostility between the totems of the phratries. This parallelism completes the proof that the mythology of the great gods and that of these totems are closely related. This relationship will appear still more evident if we notice that the rival of the god is regularly either a crow or an eagle-hawk, and that these are quite generally the totems of the phratries.[4]

So Baiame, Daramulun, Nuralie and Bunjil seem to be phratry-totems who have been deified; and we may imagine that this apotheosis took place as follows. It is obviously in the assemblies which take place in regard to the initiation that the conception was elaborated, for the great gods do not play a rôle of any importance except in these rites, and are strangers to the other religious ceremonies. Moreover, as the initiation is the principal form of the tribal cult, it is only on this occasion that a tribal mythology could arise. We have already seen how the rituals of circumcision and subincision spontaneously tend to personify themselves under the form of civilizing heroes. However, these heroes exercised no supremacy; they were on the same footing as the other legendary benefactors of society. But wherever the tribe acquired a livelier sentiment of itself, this sentiment naturally incarnated itself in some personage, who became its symbol. In order to account for the bonds uniting them to one another, no matter what clan they belonged to, men imagined that they were all descended from the same stock and that they were all descended from a single father, to whom they owe their existence, though he owed his to no one. The god of the initiation was predestined to this rôle, for, according to an expression frequently coming to the lips of the natives, the object of the initiation is to make or manufacture men. So they attributed a creative power to this god, and for all these reasons, he found himself invested with a prestige setting him well above the other heroes of the mythology. These others became his auxiliaries, subordinate to him; they were made his sons or younger brothers, as was the case with Tundun, Gayandi, Karween,

[1] Brough Smyth, I, pp. 425–427. Cf. Howitt, *Nat. Tr.*, p. 486. In this case, Karween is identified with the blue heron.

[2] Brough Smyth, I, p. 423.

[3] Ridley, *Kamilaroi*, p. 136; Howitt, *Nat. Tr.*, p 585; Mathews, *J. of R. S. of N.S. Wales*, XXVIII (1894), p. 111.

[4] See above, p. 145. Cf. Father Schmidt, *The Origin of the Idea of God*, in *Anthropos*, 1909.

Pallyan, etc. But other sacred beings already existed, who occupied an equally eminent place in the religious system of the clan: these were the totems of the phratries. Wherever these are maintained, they are believed to keep the totems of the clans dependent upon them. Thus they had all that was necessary for becoming tribal divinities themselves. So it was only natural that a partial confusion should arise between these two sorts of mythical beings; it is thus that one of the two fundamental totems of the tribe gave his traits to the great god. But as it was necessary to explain why only one of them was called to this dignity and the other excluded, they supposed that this latter, in the course of a fight against his rival, was vanquished and that his exclusion was the consequence of his defeat. This theory was the more readily admitted because it was in accord with the rest of the mythology, where the totems of the phratries are generally considered enemies of one another.

A myth observed by Mrs. Parker among the Euahlayi[1] may serve to confirm this explanation, for it merely translates it into figurative language. It is related that in this tribe, the totems were only the names given to the different parts of Baiame's body at first. So the clans were, in a sense, the fragments of the divine body. Now is this not just another way of saying that the great god is the synthesis of all the totems and consequently the personification of the tribal unity?

But at the same time, it takes an international character. In fact, the members of the tribe to which the young initiates belong are not the only ones who assist at the ceremonies of initiation; representatives from the neighbouring tribes are specially summoned to these celebrations, which thus become sorts of international fairs, at once religious and laical.[2] Beliefs elaborated in social environments thus constituted could not remain the exclusive patrimony of any special nationality. The stranger to whom they are revealed carries them back to his own tribe when he returns home; and as, sooner or later, he is forced to invite his former hosts, there is a continual exchange of ideas from tribe to tribe. It is thus that an international mythology was established, of which the great god was quite naturally the essential element, for it had its origin in the rites

[1] *Op. cit.*, p. 7. Among these same people, the principal wife of Baiame is also represented as the mother of all the totems, without belonging to any totem herself (*ibid.*, pp. 7, 79).

[2] See Howitt, *Nat. Tr.*, pp. 511 f., 513, 602 ff.; Mathews, *J. of R.S. of N.S. Wales*, XXXVIII, p. 270. They invite to these feasts not only the tribes with whom a regular *connubium* is established, but also those with whom there are quarrels to be arranged; the vendetta, half-ceremonial and half-serious, take place on these occasions.

of initiation which it is his function to personify. So his name passed from one language to another, along with the representations which were attached to it. The fact that the names of the phratries are generally the same in very different tribes could not fail to facilitate this diffusion. The internationalism of the totems opened the way for that of the great god.

V

We thus reach the highest conception to which totemism has arrived. This is the point where it touches and prepares the religions which are to follow, and aids us in understanding them. But at the same time, we are able to see that this culminating idea is united without any interruption to the crudest beliefs which we analysed to start with.

In fact, the great tribal god is only an ancestral spirit who finally won a pre-eminent place. The ancestral spirits are only entities forged in the image of the individual souls whose origin they are destined to explain. The souls, in their turn, are only the form taken by the impersonal forces which we found at the basis of totemism, as they individualize themselves in the human body. The unity of the system is as great as its complexity.

In this work of elaboration, the idea of the soul has undoubtedly played an important part: it is through it that the idea of personality has been introduced into the domain of religion. But it is not true that, as the theorists of animism maintain, it contains the germ of the whole religion. First of all, it presupposes the notion of *mana* or the totemic principle of which it is only a special form. Then, if the spirits and gods could not be conceived before the soul, they are, nevertheless, more than mere human souls, liberated by death; else whence would come their supernatural powers? The idea of the soul has merely served to direct the mythological imagination in a new way and to suggest to it constructions of a new sort. But the matter for these conceptions has been taken, not from the representation of the soul, but from this reservoir of the anonymous and diffused forces which constitute the original foundation of religions. The creation of mythical personalities has only been another way of thinking of these essential forces.

As for the notion of the great god, it is due entirely to the sentiment whose action we have already observed in the genesis of the most specifically totemic beliefs: this is the tribal sentiment. In fact, we have seen that totemism was not the work of isolated clans, but that it was always elaborated in the body of a tribe which was to some degree conscious of its unity. It is for this reason that the different cults peculiar to each clan mutually touch and complete each other in such a way as to form a unified whole.[1] Now it is this same sentiment of a tribal unity which is expressed in the conception of a supreme god, common to the tribe as a whole. So they are quite the same causes which are active at the bottom and at the top of this religious system.

However, up to the present, we have considered the religious representations as if they were self-sufficient and could be explained by themselves. But in reality, they are inseparable from the rites, not only because they manifest themselves there, but also because they, in their turn, feel the influence of these. Of course the cult depends upon the beliefs, but it also reacts upon them. So in order to understand them better, it is important to understand it better. The moment has come for undertaking its study.

[1] See above, p. 155.

BOOK III

THE PRINCIPAL RITUAL ATTITUDES

CHAPTER I

THE NEGATIVE CULT AND ITS FUNCTIONS
THE ASCETIC RITES

WE do not have the intention of attempting a complete description of the primitive cult in what is to follow. Being preoccupied especially with reaching that which is most elementary and most fundamental in the religious life, we shall not attempt to reconstruct in detail the frequently confused multiplicity of all the ritual forms. But out of the midst of this extreme diversity of practices we should like to touch upon the most characteristic attitudes which the primitive observes in the celebration of his cult, to classify the most general forms of his rites, and to determine their origins and significance, in order that we may control and, if there is occasion, make more definite the results to which the analysis of the beliefs has led us.[1]

Every cult presents a double aspect, one negative, the other positive. In reality, of course, the two sorts of rites which we denominate thus are closely associated ; we shall see that they suppose one another. But still, they are different and, if it is only to understand their connection, it is necessary to distinguish them.

I

By definition, sacred beings are separated beings. That which characterizes them is that there is a break of continuity between them and the profane beings. Normally, the first are outside the others. A whole group of rites has the object of realizing this state of separation which is essential. Since their function is to prevent undue mixings and to keep one of these two domains from encroaching upon the other, they are only able to impose abstentions or negative acts. Therefore, we propose to give the name negative cult to the system formed by these special rites. They do not prescribe certain acts to the faithful, but confine themselves to forbidding certain ways of acting ; so they all

[1] There is one form of ritual especially which we leave completely aside ; this is the oral ritual which must be studied in a special volume of the *Collection de l'Année Sociologique.*

take the form of interdictions, or as is commonly said by ethnographers, of *taboos*. This latter word is the one used in the Polynesian languages to designate the institution in virtue of which certain things are withdrawn from common use[1]; it is also an adjective expressing the distinctive characteristic of these kinds of things. We have already had occasion to show how hard it is to translate a strictly local and dialectical expression like this into a generic term. There is no religion where there are no interdictions and where they do not play a considerable part; so it is regrettable that the consecrated terminology should seem to make so universal an institution into a peculiarity of Polynesia.[2] The expression *interdicts* or *interdictions* seems to us to be much more preferable. However, the word taboo, like the word totem, is so customary that it would show an excess of purism to prohibit it systematically; also, the inconveniences it may have are attenuated when its real meaning and importance have once been definitely stated.

But there are interdictions of different sorts which it is important to distinguish; for we shall not have to treat all kinds of interdictions in this chapter.

First of all, beside those coming from religion, there are others which are due to magic. The two have this in common, that they declare certain things incompatible, and prescribe the separation of the things whose incompatibility is thus proclaimed. But there are also very grave differences between them. In the first place, the sanctions are not the same in the two cases. Of course the violation of the religious interdicts is frequently believed, as we shall presently see, to bring about material disorders mechanically, from which the guilty man will suffer, and which are regarded as a judgment on his act. But even if these really come about this spontaneous and automatic judgment is not the only one; it is always completed by another one, supposing human intervention. A real punishment is added to this, if it does not anticipate it, and this one is deliberately inflicted by men; or at least there is a blame and public reprobation. Even when the sacrilege has been punished, as it were, by the sickness or natural death of its author, it is also defamed; it offends opinion, which reacts against it; it puts the man who did it in fault. On the contrary, the magic interdiction is judged only by the material consequences which the forbidden act is

[1] See the article *Taboo* in the *Encyclopædia Britannica*, written by Frazer.

[2] Facts prove the reality of this inconvenience. There is no lack of writers who, putting their trust in the word, have believed that the institution thus designated was peculiar to primitive peoples in general, or even to the Polynesians (see Réville, *Religion des peuples primitifs*, II, p. 55; Richard, *La Femme dans l'histoire*, p. 435).

believed to produce, with a sort of physical necessity. In disobeying, a man runs risks similar to those to which an invalid exposes himself in not following the advice of his physician; but in this case disobedience is not a fault; it creates no indignation. There is no sin in magic. Moreover, this difference in sanction is due to a profound difference in the nature of the interdictions. The religious interdiction necessarily implies the notion of sacredness; it comes from the respect inspired by the sacred object, and its purpose is to keep this respect from failing. On the other hand, the interdictions of magic suppose only a wholly lay notion of property. The things which the magician recommends to be kept separate are those which, by reason of their characteristic properties, cannot be brought together and confused without danger. Even if he happens to ask his clients to keep at a distance from certain sacred things, it is not through respect for them and fear that they may be profaned, for, as we know, magic lives on profanations;[1] it is merely for reasons of temporal utility. In a word, religious interdictions are categorical imperatives; others are useful maxims, the first form of hygienic and medical interdictions. We cannot study two orders of facts as different as these simultaneously, or even under the same name, without confusion. We are only concerned with the religious interdictions here.[2]

But a new distinction is necessary between these latter.

There are religious interdictions whose object is to separate two sacred things of different species from each other. For example, it will be remembered that among the Wakelbura the scaffold upon which the corpse is exposed must be made exclusively of materials belonging to the phratry of the dead man; this is as much as to say that all contact between the corpse, which is sacred, and the things of the other phratry, which are also sacred, but differently, is forbidden. Elsewhere, the arms which one uses to hunt an animal with cannot be made out of a kind of wood that is classed in the same social group as the animal itself.[3] But the most important of these interdictions are the ones which we shall study in the next chapter; they are intended to prevent all communication between the purely sacred and the impurely sacred, between the sacredly auspicious and the sacredly inauspicious. All these interdictions have one common

[1] See above, p. 43.

[2] This is not saying that there is a radical break of continuity between the religious and the magic interdictions: on the contrary, it is one whose true nature is not decided. There are interdicts of folk-lore of which it is hard to say whether they are religious or magic. But their distinction is necessary, for we believe that the magic interdicts cannot be understood except as a function of the religious ones.

[3] See above, p. 149.

characteristic; they come, not from the fact that some things are sacred while others are not, but from the fact that there are inequalities and incompatibilities between sacred things. So they do not touch what is essential in the idea of sacredness. The observance of these prohibitions can give place only to isolated rites which are particular and almost exceptional; but it could not make a real cult, for before all, a cult is made by regular relations between the profane and the sacred as such.

But there is another system of religious interdictions which is much more extended and important; this is the one which separates, not different species of sacred things, but all that is sacred from all that is profane. So it is derived immediately from the notion of sacredness itself, and it limits itself to expressing and realizing this. Thus it furnishes the material for a veritable cult, and even of a cult which is at the basis of all the others; for the attitude which it prescribes is one from which the worshipper must never depart in all his relations with the sacred. It is what we call the negative cult. We may say that its interdicts are the religious interdicts *par excellence*.[1] It is only these that we shall discuss in the following pages.

But they take multiple forms. Here are the principal ones which we observe in Australia.

Before all are the interdictions of contact; these are the original taboos, of which the others are scarcely more than particular varieties. They rest upon the principle that the profane should never touch the sacred. We have seen already that the uninitiated may not touch the churinga or the bull-roarers under any circumstances. If adults are allowed the free use of them, it is because initiation has conferred a sacred character upon them. Blood, and especially that which flows during the initiation, has a religious virtue;[2] it is under the same interdict.[3] It is the same

[1] Many of the interdictions between sacred things can be traced back, we think, to those between the sacred and the profane. This is the case with the interdicts of age or rank. For example, in Australia, there are sacred foods which are reserved for the initiated. But these foods are not all sacred to the same degree; there is a hierarchy among them. Nor are the initiated all equal. They do not enjoy all their religious rights from the first, but only enter step by step into the domain of religious things. They must pass through a whole series of ranks which are conferred upon them one after another, after special trials and ceremonies; it requires months and sometimes even years to reach the highest rank. Now special foods are assigned to each of these ranks; the men of the lower ranks may not touch the foods which rightfully belong to the men of the superior ones (see Mathews, *Ethnol. Notes*, etc., *loc. cit.* pp. 262 ff.; Parker, *The Euahlayi*, p. 23; Spencer and Gillen, *Nor. Tr.*, pp. 611 ff.; *Nat. Tr.*, pp. 470 ff.). So the more sacred repels the less sacred; but this is because the second is profane in relation to the first. In fine, all the interdictions arrange themselves in two classes: the interdictions between the sacred and the profane and the purely sacred and the impurely sacred.

[2] See above, p. 137.

[3] Spencer and Gillen, *Nat. Tr.*, p. 463.

with the hair.[1] A dead man is sacred because the soul which animated the body stays with the corpse; for this reason it is sometimes forbidden to carry the bones of a dead man about unless they are wrapped up in a piece of bark.[2] Even the place where the death took place should be avoided, for they believe that the soul of the dead man continues to haunt the spot. That is why they break camp and move some distance away;[3] in certain cases they destroy it along with everything it contains,[4] and a certain time must elapse before they can come back to the same place.[5] Thus it comes about that a dying man creates an empty space about him; they abandon him after they have installed him as comfortably as possible.[6]

An exceptionally intimate contact is the one resulting from the absorption of food. Hence comes the interdiction against eating the sacred animals or vegetables, and especially those serving as totems.[7] Such an act appears so very sacrilegeous that the prohibition covers even adults, or at least, the majority of them; only the old men attain a sufficient religious dignity to escape this interdict sometimes. This prohibition has sometimes been explained by the mythical kinship uniting the man to the animals whose name he bears; they are protected by the sentiment of sympathy which they inspire by their position as kin.[8] But the fact that the consumption of the forbidden flesh is believed to cause sickness or death automatically shows that this interdiction does not have its origin in the simple revolt of the feeling of domestic relationship. Forces of another sort are in action which are analogous to those in all religions and which are believed to react against sacrileges.

Moreover, if certain foods are forbidden to the profane because they are sacred, certain others, on the contrary, are forbidden to persons of a sacred character, because they are profane. Thus it frequently happens that certain animals are specially designated as the food of women; for this reason, they believe that they partake of a feminine nature and that they are consequently

[1] *Nat. Tr.*, p. 538; *Nor. Tr.*, p. 640. [2] *Nor. Tr.*, p. 531.

[3] *Nor. Tr.*, pp. 518 f.; Howitt, *Nat. Tr.*, p. 449.

[4] Spencer and Gillen, *Nat. Tr.*, p. 498; Schulze, *loc. cit.*, p. 231.

[5] Spencer and Gillen, *Nat. Tr.*, p. 499. [6] Howitt, *Nat. Tr.*, p. 451.

[7] If the alimentary interdictions which concern the totemic plant or vegetable are the most important, they are far from being the only ones. We have seen that there are foods which are forbidden to the non-initiated because they are sacred; now very different causes may confer this character. For example, as we shall presently see, the birds which are seen on the tops of trees are reputed to be sacred, because they are neighbours to the great god who lives in heaven. Thus, it is possible that for different reasons the flesh of certain animals has been specially reserved for the old men and that consequently it has seemed to partake of the sacred character recognized in these latter.

[8] See Frazer, *Totemism*, p. 7.

profane. On the other hand, the young initiate is submitted to a series of rites of particular severity; to give him the virtues which will enable him to enter into the world of sacred things, from which he had up till then been excluded, they centre an exceptionally powerful group of religious forces upon him. Thus he enters into a state of sanctity which keeps all that is profane at a distance. Then he is not allowed to eat the game which is regarded as the special food of women.[1]

But contact may be established by other means than the touch. One comes into relations with a thing by merely regarding it: a look is a means of contact. This is why the sight of sacred things is forbidden to the profane in certain cases. A woman should never see the instruments of the cult; the most that is permitted her is to catch a glimpse of them from afar.[2] It is the same with the totemic paintings executed on the bodies of the officiants in the exceptionally important ceremonies.[3] The exceptional solemnity of the rites of initiation prevents the women in certain tribes from seeing the place where they were celebrated[4] or even the neophyte himself.[5] The sacred character which is imminent in the ceremony as a whole is naturally found in the persons of those who directed it or took some part in it; the result of this is that the novice may not raise his eyes to them, and this interdiction continues even after the rite is accomplished.[6] A dead man is also removed from view sometimes: his face is covered over in such a way that it cannot be seen.[7]

The word is another way of entering into relations with persons or things. The breath expired establishes a communication; this is a part of us which spreads outwards. Thus it is forbidden to the profane to address the sacred beings or simply to speak in their presence. Just as the neophyte must not regard either the operators or the assistants, so it is forbidden to him to converse with them except by signs; and this interdiction keeps the place to which it has been raised, by means of a special rite.[8]

[1] Howitt, *Nat. Tr.*, p. 674.—There is one interdiction of contact of which we say nothing because it is very hard to determine its exact nature: this is sexual contact. There are religious periods when a man cannot have commerce with a woman (*Nor. Tr.*, pp. 293, 295; *Nat. Tr.*, p. 397). Is this because the woman is profane or because the sexual act is dreaded? This question cannot be decided in passing. We set it aside along with all that concerns conjugal and sexual rites. It is too closely connected with the problems of marriage and the family to be separated from them.

[2] *Nat. Tr.*, p. 134; Howitt, *Nat. Tr.*, p. 354.

[3] Spencer and Gillen, *Nat. Tr.*, p. 624.

[4] Howitt, *Nat. Tr.*, p. 572.

[5] *Ibid.*, p. 661.

[6] *Nat. Tr.*, p. 386; Howitt, *Nat. Tr.*, pp. 655, 665.

[7] Among the Wiimbaio (Howitt, *ibid.*, p. 451).

[8] Howitt, *ibid.*, pp. 624, 661, 663, 667; Spencer and Gillen, *Nat. Tr.*, pp. 221, 382 ff.; *Nor. Tr.*, pp. 335, 344, 353, 369.

In a general way, there are, among the Arunta, moments in the course of the great ceremonies when silence is obligatory.[1] As soon as the churinga are exposed, every one keeps still, or if someone talks, he does so in a low voice or with his lips only.[2]

Besides the sacred things, there are words and sounds which have the same character; they should not pass the lips of the profane or enter their ears. There are ritual songs which women must not hear under pain of death.[3] They may hear the noise of the bull-roarers, but only from a distance. Every proper name is considered an essential element of the person who bears it; being closely associated in the mind to the idea of this person, it participates in the sentiments which this latter inspires. So if the one is sacred, the other is. Therefore, it may not be pronounced in the course of the profane life. Among the Warramunga there is one totem which is particularly venerated, this is the snake called Wollunqua; its name is taboo.[4] It is the same with Baiame, Daramulun and Bunjil; the esoteric form of their name must not be revealed to the uninitiate.[5] During mourning, the name of the dead man must not be mentioned, at least by his parents, except when there is an absolute necessity, and even in this case it must be whispered.[6] This interdiction is frequently perpetual for the widow and certain relatives.[7] Among certain peoples, this even extends beyond the family; all the individuals whose name is the same as that of the dead man must change theirs temporarily.[8] But there is more than this: the relatives and intimate friends sometimes abstain from certain words in the usual language, undoubtedly because they were employed by the dead man; these gaps are filled in by means of periphrases or words taken from some foreign dialects.[9] In addition to their public and everyday names all men have another which is kept a secret: the women and children do not know it; it is never used in the ordinary life. This is because it has a religious character.[10] There are even ceremonies during which it is necessary to speak a special language which must not be used for profane purposes. It is the beginning of a sacred language.[11]

Not only are the sacred beings separated from the profane, but also nothing which either directly or indirectly concerns the

[1] Spencer and Gillen, *Nat. Tr.*, pp. 221, 262, 288, 303, 378, 380.
[2] *Ibid.*, p. 302. [3] Howitt, *Nat. Tr.*, p. 581.
[4] *Nor. Tr.*, p. 227. [5] See above, p. 288.
[6] Spencer and Gillen, *Nat. Tr.*, p. 498; *Nor. Tr.*, p. 526; Taplin, *Narrinyeri*, p. 19.
[7] Howitt, *Nat. Tr.*, pp. 466, 469 ff.
[8] Wyatt, *Adelaide and Encounter Bay Tribes*, in Woods, p. 165.
[9] Howitt, *Nat. Tr.*, p. 470.
[10] *Ibid.*, p. 657; Spencer and Gillen, *Nat. Tr.*, p. 139; *Nor. Tr.*, pp. 580 ff.
[11] Howitt, *Nat. Tr.*, p. 537.

profane life should be confused with the religious life. Complete nudity is frequently demanded of the native as a prerequisite to being admitted to participation in the rites ;[1] he is required to strip himself of all his habitual ornaments, even those to which he is the most attached, and from which he separates himself the least willingly because of the protecting virtues he attributes to them.[2] If he is obliged to decorate himself to play his part in the ritual, this decoration has to be made specially for the occasion ; it is a ceremonial costume, a gala dress.[3] As these ornaments are sacred, owing to the use made of them, he is forbidden to use them in profane affairs ; when the ceremony is finished, they are buried or burnt ;[4] the men must even wash themselves in such a way as to carry away with them no trace of the decorations with which they were adorned.[5]

In general, all acts characteristic of the ordinary life are forbidden while those of the religious life are taking place. The act of eating is, of itself, profane ; for it takes place every day, it satisfies essentially utilitarian and material needs and it is a part of our ordinary existence.[6] This is why it is prohibited in religious times. When one totemic group has loaned its churinga to a foreign clan, it is an exceptionally solemn moment when they are brought back and put into the ertnatulunga ; all those who take part in the ceremony must fast as long as it lasts, and it lasts a long time.[7] The same rule is observed during the rites,[8] of which we shall speak in the next chapter, as well as at certain moments of the initiation.[9]

For this same reason, all temporal occupations are suspended while the great religious solemnities are taking place. According to a remark of Spencer and Gillen,[10] which we have already had occasion to cite, the life of the Australian is divided into two very distinct parts : the one is devoted to hunting, fishing and warfare ; the other is consecrated to the cult, and these two forms

[1] Howitt, *Nat. Tr.*, pp. 544, 597, 614, 620.

[2] For example, the hair belt which he ordinarily wears (Spencer and Gillen, *Nat. Tr.*, p. 171).

[3] *Ibid.*, p. 624 ff. [4] Howitt, *Nat. Tr.*, p. 556. [5] *Ibid.*, p. 587.

[6] This act takes on a sacred character, it is true, when the elements eaten are sacred. But in itself, the act is so very profane that eating a sacred food always constitutes a profanation. The profanation may be permitted or even ordered, but, as we shall see below, only on condition that rites attenuating or expiating it precede or accompany it. The existence of these rites shows that, by itself, the sacred thing should not be eaten.

[7] *Nor. Tr.*, p. 263. [8] Spencer and Gillen, *Nat. Tr.*, p. 171.

[9] Howitt, *Nat. Tr.*, p. 674. Perhaps the rule against talking during the great religious solemnities is due to the same cause. Men speak, and especially in a high voice, during ordinary life ; then, in the religious life they ought to keep still or talk in a low voice. This same consideration is not foreign to the alimentary interdictions (see above, p. 128).

[10] *Nor. Tr.*, p. 33.

of activity mutually exclude and repel one another. It is on this principle that the universal institution of religious days of rest reposes. The distinctive character of the feast-days in all known religions is the cessation of work and the suspension of public and private life, in so far as it does not have a religious objective. This repose is not merely a sort of temporary relaxation which men have given themselves in order to give themselves up more freely to the sentiments of joy ordinarily awakened by the feast-days; for they are sad feasts, consecrated to mourning and repentance, and during which this cessation is no less obligatory. This is because work is an eminent form of profane activity: it has no other apparent end than to provide for the temporal necessities of life; it puts us in relations with ordinary things only. On feast days, on the contrary, the religious life attains an exceptional degree of intensity. So the contrast between the two forms of existence is especially marked at this moment; consequently, they cannot remain near to each other. A man cannot approach his god intimately while he still bears on him marks of his profane life; inversely, he cannot return to his usual occupations when a rite has just sanctified him. So the ritual day of rest is only one particular case of the general incompatibility separating the sacred from the profane; it is the result of an interdiction.

It would be impossible to enumerate here all the different interdictions which have been observed, even in the Australian religions alone. Like the notion of sacredness upon which it rests, the system of interdicts extends into the most diverse relations; it is even used deliberately for utilitarian ends.[1]

[1] Since there is a sacred principle, the soul, within each man, from the very first, the individual is surrounded by interdicts, the original form of the moral interdicts which isolate and protect the human person to-day. Thus the corpse of his victim is considered dangerous for a murderer (Spencer and Gillen, *Nat. Tr.*, p. 492), and is taboo for him. Now the interdicts having this origin are frequently used by individuals as a means of withdrawing certain things from common use and thus establishing a property right over them. " When a man goes away from the camp, leaving his arms and food there," says Roth, speaking of the tribes on the Palmer River (North Queensland), " if he urinates near the objects he leaves, they become *tami* (equivalent to taboo) and he may be sure of finding them intact on his return " (*North Queensland Ethnography*, in *Records of the Australian Museum*, Vol. VII, No. 2, p. 75). This is because the urine, like the blood, is believed to contain some of the sacred force which is personal to the individual. So it keeps strangers at a distance. For the same reasons, the spoken word may also serve as a vehicle for these same influences; that is how it becomes possible to prevent access to an object by a mere verbal declaration. This power of making interdicts varies with different individuals; it is greater as their character is more sacred. Men have this privilege almost to the exclusion of women (Roth cites one single case of a taboo imposed by women); it is at its maximum with the chiefs and old men, who use it to monopolize whatever things they find it convenient to (Roth, *ibid.*, p. 77). Thus the religious interdict becomes a right of property and an administrative rule.

But howsoever complex it may be, it finally rests upon two fundamental interdictions, which summarize it and dominate it.

In the first place, the religious life and the profane life cannot coexist in the same place. If the former is to develop, a special spot must be placed at its disposition, from which the second is excluded. Hence comes the founding of temples and sanctuaries: these are the spots awarded to sacred beings and things and serve them as residences, for they cannot establish themselves in any place except on the condition of entirely appropriating to themselves all within a certain distance. Such arrangements are so indispensable to all religious life that even the most inferior religions cannot do without them. The ertnatulunga, the spot where the churinga are deposited, is a veritable sanctuary. So the uninitiated are not allowed to approach it. It is even forbidden to carry on any profane occupation whatsoever there. As we shall presently see, there are other holy places where important ceremonies are celebrated.[1]

Likewise, the religious life and the profane life cannot coexist in the same unit of time. It is necessary to assign determined days or periods to the first, from which all profane occupations are excluded. Thus feast days are born. There is no religion, and, consequently, no society which has not known and practised this division of time into two distinct parts, alternating with one another according to a law varying with the peoples and the civilizations; as we have already pointed out, it was probably the necessity of this alternation which led men to introduce into the continuity and homogeneity of duration, certain distinctions and differentiations which it does not naturally have.[2] Of course, it is almost impossible that the religious life should ever succeed in concentrating itself hermetically in the places and times which are thus attributed to it; it is inevitable that a little of it should filter out. There are always some sacred things outside the sanctuaries; there are some rites that can be celebrated on work-days. But these are sacred things of the second rank and rites of a lesser importance. Concentration remains the dominating characteristic of this organization. Generally this concentration is complete for all that concerns the public cult, which cannot be celebrated except in common. The individual, private cult is the only one which comes very near to the temporal life. Thus the contrast between these two successive phases of human life attains its maximum of intensity in the inferior societies; for it is there that the individual cult is the most rudimentary.[3]

[1] See below, this book, ch. ii. [2] See above, p. 10.
[3] See above, p. 219.

II

Up to the present, the negative cult has been presented to us only as a system of abstentions. So it seems to serve only to inhibit activity, and not to stimulate it or to modify it. And yet, as an unexpected reaction to this inhibitive effect, it is found to exercise a positive action of the highest importance over the religious and moral nature of the individual.

In fact, owing to the barrier which separates the sacred from the profane, a man cannot enter into intimate relations with sacred things except after ridding himself of all that is profane in him. He cannot lead a religious life of even a slight intensity unless he commences by withdrawing more or less completely from the temporal life. So the negative cult is in one sense a means in view of an end : it is a condition of access to the positive cult. It does not confine itself to protecting sacred beings from vulgar contact ; it acts upon the worshipper himself and modifies his condition positively. The man who has submitted himself to its prescribed interdictions is not the same afterwards as he was before. Before, he was an ordinary being who, for this reason, had to keep at a distance from the religious forces. Afterwards, he is on a more equal footing with them ; he has approached the sacred by the very act of leaving the profane ; he has purified and sanctified himself by the very act of detaching himself from the base and trivial matters that debased his nature. So the negative rites confer efficient powers just as well as the positive ones ; the first, like the second, can serve to elevate the religious tone of the individual. According to a very true remark which has been made, no one can engage in a religious ceremony of any importance without first submitting himself to a sort of preliminary initiation which introduces him progressively into the sacred world.[1] Unctions, lustrations, benedictions or any essentially positive operation may be used for this purpose ; but the same result may be attained by means of fasts and vigils or retreat and silence, that is to say, by ritual abstinences, which are nothing more than certain interdictions put into practice.

When there are only particular and isolated negative rites, their positive action is generally too slight to be easily perceptible. But there are circumstances when a whole system of interdictions is concentrated on one man ; in these cases, their effects accumulate, and thus become more manifest. This takes place in Australia at the time of the initiation. The neophyte is submitted to a

[1] See Hubert and Mauss, *Essai sur la nature et la fonction du sacrifice*, in *Mélanges d'histoire des religions*, pp. 22 ff.

great variety of negative rites. He must withdraw from the society in which his existence has been passed up till then, and from almost all human society. Not only is it forbidden for him to see women and uninitiated persons,[1] but he also goes to live in the brush, far from his fellows, under the direction of some old men who serve him as godfathers.[2] So very true is it that the forest is considered his natural environment, that in a certain number of tribes, the word with which the initiation is designated signifies *that which is from the forest.*[3] For this same reason, he is frequently decorated with leaves during the ceremonies at which he assists.[4] In this way he passes long months,[5] interspersed from time to time with rites in which he must take a part. This time is a period of all sorts of abstinences for him. A multitude of foods are forbidden him; he is allowed only that quantity of food which is absolutely indispensable for the maintenance of life; [6] he is even sometimes bound to a rigorous fast,[7] or must eat impure foods.[8] When he eats, he must not touch the food with his hands; his godfathers put it into his mouth for him.[9] In some cases, he must go to beg his food.[10] Likewise, he sleeps only as much as is indispensable.[11] He must abstain from talking, to the extent of not uttering a word; it is by signs that he makes known his needs.[12] He must not wash; [13] sometimes he must not move. He remains stretched out upon the earth, immobile[14] and without clothing of any sort.[15] Now the result of the numerous interdictions is to bring about a radical change of condition in the initiate. Before the initiation, he lived with the women; he was excluded from the cult. After it, he is admitted to the society of men; he takes part in the rites, and has acquired a sacred character. The metamorphosis is so complete that it is sometimes represented as a second birth. They imagine that the profane person, who was the young man up till then, has died, that he has been killed and carried away by the god of the initiation, Bunjil, Baiame or

[1] Howitt, *Nat. Tr.*, pp. 560, 657, 659, 661. Even the shadow of a woman must not fall upon him (*ibid.*, p. 633). Whatever he has touched must not be touched by a woman (*ibid.*, p. 621).

[2] *Ibid.*, pp. 561, 563, 670 f.; Spencer and Gillen, *Nat. Tr.*, p. 223; *Nor. Tr.*, pp. 340, 342.

[3] The word Jeraeil, for example, among the Kurnai, or Kuringal among the Yuin and Wolgal (Howitt, *Nat. Tr.*, pp. 518, 617).

[4] Spencer and Gillen, *Nat. Tr.*, p. 348.

[5] Howitt, p. 561.

[6] Howitt, pp. 633, 538, 560.

[7] *Ibid.*, p. 674; Parker, *Euahlayi*, p. 75.

[8] Ridley, *Kamilaroi*, p. 154.

[9] Howitt, p. 563.

[10] *Ibid.*, p. 611.

[11] *Ibid.*, pp. 549, 674.

[12] Howitt, *Nat. Tr.*, pp. 580, 596, 604, 668, 670; Spencer and Gillen, *Nat. Tr.*, pp. 223, 351.

[13] Howitt, p. 557.

[14] *Ibid.*, p. 604; Spencer and Gillen, *Nat. Tr.*, p. 351.

[15] Howitt, p. 611.

Daramulun, and that quite another individual has taken the place of the one that no longer is.[1] So here we find the very heart of the positive effects of which negative rites are capable. Of course we do not mean to say that these latter produced this great transformation all by themselves; but they certainly contributed to it, and largely.

In the light of these facts, we are able to understand what asceticism is, what place it occupies in the religious life and whence come the virtues which have generally been attributed to it. In fact, there is no interdict, the observance of which does not have an ascetic character to a certain degree. Abstaining from something which may be useful or from a form of activity which, since it is usual, should answer to some human need, is, of necessity, imposing constraints and renunciations. So in order to have real asceticism, it is sufficient for these practices to develop in such a way as to become the basis of a veritable scheme of life. Normally, the negative cult serves only as an introduction and preparation for the positive cult. But it sometimes happens that it frees itself from this subordination and passes to the first place, and that the system of interdicts swells and exaggerates itself to the point of usurping the entire existence. Thus a systematic asceticism is born which is consequently nothing more than a hypertrophy of the negative cult. The special virtues which it is believed to confer are only an amplified form of those conferred, to a lesser degree, by the practice of any interdiction. They have the same origin; for they both rest on the principle that a man sanctifies himself only by efforts made to separate himself from the profane. The pure ascetic is a man who raises himself above men and acquires a special sanctity by fasts and vigils, by retreat and silence, or in a word, by privations, rather than by acts of positive piety (offerings, sacrifices, prayers, etc.). History shows to what a high religious prestige one may attain by this method: the Buddhist saint is essentially an ascetic, and he is equal or superior to the gods.

It follows that asceticism is not a rare, exceptional and nearly abnormal fruit of the religious life, as some have supposed it to be; on the contrary, it is one of its essential elements. Every religion contains it, at least in germ, for there are none in which a system of interdicts is not found. Their only difference in this regard which there may be between cults is that this germ is more or less developed in different ones. It should also be added that there probably is not a single one in which this development does not take, at least temporarily, the characteristic traits of

[1] Howitt, p. 589.

real asceticism. This is what generally takes place at certain critical periods when, for a relatively short time, it is necessary to bring about a grave change of condition in a subject. Then, in order to introduce him more rapidly into the circle of sacred things with which he must be put in contact, he is separated violently from the profane world; but this does not come without many abstinences and an exceptional recrudescence of the system of interdicts. Now this is just what happens in Australia at the moment of initiation. In order to transform youths into men, it is necessary to make them live the life of a veritable ascetic. Mrs. Parker very justly calls them the monks of Baiame.[1]

But abstinences and privations do not come without suffering. We hold to the profane world by all the fibres of our flesh; our senses attach us to it; our life depends upon it. It is not merely the natural theatre of our activity; it penetrates us from every side; it is a part of ourselves. So we cannot detach ourselves from it without doing violence to our nature and without painfully wounding our instincts. In other words, the negative cult cannot develop without causing suffering. Pain is one of its necessary conditions. Some have been led to think of it as constituting a sort of rite in itself; they have seen in it a state of grace which is to be sought and aroused, even artificially, because of the powers and privileges which it confers in the same way as these systems of interdicts, of which it is the natural accompaniment. So far as we know, Preuss is the first who has realized the religious rôle[2] which is attributed to suffering in the inferior societies. He cites the case of the Arapahs who inflict veritable torments upon themselves in order to become immune

[1] One may compare these ascetic practices with those used at the initiation of a magician. Just like the young neophyte, the apprentice magician is submitted to a multitude of interdictions, the observation of which contributes to his acquisition of his specific powers (see *L'Origine des pouvoirs magiques*, in Hubert and Mauss, *Mélanges d'histoire des religions*, pp. 171, 173, 176). The same is true for the husband and wife on the day before and the day after the wedding (taboos of the betrothed and newly married); this is because marriage also implies a grave change of condition. We limit ourselves to mentioning these facts summarily, without stopping over them; for the first concern magic, which is not our subject, and the second have to do with that system of juridico-religious rules which relates to the commerce of the sexes, the study of which will be possible only in conjunction with the other precepts of primitive conjugal morality.

[2] It is true that Preuss interprets these facts by saying that suffering is a way of increasing a man's magic force (*die menschliche Zauberkraft*); from this expression, one might believe that suffering is a magic rite, not a religious one. But as we have already pointed out, Preuss gives the name magic, without great precision, to all anonymous and impersonal forces, whether they belong to magic or religion. Of course, there are tortures which are used to make magicians; but many of those which we have described are a part of the real religious ceremonies, and, consequently, it is the religious state of the individuals which they modify.

from the dangers of battle; of the Big Belly Indians who submit to actual tortures on the eve of military expeditions; of the Hupa who swim in icy rivers and then remain stretched out on the bank as long as possible, in order to assure themselves of success in their enterprises; of the Karaya who from time to time draw blood from their arms and legs by means of scratches made out of the teeth of fish, in order to strengthen their muscles; of the men of Dallmannhafen (Emperor William's Land in New Guinea) who combat the sterility of their women by making bloody incisions in the upper part of their thighs.[1]

But similar facts may be found without leaving Australia, especially in the course of the initiation ceremonies. Many of the rites practised on this occasion consist in systematically inflicting certain pains on the neophyte in order to modify his condition and to make him acquire the qualities characteristic of a man. Thus, among the Larakia, while the young men are in retreat in the forest, their godfathers and guardians give them violent blows at any instant, without warning and without cause.[2] Among the Urabunna, at a certain time, the novice is stretched out on the ground, his face against the earth. All the men present beat him rudely; then they make four or eight gashes on his back, arranged on each side of the dorsal spine and one on the meridial line of the nape of his neck.[3] Among the Arunta, the first rite of the initiation consists in tossing the subject in a blanket; the men throw him into the air and catch him when he comes down, to throw him up again.[4] In the same tribe, at the close of this long series of ceremonies, the young man lies down on a bed of leaves under which they have placed

[1] Preuss, *Der Ursprung der Religion und Kunst*, in *Globus*, LXXXVIII, pp. 309–400. Under this same rubric Preuss classes a great number of incongruous rites, for example, effusions of blood which act in virtue of the positive qualities attributed to blood and not because of the suffering which they imply. We retain only those in which suffering is an essential element of the rite and the cause of its efficacy.

[2] *Nor. Tr.*, pp. 331 f.

[3] *Ibid.*, p. 335. A similar practice will be found among the Dieri (Howitt, *Nat. Tr.*, pp. 658 ff.).

[4] Spencer and Gillen, *Nat. Tr.*, pp. 214 ff.—From this example we see that the rites of initiation sometimes have all the characteristics of hazing. In fact, hazing is a real social institution which arises spontaneously every time that two groups, inequal in their moral and social situation, come into intimate contact. In this case, the one considering itself superior to the other resists the intrusion of the new-comers; it reacts against them is such a way as to make them aware of the superiority it feels. This reaction, which is produced automatically and which takes the form of more or less grave cruelties quite naturally, is also destined to shape the individuals for their new existence and assimilate them into their new environment. So it is a sort of initiation. Thus it is explained how the initiation, on its side, takes the form of hazing. It is because the group of old men is superior in religious and moral dignity to that of the young men, and yet the first must assimilate the second. So all the conditions for hazing are given.

live coals; he remains there, immobile in the midst of the heat and suffocating smoke.[1] A similar rite is observed among the Urabunna; but in addition, while the patient is in this painful situation, they beat him on the back.[2] In a general way, all the exercises to which he is submitted have this same character to such an extent that when he is allowed to re-enter the ordinary life, he has a pitiful aspect and appears half stupefied.[3] It is true that all these practices are frequently represented as ordeals destined to prove the value of the neophyte and to show whether he is worthy of being admitted into the religious society or not.[4] But in reality, the probational function of the rite is only another aspect of its efficacy. For the fact that it has been undergone is proved by its producing its effect, that is to say, by its conferring the qualities which are the original reason for its existence.

In other cases, these ritual cruelties are executed, not on the organism as a whole, but on a particular organ or tissue, whose vitality it is their object to stimulate. Thus, among the Arunta, the Warramunga and many other tribes,[5] at a certain moment in the initiation, certain persons are charged with biting the novice severely in the scalp. This operation is so painful that the patient can hardly support it without uttering cries. Its object is to make the hair grow.[6] The same treatment is applied to make the beard grow. The rite of pulling out hairs, which Howitt mentions in other tribes, seems to have the same reason for existence.[7] According to Eylmann, the men and women of the Arunta and the Kaitish make small wounds on their arms with sticks red with fire, in order to become skilful in making fire or to acquire the strength necessary for carrying heavy loads of wood.[8] According to this same observer, the Warramunga girls amputate the second and third joints of the index finger on one hand, thinking that the finger thus becomes better fitted for finding yams.[9]

It is not impossible that the extraction of teeth was sometimes destined to produce effects of this sort. In any case, it is certain that the cruel rites of circumcision and subincision have the object of conferring particular powers on the genital organs. In fact, the young man is not allowed to marry until after he has undergone them; so he owes them special virtues. What makes

[1] Spencer and Gillen, *Nat. Tr.*, p. 372.
[2] *Ibid.*, p. 335.
[3] Howitt, *Nat. Tr.*, p. 675.
[4] Howitt, *Nat. Tr.*, pp. 569, 604.
[5] Spencer and Gillen, *Nat. Tr.*, p. 251; *Nor. Tr.*, 341, 352.
[6] Among the Warramunga, the operation must be made by persons favoured with beautiful hair.
[7] Howitt, *Nat. Tr.*, p. 675; this concerns the tribes on the lower Darling.
[8] Eylmann, *op. cit.*, p. 212.
[9] *Ibid.*

this initiation *sui generis* indispensable is that in all inferior societies, the union of the sexes is marked with a religious character. It is believed to put redoubtable forces into play which a man cannot approach without danger, until after he has acquired the necessary immunity, by ritual processes:[1] for this, a whole series of positive and negative practices is used, of which circumcision and subincision are the forerunners. By painfully mutilating an organ, a sacred character is given to it, since by that act, it is put into shape for resisting the equally sacred forces which it could not meet otherwise.

At the beginning of this work, we said that all the essential elements of religious thought and life ought to be found, at least in germ, in the most primitive religions: the preceding facts confirm this assertion. If there is any one belief which is believed to be peculiar to the most recent and idealistic religions, it is the one attributing a sanctifying power to sorrow. Now this same belief is at the basis of the rites which have just been observed. Of course, it is understood differently at the different moments of history when it is studied. For the Christian, it acts especially upon the soul: it purges it, ennobles it, spiritualizes it. For the Australian, it is the body over which it is efficient: it increases its vital energies; it makes its beard and hair grow; it toughens its members. But in both cases the principle is the same. In both it is admitted that suffering creates exceptional strength. And this belief is not without foundation. In fact, it is by the way in which he braves suffering that the greatness of a man is best manifested. He never rises above himself with more brilliancy than when he subdues his own nature to the point of making it follow a way contrary to the one it would spontaneously take. By this, he distinguishes himself from all the other creatures who follow blindly wherever pleasure calls them; by this, he makes a place apart for himself in the world. Suffering is the sign that certain of the bonds attaching him to his profane environment are broken; so it testifies that he is partially freed from this environment, and, consequently, it is justly considered the instrument of deliverance. So he who is thus delivered is not the victim of a pure illusion when he believes himself invested with a sort of mastery over things: he really has raised himself above them, by the very act of renouncing them; he is stronger than nature, because he makes it subside.

Moreover, it is by no means true that this virtue has only an

[1] References on this question will be found in our memoir on *La Prohibition de l'incest et ses origines* (*Année Sociol.*, I, pp. 1 ff.), and Crawley, *The Mystic Rose*, pp. 37 ff.

æsthetic value: the whole religious life supposes it. Sacrifices and privations do not come without privations which cost the worshipper dear. Even if the rites do not demand material gifts from him, they require his time and his strength. In order to serve his gods, he must forget himself; to make for them a fitting place in his own life, he must sacrifice his profane interests. The positive cult is possible only when a man is trained to renouncement, to abnegation, to detachment from self, and consequently to suffering. It is necessary that he have no dread of them: he cannot even fulfil his duties joyfully unless he loves them to some extent. But for that, it is necessary that he train himself, and it is to this that the ascetic practices tend. So the suffering which they impose is not arbitrary and sterile cruelty; it is a necessary school, where men form and temper themselves, and acquire the qualities of disinterestedness and endurance without which there would be no religion. If this result is to be obtained, it is even a good thing that the ascetic ideal be incarnated eminently in certain persons, whose speciality, so to speak, it is to represent, almost with excess, this aspect of the ritual life; for they are like so many living models, inciting to effort. Such is the historic rôle of the great ascetics. When their deeds and acts are analysed in detail, one asks himself what useful end they can have. He is struck by the fact that there is something excessive in the disdain they profess for all that ordinarily impassions men. But these exaggerations are necessary to sustain among the believers a sufficient disgust for an easy life and common pleasures. It is necessary that an elite put the end too high, if the crowd is not to put it too low. It is necessary that some exaggerate, if the average is to remain at a fitting level.

But asceticism does not serve religious ends only. Here, as elsewhere, religious interests are only the symbolic form of social and moral interests. The ideal beings to whom the cults are addressed are not the only ones who demand of their followers a certain disdain for suffering: society itself is possible only at this price. Though exalting the strength of man, it is frequently rude to individuals; it necessarily demands perpetual sacrifices from them; it is constantly doing violence to our natural appetites, just because it raises us above ourselves. If we are going to fulfil our duties towards it, then we must be prepared to do violence to our instincts sometimes and to ascend the decline of nature when it is necessary. So there is an asceticism which, being inherent in all social life, is destined to survive all the mythologies and all the dogmas; it is an integral part of all human culture. At bottom, this is the asceticism which is the reason for the existence of and the justification of that which has been taught by the religions of all times.

III

Having determined what the system of interdicts consists in and what its positive and negative functions are, we must now seek the causes which have given it birth.

In one sense, it is logically implied in the very notion of sacredness. All that is sacred is the object of respect, and every sentiment of respect is translated, in him who feels it, by movements of inhibition. In fact, a respected being is always expressed in the consciousness by a representation which, owing to the emotion it inspires, is charged with a high mental energy ; consequently, it is armed in such a way as to reject to a distance every other representation which denies it in whole or in part. Now the sacred world and the profane world are antagonistic to each other. They correspond to two forms of life which mutually exclude one another, or which at least cannot be lived at the same time with the same intensity. We cannot give ourselves up entirely to the ideal beings to whom the cult is addressed and also to ourselves and our own interests at the same time ; we cannot devote ourselves entirely to the group and entirely to our own egoism at once. Here there are two systems of conscious states which are directed and which direct our conduct towards opposite poles. So the one having the greater power of action should tend to exclude the other from the consciousness. When we think of holy things, the idea of a profane object cannot enter the mind without encountering grave resistance ; something within us opposes itself to its installation. This is because the representation of a sacred thing does not tolerate neighbours. But this psychic antagonism and this mutual exclusion of ideas should naturally result in the exclusion of the corresponding things. If the ideas are not to coexist, the things must not touch each other or have any sort of relations. This is the very principle of the interdict.

Moreover, the world of sacred things is, by definition, a world apart. Since it is opposed to the profane world by all the characteristics we have mentioned, it must be treated in its own peculiar way : it would be a misunderstanding of its nature and a confusion of it with something that it is not, to make use of the gestures, language and attitudes which we employ in our relations with ordinary things, when we have to do with the things that compose it. We may handle the former freely ; we speak freely to vulgar beings ; so we do not touch the sacred beings, or we touch them only with reserve; we do not speak in their presence, or we do not speak the common language there. All that is used in our commerce with the one must be excluded from our commerce with the other.

But if this explanation is not inexact, it is, nevertheless, insufficient. In fact, there are many beings which are the objects of respect without being protected by systems of rigorous interdictions such as those we have just described. Of course there is a general tendency of the mind to localize different things in different places, especially when they are incompatible with each other. But the profane environment and the sacred one are not merely distinct, but they are also closed to one another; between them there is an abyss. So there ought to be some particular reason in the nature of sacred things, which causes this exceptional isolation and mutual exclusion. And, in fact, by a sort of contradiction, the sacred world is inclined, as it were, to spread itself into this same profane world which it excludes elsewhere: at the same time that it repels it, it tends to flow into it as soon as it approaches. This is why it is necessary to keep them at a distance from one another and to create a sort of vacuum between them.

What makes these precautions necessary is the extraordinary contagiousness of a sacred character. Far from being attached to the things which are marked with it, it is endowed with a sort of elusiveness. Even the most superficial or roundabout contact is sufficient to enable it to spread from one object to another. Religious forces are represented in the mind in such a way that they always seem ready to escape from the points where they reside and to enter everything passing within their range. The nanja tree where the spirit of an ancestor lives is sacred for the individual who considers himself the reincarnation of this ancestor. But every bird which alights upon this tree participates in this same nature: it is also forbidden to touch it.[1] We have already had occasion to show how simple contact with a churinga is enough to sanctify men and things; [2] it is also upon this principle of the contagiousness of sacredness that all the rites of consecration repose. The sanctity of the churinga is so great that its action is even felt at a distance. It will be remembered how this extends not only to the cave where they are kept, but also to the whole surrounding district, to the animals who take refuge there, whom it is forbidden to kill, and to the plants which grow there, which must not be touched.[3] A snake totem has its centre at a place where there

[1] Spencer and Gillen, *Nat. Tr.*, p. 133.

[2] See above, p. 121.

[3] Spencer and Gillen, *Nat. Tr.*, pp. 134 f.; Strehlow, I, p. 78.

is a water-hole. The sacred character of the totem is communicated to this place, to the water-hole and even to the water itself, which is forbidden to all the members of the totemic group.[1] The initiate lives in an atmosphere charged with religiousness, and it is as though he were impregnated with it himself.[2] Consequently all that he possesses and all that he touches is forbidden to the women, and withdrawn from their contact, even down to the bird he has struck with his stick, the kangaroo he has pierced with his lance or the fish which has bit on his hook.[3] But, on the other hand, the rites to which he is submitted and the things which have a part in them have a sanctity superior to his own: this sanctity is contagiously transmitted to everything which evokes the idea of one or the other. The tooth which has been knocked out of him is considered very holy.[4] For this reason, he may not eat animals with prominent teeth, because they make him think of his own lost tooth. The ceremonies of the Kuringal terminate with a ritual washing;[5] acquatic birds are forbidden to the neophyte because they make him think of this rite. Animals that climb to the tops of trees are equally sacred for him, because they are too near to Daramulun, the god of the initiation, who lives in heaven.[6] The soul of a dead man is a sacred thing: we have already seen how this same property passes to the corpse in which the soul resided, to the spot where this is buried, to the camp in which he lived when alive, and which is either destroyed or quitted, to the name he bore, to his wife and to his relations.[7] They, too, are invested, as it were, with a sacred character; consequently, men keep at a distance from them; they do not treat them as mere profane beings. In the societies observed by Dawson, their names, like that of the dead man, cannot be pronounced during the period of mourning.[8] Certain animals which he ate may also be prohibited.[9]

This contagiousness of sacredness is too well known a

[1] Spencer and Gillen, *Nor. Tr.*, pp. 167, 299.

[2] In addition to the ascetic rites of which we have spoken, there are some positive ones whose object is to charge, or, as Howitt says, to saturate the initiate with religiousness (Howitt, *Nat. Tr.*, p. 535). It is true that instead of religiousness, Howitt speaks of magic powers, but as we know, for the majority of the ethnologists, this word merely signifies religious virtues of an impersonal nature.

[3] Howitt, *ibid.*, pp. 674 f.

[4] Spencer and Gillen, *Nat. Tr.*, p. 454. Cf. Howitt, *Nat. Tr.*, p. 561.

[5] Howitt, *Nat. Tr.*, p. 557. [6] *Ibid.*, p. 560.

[7] See above, pp. 303, 306. Cf. Spencer and Gillen, *Nat. Tr.*, p. 498; *Nor. Tr.*, pp. 506, 507, 518 f., 526; Howitt, *Nat. Tr.*, p. 449, 461, 469; Mathews, in *J. of R.S. of N.S. Wales*, XXXVIII, p. 274; Schulze, *loc. cit.*, p. 231; Wyatt, *Adelaide and Encounter Bay Tribes*, in Woods, pp. 165, 198.

[8] *Australian Aborigines*, p. 42. [9] Howitt, *Nat. Tr.*, pp. 470–471.

phenomenon[1] to require any proof of its existence from numerous examples; we only wish to show that it is as true in totemism as in the more advanced religions. When once established, it quickly explains the extreme rigour of the interdicts separating the sacred from the profane. Since, in virtue of this extraordinary power of expansion, the slightest contact, the least proximity, either material or simply moral, suffices to draw religious forces out of their domain, and since, on the other hand, they cannot leave it without contradicting their nature, a whole system of measures is indispensable for maintaining the two worlds at a respectful distance from one another. This is why it is forbidden to the profane, not only to touch, but even to see or hear that which is sacred, and why these two sorts of life cannot be mixed in their consciousnesses. Precautions are necessary to keep them apart because, though opposing one another, they tend to confuse themselves into one another.

When we understand the multiplicity of these interdicts we also understand the way in which they operate and the sanctions which are attached to them. Owing to the contagiousness inherent in all that is sacred, a profane being cannot violate an interdict without having the religious force, to which he has unduly approached, extend itself over him and establish its empire over him. But as there is an antagonism between them, he becomes dependent upon a hostile power, whose hostility cannot fail to manifest itself in the form of violent reactions which tend to destroy him. This is why sickness or death are considered the natural consequences of every transgression of this sort; and they are consequences which are believed to come by themselves, with a sort of physical necessity. The guilty man feels himself attacked by a force which dominates him and against which he is powerless. Has he eaten the totemic animal? Then he feels it penetrating him and gnawing at his vitals; he lies down on the ground and awaits death.[2] Every profanation implies a consecration, but one which is dreadful, both for the subject consecrated and for those who approach him. It is the consequences of this consecration which sanction, in part, the interdict.[3]

It should be noticed that this explanation of the interdicts

[1] On this question, see Robertson Smith, *Religion of the Semites*, pp. 152 ff., 446, 481; Frazer, art. *Taboo* in *Encyc. Brit.*, Jevons, *Introduction to the History of Religions*, pp. 59 f.; Crawley, *Mystic Rose*, ch. ii–ix; Van Gennep, *Tabou et Totemisme à Madagascar*, ch. iii.

[2] See references above, p. 128, n. 1. Cf. *Nor. Tr.*, pp. 323, 324; *Nat. Tr.*, p. 168; Taplin, *The Narrinyeri*, p. 16; Roth, *North Queensland Ethnography*. Bull. 10, *Records of Austral. Museum*, VII, p. 76.

[3] It is to be remembered that when it is a religious interdict that has been violated, these sanctions are not the only ones; there is also a real punishment or a stigma of opinion.

does not depend upon the variable symbols by the aid of which religious forces are conceived. It matters little whether these are conceived as anonymous and impersonal energies or figured as personalities endowed with consciousness and feeling. In the former case, of course, they are believed to react against profaning transgressions in an automatic and unconscious manner, while in the latter case, they are thought to obey passionate movements determined by the offence resented. But at bottom, these two conceptions, which, moreover, have the same practical effect, only express one and the same psychic mechanism in two different languages. The basis of both is the antagonism of the sacred and the profane, combined with the remarkable aptitude of the former for spreading over to the latter; now this antagonism and this contagiousness act in the same way, whether the sacred character is attributed to blind forces or to conscious ones. Thus, so far is it from being true that the real religious life commences only where there are mythical personalities, that we see that in this case the rite remains the same, whether the religious beings are personified or not. This is a statement which we shall have occasion to repeat in each of the chapters which follow.

IV

But if this contagiousness of sacredness helps to explain the system of interdicts, how is it to be explained itself?

Some have tried to explain it with the well-known laws of the association of ideas. The sentiments inspired in us by a person or a thing spread contagiously from the idea of this thing or person to the representations associated with it, and thence to the objects which these representations express. So the respect which we have for a sacred being is communicated to everything touching this being, or resembling it, or recalling it. Of course a cultivated man is not deceived by these associations; he knows that these derived emotions are due to mere plays of the images and to entirely mental combinations, so he does not give way to the superstitions which these illusions tend to bring about. But they say that the primitive naïvely objectifies his impressions, without criticising them. Does something inspire a reverential fear in him? He concludes that an august and redoubtable force really resides in it; so he keeps at a distance from this thing and treats it as though it were sacred, even though it has no right to this title.[1]

[1] See Jevons, *Introduction to the History of Religions*, pp. 67–68. We say nothing of the recent, and slightly explicit, theory of Crawley (*Mystic Rose*, ch. iv–vii), according to which the contagiousness of taboos is due to a false interpretation of the phenomena of contagion. It is arbitrary. As Jevons very truly says in the passage to which we refer, the contagious character of sacredness is affirmed *a priori*, and not on a faith in badly interpreted experiences.

But whoever says this forgets that the most primitive religions are not the only ones which have attributed this power of propagation to the sacred character. Even in the most recent cults, there is a group of rites which repose upon this principle. Does not every consecration by means of anointing or washing consist in transferring into a profane object the sanctifying virtues of a sacred one ? Yet it is difficult to regard an enlightened Catholic of to-day as a sort of retarded savage who continues to be deceived by his associations of ideas, while nothing in the nature of things explains or justifies these ways of thinking. Moreover, it is quite arbitrarily that they attribute to the primitive this tendency to objectify blindly all his emotions. In his ordinary life, and in the details of his lay occupations, he does not impute the properties of one thing to its neighbours, or *vice versa*. If he is less careful than we are about clarity and distinction, still it is far from true that he has some vague, deplorable aptitude for jumbling and confusing everything. Religious thought alone has a marked leaning towards these sorts of confusions. So it is in something special to the nature of religious things, and not in the general laws of the human intelligence, that the origin of these predispositions is to be sought.

When a force or property seems to be an integral part or constituent element of the subject in which it resides, we cannot easily imagine its detaching itself and going elsewhere. A body is defined by its mass and its atomic composition ; so we do not think that it could communicate any of these distinctive characteristics by means of contact. But, on the other hand, if we are dealing with a force which has penetrated the body from without, since nothing attaches it there and since it is foreign to the body, there is nothing inconceivable in its escaping again. Thus the heat or electricity which a body has received from some external source may be transmitted to the surrounding medium, and the mind readily accepts the possibility of this transmission. So the extreme facility with which religious forces spread out and diffuse themselves has nothing surprising about it, if they are generally thought of as outside of the beings in which they reside. Now this is just what the theory we have proposed implies.

In fact, they are only collective forces hypostatized, that is to say, moral forces ; they are made up of the ideas and sentiments awakened in us by the spectacle of society, and not of sensations coming from the physical world. So they are not homogeneous with the visible things among which we place them. They may well take from these things the outward and material forms in which they are represented, but they owe none of their efficacy to them. They are not united by external bonds to the different supports upon which they alight; they have no roots there; according to an expression we have already used [1] and which serves best for characterizing them, *they are added to them.* So there are no objects which are predestined to receive them, to the exclusion of all others; even the most insignificant and vulgar may do so; accidental circumstances decide which are the chosen ones. The terms in which Codrington speaks of the mana should be borne in mind: it is a force, he says, which "*is not fixed in anything and can be conveyed in almost anything.*" [2] Likewise, the Dakota of Miss Fletcher represented the wakan as a sort of surrounding force which is always coming and going through the world, alighting here and there, but definitely fixing itself nowhere.[3] Even the religious character inherent in men does not have a different character. There is certainly no other being in the world of experience which is closer to the very source of all religious life; none participates in it more directly, for it is in human consciousnesses that it is elaborated. Yet we know that the religious principle animating men, to wit, the soul, is partially external.

But if religious forces have a place of their own nowhere, their mobility is easily explained. Since nothing attaches them to the things in which we localize them, it is natural that they should escape on the slightest contact, in spite of themselves, so to speak, and that they should spread afar. Their intensity incites them to this spreading, which everything favours. This is why the soul itself, though holding to the body by very personal bonds, is constantly threatening to leave it: all the apertures and pores of the body are just so many ways by which it tends to spread and diffuse itself into the outside.[4]

But we shall account for this phenomenon which we are trying to understand, still better if, instead of considering the notion of religious forces as it is when completely formulated, we go back to the mental process from which it results.

We have seen, in fact, that the sacred character of a being does not rest in any of its intrinsic attributes. It is not because the totemic animal has a certain aspect or property that it inspires religious sentiments; these result from causes wholly foreign to the nature of the object upon which they fix themselves. What constitutes them are the impressions of comfort and dependence which the action of the society provokes in the mind. Of themselves, these emotions are not attached to the idea of any

[1] See above, p. 229. [2] See above, p. 194.
[3] See above, p. 190.
[4] This has been well demonstrated by Preuss in his articles in the *Globus*.

particular object; but as these emotions exist and are especially intense, they are also eminently contagious. So they make a stain of oil; they extend to all the other mental states which occupy the mind; they penetrate and contaminate those representations especially in which are expressed the various objects which the man had in his hands or before his eyes at the moment: the totemic designs covering his body, the bull-roarers which he was making roar, the rocks surrounding him, the ground under his feet, etc. It is thus that the objects themselves get a religious value which is really not inherent in them but is conferred from without. So the contagion is not a sort of secondary process by which sacredness is propagated, after it has once been acquired; it is the very process by which it is acquired. It is by contagion that it establishes itself: we should not be surprised, therefore, if it transmits itself contagiously. What makes its reality is a special emotion; if it attaches itself to some object, it is because this emotion has found this object in its way. So it is natural that from this one it should spread to all those which it finds in its neighbourhood, that is to say, to all those which any reason whatsoever, either matérial contiguity or mere similarity, has mentally connected with the first.

Thus, the contagiousness of sacredness finds its explanation in the theory which we have proposed of religious forces, and by this very fact, it serves to confirm our theory.[1] And, at the same time, it aids us in understanding a trait of primitive mentality to which we have already called the attention.

We have seen [2] the facility with which the primitive confuses kingdoms and identifies the most heterogeneous things, men, animals, plants, stars, etc. Now we see one of the causes which has contributed the most to facilitating these confusions. Since religious forces are eminently contagious, it is constantly happening that the same principle animates very different objects equally; it passes from some into others as the result of either a simple material proximity or of even a superficial similarity. It is thus that men, animals, plants and rocks come to have the same totem: the men because they bear the name of the animal: the animals because they bring the totemic emblem to mind; the plants because they nourish these animals; the rocks because they mark the place where the ceremonies are celebrated. Now religious forces are therefore considered the source of all efficacy;

[1] It is true that this contagiousness is not peculiar to religious forces; those belonging to magic have the same property; yet it is evident that they do not correspond to objectified social sentiments. It is because magic forces have been conceived on the model of religious forces. We shall come back to this point again (see p. 361).

[2] See above, p. 235.

so beings having one single religious principle ought to pass as having the same essence, and as differing from one another only in secondary characteristics. This is why it seemed quite natural to arrange them in a single category and to regard them as mere varieties of the same class, transmutable into one another.

When this relation has been established, it makes the phenomena of contagion appear under a new aspect. Taken by themselves, they seem to be quite foreign to the logical life. Is their effect not to mix and confuse beings, in spite of their natural differences? But we have seen that these confusions and participation have played a rôle of the highest utility in logic; they have served to bind together things which sensation leaves apart from one another. So it is far from true that contagion, the source of these connections and confusions, is marked with that fundamental irrationality that one is inclined to attribute it at first. It has opened the way for the scientific explanations of the future.

CHAPTER II

THE POSITIVE CULT

I.—*The Elements of the Sacrifice*

WHATEVER the importance of the negative cult may be, and though it may indirectly have positive effects, it does not contain its reason for existence in itself; it introduces one to the religious life, but it supposes this more than it constitutes it. If it orders the worshipper to flee from the profane world, it is to bring him nearer to the sacred world. Men have never thought that their duties towards religious forces might be reduced to a simple abstinence from all commerce; they have always believed that they upheld positive and bilateral relations with them, whose regulation and organization is the function of a group of ritual practices. To this special system of rites we give the name of *positive cult.*

For some time we almost completely ignored the positive cult of the totemic religion and what it consists in. We knew almost nothing more than the initiation rites, and we do not know those sufficiently well even now. But the observations of Spencer and Gillen, prepared for by those of Schulze and confirmed by those of Strehlow, on the tribes of central Australia, have partially filled this gap in our information. There is one ceremony especially which these explorers have taken particular pains to describe to us and which, moreover, seems to dominate the whole totemic cult: this is the one that the Arunta, according to Spencer and Gillen, call the *Intichiuma.* It is true that Strehlow contests the meaning of this word. According to him, intichiuma (or, as he writes it, *intijiuma*) means "to instruct" and designates the ceremonies performed before the young man to teach him the traditions of the tribe. The feast which we are going to describe bears, he says, the name *mbatjalkatiuma,* which means "to fecundate" or "to put into a good condition."[1] But we shall not try to settle this question of vocabulary, which touches the real problem but slightly, as the rites in question are all

[1] Strehlow, I, p. 4.

celebrated in the course of the initiation. On the other hand, as the word Intichiuma now belongs to the current language of ethnography, and has almost become a common noun, it seems useless to replace it with another.[1]

The date on which the Intichiuma takes place depends largely upon the season. There are two sharply separated seasons in Australia: one is dry and lasts for a long time; the other is rainy and is, on the contrary, very short and frequently irregular. As soon as the rains arrive, vegetation springs up from the ground as though by enchantment and animals multiply, so that the country which had recently been only a sterile desert is rapidly filled with a luxurious flora and fauna. It is just at the moment when the good season seems to be close at hand that the Intichiuma is celebrated. But as the rainy season is extremely variable, the date of the ceremonies cannot be fixed once for all. It varies with the climatic circumstances, which only the chief of the totemic group, the Alatunja, is qualified to judge: on a day which he considers suitable, he informs his companions that the moment has arrived.[2]

Each totemic group has its own Intichiuma. Even if this rite is general in the societies of the centre, it is not the same everywhere; among the Warramunga, it is not what it is among the Arunta; it varies, not only among the tribes, but also within the tribe, among the clans. But it is obvious that the different mechanisms in use are too closely related to each other to be dissociated completely. There is no ceremony, perhaps, which is not made up of several, though these are very unequally developed: what exists only as a germ in one, occupies the most important place in another, and inversely. Yet they must be carefully distinguished, for they constitute just so many different ritual types to be described and explained separately, but afterwards we must seek some common source from which they were derived.

Let us commence with those observed among the Arunta.

I

The celebration includes two successive phases. The object of the rites which take place in the first is to assure the prosperity of the animal or vegetable species serving the clan as totem. The means employed for this end may be reduced to two principal types.

[1] Of course the word designating these celebrations changes with the tribes. The Urabunna call them *Pitjinta* (*Nor. Tr.*, p. 284); the Warramunga *Thalaminta* (*ibid.*, p. 297), etc.

[2] Schulze, *loc. cit.*, p. 243; Spencer and Gillen, *Nat. Tr.*, pp. 169 f.

It will be remembered that the fabulous ancestors from whom each clan is supposed to be descended, formerly lived on earth and left traces of their passage there. These traces consist especially in stones and rocks which they deposited at certain places, or which were formed at the spots where they entered into the ground. These rocks and stones are considered the bodies or parts of the bodies of the ancestors, whose memory they keep alive; they represent them. Consequently, they also represent the animals and plants which served these same ancestors as totems, for an individual and his totem are only one. The same reality and the same properties are attributed to them as to the actually living plants or animals of the same species. But they have this advantage over these latter, that they are imperishable, knowing neither sickness nor death. So they are like a permanent immutable and ever-available reserve of animal and vegetable life. Also, in a certain number of cases, it is this reserve that they annually draw upon to assure the reproduction of the species.

Here, for example, is how the Witchetty grub clan, at Alice Springs, proceeds at its Intichiuma.[1]

On the day fixed by the chief, all the members of the totemic group assemble in the principal camp. The men of the other totems retire to a distance;[2] for among the Arunta, they are not allowed to be present at the celebration of the rite, which has all the characteristics of a secret ceremony. An individual of a different totem, but of the same phratry, may be invited to be present, as a favour; but this is only as a witness. In no case can he take an active part.

After the men of the totem have assembled, they leave the camp, leaving only two or three of their number behind. They advance in a profound silence, one behind another, all naked, without arms and without any of their habitual ornaments. Their attitude and their pace are marked with a religious gravity: this is because the act in which they are taking part has an exceptional importance in their eyes. Also, until the end of the ceremony they are required to observe a rigorous fast.

The country which they traverse is all filled with souvenirs left by the glorious ancestors. Thus they arrive at a spot where a huge block of quartz is found, with small round stones all around it. This block represents the witchetty grub as an adult. The Alatunja strikes it with a sort of wooden tray called *apmara*,[3]

[1] *Nat. Tr.*, pp. 170 ff.

[2] Of course the women are under the same obligation.

[3] The apmara is the only thing which he brought from the camp.

and at the same time he intones a chant, whose object is to invite the animal to lay eggs. He proceeds in the same fashion with the stones which are regarded as the eggs of the animal and with one of which he rubs the stomach of each assistant. This done, they all descend a little lower, to the foot of a cliff also celebrated in the myths of the Alcheringa, at the base of which is another stone, also representing the witchetty grub. The Alatunja strikes it with his apmara ; the men accompanying him do so as well, with branches of a gum-tree which they have gathered on the way, all of which goes on in the midst of chants renewing the invitation previously addressed to the animal. About ten different spots are visited in turn, some of which are a mile or more from the others. At each of them there is a stone at the bottom of a cave or hole, which is believed to represent the witchetty grub in one of his aspects or at one of the phases of his existence, and upon each of these stones, the same ceremonies are repeated.

The meaning of the rite is evident. When the Alatunja strikes the sacred stones, it is to detach some dust. The grains of this very holy dust are regarded as so many germs of life ; each of them contains a spiritual principle which will give birth to a new being, when introduced into an organism of the same species. The branches with which the assistants are provided serve to scatter this precious dust in all directions ; it is scattered everywhere, to accomplish its fecundating work. By this means, they assure, in their own minds, an abundant reproduction of the animal species over which the clans guard, so to speak, and upon which it depends.

The natives themselves give the rite this interpretation. Thus, in the clan of the *ilpirla* (a kind of " manna "), they proceed in the following manner. When the day of the Intichiuma arrives, the group assembles near a huge rock, about fifty feet high ; on top of this rock is another, very similar to the first in aspect and surrounded by other smaller ones. Both represent masses of manna. The Alatunja digs up the ground at the foot of this rock and uncovers a churinga which is believed to have been buried there in Alcheringa times, and which is, as it were, the quintessence of the manna. Then he climbs up to the summit of the higher rock and rubs it, first with the churinga and then with the smaller stones which surround it. Finally, he brushes away the dust which has thus been collected on the surface of the rock, with the branches of a tree ; each of the assistants does the same in his turn. Now Spencer and Gillen say that the idea of the natives is that the dust thus scattered will " settle upon the mulga trees and so produce manna." In fact, these operations are accompanied by a hymn sung by those present, in which this idea is expressed.[1]

With variations, this same rite is found in other societies. Among the Urabunna, there is a rock representing an ancestor of the Lizard clan; bits are detached from it which they throw in every direction, in order to secure an abundant production of lizards.[2] In this same tribe, there is a sand-bank which mythological souvenirs closely associate with the louse totem. At the same spot are two trees, one of which is called the ordinary louse tree, the other, the crab-louse tree. They take some of this sand, rub it on these trees, throw it about on every side and become convinced that, as a result of this, lice will be born in large numbers.[3] The Mara perform the Intichiuma of the bees by scattering dust detached from sacred rocks.[4] For the kangaroo of the plains, a slightly different method is used. They take some kangaroo-dung and wrap it up in a certain herb of which the animal is very fond, and which belongs to the kangaroo totem for this reason. Then they put the dung, thus enveloped, on the ground between two bunches of this herb and set the whole thing on fire. With the flame thus made, they light the branches of trees and then whirl them about in such a way that sparks fly in every direction. These sparks play the same rôle as the dust in the preceding cases.[5]

In a certain number of clans,[6] men mix something of their own substance with that of the stone, in order to make the rite more efficacious. Young men open their veins and let streams of blood flow on to the rock. This is the case, for example, in the Intichiuma of the Hakea flower among the Arunta. The ceremony takes place in a sacred place around an equally sacred rock which, in the eyes of the natives, represents Hakea flowers. After certain preliminary operations, " the old leader asks one of the young men to open a vein in his arm, which he does, and allows the blood to sprinkle freely, while the other men continue the singing. The blood flows until the stone is completely covered." [7] The object of this practice is to revivify the virtues of the stone, after a fashion, and to reinforce its efficacy. It should not be forgotten that the men of the clan are relatives of the plant or animal whose name they bear; the same principle of life is in them, and especially in their blood. So it is only natural that one should use this blood and the mystic germs which it carries to assure the regular reproduction of the

[1] *Nat. Tr.*, pp. 185–186. [2] *Nor. Tr.*, p. 288. [3] *Ibid.*

[4] *Nor. Tr.*, p. 312. [5] *Ibid.*

[6] We shall see below that these clans are much more numerous than Spencer and Gillen say.

[7] *Nat. Tr.*, pp. 184–185.

totemic species. It frequently happens among the Arunta that when a man is sick or tired, one of his young companions opens his veins and sprinkles him with his blood in order to re-animate him.[1] If blood is able to reawaken life in a man in this way, it is not surprising that it should also be able to awaken it in the animal or vegetable species with which the men of the clan are confounded.

The same process is employed in the Intichiuma of the Undiara kangaroo among the Arunta. The theatre of the ceremony is a water-hole vaulted over by a peaked rock. This rock represents an animal-kangaroo of the Alcheringa which was killed and deposited there by a man-kangaroo of the same epoch; many kangaroo spirits are also believed to reside there. After a certain number of sacred stones have been rubbed against each other in the way we have described, several of the assistants climb up on the rock upon which they let their blood flow.[2] "The purpose of the ceremony at the present day, so say the natives, is by means of pouring out the blood of kangaroo men upon the rock, to drive out in all directions the spirits of the kangaroo animals and so to increase the number of the animals."[3]

There is even one case among the Arunta where the blood seems to be the active principle in the rite. In the Emu group, they do not use sacred stones or anything resembling them. The Alatunja and some of his assistants sprinkle the ground with their blood; on the ground thus soaked, they trace lines in various colours, representing the different parts of the body of an emu. They kneel down around this design and chant a monotonous hymn. From the fictitious emu to which this chant is addressed, and, consequently, from the blood which has served to make it, they believe that vivifying principles go forth, which animate the embryos of the new generation, and thus prevent the species from disappearing.[4]

Among the Wonkgongaru,[5] there is one clan whose totem is a certain kind of fish; in the Intichiuma of this totem also, it is the blood that plays the principal part. The chief of the

[1] *Nat. Tr.*, pp. 438, 461, 464; *Nor. Tr.*, pp. 596 ff.

[2] *Nat. Tr.*, p. 201.

[3] *Ibid.*, p. 206. We use the words of Spencer and Gillen, and with them, we say that "spirits or spirit parts of kangaroo" are disengaged from the rocks. Strehlow (III, p. 7) contests the exactness of this expression. According to him, the rite makes real kangaroos, with living bodies, appear. But this dispute is without interest, just as the one about the notion of the *ratapa* was (see above, p. 252). The kangaroo germs thus escaping from the rock are not visible, so they are not made out of the same substance as the kangaroos which we see. This is all that Spencer and Gillen mean to say. It is quite certain, moreover, that they are not pure spirits such as a Christian might conceive. Like human souls, they have a material form.

[4] *Nat. Tr.*, p. 181.

[5] A tribe on the east of Lake Eyre.

group, after being ceremoniously painted, goes into a pool of water and sits down there. Then he pierces his scrotum and the skin around his navel with small pointed bones. " The blood from the wounds goes into the water and gives rise to fish." [1]

By a wholly similar process, the Dieri think that they assure the reproduction of two of their totems, the carpet snake and the woma snake (the ordinary snake). A Mura-mura named Minkani is thought to live under a dune. His body is represented by some fossil bones of animals or reptiles, such as the deltas of the rivers flowing into Lake Eyre contain, according to Howitt. When the day of the ceremony arrives, the men assemble and go to the home of the Minkani. There they dig until they come to a layer of damp earth which they call " the excrement of Minkani." From now on, they continue to turn up the soil with great care until they uncover " the elbow of Minkani." Then two young men open their veins and let their blood flow on to the sacred rock. They chant the hymn of Minkani while the assistants, carried away in a veritable frenzy, beat each other with their arms. The battle continues until they get back to the camp, which is about a mile away. Here, the women intervene and put an end to the combat. They collect the blood which has flown from the wounds, mix it with the " excrement of Minkani," and scatter the resulting mixture over the dune. When this rite has been accomplished, they are convinced that carpet snakes will be born in abundance.[2]

In certain cases, they use the very substance which they wish to produce as the vivifying principle. Thus among the Kaitish, in the course of a ceremony whose object is to create rain, they sprinkle water over a sacred rock which represents the mythical heroes of the Water clan. It is evident that they believe that by this means they augment the productive virtues of the rock just as well as with blood, and for the same reasons.[3] Among the Mara, the actor takes water from a sacred hole, puts it in his mouth and spits it out in every direction.[4] Among the Worgaia, when the yams begin to sprout, the chief of the Yam clan sends men of the phratry of which he is not a member himself to gather some of these plants ; these bring some to him, and ask him to intervene, in order that the species may develop well. He takes one, chews it, and throws the bits in every direction.[5] Among the Kaitish when, after various rites which we shall not describe, the grain of a certain grass called Erlipinna has reached its full

[1] *Nor. Tr.*, pp. 287 f.

[2] Howitt, *Nat. Tr.*, p. 798. Cf. Howitt, *Legends of the Dieri and Kindred Tribes of Central Australia*, in *J.A.I.*, XXIV, pp. 124 ff. Howitt believes that the ceremony is performed by the men of the totem, but is not prepared to say so definitely. [3] *Nor. Tr.*, p. 295. [4] *Ibid.*, p. 314. [5] *Ibid.*, pp. 296 f.

development, the chief of the totem brings a little of it to camp and grinds it between two stones; the dust thus obtained is piously gathered up, and a few grains are placed on the lips of the chief, who scatters them by blowing. This contact with the mouth of the chief, which has a very special sacramental virtue, undoubtedly has the object of stimulating the vitality of the germs which these grains contain and which, being blown to all the quarters of the horizon, go to communicate these fecundating virtues which they possess to the plants.[1]

The efficacy of these rites is never doubted by the native: he is convinced that they must produce the results he expects, with a sort of necessity. If events deceive his hopes, he merely concludes that they were counteracted by the sorcery of some hostile group. In any case, it never enters his mind that a favourable result could be obtained by any other means. If by chance the vegetation grows or the animals produce before he has performed his Intichiuma, he supposes that another Intichiuma has been celebrated under the ground by the ancestors and that the living reap the benefits of this subterranean ceremony.[2]

II

This is the first act of the celebration.

During the period immediately following, there are no regular

[1] *Nat. Tr.*, p. 170.

[2] *Ibid.*, p. 519.—The analysis of the rites which have just been studied is based solely on the observations of Spencer and Gillen. Since this chapter was written, Strehlow has published the third fascicule of his work, which deals with the positive cult and especially the Intichiuma, or, as he says, the rites of the *mbatjalkatiuma*. But we have found nothing in this publication which obliges us to modify the preceding description or even to complete it with important additions. The most interesting thing taught by Strehlow on this subject is that the effusions and oblations of blood are much more frequent than one would suspect from the account of Spencer and Gillen (see Strehlow, III, pp. 13, 14, 19, 29, 39, 43, 46, 56, 67, 80, 89).

Moreover, the information given by Strehlow in regard to the cult must be taken carefully, for he was not a witness of the rites he describes; he confined himself to collecting oral testimony, which is generally rather summary (see fasc. III, Preface of Leonhardi, p. v). It may even be asked if he has not confused the totemic ceremonies of initiation with those which he calls *mbatjalkatiuma*, to an excessive degree. Of course, he has made a praiseworthy attempt to distinguish them and has made two of their distinctive characteristics very evident. In the first place, the Intichiuma always takes place at a sacred spot to which the souvenir of some ancestor is attached, while the initiation ceremonies may be celebrated anywhere. Secondly, the oblations of blood are special to the Intichiuma, which proves that they are close to the heart of the ritual (III, p. 7). But in the description which he gives us of the rites, we find facts belonging indifferently to each species of ceremony. In fact, in what he describes under the name mbatjalkatiuma, the young men generally take an important part (for example, see pp. 11, 13, etc.), which is characteristic of the initiation. Also, it seems as though the place of the rite is arbitrary, for the actors construct their scene artificially. They dig a hole into which they go; he seldom makes any allusion to sacred trees or rocks and their ritual rôle.

ceremonies. However, the religious life remains intense: this is manifested especially by an aggravation of the system of interdicts. It is as though the sacred character of the totem were reinforced: they do not even dare to touch it. In ordinary times, the Arunta may eat the animal or plant which serves as totem, provided they do so with moderation, but on the morrow of the Intichiuma this right is suspended; the alimentary interdiction is strict and without exceptions. They believe that any violation of this interdict would result in neutralizing the good effects of the rite and in preventing the increase of the species. It is true that the men of other totems who happen to be in the same locality are not submitted to the same prohibition. However, their liberty is less than ordinary at this time. They may not consume the totemic animal wherever they place, in the brush, for example; they must bring it to camp, and it is there only that it may be cooked.[1]

A final ceremony terminates this period of extraordinary interdictions and definitely closes this long series of rites. It varies somewhat in different clans, but the essential elements are the same everywhere. Here are the two principal forms which it takes among the Arunta. One of these is in connection with the witchetty grub, the other with the kangaroo.

When the grubs have attained full maturity and appear in abundance, the men of the totem, as well as others, collect as many of them as possible; then they all bring those they have found back to camp and cook them until they become hard and brittle. They are then preserved in wooden vessels called *pitchi*. The harvest of grubs is possible only during a very short time, for they appear only after the rain. When they begin to be less numerous, the Alatunja summons everybody to the camp; on his invitation, each one brings his supply. The others place theirs before the men of that totem. The Alatunja takes one of these *pitchi* and, with the aid of his companions, he grinds its contents between two stones; after this, he eats a little of the powder thus obtained, his assistants do the same, and what remains is given to the men of the other clans, who may now dispose of it freely. They proceed in exactly the same manner with the supply provided by the Alatunja. From now on, the men and women of the totem may eat it, but only a little at a time; if they went beyond the limits allowed, they would lose the powers necessary to celebrate the Intichiuma and the species would not reproduce. Yet, if they did not eat any at all, and especially if the Alatunja ate none in the circumstances we have just described, they would be overtaken by the same incapacity.

[1] *Nat. Tr.*, p. 203. Cf. Meyer, *The Encounter Bay Tribe*, in Woods, p. 187.

In the totemic group of the Kangaroo, which has its centre at Undiara, certain characteristics of the ceremony are more clearly marked. After the rites which we have described have been accomplished on the sacred rock, the young men go and hunt the kangaroo, bringing their game back to the camp. Here, the old men, with the Alatunja in their midst, eat a little of the flesh of the animal, and anoint the bodies of those who took part in the Intichiuma with its fat. The rest is divided up among the men assembled. Next, the men of the totem decorate themselves with totemic designs and the night is passed in songs commemorating the exploits accomplished by men and animal kangaroos in the times of the Alcheringa. The next day, the young men go hunting again in the forest and bring back a larger number of kangaroos than the first time, and the ceremonies of the day before recommence.[1]

With variations of detail, the same rite is found in other Arunta clans,[2] among the Urabunna,[3] the Kaitish,[4] the Unmatjera,[5] and in the Encounter Bay Tribe.[6] Everywhere, it is made up of the same essential elements. A few specimens of the totemic animal or plant are presented to the chief of the clan, who solemnly eats them and who must eat them. If he did not fulfil this duty, he would lose the power of celebrating the Intichiuma efficaciously, that is to say, so as to recreate the species annually. Sometimes the ritual consumption is followed by an unction made with the fat of the animal or certain parts of the plant.[7] This rite is generally repeated by the men of the totem, or at least by the old men, and after it has been accomplished, the exceptional interdictions are raised.

In the tribes located farther north, among the Warramunga and neighbouring societies,[8] this ceremony is no longer found. However, traces are found which seem to indicate that there was a time when it was known. It is true that the chief of the clan never eats the totem ritually and obligatorily. But in certain cases, men who are not of the totem whose Intichiuma has just been celebrated, must bring the animal or plant to camp and offer it to the chief, asking him if he wants to eat it. He refuses and adds, " I have made this for you ; you may eat it freely." [9] So the custom of the presentation remains and the question asked

[1] Spencer and Gillen, *Nat. Tr.*, p. 204.
[2] *Nat. Tr.*, pp. 205–207.
[3] *Nor. Tr.*, pp. 286 f. [4] *Ibid.*, p. 294.
[5] *Ibid.*, p. 296.
[6] Meyer, *in* Woods, p. 187.
[7] We have already cited one case ; others will be found in Spencer and Gillen, *Nat. Tr.*, p. 208 ; *Nor. Tr.*, p. 286.
[8] The Walpari, Wulmala, Tjingilli, Umbaia.
[9] *Nor. Tr.*, p. 318.

of the chief seems to date back to an epoch when the ritual consumption was practised.[1]

III

The interest of the system of rites which has just been described lies in the fact that in them we find, in the most elementary form that is actually known, all the essential principles of a great religious institution which was destined to become one of the foundation stones of the positive cult in the superior religions: this is the institution of sacrifice.

We know what a revolution the work of Robertson Smith brought about in the traditional theory of sacrifice.[2] Before him, sacrifice was regarded as a sort of tribute or homage, either obligatory or optional, analogous to that which subjects owe to their princes. Robertson Smith was the first to remark that this classic explanation did not account for two essential characteristics of the rite. In the first place, it is a repast: its substance is food. Secondly, it is a repast in which the worshippers who offer it take part, along with the god to whom it is offered. Certain parts of the victim are reserved for the divinity; others are

[1] For the second part of the ceremony as for the first, we have followed Spencer and Gillen. On this subject, the recent fascicule of Strehlow only confirms the observations of his predecessors, at least on all essential points. He recognizes that after the first ceremony (two months afterwards, he says, p. 13), the chief of the clan eats the totemic animal or plant ritually and that after this he raises the interdicts; he calls this operation *die Freigabe des Totems zum allgemeinen Gebrauch* (III, p. 7). He even tells us that this operation is important enough to have a special word for it in the Arunta language. He adds, it is true, that this ritual consummation is not the only one, but that the chiefs and old men sometimes eat the sacred plant or animal before the first ceremony and that the performer of the rite does so after the celebration. The fact is not improbable; these consummations are means employed by the officiants or assistants to acquire virtues which they acquire; it is not surprising if they are numerous. It does not invalidate the account of Spencer and Gillen at all, for the rite upon which they insist, and not without reason, is the *Freigabe des Totems*.

On only two points does Strehlow contest the allegations of Spencer and Gillen. In the first place, he declares that the ritual consumption does not take place in every case. This cannot be doubted, for there are some animals and plants which are not edible. But still, the rite is very frequent; Strehlow himself cites numerous examples (pp. 13, 14, 19, 23, 33, 36, 50, 59, 67, 68, 71, 75, 80, 84, 89, 93). Secondly, we have seen that according to Spencer and Gillen, if the chief does not eat the totemic animal or plant, he will lose his powers. Strehlow assures us that the testimony of natives does not confirm this assertion. But this question seems to us to be quite secondary. The assured fact is that the ritual consumption is required, so it must be thought useful or necessary. Now, like every communion, it can only serve to confer needed virtues upon the person communicating. It does not follow from the fact that the natives, or some of them, have forgotten this function of the rite, that it is not real. Is it necessary to repeat that worshippers are generally ignorant of the real reasons for their practices?

[2] See *The Religion of the Semites*, Lectures vi–xi, and the article *Sacrifice* in the *Encyclopædia Britannica* (Ninth Edition).

attributed to the sacrificers, who consume them; this is why the Bible often speaks of the sacrifice as a repast in the presence of Jahveh. Now in a multitude of societies, meals taken in common are believed to create a bond of artificial kinship between those who assist at them. In fact, relatives are people who are naturally made of the same flesh and blood. But food is constantly remaking the substance of the organism. So a common food may produce the same effects as a common origin. According to Smith, sacrificial banquets have the object of making the worshipper and his god communicate in the same flesh, in order to form a bond of kinship between them. From this point of view, sacrifice takes on a wholly new aspect. Its essential element is no longer the act of renouncement which the word sacrifice ordinarily expresses; before all, it is an act of alimentary communion.

Of course there are some reservations to be made in the details of this way of explaining the efficacy of sacrificial banquets. This does not result exclusively from the act of eating together. A man does not sanctify himself merely by sitting down, in some way, at the same table with a god, but especially by eating food at this ritual repast which has a sacred character. It has been shown how a whole series of preliminary operations, lustrations, unctions, prayers, etc., transform the animal to be immolated into a sacred thing, whose sacredness is subsequently transferred to the worshipper who eats it.[1] But it is true, none the less, that the alimentary communion is one of the essential elements of the sacrifice. Now when we turn to the rite which terminates the ceremonies of the Intichiuma, we find that it, too, consists in an act of this sort. After the totemic animal has been killed, the Alatunja and the old men solemnly eat it. So they communicate with the sacred principle residing in it and they assimilate it. The only difference we find here is that the animal is naturally sacred while it ordinarily acquires this character artificially in the course of the sacrifice.

Moreover, the object of this communion is manifest. Every member of a totemic clan contains a mystic substance within him which is the pre-eminent part of his being, for his soul is made out of it. From it come whatever powers he has and his social position, for it is this which makes him a person. So he has a vital interest in maintaining it intact and in keeping it, as far as is possible, in a state of perpetual youth. Unfortunately all forces, even the most spiritual, are used up in the course of time if nothing comes to return to them the energy they lose

[1] See Hubert and Mauss, *Essai sur la nature et la fonction du sacrifice*, in *Mélanges d'histoire des religions*, pp. 40 ff.

through the normal working of things; there is a necessity of the first importance here which, as we shall see, is the real reason for the positive cult. Therefore the men of a totem cannot retain their position unless they periodically revivify the totemic principle which is in them; and as they represent this principle in the form of a vegetable or animal, it is to the corresponding animal or vegetable species that they go to demand the supplementary forces needed to renew this and to rejuvenate it. A man of the Kangaroo clan believes himself and feels himself a kangaroo; it is by this quality that he defines himself; it is this which marks his place in the society. In order to keep it, he takes a little of the flesh of this same animal into his own body from time to time. A small bit is enough, owing to the rule: *the part is equal to the whole.*[1]

If this operation is to produce all the desired effects, it may not take place at no matter what moment. The most opportune time is when the new generation has just reached its complete development, for this is also the moment when the forces animating the totemic species attain their maximum intensity. They have just been drawn with great difficulty from those rich reservoirs of life, the sacred trees and rocks. Moreover, all sorts of means have been employed to increase their intensity still more; this is the use of the rites performed during the first part of the Intichiuma. Also, by their very aspect, the firstfruits of the harvest manifest the energy which they contain: here the totemic god acclaims himself in all the glory of his youth. This is why the firstfruits have always been regarded as a very sacred fruit, reserved for very holy beings. So it is natural that the Australian uses it to regenerate himself spiritually. Thus both the date and the circumstances of the ceremonies are explained.

Perhaps some will be surprised that so sacred a food may be eaten by ordinary profane persons. But in the first place, there is no positive cult which does not face this contradiction. Every sacred being is removed from profane touch by this very character with which it is endowed; but, on the other hand, they would serve for nothing and have no reason whatsoever for their existence if they could not come in contact with these same worshippers who, on another ground, must remain respectfully distant from them. At bottom, there is no positive rite which does not constitute a veritable sacrilege, for a man cannot hold commerce with the sacred beings without crossing the barrier which should ordinarily keep them separate. But the important thing is that the sacrilege should be accompanied

[1] See the explanation of this rule, above, p. 229.

with precautions which attenuate it. Among those employed, the most usual one consists in arranging the transition so as to introduce the worshipper slowly and gradually into the circle of sacred things. When it has been broken and diluted in this fashion, the sacrilege does not offend the religious conscience so violently; it is not regarded as a sacrilege and so vanishes. This is what happens in the case now before us. The effect of the whole series of rites which has preceded the moment when the totem is solemnly eaten has been to sanctify those who took an active part in them. They constitute an essentially religious period, through which no one could go without a transformation of his religious state. The fasts, the contact with sacred rocks, the churinga,[1] the totemic decorations, etc., have gradually conferred upon him a character which he did not have before and which enables him to approach, without a shocking and dangerous profanation, this desirable and redoubtable food which is forbidden him in ordinary times.[2]

If the act by which a sacred being is first immolated and then eaten by those who adore it may be called a sacrifice, the rite of which we have just been speaking has a right to this same name. Moreover, its significance is well shown by the striking analogies it presents with so many practices met with in a large number of agrarian cults. It is a very general rule that even among peoples who have attained a high degree of civilization, the firstfruits of the harvest are used in the ritual repasts, of which the pascal feast is the best known example.[3] On the other hand, as the agrarian rites are at the very basis of the most advanced forms of the cult, we see that the Intichiuma of the Australian societies is closer to us than one might imagine from its apparent crudeness.

By an intuition of genius, Smith had an intuition of all this, though he was not acquainted with the facts. By a series of ingenious deductions—which need not be reproduced here, for their interest is now only historical[4]—he thought that he could establish the fact that at the beginning the animal immolated in the sacrifice must have been regarded as quasi-divine and as a close relative of those who immolated it: now these characteristics are just the ones with which the totemic species is defined. Smith even went so far as to suppose that totemism must have known and practised a rite wholly similar to the one we have been studying; he was even inclined to see the original source

[1] See Strehlow, III, p. 3.

[2] We must not forget that among the Arunta it is not completely forbidden to eat the totemic animal.

[3] See other facts in Frazer, *Golden Bough*, pp. 348 ff.

[4] *The Religion of the Semites*, pp. 275 ff.

of the whole sacrificial institution in a sacrifice of this sort.[1] Sacrifice was not founded to create a bond of artificial kinship between a man and his gods, but to maintain and renew the natural kinship which primitively united them. Here, as elsewhere, the artifice was born only to imitate nature. But in the book of Smith this hypothesis was presented as scarcely more than a theory which the then known facts supported very imperfectly. The rare cases of totemic sacrifice which he cites in support of his theory do not have the significance he attributed to them ; the animals which figure in them are not real totems.[2] But to-day we are able to state that on at least one point the demonstration is made : in fact, we have just seen that in an important number of societies the totemic sacrifice, such as Smith conceived it, is or has been practised. Of course, we have no proof that this practice is necessarily inherent to totemism or that it is the germ out of which all the other types of sacrifices have developed. But if the universality of the rite is hypothetical, its existence is no longer to be contested. Hereafter it is to be regarded as established that the most mystical form of the alimentary communion is found even in the most rudimentary cults known to-day.

IV

But on another point the new facts at our disposal invalidate the theories of Smith.

According to him, the communion was not only an essential element of the sacrifice, but at the beginning, at least, it was the unique element. Not only is one mistaken when he reduces sacrifice to nothing more than a tribute or offering, but the very idea of an offering was originally absent from it ; this intervened only at a late period and under the influence of external circumstances ; so instead of being able to aid us in understanding it, it has rather masked the real nature of the ritual mechanism. In fact, Smith claimed to find in the very notion of oblation an absurdity so revolting that it could never have been the fundamental reason for so great an institution. One of the most important functions incumbent upon the divinity is to assure to men that food which is necessary for life ; so it seems impossible that the sacrifice, in its turn, should consist in a presentation of food to the divinity. It even seems self-contradictory that the gods should expect their food from a man, when it is from them that he gets his. Why should they have need of his aid in order to deduct beforehand their just share of the things which he

[1] *The Religion of the Semites*, pp. 318–319.

[2] On this point, see Hubert and Mauss, *Mélanges d'histoire des religions*, preface, p. v ff.

receives from their hands? From these considerations Smith concluded that the idea of a sacrifice-offering could have been born only in the great religions, where the gods, removed from the things with which they were primitively confused, were thought of as sorts of kings and the eminent proprietors of the earth and its products. From this moment onwards, the sacrifice was associated with the tribute which subjects paid to their prince, as a price of the rights which were conceded to them. But this new interpretation was really an alteration and even a corruption of the primitive conception. For "the idea of property materializes all that it touches"; by introducing itself into the sacrifice, it denatured it and made it into a sort of bargain between the man and the divinity.[1]

But the facts which we have described overthrow this argumentation. These rites are certainly among the most primitive that have ever been observed. No determined mythical personality appears in them; there is no question of gods or spirits that are properly so called; it is only vaguely anonymous and impersonal forces which they put into action. Yet the reasoning which they suppose is exactly the one that Smith declared impossible because of its absurdity.

Let us return to the first act of the Intichiuma, to the rites destined to assure the fecundity of the animal or vegetable species which serves the clan as totem. This species is the pre-eminently sacred thing; in it is incarnated that which we have been able to call, by metaphor, the totemic divinity. Yet we have seen that to perpetuate itself it has need of the aid of men. It is they who dispense the life of the new generation each year; without them, it would never be born. If they stopped celebrating the Intichiuma, the sacred beings would disappear from the face of the earth. So in one sense, it is from men that they get their existence; yet in another way, it is from them that men get theirs; for after they have once arrived at maturity, it is from them that men acquire the force needed to support and repair their spiritual beings. Thus we are able to say that men make their gods, or, at least, make them live; but at the same time, it is from them that they live themselves. So they are regularly guilty of the circle which, according to Smith, is implied in the very idea of a sacrificial tribute: they give to the sacred beings a little of what they receive from them, and they receive from them all that they give.

But there is still more to be said: the oblations which he is thus forced to make every year do not differ in nature from those which are made later in the rites properly called sacrifices.

[1] *The Religion of the Semites*, pp. 390 ff.

If the sacrificer immolates an animal, it is in order that the living principles within it may be disengaged from the organism and go to nourish the divinity. Likewise, the grains of dust which the Australian detaches from the sacred rock are so many sacred principles which he scatters into space, so that they may go to animate the totemic species and assure its renewal. The gesture with which this scattering is made is also that which normally accompanies offerings. In certain cases, the resemblance between the two rites may be followed even to the details of the movements effected. We have seen that in order to have rain the Kaitish pour water over the sacred stone; among certain peoples, the priest pours water over the altar, with the same end in view.[1] The effusions of blood which are usual in a certain number of Intichiuma are veritable oblations. Just as the Arunta or Dieri sprinkle the sacred rock or the totemic design with blood, so it frequently happens that in the more advanced cults, the blood of the sacrificed victim or of the worshipper himself is spilt before or upon the altar.[2] In these cases, it is given to the gods, of whom it is the preferred food; in Australia, it is given to the sacred species. So we have no ground for saying that the idea of oblation is a late product of civilization.

A document which we owe to Strehlow puts this kinship of the Intichiuma and the sacrifice clearly into evidence. This is a hymn which accompanies the Intichiuma of the Kangaroo; the ceremony is described at the same time that its expected effects are announced. A morsel of kangaroo fat has been placed by the chief upon a support made of branches. The text says that this fat makes the fat of the kangaroos increase.[3] This time, they do not confine themselves to sprinkling sacred dust or human blood about; the animal itself is immolated, or sacrificed as one might say, placed upon a sort of altar, and offered to the species, whose life it should maintain.

Now we see the sense in which we may say that the Intichiuma contains the germs of the sacrificial system. In the form which it takes when fully constituted, a sacrifice is composed of two essential elements: an act of communion and an act of oblation. The worshipper communes with his god by taking in a sacred food, and at the same time he makes an offering to this god. We find these two acts in the Intichiuma, as we have described it. The only difference is that in the ordinary sacrifice[4] they are

[1] Smith cites some cases himself in *The Rel. of the Semites*, p. 231.

[2] For example, see Exodus xxix. 10–14; Leviticus ix. 8–11; it is their own blood which the priests of Baal pour over the altar (1 Kings xviii. 28).

[3] Strehlow, III, p. 12, verse 7.

[4] At least when it is complete: in certain cases, it may be reduced to one of its elements.

made simultaneously or else follow one another immediately, while in the Australian ceremony they are separated. In the former case, they are parts of one undivided rite; here, they take place at different times, and may even be separated by a rather long interval. But, at bottom, the mechanism is the same. Taken as a whole, the Intichiuma is a sacrifice, but one whose parts are not yet articulated and organized.

The relating of these two ceremonies has the double advantage of enabling us to understand better the nature of the Intichiuma and that of sacrifice.

We understand the Intichiuma better. In fact, the conception of Frazer, which made it a simple magic operation[1] with no religious character at all, is now seen to be unsupportable. One cannot dream of excluding from religion a rite which is the forerunner of so great a religious institution.

But we also understand what the sacrifice itself is better. In the first place, the equal importance of the two elements entering into it is now established. If the Australian makes offerings to his sacred beings, there is no reason for supposing that the idea of oblation was foreign to the primitive organization of the sacrificial institution and later upset its natural arrangement. The theory of Smith must be revised on this point.[2] Of course the sacrifice is partially a communion; but it is also, and no less essentially, a gift and an act of renouncement. It always presupposes that the worshipper gives some of his substance or his goods to his gods. Every attempt to deduce one of these elements from the other is hopeless. Perhaps the oblation is even more permanent than the communion.[3]

In the second place, it ordinarily seems as though the sacrifice, and especially the sacrificial oblation, could only be addressed to personal beings. But the oblations which we have met with in Australia imply no notion of this sort. In other words, the sacrifice is independent of the varying forms in which the religious forces are conceived; it is founded upon more profound reasons, which we shall seek presently.

In any case, it is clear that the act of offering naturally arouses in the mind the idea of a moral subject, whom this offering is destined to please. The ritual acts which we have described

[1] Strehlow says that the natives "regard these ceremonies as a sort of divine service, just as a Christian regards the exercises of his religion" (III, p. 9).

[2] It should be asked, for example, whether the effusions of blood and the offerings of hair which Smith regards as acts of communion are not real oblations (see Smith, *op. cit.*, pp. 320 ff.).

[3] The expiatory rites, of which we shall speak more fully in the fifth chapter of this same book, are almost exclusively oblations. They are communions only secondarily.

become more intelligible when it is believed that they are addressed to persons. So the practices of the Intichiuma, while actually putting only impersonal forces into play, prepare the way for a different conception.[1] Of course they were not sufficient to form the idea of mythical personalities by themselves, but when this idea had once been formed, the very nature of these rites made it enter into the cult ; thus, taking a more direct interest in action and life, it also acquired a greater reality. So we are even able to believe that the cult favoured, in a secondary manner, no doubt, but nevertheless one which is worthy of attention, the personification of the religious forces.

V

But we still have to explain the contradiction in which Robertson Smith saw an inadmissible logical scandal.

If the sacred beings always manifested their powers in a perfectly equal manner, it would appear inconceivable that men should dream of offering them services, for we cannot see what need they could have of them. But in the first place, in so far as they are confused with things, and in so far as they are regarded as principles of the cosmic life, they are themselves submitted to the rhythm of this life. Now this goes in oscillations in contrary directions, which succeed one another according to a determined law. Sometimes it is affirmed in all its glory; sometimes it weakens to such an extent that one may ask himself whether it is not going to fade away. Vegetation dies every year ; will it be reborn ? Animal species tend to become extinguished by the effect of natural and violent death ; will they be renewed at such a time and in such a way as is proper ? Above all, the rain is capricious ; there are long periods during which it seems to have disappeared for ever. These periodical variations of nature bear witness to the fact that at the corresponding periods, the sacred beings upon whom the plants, animals, rain, etc., depend are themselves passing through grave crises ; so they, too, have their periods of giving way. But men could not regard these spectacles as indifferent spectators. If he is to live, the universal life must continue, and consequently the gods must not die. So he seeks to sustain and aid them ; for this, he puts at their service whatever forces he has at his disposition, and mobilizes them for this purpose. The blood flowing in his veins has fecundating virtues ; he pours it forth. From the sacred rocks

[1] This is why we frequently speak of the ceremonies as if they were addressed to living personalities (see, for example, texts by Krichauff and Kemp, in Eylmann, p. 202).

possessed by his clan he takes those germs of life which lie dormant there, and scatters them into space. In a word, he makes oblations.

The external and physical crises, moreover, duplicate internal and mental crises which tend toward the same result. Sacred beings exist only when they are represented as such in the mind. When we cease to believe in them, it is as though they did not exist. Even those which have a material form and are given by sensible experience, depend upon the thought of the worshippers who adore them; for the sacred character which makes them objects of the cult is not given by their natural constitution; it is added to them by belief. The kangaroo is only an animal like all others; yet, for the men of the Kangaroo, it contains within it a principle which puts it outside the company of others, and this principle exists only in the minds of those who believe in it.[1] If these sacred beings, when once conceived, are to have no need of men to continue, it would be necessary that the representations expressing them always remain the same. But this stability is impossible. In fact, it is in the communal life that they are formed, and this communal life is essentially intermittent. So they necessarily partake of this same intermittency. They attain their greatest intensity at the moment when the men are assembled together and are in immediate relations with one another, when they all partake of the same idea and the same sentiment. But when the assembly has broken up and each man has returned to his own peculiar life, they progressively lose their original energy. Being covered over little by little by the rising flood of daily experiences, they would soon fall into the unconscious, if we did not find some means of calling them back into consciousness and revivifying them. If we think of them less forcefully, they amount to less for us and we count less upon them; they exist to a lesser degree. So here we have another point of view, from which the services of men are necessary to them. This second reason for their existence is even more important than the first, for it exists all the time. The intermittency of the physical life can affect religious beliefs only when religions are not yet detached from their cosmic basis. The intermittency of the social life, on the other hand, is inevitable; even the most idealistic religions cannot escape it.

Moreover, it is owing to this state of dependency upon the

[1] In a philosophical sense, the same is true of everything, for nothing exists except in representation. But as we have shown (p. 227), this proposition is doubly true for religious forces, for there is nothing in the constitution of things which corresponds to sacredness.

thought of men, in which the gods find themselves, that the former are able to believe in the efficacy of their assistance. The only way of renewing the collective representations which relate to sacred beings is to retemper them in the very source of the religious life, that is to say, in the assembled groups. Now the emotions aroused by these periodical crises through which external things pass induce the men who witness them to assemble, to see what should be done about it. But by the very fact of uniting, they are mutually comforted; they find a remedy because they seek it together. The common faith becomes reanimated quite naturally in the heart of this reconstituted group; it is born again because it again finds those very conditions in which it was born in the first place. After it has been restored, it easily triumphs over all the private doubts which may have arisen in individual minds. The image of the sacred things regains power enough to resist the internal or external causes which tended to weaken it. In spite of their apparent failure, men can no longer believe that the gods will die, because they feel them living in their own hearts. The means employed to succour them, howsoever crude these may be, cannot appear vain, for everything goes on as if they were really effective. Men are more confident because they feel themselves stronger; and they really are stronger, because forces which were languishing are now reawakened in the consciousness.

So we must be careful not to believe, along with Smith, that the cult was founded solely for the benefit of men and that the gods have nothing to do with it: they have no less need of it than their worshippers. Of course men would be unable to live without gods, but, on the other hand, the gods would die if their cult were not rendered. This does not have the sole object of making profane subjects communicate with sacred beings, but it also keeps these latter alive and is perpetually remaking and regenerating them. Of course it is not the material oblations which bring about this regeneration by their own virtues; it is the mental states which these actions, though vain in themselves, accompany or reawaken. The real reason for the existence of the cults, even of those which are the most materialistic in appearance, is not to be sought in the acts which they prescribe, but in the internal and moral regeneration which these acts aid in bringing about. The things which the worshipper really gives his gods are not the foods which he places upon the altars, nor the blood which he lets flow from his veins: it is his thought. Nevertheless, it is true that there is an exchange of services, which are mutually demanded, between the divinity and its worshippers. The rule *do ut des*, by which the principle of sacrifice has sometimes been defined, is not a late invention of utilitarian theorists: it only expresses in an explicit way the very mechanism of the sacrificial system and, more generally, of the whole positive cult. So the circle pointed out by Smith is very real; but it contains nothing humiliating for the reason. It comes from the fact that the sacred beings, though superior to men, can live only in the human consciousness.

But this circle will appear still more natural to us, and we shall understand its meaning and the reason for its existence still better if, carrying our analysis still farther and substituting for the religious symbols the realities which they represent, we investigate how these behave in the rite. If, as we have attempted to establish, the sacred principle is nothing more nor less than society transfigured and personified, it should be possible to interpret the ritual in lay and social terms. And, as a matter of fact, social life, just like the ritual, moves in a circle. On the one hand, the individual gets from society the best part of himself, all that gives him a distinct character and a special place among other beings, his intellectual and moral culture. If we should withdraw from men their language, sciences, arts and moral beliefs, they would drop to the rank of animals. So the characteristic attributes of human nature come from society. But, on the other hand, society exists and lives only in and through individuals. If the idea of society were extinguished in individual minds and the beliefs, traditions and aspirations of the group were no longer felt and shared by the individuals, society would die. We can say of it what we just said of the divinity: it is real only in so far as it has a place in human consciousnesses, and this place is whatever one we may give it. We now see the real reason why the gods cannot do without their worshippers any more than these can do without their gods; it is because society, of which the gods are only a symbolic expression, cannot do without individuals any more than these can do without society.

Here we touch the solid rock upon which all the cults are built and which has caused their persistence ever since human societies have existed. When we see what religious rites consist of and towards what they seem to tend, we demand with astonishment how men have been able to imagine them, and especially how they can remain so faithfully attached to them. Whence could the illusion have come that with a few grains of sand thrown to the wind, or a few drops of blood shed upon a rock or the stone of an altar, it is possible to maintain the life of an animal species or of a god? We have undoubtedly made a step in advance towards the solution of this problem when we have discovered, behind these outward and apparently unreasonable movements, a mental mechanism which gives them a meaning and a moral significance. But we are in no way assured that this mechanism itself does not consist in a simple play of hallucinatory images. We have pointed out the psychological process which leads the believers to imagine that the rite causes the spiritual forces of which they have need to be reborn about them; but it does not follow from the fact that this belief is psychologically explicable that it has any objective value. If we are to see in the efficacy attributed to the rites anything more than the product of a chronic delirium with which humanity has abused itself, we must show that the effect of the cult really is to recreate periodically a moral being upon which we depend as it depends upon us. Now this being does exist: it is society.

Howsoever little importance the religious ceremonies may have, they put the group into action; the groups assemble to celebrate them. So their first effect is to bring individuals together, to multiply the relations between them and to make them more intimate with one another. By this very fact, the contents of their consciousnesses is changed. On ordinary days, it is utilitarian and individual avocations which take the greater part of the attention. Every one attends to his own personal business; for most men, this primarily consists in satisfying the exigencies of material life, and the principal incentive to economic activity has always been private interest. Of course social sentiments could never be totally absent. We remain in relations with others; the habits, ideas and tendencies which education has impressed upon us and which ordinarily preside over our relations with others, continue to make their action felt. But they are constantly combated and held in check by the antagonistic tendencies aroused and supported by the necessities of the daily struggle. They resist more or less successfully, according to their intrinsic energy: but this energy is not renewed. They live upon their past, and consequently they would be used up in the course of time, if nothing returned to them a little of the force that they lose through these incessant conflicts and frictions. When the Australians, scattered in little groups, spend their time in hunting and fishing, they lose sight of what concerns their clan or tribe: their only thought is to catch as much game as possible. On feast days, on the contrary, these preoccupations are necessarily eclipsed; being essentially profane, they are excluded from these sacred periods. At this time, their thoughts are centred upon their common beliefs, their common traditions, the memory of their great ancestors, the collective ideal of which they are the incarnation; in a word, upon social things. Even the material interests which these great religious ceremonies are designed to satisfy concern the public order and are therefore social. Society as a whole is interested that the harvest be abundant, that the rain fall at the right time and not excessively, that the animals reproduce regularly. So it is society that is in the foreground of every consciousness; it dominates and directs all conduct; this is equivalent to saying that it is more living and active, and consequently more real, than in profane times. So men do not deceive themselves when they feel at this time that there is something outside of them which is born again, that there are forces which are reanimated and a life which reawakens. This renewal is in no way imaginary and the individuals themselves profit from it. For the spark of a social being which each bears within him necessarily participates in this collective renovation. The individual soul is regenerated too, by being dipped again in the source from which its life comes; consequently it feels itself stronger, more fully master of itself, less dependent upon physical necessities.

We know that the positive cult naturally tends to take periodic forms; this is one of its distinctive features. Of course there are rites which men celebrate occasionally, in connection with passing situations. But these episodic practices are always merely accessory, and in the religions studied in this book, they are almost exceptional. The essential constituent of the cult is the cycle of feasts which return regularly at determined epochs. We are now able to understand whence this tendency towards periodicity comes; the rhythm which the religious life follows only expresses the rhythm of the social life, and results from it. Society is able to revivify the sentiment it has of itself only by assembling. But it cannot be assembled all the time. The exigencies of life do not allow it to remain in congregation indefinitely; so it scatters, to assemble anew when it again feels the need of this. It is to these necessary alternations that the regular alternations of sacred and profane times correspond. Since the apparent object, at least, of the cult was at first to regularize the course of natural phenomena, the rhythm of the cosmic life has put its mark on the rhythm of the ritual life. This is why the feasts have long been associated with the seasons; we have seen this characteristic already in the Intichiuma of Australia. But the seasons have only furnished the outer frame-work for this organization, and not the principle upon which it rests; for even the cults which aim at exclusively spiritual ends have remained periodical. So this periodicity must be due to other causes. Since the seasonal changes are critical periods for nature, they are a natural occasion for assembling, and consequently for religious ceremonies. But other events can and have successfully fulfilled this function of occasional cause. However, it must be recognized that this frame-work, though purely external, has given proof of a singular resistive force, for traces of it are found even in the religions which are the most fully detached from all physical bases. Many Christian celebrations are founded, with no break of continuity, on the pastoral and agrarian feasts of the ancient Hebrews, although in themselves they are neither pastoral nor agrarian.

Moreover, this rhythm is capable of varying in different societies. Where the period of dispersion is long, and the dispersion itself is extreme, the period of congregation, in its turn, is very prolonged, and produces veritable debauches of collective and religious life. Feasts succeed one another for weeks or even for months, while the ritual life sometimes attains to a sort of frenzy. This is what happens among the Australian tribes and many of the tribes of North-western America.[1] Elsewhere, on the contrary, these two phases of the social life succeed one another after shorter intervals, and then the contrast between them is less marked. The more societies develop, the less they seem to allow of too great intermittences.

[1] See Mauss, *Essai sur les variations saisonnières des sociétés Eskimos*, in *Année Sociol.*, IX, pp. 96 ff.

CHAPTER III

THE POSITIVE CULT—*continued*

II.—*Imitative Rites and the Principle of Causality*

BUT the processes which we have just been describing are not the only ones employed to assure the fecundity of the totemic species. There are others which serve for the same end, whether they accompany the preceding ones or replace them.

I

In the very ceremonies which we have been describing, in addition to the oblations, whether bloody or otherwise, there are other rites which are frequently celebrated, whose object is to complete the former ones and to consolidate their effects. They consist in movements and cries whose object is to imitate the different attitudes and aspects of the animal whose reproduction is desired; therefore, we shall call them *imitative*.

Thus the Intichiuma of the Witchetty grub among the Arunta includes more than the rites performed upon the sacred rocks, of which we have already spoken. When these are finished, the men set out to return to camp; but when they still are about a mile away, they halt and all decorate themselves ritually; after this, the march is resumed. The decorations with which they thus adorn themselves announce that an important ceremony is going to take place. And, in fact, while the company was absent, one of the old men who had been left to guard the camp had built a shelter out of branches, called *Umbana*, which represented the chrysalis out of which the insect comes. All of those who had taken part in the previous ceremonies assemble near the spot where this construction has been raised; then they advance slowly, stopping from time to time, until they reach the *Umbana*, which they enter. At once all the men who do not belong to the phratry of the Witchetty grub totem, and who assist at the scene, though from a distance, lie down on the ground, with their faces against the earth; they must remain in this position without moving until they are allowed to get up again. Meanwhile, a chant arises from the interior of the *Umbana*, which describes the different phases through which the animal passes in the course of its development, and the myths of which the sacred rocks are the subject. When this hymn ceases, the Alatunja glides out of the *Umbana*, though remaining in a squatting position, and advances slowly over the ground before him; he is followed by all his companions who reproduce gestures whose evident object is to represent the insect as it leaves the chrysalis. Also, a hymn which is heard at just this moment and which is like an oral commentary on the rite, consists in a description of the movements made by the insect at this stage of its development.[1]

Another Intichiuma,[2] celebrated in connection with another kind of grub, the *unchalka* [3] grub, has this character still more clearly. The actors of this rite decorate themselves with designs representing the *unchalka* bush upon which this grub lives at the beginning of its existence. Then they cover a buckler with concentric circles of down, representing another kind of bush upon which the insect lays its eggs when it has become adult. When all these preparations are finished, they all sit down on the ground in a semicircle facing the principal officiant. He alternately bends his body double by leaning towards the ground and then rises on his knees; at the same time, he shakes his stretched-out arms, which is a way of representing the wings of the insect. From time to time, he leans over the buckler, imitating the way in which the butterfly flies over the trees where it lays its eggs. When this ceremony is finished, another commences at a different spot, to which they go in silence. This time they use two bucklers. Upon one the tracks of the grub are represented by zigzag lines; upon the other, concentric circles of uneven dimensions represent the eggs of the insect and the seed of the Eremophile bush, upon which it is nourished. As in the former ceremony, they all sit down in silence while the officiant acts, representing the movements of the animal when leaving its chrysalis and taking its first flight.

Spencer and Gillen also point out certain analogous facts among the Arunta, though these are of a minor importance: in the Intichiuma of the Emu, for example, at a certain moment the actors try to reproduce by their attitude the air and aspect of this bird; [4] in the Intichiuma of water, the men of the totem

[1] *Nat. Tr.*, p. 176.

[2] *Nor. Tr.*, p. 179. It is true that Spencer and Gillen do not say expressly that this is an Intichiuma. But the context allow of no doubt on this point.

[3] In the index of totem names, Spencer and Gillen write *Untjalka* (*Nor. Tr.*, p. 772).

[4] *Nat. Tr.*, p. 182.

utter the characteristic cry of the plover, a cry which is naturally associated in the mind with the rainy season.[1] But in all, the examples of imitative rites which these two explorers have noted are rather few in number. However, it is certain that their relative silence on this point is due either to their not having observed the Intichiuma sufficiently or else to their having neglected this side of the ceremonies. Schulze, on the other hand, has been struck by the essentially imitative nature of the Arunta rites. "The sacred corrobbori," he says, "are generally ceremonies representing animals": he calls them *animal tjurunga*[2] and his testimony is now confirmed by the documents collected by Strehlow. The examples given by this latter author are so numerous that it is impossible to cite them all: there are scarcely any ceremonies in which some imitating gesture is not pointed out. According to the nature of the animals whose feast is celebrated, they jump after the manner of kangaroos, or imitate the movements they make in eating, the flight of winged ants, the characteristic noise of the bat, the cry of the wild turkey, the hissing of the snake, the croaking of the frog, etc.[3] When the totem is a plant, they make the gesture of plucking it,[4] or eating it,[5] etc.

Among the Warramunga, the Intichiuma generally takes a special form, which we shall describe in the next chapter and which differs from those which we have studied up to the present. However, there is one typical case of a purely imitative Intichiuma among this people; it is that of the black cockatoo. The ceremony described by Spencer and Gillen commenced at ten o'clock in the evening. All night long the chief of the clan imitated the cry of the bird with a disheartening monotony. He stopped only when he had come to the end of his force, and then his son replaced him; then he commenced again as soon as he felt a little refreshed. These exhausting exercises continued until morning without interruption.[6]

Living beings are not the only ones which they try to imitate. In a large number of tribes, the Intichiuma of rain consists essentially in imitative rites. One of the most simple of these is that celebrated among the Arabunna. The chief of the clan is seated on the ground, all covered with white down and holding a lance in his hands. He shakes himself, undoubtedly in order to detach from his body the down which is fixed there and which represents clouds when scattered about in the air. Thus he imitates the men-clouds of the Alcheringa who, according to

[1] *Nat. Tr.*, p. 193. [2] Schulze, *loc. cit.*, p. 221; cf. p. 243.
[3] Strehlow, III, pp. 11, 31, 36, 37, 68, 72, 84. [4] *Ibid.*, p. 100.
[5] *Ibid.*, pp. 81, 100, 112, 115. [6] *Nor. Tr.*, p. 310.

the legend, had the habit of ascending to heaven and forming clouds there, from which the rain then fell. In a word, the object of the whole rite is to represent the formation and ascension of clouds, the bringers of rain.[1]

The ceremony is much more complicated among the Kaitish. We have already spoken of one of the means employed: the officiant pours water over the sacred stones and himself. But the action of this sort of oblation is reinforced by other rites. The rainbow is considered to have a close connection with rain: they say that it is its son and that it is always urged to appear to make the rain stop. To make the rain fall, it is therefore necessary that it should not appear; they believe that this result can be obtained in the following manner. A design representing a rainbow is made upon a buckler. They carry this buckler to camp, taking care to keep it hidden from all eyes. They are convinced that by making this image of the rainbow invisible, they keep the rainbow itself from appearing. Meanwhile, the chief of the clan, having beside him a *pitchi* full of water, throws in all directions flakes of down which represent clouds. Repeated imitations of the cry of the plover complete this ceremony, which seems to have an especial gravity; for as long as it lasts, all those who participate in it, either as actors or assistants, may have no relations whatsoever with their wives; they may not even speak to them.[2]

The processes of figuration are different among the Dieri. Rain is not represented by water, but by blood, which the men cause to flow from their veins on to the assistants.[3] At the same time they throw handfuls of white down about, which represent clouds. A hut has been constructed previously, in which they now place two large stones representing piles of clouds, a sign of rain. After they have been left there for a little while, they are carried a little distance away and placed as high as possible in the loftiest tree to be found; this is a way of making the clouds mount into the sky. Powdered gypsum is then thrown into a water-hole, for when he sees this, the rain spirit soon makes the clouds appear. Finally all the men, young and old, assemble around the hut and with heads lowered, they charge upon it; they rush violently through it, repeating the operation several times, until nothing remains of the whole construction except

[1] *Nor. Tr.*, pp. 285–286. Perhaps the object of these movements of the lance is to pierce the clouds.

[2] *Nor. Tr.*, pp. 294–296. It is curious that, on the contrary, the Anula regard the rainbow as productive of rain (*ibid.*, p. 314).

[3] The same process is employed among the Arunta (Strehlow, III, p. 132). Of course we may ask if this effusion of blood is not an oblation designed to win the powers which produce rain. However, Gason says distinctly that this is a way of imitating the water which falls.

the supporting posts. Then they fall upon these and shake and pull at them until the whole thing has tumbled down. The operation consisting in running through the hut is supposed to represent clouds bursting; the tumbling down of the construction, the fall of rain.[1]

In the north-western tribes studied by Clement,[2] which occupy the district included between the Fontescue and Fitzroy rivers, certain ceremonies are celebrated whose object is exactly the same as that of the Intichiuma of the Arunta, and which seem to be, for the most part, essentially imitative.

These peoples give the name *tarlow* to certain piles of stones which are evidently sacred, for, as we shall see, they are the object of important rites. Every animal, every plant, and in fact, every totem or sub-totem,[3] is represented by a *tarlow* which a special clan [4] guards. The analogy between these *tarlow* and the sacred rocks of the Arunta is easily seen.

When kangaroos, for example, become rare, the chief of the clan to which the *tarlow* of the kangaroo belongs goes to it with a certain number of companions. Here various rites are performed, the chief of which consist in jumping around the *tarlow* as kangaroos jump, in drinking as they drink and, in a word, in imitating all their most characteristic movements. The weapons used in hunting the animal have an important part in these rites. They brandish them, throw them against the stones, etc. When they are concerned for emus, they go to the *tarlow* of the emu, and walk and run as these birds do. The skill which the natives show in these imitations is, as it appears, really remarkable.

Other *tarlow* are consecrated to plants, such as the cereals. In this case, they imitate the actions of threshing and grinding the grain. Since in ordinary life it is the women who are normally charged with these tasks, it is also they who perform the rite, in the midst of songs and dances.

II

All these rites belong to the same type. The principle upon which they rest is one of those at the basis of what is commonly and incorrectly called sympathetic[5] magic.

[1] Gason, *The Dieri Tribe*, in Curr, II, pp. 66–68. Howitt (*Nat. Tr.*, pp. 798–800) mentions other rites of the Dieri for obtaining rain.

[2] *Ethnological Notes on the Western Australian Aborigines*, in *Internationales Archiv. f. Ethnographie*, XVI, pp. 6–7. Cf. Withnal, *Marriage Rites and Relationship* in *Man*, 1903, p. 42.

[3] We presume that sub-totems may have *tarlow*, for, according to Clement, certain clans have several totems.

[4] Clement says a tribal family.

[5] We shall explain below (p. 362) why this is incorrect.

These principles are ordinarily reduced to two.[1]

The first may be stated thus: *anything touching an object also touches everything which has any relation of proximity or unity whatsoever with this object.* Thus, whatever affects the part also affects the whole; any action exercised over an individual is transmitted to his neighbours, relatives and all those to whom he is united in any way. All these cases are simple applications of the law of contagion, which we have already studied. A condition or a good or bad quality are communicated contagiously from one subject to another who has some connection with the former.

The second principle is ordinarily summed up in the formula: *like produces like.* The representation of a being or condition produces this being or condition. This is the maxim which brings about the rites which we have just been describing, and it is in them that we can best observe its characteristics. The classical example of the magic charm, which is ordinarily given as the typical application of this same precept, is much less significant. The charm is, to a large extent, a simple phenomenon of transfer. The idea of the image is associated in the mind with that of the model; consequently the effects of an action performed upon a statue are transmitted contagiously to the person whose traits it reproduces. The function of the image is for its original what that of a part is for the whole: it is an agent of transmission. Therefore men think that they can obtain the same result by burning the hair of the person whom they wish to injure: the only difference between these two sorts of operations is that in one, the communication is made through similarity, while in the other it is by means of contiguity. It is different with the rites which concern us. They suppose not only the displacement of a given condition or quality, which passes from one object into the other, but also the creation of something entirely new. The mere act of representing the animal gives birth to this animal and creates it; by imitating the sound of wind or falling water, they cause clouds to form, rain to fall, etc. Of course resemblance plays an important part in each case, but not at all the same one. In a charm, it only gives a special direction to the action exercised; it directs in a certain way an action not originating in it. In the rites of which we have just been speaking, it acts by itself and is directly efficacious. So, in contradiction to the usual definitions, the real difference between the two principles of the so-called sympathetic magic and the corresponding practices is not that

[1] On this classification, see Frazer, *Lectures on the Early History of Kingship*, pp. 37 ff.; Hubert and Mauss, *Théorie générale de la Magie*, pp. 61 ff.

it is contiguity acts in one case and resemblance in the other, but that in the former there is a simple contagious communication, while there is production and creation in the latter.[1]

The explanation of imitative rites therefore implies the explanation of the second of these principles, and reciprocally.

We shall not tarry long to discuss the explanation proposed by the anthropological school, and especially by Tylor and Frazer. Just as in their attempts to account for the contagiousness of a sacred character, they invoke the association of ideas. " Homœopathic magic," says Frazer, who prefers this expression to imitative magic, " is founded on the association of ideas by similarity ; contagious magic is founded on the association of ideas by contiguity. Homœopathic magic commits the mistake of assuming that things which resemble each other are the same."[2] But this is a misunderstanding of the special nature of the practices under discussion. On the one hand, the formula of Frazer may be applied with some fitness to the case of charms ;[3] here, in fact, two distinct things are associated with each other, owing to their partial resemblance : these are the image and the model which it represents more or less systematically. But in the imitative rites, which we have just been observing, the image alone is given ; as for the model, it does not exist, for the new generation of the totemic species is as yet only a hope and even an uncertain hope at that. So there could be no question of association, whether correct or not ; there is a real creation, and we cannot see how the association of ideas could possibly lead to a belief in this creation. How could the mere act of representing the movements of an animal bring about the certitude that this animal will be born, and born in abundance ?

The general properties of human nature cannot explain such special practices. So instead of considering the principle upon which they rest in its general and abstract form, let us replace it in the environment of which it is a part and where we have been observing it, and let us connect it with the system of ideas and sentiments which the above rites put into practice, and then we shall be better able to perceive the causes from which it results.

The men who assemble on the occasion of these rites believe that they are really animals or plants of the species whose name

[1] We say nothing of what has been called the law of opposition, for, as MM. Hubert and Mauss have shown, a contrary produces its opposite only through the intermediacy of a similar (*Théorie générale de la Magie*, p. 70).

[2] *Lectures on the History of Kingship*, p. 39.

[3] It is applicable in the sense that there is really an association of the statue and the person encharmed. But it is true that this association is the simple product of an association of ideas by similarity. The true determining cause of the phenomenon is the contagiousness peculiar to religious forces, as we have shown.

they bear. They feel within them an animal or vegetable nature, and in their eyes, this is what constitutes whatever is the most essential and the most excellent in them. So when they assemble, their first movement ought to be to show each other this quality which they attribute to themselves and by which they are defined. The totem is their rallying sign; for this reason, as we have seen, they design it upon their bodies; but it is no less natural that they should seek to resemble it in their gestures, their cries, their attitude. Since they are emus or kangaroos, they comport themselves like the animals of the same name. By this means, they mutually show one another that they are all members of the same moral community and they become conscious of the kinship uniting them. The rite does not limit itself to expressing this kinship; it makes it or remakes it. For it exists only in so far as it is believed in, and the effect of all these collective demonstrations is to support the beliefs upon which they are founded. Therefore, these leaps, these cries and these movements of every sort, though bizarre and grotesque in appearance, really have a profound and human meaning. The Australian seeks to resemble his totem just as the faithful in more advanced religions seek to resemble their God. For the one as for the other, this is a means of communicating with the sacred being, that is to say, with the collective ideal which this latter symbolizes. This is an early form of the ὁμοίωσις τῷ θεῷ.

However, as this first reason is connected with the most specialized portions of the totemic beliefs, the principle by which like produces like should not have survived totemism, if this had been the only one in operation. Now there is probably no religion in which rites derived from it are not found. So another reason must co-operate with this first one.

And, in fact, the ceremonies where we have seen it applied do not merely have the very general object which we have just mentioned, howsoever essential this may be; they also aim at a more immediate and more conscious end, which is the assurance of the reproduction of the totemic species. The idea of this necessary reproduction haunts the minds of the worshippers: upon it the forces of their attention and will are concentrated. Now a single preoccupation cannot possess a group of men to this point without being externalized in a material form. Since all think of the animal or plant to whose destinies the clan is united, it is inevitable that this common thought should not be manifested outwardly by gestures,[1] and those naturally designated for this office are those which represent this animal or plant in one of its most characteristic attitudes; there are no other movements

[1] For the causes determining this outward manifestation, see above, pp. 230 ff.

so close to the idea filling every mind, for these are an immediate and almost automatic translation of it. So they make themselves imitate the animal; they cry like it, they jump like it; they reproduce the scenes in which they make daily use of the plant. All these ways of representation are just so many means of ostensibly showing the end towards which all minds are directed, of telling the thing which they wish to realize, of calling it up and of evoking it. And this need belongs to no one time, nor does it depend upon the beliefs of any special religion; it is essentially human. This is why, even in religions very far removed from those we have been studying, the worshippers, when assembled to ask their gods for some event which they ardently desire, are forced to figure it. Of course, the word is also a way of expressing it; but the gesture is no less natural; it bursts out from the organism just as spontaneously; it even precedes the word, or, in any case, accompanies it.

But if we can thus understand how the gestures acquired a place in the ceremony, we still must explain the efficacy attributed to them. If the Australian repeats them regularly each new season, it is because he believes them essential to the success of the rite. Where could he have gotten the idea that by imitating an animal, one causes it to reproduce?

So manifest an error seems hardly intelligible so long as we see in the rite only the material end towards which it seems to aim. But we know that in addition to the effect which it is thought to have on the totemic species, it also exercises a profound influence over the souls of the worshippers who take part in it. They take away with them a feeling of well-being, whose causes they cannot clearly see, but which is well founded. They feel that the ceremony is good for them; and, as a matter of fact, they reforge their moral nature in it. How could this sort of well-being fail to give them a feeling that the rite has succeeded, that it has been what it set out to be, and that it has attained the ends at which it was aimed? As the only end which was consciously sought was the reproduction of the totemic species, this seems to be assured by the means employed, the efficacy of which is thus proven. Thus it comes about that men attribute creative virtues to their gestures, which in themselves are vain. The moral efficacy of the rite, which is real, leads to the belief in its physical efficacy, which is imaginary; that of the whole, to the belief in that of each part by itself. The truly useful effects produced by the whole ceremony are like an experimental justification of the elementary practices out of which it is made, though in reality, all these practices are in no way indispensable to its success. A certain proof, moreover, that they do not act by themselves is that they may be replaced by others, of a very different nature, without any modification of the final result. It appears that there are Intichiuma which include only oblations, with no imitative rites; others are purely imitative, and include no oblations. However, both are believed to have the same efficacy. So if a price is attached to these various manœuvres, it is not because of their intrinsic value, but because they are a part of a complex rite, whose utility as a whole is realized.

We are able to understand this state of mind all the easier because we can still observe it about us. Especially among the most cultivated peoples and environments, we frequently meet with believers who, though having doubts as to the special efficacy attributed by dogma to each rite considered separately, still continue to participate in the cult. They are not sure that the details of the prescribed observances are rationally justifiable; but they feel that it would be impossible to free oneself of them without falling into a moral confusion before which they recoil. The very fact that in them the faith has lost its intellectual foundations throws into eminence the profound reasons upon which they rest. This is why the easy criticisms to which an unduly simple rationalism has sometimes submitted ritual prescriptions generally leave the believer indifferent: it is because the true justification of religious practices does not lie in the apparent ends which they pursue, but rather in the invisible action which they exercise over the mind and in the way in which they affect our mental status. Likewise, when preachers undertake to convince, they devote much less attention to establishing directly and by methodical proofs the truth of any particular proposition or the utility of such and such an observance, than to awakening or reawakening the sentiment of the moral comfort attained by the regular celebration of the cult. Thus they create a predisposition to belief, which precedes proofs, which leads the mind to overlook the insufficiency of the logical reasons, and which thus prepares it for the proposition whose acceptance is desired. This favourable prejudice, this impulse towards believing, is just what constitutes faith; and it is faith which makes the authority of the rites, according to the believer, whoever he may be, Christian or Australian. The only superiority of the former is that he better accounts for the psychological process from which his faith results; he knows that " it is faith that saves."

It is because faith has this origin that it is, in a sense, " impermeable to experience."[1] If the intermittent failures of the Intichiuma do not shake the confidence of the Australian in his

[1] M. Lévy-Bruhl, *Les Fonctions mentales dans les sociétés inférieures*, pp. 61–68.

rite, it is because he holds with all the strength of his soul to these practices in which he periodically recreates himself; he could not deny their principle without causing an upheaval of his own being, which resists. But howsoever great this force of resistance may be, it cannot radically distinguish religious mentality from the other forms of human mentality, even those which are the most habitually opposed to it. In this connection, that of a scholar differs from the preceding only in degree. When a scientific law has the authority of numerous and varied experiments, it is against all method to renounce it too quickly upon the discovery of a fact which seems to contradict it. It is still necessary to make sure that the fact does not allow of a single interpretation, and that it is impossible to account for it, without abandoning the proposition which it seems to invalidate. Now the Australian does not proceed otherwise when he attributes the failure of the Intichiuma to some sorcery, or the abundance of a premature crop to a mystic Intichiuma celebrated in the beyond. He has all the more reason for not doubting his rite on the belief in a contrary fact, since its value is, or seems to be, established by a larger number of harmonizing facts. In the first place, the moral efficacy of the ceremony is real and is felt directly by all who participate in it; there is a constantly renewed experience in it, whose importance no contradictory experience can diminish. Also, the physical efficacy itself is not unable to find an at least apparent confirmation in the data of objective observation. As a matter of fact, the totemic species normally does reproduce regularly; so in the great majority of cases, everything happens just as if the ritual gestures really did produce the effects expected of them. Failures are the exception. As the rites, and especially those which are periodical, demand nothing more of nature than that it follow its ordinary course, it is not surprising that it should generally have the air of obeying them. So if the believer shows himself indocile to certain lessons of experience, he does so because of other experiences which seem more demonstrative. The scholar does not do otherwise; only he introduces more method.

So magic is not, as Frazer has held,[1] an original fact, of which religion is only a derived form. Quite on the contrary, it was under the influence of religious ideas that the precepts upon which the art of the magician is based were established, and it was only through a secondary extension that they were applied to purely lay relations. Since all the forces of the universe have been conceived on the model of the sacred forces, the

[1] *Golden Bough*², I, pp. 69–75.

contagiousness inherent in the second was extended to the first, and men have believed that all the properties of a body could be transmitted contagiously. Likewise, when the principle according to which like produces like had been established, in order to satisfy certain religious needs, it detached itself from its ritual origins to become, through a sort of spontaneous generalization, a law of nature.[1] But in order to understand these fundamental axioms of magic, they must be replaced in the religious atmosphere in which they arose and which alone enables us to account for them. When we regard them as the work of isolated individuals or solitary magicians, we ask how they could ever have occurred to the mind of man, for nothing in experience could either suggest or verify them ; and especially we do not explain how so deceiving an art has been able to impose itself for so long a time in the confidence of men. But this problem disappears when we realize that the faith inspired by magic is only a particular case of religious faith in general, and that it is itself the product, at least indirectly, of a collective effervescence. This is as much as to say that the use of the expression sympathetic magic to designate the system of rites which we have just been speaking is not very exact. There are sympathetic rites, but they are not peculiar to magic ; not only are they to be found in religion, but it was from religion that magic received them. So we only risk confusion when, by the name we give them, we have the air of making them something which is specifically magic.

The results of our analysis thus attach themselves to and and confirm those attained by MM. Hubert and Mauss when they studied magic directly.[2] They have shown that this is nothing more nor less than crude industry based on incomplete science. Behind the mechanisms, purely laical in appearance, which are used by the magician, they point out a background of religious conceptions and a whole world of forces, the idea of which has been taken by magic from religion. We are now able to understand how it comes that magic is so full of religious elements : it is because it was born of religion.

III

But the principle which has just been set forth does not merely have a function in the ritual ; it is of direct interest for the theory

[1] We do not wish to say that there was ever a time when religion existed without magic. Probably as religion took form, certain of its principles were extended to non-religious relations, and it was thus supplemented by a more or less developed magic. But if these two systems of ideas and practices do not correspond to distinct historical phases, they have a relation of definite derivation between them. This is all we have sought to establish.

[2] *Loc. cit.*, pp. 108 ff.

of knowledge. In fact, it is a concrete statement of the law of causality and, in all probability, one of the most primitive statements of it which has ever existed. A full conception of the causal relation is implied in the power thus attributed to the like to produce the like; and this conception dominates primitive thought, for it is the basis both of the practices of the cult and the technique of the magician. So the origins of the precept upon which the imitative rites depend are able to clarify those of the principle of causality. The genesis of one should aid us in understanding the genesis of the other. Now we have shown how the former is a product of social causes: it was elaborated by groups having collective ends in view, and it translates collective sentiments. So we may assume that the same is true for the second.

In fact, an analysis of the principle of causality is sufficient to assure us that the diverse elements of which it is composed really did have this origin.

The first thing which is implied in the notion of the causal relation is the idea of efficacy, of productive power, of active force. By cause we ordinarily mean something capable of producing a certain change. The cause is the force before it has shown the power which is in it; the effect is this same power, only actualized. Men have always thought of causality in dynamic terms. Of course certain philosophers had refused all objective value to this conception; they see in it only an arbitrary construction of the imagination, which corresponds to nothing in the things themselves. But, at present, we have no need of asking whether it is founded in reality or not; it is enough for us to state that it exists and that it constitutes and always has constituted an element of ordinary mentality; and this is recognized even by those who criticize it. Our immediate purpose is to seek, not what it may be worth logically, but how it is to be explained.

Now it depends upon social causes. Our analysis of facts has already enabled us to see that the prototype of the idea of force was the mana, wakan, orenda, the totemic principle or any of the various names given to collective force objectified and projected into things.[1] The first power which men have thought of as such seems to have been that exercised by humanity over its members. Thus reason confirms the results of observation; in fact, it is even possible to show why this notion of power, efficacy or active force could not have come from any other source.

In the first place, it is evident and recognized by all that it could not be furnished to us by external experience. Our senses

[1] See above, pp. 203 f.

only enable us to perceive phenomena which coexist or which follow one another, but nothing perceived by them could give us the idea of this determining and compelling action which is characteristic of what we call a power or force. They can touch only realized and known conditions, each separate from the others; the internal process uniting these conditions escapes them. Nothing that we learn could possibly suggest to us the idea of what an influence or efficaciousness is. It is for this very reason that the philosophers of empiricism have regarded these different conceptions as so many mythological aberrations. But even supposing that they all are hallucinations, it is still necessary to show how they originated.

If external experience counts for nothing in the origin of these ideas, and it is equally inadmissible that they were given us ready-made, one might suppose that they come from internal experience. In fact, the notion of force obviously includes many spiritual elements which could only have been taken from our psychic life.

Some have believed that the act by which our will brings a deliberation to a close, restrains our impulses and commands our organism, might have served as the model of this construction. In willing, it is said, we perceive ourselves directly as a power in action. So when this idea had once occurred to men, it seems that they only had to extend it to things to establish the conception of force.

As long as the animist theory passed as a demonstrated truth, this explanation was able to appear to be confirmed by history. If the forces with which human thought primitively populated the world really had been spirits, that is to say, personal and conscious beings more or less similar to men, it was actually possible to believe that our individual experience was enough to furnish us with the constituent elements of the notion of force. But we know that the first forces which men imagined were, on the contrary, anonymous, vague and diffused powers which resemble cosmic forces in their impersonality, and which are therefore most sharply contrasted with the eminently personal power, the human will. So it is impossible that they should have been conceived in its image.

Moreover, there is one essential characteristic of the impersonal forces which would be inexplicable under this hypothesis: this is their communicability. The forces of nature have always been thought of as capable of passing from one object to another, of mixing, combining and transforming themselves into one another. It is even this property which gives them their value as an explanation, for it is through this that effects can be connected with their causes without a break of continuity. Now the self has just the opposite characteristic : it is incommunicable. It cannot change its material substratum or spread from one to another ; it spreads out in metaphor only. So the way in which it decides and executes its decisions could never have suggested the idea of an energy which communicates itself and which can even confound itself with others and, through these combinations and mixings, give rise to new effects.

Therefore, the idea of force, as implied in the conception of the causal relation, must present a double character. In the first place, it can come only from our internal experience ; the only forces which we can directly learn about are necessarily moral forces. But, at the same time, they must be impersonal, for the notion of an impersonal power was the first to be constituted. Now the only ones which satisfy these two conditions are those coming from life together : they are collective forces. In fact, these are, on the one hand, entirely psychical ; they are made up exclusively of objectified ideas and sentiments. But, on the other hand, they are impersonal by definition, for they are the product of a co-operation. Being the work of all, they are not the possession of anybody in particular. They are so slightly attached to the personalities of the subjects in whom they reside that they are never fixed there. Just as they enter them from without, they are also always ready to leave them. Of themselves, they tend to spread further and further and to invade ever new domains : we know that there are none more contagious, and consequently more communicable. Of course physical forces have the same property, but we cannot know this directly ; we cannot even become acquainted with them as such, for they are outside us. When I throw myself against an obstacle, I have a sensation of hindrance and trouble ; but the force causing this sensation is not in me, but in the obstacle, and is consequently outside the circle of my perception. We perceive its effects, but we cannot reach the cause itself. It is otherwise with social forces : they are a part of our internal life, as we know, more than the products of their action ; we see them acting. The force isolating the sacred being and holding profane beings at a distance is not really in this being ; it lives in the minds of the believers. So they perceive it at the very moment when it is acting upon their wills, to inhibit certain movements or command others. In a word, this constraining and necessitating action, which escapes us when coming from an external object, is readily perceptible here because everything is inside us. Of course we do not always interpret it in an adequate manner, but at least we cannot fail to be conscious of it.

Moreover, the idea of force bears the mark of its origin in an apparent way. In fact, it implies the idea of power which, in its turn, does not come without those of ascendancy, mastership and domination, and their corollaries, dependence and subordination; now the relations expressed by all these ideas are eminently social. It is society which classifies beings into superiors and inferiors, into commanding masters and obeying servants; it is society which confers upon the former the singular property which makes the command efficacious and which makes *power*. So everything tends to prove that the first powers of which the human mind had any idea were those which societies have established in organizing themselves: it is in their image that the powers of the physical world have been conceived. Also, men have never succeeded in imagining themselves as forces mistress over the bodies in which they reside, except by introducing concepts taken from social life. In fact, these must be distinguished from their physical doubles and must be attributed a dignity superior to that of these latter; in a word, they must think of themselves as souls. As a matter of fact, men have always given the form of souls to the forces which they believe that they are. But we know that the soul is quite another thing from a name given to the abstract faculty of moving, thinking and feeling; before all, it is a religious principle, a particular aspect of the collective force. In fine, a man feels that he has a soul, and consequently a force, because he is a social being. Though an animal moves its members just as we do, and though it has the same power as we over its muscles, nothing authorizes us to suppose that it is conscious of itself as an active and efficacious cause. This is because it does not have, or, to speak more exactly, does not attribute to itself a soul. But if it does not attribute a soul to itself, it is because it does not participate in a social life comparable to that of men. Among animals, there is nothing resembling a civilization.[1]

But the notion of force is not all of the principle of causality. This consists in a judgment stating that every force develops in a definite manner, and that the state in which it is at each particular moment of its existence predetermines the next state. The former is called cause, the latter, effect, and the causal judgment affirms the existence of a necessary connection between these two moments for every force. The mind posits this connection before having any proofs of it, under the empire of a sort of constraint from which it cannot free itself; it postulates it, as they say, *a priori*.

[1] Of course animal societies do exist. However, the word does not have exactly the same sense when applied to men and to animals. The institution is a characteristic fact of human societies; but animals have no institutions.

Empiricism has never succeeded in accounting for this apriorism and necessity. Philosophers of this school have never been able to explain how an association of ideas, reinforced by habit, could produce more than an expectation or a stronger or weaker predisposition on the part of ideas to appear in a determined order. But the principle of causality has quite another character. It is not merely an imminent tendency of our thought to take certain forms; it is an external norm, superior to the flow of our representations, which it dominates and rules imperatively. It is invested with an authority which binds the mind and surpasses it, which is as much as to say that the mind is not its artisan. In this connection, it is useless to substitute hereditary habit for individual habit, for habit does not change its nature by lasting longer than one man's life; it is merely stronger. An instinct is not a rule.

The rites which we have been studying allow us to catch a glimpse of another source of this authority, which, up to the present, has scarcely been suspected. Let us bear in mind how the law of causality, which the imitative rites put into practice, was born. Being filled with one single preoccupation, the group assembles: if the species whose name it bears does not reproduce, it is a matter of concern to the whole clan. The common sentiment thus animating all the members is outwardly expressed by certain gestures, which are always the same in the same circumstances, and after the ceremony has been performed, it happens, for the reasons set forth, that the desired result seems obtained. So an association arises between the idea of this result and that of the gestures preceding it; and this association does not vary from one subject to another; it is the same for all the participators in the rite, since it is the product of a collective experience. However, if no other factor intervened, it would produce only a collective expectation; after the imitative gestures had been accomplished, everybody would await the subsequent appearance of the desired event, with more or less confidence; an imperative rule of thought could never be established by this. But since a social interest of the greatest importance is at stake, society cannot allow things to follow their own course at the whim of circumstances; it intervenes actively in such a way as to regulate their march in conformity with its needs. So it demands that this ceremony, which it cannot do without, be repeated every time that it is necessary, and consequently, that the movements, a condition of its success, be executed regularly: it imposes them as an obligation. Now they imply a certain definite state of mind which, in return, participates in this same obligatory character. To prescribe that one must imitate an animal or plant to make them reproduce, is equivalent to stating it as an axiom which is above all doubt, that like produces like. Opinion cannot allow men to deny this principle in theory without also allowing them to violate it in their conduct. So society imposes it, along with the practices which are derived from it, and thus the ritual precept is doubled by a logical precept which is only the intellectual aspect of the former. The authority of each is derived from the same source: society. The respect which this inspires is communicated to the ways of thought to which it attaches a value, just as much as to ways of action. So a man cannot set aside either the ones or the others without hurling himself against public opinion. This is why the former require the adherence of the intelligence before examination, just as the latter require the submission of the will.

From this example, we can show once more how the sociological theory of the idea of causality, and of the categories in general, sets aside the classical doctrines on the question, while conciliating them. Together with apriorism, it maintains the prejudicial and necessary character of the causal relation; but it does not limit itself to affirming this; it accounts for it, yet without making it vanish under the pretext of explaining it, as empiricism does. On the other hand, there is no question of denying the part due to individual experience. There can be no doubt that by himself, the individual observes the regular succession of phenomena and thus acquires a certain *feeling* of regularity. But this feeling is not the *category* of causality. The former is individual, subjective, incommunicable; we make it ourselves, out of our own personal observations. The second is the work of the group, and is given to us ready-made. It is a frame-work in which our empirical ascertainments arrange themselves and which enables us to think of them, that is to say, to see them from a point of view which makes it possible for us to understand one another in regard to them. Of course, if this frame can be applied to the contents, that shows that it is not out of relation with the matter which it contains; but it is not to be confused with this. It surpasses it and dominates it. This is because it is of a different origin. It is not a mere summary of individual experiences; before all else, it is made to fulfil the exigencies of life in common.

In fine, the error of empiricism has been to regard the causal bond as merely an intellectual construction of speculative thought and the product of a more or less methodical generalization. Now, by itself, pure speculation can give birth only to provisional, hypothetical and more or less plausible views, but ones which must always be regarded with suspicion, for we can never be sure that some new observation in the future will not invalidate them. An axiom which the mind accepts and must accept, without control and without reservation, could never come from this source. Only the necessities of action, and especially of collective action, can and must express themselves in categorical formulæ, which are peremptory and short, and admit of no contradiction, for collective movements are possible only on condition of being in concert and, therefore, regulated and definite. They do not allow of any fumbling, the source of anarchy; by themselves, they tend towards an organization which, when once established, imposes itself upon individuals. And as action cannot go beyond intelligence, it frequently happens that the latter is drawn into the same way and accepts without discussion the theoretical postulates demanded by action. The imperatives of thought are probably only another side of the imperatives of action.

It is to be borne in mind, moreover, that we have never dreamed of offering the preceding observations as a complete theory of the concept of causality. The question is too complex to be resolved thus. The principle of causality has been understood differently in different times and places; in a single society, it varies with the social environment and the kingdoms of nature to which it is applied.[1] So it would be impossible to determine with sufficient precision the causes and conditions upon which it depends, after a consideration of only one of the forms which it has presented during the course of history. The views which we have set forth should be regarded as mere indications, which must be controlled and completed. However, as the causal law which we have been considering is certainly one of the most primitive which exists, and as it has played a considerable part in the development of human thought and industry, it is a privileged experiment, so we may presume that the remarks of which it has been the occasion may be generalized to a certain degree.

[1] The conception of cause is not the same for a scholar and for a man with no scientific culture. Also, many of our contemporaries understand the principle of causality differently, as they apply it to social facts and to physico-chemical facts. In the social order, men frequently exhibit a conception of causality singularly like that which was at the basis of magic for a long time. One might even ask if a physicist and a biologist represent the causal relation in the same fashion.

CHAPTER IV

THE POSITIVE CULT—*continued*

III.—*Representative or Commemorative Rites*

THE explanation which we have given of the positive rites of which we have been speaking in the two preceding chapters attributes to them a significance which is, above all, moral and social. The physical efficaciousness assigned to them by the believer is the product of an interpretation which conceals the essential reason for their existence: it is because they serve to remake individuals and groups morally that they are believed to have a power over things. But even if this hypothesis has enabled us to account for the facts, we cannot say that it has been demonstrated directly; at first view, it even seems to conciliate itself rather badly with the nature of the ritual mechanisms which we have analysed. Whether they consist in oblations or imitative acts, the gestures composing them have purely material ends in view; they have, or seem to have, the sole object of making the totemic species reproduce. Under these circumstances, is it not surprising that their real function should be to serve moral ends?

It is true that their physical function may have been exaggerated by Spencer and Gillen, even in the cases where it is the most incontestable. According to these authors, each clan celebrates its Intichiuma for the purpose of assuring a useful food to the other clans, and the whole cult consists in a sort of economic co-operation of the different totemic groups; each works for the others. But according to Strehlow, this conception of Australian totemism is wholly foreign to the native mind. "If," he says, "the members of one totemic group set themselves to multiplying the animals or plants of the consecrated species, and seem to work for their companions of other totems, we must be careful not to regard this collaboration as the fundamental principle of Arunta or Loritja totemism. The blacks themselves have never told me that this was the object of their ceremonies. Of course, when I suggested and explained the idea to them, they understood it and acquiesced. But I should not be blamed for having some distrust of replies gained in this fashion." Strehlow also remarks that this way of interpreting the rite is contradicted by the fact that the totemic animals and plants are not all edible or useful; some are good for nothing; some are even dangerous. So the ceremonies which concern them could not have any such end in view.[1] "When some one asks the natives what the determining reason for these ceremonies is," concludes our author, "they are unanimous in replying: 'It is because our ancestors arranged things thus. This is why we do thus and not differently.'"[2] But in saying that the rite is observed because it comes from the ancestors, it is admitted that its authority is confounded with the authority of tradition, which is a social affair of the first order. Men celebrate it to remain faithful to the past, to keep for the group its normal physiognomy, and not because of the physical effects which it may produce. Thus, the way in which the believers themselves explain them show the profound reasons upon which the rites proceed.

But there are cases when this aspect of the ceremonies is immediately apparent.

I

These may be observed the best among the Warramunga.[3]

Among this people, each clan is thought to be descended from a single ancestor who, after having been born in some determined spot, passed his terrestrial existence in travelling over the country in every direction. It is he who, in the course of his voyages, gave to the land the form which it now has; it is he who made the mountains and plains, the water-holes and streams, etc. At the same time, he sowed upon his route living germs which were disengaged from his body and, after many successive reincarnations, became the actual members of the clan. Now the ceremony of the Warramunga which corresponds exactly to the Intichiuma of the Arunta, has the object of commemorating and representing the mythical history

[1] Of course these ceremonies are not followed by an alimentary communion. According to Strehlow, they have another name, at least when they concern non-edible plants: they are called, not mbatjalkatiuma, but *knujilelama* (Strehlow, III, p. 96).

[2] Strehlow, III, p. 8.

[3] The Warramunga are not the only ones among whom the Intichiuma takes the form of a dramatic representation. It is also found among the Tjingilli, the Umbaia, the Wulmala, the Walpari and even the Kaitish, though in certain of its features the ritual of these latter resembles that of the Arunta (*Nor. Tr.*, p. 291, 309, 311, 317). If we take the Warramunga as a type, it is because they have been studied the best by Spencer and Gillen.

of this ancestor. There is no question of oblations or, except in one single case,[1] of imitative practices. The rite consists solely in recollecting the past and, in a way, making it present by means of a veritable dramatic representation. This word is the more exact because in this ceremony, the officiant is in no way considered an incarnation of the ancestor, whom he represents ; he is an actor playing a rôle.

As an example, let us describe the Intichiuma of the Black Snake, as Spencer and Gillen observed it.[2]

An initial ceremony does not seem to refer to the past ; at least the description of it which is given us gives no authorization for interpreting it in this sense. It consists in running and leaping on the part of two officiants,[3] who are decorated with designs representing the black snake. When they finally fall exhausted on the ground, the assistants gently pass their hands over the emblematic designs with which the backs of the two actors are covered. They say that this act pleases the black snake. It is only afterwards that the series of commemorative ceremonies commences.

They put into action the mythical history of the ancestor Thalaualla, from the moment he emerged from the ground up to his definite return thither. They follow him through all his voyages. The myth says that in each of the localities where he sojourned, he celebrated totemic ceremonies ; they now repeat them in the same order in which they are supposed to have taken place originally. The movement which is acted the most frequently consists in twisting the entire body about rhythmically and violently ; this is because the ancestor did the same thing to make the germs of life which were in him come out. The actors have their bodies covered with down, which is detached and flies away during these movements ; this is a way of representing the flight of these mystic germs and their dispersion into space.

It will be remembered that among the Arunta, the scene of the ceremony is determined by the ritual : it is the spot where the sacred rocks, trees and water-holes are found, and the worshippers must go there to celebrate the cult. Among the Warramunga, on the contrary, the ceremonial ground is arbitrarily chosen according to convenience. It is a conventional scene. However, the original scene of the events whose reproduction constitutes the theme of the rite is itself represented by

[1] This is the case with the Intichiuma of the black cockatoo (see above, p. 353).

[2] *Nor. Tr.*, pp. 300 ff.

[3] One of these two actors does not belong to the Black Snake clan, but to that of the Crow. This is because the Crow is supposed to be an " associate " of the Black Snake : in other words, it is a sub-totem.

means of designs. Sometimes these designs are made upon the very bodies of the actors. For example, a small circle coloured red, painted on the back and stomach, represents a water-hole.[1] In other cases, the image is traced on the soil. Upon a ground previously soaked and covered with red ochre, they draw curved lines, made up of a series of white points, which symbolize a stream or a mountain. This is a beginning of decoration.

In addition to the properly religious ceremonies which the ancestor is believed to have celebrated long ago, they also represent simple episodes of his career, either epic or comic. Thus, at a given moment, while three actors are on the scene, occupied in an important rite, another one hides behind a bunch of trees situated at some distance. A packet of down is attached about his neck which represents a *wallaby*. As soon as the principal ceremony is finished, an old man traces a line upon the ground which is directed towards the spot where the fourth actor is hidden. The others march behind him, with eyes lowered and fixed upon this line, as though following a trail. When they discover the man, they assume a stupefied air and one of them beats him with a club. This represents an incident in the life of the great black snake. One day, his son went hunting, caught a *wallaby* and ate it without giving his father any. The latter followed his tracks, surprised him and forced him to disgorge; it is to this that the beating at the end of the representation alludes.[2]

We shall not relate here all the mythical events which are represented successively. The preceding examples are sufficient to show the character of these ceremonies: they are dramas, but of a particular variety; they act, or at least they are believed to act, upon the course of nature. When the commemoration of Thalaualla is terminated, the Warramunga are convinced that black snakes cannot fail to increase and multiply. So these dramas are rites, and even rites which, by the nature of their efficacy, are comparable on every point to those which constitute the Intichiuma of the Arunta.

Therefore each is able to clarify the other. It is even more legitimate to compare them than if there were no break of continuity between them. Not only is the end pursued identical in each case, but the most characteristic part of the Warramunga ritual is found in germ in the other. In fact, the Intichiuma, as the Arunta generally perform it, contains within it a sort of implicit commemoration. The places where it is celebrated are necessarily those which the ancestor made illustrious. The roads over which the worshippers pass in the course of their pious

[1] *Nor. Tr.*, p. 302. [2] *Ibid.*, p. 305.

pilgrimages are those which the heroes of the Alcheringa traversed; the places where they stop to proceed with the rites are those where their fathers sojourned themselves, where they vanished into the ground, etc. So everything brings their memory to the minds of the assistants. Moreover, to the manual rites they frequently add hymns relating the exploits of their ancestors.[1] If, instead of being told, these stories are acted, and if, in this new form, they develop in such a way as to become an essential part of the ceremony, then we have the ceremony of the Warramunga. But even more can be said, for on one side, the Arunta Intichiuma is already a sort of representation. The officiant is one with the ancestor from whom he is descended and whom he reincarnates.[2] The gestures he makes are those which this ancestor made in the same circumstances. Speaking exactly, of course he does not play the part of the ancestral personage as an actor might do it; he is this personage himself. But it is true, notwithstanding, that, in one sense, it is the hero who occupies the scene. In order to accentuate the representative character of the rite, it would be sufficient for the duality of the ancestor and the officiant to become more marked; this is just what happens among the Warramunga.[3] Even among the Arunta, at least one Intichiuma is mentioned in which certain persons are charged with representing ancestors with whom they have no relationship of mythical descent, and in which there is consequently a proper dramatic representation: this is the Intichiuma of the Emu.[4] It seems that in this case, also, contrarily to the general rule among this people, the theatre of the ceremony is artificially arranged.[5]

[1] See Spencer and Gillen, *Nat. Tr.*, p. 188; Strehlow, III, p. 5.

[2] Strehlow himself recognizes this: " The totemic ancestor and his descendant, who represents him (*der Darsteller*) are presented as one in these sacred hymns." (III, p. 6). As this incontestable fact contradicts the theory according to which ancestral souls do not reincarnate themselves, Strehlow adds, it is true, in a note, that " in the course of the ceremony there is no real incarnation of the ancestor in the person who represents him." If Strehlow wishes to say that the incarnation does not take place on the occasion of the ceremony, then nothing is more certain. But if he means that there is no incarnation at all, we do not understand how the officiant and the ancestor can be confounded.

[3] Perhaps this difference is partially due to the fact that among the Warramunga each clan is thought to be descended from one single ancestor about whom the legendary history of the clan centres. This is the ancestor whom the rite commemorates; now the officiant need not be descended from him. One might even ask if these mythical chiefs, who are sorts of demigods, are submitted to reincarnation.

[4] In this Intichiuma, three assistants represent ancestors " of a considerable antiquity "; they play a real part (*Nat. Tr.*, pp. 181–182). It is true that Spencer and Gillen add that these are ancestors posterior to the Alcheringa. Nevertheless, mythical personages are represented in the course of the rite.

[5] Sacred rocks and water-holes are not mentioned. The centre of the ceremony is the image of an emu drawn on the ground, which can be made anywhere.

It does not follow from the fact that, in spite of the differences separating them, these two varieties of ceremony thus have an air of kinship, as it were, that there is a definite relation of succession between them, and that one is a transformation of the other. It may very well be that the resemblances pointed out come from the fact that the two sprang from the same source, that is, from the same original ceremony, of which they are only divergent forms: we shall even see that this hypothesis is the most probable one. But even without taking sides on this question, what has already been said is enough to show that they are rites of the same nature. So we may be allowed to compare them, and to use the one to enable us to understand the other better.

Now the peculiar thing in the ceremonies of the Warramunga of which we have been speaking, is that not a gesture is made whose object is to aid or to provoke directly the increase of the totemic species.[1] If we analyse the movements made, as well as the words spoken, we generally find nothing which betrays any intention of this sort. Everything is in representations whose only object can be to render the mythical past of the clan present to the mind. But the mythology of a group is the system of beliefs common to this group. The traditions whose memory it perpetuates express the way in which society represents man and the world; it is a moral system and a cosmology as well as a history. So the rite serves and can serve only to sustain the vitality of these beliefs, to keep them from being effaced from memory and, in sum, to revivify the most essential elements of the collective consciousness. Through it, the group periodically renews the sentiment which it has of itself and of its unity; at the same time, individuals are strengthened in their social natures. The glorious souvenirs which are made to live again before their eyes, and with which they feel that they have a kinship, give them a feeling of strength and confidence: a man is surer of his faith when he sees to how distant a past it goes back and what great things it has inspired. This is the characteristic of the ceremony which makes it instructive. Its tendency is to act entirely upon the mind and upon it alone. So if men believe nevertheless that it acts upon things and that it assures the prosperity of the species, this can be only as a reaction to the moral action which it exercises and which is obviously the only one which is real. Thus the hypothesis which we have proposed is verified by a significant experiment, and this

[1] We do not mean to say that all the ceremonies of the Warramunga are of this type. The example of the white cockatoo, of which we spoke above, proves that there are exceptions.

verification is the more convincing because, as we have shown, there is no difference in nature between the ritual system of the Warramunga and that of the Arunta. The one only makes more evident what we had already conjectured from the other.

II

But there are ceremonies in which this representative and idealistic character is still more accentuated.

In those of which we have been speaking, the dramatic representation did not exist for itself; it was only a means having a very material end in view, namely, the reproduction of the totemic species. But there are others which do not differ materially from the preceding ones, but from which, nevertheless, all preoccupations of this sort are absent. The past is here represented for the mere sake of representing it and fixing it more firmly in the mind, while no determined action over nature is expected of the rite. At least, the physical effects sometimes imputed to it are wholly secondary and have no relation with the liturgical importance attributed to it.

This is the case notably with the ceremonies which the Warramunga celebrate in honour of the snake Wollunqua.[1]

As we have already said, the Wollunqua is a totem of a very especial sort. It is not an animal or vegetable species, but a unique being: there is only one Wollunqua. Moreover, this being is purely mythical. The natives represent it as a colossal snake whose length is such that when it rises on its tail its head is lost in the clouds. It resides, they believe, in a water-hole called Thapauerlu, which is hidden in the bottom of a solitary valley. But if it differs in certain ways from the ordinary totems, it has all their distinctive characteristics nevertheless. It serves as the collective name and emblem of a whole group of individuals who regard it as their common ancestor, while the relations which they sustain with this mythical beast are identical with those which the members of other totems believe that they sustain with the founders of their respective clans. In the Alcheringa[2] times, the Wollunqua traversed the country in every direction. In the different localities where it stopped, it scattered "spirit-children," the spiritual principles which

[1] *Nor. Tr.*, pp. 226 ff. On this same subject, cf. certain passages of Eylmann which evidently refer to the same mythical being (*Die Eingeborenen*, etc., p. 185). Strehlow also mentions a mythical snake among the Arunta (*Kulaia*, water-snake) which may not differ greatly from the Wollunqua (Strehlow, I, p. 78; cf. II, p. 71, where the Kulaia is found in a list of totems).

[2] We use the Arunta words, in order not to complicate our terminology; the Warramunga call this mythical period Wingara.

still serve as the souls of the living of to-day. The Wollunqua is even considered as a sort of pre-eminent totem. The Warramunga are divided into two phratries, called Uluuru and Kingilli. Nearly all the totems of the former are snakes of different kinds. Now they are all believed to be descended from the Wollunqua; they say that it was their grandfather.[1] From this, we can catch a glimpse of how the myth of the Wollunqua probably arose. In order to explain the presence of so many similar totems in the same phratry, they imagined that all were derived from one and the same totem; it was necessary to give it a gigantic form so that in its very appearance it might conform to the considerable rôle assigned to it in the history of the tribe.

Now the Wollunqua is the object of ceremonies not differing in nature from those which we have already studied: they are representations in which are portrayed the principal events of its fabulous life. They show it coming out of the ground and passing from one locality to another; they represent different episodes in its voyages, etc. Spencer and Gillen assisted at fifteen ceremonies of this sort which took place between the 27th of July and the 23rd of August, all being linked together in a determined order, in such a way as to form a veritable cycle.[2] In the details of the rites constituting it, this long celebration is therefore indistinct from the ordinary Intichiuma of the Warramunga, as is recognized by the authors who have described it to us.[3] But, on the other hand, it is an Intichiuma which could not have the object of assuring the fecundity of an animal or vegetable species, for the Wollunqua is a species all by itself and does not reproduce. It exists, and the natives do not seem to feel that it has need of a cult to preserve it in its existence. These ceremonies not only seem to lack the efficacy of the classic Intichiuma, but it even seems as though they have no material efficacy of any sort. The Wollunqua is not a divinity set over a special order of natural phenomena, so they expect no definite service from him in exchange for the cult. Of course they say that if the ritual prescriptions are badly observed, the Wollunqua becomes angry, leaves his retreat and comes to punish his worshippers for their negligence; and inversely, when everything passes regularly, they are led to

[1] "It is not easy to express in words what is in reality rather a vague feeling amongst the natives, but after carefully watching the different series of ceremonies, we were impressed with the feeling that the Wollunqua represented to the native mind the idea of a dominant totem" (*Nor. Tr.*, p. 248).

[2] One of the most solemn of these ceremonies is the one which we have had occasion to describe above (p. 217), in the course of which, an image of the Wollunqua is designed on a sort of hillock which is then torn to pieces in the midst of a general effervescence.

[3] *Nor. Tr.*, pp. 227, 248.

believe that they will be fortunate and that some happy event will take place; but it is quite evident that these possible sanctions are an after-thought to explain the rite. After the ceremony had been established, it seemed natural that it should serve for something, and that the omission of the prescribed observances should therefore expose one to grave dangers. But it was not established to forestall these mythical dangers or to assure particular advantages. The natives, moreover, have only the very haziest ideas of them. When the whole ceremony is completed, the old men announce that if the Wollunqua is pleased, he will send rain. But it is not to have rain that they go through with the celebration.[1] They celebrate it because their ancestors did, because they are attached to it as to a highly respected tradition and because they leave it with a feeling of moral well-being. Other considerations have only a complimentary part; they may serve to strengthen the worshippers in the attitude prescribed by the rite, but they are not the reason for the existence of this attitude.

So we have here a whole group of ceremonies whose sole purpose is to awaken certain ideas and sentiments, to attach the present to the past or the individual to the group. Not only are they unable to serve useful ends, but the worshippers themselves demand none. This is still another proof that the psychical

[1] Here are the terms of Spencer and Gillen in the only passage in which they speak of a possible connection between the Wollunqua and rain. A few days after the rite about the hillock, " the old men say that they have heard Wollunqua speak, that he was satisfied with what had passed and that he was going to send rain. The reason for this prophecy was that they, as well as ourselves, had heard thunder rolling at a distance." To such a slight extent is the production of rain the immediate object of the ceremony that they did not attribute it to Wollunqua until several days later, and then after accidental circumstances. Another fact shows how vague the ideas of the natives are on this point. A few lines below, thunder is spoken of as a sign, not of the Wollunqua's satisfaction, but of its discontent. In spite of these prognostics, continue our authors, " the rain did not fall. But some days later, they heard the thunder rolling in the distance again. The old men said that the Wollunqua was grumbling because he was not contented" with the way in which the rite had been celebrated. Thus a single phenomenon, the noise of thunder, is sometimes interpreted as a sign of a favouring disposition, and sometimes as a mark of evil intentions.

However, there is one detail of the ritual which, if we accept the explanation of it proposed by Spencer and Gillen, is directly efficient. According to them, the destruction of the hillock was intended to frighten the Wollunqua and to prevent it, by magic constraint, from leaving its retreat. But this interpretation seems very doubtful to us. In fact, in the very case of which we were speaking, where it was announced that the Wollunqua was dissatisfied, this dissatisfaction was attributed to the fact that they had neglected to take away the debris of the hillock. So this removal is demanded by the Wollunqua itself, and in no way intended to intimidate it and exercise a coercive influence over it. This is probably merely one case of a more general rule which is in force among the Warramunga: the instruments of the cult must be destroyed after each ceremony. Thus the ritual ornamentations with which the officiants are decorated are violently torn off from them when the rite is terminated (*Nor. Tr.*, p. 205).

state in which the assembled group happens to be constitutes the only solid and stable basis of what we may call the ritual mentality. The beliefs which attribute such or such a physical efficaciousness to the rites are wholly accessory and contingent, for they may be lacking without causing any alteration in the essentials of the rite. Thus the ceremonies of the Wollunqua show even better than the preceding ones the fundamental function of the positive cult.

If we have insisted especially upon these solemnities, it is because of their exceptional importance. But there are others with exactly the same character. Thus, the Warramunga have a totem "of the laughing boy." Spencer and Gillen say that the clan bearing this name has the same organization as the other totemic groups. Like them, it has its sacred places (*mungai*) where the founder-ancestor celebrated ceremonies in the fabulous times, and where he left behind him spirit-children who became the men of the clan; the rites connected with this totem are indistinguishable from those relating to the animal or vegetable totems.[1] Yet it is evident that they could not have any physical efficaciousness. They consist in a series of four ceremonies which repeat one another more or less, but which are intended only to amuse and to provoke laughter by laughter, in fine, to maintain the gaiety and good-humour which the group has as its speciality.[2]

We find more than one totem among the Arunta themselves which has no other Intichiuma. We have seen that among this people, the irregularities and depressions of the land, which mark the places where some ancestor sojourned, sometimes serve as totems.[3] Ceremonies are attached to these totems which are manifestly incapable of physical effects of any sort. They can consist only in representations whose object is to commemorate the past, and they can aim at no end beyond this commemoration.[4]

While they enable us to understand the nature of the cult better, these ritual representations also put into evidence an important element of religion: this is the recreative and esthetic element.

We have already had occasion to show that they are closely akin to dramatic representations.[5] This kinship appears with still greater clarity in the latter ceremonies of which we have

[1] *Nor. Tr.*, pp. 207–208. [2] *Ibid.*, p. 210.

[3] See, in the list of totems drawn up by Strehlow, Nos. 432–442 (II, p. 72).

[4] See Strehlow, III, p, 8. Among the Arunta there is also a totem *Worra* which greatly resembles the "laughing boy" totem of Warramunga (*ibid.*, and III, p. 124). *Worra* means young men. The object of the ceremony is to make the young men take more pleasure in the game *labara* (for this game, see Strehlow, I, p. 55, n. 1).

[5] See above, p. 373.

spoken. Not only do they employ the same processes as the real drama, but they also pursue an end of the same sort: being foreign to all utilitarian ends, they make men forget the real world and transport them into another where their imagination is more at ease; they distract. They sometimes even go so far as to have the outward appearance of a recreation: the assistants may be seen laughing and amusing themselves openly.[1]

Representative rites and collective recreations are even so close to one another that men pass from one sort to the other without any break of continuity. The characteristic feature of the properly religious ceremonies is that they must be celebrated on a consecrated ground, from which women and non-initiated persons are excluded.[2] But there are others in which this religious character is somewhat effaced, though it has not disappeared completely. They take place outside the ceremonial ground, which proves that they are already laicized to a certain degree; but profane persons, women and children, are not yet admitted to them. So they are on the boundary between the two domains. They generally deal with legendary personages, but ones having no regular place in the frame-work of the totemic religion. They are spirits, more generally malevolent ones, having relations with the magicians rather than the ordinary believers, and sorts of bugbears, in whom men do not believe with the same degree of seriousness and firmness of conviction as in the proper totemic beings and things.[3] As the bonds by which the events and personages represented are attached to the history of the tribe relax, these take on a proportionately more unreal appearance, while the corresponding ceremonies change in nature. Thus men enter into the domain of pure fancy, and pass from the commemorative rite to the ordinary corrobbori, a simple public merry-making, which has nothing religious about it and in which all may take part indifferently. Perhaps some of these representations, whose sole object now is to distract, are ancient rites, whose character has been changed. In fact, the distinction between these two sorts of ceremonies is so variable that it is impossible to state with precision to which of the two kinds they belong.[4]

[1] A case of this sort will be found in *Nor. Tr.*, p. 204.

[2] *Nat. Tr.*, p. 118 and n. 2, pp. 618 ff.; *Nor. Tr.*, pp. 716 ff. There are some sacred ceremonies from which women are not wholly excluded (see, for example, *Nor. Tr.*, pp. 375 ff.); but this is exceptional.

[3] See *Nat. Tr.*, pp. 329 ff.; *Nor. Tr.*, pp. 210 ff.

[4] This is the case, for example, with the corrobbori of the Molonga among the Pitta-Pitta of Queensland and the neighbouring tribes (see Roth, *Ethnog. Studies among the N.W. Central Queensland Aborigines*, pp. 120 ff.).—References for the ordinary corrobbori will be found in Stirling, *Rep. of the Horn Expedition to Central Australia*, Part IV, p. 72, and in Roth, *op. cit.*, pp. 117 ff.

It is a well-known fact that games and the principal forms of art seem to have been born of religion and that for a long time they retained a religious character.[1] We now see what the reasons for this are : it is because the cult, though aimed primarily at other ends, has also been a sort of recreation for men. Religion has not played this rôle by hazard or owing to a happy chance, but through a necessity of its nature. Though, as we have established, religious thought is something very different from a system of fictions, still the realities to which it corresponds express themselves religiously only when religion transfigures them. Between society as it is objectively and the sacred things which express it symbolically, the distance is considerable. It has been necessary that the impressions really felt by men, which served as the original matter of this construction, should be interpreted, elaborated and transformed until they became unrecognizable. So the world of religious things is a partially imaginary world, though only in its outward form, and one which therefore lends itself more readily to the free creations of the mind. Also, since the intellectual forces which serve to make it are intense and tumultuous, the unique task of expressing the real with the aid of appropriate symbols is not enough to occupy them. A surplus generally remains available which seeks to employ itself in supplementary and superfluous works of luxury, that is to say, in works of art. There are practices as well as beliefs of this sort. The state of effervescence in which the assembled worshippers find themselves must be translated outwardly by exuberant movements which are not easily subjected to too carefully defined ends. In part, they escape aimlessly, they spread themselves for the mere pleasure of so doing, and they take delight in all sorts of games. Besides, in so far as the beings to whom the cult is addressed are imaginary, they are not able to contain and regulate this exuberance ; the pressure of tangible and resisting realities is required to confine activities to exact and economical forms. Therefore one exposes oneself to grave misunderstandings if, in explaining rites, he believes that each gesture has a precise object and a definite reason for its existence. There are some which serve nothing ; they merely answer the need felt by worshippers for action, motion, gesticulation. They are to be seen jumping, whirling, dancing, crying and singing, though it may not always be possible to give a meaning to all this agitation.

Therefore religion would not be itself if it did not give some place to the free combinations of thought and activity, to play,

[1] On this question see the excellent work of Culin, *Games of the North American Indians* (*XXIVth Rep. of the Bureau of Am. Ethnol.*).

to art, to all that recreates the spirit that has been fatigued by the too great slavishness of daily work: the very same causes which called it into existence make it a necessity. Art is not merely an external ornament with which the cult has adorned itself in order to dissimulate certain of its features which may be too austere and too rude; but rather, in itself, the cult is something æsthetic. Owing to the well-known connection which mythology has with poetry, some have wished to exclude the former from religion;[1] the truth is that there is a poetry inherent in all religion. The representative rites which have just been studied make this aspect of the religious life manifest; but there are scarcely any rites which do not present it to some degree.

One would certainly commit the gravest error if he saw only this one aspect of religion, or if he even exaggerated its importance. When a rite serves only to distract, it is no longer a rite. The moral forces expressed by religious symbols are real forces with which we must reckon and with which we cannot do what we will. Even when the cult aims at producing no physical effects, but limits itself to acting on the mind, its action is in quite a different way from that of a pure work of art. The representations which it seeks to awaken and maintain in our minds are not vain images which correspond to nothing in reality, and which we call up aimlessly for the mere satisfaction of seeing them appear and combine before our eyes. They are as necessary for the well working of our moral life as our food is for the maintenance of our physical life, for it is through them that the group affirms and maintains itself, and we know the point to which this is indispensable for the individual. So a rite is something different from a game; it is a part of the serious life. But if its unreal and imaginary element is not essential, nevertheless it plays a part which is by no means negligible. It has its share in the feeling of comfort which the worshipper draws from the rite performed; for recreation is one of the forms of the moral remaking which is the principal object of the positive rite. After we have acquitted ourselves of our ritual duties, we enter into the profane life with increased courage and ardour, not only because we come into relations with a superior source of energy, but also because our forces have been reinvigorated by living, for a few moments, in a life that is less strained, and freer and easier. Hence religion acquires a charm which is not among the slightest of its attractions.

This is why the very idea of a religious ceremony of some importance awakens the idea of a feast. Inversely, every feast,

[1] See above, p. 81.

even when it has purely lay origins, has certain characteristics of the religious ceremony, for in every case its effect is to bring men together, to put the masses into movement and thus to excite a state of effervescence, and sometimes even of delirium, which is not without a certain kinship with the religious state. A man is carried outside himself and diverted from his ordinary occupation and preoccupations. Thus the same manifestations are to be observed in each case: cries, songs, music, violent movements, dances, the search for exciteants which raise the vital level, etc. It has frequently been remarked that popular feasts lead to excesses, and cause men to lose sight of the distinction separating the licit from the illicit;[1] there are also religious ceremonies which make it almost necessary to violate the rules which are ordinarily the most respected.[2] Of course this does not mean that there is no way to distinguish these two forms of public activity. The simple merry-making, the profane corrobbori, has no serious object, while, as a whole, a ritual ceremony always has an important end. Still it is to be remembered that there is perhaps no merry-making in which the serious life does not have some echo. The difference consists rather in the unequal proportions in which the two elements are combined.

III

A more general fact confirms the views which precede.

In their first book, Spencer and Gillen presented the Intichiuma as a perfectly definite ritual entity: they spoke of it as though it were an operation destined exclusively for the assurance of the reproduction of the totemic species, and it seemed as though it ought to lose all meaning, if this unique function were set aside. But in their *Northern Tribes of Central Australia*, the same authors use a different language, though perhaps without noticing it. They recognize that these same ceremonies may take place either in the regular Intichiuma or in the initiation

[1] Especially in sexual matters. In the ordinary corrobbori, sexual licence is frequent (see Spencer and Gillen, *Nat. Tr.*, pp. 96–97, and *Nor. Tr.*, pp. 136–137). On sexual licence in popular feasts in general, see Hagelstrange, *Süddeutsches Bauernleben im Mittelalter*, pp. 221 ff.

[2] Thus the exogamic rules must be violated in the course of certain religious ceremonies (see above, p. 216, n. 1). A precise ritual meaning probably could not be found for these excesses. It is merely a mechanical consequence of the state of super-excitation provoked by the ceremony. It is an example of rites having no definite object themselves, but which are mere discharges of energy (see above, p. 381). The native does not assign them a definite end either; he merely says that if these licences are not committed, the rite will not produce its effects; the ceremony will fail.

rites.[1] So they serve equally in the making of animals or plants of the totemic species, or in conferring upon novices the qualities necessary to make them regular members of the men's society.[2] From this point of view, the Intichiuma takes on a new aspect. It is no longer a distinct ritual mechanism, resting upon principles of its own, but a particular application of more general ceremonies which may be utilized for very different ends. For this reason, in their later work, before speaking of the Intichiuma and the initiation they consecrate a special chapter to the totemic ceremonies in general, making abstraction of the diverse forms which they may take, according to the ends for which they are employed.[3]

This fundamental indetermination of the totemic ceremonies was only indicated by Spencer and Gillen, and rather indirectly at that; but it has now been confirmed by Strehlow in more explicit terms. "When they lead the young novices through the different feasts of the initiation," he says, "they perform before them a series of ceremonies which, though reproducing, even in their most characteristic details, the rites of the regular cult (viz. *the rites which Spencer and Gillen call the Intichiuma*), do not have, nevertheless, the end of multiplying the corresponding totem and causing it to prosper." [4] It is the same ceremony which serves in the two cases; the name alone is not the same. When its special object is the reproduction of the species, they call it *mbatjalkatiuma* and it is only when it is a part of the process of initiation that they give it the name Intichiuma.[5]

Moreover, these two sorts of ceremonies are distinguished from one another among the Arunta by certain secondary characteristics. Though the structure of the rite is the same in both cases, still we know that the effusions of blood and, more generally, the oblations characteristic of the Arunta Intichiuma are not found in the initiation ceremonies. Moreover, among this same people, the Intichiuma takes place at a spot regularly fixed by tradition, to which men must make a pilgrimage, while

[1] Here are the very words used by Spencer and Gillen: "They (the ceremonies connected with the totems) are often, though by no means always, associated with the performance of the ceremonies attendant upon initiation of young men, or are connected with the Intichiuma" (*Nor. Tr.*, p. 178).

[2] We leave aside the question of what this character consists in. It is a problem which would lead us into a very long and technical development and which must therefore be treated by itself. Moreover, it does not concern the propositions established in this present work.

[3] This is chapter vi, entitled *Ceremonies Connected with the Totems.*

[4] Strehlow, III, pp. 1–2.

[5] This explains the error of which Strehlow accuses Spencer and Gillen: that they applied to one form of the ceremony the term which is more appropriate for the other. But in these conditions, the error hardly seems to have the gravity attributed to it by Strehlow.

the scene of the initiation ceremonies is purely conventional.[1] But when the Intichiuma consists in a simple dramatic representation, as is the case among the Warramunga, the lack of distinction between the two rites is complete. In the one as in the other, they commemorate the past, they put the myth into action, they play—and one cannot play in two materially different ways. So, according to the circumstances, one and the same ceremony serves two distinct functions.[2]

It may even lend itself to other uses. We know that as blood is a sacred thing, women must not see it flow. Yet it happens sometimes that a quarrel breaks out in their presence and ends in the shedding of blood. Thus an infraction of the ritual is committed. Among the Arunta, the man whose blood flowed first must, to atone for this fault, " celebrate a ceremony connected with the totem either of his father or of his mother " ;[3] this ceremony has a special name, *Alua uparilima,* which means the washing away of blood. But in itself, it does not differ from those celebrated at the time of the initiation or in the Intichiuma : it represents an event of ancestral history. So it may serve equally to initiate, to act upon the totemic species or to expiate a sacrilege. We shall see that a totemic ceremony may also take the place of a funeral rite.[4]

MM. Hubert and Mauss have already pointed out a functional ambiguity of this same sort in the case of sacrifice, and more especially, in that of Hindu sacrifice.[5] They have shown how the sacrifice of communion, that of expiation, that of a vow and that of a contract are only variations of one and the same mechanism. We now see that the fact is much more primitive,

[1] It cannot be otherwise. In fact, as the initiation is a tribal feast, novices of different totems are initiated at the same time. So the ceremonies which thus succeed one another in the same place have to do with several totems, and, therefore, they must take place away from the places with which they are connected by the myth.

[2] It will now be understood why we have never studied the initiation rites by themselves : it is because they are not a ritual entity, but are formed by the conglomeration of rites of different sorts. There are interdictions, ascetic rites and representative ceremonies which cannot be distinguished from those celebrated at the time of the Intichiuma. So we had to dismember this composite system and treat each of the different rites composing it separately, classifying them with the similar rites to which they are to be related. We have also seen (pp. 285 ff.) that the initiation has served as the point of departure for a new religion which tends to surpass totemism. But it has been sufficient for us to show that totemism contained the germs of this religion ; we have had no need of following out its development. The object of this book is to study the elementary beliefs and practices ; so we must stop at the moment when they give birth to more complex forms.

[3] *Nat. Tr.*, p. 463. If the individual may choose between the ceremonies of his paternal and maternal totems, it is because, owing to reasons which we have set forth above (p. 183), he participates in both.

[4] See below, ch. v, p. 395.

[5] See *Essai sur le Sacrifice*, in *Mélanges d'histoire des Religions*, p. 83.

and in no way limited to the institution of sacrifice. Perhaps no rite exists which does not present a similar indetermination. The mass serves for marriages as for burials; it redeems the faults of the dead and wins the favours of the deity for the living, etc. Fasting is an expiation and a penance; but it is also a preparation for communion; it even confers positive virtues. This ambiguity shows that the real function of a rite does not consist in the particular and definite effects which it seems to aim at and by which it is ordinarily characterized, but rather in a general action which, though always and everywhere the same, is nevertheless capable of taking on different forms according to the circumstances. Now this is just what is demanded by the theory which we have proposed. If the real function of the cult is to awaken within the worshippers a certain state of soul, composed of moral force and confidence, and if the various effects imputed to the rites are due only to a secondary and variable determination of this fundamental state, it is not surprising if a single rite, while keeping the same composition and structure, seems to produce various effects. For the mental dispositions, the excitation of which is its permanent function, remain the same in every case; they depend upon the fact that the group is assembled, and not upon the special reasons for which it is assembled. But, on the other hand, they are interpreted differently according to the circumstances to which they are applied. Is it a physical result which they wish to obtain? The confidence they feel convinces them that the desired result is or will be obtained by the means employed. Has some one committed a fault for which he wishes to atone? The same state of moral assurance will lead him to attribute expiatory virtues to these same ritual gestures. Thus, the apparent efficacy will seem to change while the real efficacy remains invariable, and the rite will seem to fulfil various functions though in fact it has only one, which is always the same.

Inversely, just as a single rite may serve many ends, so many rites may produce the same effect and mutually replace one another. To assure the reproduction of the totemic species, one may have recourse equally to oblations, to imitative practices or to commemorative representations. This aptitude of rites for substituting themselves for one another proves once more both their plasticity and the extreme generality of the useful action which they exercise. The essential thing is that men are assembled, that sentiments are felt in common and expressed in common acts; but the particular nature of these sentiments and acts is something relatively secondary and contingent.

To become conscious of itself, the group does not need to perform certain acts in preference to all others. The necessary thing is that it partakes of the same thought and the same action ; the visible forms in which this communion takes place matter but little. Of course, these external forms do not come by chance ; they have their reasons ; but these reasons do not touch the essential part of the cult.

So everything leads us back to this same idea : before all, rites are means by which the social group reaffirms itself periodically. From this, we may be able to reconstruct hypothetically the way in which the totemic cult should have arisen originally. Men who feel themselves united, partially by bonds of blood, but still more by a community of interest and tradition, assemble and become conscious of their moral unity. For the reasons which we have set forth, they are led to represent this unity in the form of a very special kind of consubstantiality : they think of themselves as all participating in the nature of some determined animal. Under these circumstances, there is only one way for them to affirm their collective existence : this is to affirm that they are like the animals of this species, and to do so not only in the silence of their own thoughts, but also by material acts. These are the acts which make up the cult, and they obviously can consist only in movements by which the man imitates the animal with which he identifies himself. When understood thus, the imitative rites appear as the first form of the cult. It will be thought that this is attributing a very considerable historical importance to practices which, at first view, give the effect of childish games. But, as we have shown, these naïve and awkward gestures and these crude processes of representation translate and maintain a sentiment of pride, confidence and veneration wholly comparable to that expressed by the worshippers in the most idealistic religions when, being assembled, they proclaim themselves the children of the almighty God. For in the one case as in the other, this sentiment is made up of the same impressions of security and respect which are awakened in individual consciousnesses by this great moral force which dominates them and sustains them, and which is the collective force.

The other rites which we have been studying are probably only variations of this essential rite. When the close union of the animal and men has once been admitted, men feel acutely the necessity of assuring the regular reproduction of the principal object of the cult. These imitative practices, which probably had only a moral end at first, thus became subordinated to utilitarian and material ends and they were thought of as means of producing the desired result. But proportionately as, through the development of mythology, the ancestral hero, who was at first confused with the totemic animal, distinguished himself more and more, and became a more personal figure, the imitation of the ancestor was substituted for the imitation of the animal, or took a place beside it, and then representative ceremonies replaced or completed the imitative rites. Finally, to be surer of attaining the end they sought, men felt the need of putting into action all the means at their disposal. Close at hand they had reserves of living forces accumulated in the sacred rocks, so they utilized them; since the blood of the men was of the same nature as that of the animal, they used it for the same purpose and shed it. Inversely, owing to this same kinship, men used the flesh of the animal to remake their own substance. Hence came the rites of oblation and communion. But, at bottom, all these different practices are only variations of one and the same theme: everywhere their basis is the same state of mind, interpreted differently according to the situations, the moments of history and the dispositions of the worshippers.

CHAPTER V

PIACULAR RITES AND THE AMBIGUITY OF THE NOTION OF SACREDNESS

HOWSOEVER much they may differ from one another in the nature of the gestures they imply, the positive rites which we have been passing under review have one common characteristic: they are all performed in a state of confidence, joy and even enthusiasm. Though the expectation of a future and contingent event is not without a certain uncertainty, still it is normal that the rain fall when the season for it comes, and that the animal and vegetable species reproduce regularly. Oft-repeated experiences have shown that the rites generally do produce the effects which are expected of them and which are the reason for their existence. Men celebrate them with confidence, joyfully anticipating the happy event which they prepare and announce. Whatever movements men perform participate in this same state of mind: of course, they are marked with the gravity which a religious solemnity always supposes, but this gravity excludes neither animation nor joy.

These are all joyful feasts. But there are sad celebrations as well, whose object is either to meet a calamity, or else merely to commemorate and deplore it. These rites have a special aspect, which we are going to attempt to characterize and explain. It is the more necessary to study them by themselves since they are going to reveal a new aspect of the religious life to us.

We propose to call the ceremonies of this sort piacular. The term *piaculum* has the advantage that while it suggests the idea of expiation, it also has a much more extended signification. Every misfortune, everything of evil omen, everything that inspires sentiments of sorrow or fear necessitates a *piaculum* and is therefore called piacular.[1] So this word seems to be very well adapted for designating the rites which are celebrated by those in a state of uneasiness or sadness.

[1] *Piacularia auspicia appellabant quæ sacrificantibus tristia portendebant* (Paul ex Fest., p. 244, ed. Müller). The word *piaculum* is even used as a synonym of misfortune. "*Vetonica herba,*" says Pliny, "*tantum gloriæ habet ut domus in qua sita sit tuta existimetur a piaculis omnibus*" (XXV, 8, 46).

I

Mourning offers us a first and important example of piacular rites. However, a distinction is necessary between the different rites which go to make up mourning. Some consist in mere abstentions: it is forbidden to pronounce the name of the dead,[1] or to remain near the place where the death occurred;[2] relatives, especially the female ones, must abstain from all communication with strangers;[3] the ordinary occupations of life are suspended, just as in feast-time,[4] etc. All these practices belong to the negative cult and are explained like the other rites of the same sort, so they do not concern us at present. They are due to the fact that the dead man is a sacred being. Consequently, everything which is or has been connected with him is, by contagion, in a religious state excluding all contact with things from profane life.

But mourning is not made up entirely of interdicts which have to be observed. Positive acts are also demanded, in which the relatives are both the actors and those acted upon.

Very frequently these rites commence as soon as the death appears imminent. Here is a scene which Spencer and Gillen witnessed among the Warramunga. A totemic ceremony had just been celebrated and the company of actors and spectators was leaving the consecrated ground when a piercing cry suddenly came from the camp: a man was dying there. At once, the whole company commenced to run as fast as they could, while most of them commenced to howl. " Between us and the camp," say these observers, " lay a deep creek, and on the bank of this, some of the men, scattered about here and there, sat down, bending their heads forwards between their knees, while they wept and moaned. Crossing the creek we found that, as usual, the men's camp had been pulled to pieces. Some of the women, who had come from every direction, were lying prostrate on the body, while others were standing or kneeling around, digging the sharp ends of yam-sticks into the crown of their heads, from which the blood streamed down over their faces, while all the time they kept up a loud, continuous wail. Many of the men, rushing up to the spot, threw themselves upon the body, from which the women arose when the men approached, until in a few minutes we could see nothing but a struggling mass of bodies all mixed up together. To one side, three men of the Thapungarti class, who still wore their ceremonial decorations, sat down wailing loudly, with their backs towards the dying man, and in

[1] *Nor. Tr.*, p. 526; Eylmann, p. 239. Cf. above, p. 305.
[2] Brough Smyth, I, p. 106; Dawson, p. 64; Eylmann, p. 239.
[3] Dawson, p. 66; Eylmann, p. 241.
[4] *Nat. Tr.*, p. 502; Dawson, p. 67.

a minute or two another man of the same class rushed on to the ground yelling and brandishing a stone knife. Reaching the camp, he suddenly gashed both thighs deeply, cutting right across the muscles, and, unable to stand, fell down into the middle of the group, from which he was dragged out after a time by three or four female relatives, who immediately applied their mouths to the gaping wounds while he lay exhausted on the ground." The man did not actually die until late in the evening. As soon as he had given up his last breath, the same scene was re-enacted, only this time the wailing was still louder, and men and women, seized by a veritable frenzy, were rushing about cutting themselves with knives and sharp-pointed sticks, the women battering one another's heads with fighting clubs, no one attempting to ward off either cuts or blows. Finally, after about an hour, a torchlight procession started off across the plain, to a tree in whose branches the body was left.[1]

Howsoever great the violence of these manifestations may be, they are strictly regulated by etiquette. The individuals who make bloody incisions in themselves are designated by usage: they must have certain relations of kinship with the dead man. Thus, in the case observed by Spencer and Gillen among the Warramunga, those who slashed their thighs were the maternal grandfather of the deceased, his maternal uncle, and the maternal uncle and brother of his wife.[2] Others must cut their whiskers and hair, and then smear their scalps with pipe-clay. Women have particularly severe obligations. They must cut their hair and cover the whole body with pipe-clay; in addition to this, a strict silence is imposed upon them during the whole period of mourning, which may last as long as two years. It is not rare among the Warramunga that, as a result of this interdiction, all the women of a camp are condemned to the most absolute silence. This becomes so habitual to them that even after the expiration of the period of mourning, they voluntarily renounce all spoken language and prefer to communicate with gestures—in which, by the way, they acquire a remarkable ability. Spencer and Gillen knew one old woman who had not spoken for over twenty-four years.[3]

[1] *Nor. Tr.*, pp. 516–517.

[2] *Ibid.*, pp. 520–521. The authors do not say whether these were tribal or blood relatives. The former hypothesis is the more probable one.

[3] *Nor. Tr.*, pp. 525 f. This interdiction against speaking, which is peculiar to women, though it consists in a simple abstention, has all the appearance of a piacular rite: it is a way of incommoding one's self. Therefore we mention it here. Also, fasting may be a piacular rite or an ascetic one, according to the circumstances. Everything depends upon the conditions in which it takes place and the end pursued (for the difference between these two sorts of rites, see below, p. 396).

The ceremony which we have described opens a long series of rites which succeed one another for weeks and even for months. During the days which follow, they are renewed in various forms. Groups of men and women sit on the ground, weeping and lamenting, and kissing each other at certain moments. These ritual kissings are repeated frequently during the period of mourning. It seems as though men felt a need of coming close together and communicating most closely; they are to be seen holding to each other and wound together so much as to make one single mass, from which loud groans escape.[1] Meanwhile, the women commence to lacerate their heads again, and, in order to intensify the wounds they make, they even go so far as to burn them with the points of fiery sticks.[2]

Practices of this sort are general in all Australia. The funeral rites, that is, the ritual cares given to the corpse, the way in which it is buried, etc., change with different tribes,[3] and in a single tribe they vary with the age, sex and social importance of the individual.[4] But the real ceremonies of mourning repeat the same theme everywhere; the variations are only in the details. Everywhere we find this same silence interrupted by groans,[5] the same obligation of cutting the hair and beard,[6] or of covering one's head with pipe-clay or cinders, or perhaps even with excrements;[7] everywhere, finally, we find this same frenzy for beating one's self, lacerating one's self and burning one's self. In central Victoria, "when death visits a tribe there is great weeping and lamentation amongst the women, the elder portion of whom lacerate their temples with their nails. The parents of the deceased lacerate themselves fearfully, especially if it be an only son whose loss they deplore. The father beats and cuts his head with a tomahawk until he utters bitter groans, the mother sits by the fire and burns her breasts and abdomen with a small fire-stick. Sometimes the burns thus inflicted are so severe as to cause death."[8]

[1] A very expressive illustration showing this rite will be found in *Nor. Tr.*, p. 525.

[2] *Ibid.*, p. 522.

[3] For the principal forms of funeral rites, see Howitt, *Nat. Tr.*, pp. 446–508, for the tribes of the South-East; Spencer and Gillen, *Nor. Tr.*, p. 505, and *Nat. Tr.*, pp. 497 ff., for those of the centre; Roth, *Nor. Queensland Ethnog.*, Bull. 9, in *Records of the Australian Museum*, VI, No. 5, pp. 365 ff. (*Burial Customs and Disposal of the Dead*).

[4] See, for example, Roth, *loc. cit.*, p. 368; Eyre, *Journals of Exped. into Central Aust.*, II, pp. 344 f.

[5] Spencer and Gillen, *Nat. Tr.*, p. 500; *Nor. Tr.*, pp. 507, 508; Eylmann, p. 241; Parker, *Euahlayi*, pp. 83 ff.; Brough Smyth, I, p. 118.

[6] Dawson, p. 66; Howitt, *Nat. Tr.*, p. 466; Eylmann, pp. 239–240.

[7] Brough Smyth, I, p. 113.

[8] W. E. Stanbridge, *Trans. Ethnological Society of London*, N.S., Vol. I, p. 286.

According to an account of Brough Smyth, here is what happens in one of the southern tribes of the same state. As the body is lowered into the grave, " the widow begins her sad ceremonies. She cuts off her hair above her forehead, and becoming frantic, seizes fire-sticks, and burns her breasts, arms, legs and thighs. She seems to delight in the self-inflicted torture. It would be rash and vain to interrupt her. When exhausted, and when she can hardly walk, she yet endeavours to kick the embers of the fire, and to throw them about. Sitting down, she takes the ashes into her hands, rubs them into her wounds, and then scratches her face (the only part not touched by the fire-sticks) until the blood mingles with the ashes, which partly hide her cruel wounds. In this plight, scratching her face continually, she utters howls and lamentations."[1]

The description which Howitt gives of the rites of mourning among the Kurnai is remarkably similar to these others. After the body has been wrapped up in opossum skins and put in a shroud of bark, a hut is built in which the relatives assemble. " There they lay lamenting their loss, saying, for instance, 'Why did you leave us ? ' Now and then their grief would be intensified by some one, for instance, the wife, uttering an ear-piercing wail, ' My spouse is dead,' or another would say, ' My child is dead.' All the others would then join in with the proper term of relationship, and they would gash themselves with sharp stones and tomahawks until their heads and bodies streamed with blood. This bitter wailing and weeping continued all night."[2]

Sadness is not the only sentiment expressed during these ceremonies ; a sort of anger is generally mixed with it. The relatives feel a need of avenging the death in some way or other. They are to be seen throwing themselves upon one another and trying to wound each other. Sometimes the attack is real ; sometimes it is only pretended.[3] There are even cases when these peculiar combats are organized. Among the Kaitish, the hair of the deceased passes by right to his son-in-law. But he, in return, must go, in company with some of his relatives and friends, and provoke a quarrel with one of his tribal brothers, that is, with a man belonging to the same matrimonial class as himself and one who might therefore have married the daughter of the dead man. This provocation cannot be refused and the two combatants inflict serious wounds upon each other's

[1] Brough Smyth, I, p. 104.

[2] Howitt, *Nat. Tr.*, p. 459. Similar scenes will be found in Eyre, *op. cit.*, II, p. 255, n., and p. 347 ; Roth, *loc. cit.*, pp. 394, 395, for example ; Grey, II, pp. 320 ff.

[3] Brough Smyth, I, pp. 104, 112 ; Roth, *loc. cit.*, p. 382.

shoulders and thighs. When the duel is terminated, the challenger passes on to his adversary the hair which he had temporarily inherited. This latter then provokes and fights with another of his tribal brothers, to whom the precious relic is next transmitted, but only provisionally; thus it passes from hand to hand and circulates from group to group.[1] Also, something of these same sentiments enters into that sort of rage with which each relative beats himself, burns himself or slashes himself: a sorrow which reaches such a paroxysm is not without a certain amount of anger. One cannot fail to be struck by the resemblances which these practices present to those of the vendetta. Both proceed from the same principle that death demands the shedding of blood. The only difference is that in one case the victims are the relatives, while in the other they are strangers. We do not have to treat especially of the vendetta, which belongs rather to the study of juridic institutions; but it should be pointed out, nevertheless, how it is connected with the rites of mourning, whose end it announces.[2]

In certain societies, the mourning is terminated by a ceremony whose effervescence reaches or surpasses that produced by the inaugural ceremonies. Among the Arunta, this closing rite is called *Urpmilchima*. Spencer and Gillen assisted at two of these rites. One was celebrated in honour of a man, the other of a woman. Here is the description they give of the latter.[3]

They commence by making some ornaments of a special sort, called *Chimurilia* by the men and *Aramurilia* by the women. With a kind of resin, they fixed small animal bones, which had previously been gathered and set aside, to locks of hair furnished by the relatives of the dead woman. These are then attached to one of the head-bands which women ordinarily wear and the feathers of black cockatoos and parrots are added to it. When these preparations are completed, the women assemble in their camp. They paint their bodies different colours, according to their degree of kinship with the deceased. After being embraced by one another for some ten minutes, while uttering uninterrupted groans, they set out for the tomb. At a certain distance, they meet a brother by blood of the dead woman, who is accompanied by some of his tribal brothers. Everybody sits down on the ground, and the lamentations recommence. A *pitchi*[4] containing the Chimurilia is then presented to the elder brother, who presses it against his stomach; they say that this is a way of lessening his sorrow. They take out one of the Chimurilia and the dead

[1] *Nor. Tr.*, pp. 511–512.
[2] Dawson, p. 67; Roth, *loc. cit.*, pp. 366–367. [3] *Nat. Tr.*, pp. 508–510.
[4] A little wooden vessel, of which we spoke above, p. 334.

woman's mother puts it on her head for a little while ; then it is put back into the *pitchi*, which each of the other men presses against his breast, in his turn. Finally, the brother puts the Chimurilia on the heads of two elder sisters and they set out again for the tomb. On the way, the mother throws herself on the ground several times, and tries to slash her head with a pointed stick. Every time, the other women pick her up, and seem to take care that she does not hurt herself too much. When they arrive at the tomb, she throws herself on the knoll and endeavours to destroy it with her hands, while the other women literally dance upon her. The tribal mothers and aunts (sisters of the dead woman's father) follow her example ; they also throw themselves on the ground, and mutually beat and tear each other ; finally their bodies are all streaming with blood. After a while, they are dragged aside. The elder sisters then make a hole in the earth of the tomb, in which they place the Chimurilia, which had previously been torn to pieces. Once again the tribal mothers throw themselves on the ground and slash each other's heads. At this moment, " the weeping and wailing of the women who were standing round seemed to drive them almost frenzied, and the blood, streaming down their bodies over the white pipe-clay, gave them a ghastly appearance. At last only the old mother was left crouching alone, utterly exhausted and moaning weakly on the grave."[1] Then the others raised her up and rubbed off the pipe-clay with which she was covered ; this was the end of the ceremony and of the mourning.[1]

Among the Warramunga, the final rite presents some rather particular characteristics. There seems to be no shedding of blood here, but the collective effervescence is translated in another manner.

Among his people, before the body is definitely interred, it is exposed upon a platform placed in the branches of a tree ; it is left there to decompose slowly, until nothing remains but the bones. Then these are gathered together and, with the exception of the humerus, they are placed inside an ant-hill. The humerus is wrapped up in a bark box, which is decorated in different manners. The box is then brought to camp, amid the cries and groans of the women. During the following days, they celebrate a series of totemic rites, concerning the totem of the deceased and the mythical history of the ancestors from whom the clan is descended. When all these ceremonies have been terminated, they proceed to the closing rite.

[1] *Nat. Tr.*, pp. 508–510. The other final rite at which Spencer and Gillen assisted is described on pp. 503–508 of the same work. It does not differ essentially from the one we have analysed.

A trench one foot deep and fifteen feet long is dug in the field of the ceremony. A design representing the totem of the deceased and certain spots where the ancestor stopped is made on the ground a little distance from it. Near this design, a little ditch is dug in the ground. Ten decorated men then advance, one behind another, and with their hands crossed behind their heads and their legs wide apart they stand astraddle the trench. At a given signal, the women run from the camp in a profound silence ; when they are near, they form in Indian file, the last one holding in her hands the box containing the humerus. Then, after throwing themselves on the ground, they advance on their hands and knees, and pass all along the trench, between the legs of the men. The scene shows a state of great sexual excitement. As soon as the last woman has passed, they take the box from her, and take it to the ditch, near which is an old man ; he breaks the bone with a sharp blow, and hurriedly buries it in the debris. During this time, the women have remained at a distance, with their backs turned upon the scene, for they must not see it. But when they hear the blow of the axe, they flee, uttering cries and groans. The rite is accomplished ; the mourning is terminated.[1]

II

These rites belong to a very different type from those which we have studied hitherto. We do not mean to say that important resemblances cannot be found between the two, which we shall have to note ; but the differences are more apparent. Instead of happy dances, songs and dramatic representations which distract and relax the mind, they are tears and groans and, in a word, the most varied manifestations of agonized sorrow and a sort of mutual pity, which occupy the whole scene. Of course the shedding of blood also takes place in the Intichiuma, but this is an oblation made with a movement of pious enthusiasm. Even though the motions may be the same, the sentiments expressed are different and even opposed. Likewise, the ascetic rites certainly imply privations, abstinences and mutilations, but ones which must be borne with an impassive firmness and serenity. Here, on the contrary, dejection, cries and tears are the rule. The ascetic tortures himself in order to prove, in his own eyes and those of his fellows, that he is above suffering. During mourning, men injure themselves to prove that they suffer. By all these signs, the characteristic traits of the piacular rites are to be recognized.

But how are they to be explained ?

[1] *Nor. Tr.*, pp. 531–540.

One initial fact is constant : mourning is not the spontaneous expression of individual emotions.[1] If the relations weep, lament, mutilate themselves, it is not because they feel themselves personally affected by the death of their kinsman. Of course, it may be that in certain particular cases, the chagrin expressed is really felt.[2] But it is more generally the case that there is no connection between the sentiments felt and the gestures made by the actors in the rite.[3] If, at the very moment when the weepers seem the most overcome by their grief, some one speaks to them of some temporal interest, it frequently happens that they change their features and tone at once, take on a laughing air and converse in the gayest fashion imaginable.[4] Mourning is not a natural movement of private feelings wounded by a cruel loss ; it is a duty imposed by the group. One weeps, not simply because he is sad, but because he is forced to weep. It is a ritual attitude which he is forced to adopt out of respect for custom, but which is, in a large measure, independent of his affective state. Moreover, this obligation is sanctioned by mythical or social penalties. They believe, for example, that if a relative does not mourn as is fitting, then the soul of the departed follows upon his steps and kills him.[5] In other cases, society does not leave it to the religious forces to punish the negligent ; it intervenes itself, and reprimands the ritual faults. If a son-in-law does not render to his father-in-law the funeral attentions which are due him, and if he does not make the prescribed incisions, then his tribal fathers-in-law take his wife away from him and give him another.[6] Therefore, in order to square himself with usage, a man sometimes forces tears to flow by artificial means.[7]

Whence comes this obligation ?

Ethnographers and sociologists are generally satisfied with the reply which the natives themselves give to this question. They say that the dead wish to be lamented, that by refusing them the tribute of sorrow which is their right, men offend them, and that the only way of preventing their anger is to conform to their will.[8]

But this mythological interpretation merely modifies the terms of the problem, without resolving it ; it is still necessary to explain why the dead imperatively reclaim the mourning. It

[1] Contrarily to what Jevons says, *Introduction to the History of Religion*, pp. 46 ff.

[2] This makes Dawson say that the mourning is sincere (p. 66). But Eylmann assures us that he never knew a single case where there was a wound from sorrow really felt (*op. cit.*, p. 113).

[3] *Nat. Tr.*, p. 510.

[4] Eylmann, pp. 238–239.

[5] *Nor. Tr.*, p. 507 ; *Nat. Tr.*, p. 498.

[6] *Nat. Tr.*, p. 500 ; Eylmann, p. 227.

[7] Brough Smyth, I, p. 114.

[8] *Nat. Tr.*, p. 510.

may be said that it is natural for men to wish to be mourned and regretted. But in making this sentiment explain the complex system of rites which make up mourning, we attribute to the Australian affective exigencies of which the civilized man himself does not always give evidence. Let us admit—as is not evident *a priori*—that the idea of not being forgotten too readily is pleasing to a man who thinks of the future. It is still to be established that it has ever had enough importance in the minds of the living for one to attribute to the dead a state of mind proceeding almost entirely from this preoccupation. It seems especially improbable that such a sentiment could obsess and impassion men who are seldom accustomed to thinking beyond the present moment. So far is it from being a fact that the desire to survive in the memory of those who are still alive is to be regarded as the origin of mourning, that we may even ask ourselves whether it was not rather mourning itself which, when once established, aroused the idea of and the taste for posthumous regrets.

The classic interpretation appears still more unsustainable when we know what the primitive mourning consists in. It is not made up merely of pious regrets accorded to him who no longer is, but also of severe abstinences and cruel sacrifices. The rite does not merely demand that one think of the deceased in a melancholy way, but also that he beat himself, bruise himself, lacerate himself and burn himself. We have even seen that persons in mourning sometimes torture themselves to such a degree that they do not survive their wounds. What reason has the dead man for imposing such torments upon them ? Such a cruelty on his part denotes something more than a desire not to be forgotten. If he is to find pleasure in seeing his own suffer, it is necessary that he hate them, that he be thirsty for their blood. This ferocity would undoubtedly appear natural to those for whom every spirit is necessarily an evil and redoubted power. But we know that there are spirits of every sort ; how does it happen that the soul of the dead man is necessarily an evil spirit ? As long as the man is alive, he loves his relatives and exchanges services with them. Is it not strange that as soon as it is freed from his body, his soul should instantly lay aside its former sentiments and become an evil and tormenting genius ? It is a general rule that the dead man retains the personality of the living, and that he has the same character, the same hates and the same affections. So this metamorphosis is not easily understandable by itself. It is true that the natives admit it implicitly when they explain the rite by the exigencies of the dead man, but the question now before us is to know whence this conception came. Far from being capable of being regarded as a truism, it is as obscure as the rite itself, and consequently cannot account for it.

Finally, even if we had found the reasons for this surprising transformation, we would still have to explain why it is only temporary. For it does not last beyond the period of mourning; after the rites have once been accomplished, the dead man becomes what he was when alive, an affectionate and devoted relation. He puts the new powers which he receives from his new condition at the service of his friends.[1] Thenceforth, he is regarded as a good genius, always ready to aid those whom he was recently tormenting. Whence come these successive transfers? If the evil sentiments attributed to the soul come solely from the fact that it is no longer in life, they should remain invariable, and if the mourning is due to this, it should be interminable.

These mythical explanations express the idea which the native has of the rite, and not the rite itself. So we may set them aside and face the reality which they translate, though disfiguring it in doing so. If mourning differs from the other forms of the positive cult, there is one feature in which it resembles them: it, too, is made up out of collective ceremonies which produce a state of effervescence among those who take part in them. The sentiments aroused are different; but the arousal is the same. So it is presumable that the explanation of the joyous rites is capable of being applied to the sad rites, on condition that the terms be transposed.

When some one dies, the family group to which he belongs feels itself lessened and, to react against this loss, it assembles. A common misfortune has the same effects as the approach of a happy event: collective sentiments are renewed which then lead men to seek one another and to assemble together. We have even seen this need for concentration affirm itself with a particular energy: they embrace one another, put their arms round one another, and press as close as possible to one another. But the affective state in which the group then happens to be only reflects the circumstances through which it is passing. Not only do the relatives, who are effected the most directly, bring their own personal sorrow to the assembly, but the society exercises a moral pressure over its members, to put their sentiments in harmony with the situation. To allow them to remain indifferent to the blow which has fallen upon it and diminished it, would be equivalent to proclaiming that it does not hold the place in their hearts which is due it; it would be denying itself. A family

[1] Several examples of this belief are to be found in Howitt, *Nat. Tr.*, p. 435. Cf. Strehlow, I, 15–16; II, p. 7.

which allows one of its members to die without being wept for shows by that very fact that it lacks moral unity and cohesion: it abdicates; it renounces its existence. An individual, in his turn, if he is strongly attached to the society of which he is a member, feels that he is morally held to participating in its sorrows and joys; not to be interested in them would be equivalent to breaking the bonds uniting him to the group; it would be renouncing all desire for it and contradicting himself. When the Christian, during the ceremonies commemorating the Passion, and the Jew, on the anniversary of the fall of Jerusalem, fast and mortify themselves, it is not in giving way to a sadness which they feel spontaneously. Under these circumstances, the internal state of the believer is out of all proportion to the severe abstinences to which they submit themselves. If he is sad, it is primarily because he consents to being sad, and he consents to it in order to affirm his faith. The attitude of the Australian during mourning is to be explained in the same way. If he weeps and groans, it is not merely to express an individual chagrin; it is to fulfil a duty of which the surrounding society does not fail to remind him.

We have seen elsewhere how human sentiments are intensified when affirmed collectively. Sorrow, like joy, becomes exalted and amplified when leaping from mind to mind, and therefore expresses itself outwardly in the form of exuberant and violent movements. But these are no longer expressive of the joyful agitation which we observed before; they are shrieks and cries of pain. Each is carried along by the others; a veritable panic of sorrow results. When pain reaches this degree of intensity, it is mixed with a sort of anger and exasperation. One feels the need of breaking something, of destroying something. He takes this out either upon himself or others. He beats himself, burns himself, wounds himself or else he falls upon others to beat, burn and wound them. Thus it became the custom to give one's self up to the veritable orgies of tortures during mourning. It seems very probable that blood-revenge and head-hunting have their origin in this. If every death is attributed to some magic charm, and for this reason it is believed that the dead man ought to be avenged, it is because men must find a victim at any price, upon whom the collective pain and anger may be discharged. Naturally this victim is sought outside the group; a stranger is a subject *minoris resistentiæ;* as he is not protected by the sentiments of sympathy inspired by a relative or neighbour, there is nothing in him which subdues and neutralizes the evil and destructive sentiments aroused by the death. It is undoubtedly for this same reason that women serve more frequently than men as the passive objects of the cruellest rites of mourning; since they have a smaller social value, they are more obviously designated as scapegoats.

We see that this explanation of mourning completely leaves aside all ideas of souls or spirits. The only forces which are really active are of a wholly impersonal nature: they are the emotions aroused in the group by the death of one of its members. But the primitive does not know the psychical mechanism from which these practices result. So when he tries to account for them, he is obliged to forge a wholly different explanation. All he knows is that he must painfully mortify himself. As every obligation suggests the notion of a will which obliges, he looks about him to see whence this constraint which he feels may come. Now, there is one moral power, of whose reality he is assured and which seems designated for this rôle: this is the soul which the death has liberated. For what could have a greater interest than it in the effects which its own death has on the living? So they imagine that if these latter inflict an unnatural treatment upon themselves, it is to conform to its exigencies. It was thus that the idea of the soul must have intervened at a later date into the mythology of mourning. But also, since it is thus endowed with inhuman exigencies, it must be supposed that in leaving the body which it animated, the soul lays aside every human sentiment. Hence the metamorphosis which makes a dreaded enemy out of the relative of yesterday. This transformation is not the origin of mourning; it is rather its consequence. It translates a change which has come over the affective state of the group: men do not weep for the dead because they fear them; they fear them because they weep for them.

But this change of the affective state can only be a temporary one, for while the ceremonies of mourning result from it, they also put an end to it. Little by little, they neutralize the very causes which have given rise to them. The foundation of mourning is the impression of a loss which the group feels when it loses one of its members. But this very impression results in bringing individuals together, in putting them into closer relations with one another, in associating them all in the same mental state, and therefore in disengaging a sensation of comfort which compensates the original loss. Since they weep together, they hold to one another and the group is not weakened, in spite of the blow which has fallen upon it. Of course they have only sad emotions in common, but communicating in sorrow is still communicating, and every communion of mind, in whatever form it may be made, raises the social vitality. The exceptional violence of the manifestations by which the common pain is necessarily and obligatorily expressed even testifies to the fact that at this moment, the society is more alive and active than ever. In fact, whenever the social sentiment is painfully wounded, it reacts with greater force than ordinarily: one never holds so closely to his family as when it has just suffered. This surplus energy effaces the more completely the effects of the interruption which was felt at first, and thus dissipates the feeling of coldness which death always brings with it. The group feels its strength gradually returning to it; it begins to hope and to live again. Presently one stops mourning, and he does so owing to the mourning itself. But as the idea formed of the soul reflects the moral state of the society, this idea should change as this state changes. When one is in the period of dejection and agony, he represents the soul with the traits of an evil being, whose sole occupation is to persecute men. But when he feels himself confident and secure once more, he must admit that it has retaken its former nature and its former sentiments of tenderness and solidarity. Thus we explain the very different ways in which it is conceived at different moments of its existence.[1]

Not only do the rites of mourning determine certain of the secondary characteristics attributed to the soul, but perhaps they are not foreign to the idea that it survives the body. If he is to understand the practices to which he submits on the death of a parent, a man is obliged to believe that these are not an indifferent matter for the deceased. The shedding of blood which is practised so freely during mourning is a veritable sacrifice offered to the dead man.[2] So something of the dead man must survive, and as this is not the body, which is manifestly immobile and decomposed, it can only be the soul. Of course it is impossible to say with any exactness what part these considerations have had in the origin of the idea of immortality. But it is probable that here the influence of the cult is the same as it is elsewhere. Rites are more easily explicable when one imagines that they are addressed to personal beings;

[1] It may be asked why repeated ceremonies are necessary to produce the relief which follows upon mourning. The funeral ceremonies are frequently very long; they include many operations which take place at intervals during many months. Thus they prolong and support the moral disturbance brought about by the death (cf. Hertz, *La Réprésentation collective de la mort*, in *Année Sociol.*, X, pp. 48 ff.). In a general way, a death marks a grave change of condition which has extended and enduring effects upon the group. It takes a long time to neutralize these effects.

[2] In a case reported by Grey from the observations of Bussel, the rite has all the aspects of a sacrifice: the blood is sprinkled over the body itself (Grey, II, p. 330). In other cases, there is something like an offering of the beard: men in mourning cut off a part of their beards, which they throw on to the corpse (*ibid.*, p. 335).

so men have been induced to extend the influence of the mythical personalities in the religious life. In order to account for mourning, they have prolonged the existence of the soul beyond the tomb. This is one more example of the way in which rites react upon beliefs.

III

But death is not the only event which may disturb a community. Men have many other occasions for being sorry and lamenting, so we might foresee that even the Australians would know and practise other piacular rites besides mourning. However, it is a remarkable fact that only a small number of examples are to be found in the accounts of the observers.

One rite of this sort greatly resembles those which have just been studied. It will be remembered that among the Arunta, each local group attributes exceptionally important virtues to its collection of churinga: this is this collective palladium, upon whose fate the fate of the community itself is believed to depend. So when enemies or white men succeed in stealing one of these religious treasures, this loss is considered a public calamity. This misfortune is the occasion of a rite having all the characteristics of mourning: men smear their bodies with white pipe-clay and remain in camp, weeping and lamenting, during a period of two weeks.[1] This is a new proof that mourning is determined, not by the way in which the soul of the dead is conceived, but by impersonal causes, by the moral state of the group. In fact, we have here a rite which, in its structure, is indistinguishable from the real mourning, but which is, nevertheless, independent of every notion of spirits or evil-working demons.[2]

Another circumstance which gives occasion for ceremonies of the same nature is the distress in which the society finds itself after an insufficient harvest. "The natives who live in the vicinity of Lake Eyre," says Eylmann, "also seek to prevent an insufficiency of food by means of secret ceremonies. But many of the ritual practices observed in this region are to be distinguished from those which have been mentioned already: it is not by symbolic dances, by imitative movements nor dazzling decorations that they try to act upon the religious powers or the forces of nature, but by means of the suffering which individuals inflict upon themselves. In the northern territories,

[1] *Nat. Tr.*, pp. 135–136.

[2] Of course each churinga is believed to be connected with an ancestor. But it is not to appease the spirits of the ancestors that they mourn for the lost churinga. We have shown elsewhere (p. 123) that the idea of the ancestor only entered into the conception of the churinga secondarily and late.

it is by means of tortures, such as prolonged fasts, vigils, dances persisted up to the exhaustion of the dancers, and physical pains of every sort, that they attempt to appease the powers which are ill-disposed towards men." [1] The torments to which the natives submit themselves for this purpose sometimes leave them in such a state of exhaustion that they are unable to follow the hunt for some days to come.[2]

These practices are employed especially for fighting against drought. This is because a scarcity of water results in a general want. To remedy this evil, they have recourse to violent methods. One which is frequently used is the extraction of a tooth. Among the Kaitish, for example, they pull out an incisor from one man, and hang it on a tree.[3] Among the Dieri, the idea of rain is closely associated with that of bloody incisions made in the skin of the chest and arms.[4] Among this same people, whenever the drought is very great, the great council assembles and summons the whole tribe. It is really a tribal event. Women are sent in every direction to notify men to assemble at a given place and time. After they have assembled, they groan and cry in a piercing voice about the miserable state of the land, and they beg the *Mura-mura* (the mythical ancestors) to give them the power of making an abundant rain fall.[5] In the cases, which, by the way, are very rare, when there has been an excessive rainfall, an analogous ceremony takes place to stop it. Old men then enter into a veritable frenzy,[6] while the cries uttered by the crowd are really painful to hear.[7]

Spencer and Gillen describe, under the name of Intichiuma, a ceremony which may well have the same object and the same origin as the preceding ones: a physical torture is applied to make an animal species multiply. Among the Urabunna, there is one clan whose totem is a variety of snake called *wadnungadni*. This is how the chief of the clan proceeds, to make sure that these snakes may never be lacking. After having been decorated, he kneels down on the ground, holding his arms straight out. An assistant pinches the skin of his right arm between his fingers, and the officiant forces a pointed bone five inches long through the fold thus formed. This self-mutilation is believed to produce the desired result.[8] An analogous rite is used among the Dieri to make the wild-hens lay: the operators pierce their scrotums.[9]

[1] *Op. cit.*, p. 207; cf. p. 116.
[2] Eylmann, p. 208.
[3] *Ibid.*, p. 211.
[4] Howitt, *The Dieri*, in *J.A.I.*, XX (1891), p. 93.
[5] Howitt, *Nat. Tr.*, p. 394.
[6] Howitt, *ibid.*, p. 396.
[7] Communication of Gason in *J.A.I.*, XXIV (1895), p. 175.
[8] *Nor. Tr.*, p. 286.
[9] Gason, *The Dieri Tribe*, in Curr, II, p. 68.

In certain of the Lake Eyre tribes, men pierce their ears to make yams reproduce.[1]

But these partial or total famines are not the only plagues which may fall upon a tribe. Other events happen more or less periodically which menace, or seem to menace, the existence of the group. This is the case, for example, with the southern lights. The Kurnai believe that this is a fire lighted in the heavens by the great god Mungan-ngaua ; therefore, whenever they see it, they are afraid that it may spread to the earth and devour them, so a great effervescence results in the camp. They shake a withered hand, to which the Kurnai attribute various virtues, and utter such cries as "Send it away ; do not let us be burned." At the same time, the old men order an exchange of wives, which always indicates a great excitement.[2] The same sexual licence is mentioned among the Wiimbaio whenever a plague appears imminent, and especially in times of an epidemic.[3]

Under the influence of these ideas, mutilations and the shedding of blood are sometimes considered an efficient means of curing maladies. If an accident happens to a child among the Dieri, his relations beat themselves on the head with clubs or boomerangs until the blood flows down over their faces. They believe that by this process, they relieve the child of the suffering.[4] Elsewhere, they imagine that they can obtain the same end by means of a supplementary totemic ceremony.[5] We may connect with these the example already given of a ceremony celebrated specially to efface the effects of a ritual fault.[6] Of course there are neither wounds nor blows nor physical suffering of any sort in these two latter cases, yet the rite does not differ in nature from the others : the end sought is always the turning aside of an evil or the expiation of a fault by means of an extraordinary ritual prestation.

Outside of mourning, such are the only cases of piacular rites which we have succeeded in finding in Australia. To be sure, it is probable that some have escaped us, while we may presume equally well that others have remained unperceived by the observers. But if those discovered up to the present are few in number, it is probably because they do not hold a

[1] Gason, *The Dieri Tribe*: Eylmann, p. 208.

[2] Howitt, *Nat. Tr.*, pp. 277 and 430.

[3] *Ibid.*, p. 195.

[4] Gason, *The Dieri Tribe*, in Curr, II, p. 69. The same process is used to expiate a ridiculous act. Whenever anybody, by his awkwardness or otherwise, has caused the laughter of others, he asks one of them to beat him on the head until blood flows. Then things are all right again, and the one who was laughed at joins in the general gaiety (*ibid.*, p. 70).

[5] Eylmann, pp. 212 and 447.

[6] See above, p. 385.

large place in the cult. We see how far primitive religions are from being the daughters of agony and fear from the fact that the rites translating these painful emotions are relatively rare. Of course this is because the Australian, while leading a miserable existence as compared with other more civilized peoples, demands so little of life that he is easily contented. All that he asks is that nature follow its normal course, that the seasons succeed one another regularly, that the rain fall, at the ordinary time, in abundance and without excess. Now great disturbances in the cosmic order are always exceptional; thus it is noticeable that the majority of the regular piacular rites, examples of which we have given above, have been observed in the tribes of the centre, where droughts are frequent and constitute veritable disasters. It is still surprising, it is true, that piacular rites specially destined to expiate sins, seem to be completely lacking. However, the Australian, like every other man, must commit ritual faults, which he has an interest in redeeming; so we may ask if the silence of the texts on this point may not be due to insufficient observation.

But howsoever few the facts which we have been able to gather may be, they are, nevertheless, instructive.

When we study piacular rites in the more advanced religions, where the religious forces are individualized, they appear to be closely bound up with anthropomorphic conceptions. When the believer imposes privations upon himself and submits himself to austerities, it is in order to disarm the malevolence attributed by him to certain of the sacred beings upon whom he thinks that he is dependent. To appease their hatred or anger, he complies with their exigencies; he beats himself in order that he may not be beaten by them. So it seems as though these practices could not arise until after gods and spirits were conceived as moral persons, capable of passions analogous to those of men. For this reason, Robertson Smith thought it possible to assign a relatively late date to expiatory sacrifices, just as to sacrificial oblations. According to him, the shedding of blood which characterizes these rites was at first a simple process of communion: men poured forth their blood upon the altar in order to strengthen the bonds uniting them to their god. The rite acquired a piacular and penal character only when its original significance was forgotten and when the new idea which was formed of sacred beings allowed men to attribute another function to it.[1]

But as piacular rites are met with even in the Australian societies, it is impossible to assign them so late an origin.

[1] *The Religion of the Semites*, lect. XI.

Moreover, all that we have observed, with one single exception,[1] are independent of all anthropomorphic conceptions: there is no question of either spirits or gods. Abstinences and effusions of blood stop famines and cure sicknesses directly and by themselves. No spiritual being introduces his action between the rite and the effect it is believed to produce. So mythical personalities intervened only at a late date. After the mechanism of the ritual had once been established, they served to make it more easily representable in the mind, but they are not conditions of its existence. It is for other reasons that it was founded; it is to another cause that it owes its efficacy.

It acts through the collective forces which it puts into play. Does a misfortune which menaces the group appear imminent? Then the group unites, as in the case of mourning, and it is naturally an impression of uneasiness and perplexity which dominates the assembled body. Now, as always, the pooling of these sentiments results in intensifying them. By affirming themselves, they exalt and impassion themselves and attain a degree of violence which is translated by the corresponding violence of the gestures which express them. Just as at the death of a relative, they utter terrible cries, fly into a passion and feel that they must tear and destroy; it is to satisfy this need that they beat themselves, wound themselves, and make their blood flow. When emotions have this vivacity, they may well be painful, but they are not depressing; on the contrary, they denote a state of effervescence which implies a mobilization of all our active forces, and even a supply of external energies. It matters little that this exaltation was provoked by a sad event, for it is real, notwithstanding, and does not differ specifically from what is observed in the happy feasts. Sometimes it is even made manifest by movements of the same nature: there is the same frenzy which seizes the worshippers and the same tendency towards sexual debauches, a sure sign of great nervous over-excitement. Robertson Smith had already noticed this curious influence of sad rites in the Semitic cults: "in evil times," he says, "when men's thoughts were habitually sombre, they betook themselves to the physical excitement of religion as men now take refuge in wine. . . . And so in general when an act of Semitic worship began with sorrow and lamentation—as in the mourning for Adonis, or the great atoning ceremonies which became common in later times—a swift revulsion of feeling followed, and the gloomy part of the service was presently

[1] This is the case in which the Dieri, according to Jason, invoke the Mura-mura of water during a drought.

succeeded by a burst of hilarious revelry."[1] In a word, even when religious ceremonies have a disquieting or saddening event as their point of departure, they retain their stimulating power over the affective state of the group and individuals. By the mere fact that they are collective, they raise the vital tone. When one feels life within him—whether it be in the form of painful irritation or happy enthusiasm—he does not believe in death; so he becomes reassured and takes courage again, and subjectively, everything goes on as if the rite had really driven off the danger which was dreaded. This is how curing or preventive virtues come to be attributed to the movements which one makes, to the cries uttered, to the blood shed and to the wounds inflicted upon one's self or others; and as these different tortures necessarily make one suffer, suffering by itself is finally regarded as a means of conjuring evil or curing sickness.[2] Later, when the majority of the religious forces had taken the form of moral personalities, the efficacy of these practices was explained by imagining that their object was to appease an evil-working or irritated god. But these conceptions only reflect the rite and the sentiments it arouses; they are an interpretation of it, not its determining cause.

A negligence of the ritual acts in the same way. It, too, is a menace for the group; it touches it in its moral existence for it touches it in its beliefs. But if the anger which it causes is affirmed ostensibly and energetically, it compensates the evil which it has caused. For if it is acutely felt by all, it is because the infraction committed is an exception and the common faith remains entire. So the moral unity of the group is not endangered. Now the penalty inflicted as an expiation is only a manifestation of the public anger, the material proof of its unanimity. So it really does have the healing effect attributed to it. At bottom, the sentiment which is at the root of the real expiatory rites does not differ in nature from that which we have found at the basis of the other piacular rites: it is a sort of irritated sorrow which tends to manifest itself by acts of destruction. Sometimes it is assuaged to the detriment of him who feels it; sometimes it is at the expense of some foreign third party. But in either case, the psychic mechanism is essentially the same.[3]

[1] *Op. cit.*, p. 262.

[2] It is also possible that the belief in the morally tempering virtues of suffering (see above, p. 312) has added something here. Since sorrow sanctifies and raises the religious level of the worshipper, it may also raise him up again when he falls lower than usual.

[3] Cf. what we have said of expiation in our *Division du travail social*[3], pp. 64 ff.

IV

One of the greatest services which Robertson Smith has rendered to the science of religions is to have pointed out the ambiguity of the notion of sacredness.

Religious forces are of two sorts. Some are beneficent, guardians of the physical and moral order, dispensers of life and health and all the qualities which men esteem: this is the case with the totemic principle, spread out in the whole species, the mythical ancestor, the animal-protector, the civilizing heroes and the tutelar gods of every kind and degree. It matters little whether they are conceived as distinct personalities or as diffused energies; under either form they fulfil the same function and affect the minds of the believers in the same way: the respect which they inspire is mixed with love and gratitude. The things and the persons which are normally connected with them participate in the same sentiments and the same character: these are holy things and persons. Such are the spots consecrated to the cult, the objects which serve in the regular rites, the priests, the ascetics, etc.—On the other hand, there are evil and impure powers, productive of disorders, causes of death and sickness, instigators of sacrilege. The only sentiments which men have for them are a fear into which horror generally enters. Such are the forces upon which and by which the sorcerer acts, those which arise from corpses or the menstrual blood, those freed by every profanation of sacred things, etc. The spirits of the dead and malign genii of every sort are their personified forms.

Between these two categories of forces and beings, the contrast is as complete as possible and even goes into the most radical antagonism. The good and salutary powers repel to a distance these others which deny and contradict them. Therefore the former are forbidden to the latter: any contact between them is considered the worst of profanations. This is the typical form of those interdicts between sacred things of different species, the existence of which we have already pointed out.[1] Women during menstruation, and especially at its beginning, are impure; so at this moment they are rigorously sequestered; men may have no relations with them.[2] Bull-roarers and churinga never come near a dead man.[3] A sacrilegious

[1] See above, p. 301.

[2] Spencer and Gillen, *Nat. Tr.*, p. 460; *Nor. Tr.*, p. 601; Roth, *North Queensland Ethnography*, Bulletin No. 5, p. 24. It is useless to multiply references for so well-known a fact.

[3] However, Spencer and Gillen cite one case where churinga are placed on the head of the dead man (*Nat. Tr.*, p. 156). But they admit that the fact is unique and abnormal (*ibid.*, p. 157), while Strehlow energetically denies it (II, p. 79).

person is excluded from the society of the faithful; access to the cult is forbidden him. Thus the whole religious life gravitates about two contrary poles between which there is the same opposition as between the pure and the impure, the saint and the sacrilegious, the divine and the diabolic.

But while these two aspects of the religious life oppose one another, there is a close kinship between them. In the first place, both have the same relation towards profane beings: these must abstain from all contact with impure things just as from the most holy things. The former are no less forbidden than the latter: they are withdrawn from circulation alike. This shows that they too are sacred. Of course the sentiments inspired by the two are not identical: respect is one thing, disgust and horror another. Yet, if the gestures are to be the same in both cases, the sentiments expressed must not differ in nature. And, in fact, there is a horror in religious respect, especially when it is very intense, while the fear inspired by malign powers is generally not without a certain reverential character. The shades by which these two attitudes are differentiated are even so slight sometimes that it is not always easy to say which state of mind the believers actually happen to be in. Among certain Semitic peoples, pork was forbidden, but it was not always known exactly whether this was because it was a pure or an impure thing [1] and the same may be said of a very large number of alimentary interdictions.

But there is more to be said; it very frequently happens that an impure thing or an evil power becomes a holy thing or a guardian power, without changing its nature, through a simple modification of external circumstances. We have seen how the soul of a dead man, which is a dreaded principle at first, is transformed into a protecting genius as soon as the mourning is finished. Likewise, the corpse, which begins by inspiring terror and aversion, is later regarded as a venerated relic: funeral anthropophagy, which is frequently practised in the Australian societies, is a proof of this transformation.[2] The totemic animal is the pre-eminently sacred being; but for him who eats its flesh unduly, it is a cause of death. In a general way, the sacrilegious person is merely a profane one who has been infected with a benevolent religious force. This changes its nature in changing its habitat; it defiles rather than sanctifies.[3] The

[1] Smith, *Rel. of Semites*, p. 153; cf. p. 446, the additional note, *Holiness, Uncleanness and Taboo*.

[2] Howitt, *Nat. Tr.*, pp. 448–450; Brough Smyth, I, pp. 118, 120; Dawson, p. 67; Eyre, II, p. 251; Roth, *North Queensland Ethn.*, Bull. Mo. 9, in *Rec. of the Austral. Museum*, VI, No. 5, p. 367.

[3] See above, p. 320.

blood issuing from the genital organs of a woman, though it is evidently as impure as that of menstruation, is frequently used as a remedy against sickness.[1] The victim immolated in expiatory sacrifices is charged with impurities, for they have concentrated upon it the sins which were to be expiated. Yet, after it has been slaughtered, its flesh and blood are employed for the most pious uses.[2] On the contrary, though the communion is generally a religious operation whose normal function is to consecrate, it sometimes produces the effects of a sacrilege. In certain cases, the persons who have communicated are forced to flee from one another as from men infected with a plague. One would say that they have become a source of dangerous contamination for one another: the sacred bond which unites them also separates them. Examples of this sort of communion are numerous in Australia. One of the most typical has been observed among the Narrinyeri and the neighbouring tribes. When an infant arrives in the world, its parents carefully preserve its umbilical cord, which is believed to conceal a part of its soul. Two persons who exchange the cords thus preserved communicate together by the very act of this exchange, for it is as though they exchanged their souls. But, at the same time, they are forbidden to touch or speak to or even to see one another. It is just as though they were each an object of horror for the other.[3]

So the pure and the impure are not two separate classes, but two varieties of the same class, which includes all sacred things. There are two sorts of sacredness, the propitious and the unpropitious, and not only is there no break of continuity between these two opposed forms, but also one object may pass from the one to the other without changing its nature. The pure is made out of the impure, and reciprocally. It is in the possibility of these transmutations that the ambiguity of the sacred consists.

But even if Robertson Smith did have an active sentiment of this ambiguity, he never gave it an express explanation. He confined himself to remarking that, as all religious forces are indistinctly intense and contagious, it is wise not to approach them except with respectful precautions, no matter what direction their action may be exercised in. It seemed to him that he could thus account for the air of kinship which they all present, in

[1] *Nor. Tr.*, p. 599; *Nat. Tr.*, p. 464.

[2] Among the Hebrews, for example, they sprinkled the altar with the blood of the expiatory victim (Lev. iv, 5 ff.); they burned the flesh and used products of this combustion to make water of purification (Numb. xix).

[3] Taplin, *The Narrinyeri*, pp. 32–34. When two persons who have thus exchanged their umbilical cords belong to different tribes, they are used as inter-tribal messengers. In this case, the exchange of cords took place shortly after birth, through the intermediary of their respective parents.

spite of the contrasts which oppose them otherwise. But the question was only put off; it still remains to be shown how it comes that the powers of evil have the same intensity and contagiousness as the others. In other words, how does it happen that they, too, are of a religious nature? Also, the energy and force of expansion which they have in common do not enable us to understand how, in spite of the conflict which divides them, they may be transformed into one another or substituted for each other in their respective functions, and how the pure may contaminate while the impure sometimes serves to sanctify.[1]

The explanation of piacular rites which we have proposed enables us to reply to this double question.

We have seen, in fact, that the evil powers are the product of these rites and symbolize them. When a society is going through circumstances which sadden, perplex or irritate it, it exercises a pressure over its members, to make them bear witness, by significant acts, to their sorrow, perplexity or anger. It imposes upon them the duty of weeping, groaning or inflicting wounds upon themselves or others, for these collective manifestations, and the moral communion which they show and strengthen, restore to the group the energy which circumstances threaten to take away from it, and thus they enable it to become settled. This is the experience which men interpret when they imagine that outside them there are evil beings whose hostility, whether constitutional or temporary, can be appeased only by human suffering. These beings are nothing other than collective states objectified; they are society itself seen under one of its aspects. But we also know that the benevolent powers are constituted in the same way; they, too, result from the collective life and express it; they, too, represent the society, but seen from a very different attitude, to wit, at the moment when it confidently affirms itself and ardently presses on towards the realization of the ends which it pursues. Since

[1] It is true that Smith did not admit the reality of these substitutions and transformations. According to him, if the expiatory victim served to purify, it was because it had nothing impure in itself. At first, it was a holy thing; it was destined to re-establish, by means of a communion, the bonds of kinship uniting the worshipper to his god, when a ritual fault had strained or broken them. An exceptionally holy animal was chosen for this operation in order that the communion might be as efficacious as possible, and efface the effects of the fault as completely as possible. It was only when they no longer understood the meaning of the rite that the sacrosanct animal was considered impure (*op. cit.*, pp. 347 ff.). But it is inadmissible that beliefs and practices as universal as these, which we find at the foundation of the expiatory sacrifice, should be the product of a mere error of interpretation. In fact, we cannot doubt that the expiatory victim was charged with the impurity of the sin. We have shown, moreover, that these transformations of the pure into the impure, or the contrary, are to be found in the most inferior societies which we know.

these two sorts of forces have a common origin, it is not at all surprising that, though facing in opposite directions, they should have the same nature, that they are equally intense and contagious and consequently forbidden and sacred.

From this we are able to understand how they change into one another. Since they reflect the abjective state in which the group happens to be, it is enough that this state change for their character to change. After the mourning is over, the domestic group is re-calmed by the mourning itself; it regains confidence; the painful pressure which they felt exercised over them is relieved; they feel more at their ease. So it seems to them as though the spirit of the deceased had laid aside its hostile sentiments and become a benevolent protector. The other transmutations, examples of which we have cited, are to be explained in the same way. As we have already shown, the sanctity of a thing is due to the collective sentiment of which it is the object. If, in violation of the interdicts which isolate it, it comes in contact with a profane person, then this same sentiment will spread contagiously to this latter and imprint a special character upon him. But in spreading, it comes into a very different state from the one it was in at first. Offended and irritated by the profanation implied in this abusive and unnatural extension, it becomes aggressive and inclined to destructive violences: it tends to avenge itself for the offence suffered. Therefore the infected subject seems to be filled with a mighty and harmful force which menaces all that approaches him; it is as though he were marked with a stain or blemish. Yet the cause of this blemish is the same psychic state which, in other circumstances, consecrates and sanctifies. But if the anger thus aroused is satisfied by an expiatory rite, it subsides, alleviated; the offended sentiment is appeased and returns to its original state. So it acts once more as it acted in the beginning; instead of contaminating, it sanctifies. As it continues to infect the object to which it is attached, this could never become profane and religiously indifferent again. But the direction of the religious force with which it seems to be filled is inverted: from being impure, it has become pure and an instrument of purification.

In résumé, the two poles of the religious life correspond to the two opposed states through which all social life passes. Between the propitiously sacred and the unpropitiously sacred there is the same contrast as between the states of collective well-being and ill-being. But since both are equally collective, there is, between the mythological constructions symbolizing them, an intimate kinship of nature. The sentiments held in common vary from extreme dejection to extreme joy, from painful irritation to ecstatic enthusiasm; but, in any case, there is a communion of minds and a mutual comfort resulting from this communion. The fundamental process is always the same; only circumstances colour it differently. So, at bottom, it is the unity and the diversity of social life which make the simultaneous unity and diversity of sacred beings and things.

This ambiguity, moreover, is not peculiar to the idea of sacredness alone; something of this characteristic has been found in all the rites which we have been studying. Of course it was essential to distinguish them; to confuse them would have been to misunderstand the multiple aspects of the religious life. But, on the other hand, howsoever different they may be, there is no break of continuity between them. Quite on the contrary, they overlap one another and may even replace each other mutually. We have already shown how the rites of oblation and communion, the imitative rites and the commemorative rites frequently fulfil the same function. One might imagine that the negative cult, at least, would be more sharply separated from the positive cult; yet we have seen that the former may produce positive effects, identical with those produced by the latter. The same results are obtained by fasts, abstinences and self-mutilations as by communions, oblations and commemorations. Inversely, offerings and sacrifices imply privations and renunciations of every sort. The continuity between ascetic and piacular rites is even more apparent: both are made up of sufferings, accepted or undergone, to which an analogous efficacy is attributed. Thus the practices, like the beliefs, are not arranged in two separate classes. Howsoever complex the outward manifestations of the religious life may be, at bottom it is one and simple. It responds everywhere to one and the same need, and is everywhere derived from one and the same mental state. In all its forms, its object is to raise man above himself and to make him lead a life superior to that which he would lead, if he followed only his own individual whims: beliefs express this life in representations; rites organize it and regulate its working.

CONCLUSION

AT the beginning of this work we announced that the religion whose study we were taking up contained within it the most characteristic elements of the religious life. The exactness of this proposition may now be verified. Howsoever simple the system which we have studied may be, we have found within it all the great ideas and the principal ritual attitudes which are at the basis of even the most advanced religions: the division of things into sacred and profane, the notions of the soul, of spirits, of mythical personalities, and of a national and even international divinity, a negative cult with ascetic practices which are its exaggerated form, rites of oblation and communion, imitative rites, commemorative rites and expiatory rites; nothing essential is lacking. We are thus in a position to hope that the results at which we have arrived are not peculiar to totemism alone, but can aid us in an understanding of what religion in general is.

It may be objected that one single religion, whatever its field of extension may be, is too narrow a base for such an induction. We have not dreamed for a moment of ignoring the fact that an extended verification may add to the authority of a theory, but it is equally true that when a law has been proven by one well-made experiment, this proof is valid universally. If in one single case a scientist succeeded in finding out the secret of the life of even the most protoplasmic creature that can be imagined, the truths thus obtained would be applicable to all living beings, even the most advanced. Then if, in our studies of these very humble societies, we have really succeeded in discovering some of the elements out of which the most fundamental religious notions are made up, there is no reason for not extending the most general results of our researches to other religions. In fact, it is inconceivable that the same effect may be due now to one cause, now to another, according to the circumstances, unless the two causes are at bottom only one. A single idea cannot express one reality here and another one there, unless the duality is only apparent. If among certain peoples the ideas of sacredness, the soul and God are to be explained sociologically, it should be presumed scientifically that, in principle, the same explanation is valid for all the peoples among whom these same ideas are found with the same essential characteristics. Therefore, supposing that we have not been deceived, certain at least of our conclusions can be legitimately generalized. The moment has come to disengage these. And an induction of this sort, having at its foundation a clearly defined experiment, is less adventurous than many summary generalizations which, while attempting to reach the essence of religion at once, without resting upon the careful analysis of any religion in particular, greatly risk losing themselves in space.

I

The theorists who have undertaken to explain religion in rational terms have generally seen in it before all else a system of ideas, corresponding to some determined object. This object has been conceived in a multitude of ways: nature, the infinite, the unknowable, the ideal, etc.; but these differences matter but little. In any case, it was the conceptions and beliefs which were considered as the essential elements of religion. As for the rites, from this point of view they appear to be only an external translation, contingent and material, of these internal states which alone pass as having any intrinsic value. This conception is so commonly held that generally the disputes of which religion is the theme turn about the question whether it can conciliate itself with science or not, that is to say, whether or not there is a place beside our scientific knowledge for another form of thought which would be specifically religious.

But the believers, the men who lead the religious life and have a direct sensation of what it really is, object to this way of regarding it, saying that it does not correspond to their daily experience. In fact, they feel that the real function of religion is not to make us think, to enrich our knowledge, nor to add to the conceptions which we owe to science others of another origin and another character, but rather, it is to make us act, to aid us to live. The believer who has communicated with his god is not merely a man who sees new truths of which the unbeliever is ignorant; he is a man who is *stronger*. He feels within him more force, either to endure the trials of existence, or to conquer them. It is as though he were raised above the miseries of the world, because he is raised above his condition as a mere man; he believes that he is saved from evil, under whatever form he may conceive this evil. The first article in every creed is the belief in salvation by faith. But it is hard to see how a mere idea could have this efficacy. An idea is in reality only a part of ourselves; then how could it confer upon us powers superior to those which we have of our own nature? Howsoever rich it might be in affective virtues, it could add nothing to our natural vitality; for it could only release the motive powers which are within us, neither creating them nor increasing them. From the mere fact that we consider an object worthy of being loved and sought after, it does not follow that we feel ourselves stronger afterwards; it is also necessary that this object set free energies superior to these which we ordinarily have at our command and also that we have some means of making these enter into us and unite themselves to our interior lives. Now for that, it is not enough that we think of them; it is also indispensable that we place ourselves within their sphere of action, and that we set ourselves where we may best feel their influence; in a word, it is necessary that we act, and that we repeat the acts thus necessary every time we feel the need of renewing their effects. From this point of view, it is readily seen how that group of regularly repeated acts which form the cult get their importance. In fact, whoever has really practised a religion knows very well that it is the cult which gives rise to these impressions of joy, of interior peace, of serenity, of enthusiasm which are, for the believer, an experimental proof of his beliefs. The cult is not simply a system of signs by which the faith is outwardly translated; it is a collection of the means by which this is created and recreated periodically. Whether it consists in material acts or mental operations, it is always this which is efficacious.

Our entire study rests upon this postulate that the unanimous sentiment of the believers of all times cannot be purely illusory. Together with a recent apologist of the faith [1] we admit that these religious beliefs rest upon a specific experience whose demonstrative value is, in one sense, not one bit inferior to that of scientific experiments, though different from them. We, too, think that "a tree is known by its fruits," [2] and that fertility is the best proof of what the roots are worth. But from the fact that a "religious experience," if we choose to call it this, does exist and that it has a certain foundation—and, by the way, is there any experience which has none?—it does not follow that the reality which is its foundation conforms objectively to the idea which believers have of it. The very fact that the fashion in which it has been conceived has varied infinitely in different times is enough to prove that none of these conceptions express it adequately. If a scientist states it as an axiom

[1] William James, *The Varieties of Religious Experience.*
[2] Quoted by James, *op. cit.*, p. 20.

that the sensations of heat and light which we feel correspond to some objective cause, he does not conclude that this is what it appears to the senses to be. Likewise, even if the impressions which the faithful feel are not imaginary, still they are in no way privileged intuitions; there is no reason for believing that they inform us better upon the nature of their object than do ordinary sensations upon the nature of bodies and their properties. In order to discover what this object consists of, we must submit them to an examination and elaboration analogous to that which has substituted for the sensuous idea of the world another which is scientific and conceptual.

This is precisely what we have tried to do, and we have seen that this reality, which mythologies have represented under so many different forms, but which is the universal and eternal objective cause of these sensations *sui generis* out of which religious experience is made, is society. We have shown what moral forces it develops and how it awakens this sentiment of a refuge, of a shield and of a guardian support which attaches the believer to his cult. It is that which raises him outside himself; it is even that which made him. For that which makes a man is the totality of the intellectual property which constitutes civilization, and civilization is the work of society. Thus is explained the preponderating rôle of the cult in all religions, whichever they may be. This is because society cannot make its influence felt unless it is in action, and it is not in action unless the individuals who compose it are assembled together and act in common. It is by common action that it takes consciousness of itself and realizes its position; it is before all else an active co-operation. The collective ideas and sentiments are even possible only owing to these exterior movements which symbolize them, as we have established.[1] Then it is action which dominates the religious life, because of the mere fact that it is society which is its source.

In addition to all the reasons which have been given to justify this conception, a final one may be added here, which is the result of our whole work. As we have progressed, we have established the fact that the fundamental categories of thought, and consequently of science, are of religious origin. We have seen that the same is true for magic and consequently for the different processes which have issued from it. On the other hand, it has long been known that up until a relatively advanced moment of evolution, moral and legal rules have been indistinguishable from ritual prescriptions. In summing up, then, it may be said that nearly all the great social institutions have

[1] See above, pp. 230 ff.

been born in religion.[1] Now in order that these principal aspects of the collective life may have commenced by being only varied aspects of the religious life, it is obviously necessary that the religious life be the eminent form and, as it were, the concentrated expression of the whole collective life. If religion has given birth to all that is essential in society, it is because the idea of society is the soul of religion.

Religious forces are therefore human forces, moral forces. It is true that since collective sentiments can become conscious of themselves only by fixing themselves upon external objects, they have not been able to take form without adopting some of their characteristics from other things: they have thus acquired a sort of physical nature; in this way they have come to mix themselves with the life of the material world, and then have considered themselves capable of explaining what passes there. But when they are considered only from this point of view and in this rôle, only their most superficial aspect is seen. In reality, the essential elements of which these collective sentiments are made have been borrowed by the understanding. It ordinarily seems that they should have a human character only when they are conceived under human forms;[2] but even the most impersonal and the most anonymous are nothing else than objectified sentiments.

It is only by regarding religion from this angle that it is possible to see its real significance. If we stick closely to appearances, rites often give the effect of purely manual operations: they are anointings, washings, meals. To consecrate something, it is put in contact with a source of religious energy, just as to-day a body is put in contact with a source of heat or electricity to warm or electrize it; the two processes employed are not essentially different. Thus understood, religious technique seems to be a sort of mystic mechanics. But these material manœuvres are only the external envelope under which the mental operations are hidden. Finally, there is no question of exercising a physical constraint upon blind and, incidentally, imaginary forces, but rather of reaching individual consciousnesses, of giving them a direction and of disciplining them. It is sometimes said

[1] Only one form of social activity has not yet been expressly attached to religion: that is economic activity. Sometimes processes that are derived from magic have, by that fact alone, an origin that is indirectly religious. Also, economic value is a sort of power or efficacy, and we know the religious origins of the idea of power. Also, richness can confer *mana*; therefore it has it. Hence it is seen that the ideas of economic value and of religious value are not without connection. But the question of the nature of these connections has not yet been studied.

[2] It is for this reason that Frazer and even Preuss set impersonal religious forces outside of, or at least on the threshold of religion, to attach them to magic.

that inferior religions are materialistic. Such an expression is inexact. All religions, even the crudest, are in a sense spiritualistic: for the powers they put in play are before all spiritual, and also their principal object is to act upon the moral life. Thus it is seen that whatever has been done in the name of religion cannot have been done in vain: for it is necessarily the society that did it, and it is humanity that has reaped the fruits.

But, it is said, what society is it that has thus made the basis of religion? Is it the real society, such as it is and acts before our very eyes, with the legal and moral organization which it has laboriously fashioned during the course of history? This is full of defects and imperfections. In it, evil goes beside the good, injustice often reigns supreme, and the truth is often obscured by error. How could anything so crudely organized inspire the sentiments of love, the ardent enthusiasm and the spirit of abnegation which all religions claim of their followers? These perfect beings which are gods could not have taken their traits from so mediocre, and sometimes even so base a reality.

But, on the other hand, does someone think of a perfect society, where justice and truth would be sovereign, and from which evil in all its forms would be banished for ever? No one would deny that this is in close relations with the religious sentiment; for, they would say, it is towards the realization of this that all religions strive. But that society is not an empirical fact, definite and observable; it is a fancy, a dream with which men have lightened their sufferings, but in which they have never really lived. It is merely an idea which comes to express our more or less obscure aspirations towards the good, the beautiful and the ideal. Now these aspirations have their roots in us; they come from the very depths of our being; then there is nothing outside of us which can account for them. Moreover, they are already religious in themselves; thus it would seem that the ideal society presupposes religion, far from being able to explain it.[1]

But, in the first place, things are arbitrarily simplified when religion is seen only on its idealistic side: in its way, it is realistic. There is no physical or moral ugliness, there are no vices or evils which do not have a special divinity. There are gods of theft and trickery, of lust and war, of sickness and of death. Christianity itself, howsoever high the idea which it has made of the divinity may be, has been obliged to give the spirit of evil a place in its mythology. Satan is an essential piece of the Christian system; even if he is an impure being, he is not a profane one. The anti-god is a god, inferior and subordinated, it is true, but

[1] Boutroux, *Science et Religion*, pp. 206–207.

nevertheless endowed with extended powers; he is even the object of rites, at least of negative ones. Thus religion, far from ignoring the real society and making abstraction of it, is in its image; it reflects all its aspects, even the most vulgar and the most repulsive. All is to be found there, and if in the majority of cases we see the good victorious over evil, life over death, the powers of light over the powers of darkness, it is because reality is not otherwise. If the relation between these two contrary forces were reversed, life would be impossible; but, as a matter of fact, it maintains itself and even tends to develop.

But if, in the midst of these mythologies and theologies we see reality clearly appearing, it is none the less true that it is found there only in an enlarged, transformed and idealized form. In this respect, the most primitive religions do not differ from the most recent and the most refined. For example, we have seen how the Arunta place at the beginning of time a mythical society whose organization exactly reproduces that which still exists to-day; it includes the same clans and phratries, it is under the same matrimonial rules and it practises the same rites. But the personages who compose it are ideal beings, gifted with powers and virtues to which common mortals cannot pretend. Their nature is not only higher, but it is different, since it is at once animal and human. The evil powers there undergo a similar metamorphosis: evil itself is, as it were, made sublime and idealized. The question now raises itself of whence this idealization comes.

Some reply that men have a natural faculty for idealizing, that is to say, of substituting for the real world another different one, to which they transport themselves by thought. But that is merely changing the terms of the problem; it is not resolving it or even advancing it. This systematic idealization is an essential characteristic of religions. Explaining them by an innate power of idealization is simply replacing one word by another which is the equivalent of the first; it is as if they said that men have made religions because they have a religious nature. Animals know only one world, the one which they perceive by experience, internal as well as external. Men alone have the faculty of conceiving the ideal, of adding something to the real. Now where does this singular privilege come from? Before making it an initial fact or a mysterious virtue which escapes science, we must be sure that it does not depend upon empirically determinable conditions.

The explanation of religion which we have proposed has precisely this advantage, that it gives an answer to this question.

For our definition of the sacred is that it is something added to and above the real: now the ideal answers to this same definition; we cannot explain one without explaining the other. In fact, we have seen that if collective life awakens religious thought on reaching a certain degree of intensity, it is because it brings about a state of effervescence which changes the conditions of psychic activity. Vital energies are over-excited, passions more active, sensations stronger; there are even some which are produced only at this moment. A man does not recognize himself; he feels himself transformed and consequently he transforms the environment which surrounds him. In order to account for the very particular impressions which he receives, he attributes to the things with which he is in most direct contact properties which they have not, exceptional powers and virtues which the objects of every-day experience do not possess. In a word, above the real world where his profane life passes he has placed another which, in one sense, does not exist except in thought, but to which he attributes a higher sort of dignity than to the first. Thus, from a double point of view it is an ideal world.

The formation of the ideal world is therefore not an irreducible fact which escapes science; it depends upon conditions which observation can touch; it is a natural product of social life. For a society to become conscious of itself and maintain at the necessary degree of intensity the sentiments which it thus attains, it must assemble and concentrate itself. Now this concentration brings about an exaltation of the mental life which takes form in a group of ideal conceptions where is portrayed the new life thus awakened; they correspond to this new set of psychical forces which is added to those which we have at our disposition for the daily tasks of existence. A society can neither create itself nor recreate itself without at the same time creating an ideal. This creation is not a sort of work of supererogation for it, by which it would complete itself, being already formed; it is the act by which it is periodically made and remade. Therefore when some oppose the ideal society to the real society, like two antagonists which would lead us in opposite directions, they materialize and oppose abstractions. The ideal society is not outside of the real society; it is a part of it. Far from being divided between them as between two poles which mutually repel each other, we cannot hold to one without holding to the other. For a society is not made up merely of the mass of individuals who compose it, the ground which they occupy, the things which they use and the movements which they perform, but above all is the idea which it forms of itself. It is un-

HINTS TO SINGERS, Lillian Nordica. Selecting the right teacher, developing confidence, overcoming stage fright, and many other important skills receive thoughtful discussion in this indispensible guide, written by a world-famous diva of four decades' experience. 96pp. 5⅜ x 8½. 0-486-40094-8

THE COMPLETE NONSENSE OF EDWARD LEAR, Edward Lear. All nonsense limericks, zany alphabets, Owl and Pussycat, songs, nonsense botany, etc., illustrated by Lear. Total of 320pp. 5⅜ x 8½. (Available in U.S. only.) 0-486-20167-8

VICTORIAN PARLOUR POETRY: An Annotated Anthology, Michael R. Turner. 117 gems by Longfellow, Tennyson, Browning, many lesser-known poets. "The Village Blacksmith," "Curfew Must Not Ring Tonight," "Only a Baby Small," dozens more, often difficult to find elsewhere. Index of poets, titles, first lines. xxiii + 325pp. 5⅜ x 8¼. 0-486-27044-0

DUBLINERS, James Joyce. Fifteen stories offer vivid, tightly focused observations of the lives of Dublin's poorer classes. At least one, "The Dead," is considered a masterpiece. Reprinted complete and unabridged from standard edition. 160pp. 5$\frac{3}{16}$ x 8¼. 0-486-26870-5

GREAT WEIRD TALES: 14 Stories by Lovecraft, Blackwood, Machen and Others, S. T. Joshi (ed.). 14 spellbinding tales, including "The Sin Eater," by Fiona McLeod, "The Eye Above the Mantel," by Frank Belknap Long, as well as renowned works by R. H. Barlow, Lord Dunsany, Arthur Machen, W. C. Morrow and eight other masters of the genre. 256pp. 5⅜ x 8½. (Available in U.S. only.) 0-486-40436-6

THE BOOK OF THE SACRED MAGIC OF ABRAMELIN THE MAGE, translated by S. MacGregor Mathers. Medieval manuscript of ceremonial magic. Basic document in Aleister Crowley, Golden Dawn groups. 268pp. 5⅜ x 8½. 0-486-23211-5

THE BATTLES THAT CHANGED HISTORY, Fletcher Pratt. Eminent historian profiles 16 crucial conflicts, ancient to modern, that changed the course of civilization. 352pp. 5⅜ x 8½. 0-486-41129-X

NEW RUSSIAN-ENGLISH AND ENGLISH-RUSSIAN DICTIONARY, M. A. O'Brien. This is a remarkably handy Russian dictionary, containing a surprising amount of information, including over 70,000 entries. 366pp. 4½ x 6⅛. 0-486-20208-9

NEW YORK IN THE FORTIES, Andreas Feininger. 162 brilliant photographs by the well-known photographer, formerly with *Life* magazine. Commuters, shoppers, Times Square at night, much else from city at its peak. Captions by John von Hartz. 181pp. 9¼ x 10¾. 0-486-23585-8

INDIAN SIGN LANGUAGE, William Tomkins. Over 525 signs developed by Sioux and other tribes. Written instructions and diagrams. Also 290 pictographs. 111pp. 6⅛ x 9¼. 0-486-22029-X

ANATOMY: A Complete Guide for Artists, Joseph Sheppard. A master of figure drawing shows artists how to render human anatomy convincingly. Over 460 illustrations. 224pp. 8⅜ x 11¼. 0-486-27279-6

MEDIEVAL CALLIGRAPHY: Its History and Technique, Marc Drogin. Spirited history, comprehensive instruction manual covers 13 styles (ca. 4th century through 15th). Excellent photographs; directions for duplicating medieval techniques with modern tools. 224pp. 8⅜ x 11¼. 0-486-26142-5

CATALOG OF DOVER BOOKS

HOW TO DO BEADWORK, Mary White. Fundamental book on craft from simple projects to five-bead chains and woven works. 106 illustrations. 142pp. 5⅜ x 8. 0-486-20697-1

THE 1912 AND 1915 GUSTAV STICKLEY FURNITURE CATALOGS, Gustav Stickley. With over 200 detailed illustrations and descriptions, these two catalogs are essential reading and reference materials and identification guides for Stickley furniture. Captions cite materials, dimensions and prices. 112pp. 6½ x 9¼. 0-486-26676-1

EARLY AMERICAN LOCOMOTIVES, John H. White, Jr. Finest locomotive engravings from early 19th century: historical (1804–74), main-line (after 1870), special, foreign, etc. 147 plates. 142pp. 11⅜ x 8¼. 0-486-22772-3

LITTLE BOOK OF EARLY AMERICAN CRAFTS AND TRADES, Peter Stockham (ed.). 1807 children's book explains crafts and trades: baker, hatter, cooper, potter, and many others. 23 copperplate illustrations. 140pp. 4⅝ x 6. 0-486-23336-7

VICTORIAN FASHIONS AND COSTUMES FROM HARPER'S BAZAR, 1867–1898, Stella Blum (ed.). Day costumes, evening wear, sports clothes, shoes, hats, other accessories in over 1,000 detailed engravings. 320pp. 9⅜ x 12¼. 0-486-22990-4

THE LONG ISLAND RAIL ROAD IN EARLY PHOTOGRAPHS, Ron Ziel. Over 220 rare photos, informative text document origin (1844) and development of rail service on Long Island. Vintage views of early trains, locomotives, stations, passengers, crews, much more. Captions. 8⅞ x 11¾. 0-486-26301-0

VOYAGE OF THE LIBERDADE, Joshua Slocum. Great 19th-century mariner's thrilling, first-hand account of the wreck of his ship off South America, the 35-foot boat he built from the wreckage, and its remarkable voyage home. 128pp. 5⅜ x 8½. 0-486-40022-0

TEN BOOKS ON ARCHITECTURE, Vitruvius. The most important book ever written on architecture. Early Roman aesthetics, technology, classical orders, site selection, all other aspects. Morgan translation. 331pp. 5⅜ x 8½. 0-486-20645-9

THE HUMAN FIGURE IN MOTION, Eadweard Muybridge. More than 4,500 stopped-action photos, in action series, showing undraped men, women, children jumping, lying down, throwing, sitting, wrestling, carrying, etc. 390pp. 7⅞ x 10⅝. 0-486-20204-6 Clothbd.

TREES OF THE EASTERN AND CENTRAL UNITED STATES AND CANADA, William M. Harlow. Best one-volume guide to 140 trees. Full descriptions, woodlore, range, etc. Over 600 illustrations. Handy size. 288pp. 4½ x 6⅜. 0-486-20395-6

GROWING AND USING HERBS AND SPICES, Milo Miloradovich. Versatile handbook provides all the information needed for cultivation and use of all the herbs and spices available in North America. 4 illustrations. Index. Glossary. 236pp. 5⅜ x 8½. 0-486-25058-X

BIG BOOK OF MAZES AND LABYRINTHS, Walter Shepherd. 50 mazes and labyrinths in all–classical, solid, ripple, and more–in one great volume. Perfect inexpensive puzzler for clever youngsters. Full solutions. 112pp. 8⅛ x 11. 0-486-22951-3

PIANO TUNING, J. Cree Fischer. Clearest, best book for beginner, amateur. Simple repairs, raising dropped notes, tuning by easy method of flattened fifths. No previous skills needed. 4 illustrations. 201pp. 5⅜ x 8½. 0-486-23267-0

PSYCHOLOGY OF MUSIC, Carl E. Seashore. Classic work discusses music as a medium from psychological viewpoint. Clear treatment of physical acoustics, auditory apparatus, sound perception, development of musical skills, nature of musical feeling, host of other topics. 88 figures. 408pp. 5⅜ x 8½. 0-486-21851-1

LIFE IN ANCIENT EGYPT, Adolf Erman. Fullest, most thorough, detailed older account with much not in more recent books, domestic life, religion, magic, medicine, commerce, much more. Many illustrations reproduce tomb paintings, carvings, hieroglyphs, etc. 597pp. 5⅜ x 8½. 0-486-22632-8

SUNDIALS, Their Theory and Construction, Albert Waugh. Far and away the best, most thorough coverage of ideas, mathematics concerned, types, construction, adjusting anywhere. Simple, nontechnical treatment allows even children to build several of these dials. Over 100 illustrations. 230pp. 5⅜ x 8½. 0-486-22947-5

THEORETICAL HYDRODYNAMICS, L. M. Milne-Thomson. Classic exposition of the mathematical theory of fluid motion, applicable to both hydrodynamics and aerodynamics. Over 600 exercises. 768pp. 6⅛ x 9¼. 0-486-68970-0

OLD-TIME VIGNETTES IN FULL COLOR, Carol Belanger Grafton (ed.). Over 390 charming, often sentimental illustrations, selected from archives of Victorian graphics–pretty women posing, children playing, food, flowers, kittens and puppies, smiling cherubs, birds and butterflies, much more. All copyright-free. 48pp. 9¼ x 12¼. 0-486-27269-9

PERSPECTIVE FOR ARTISTS, Rex Vicat Cole. Depth, perspective of sky and sea, shadows, much more, not usually covered. 391 diagrams, 81 reproductions of drawings and paintings. 279pp. 5⅜ x 8½. 0-486-22487-2

DRAWING THE LIVING FIGURE, Joseph Sheppard. Innovative approach to artistic anatomy focuses on specifics of surface anatomy, rather than muscles and bones. Over 170 drawings of live models in front, back and side views, and in widely varying poses. Accompanying diagrams. 177 illustrations. Introduction. Index. 144pp. 8⅜ x11¼. 0-486-26723-7

GOTHIC AND OLD ENGLISH ALPHABETS: 100 Complete Fonts, Dan X. Solo. Add power, elegance to posters, signs, other graphics with 100 stunning copyright-free alphabets: Blackstone, Dolbey, Germania, 97 more–including many lower-case, numerals, punctuation marks. 104pp. 8⅛ x 11. 0-486-24695-7

THE BOOK OF WOOD CARVING, Charles Marshall Sayers. Finest book for beginners discusses fundamentals and offers 34 designs. "Absolutely first rate . . . well thought out and well executed."–E. J. Tangerman. 118pp. 7¾ x 10⅝. 0-486-23654-4

ILLUSTRATED CATALOG OF CIVIL WAR MILITARY GOODS: Union Army Weapons, Insignia, Uniform Accessories, and Other Equipment, Schuyler, Hartley, and Graham. Rare, profusely illustrated 1846 catalog includes Union Army uniform and dress regulations, arms and ammunition, coats, insignia, flags, swords, rifles, etc. 226 illustrations. 160pp. 9 x 12. 0-486-24939-5

WOMEN'S FASHIONS OF THE EARLY 1900s: An Unabridged Republication of "New York Fashions, 1909," National Cloak & Suit Co. Rare catalog of mail-order fashions documents women's and children's clothing styles shortly after the turn of the century. Captions offer full descriptions, prices. Invaluable resource for fashion, costume historians. Approximately 725 illustrations. 128pp. 8⅜ x 11¼. 0-486-27276-1

CATALOG OF DOVER BOOKS

ANIMALS: 1,419 Copyright-Free Illustrations of Mammals, Birds, Fish, Insects, etc., Jim Harter (ed.). Clear wood engravings present, in extremely lifelike poses, over 1,000 species of animals. One of the most extensive pictorial sourcebooks of its kind. Captions. Index. 284pp. 9 x 12. 0-486-23766-4

1001 QUESTIONS ANSWERED ABOUT THE SEASHORE, N. J. Berrill and Jacquelyn Berrill. Queries answered about dolphins, sea snails, sponges, starfish, fishes, shore birds, many others. Covers appearance, breeding, growth, feeding, much more. 305pp. 5¼ x 8¼. 0-486-23366-9

ATTRACTING BIRDS TO YOUR YARD, William J. Weber. Easy-to-follow guide offers advice on how to attract the greatest diversity of birds: birdhouses, feeders, water and waterers, much more. 96pp. $5\frac{3}{16}$ x 8¼. 0-486-28927-3

MEDICINAL AND OTHER USES OF NORTH AMERICAN PLANTS: A Historical Survey with Special Reference to the Eastern Indian Tribes, Charlotte Erichsen-Brown. Chronological historical citations document 500 years of usage of plants, trees, shrubs native to eastern Canada, northeastern U.S. Also complete identifying information. 343 illustrations. 544pp. 6½ x 9¼. 0-486-25951-X

STORYBOOK MAZES, Dave Phillips. 23 stories and mazes on two-page spreads: Wizard of Oz, Treasure Island, Robin Hood, etc. Solutions. 64pp. 8¼ x 11. 0-486-23628-5

AMERICAN NEGRO SONGS: 230 Folk Songs and Spirituals, Religious and Secular, John W. Work. This authoritative study traces the African influences of songs sung and played by black Americans at work, in church, and as entertainment. The author discusses the lyric significance of such songs as "Swing Low, Sweet Chariot," "John Henry," and others and offers the words and music for 230 songs. Bibliography. Index of Song Titles. 272pp. 6½ x 9¼. 0-486-40271-1

MOVIE-STAR PORTRAITS OF THE FORTIES, John Kobal (ed.). 163 glamor, studio photos of 106 stars of the 1940s: Rita Hayworth, Ava Gardner, Marlon Brando, Clark Gable, many more. 176pp. 8⅜ x 11¼. 0-486-23546-7

YEKL and THE IMPORTED BRIDEGROOM AND OTHER STORIES OF YIDDISH NEW YORK, Abraham Cahan. Film Hester Street based on *Yekl* (1896). Novel, other stories among first about Jewish immigrants on N.Y.'s East Side. 240pp. 5⅜ x 8½. 0-486-22427-9

SELECTED POEMS, Walt Whitman. Generous sampling from *Leaves of Grass*. Twenty-four poems include "I Hear America Singing," "Song of the Open Road," "I Sing the Body Electric," "When Lilacs Last in the Dooryard Bloom'd," "O Captain! My Captain!"–all reprinted from an authoritative edition. Lists of titles and first lines. 128pp. $5\frac{3}{16}$ x 8¼. 0-486-26878-0

SONGS OF EXPERIENCE: Facsimile Reproduction with 26 Plates in Full Color, William Blake. 26 full-color plates from a rare 1826 edition. Includes "The Tyger," "London," "Holy Thursday," and other poems. Printed text of poems. 48pp. 5¼ x 7. 0-486-24636-1

THE BEST TALES OF HOFFMANN, E. T. A. Hoffmann. 10 of Hoffmann's most important stories: "Nutcracker and the King of Mice," "The Golden Flowerpot," etc. 458pp. 5⅜ x 8½. 0-486-21793-0

THE BOOK OF TEA, Kakuzo Okakura. Minor classic of the Orient: entertaining, charming explanation, interpretation of traditional Japanese culture in terms of tea ceremony. 94pp. 5⅜ x 8½. 0-486-20070-1

THE CLARINET AND CLARINET PLAYING, David Pino. Lively, comprehensive work features suggestions about technique, musicianship, and musical interpretation, as well as guidelines for teaching, making your own reeds, and preparing for public performance. Includes an intriguing look at clarinet history. "A godsend," *The Clarinet,* Journal of the International Clarinet Society. Appendixes. 7 illus. 320pp. 5⅜ x 8½. 0-486-40270-3

HOLLYWOOD GLAMOR PORTRAITS, John Kobal (ed.). 145 photos from 1926-49. Harlow, Gable, Bogart, Bacall; 94 stars in all. Full background on photographers, technical aspects. 160pp. 8⅜ x 11¼. 0-486-23352-9

THE RAVEN AND OTHER FAVORITE POEMS, Edgar Allan Poe. Over 40 of the author's most memorable poems: "The Bells," "Ulalume," "Israfel," "To Helen," "The Conqueror Worm," "Eldorado," "Annabel Lee," many more. Alphabetic lists of titles and first lines. 64pp. 5$^{3}/_{16}$ x 8¼. 0-486-26685-0

PERSONAL MEMOIRS OF U. S. GRANT, Ulysses Simpson Grant. Intelligent, deeply moving firsthand account of Civil War campaigns, considered by many the finest military memoirs ever written. Includes letters, historic photographs, maps and more. 528pp. 6⅛ x 9¼. 0-486-28587-1

ANCIENT EGYPTIAN MATERIALS AND INDUSTRIES, A. Lucas and J. Harris. Fascinating, comprehensive, thoroughly documented text describes this ancient civilization's vast resources and the processes that incorporated them in daily life, including the use of animal products, building materials, cosmetics, perfumes and incense, fibers, glazed ware, glass and its manufacture, materials used in the mummification process, and much more. 544pp. 6$^{1}/_{8}$ x 9$^{1}/_{4}$. (Available in U.S. only.) 0-486-40446-3

RUSSIAN STORIES/RUSSKIE RASSKAZY: A Dual-Language Book, edited by Gleb Struve. Twelve tales by such masters as Chekhov, Tolstoy, Dostoevsky, Pushkin, others. Excellent word-for-word English translations on facing pages, plus teaching and study aids, Russian/English vocabulary, biographical/critical introductions, more. 416pp. 5⅜ x 8½. 0-486-26244-8

PHILADELPHIA THEN AND NOW: 60 Sites Photographed in the Past and Present, Kenneth Finkel and Susan Oyama. Rare photographs of City Hall, Logan Square, Independence Hall, Betsy Ross House, other landmarks juxtaposed with contemporary views. Captures changing face of historic city. Introduction. Captions. 128pp. 8¼ x 11. 0-486-25790-8

NORTH AMERICAN INDIAN LIFE: Customs and Traditions of 23 Tribes, Elsie Clews Parsons (ed.). 27 fictionalized essays by noted anthropologists examine religion, customs, government, additional facets of life among the Winnebago, Crow, Zuni, Eskimo, other tribes. 480pp. 6⅛ x 9¼. 0-486-27377-6

TECHNICAL MANUAL AND DICTIONARY OF CLASSICAL BALLET, Gail Grant. Defines, explains, comments on steps, movements, poses and concepts. 15-page pictorial section. Basic book for student, viewer. 127pp. 5⅜ x 8½. 0-486-21843-0

THE MALE AND FEMALE FIGURE IN MOTION: 60 Classic Photographic Sequences, Eadweard Muybridge. 60 true-action photographs of men and women walking, running, climbing, bending, turning, etc., reproduced from rare 19th-century masterpiece. vi + 121pp. 9 x 12. 0-486-24745-7

STICKLEY CRAFTSMAN FURNITURE CATALOGS, Gustav Stickley and L. & J. G. Stickley. Beautiful, functional furniture in two authentic catalogs from 1910. 594 illustrations, including 277 photos, show settles, rockers, armchairs, reclining chairs, bookcases, desks, tables. 183pp. 6½ x 9¼. 0-486-23838-5

AMERICAN LOCOMOTIVES IN HISTORIC PHOTOGRAPHS: 1858 to 1949, Ron Ziel (ed.). A rare collection of 126 meticulously detailed official photographs, called "builder portraits," of American locomotives that majestically chronicle the rise of steam locomotive power in America. Introduction. Detailed captions. xi+ 129pp. 9 x 12. 0-486-27393-8

AMERICA'S LIGHTHOUSES: An Illustrated History, Francis Ross Holland, Jr. Delightfully written, profusely illustrated fact-filled survey of over 200 American lighthouses since 1716. History, anecdotes, technological advances, more. 240pp. 8 x 10¾. 0-486-25576-X

TOWARDS A NEW ARCHITECTURE, Le Corbusier. Pioneering manifesto by founder of "International School." Technical and aesthetic theories, views of industry, economics, relation of form to function, "mass-production split" and much more. Profusely illustrated. 320pp. 6⅛ x 9¼. (Available in U.S. only.) 0-486-25023-7

HOW THE OTHER HALF LIVES, Jacob Riis. Famous journalistic record, exposing poverty and degradation of New York slums around 1900, by major social reformer. 100 striking and influential photographs. 233pp. 10 x 7⅞. 0-486-22012-5

FRUIT KEY AND TWIG KEY TO TREES AND SHRUBS, William M. Harlow. One of the handiest and most widely used identification aids. Fruit key covers 120 deciduous and evergreen species; twig key 160 deciduous species. Easily used. Over 300 photographs. 126pp. 5⅜ x 8½. 0-486-20511-8

COMMON BIRD SONGS, Dr. Donald J. Borror. Songs of 60 most common U.S. birds: robins, sparrows, cardinals, bluejays, finches, more–arranged in order of increasing complexity. Up to 9 variations of songs of each species. Cassette and manual 0-486-99911-4

ORCHIDS AS HOUSE PLANTS, Rebecca Tyson Northen. Grow cattleyas and many other kinds of orchids–in a window, in a case, or under artificial light. 63 illustrations. 148pp. 5⅜ x 8½. 0-486-23261-1

MONSTER MAZES, Dave Phillips. Masterful mazes at four levels of difficulty. Avoid deadly perils and evil creatures to find magical treasures. Solutions for all 32 exciting illustrated puzzles. 48pp. 8¼ x 11. 0-486-26005-4

MOZART'S DON GIOVANNI (DOVER OPERA LIBRETTO SERIES), Wolfgang Amadeus Mozart. Introduced and translated by Ellen H. Bleiler. Standard Italian libretto, with complete English translation. Convenient and thoroughly portable–an ideal companion for reading along with a recording or the performance itself. Introduction. List of characters. Plot summary. 121pp. 5¼ x 8½. 0-486-24944-1

FRANK LLOYD WRIGHT'S DANA HOUSE, Donald Hoffmann. Pictorial essay of residential masterpiece with over 160 interior and exterior photos, plans, elevations, sketches and studies. 128pp. 9¼ x 10¾. 0-486-29120-0

A CATALOG OF SELECTED

DOVER BOOKS

IN ALL FIELDS OF INTEREST

doubtedly true that it hesitates over the manner in which it ought to conceive itself; it feels itself drawn in divergent directions. But these conflicts which break forth are not between the ideal and reality, but between two different ideals, that of yesterday and that of to-day, that which has the authority of tradition and that which has the hope of the future. There is surely a place for investigating whence these ideals evolve; but whatever solution may be given to this problem, it still remains that all passes in the world of the ideal.

Thus the collective ideal which religion expresses is far from being due to a vague innate power of the individual, but it is rather at the school of collective life that the individual has learned to idealize. It is in assimilating the ideals elaborated by society that he has become capable of conceiving the ideal. It is society which, by leading him within its sphere of action, has made him acquire the need of raising himself above the world of experience and has at the same time furnished him with the means of conceiving another. For society has constructed this new world in constructing itself, since it is society which this expresses. Thus both with the individual and in the group, the faculty of idealizing has nothing mysterious about it. It is not a sort of luxury which a man could get along without, but a condition of his very existence. He could not be a social being, that is to say, he could not be a man, if he had not acquired it. It is true that in incarnating themselves in individuals, collective ideals tend to individualize themselves. Each understands them after his own fashion and marks them with his own stamp; he suppresses certain elements and adds others. Thus the personal ideal disengages itself from the social ideal in proportion as the individual personality develops itself and becomes an autonomous source of action. But if we wish to understand this aptitude, so singular in appearance, of living outside of reality, it is enough to connect it with the social conditions upon which it depends.

Therefore it is necessary to avoid seeing in this theory of religion a simple restatement of historical materialism: that would be misunderstanding our thought to an extreme degree. In showing that religion is something essentially social, we do not mean to say that it confines itself to translating into another language the material forms of society and its immediate vital necessities. It is true that we take it as evident that social life depends upon its material foundation and bears its mark, just as the mental life of an individual depends upon his nervous system and in fact his whole organism. But collective consciousness is something more than a mere epiphenomenon of its

morphological basis, just as individual consciousness is something more than a simple efflorescence of the nervous system. In order that the former may appear, a synthesis *sui generis* of particular consciousnesses is required. Now this synthesis has the effect of disengaging a whole world of sentiments, ideas and images which, once born, obey laws all their own. They attract each other, repel each other, unite, divide themselves, and multiply, though these combinations are not commanded and necessitated by the condition of the underlying reality. The life thus brought into being even enjoys so great an independence that it sometimes indulges in manifestations with no purpose or utility of any sort, for the mere pleasure of affirming itself. We have shown that this is often precisely the case with ritual activity and mythological thought.[1]

But if religion is the product of social causes, how can we explain the individual cult and the universalistic character of certain religions ? If it is born *in foro externo,* how has it been able to pass into the inner conscience of the individual and penetrate there ever more and more profoundly ? If it is the work of definite and individualized societies, how has it been able to detach itself from them, even to the point of being conceived as something common to all humanity ?

In the course of our studies, we have met with the germs of individual religion and of religious cosmopolitanism, and we have seen how they were formed ; thus we possess the more general elements of the reply which is to be given to this double question.

We have shown how the religious force which animates the clan particularizes itself, by incarnating itself in particular consciousnesses. Thus secondary sacred beings are formed ; each individual has his own, made in his own image, associated to his own intimate life, bound up with his own destiny ; it is the soul, the individual totem, the protecting ancestor, etc. These beings are the object of rites which the individual can celebrate by himself, outside of any group ; this is the first form of the individual cult. To be sure, it is only a very rudimentary cult ; but since the personality of the individual is still only slightly marked, and but little value is attributed to it, the cult which expresses it could hardly be expected to be very highly developed as yet. But as individuals have differentiated themselves more and more and the value of an individual

[1] See above, pp. 379 ff. On this same question, see also our article, "Représentations individuelles et représentations collectives," in the *Revue de Métaphysique*, May, 1898.

has increased, the corresponding cult has taken a relatively greater place in the totality of the religious life and at the same time it is more fully closed to outside influences.

Thus the existence of individual cults implies nothing which contradicts or embarrasses the sociological interpretation of religion; for the religious forces to which it addresses itself are only the individualized forms of collective forces. Therefore, even when religion seems to be entirely within the individual conscience, it is still in society that it finds the living source from which it is nourished. We are now able to appreciate the value of the radical individualism which would make religion something purely individual: it misunderstands the fundamental conditions of the religious life. If up to the present it has remained in the stage of theoretical aspirations which have never been realized, it is because it is unrealizable. A philosophy may well be elaborated in the silence of the interior imagination, but not so a faith. For before all else, a faith is warmth, life, enthusiasm, the exaltation of the whole mental life, the raising of the individual above himself. Now how could he add to the energies which he possesses without going outside himself? How could he surpass himself merely by his own forces? The only source of life at which we can morally reanimate ourselves is that formed by the society of our fellow beings; the only moral forces with which we can sustain and increase our own are those which we get from others. Let us even admit that there really are beings more or less analogous to those which the mythologies represent. In order that they may exercise over souls the useful direction which is their reason for existence, it is necessary that men believe in them. Now these beliefs are active only when they are partaken by many. A man cannot retain them any length of time by a purely personal effort; it is not thus that they are born or that they are acquired; it is even doubtful if they can be kept under these conditions. In fact, a man who has a veritable faith feels an invincible need of spreading it: therefore he leaves his isolation, approaches others and seeks to convince them, and it is the ardour of the convictions which he arouses that strengthens his own. It would quickly weaken if it remained alone.

It is the same with religious universalism as with this individualism. Far from being an exclusive attribute of certain very great religions, we have found it, not at the base, it is true, but at the summit of the Australian system. Bunjil, Daramulun or Baiame are not simple tribal gods; each of them is recognized by a number of different tribes. In a sense, their cult is international. This conception is therefore very near to that found

in the most recent theologies. So certain writers have felt it their duty to deny its authenticity, howsoever incontestable this may be.

And we have been able to show how this has been formed.

Neighbouring tribes of a similar civilization cannot fail to be in constant relations with each other. All sorts of circumstances give an occasion for it: besides commerce, which is still rudimentary, there are marriages; these international marriages are very common in Australia. In the course of these meetings, men naturally become conscious of the moral relationship which united them. They have the same social organization, the same division into phratries, clans and matrimonial classes; they practise the same rites of initiation, or wholly similar ones. Mutual loans and treaties result in reinforcing these spontaneous resemblances. The gods to which these manifestly identical institutions were attached could hardly have remained distinct in their minds. Everything tended to bring them together and consequently, even supposing that each tribe elaborated the notion independently, they must necessarily have tended to confound themselves with each other. Also, it is probable that it was in inter-tribal assemblies that they were first conceived. For they are chiefly the gods of initiation, and in the initiation ceremonies, the different tribes are usually represented. So if sacred beings are formed which are connected with no geographically determined society, that is not because they have an extra-social origin. It is because there are other groups above these geographically determined ones, whose contours are less clearly marked: they have no fixed frontiers, but include all sorts of more or less neighbouring and related tribes. The particular social life thus created tends to spread itself over an area with no definite limits. Naturally the mythological personages who correspond to it have the same character; their sphere of influence is not limited; they go beyond the particular tribes and their territory. They are the great international gods.

Now there is nothing in this situation which is peculiar to Australian societies. There is no people and no state which is not a part of another society, more or less unlimited, which embraces all the peoples and all the States with which the first comes in contact, either directly or indirectly; there is no national life which is not dominated by a collective life of an international nature. In proportion as we advance in history, these international groups acquire a greater importance and extent. Thus we see how, in certain cases, this universalistic tendency has been able to develop itself to the point of affecting

not only the higher ideas of the religious system, but even the principles upon which it rests.

II

Thus there is something eternal in religion which is destined to survive all the particular symbols in which religious thought has successively enveloped itself. There can be no society which does not feel the need of upholding and reaffirming at regular intervals the collective sentiments and the collective ideas which make its unity and its personality. Now this moral remaking cannot be achieved except by the means of reunions, assemblies and meetings where the individuals, being closely united to one another, reaffirm in common their common sentiments; hence come ceremonies which do not differ from regular religious ceremonies, either in their object, the results which they produce, or the processes employed to attain these results. What essential difference is there between an assembly of Christians celebrating the principal dates of the life of Christ, or of Jews remembering the exodus from Egypt or the promulgation of the decalogue, and a reunion of citizens commemorating the promulgation of a new moral or legal system or some great event in the national life?

If we find a little difficulty to-day in imagining what these feasts and ceremonies of the future could consist in, it is because we are going through a stage of transition and moral mediocrity. The great things of the past which filled our fathers with enthusiasm do not excite the same ardour in us, either because they have come into common usage to such an extent that we are unconscious of them, or else because they no longer answer to our actual aspirations; but as yet there is nothing to replace them. We can no longer impassionate ourselves for the principles in the name of which Christianity recommended to masters that they treat their slaves humanely, and, on the other hand, the idea which it has formed of human equality and fraternity seems to us to-day to leave too large a place for unjust inequalities. Its pity for the outcast seems to us too Platonic; we desire another which would be more practicable; but as yet we cannot clearly see what it should be nor how it could be realized in facts. In a word, the old gods are growing old or already dead, and others are not yet born. This is what rendered vain the attempt of Comte with the old historic souvenirs artificially revived: it is life itself, and not a dead past which can produce a living cult. But this state of incertitude and confused agitation cannot last for ever. A day will come when our societies will

know again those hours of creative effervescence, in the course of which new ideas arise and new formulæ are found which serve for a while as a guide to humanity; and when these hours shall have been passed through once, men will spontaneously feel the need of reliving them from time to time in thought, that is to say, of keeping alive their memory by means of celebrations which regularly reproduce their fruits. We have already seen how the French Revolution established a whole cycle of holidays to keep the principles with which it was inspired in a state of perpetual youth. If this institution quickly fell away, it was because the revolutionary faith lasted but a moment, and deceptions and discouragements rapidly succeeded the first moments of enthusiasm. But though the work may have miscarried, it enables us to imagine what might have happened in other conditions; and everything leads us to believe that it will be taken up again sooner or later. There are no gospels which are immortal, but neither is there any reason for believing that humanity is incapable of inventing new ones. As to the question of what symbols this new faith will express itself with, whether they will resemble those of the past or not, and whether or not they will be more adequate for the reality which they seek to translate, that is something which surpasses the human faculty of foresight and which does not appertain to the principal question.

But feasts and rites, in a word, the cult, are not the whole religion. This is not merely a system of practices, but also a system of ideas whose object is to explain the world; we have seen that even the humblest have their cosmology. Whatever connection there may be between these two elements of the religious life, they are still quite different. The one is turned towards action, which it demands and regulates; the other is turned towards thought, which it enriches and organizes. Then they do not depend upon the same conditions, and consequently it may be asked if the second answers to necessities as universal and as permanent as the first.

When specific characteristics are attributed to religious thought, and when it is believed that its function is to express, by means peculiar to itself, an aspect of reality which evades ordinary knowledge as well as science, one naturally refuses to admit that religion can ever abandon its speculative rôle. But our analysis of the facts does not seem to have shown this specific quality of religion. The religion which we have just studied is one of those whose symbols are the most disconcerting for the reason. There all appears mysterious. These beings which belong to the most heterogeneous groups at the same time, who multiply

without ceasing to be one, who divide without diminishing, all seem, at first view, to belong to an entirely different world from the one where we live; some have even gone so far as to say that the mind which constructed them ignored the laws of logic completely. Perhaps the contrast between reason and faith has never been more thorough. Then if there has ever been a moment in history when their heterogeneousness should have stood out clearly, it is here. But contrary to all appearances, as we have pointed out, the realities to which religious speculation is then applied are the same as those which later serve as the subject of reflection for philosophers: they are nature, man, society. The mystery which appears to surround them is wholly superficial and disappears before a more painstaking observation: it is enough merely to set aside the veil with which mythological imagination has covered them for them to appear such as they really are. Religion sets itself to translate these realities into an intelligible language which does not differ in nature from that employed by science; the attempt is made by both to connect things with each other, to establish internal relations between them, to classify them and to systematize them. We have even seen that the essential ideas of scientific logic are of religious origin. It is true that in order to utilize them, science gives them a new elaboration; it purges them of all accidental elements; in a general way, it brings a spirit of criticism into all its doings, which religion ignores; it surrounds itself with precautions to "escape precipitation and bias," and to hold aside the passions, prejudices and all subjective influences. But these perfectionings of method are not enough to differentiate it from religion. In this regard, both pursue the same end; scientific thought is only a more perfect form of religious thought. Thus it seems natural that the second should progressively retire before the first, as this becomes better fitted to perform the task.

And there is no doubt that this regression has taken place in the course of history. Having left religion, science tends to substitute itself for this latter in all that which concerns the cognitive and intellectual functions. Christianity has already definitely consecrated this substitution in the order of material things. Seeing in matter that which is profane before all else, it readily left the knowledge of this to another discipline, *tradidit mundum hominum disputationi*, "He gave the world over to the disputes of men"; it is thus that the natural sciences have been able to establish themselves and make their authority recognized without very great difficulty. But it could not give up the world of souls so easily; for it is before all over souls that the god of

the Christians aspires to reign. That is why the idea of submitting the psychic life to science produced the effect of a sort of profanation for a long time; even to-day it is repugnant to many minds. However, experimental and comparative psychology is founded and to-day we must reckon with it. But the world of the religious and moral life is still forbidden. The great majority of men continue to believe that here there is an order of things which the mind cannot penetrate except by very special ways. Hence comes the active resistance which is met with every time that someone tries to treat religious and moral phenomena scientifically. But in spite of these oppositions, these attempts are constantly repeated and this persistence even allows us to foresee that this final barrier will finally give way and that science will establish herself as mistress even in this reserved region.

That is what the conflict between science and religion really amounts to. It is said that science denies religion in principle. But religion exists; it is a system of given facts; in a word, it is a reality. How could science deny this reality? Also, in so far as religion is action, and in so far as it is a means of making men live, science could not take its place, for even if this expresses life, it does not create it; it may well seek to explain the faith, but by that very act it presupposes it. Thus there is no conflict except upon one limited point. Of the two functions which religion originally fulfilled, there is one, and only one, which tends to escape it more and more: that is its speculative function. That which science refuses to grant to religion is not its right to exist, but its right to dogmatize upon the nature of things and the special competence which it claims for itself for knowing man and the world. As a matter of fact, it does not know itself. It does not even know what it is made of, nor to what need it answers. It is itself a subject for science, so far is it from being able to make the law for science! And from another point of view, since there is no proper subject for religious speculation outside that reality to which scientific reflection is applied, it is evident that this former cannot play the same rôle in the future that it has played in the past.

However, it seems destined to transform itself rather than to disappear.

We have said that there is something eternal in religion: it is the cult and the faith. Men cannot celebrate ceremonies for which they see no reason, nor can they accept a faith which they in no way understand. To spread itself or merely to maintain itself, it must be justified, that is to say, a theory must be made of it. A theory of this sort must undoubtedly be founded

upon the different sciences, from the moment when these exist; first of all, upon the social sciences, for religious faith has its origin in society; then upon psychology, for society is a synthesis of human consciousnesses; and finally upon the sciences of nature, for man and society are a part of the universe and can be abstracted from it only artificially. But howsoever important these facts taken from the constituted sciences may be, they are not enough; for faith is before all else an impetus to action, while science, no matter how far it may be pushed, always remains at a distance from this. Science is fragmentary and incomplete; it advances but slowly and is never finished; but life cannot wait. The theories which are destined to make men live and act are therefore obliged to pass science and complete it prematurely. They are possible only when the practical exigencies and the vital necessities which we feel without distinctly conceiving them push thought in advance, beyond that which science permits us to affirm. Thus religions, even the most rational and laicized, cannot and never will be able to dispense with a particular form of speculation which, though having the same subjects as science itself, cannot be really scientific: the obscure intuitions of sensation and sentiment too often take the place of logical reasons. On one side, this speculation resembles that which we meet with in the religions of the past; but on another, it is different. While claiming and exercising the right of going beyond science, it must commence by knowing this and by inspiring itself with it. Ever since the authority of science was established, it must be reckoned with; one can go farther than it under the pressure of necessity, but he must take his direction from it. He can affirm nothing that it denies, deny nothing that it affirms, and establish nothing that is not directly or indirectly founded upon principles taken from it. From now on, the faith no longer exercises the same hegemony as formerly over the system of ideas that we may continue to call religion. A rival power rises up before it which, being born of it, ever after submits it to its criticism and control. And everything makes us foresee that this control will constantly become more extended and efficient, while no limit can be assigned to its future influence.

III

But if the fundamental notions of science are of a religious origin, how has religion been able to bring them forth? At first sight, one does not see what relations there can be between religion and logic. Or, since the reality which religious thought expresses is society, the question can be stated in the following

terms, which make the entire difficulty appear even better: what has been able to make social life so important a source for the logical life? It seems as though nothing could have predestined it to this rôle, for it certainly was not to satisfy their speculative needs that men associated themselves together.

Perhaps we shall be found over bold in attempting so complex a question here. To treat it as it should be treated, the sociological conditions of knowledge should be known much better than they actually are; we are only beginning to catch glimpses of some of them. However, the question is so grave, and so directly implied in all that has preceded, that we must make an effort not to leave it without an answer. Perhaps it is not impossible, even at present, to state some general principles which may at least aid in the solution.

Logical thought is made up of concepts. Seeking how society can have played a rôle in the genesis of logical thought thus reduces itself to seeking how it can have taken a part in the formation of concepts.

If, as is ordinarily the case, we see in the concept only a general idea, the problem appears insoluble. By his own power, the individual can compare his conceptions and images, disengage that which they have in common, and thus, in a word, generalize. Then it is hard to see why this generalization should be possible only in and through society. But, in the first place, it is inadmissible that logical thought is characterized only by the greater extension of the conceptions of which it is made up. If particular ideas have nothing logical about them, why should it be different with general ones? The general exists only in the particular; it is the particular simplified and impoverished. Then the first could have no virtues or privileges which the second has not. Inversely, if conceptual thought can be applied to the class, species or variety, howsoever restricted these may be, why can it not be extended to the individual, that is to say, to the limit towards which the conception tends, proportionately as its extension diminishes? As a matter of fact, there are many concepts which have only individuals as their object. In every sort of religion, gods are individualities distinct from each other; however, they are conceived, not perceived. Each people represents its historic or legendary heroes in fashions which vary with the time. Finally, every one of us forms an idea of the individuals with whom he comes in contact, of their character, of their appearance, their distinctive traits and their moral and physical temperaments: these notions, too, are real concepts. It is true that in general they are formed crudely enough; but even among

scientific concepts, are there a great many that are perfectly adequate for their object? In this direction, there are only differences of degree between them.

Therefore the concept must be defined by other characteristics. It is opposed to sensual representations of every order—sensations, perceptions or images—by the following properties.

Sensual representations are in a perpetual flux; they come after each other like the waves of a river, and even during the time that they last, they do not remain the same thing. Each of them is an integral part of the precise instant when it takes place. We are never sure of again finding a perception such as we experienced it the first time; for if the thing perceived has not changed, it is we who are no longer the same. On the contrary, the concept is, as it were, outside of time and change; it is in the depths below all this agitation; it might be said that it is in a different portion of the mind, which is serener and calmer. It does not move of itself, by an internal and spontaneous evolution, but, on the contrary, it resists change. It is a manner of thinking that, at every moment of time, is fixed and crystallized.[1] In so far as it is what it ought to be, it is immutable. If it changes, it is not because it is its nature to do so, but because we have discovered some imperfection in it; it is because it had to be rectified. The system of concepts with which we think in everyday life is that expressed by the vocabulary of our mother tongue; for every word translates a concept. Now language is something fixed; it changes but very slowly, and consequently it is the same with the conceptual system which it expresses. The scholar finds himself in the same situation in regard to the special terminology employed by the science to which he has consecrated himself, and hence in regard to the special scheme of concepts to which this terminology corresponds. It is true that he can make innovations, but these are always a sort of violence done to the established ways of thinking.

And at the same time that it is relatively immutable, the concept is universal, or at least capable of becoming so. A concept is not my concept; I hold it in common with other men, or, in any case, can communicate it to them. It is impossible for me to make a sensation pass from my consciousness into that of another; it holds closely to my organism and personality and cannot be detached from them. All that I can do is to invite others to place themselves before the same object as myself and to leave themselves to its action. On the other hand, conversation and all intellectual communication between men is an exchange of concepts. The concept is an essentially

[1] William James, *Principles of Psychology*, I, p. 464.

impersonal representation; it is through it that human intelligences communicate.[1]

The nature of the concept, thus defined, bespeaks its origin. If it is common to all, it is the work of the community. Since it bears the mark of no particular mind, it is clear that it was elaborated by a unique intelligence, where all others meet each other, and after a fashion, come to nourish themselves. If it has more stability than sensations or images, it is because the collective representations are more stable than the individual ones; for while an individual is conscious even of the slight changes which take place in his environment, only events of a greater gravity can succeed in affecting the mental status of a society. Every time that we are in the presence of a *type* [2] of thought or action which is imposed uniformly upon particular wills or intelligences, this pressure exercised over the individual betrays the intervention of the group. Also, as we have already said, the concepts with which we ordinarily think are those of our vocabulary. Now it is unquestionable that language, and consequently the system of concepts which it translates, is the product of a collective elaboration. What it expresses is the manner in which society as a whole represents the facts of experience. The ideas which correspond to the diverse elements of language are thus collective representations.

Even their contents bear witness to the same fact. In fact, there are scarcely any words among those which we usually employ whose meaning does not pass, to a greater or less extent, the limits of our personal experience. Very frequently a term expresses things which we have never perceived or experiences which we have never had or of which we have never been the witnesses. Even when we know some of the objects which it concerns, it is only as particular examples that they serve to illustrate the idea which they would never have been able to form by themselves. Thus there is a great deal of knowledge

[1] This universality of the concept should not be confused with its generality: they are very different things. What we mean by universality is the property which the concept has of being communicable to a number of minds, and in principle, to all minds; but this communicability is wholly independent of the degree of its extension. A concept which is applied to only one object, and whose extension is consequently at the minimum, can be the same for everybody: such is the case with the concept of a deity.

[2] It may be objected that frequently, as the mere effect of repetition, ways of thinking and acting become fixed and crystallized in the individual, in the form of habits which resist change. But a habit is only a tendency to repeat an act or idea automatically every time that the same circumstances appear; it does not at all imply that the idea or act is in the form of an exemplary type, proposed to or imposed upon the mind or will. It is only when a type of this sort is set up, that is to say, when a rule or standard is established, that social action can and should be presumed.

condensed in the word which I never collected, and which is not individual; it even surpasses me to such an extent that I cannot even completely appropriate all its results. Which of us knows all the words of the language he speaks and the entire signification of each?

This remark enables us to determine the sense in which we mean to say that concepts are collective representations. If they belong to a whole social group, it is not because they represent the average of the corresponding individual representations; for in that case they would be poorer than the latter in intellectual content, while, as a matter of fact, they contain much that surpasses the knowledge of the average individual. They are not abstractions which have a reality only in particular consciousnesses, but they are as concrete representations as an individual could form of his own personal environment: they correspond to the way in which this very special being, society, considers the things of its own proper experience. If, as a matter of fact, the concepts are nearly always general ideas, and if they express categories and classes rather than particular objects, it is because the unique and variable characteristics of things interest society but rarely; because of its very extent, it can scarcely be affected by more than their general and permanent qualities. Therefore it is to this aspect of affairs that it gives its attention: it is a part of its nature to see things in large and under the aspect which they ordinarily have. But this generality is not necessary for them, and, in any case, even when these representations have the generic character which they ordinarily have, they are the work of society and are enriched by its experience.

That is what makes conceptual thought so valuable for us. If concepts were only general ideas, they would not enrich knowledge a great deal, for, as we have already pointed out, the general contains nothing more than the particular. But if before all else they are collective representations, they add to that which we can learn by our own personal experience all that wisdom and science which the group has accumulated in the course of centuries. Thinking by concepts is not merely seeing reality on its most general side, but it is projecting a light upon the sensation which illuminates it, penetrates it and transforms it. Conceiving something is both learning its essential elements better and also locating it in its place; for each civilization has its organized system of concepts which characterizes it. Before this scheme of ideas, the individual is in the same situation as the νοῦς of Plato before the world of Ideas. He must assimilate them to himself, for he must have them to hold intercourse with others; but the assimilation is always imperfect.

Each of us sees them after his own fashion. There are some which escape us completely and remain outside of our circle of vision; there are others of which we perceive certain aspects only. There are even a great many which we pervert in holding, for as they are collective by nature, they cannot become individualized without being retouched, modified, and consequently falsified. Hence comes the great trouble we have in understanding each other, and the fact that we even lie to each other without wishing to: it is because we all use the same words without giving them the same meaning.

We are now able to see what the part of society in the genesis of logical thought is. This is possible only from the moment when, above the fugitive conceptions which they owe to sensuous experience, men have succeeded in conceiving a whole world of stable ideas, the common ground of all intelligences. In fact, logical thinking is always impersonal thinking, and is also thought *sub species æternitatis*—as though for all time. Impersonality and stability are the two characteristics of truth. Now logical life evidently presupposes that men know, at least confusedly, that there is such a thing as truth, distinct from sensuous appearances. But how have they been able to arrive at this conception? We generally talk as though it should have spontaneously presented itself to them from the moment they opened their eyes upon the world. However, there is nothing in immediate experience which could suggest it; everything even contradicts it. Thus the child and the animal have no suspicion of it. History shows that it has taken centuries for it to disengage and establish itself. In our Western world, it was with the great thinkers of Greece that it first became clearly conscious of itself and of the consequences which it implies; when the discovery was made, it caused an amazement which Plato has translated into magnificent language. But if it is only at this epoch that the idea is expressed in philosophic formulæ, it was necessarily pre-existent in the stage of an obscure sentiment. Philosophers have sought to elucidate this sentiment, but they have not succeeded. In order that they might reflect upon it and analyse it, it was necessary that it be given them, and that they seek to know whence it came, that is to say, in what experience it was founded. This is in collective experience. It is under the form of collective thought that impersonal thought is for the first time revealed to humanity; we cannot see by what other way this revelation could have been made. From the mere fact that society exists, there is also, outside of the individual sensations and images, a whole system of representations which enjoy marvellous properties. By means of them, men understand

each other and intelligences grasp each other. They have within them a sort of force or moral ascendancy, in virtue of which they impose themselves upon individual minds. Hence the individual at least obscurely takes account of the fact that above his private ideas, there is a world of absolute ideas according to which he must shape his own ; he catches a glimpse of a whole intellectual kingdom in which he participates, but which is greater than he. This is the first intuition of the realm of truth. From the moment when he first becomes conscious of these higher ideas, he sets himself to scrutinizing their nature ; he asks whence these pre-eminent representations hold their prerogatives and, in so far as he believes that he has discovered their causes, he undertakes to put these causes into action for himself, in order that he may draw from them by his own force the effects which they produce ; that is to say, he attributes to himself the right of making concepts. Thus the faculty of conception has individualized itself. But to understand its origins and function, it must be attached to the social conditions upon which it depends.

It may be objected that we show the concept in one of its aspects only, and that its unique rôle is not the assuring of a harmony among minds, but also, and to a greater extent, their harmony with the nature of things. It seems as though it had a reason for existence only on condition of being true, that is to say, objective, and as though its impersonality were only a consequence of its objectivity. It is in regard to things, thought of as adequately as possible, that minds ought to communicate. Nor do we deny that the evolution of concepts has been partially in this direction. The concept which was first held as true because it was collective tends to be no longer collective except on condition of being held as true: we demand its credentials of it before according it our confidence. But we must not lose sight of the fact that even to-day the great majority of the concepts which we use are not methodically constituted; we get them from language, that is to say, from common experience, without submitting them to any criticism. The scientifically elaborated and criticized concepts are always in the very slight minority. Also, between them and those which draw all their authority from the fact that they are collective, there are only differences of degree. A collective representation presents guarantees of objectivity by the fact that it is collective : for it is not without sufficient reason that it has been able to generalize and maintain itself with persistence. If it were out of accord with the nature of things, it would never have been able to acquire an extended

and prolonged empire over intellects. At bottom, the confidence inspired by scientific concepts is due to the fact that they can be methodically controlled. But a collective representation is necessarily submitted to a control that is repeated indefinitely; the men who accept it verify it by their own experience. Therefore, it could not be wholly inadequate for its subject. It is true that it may express this by means of imperfect symbols; but scientific symbols themselves are never more than approximative. It is precisely this principle which is at the basis of the method which we follow in the study of religious phenomena: we take it as an axiom that religious beliefs, howsoever strange their appearance may be at times, contain a truth which must be discovered.[1]

On the other hand, it is not at all true that concepts, even when constructed according to the rules of science, get their authority uniquely from their objective value. It is not enough that they be true to be believed. If they are not in harmony with the other beliefs and opinions, or, in a word, with the mass of the other collective representations, they will be denied; minds will be closed to them; consequently it will be as though they did not exist. To-day it is generally sufficient that they bear the stamp of science to receive a sort of privileged credit, because we have faith in science. But this faith does not differ essentially from religious faith. In the last resort, the value which we attribute to science depends upon the idea which we collectively form of its nature and rôle in life; that is as much as to say that it expresses a state of public opinion. In all social life, in fact, science rests upon opinion. It is undoubtedly true that this opinion can be taken as the object of a study and a science made of it; this is what sociology principally consists in. But the science of opinion does not make opinions; it can only observe them and make them more conscious of themselves. It is true that by this means it can lead them to change, but science continues to be dependent upon opinion at the very moment when it seems to be making its laws; for, as we have already shown, it is from opinion that it holds the force necessary to act upon opinion.[2]

Saying that concepts express the manner in which society represents things is also saying that conceptual thought is coeval with humanity itself. We refuse to see in it the product of a more or less retarded culture. A man who did not think

[1] Thus we see how far it is from being true that a conception lacks objective value merely because it has a social origin.

[2] See also above, p. 208.

with concepts would not be a man, for he would not be a social being. If reduced to having only individual perceptions, he would be indistinguishable from the beasts. If it has been possible to sustain the contrary thesis, it is because concepts have been defined by characteristics which are not essential to them. They have been identified with general ideas[1] and with clearly limited and circumscribed general ideas.[2] In these conditions it has possibly seemed as though the inferior societies had no concepts properly so called; for they have only rudimentary processes of generalization and the ideas which they use are not generally very well defined. But the greater part of our concepts are equally indetermined; we force ourselves to define them only in discussions or when doing careful work. We have also seen that conceiving is not generalizing. Thinking conceptually is not simply isolating and grouping together the common characteristics of a certain number of objects; it is relating the variable to the permanent, the individual to the social. And since logical thought commences with the concept, it follows that it has always existed; there is no period in history when men have lived in a chronic confusion and contradiction. To be sure, we cannot insist too much upon the different characteristics which logic presents at different periods in history; it develops like the societies themselves. But howsoever real these differences may be, they should not cause us to neglect the similarities, which are no less essential.

IV

We are now in a position to take up a final question which has already been raised in our introduction[3] and which has been taken as understood in the remainder of this work. We have seen that at least some of the categories are social things. The question is where they got this character.

Undoubtedly it will be easily understood that since they are themselves concepts, they are the work of the group. It can even be said that there are no other concepts which present to an equal degree the signs by which a collective representation is recognized. In fact, their stability and impersonality are such that they have often passed as being absolutely universal and immutable. Also, as they express the fundamental conditions for an agreement between minds, it seems evident that they have been elaborated by society.

[1] Lévy-Bruhl, *Les fonctions mentales dans les sociétés inférieures*, pp. 131–138.
[2] *Ibid.*, p. 446.
[3] See above, p. 18.

But the problem concerning them is more complex, for they are social in another sense and, as it were in the second degree. They not only come from society, but the things which they express are of a social nature. Not only is it society which has founded them, but their contents are the different aspects of the social being: the category of class was at first indistinct from the concept of the human group; it is the rhythm of social life which is at the basis of the category of time; the territory occupied by the society furnished the material for the category of space; it is the collective force which was the prototype of the concept of efficient force, an essential element in the category of causality. However, the categories are not made to be applied only to the social realm; they reach out to all reality. Then how is it that they have taken from society the models upon which they have been constructed?

It is because they are the pre-eminent concepts, which have a preponderating part in our knowledge. In fact, the function of the categories is to dominate and envelop all the other concepts: they are permanent moulds for the mental life. Now for them to embrace such an object, they must be founded upon a reality of equal amplitude.

Undoubtedly the relations which they express exist in an implicit way in individual consciousnesses. The individual lives in time, and, as we have said, he has a certain sense of temporal orientation. He is situated at a determined point in space, and it has even been held, and sustained with good reasons, that all sensations have something special about them.[1] He has a feeling of resemblances; similar representations are brought together and the new representation formed by their union has a sort of generic character. We also have the sensation of a certain regularity in the order of the succession of phenomena; even an animal is not incapable of this. However, all these relations are strictly personal for the individual who recognizes them, and consequently the notion of them which he may have can in no case go beyond his own narrow horizon. The generic images which are formed in my consciousness by the fusion of similar images represent only the objects which I have perceived directly; there is nothing there which could give me the idea of a class, that is to say, of a mould including the *whole* group of all possible objects which satisfy the same condition. Also, it would be necessary to have the idea of group in the first place, and the mere observations of our interior life could

[1] William James, *Principles of Psychology*, I, p. 134.

never awaken that in us. But, above all, there is no individual experience, howsoever extended and prolonged it may be, which could give a suspicion of the existence of a whole class which would embrace every single being, and to which other classes are only co-ordinated or subordinated species. This idea of *all*, which is at the basis of the classifications which we have just cited, could not have come from the individual himself, who is only a part in relation to the whole and who never attains more than an infinitesimal fraction of reality. And yet there is perhaps no other category of greater importance; for as the rôle of the categories is to envelop all the other concepts, the category *par excellence* would seem to be this very concept of *totality*. The theorists of knowledge ordinarily postulate it as if it came of itself, while it really surpasses the contents of each individual consciousness taken alone to an infinite degree.

For the same reasons, the space which I know by my senses, of which I am the centre and where everything is disposed in relation to me, could not be space in general, which contains all extensions and where these are co-ordinated by personal guide-lines which are common to everybody. In the same way, the concrete duration which I feel passing within me and with me could not give me the idea of time in general: the first expresses only the rhythm of my individual life; the second should correspond to the rhythm of a life which is not that of any individual in particular, but in which all participate.[1] In the same way, finally, the regularities which I am able to conceive in the manner in which my sensations succeed one another may well have a value for me; they explain how it comes about that when I am given the first of two phenomena whose concurrence I have observed, I tend to expect the other. But this personal state of expectation could not be confounded with the conception of a universal order of succession which imposes itself upon all minds and all events.

Since the world expressed by the entire system of concepts is the one that society regards, society alone can furnish the most general notions with which it should be represented. Such an object can be embraced only by a subject which contains all the individual subjects within it. Since the universe does not exist except in so far as it is thought of, and since it is not

[1] Men frequently speak of space and time as if they were only concrete extent and duration, such as the individual consciousness can feel, but enfeebled by abstraction. In reality, they are representations of a wholly different sort, made out of other elements, according to a different plan, and with equally different ends in view.

completely thought of except by society, it takes a place in this latter; it becomes a part of society's interior life, while this is the totality, outside of which nothing exists. The concept of totality is only the abstract form of the concept of society: it is the whole which includes all things, the supreme class which embraces all other classes. Such is the final principle upon which repose all these primitive classifications where beings from every realm are placed and classified in social forms, exactly like men.[1] But if the world is inside of society, the space which this latter occupies becomes confounded with space in general. In fact, we have seen how each thing has its assigned place in social space, and the degree to which this space in general differs from the concrete expanses which we perceive is well shown by the fact that this localization is wholly ideal and in no way resembles what it would have been if it had been dictated to us by sensuous experience alone.[2] For the same reason, the rhythm of collective life dominates and embraces the varied rhythms of all the elementary lives from which it results; consequently the time which it expresses dominates and embraces all particular durations. It is time in general. For a long time the history of the world has been only another aspect of the history of society. The one commences with the other; the periods of the first are determined by the periods of the second. This impersonal and total duration is measured, and the guide-lines in relation to which it is divided and organized are fixed by the movements of concentration or dispersion of society; or, more generally, the periodical necessities for a collective renewal. If these critical instants are generally attached to some material phenomenon, such as the regular recurrence of such or such a star or the alternation of the seasons, it is because objective signs are necessary to make this essentially social organization intelligible to all. In the same way, finally, the causal relation, from the moment when it is collectively stated by the group, becomes independent of every individual consciousness; it rises above all particular minds and events. It is a law whose value depends upon no person. We have already shown how it is clearly thus that it seems to have originated.

Another reason explains why the constituent elements of the categories should have been taken from social life: it is because the relations which they express could not have been learned except in and through society. If they are in a sense

[1] At bottom, the concept of totality, that of society and that of divinity are very probably only different aspects of the same notion.

[2] See our *Classifications primitives, loc. cit.*, pp. 40 ff.

immanent in the life of an individual, he has neither a reason nor the means for learning them, reflecting upon them and forming them into distinct ideas. In order to orient himself personally in space and to know at what moments he should satisfy his various organic needs, he has no need of making, once and for all, a conceptual representation of time and space. Many animals are able to find the road which leads to places with which they are familiar; they come back at a proper moment without knowing any of the categories; sensations are enough to direct them automatically. They would also be enough for men, if their sensations had to satisfy only individual needs. To recognize the fact that one thing resembles another which we have already experienced, it is in no way necessary that we arrange them all in groups and species: the way in which similar images call up each other and unite is enough to give the feeling of resemblance. The impression that a certain thing has already been seen or experienced implies no classification. To recognize the things which we should seek or from which we should flee, it would not be necessary to attach the effects of the two to their causes by a logical bond, if individual conveniences were the only ones in question. Purely empirical sequences and strong connections between the concrete representations would be as sure guides for the will. Not only is it true that the animal has no others, but also our own personal conduct frequently supposes nothing more. The prudent man is the one who has a very clear sensation of what must be done, but which he would ordinarily be quite incapable of stating as a general law.

It is a different matter with society. This is possible only when the individuals and things which compose it are divided into certain groups, that is to say, classified, and when these groups are classified in relation to each other. Society supposes a self-conscious organization which is nothing other than a classification. This organization of society naturally extends itself to the place which this occupies. To avoid all collisions, it is necessary that each particular group have a determined portion of space assigned to it: in other terms, it is necessary that space in general be divided, differentiated, arranged, and that these divisions and arrangements be known to everybody. On the other hand, every summons to a celebration, a hunt or a military expedition implies fixed and established dates, and consequently that a common time is agreed upon, which everybody conceives in the same fashion. Finally, the co-operation of many persons with the same end in view is possible only when they are in agreement as to

the relation which exists between this end and the means of attaining it, that is to say, when the same causal relation is admitted by all the co-operators in the enterprise. It is not surprising, therefore, that social time, social space, social classes and causality should be the basis of the corresponding categories, since it is under their social forms that these different relations were first grasped with a certain clarity by the human intellect.

In summing up, then, we must say that society is not at all the illogical or a-logical, incoherent and fantastic being which it has too often been considered. Quite on the contrary, the collective consciousness is the highest form of the psychic life, since it is the consciousness of the consciousnesses. Being placed outside of and above individual and local contingencies, it sees things only in their permanent and essential aspects, which it crystallizes into communicable ideas. At the same time that it sees from above, it sees farther; at every moment of time, it embraces all known reality; that is why it alone can furnish the mind with the moulds which are applicable to the totality of things and which make it possible to think of them. It does not create these moulds artificially; it finds them within itself; it does nothing but become conscious of them. They translate the ways of being which are found in all the stages of reality but which appear in their full clarity only at the summit, because the extreme complexity of the psychic life which passes there necessitates a greater development of consciousness. Attributing social origins to logical thought is not debasing it or diminishing its value or reducing it to nothing more than a system of artificial combinations; on the contrary, it is relating it to a cause which implies it naturally. But this is not saying that the ideas elaborated in this way are at once adequate for their object. If society is something universal in relation to the individual, it is none the less an individuality itself, which has its own personal physiognomy and its idiosyncrasies; it is a particular subject and consequently particularizes whatever it thinks of. Therefore collective representations also contain subjective elements, and these must be progressively rooted out, if we are to approach reality more closely. But howsoever crude these may have been at the beginning, the fact remains that with them the germ of a new mentality was given, to which the individual could never have raised himself by his own efforts: by them the way was opened to a stable, impersonal and organized thought which then had nothing to do except to develop its nature.

Also, the causes which have determined this development do not seem to be specifically different from those which gave it its initial impulse. If logical thought tends to rid itself more and more of the subjective and personal elements which it still retains from its origin, it is not because extra-social factors have intervened; it is much rather because a social life of a new sort is developing. It is this international life which has already resulted in universalizing religious beliefs. As it extends, the collective horizon enlarges; the society ceases to appear as the only whole, to become a part of a much vaster one, with indetermined frontiers, which is susceptible of advancing indefinitely. Consequently things can no longer be contained in the social moulds according to which they were primitively classified; they must be organized according to principles which are their own, so logical organization differentiates itself from the social organization and becomes autonomous. Really and truly human thought is not a primitive fact; it is the product of history; it is the ideal limit towards which we are constantly approaching, but which in all probability we shall never succeed in reaching.

Thus it is not at all true that between science on the one hand, and morals and religion on the other, there exists that sort of antinomy which has so frequently been admitted, for the two forms of human activity really come from one and the same source. Kant understood this very well, and therefore he made the speculative reason and the practical reason two different aspects of the same faculty. According to him, what makes their unity is the fact that the two are directed towards the universal. Rational thinking is thinking according to the laws which are imposed upon all reasonable beings; acting morally is conducting one's self according to those maxims which can be extended without contradiction to all wills. In other words, science and morals imply that the individual is capable of raising himself above his own peculiar point of view and of living an impersonal life. In fact, it cannot be doubted that this is a trait common to all the higher forms of thought and action. What Kant's system does not explain, however, is the origin of this sort of contradiction which is realized in man. Why is he forced to do violence to himself by leaving his individuality, and, inversely, why is the impersonal law obliged to be dissipated by incarnating itself in individuals? Is it answered that there are two antagonistic worlds in which we participate equally, the world of matter and sense on the one hand, and the world of pure and impersonal reason on the other? That is merely repeating the

question in slightly different terms, for what we are trying to find out is why we must lead these two existences at the same time. Why do these two worlds, which seem to contradict each other, not remain outside of each other, and why must they mutually penetrate one another in spite of their antagonism? The only explanation which has ever been given of this singular necessity is the hypothesis of the Fall, with all the difficulties which it implies, and which need not be repeated here. On the other hand, all mystery disappears the moment that it is recognized that impersonal reason is only another name given to collective thought. For this is possible only through a group of individuals; it supposes them, and in their turn, they suppose it, for they can continue to exist only by grouping themselves together. The kingdom of ends and impersonal truths can realize itself only by the co-operation of particular wills, and the reasons for which these participate in it are the same as those for which they co-operate. In a word, there is something impersonal in us because there is something social in all of us, and since social life embraces at once both representations and practices, this impersonality naturally extends to ideas as well as to acts.

Perhaps some will be surprised to see us connect the most elevated forms of thought with society: the cause appears quite humble, in consideration of the value which we attribute to the effect. Between the world of the senses and appetites on the one hand, and that of reason and morals on the other, the distance is so considerable that the second would seem to have been able to add itself to the first only by a creative act. But attributing to society this preponderating rôle in the genesis of our nature is not denying this creation; for society has a creative power which no other observable being can equal. In fact, all creation, if not a mystical operation which escapes science and knowledge, is the product of a synthesis. Now if the synthesis of particular conceptions which take place in each individual consciousness are already and of themselves productive of novelties, how much more efficacious these vast syntheses of complete consciousnesses which make society must be! A society is the most powerful combination of physical and moral forces of which nature offers us an example. Nowhere else is an equal richness of different materials, carried to such a degree of concentration, to be found. Then it is not surprising that a higher life disengages itself which, by reacting upon the elements of which it is the product, raises them to a higher plane of existence and transforms them.

Thus sociology appears destined to open a new way to the science of man. Up to the present, thinkers were placed before this double alternative: either explain the superior and specific faculties of men by connecting them to the inferior forms of his being, the reason to the senses, or the mind to matter, which is equivalent to denying their uniqueness; or else attach them to some super-experimental reality which was postulated, but whose existence could be established by no observation. What put them in this difficulty was the fact that the individual passed as being the *finis naturæ*—the ultimate creation of nature; it seemed that there was nothing beyond him, or at least nothing that science could touch. But from the moment when it is recognized that above the individual there is society, and that this is not a nominal being created by reason, but a system of active forces, a new manner of explaining men becomes possible. To conserve his distinctive traits it is no longer necessary to put them outside experience. At least, before going to this last extremity, it would be well to see if that which surpasses the individual, though it is within him, does not come from this super-individual reality which we experience in society. To be sure, it cannot be said at present to what point these explanations may be able to reach, and whether or not they are of a nature to resolve all the problems. But it is equally impossible to mark in advance a limit beyond which they cannot go. What must be done is to try the hypothesis and submit it as methodically as possible to the control of facts. This is what we have tried to do.

INDEX